The media reader:
continuity and transformation

The Media Reader: Continuity and Transformation
This Reader provides some of the set readings for a 16-week module (D852 *Transformations in Media Culture*) which is offered by The Open University Masters in Social Sciences Programme.

The Open University Masters in Social Sciences
The MA Programme enables students to select from a range of modules to create a programme to suit their own professional or personal development. Students can choose from a range of social science modules to obtain an MA in Social Sciences, or may specialize in a particular subject area. D852 *Transformations in Media Culture* is one of the modules leading to an MA in Cultural and Media Studies.

At present there are three study lines leading to:

an MA in Cultural and Media Studies
an MA in Environmental Policy and Society
an MA in Psychological Research Methods.

Other study lines being planned include an MSc in Psychology and an MA in Social Policy/MA in Social Policy and Criminology.

OU Supported Learning
The Open University's unique, supported open ('distance') learning Masters Programme in Social Sciences is designed to introduce the concepts, approaches, theories and techniques associated with a number of academic areas of study. The MA in Social Sciences programme provides great flexibility. Students study in their own environments, in their own time, anywhere in the European Union. They receive specially prepared course materials, benefit from structured tutorial support throughout all the coursework and assessment assignments, and have the chance to work with other students.

How to apply
If you would like to register for this programme, or simply find out more information, please write for the Masters in Social Sciences prospectus to the Course Reservations Centre, PO Box 724, The Open University, Walton Hall, Milton Keynes, MK7 6ZW, UK (Telephone +44 (0) 1908 653232).

The media reader:
continuity and transformation

edited by
Hugh Mackay and
Tim O'Sullivan

SAGE Publications
London • Thousand Oaks • New Delhi

in association with The Open University

Editorial material Hugh Mackay and Tim O'Sullivan © 1999

First published 1999

 SAGE Publications Ltd
6 Bonhill Street
London EC2A 4PU

SAGE Publications Inc.
2455 Teller Road
Thousand Oaks, California 91320

SAGE Publications India Pvt Ltd
32, M-Block Market
Greater Kailash – I
New Delhi 110 048

British Library Cataloguing in Publication data

A catalogue record for this book is available
from the British Library

ISBN 0 7619 6249 2
ISBN 0 7619 6250 6 (pbk)

Library of Congress catalog record available

Text and cover design: Barker/Hilsdon
Typeset by Mayhew Typesetting, Rhayader, Powys
Printed in Great Britain by The Cromwell Press Ltd,
Trowbridge, Wiltshire

Contents

Notes on contributors

Ien Ang is Professor in the Department of Communication at the University of Western Sydney. She is author of *Watching Dallas: Soap Opera and the Melodramatic Imagination* (1985), *Desperately Seeking the Audience* (1991) and *Living Room Wars: Rethinking Media Audiences for a Postmodern World* (1996).

Manuel Castells is Professor of Sociology and of Planning at the University of California, Berkeley. He is author of *The Urban Question: a Marxist Approach* (1977) and the trilogy *The Information Age: Economy, Society and Culture* – *Volume 1 The Rise of the Network Society* (1996), *Volume 2 The Power of Identity* (1997) and *Volume 3 End of Millennium* (1997).

Simon During is Robert Wallace Professor of English at the University of Melbourne, Australia. He is author of *Foucault and Literature* (1992) and *Patrick White* (1996) and editor of *The Cultural Studies Reader* (1993).

Patrice Flichy is Head of the Communications Research Group at the Centre National d'Études des Telecommunications, France. He is author of *European Telematics* (1991, with J. Jouet and P. Beaud) and *Dynamics of Modern Communication: The Shaping and Impact of New Communication Technologies* (1995).

Leslie Haddon is visiting Research Associate in Sociology at the London School of Economics. He is author of *The Shape of Things to Consume: Bringing Information Technology into the Home* (1995, with A. Cawson and I. Miles) and editor of *Communications on the Move: The Experience of Mobile Telephony in the 1990s* (1997).

Edward Herman is Professor Emeritus of Finance at the University of Pennsylvania and author of *Manufacturing Consent: The Political Economy of the Mass Media* (1988, with Noam Chomsky), *Triumph of the Market: Essays in Economics, Politics and the Media* (1995) and *The Global Media:*

the New Missionaries of Corporate Capitalism (1997, with Robert McChesney).

David Lyon is Professor of Sociology at Queen's University, Ontario. He is editor of *Computers, Surveillance and Privacy* (1996, with E.T. Zuriek) and author of *The Information Society. Issues and Illusions* (1988) and *The Electronic Eye. The Rise of Surveillance Society* (1994) and *Postmodernity* (1994).

Brent MacGregor is Professor of Visual Communication at Edinburgh College of Art, Heriot-Watt University. A former television producer, he is author of *Live, Direct and Biased? Making Television News in the Satellite Age* (1997).

Carolyn Marvin is Associate Professor of Communications at The Annenberg School of Communication, University of Pennsylvania and author of *When Old Technologies Were New: Thinking about Electric Communication in the Late Nineteenth Century* (1988) and *Blood Sacrifice and the Nation: Totem Rituals and the American Flag* (1998).

Robert McChesney is Research Associate Professor at the University of Illinois. He is author of *Telecommunications, Mass Media and Democracy*, (1993), *The Global Media: The New Missionaries of Corporate Capitalism* (1997, with Edward Herman) and *Capitalism and the Information Age* (1998).

Joshua Meyrowitz is Professor of Communications at the University of New Hampshire. He is author of *No Sense of Place: The Impact of Electronic Media on Social Behaviour* (1985).

David Morley is Professor of Communications at Goldsmiths College, London. He is editor of *Stuart Hall: Critical Dialogues in Cultural Studies* (1996 with Kuan-Hsing Chen) and author of *The Nationwide Audience* (1980), *Family Television* (1986) and *Television, Audiences and Cultural Studies* (1992).

Graham Murdock is Reader in the Sociology of Culture at Loughborough University. He is editor of *Communicating Politics: Mass Communication and the Political Process* (1986, with P. Golding and P. Schlesinger) and *The Political Economy of the Media* (1997, with Peter Golding).

Howard Rheingold is a journalist and writer. He is editor of *The Millennium Whole Earth Catalog* (1994) and author of *Virtual Reality* (1991) and *The Virtual Community: Finding Connection in a Computerized World* (1993).

Kevin Robins is Professor of Cultural Geography at the University of Newcastle upon Tyne. He is author of *Information Technology: A Luddite*

Analysis (1986, with Frank Webster), *Spaces of Identity. Global Media, Electronic Landscapes and Cultural Boundaries* (1995, with David Morley) and *Into the Image: Cultural and Politics in the Field of Vision* (1996).

Anthony Smith, formerly a television producer and Director of the British Film Institute, is President of Magdalen College, Oxford. He is author of *Goodbye Gutenberg: The Newspaper Revolution of the 1980s* (1980), *The Age of Behemoths: The Globalization of Mass Media Firms* (1991), *Books to Bytes: Knowledge and Information in the Postmodern Era* (1993) and *Software for the Self: Technology and Culture* (1996).

Jeanette Steemers is Senior Lecturer in Media Arts at the University of Luton. She has a professional background in international television and is editor of *Changing Channels: The Prospects for Television in a Digital World* (1998).

John Street is Senior Lecturer in Politics at the University of East Anglia. He is author of *Rebel Rock: The Politics of Popular Music* (1986), *Politics and Technology* (1992) and *Politics and Popular Culture* (1996).

John Thompson is Reader in Sociology at the University of Cambridge and author of *Ideology and Modern Culture: Critical Social Theory in the Era of Mass Communication* (1990) and *The Media and Modernity: A Social Theory of the Media* (1995).

John Tomlinson is Principal Lecturer in Social and Cultural Theory at Nottingham Trent University. He is author of *Cultural Imperialism. A Critical Introduction* (1991) and *Globalisation and Culture* (1999).

Sherry Turkle is Professor of Sociology of Science at Massachussetts Institute of Technology and a licensed clinical psychologist. She is the author of *The Second Self: Computers and the Human Spirit* (1984) and *Life on the Screen: Identity in the Age of the Internet* (1996).

Frank Webster is Professor of Sociology at the University of Birmingham. He is editor of *The Postmodern University? Contested Visions of Higher Education in Society* (1997, with Anthony Smith) and author of *Information Technology: A Luddite Analysis* (1986, with Kevin Robins) and *Theories of the Information Society* (1995).

Raymond Williams died in 1988. He was a Fellow of Jesus College, Cambridge, one of the most influential socialist writers in the post-war period and a founder of British cultural and media studies. His publications include *Culture and Society 1780–1950* (1958), *The Long Revolution* (1961), *Keywords* (1976), *Politics and Letters* (1979), *Culture* (1981) and *Towards 2000* (1983).

Acknowledgements

The authors and publishers wish to thank the following for permission to use copyright material.

Chapter 1: Blackwell Publishers and Stanford University Press for extracts from John B. Thompson (1995) *The Media and Modernity* (Chapters 1 and 2, pp. 23–37, 75–80).

Chapter 2: Manchester University Press for 'Corporate dynamics and broadcasting futures' by Graham Murdock from *Controlling Broadcasting*, edited by Meryl Aldridge and Nicholas Hewitt (Fulbright Papers 13), 1994. Manchester University Press, Manchester, UK.

Chapter 3: Routledge for 'The technology and the society' from Raymond Williams and Ederyn Williams, *Television: Technology and Cultural Form*, 1989. Routledge, London.

Chapter 4: Oxford University Press Inc., New York, for excerpts from 'Implementing the future' in *When Old Technologies Were New: Thinking About Electric Communication in the Late Nineteenth Century*. © 1988 Carolyn Marvin.

Chapter 5: Sage Publications Ltd for 'The wireless age: radio broadcasting' from *Dynamics of Modern Communication*, Patrice Flichy, 1995.

Chapter 6: Oxford University Press Inc., New York, for 'Where have we been? Where are we going?' from *No Sense of Place: The Impact of Electronic Media on Social Behaviour*. © 1985 Joshua Meyrowitz.

Chapter 7: BFI Information and Education for 'Information technology and the myth of abundance' from *Books to Bytes: Knowledge and Information in the Postmodern Era* by Anthony Smith, 1993. London.

Chapter 8: Taylor & Francis for Frank Webster (1994) 'What information society?', *The Information Society*, 10: 1–23.

Chapter 9: Frank Cass & Co Ltd for John Tomlinson (1996) 'Placing and displacing the West', *The European Journal of Development Research*, 8 (2): 22–35.

Chapter 10: Cassell for permission to reproduce 'The global media in the late 1990s' from *The Global Media: The New Missionaries of Corporate Capitalism*, Edward Herman and Robert McChesney, 1993. Cassell, Wellington House, 125 Strand, London WC2R 0BB, England.

Chapter 11: The University of Chicago Press for Simon During (1997) 'Popular culture on a global scale: a challenge for cultural studies?', *Critical Inquiry*, 23 (4): 808–21.

Chapter 12: John Libbey Media at the University of Luton Press for Jeanette Steemers (1997) 'Broadcasting is dead. Long live digital choice', *Convergence*, 3 (1): 51–71.

Chapter 13: Arnold for extracts from 'The technology of newsgathering and production', Chapter 6 in *Live, Direct and Biased? Making Television News in the Satellite Age*, Brent MacGregor, 1997. Arnold, London.

Chapter 14: Random House for extracts from 'Introduction' in *The Virtual Community*, Howard Rheingold, 1994. Secker and Warburg, London.

Chapter 15: The Orion Publishing Group for the 'Introduction' to *Life on the Screen: Identity in the Age of the Internet*, Sherry Turkle, 1996. Weidenfeld and Nicolson.

Chapter 16: The British Film Institute for Leslie Haddon's chapter 'Interactive games' from *Future Visions: New Technologies of the Screen* edited by P. Haywood and T. Wollen, 1993.

Chapter 17: Routledge for 'Reimagined communities: New media, new possibilities' from *Spaces of Identity: Global Media, Electronic Landscapes and Cultural Boundaries*, David Morley and Kevin Robins, 1995. Routledge, London.

Chapter 18: Routledge for David Lyon (1998) 'The world wide web of surveillance: the internet and off-world power flows', *Information, Communication & Society*, 1 (1): 91–105.

Chapter 19: Routledge for 'In the realm of uncertainty: the global village and capitalist postmodernity' from *Living Room Wars: Rethinking Media Audiences for a Postmodern World*, Ien Ang, 1996. Routledge, London.

Chapter 20: Sage Publications Ltd for John Street (1997) 'Remote control politics? Politics, Technology and "Electronic Democracy"', *European Journal of Communication*, 12: 27–42.

Chapter 21: Bob Catterell for Manuel Castells (1997) 'An introduction to the information age', *City*, 7: 6–16.

Introduction

For about 500 years after the invention of the printing press, print remained the predominant medium of communication. This changed following the development of the electric telegraph around the middle of the nineteenth century and of the telephone a couple of decades later. These were followed by the rapid development and application of a succession of communication technologies which have had a profound impact on communication and culture – notably film, radio and television. Today, however, many claim that society stands on the threshold of an era of media transformations of a particularly far-reaching and overwhelming nature – what Mark Poster (1995) has called 'the second media age'. With the development of digital and other new technologies of production, distribution and reception, the established media landscape is changing rapidly.

Television, for example, is being transformed with digital, widescreen and high definition (HDTV), offering improved sound and picture quality and, with the growth of cable and satellite, a growing multiplicity of channels. More radically, the computer and the Internet threaten both to replace existing forms of media delivery – with Internet radio, the transmission of moving images and on-line newspapers – and to provide new interactive entertainment and other services. In this way, it is set to disrupt profoundly some of the fundamental features of the media since the Second World War.

Communications networks have been of enormous and growing importance in the development of modern, global capitalism. Today, no sector of the economy operates without the use of sophisticated communications technologies. In this way, much of modern life is inconceivable without mass communication systems, which can be seen as both cause and symptom of industrialization and modernization. The development and growth of communications and the media have been accompanied by the emergence of massive, global, multimedia corporations. Increasingly, these are to be found among the giants of corporate capitalism: of the 80 largest corporations in the world in terms of market capitalization, 16 are in the information–communication sector – and many more if one adds consumer electronics to the category (see Herman and McChesney, Chapter 10). The importance of the media and media corporations, however, is much greater than their significance as powerful economic and productive forces. It is widely acknowledged that the media are different from other industries because of the special nature of their activity and product. It is via the media that symbolic culture is communicated; through them, societal values and ways of making sense of everyday lives and culture are disseminated. Thus, as well as being major industries in the modern economy, the media occupy a very significant role in the symbolic environment, as cultural institutions.

Communication systems and the media, as John Thompson argues in Chapter 1, have been implicated deeply in the development of modernity not only because they are central to the growth of the capitalist economy but also because of their key role in political and cultural life. Modern culture is, to a great extent, 'mediated': 'media' and 'culture' are deeply interdependent. Culture cannot be understood without foregrounding the media. The dramatic expansion of the media and their assumption of a role of unparalleled significance have led to new forms of social interaction and new ways of understanding ourselves. Modern times, it is argued by Arjun Appadurai (1990), are constituted partly through their *mediascapes*, as the media not only provide information but also have profound implications for forms of identity.

As a result of the cultural significance of the media, for hundreds of years it has been acknowledged that there is a need for state regulation of the media – over and above the regulation of other industries, for example, in relation to monopolies. From taxation of the press and printing licences to the plethora of organizations and policies of the contemporary era, the importance of the media in providing a platform for expression and communication has been considered a key element in the democratic process. Thus people confront the media not just as consumers but also as citizens, and the media are regulated to ensure that they provide a forum for informing citizens and for public debate. Graham Murdock in Chapter 2 explores the relationship between communication and democracy, examining public service broadcasting and its significance for the public sphere.

As to whether new media and communication technologies are contributing to the processes of democratization or to the concentration of power and voices heard, a polarization of the positions of researchers and commentators can be identified. On the one hand are techno-enthusiasts, of various persuasions, who extol the progressive or liberating characteristics of the new communication technologies, for example, in relation to new creative production practices (Ascott, 1998), revitalizing community, reinvigorating the public sphere, democratizing communication (see Rheingold in Chapter 14), increasing the diversity of voices which can be heard, offering a space for women's networks and forms of communication to blossom (Plant, 1996), breaking down obsolete modernist conceptions of the self and enabling new, multiple identities (see Turkle in Chapter 15) and empowering consumers through enhanced interactivity and choice. The Internet is celebrated as the vanguard in the dawning of the new media age, offering interactivity, the end of any notion of information shortage and instant, inexpensive, global communication.

On the other hand are those who point to the continuities of production for profit, the increasing deregulation of the market and the rise to the fore of market forces, and the continuation and growth of global media corporations, operating in the interests of their shareholders for profit and domination rather than to enhance democracy (for example, Golding, 1998a). They point to the continuation and exacerbation of global and national inequalities of income and wealth and to ways in which new media are reinforcing divisions between rich and poor (Golding, 1998b). The reality of using the Web is seen as endless waiting, unintended disconnection, a plethora of unwanted information and high telephone charges. For some this is the latest in a series of technologies, including artificial intelligence, virtual reality and multimedia, which have been the focus of the discourses of emerging information technologies, drawn on and constructed by utopian writers, politicians, decision-makers and the media (Webster and Robins, 1986). In this debate there seems to be an increasing polarization or duality of perspectives on the value and consequences of new information and communication technologies, a division of some significance among researchers of, and commentators on, the emerging media landscape.

The history of the arrival of new communication technologies shows that new media are shaped profoundly by the context of their arrival – as demonstrated, for instance, by the domestication of television with the frameworks which had been established by radio broadcasting. Consideration of new media technologies therefore needs to pay considerable attention to the prevailing media contexts, and also to the important ways in which traditional media are being transformed by new media technologies. What is missed by both enthusiasts' and sceptics' arguments and the polarization of the debate is that in many ways the greatest significance of the new communication technologies lies in their impact on existing media, in their displacement effects. It seems quite plausible that, unlike the apocalyptic visions of the techno-enthusiasts, the home computer and the Internet will take their place beside the television and the newspaper as additional rather than replacement media. Elisabeth Murdoch, Managing Director of Sky Networks, for instance, recently argued that there are limits to the much-vaunted notions of convergence between television and computer screens. For the foreseeable future, she argues, television will be the dominant medium for 'lean-back' leisure in contrast with the home computer's 'lean-forward' interaction, refuting notions of convergence. 'Both pieces of technology will happily sit together in the home of the future' (quoted by Horsman, 1998).

Thus, in analysing continuities and transformation, it is important to distinguish between 'old media in new times' and 'new media', to grasp the complex relations between residual, dominant and emergent cultural forms, and to avoid an exclusive focus on the 'new' media transformations (Livingstone, 1998). The history of the press, film, radio and television demonstrates that each has been transformed continuously, with new technologies, organizations, practices and forms. Although these media embody and reflect deep continuities, they are also experiencing radical transformations.

Crucial to these transformations have been new technologies. While the relationships between technologies and culture are complex, Raymond Williams (Chapter 3) argues that the trajectory of the development of a technology is profoundly social. He shows how television was a technology *looking for a use*, and one developed without prior conceptions as to how it would be used, with little previous thought of programming. Williams rejects the dominant paradigm of technological determinism, whereby technology is developed in an asocial vacuum and then arrives in society to have 'effects'. Television, he suggests, emerged as a result of deep and long-running processes of 'mobile privatization', the break-up of rural communities and the shift to the cities in the era of industrialization, and the consequent demand for privatized leisure. At the same time as pointing to 'the social shaping of technology', it is important, however, not to lose sight of the materiality of technologies: as well as offering possibilities, they are constraining in that, designed for particular purposes, there are limits to the possible uses to which they can be put.

While much of the rhetoric and debate about contemporary media transformations focuses on the assessment of new technologies of the 'communications revolution', quite as important are three other issues. First are ownership patterns, which are developing fast with increasing concentration and globalization. In this process there is a growing overlap between and across new and old media corporations and other entertainment and information sectors.

Second are the new regimes of regulation which are developing. Systems of regulation which were developed principally in the context of national systems are challenged not just by the new technologies which by-pass and over-ride national boundaries, but also by processes of globalization and the liberalization of markets, the deregulation of the media. Rather than being static, state regulation has been subject to profound changes in late modernity.

Third are consumers. Whatever the aspirations of global media corporations, consumer electronics industries and national regulatory agencies, consumer sovereignty and demand has been crucial in shaping the contemporary media landscapes. Digital television, satellite broadcasting and mobile telephony are the focus of huge and concerted marketing campaigns. But the future of broadcasting and communication lies very much in the hands and pockets of consumers. Today, the cost of using new media requires far higher personal capital investment than earlier media, calling into doubt the optimistic forecasts of major industry players. Ultimately, the shape and form of a society's communications media will be determined by how the new technologies are taken up and incorporated into the everyday practices and routines of domestic and other settings. Historical evidence indicates that domestic consumption has been a critical area in which the actual trajectory of new communication technologies has often been unanticipated, with profound consequences for their direction and shape.

This book comprises a selection of chapters which offer conceptual analyses and empirical accounts of key continuities and transformations in media at the end of the twentieth century. Between them they explore and illustrate some key themes, issues and concepts for dissecting and understanding contemporary media, addressing the economic, social and cultural conditions and processes which are implicated in the inter-related moments of the production, circulation and consumption of media forms and messages. They provide a framework for making sense of the contemporary media landscape and its continuities and transformations.

References

Appadurai, Arjun (1990) 'Disjuncture and difference in the global cultural economy', *Theory, Culture and Society*, 7: 295–310.

Ascott, Roy (1998) 'Art, technology and consciousness: the technoetic paradigm', *Convergence*, 4 (3): 110–13.

Golding, Peter (1998a) 'Worldwide wedge: divisions and contradictions in the global information infrastructure', in Daya Kishan Thussu (ed.), *Electronic Empires: Global Media and Local Resistance*. London: Arnold.

Golding, Peter (1998b) 'New technologies and old problems', in Kees Brants, Joke Hermes and Lisbet van Zoonen (eds), *The Media in Question: Popular Cultures and Public Interests*. London: Sage.

Horsman, Mathew. (1998) 'Her big play', *Media Guardian*, 31 August, pp. 2–3.

Livingstone, Sonia (1998) 'Mediated childhoods: a comparative approach to young people's changing media environment in Europe', *European Journal of Communication*, 13 (4): 435–56.

Plant, Sadie (1996) 'On the matrix: cyberfeminist simulations', in Rob Shields (ed.), *Cultures of Internet: Virtual Spaces, Real Histories, Living Bodies*. London: Sage.

Poster, Mark (1995) *The Second Media Age*. Cambridge: Polity Press.

Webster, Frank and Robins, Kevin (1986) *Information Technology: a Luddite Analysis*. Norwood, NJ: Ablex.

Mass communication and the modern world

Introduction

This first part explores the importance of systems of mass communication and of the links between the development of mass communication technologies and modern society. In Chapter 1, John Thompson discusses the centrality of the media in historical processes of social and cultural transformation. He compares and contrasts pre-industrial cultures and forms of communication with industrial societies and systems of mass communication, exploring the centrality of communications to modernity and the 'transformed' nature of modern, mediated cultures and identities. In particular, he argues that a number of important consequences resulted from mass communication.

Any study of the mass media, implicitly or otherwise, is concerned with their role in contemporary society (Williams, 1962; McQuail, 1994). Crucial to this role is their contribution to the public interest. Any media transformation can be assessed in terms of its contribution to processes of democratization – in providing a forum for informing citizens, for public debate and for the expression of a multiplicity of voices and perspectives; or, on the other hand, in serving the interests of the state for control or corporate capital for profit. For Graham Murdock this is the key question to ask of any communications medium. In Chapter 2, in relation to both early broadcasting and developments in contemporary media, he examines the relationship of the communications environment to communicative and cultural rights. In doing so he raises fundamental questions about the significance of the media in democratic societies and the purposes of regulation in the context of commercial and corporate power and the often opposing values and ideals of national cultures. Communicative rights, he argues, should be understood as a prerequisite of modern citizenship: to make informed judgements in the exercise of choice as citizens requires access to the fullest possible range of information and the broadest spectrum of views, analysis and interpretation. Information and cultural rights require open discursive spaces, independent of the state and insulated from commercial interests. Broadcasting provided this arena in the post-war period, but with privatization and deregulation in the 1980s the power and influence of private corporations have been enhanced. Whereas notions of citizenship were embedded in earlier broadcasting eras and countered commercial forces, more recently there has been a shift in the conception of media users from citizens to consumers.

How is one to understand the role and impact of technologies, so crucial to contemporary transformations? Routinely, assumptions and predictions are made about the inevitability of some new technological development (digital at the moment of writing) and of the dramatic impact it will have on existing social formations and relations. In Chapter 3, Raymond Williams examines the relationship between technology and culture, developing a critique of the orthodoxy of technological determinism. Outlining a more radical approach, he raises the question of the intent which lies behind all technical research and development, debunking popular notions that technology is simply the 'appliance of science', the result of the work of isolated, heroic inventors. On the contrary, all new technologies are the result of cultural priorities. He explains that there was nothing implicit or fixed in television technology to make it inevitable that it should be transmitted to individual households; and that state regulation of broadcasting is essentially a social and political rather than a technical necessity.

Although the telephone is commonly thought of as a medium for one-to-one communication, in its earliest days it was employed as a medium for broadcasting – the only instrument which transmitted live voices across space in the nineteenth century, bar the earliest experiments with radio at the very end of the century. In Chapter 4, Carolyn Marvin explores the history and early use of the telephone for broadcasting music, theatre, politics, sport and church services. She shows how, at this historical conjuncture (1880–1900), before the stabilization of the artefact, the boundaries between competing technologies were blurred. Like Raymond

Williams's account of television, she shows how the eventual trajectory of the telephone was far from inevitable. To this end she discusses a diversity of early uses of the telephone – some of them quite extraordinary. She demonstrates the transformation of the telephone by consumers as it was brought into the home, as well as the constraints or impact of technical, regulatory and market factors. Her account shows clearly how the technological trajectory was shaped, constrained and directed by pre-existing needs and structures. As late as 1921, the American Bell Corporation considered that broadcasting would be confined to the transmission of important occasions, such as presidential inaugurations, to town halls equipped with loudspeakers. Broadcasting, Marvin explains, was seen as a vulgar activity.

While in its early years the telephone was used for broadcasting, radio was used for point-to-point communication, again showing us that there is nothing necessarily immanent in the technology to determine how it will be used, institutionalized or domesticated. Broadcasting is seen by many as one of the key innovations in twentieth-century communication and in its consequences one of the defining characteristics of modernity. Popular understandings of the origins of radio, like television, tend to conform to one-dimensional technological determinist notions of 'invention' and inevitable 'effects'. In Chapter 5, Patrice Flichy examines the moment of arrival of another 'new' media technology, radio. In this case study, he examines the dynamics – scientific, technological, economic, regulatory and market – which were involved in the social shaping of what is now understood as radio broadcasting. He argues that one cannot separate scientific discovery from technological development, but that the two proceeded hand in hand. Further, discovering social uses for the technology was part and parcel – and a key impetus for – its technical development. Flichy's account weaves together seamlessly the various actors, groups, artefacts and knowledges involved in the development of radio. Like accounts of the television and telephone, it explains the emergence and stabilization of a media technology. Comparable processes are beginning to be identified today in relation to digital multimedia technologies.

References

McQuail, Denis (1994) *Mass Communication Theory: an Introduction*. London: Sage.
Williams, Raymond (1962) *Communications*. London: Penguin.

The media and modernity **John Thompson**

Some characteristics of 'mass communication'

When we use the term 'communication media' we often think of a specific set of institutions and products: we think of books, newspapers, television and radio programmes, films, tapes, compact discs and so on. That is, we think of a set of institutions and products which are commonly subsumed under the label 'mass communication'. But what is 'mass communication'? Is this a term we can give a clear and coherent sense?

It has often been noted that 'mass communication' is an infelicitous phrase. The term 'mass' is especially misleading. It conjures up the image of a vast audience comprising many thousands, even millions of individuals. This may be an accurate image in the case of some media products, such as the most popular modern-day newspapers, films and television programmes; but it is hardly an accurate representation of the circumstance of most media products, past or present. During the early development of the periodical press, and in some sectors of the media industries today (for instance, some book and magazine publishers), the audiences were and remain relatively small and specialized. So if the term 'mass' is to be used, it should not be construed in narrowly quantitative terms. The important point about mass communication is not that a given number of individuals (or a specifiable proportion of the population) receives the products, but rather that the products are available in principle to a plurality of recipients.

There is another respect in which the expression 'mass' may be misleading. It suggests that the recipients of media products constitute a vast sea of passive, undifferentiated individuals. This is an image associated with some earlier critiques of 'mass culture' and 'mass society', critiques which generally assumed that the development of mass communication has

This chapter is taken from chapters 1 and 2 of John Thompson's *The Media and Modernity* (Cambridge, Polity Press, 1995), pp. 23–37 and 75–80.

had a largely negative impact on modern social life, creating a kind of bland and homogeneous culture which entertains individuals without challenging them, which absorbs their attention without engaging their critical faculties, which provides instant gratification without questioning the grounds on which that gratification is based. This traditional line of cultural criticism is not without interest; it has raised some important issues which still deserve to be addressed today, albeit in a rather different fashion. But this critical perspective is also imbued with a set of assumptions which are untenable, and which can only hinder an understanding of the media and their impact in the modern world. We must abandon the assumption that the recipients of media products are passive onlookers whose senses have been permanently dulled by the continuous reception of similar messages. We must also abandon the assumption that the process of reception itself is an unproblematic, uncritical process through which products are absorbed by individuals, like a sponge absorbing water. Assumptions of this kind have little to do with the actual character of reception activities and with the complex ways in which media products are taken up by individuals, interpreted by them and incorporated into their lives.

If the term 'mass' may be misleading in certain respects, the term 'communication' may be as well, since the kinds of communication generally involved in mass communication are quite different from those involved in ordinary conversation. In the communicative exchanges which take place in face-to-face interaction, the flow of communication is generally two-way: one person speaks, another replies, and so on. In other words, the communicative exchanges of face-to-face interaction are fundamentally dialogical. With most forms of mass communication, by contrast, the flow of communication is overwhelmingly one-way. Messages are produced by one set of individuals and transmitted to others who are typically situated in settings that are spatially and temporally remote from the original context of production. Hence the recipients of media messages are not so much partners in a reciprocal process of communicative exchange but rather participants in a structured process of symbolic transmission. Hence I shall generally speak of the 'transmission' or 'diffusion' of media messages rather than of 'communication' as such. Yet even in the structured circumstances of mass communication, recipients do have some capacity to intervene in and contribute to the course and content of the communicative process. They can, for instance, write letters to the editor, phone television companies and express their views, or simply refuse to purchase or receive the products concerned. Hence, while the communicative process is fundamentally asymmetrical, it is not entirely monological or one-way.

There is a further reason why the term 'mass communication' may seem somewhat inappropriate today. We generally associate this term with certain kinds of media transmission – for example, with the diffusion of mass-circulation newspapers, with radio and television broadcasting, and so on. Yet today we seem to be witnessing changes of a fundamental kind in the nature of mediated communication. The shift from analog to digital systems of information codification, combined with the development of new systems of transmission (including high-powered satellites and high-capacity cables), are creating a new technical scenario in which information and communication can be handled in more flexible ways. [. . .] [I]f the term 'mass communication' is misleading as a description of the more traditional forms of media transmission, then it seems particularly ill-suited to the new kinds of information and communication network which are becoming increasingly common today.

In view of these considerations, the term 'mass communication' should be used with a good deal of circumspection. I shall generally use other terms – such as 'mediated communication' or, more simply, 'the media' – which are less laden with misleading assumptions. Nevertheless, we should not let these conceptual difficulties obscure the fact that, through a series of historical developments which can be documented quite precisely, a new range of communicative phenomena emerged. In so far as I use the term 'mass communication', I shall use it to refer to this inter-related set of historical developments and communicative phenomena. What we now describe rather loosely as 'mass communication' is a range of phenomena that emerged historically through the development of institutions seeking to exploit new opportunities for gathering and recording information, for producing and reproducing symbolic forms, and for transmitting information and symbolic content to a plurality of recipients in return for some kind of financial remuneration.

Let me be more precise: I shall use the term 'mass communication' to refer to *the institutionalized production and generalized diffusion of symbolic goods via the fixation and transmission of information or symbolic content*. I shall unpack this account by elaborating on five characteristics: the technical and institutional means of production and diffusion; the commodification of symbolic forms; the structured break between production and reception; the extended availability of media products in time and space; and the public circulation of mediated symbolic forms. Not all of these characteristics are unique to what we would call 'mass communication'. But together they highlight a set of features which are typical and important aspects of the kind of communicative phenomena to which we have come to refer with this term.

The first characteristic of mass communication is that it involves a certain technical and institutional means of production and diffusion. It is this characteristic that has received most attention in the specialist literature on the media. For it is clear that the development of the media, from early forms of printing to the most recent developments in the field of telecommunications, has been based on a series of technical innovations which were capable of being exploited commercially. It is also clear that the exploitation of these innovations is a process that has taken place within a range of institutions and institutional frameworks, and that these institutions continue to shape the ways in which the media operate today. In other words, the development of mass communication is inseparable from the development of the *media industries* – that is, the array of organizations which, from the late Middle Ages to the present day, have been concerned with the commercial exploitation of technical innovations that enabled symbolic forms to be produced and diffused in a generalized fashion. [. . .]

The fact that mass communication typically involves the commercial exploitation of technical innovations is made explicit by the second characteristic – what I have called the commodification of symbolic forms. [. . .] I regard commodification as a particular type of 'valorization', that is, as one of the ways in which objects can be ascribed a certain value. Symbolic forms can be subjected to two principal types of valorization.[1] 'Symbolic valorization' is the process through which symbolic forms are ascribed 'symbolic value'. This is the value that objects have by virtue of the ways in which, and the extent to which, they are esteemed by individuals – that is, praised or denounced, cherished or despised by them. 'Economic valorization' is the process through which symbolic forms are ascribed 'economic value', a value for which they can be exchanged in a market. By virtue of economic valorization, symbolic forms are constituted as *commodities*: they become objects which can be bought and sold in a market for a price. I shall refer to commodified symbolic forms as 'symbolic goods'.

Mass communication typically involves the commodification of symbolic forms in the sense that the objects produced by media institutions are symbolic forms subjected, in one way or another, to the process of economic valorization. The modes of valorizing symbolic forms vary greatly, depending on the technical media and the institutional frameworks within which they are deployed. The commodification of some printed materials, such as books and pamphlets, relies largely on the capacity to produce and sell multiple copies of the work. Other printed materials (newspapers, for instance) combine this mode of valorization with other modes, such as the capacity to sell advertising space. In the case of radio and television broadcasting, the sale of air-time to advertisers has played an important role in some national contexts as a means of economic valorization. In other national contexts the recipients of radio and television programmes have been charged directly (through a licence fee) or indirectly (through taxation) for the right to receive broadcast material. Recent technological developments associated with cable and satellite transmission have created new opportunities for economic valorization, such as the payment of subscription fees or the use of credit cards which enable viewers to decode scrambled messages.

Of course, the commodification of symbolic forms is not unique to mass communication. There are other kinds of symbolic forms, such as paintings and other works of art, which are routinely subjected to the process of economic valorization. The development of a market for works of art – the art galleries, auction houses, etc. – can be seen as the development of a set of institutions which govern the economic valorization of works of art, and within which these works can be bought and sold as commodities. The more symbolic value has been ascribed to these works and their producers, that is, the more they are regarded as 'great works' and 'great artists', the greater the price, generally speaking, for which the works change hands in the art market. So the media industries are not the only institutions concerned with the economic valorization of symbolic forms. But in the modern world they are certainly among the most important of these institutions, and those most likely to impinge on the day-to-day lives of most individuals.

The third characteristic of mass communication is that it institutes a structured break between the production of symbolic forms and their reception. In all types of mass communication, the context of production is generally separate from the context or contexts of reception. Symbolic goods are produced in one context or set of contexts (namely, the institutions which form the media industries) and transmitted to recipients located in contexts which are distant and diverse (such as the varied settings of domestic households). Moreover, unlike many other cases of communication involving a separation of contexts, in the case of mass communication the flow of messages is, as I noted earlier, predominantly one-way. The context of production is not also (or not to the same extent) a context of reception, nor are the contexts of reception also (or to the same extent) contexts of production. Hence the flow of messages is a *structured* flow in which the capacity of recipients to intervene in or contribute to the process of production is strictly circumscribed.

This characteristic of mass communication has important implications for processes of production and reception. On the side of production, it means that the personnel involved in producing and transmitting media messages are generally deprived of the direct and continuous forms of feedback characteristic of face-to-face interaction. Hence the processes of production and transmission are characterized by a distinctive kind of *indeterminacy*, since these processes take place in the absence of cues provided by recipients. (Compare the difference between a speech delivered to an assembled audience, which can express approval or disapproval by laughing, clapping or remaining silent, and a speech delivered to a television camera.) Of course, media personnel have developed a variety of techniques to cope with this indeterminacy, from the use of well-tried formulae which have a predictable audience appeal (such as television series and film sequels) to market research and the regular monitoring of audience size and response.[2]

On the side of reception, the structured break implies that the recipients of mediated messages are, so to speak, left to their own devices. Recipients can make of a message more or less what they will, and the producer is not there to elaborate or to correct possible misunderstanding. It also implies that recipients are in a fundamentally unequal position with regard to the communicative process. They are, by the very nature of mass communication, unequal partners in the process of symbolic exchange. Compared with the individuals involved in the processes of production and transmission, the recipients of mediated messages have relatively little power to determine the topic and content of communication. But this does not imply that they are powerless, nor does it imply that they are simply the passive spectators of a show over which they have little or no control.

A fourth characteristic of mass communication is that it extends the availability of symbolic forms in space and time. This characteristic is closely connected to the previous one: since the media institute a separation between contexts of production and contexts of reception, it follows that mediated messages are available in contexts that are remote from the contexts in which they were originally produced. They can be, and generally are, received by individuals who are far removed in space, and perhaps also in time, from the individuals who produced them. The extended availability of mediated messages is a feature which has far reaching consequences [. . .]. Once again, the extended availability of symbolic forms is not unique to mass communication. All symbolic forms, simply by virtue of being exchanged between individuals who do not occupy identical positions in space and time, involve some degree of space–time distanciation. But with the development of institutions oriented towards the large-scale production and generalized diffusion of symbolic goods, the extended availability of symbolic forms becomes a much more significant and pervasive social phenomenon. Information and symbolic content are made available to more individuals across larger expanses of space and at greater speeds. The extended availability of symbolic forms becomes both more pronounced and more routine, in the sense that it becomes increasingly taken for granted as a routine feature of social life.

This brings us to a fifth characteristic of mass communication: it involves the public circulation of symbolic forms. The products of the media industries are available in principle to a plurality of recipients. They are produced in multiple copies or transmitted to a multiplicity of receivers in such a way that they are available in principle to anyone who has the technical means, abilities and resources to acquire them. In this respect, mass communication differs from forms of communication – such as telephone conversations, teleconferencing, or private video recordings of various kinds – which employ the same technical media of fixation and transmission but which are oriented towards a single or highly restricted range of recipients. The line to be drawn here is not clear-cut, and the distinction may be increasingly blurred in the coming decades by the deployment of new communication technologies which allow for more personalized services. Nevertheless, it is characteristic of mass communication as it has developed hitherto that its products are available in principle to a plurality of recipients – even if in fact, for a variety of reasons, these products may circulate among a relatively small and restricted sector of the population.

The availability of the products of mass communication has important implications for the ways in which we think about the distinction between the public and private domains. The fact that media products are available in principle to a plurality of recipients means that they have an intrinsically *public* character, in the sense that they are 'open' or 'available to the public'. The content of media messages is thereby rendered public, that is, made visible and observable to a multiplicity of individuals who may be, and typically are, scattered across diverse and dispersed contexts. [. . .]

The reordering of space and time

We noted earlier how the use of technical media of communication can alter the spatial and temporal dimensions of social life. By enabling individuals to communicate across extended stretches of space and time, the use of technical media enables individuals to transcend the spatial and temporal boundaries characteristic of face-to-face interaction. At the same time, it enables individuals to reorder the spatial and temporal features of social organization, and to use these reordered features as a means of pursuing their objectives.

All technical media have a bearing on the spatial and temporal aspects of social life, but the development of telecommunication technology in the second half of the nineteenth century was particularly significant in this regard. Prior to the advent of telecommunication, the extension of availability of symbolic forms in space generally required their physical transportation: with a few notable exceptions (for instance, semaphore), significant spatial distanciation could be achieved only by transporting symbolic forms from one place to another. But with the development of early forms of telecommunication, such as the telegraph and telephone, significant spatial distanciation could be achieved without physically transporting symbolic forms, and hence without incurring the temporal delays involved in transportation. The advent of telecommunication thus resulted in *the uncoupling of space and time*, in the sense that spatial distanciation no longer required temporal distanciation. Information and symbolic content could be transmitted over vast distances with relatively little delay; once the transmission wires had been installed, messages could be relayed in little more than the time required to encode and decode the information. Spatial distanciation was greatly enhanced, while temporal delays were virtually eliminated.

The uncoupling of space and time prepared the way for another transformation, closely linked to the development of telecommunication: *the discovery of despatialized simultaneity*.[3] In earlier historical periods the experience of simultaneity – that is, of events occurring 'at the same time' – presupposed a specific locale in which the simultaneous events could be experienced by the individual. Simultaneity presupposed locality; 'the same time' presupposed 'the same place'. But with the uncoupling of space and time brought about by telecommunication, the experience of simultaneity was detached from the spatial condition of common locality. It became possible to experience events as simultaneous despite the fact that they occurred in locales that were spatially remote. In contrast to the concreteness of the here and now, there emerged a sense of 'now' which was no longer bound to a particular locale. Simultaneity was extended in space and became ultimately global in scope.

The transformations of space and time brought about in part by the development of new communication technologies, and in part by the development of quicker means of transport, gave rise to increasingly acute problems of space–time coordination, problems that were eventually resolved through a series of conventions on the standardization of world time.[4] Until the mid-nineteenth century, each city, town or village had its own standard of time; there was a plurality of local times which were not coordinated with one another. But with the development of mail-coach services in the late eighteenth century and the construction of the railways in the early nineteenth, there was growing pressure for the standardization of time reckoning on a supralocal level. The introduction of the standardized railway timetable, based on Greenwich Mean Time, gradually led to the adoption of GMT as the uniform standard of time throughout Britain. The task of standardizing time reckoning on a larger territorial scale gave rise to new problems which were resolved through the introduction of standard time zones. Time zones were initially established on the North American continent in the 1870s and early 1880s, and in 1884 an International Meridian Conference was convened in Washington, DC, for the purpose of establishing a global system for the standardization of time. The world was divided into 24 one-hour time zones and an international date line was established. The date line was agreed to be the 180th meridian at the same distance east and west of Greenwich; travellers crossing it eastwards gain a day, while those crossing it westwards lose a day. Thenceforth, the standardized system of world time provided a framework for the coordination of local times and for the organization of networks of communication and transport.

The development of new media of communication and new means of transport also affected the ways in which individuals *experienced* the spatial and temporal characteristics of social life. The standardization of world time was accompanied by a growing interest in the personal experience of time and space, of speed and simultaneity, and of the uncoupling of space and time. This interest found expression in the art and literature of the late nineteenth and early twentieth centuries, from Proust and Baudelaire to James Joyce, from cubism and futurism to surrealism. The literary and artistic impact of these developments has been explored perceptively by Stephen Kern, Marshall Berman and others.[5] Here I wish to consider in a more general fashion some of the ways in which the development of communication media has affected the sense of space and time of ordinary individuals.

Prior to the development of the media industries, most people's sense of the past and of distant places was shaped primarily through the symbolic content exchanged in face-to-face interaction. The telling of stories played a central role in forming people's sense of the past and of the world beyond their immediate locales. For most people the sense of the past and the sense of distant places, as well as the sense of the spatially delimited and historically continuous communities to which they belonged, were constituted primarily by oral traditions that were produced and handed down in the social contexts of everyday life. But the increasing availability of mediated symbolic forms has gradually altered the ways in which most people acquire a sense of the past and of the world beyond their immediate milieu. The role of oral traditions was not eliminated, but these traditions were supplemented, and to some extent reconstituted, by the diffusion of media products.

The development of communication media has thus created what we may describe as a 'mediated historicity': our sense of the past, and our sense of the ways in which the past impinges on us today, become increasingly dependent on an ever expanding reservoir of mediated symbolic forms. Most individuals in Western societies today have derived their sense of the major events of the past, and even the major events of the twentieth century (the two world wars, the Russian revolution, the Holocaust, etc.), primarily from books, newspapers, films and television programmes. As events recede further and further into the past, it becomes less and less likely that individuals will derive their understanding of these events from personal experience, or from the personal experience of others whose accounts are handed down to them through face-to-face interaction. Oral tradition and face-to-face interaction continue to play important roles in shaping our sense of the past, but they operate increasingly in conjunction with a process of understanding which draws its symbolic content from the products of the media industries.

If the media have altered our sense of the past, they have also created what we could call a 'mediated worldliness': our sense of the world which lies beyond the sphere of our personal experience, and our sense of our place within this world, are increasingly shaped by mediated symbolic forms. The diffusion of media products enables us in a certain sense to experience events, observe others and, in general, learn about a world that extends beyond the sphere of our day-to-day encounters. The spatial horizons of our understanding are thereby greatly expanded, for they are no longer restricted by the need to be physically present at the places where the observed events, etc., occur. So profound is the extent to which our sense of the world is shaped by media products today that, when we travel to distant parts of the world as a visitor or tourist, our lived experience is often preceded by a set of images and expectations acquired through extended exposure to media products. Even in those cases where our experience of distant places does not concur with our expectations, the feeling of novelty or surprise often attests to the fact that our lived experience is preceded by a set of preconceptions derived, at least to some extent, from the words and images conveyed by the media.

By altering their sense of place and of the past, the development of communication media also has some bearing on individuals' sense of belonging – that is, on their sense of the groups and communities to which they feel they belong. The sense of belonging derives, to some extent, from a feeling of sharing a common history and a common locale, a common trajectory in time and space. But as our sense of the past becomes increasingly dependent on mediated symbolic forms, and as our sense of the world and our place within it becomes increasingly nourished by media products, so too our sense of the groups and communities with which we share a common path through time and space, a common origin and a common fate, is altered: we feel ourselves to belong to groups and communities which are constituted in part through the media. [. . .]

So far we have been considering some of the ways in which the development of communication media has altered individuals' sense of the past and of the world beyond their immediate locales. But let us now consider a somewhat different issue. Our sense of space and time is closely linked to our sense of *distance*, of what is near and what is far away; and our sense of distance is shaped profoundly by the means at our disposal to move through space and time. The means of transport are clearly crucial in this regard. For rural peasants in earlier centuries, London was much more distant than it is for country dwellers in Britain today. In the seventeenth century, when roads were poor and the average speed of horse-drawn carriages in provincial regions was probably around 30 miles a day, a journey to London from a county like Norfolk would have taken several days,[6] today it can be done in a couple of hours. The means of communication also play a crucial role in shaping our sense of distance. When communication was dependent on the physical transportation of messages, then the sense of distance was dependent on the time taken to travel between the origin and destination. As the speed of transportation-communication increased, the distance seemed to diminish. But with the uncoupling of space and time brought about by telecommunication, the sense of distance was gradually prised apart from its exclusive dependence on travel time. From then on, the sense of distance was dependent on two variables – travel time and speed of communication – which did not necessarily coincide. The world was shrinking in both dimensions, but more quickly in one than the other.

It is this transformation in the sense of distance that underlies what has been aptly described as 'space–time compression'.[7] With the development of new means of transportation and communication, coupled with the ever more intensive and extensive expansion of a capitalist economy oriented towards the rapid turnover of capital and goods, the significance of spatial barriers has declined and the pace of social life has speeded up. Previously remote parts of the world are drawn into global networks of interdependency. Travel time is steadily reduced and, with the development of telecommunication, the speed of communication becomes virtually instantaneous. The world seems like a smaller place: no longer a vast expanse of unchartered territories but a globe thoroughly explored, carefully mapped out and vulnerable to the meddlings of human beings.

We have yet to gain a clear understanding of the impact of these transformations on the ways in which individuals experience the flow of history and their place within it. In earlier forms of society, when most individuals lived on the land and derived their subsistence from it, the experience of the flow of time was closely connected to the natural rhythms of the seasons and to the cycles of birth and death. As individuals were increasingly drawn into an urban, factory-based system of employment, the experience of the flow of time became increasingly linked to the time-keeping mechanisms required for the synchronization of labour and the organization of the working week.[8] As time was disciplined for the purposes of increasing commodity production, there was a certain trade-off: sacrifices made in the present were exchanged for the promise of a better future. The notion of progress, elaborated in Enlightenment philosophies of history and in evolutionary social theories, was experienced in day-to-day life as the gap between past and present experience, on the one hand, and the continuously shifting horizon of expectation associated with the future, on the other.[9]

This way of experiencing the flow of time may be changing today. As the pace of life speeds up, the future no longer stretches out ahead of us like a promised land. The continuously shifting horizon of expectation begins to collapse, as it runs up against a future that repeatedly falls short of past and present expectations. It becomes more and more difficult to hold on to a linear conception of history as progress. The idea of progress is a way of colonizing the future, a way of subsuming the future to our present plans and expectations. But as the shortcomings of this strategy become clearer day by day, as the future repeatedly confounds our plans and expectations, the idea of progress begins to lose its hold on us.

It is too early to say whether this shift will continue and, if so, what its consequences will be. There can be no doubt that, thanks in part to the development of new forms of communication and transportation, our ways of experiencing space and time have changed in a quite profound manner. [. . .] But how far the developments discussed here have begun to reshape our experience of the flow of history and our place within it, our sense of the future and our orientation towards it: these are questions that I shall, for the most part, leave open. [. . .]

The growth of the media industries: an overview

I want to conclude [. . .] by highlighting some of the central trends in the development of the media industries since the early nineteenth century. I shall highlight three trends: (1) the transformation of media institutions into large-scale commercial concerns; (2) the globalization of communication; and (3) the development of electronically mediated forms of communication. My discussion of these trends will be brief. Some of the developments have been extensively documented elsewhere in the literature [. . .].

(1) The transformation of media institutions into large-scale commercial concerns is a process that began in the early nineteenth century. Of course, the commercialization of media products was not a new phenomenon; the early presses [. . .] were primarily commercial organizations oriented towards the commodification of symbolic forms. But in the course of the nineteenth century the scale of commercialization increased significantly. This was due partly to a series of technical innovations in the printing industry, and partly to a gradual transformation in the financial basis of the media industries and their methods of economic valorization. Technical innovations, such as the development of Koenig's steam press and, subsequently, the rotary printing press, greatly increased the reproductive capacity of the printing industry. They enabled the production of newspapers and other printed materials to be subjected to a set of processes – including the use of power machinery, the ramified division of labour within a factory system, etc. – which were revolutionizing other spheres of commodity

production. At the same time, many Western societies experienced substantial growth of urban populations and, during the second half of the nineteenth century, significant increases in rates of literacy, so that there was a steadily expanding market for printed materials.

As the printing industry became increasingly industrialized and the market expanded, the financial basis of the press began to change. Whereas the newspapers of the seventeenth and eighteenth centuries had been aimed primarily at a restricted, relatively well-off and well-educated sector of the population, the newspaper industry of the nineteenth and twentieth centuries became increasingly oriented towards a broader public. Technological developments and the abolition of taxes enabled prices to be reduced, and many newspapers adopted a lighter and livelier style of journalism, as well as a more vivid style of presentation, in order to attract a wider readership.[10] As the readership expanded, commercial advertising assumed an increasingly important role in the financial organization of the industry; newspapers became a vital medium for the sale of other goods and services, and their capacity to secure advertising revenue was directly linked to the size and profile of their readership. Newspapers – and to some extent other sectors of the press – increasingly became large-scale commercial ventures which required relatively large quantities of capital in order to be initiated and sustained in the face of increasingly intense competition. The traditional proprietor-publisher who owned one or two newspapers as a family concern gradually gave way to the development of large-scale, multi-newspaper and multimedia organizations.

The social and economic history of the media industries in the twentieth century is well documented and there is no need to describe it in detail here.[11] Processes of growth and consolidation have led to the increasing concentration of resources in many sectors of the industry, with fewer organizations commanding larger shares of the market. The degree of concentration is particularly striking in the newspaper industry (although by no means unique to it); by the early 1990s in Britain, for instance, four large media groups controlled around 92 per cent of the circulation of national daily newspapers and around 89 per cent of the circulation of Sunday papers.[12] Moreover, the processes of growth and consolidation are increasingly assuming a multimedia character as large corporations acquire extensive interests in various sectors of the media industries, from local and national newspapers to terrestrial and satellite television, from book and magazine publishing to film production and distribution. Faced with the economic power of large corporations, many smaller media organizations have been squeezed out of existence or forced into defensive mergers. But the growing concentration of resources has not eliminated all smaller organizations or stifled the development of new enterprises capable of exploiting technological innovations, catering for specialist markets and providing a range of information- and communication-related services. In many sectors of the media industries today, the dominance of large corporations coexists with a diverse array of smaller production and service organizations, many of which are interconnected through subcontracting and out-sourcing arrangements.[13]

Partly through mergers, takeovers and other forms of diversification, large-scale communication conglomerates have emerged and assumed an increasingly important role in the media domain. Communication conglomerates are transnational, multimedia organizations which have interests in a variety of industries concerned with information and communication. Diversification on a global scale enables large corporations to expand in ways that avoid the restrictions on ownership which apply in many national contexts; it also enables corporations to benefit from certain kinds of cross-subsidization. Today the major communication conglomerates – such as Time Warner, the Bertelsmann group, Rupert Murdoch's News Corporation, Silvio Berlusconi's Fininvest – have become key players in the media industries. These huge concentrations of economic and symbolic power provide institutional bases for the production of information and symbolic content and its circulation on a global scale.

(2) The globalization of communication is a process whose origins can be traced back to the mid-nineteenth century. In earlier centuries, printed materials were commonly transported over large distances and across the boundaries of states, kingdoms and principalities. But in the course of the nineteenth century the international flow of information and communication assumed a much more extensive and organized form. The development of international news agencies based in the major commercial cities of Europe, together with the expansion of communication networks linking the peripheral regions of empires with their European centres, established the beginnings of a global system of communication and information processing which has become increasingly ramified and complex. [. . .]

(3) The uses of electrical energy for the purposes of communication were among the great discoveries of the nineteenth century. The key technical innovations are well known.[14] The first experiments with electromagnetic telegraphy were carried out in the 1830s in the United States, England and Germany, and the first viable telegraph systems were established in the 1840s. Electromagnetic transmission was successfully adapted for the purposes of conveying speech in the 1870s, paving the way for the development of telephone systems on a commercial scale. During the last decade of the nineteenth century Marconi and others began experimenting with the transmission of signals via electromagnetic waves, thereby dispensing with the need for conduction wires. In 1898 Marconi successfully transmitted signals across 23 km of sea, and in 1899 he transmitted signals across the English Channel. The technology for transmitting speech via electromagnetic waves was developed during the first decade of the twentieth century by Fessenden and others. Following the First World War, Westinghouse in the United States and Marconi in England began experimenting with broadcasting – that is, the transmission of messages via electromagnetic waves to an indeterminate and potentially vast audience. The subsequent development of broadcasting systems – radio from the 1920s on, television from the late 1940s on – rapid and pervasive.

The development and exploitation of these various technologies were interwoven in complex ways with economic, political and coercive power. Commercial, political and military interests played a vital role in the expansion of cable networks during the second half of the nineteenth century [. . .]. Marconi's early experiments in wireless telegraphy were supported by the British Post Office, the Admiralty and the War Office, and his first commercial contracts were with the British navy. Recognizing the commercial potential and strategic significance of radio, the British, German and American governments and military establishments played an active role in its development.[15] The subsequent evolution of broadcasting systems took place within institutional frameworks which varied greatly from one national context to another and which generally represented some kind of settlement – subject to continuous review and renegotiation – between the commercial interests of the media industries, on the one hand, and the political concern to regulate, cultivate and control the new media, on the other.

The media environment bequeathed to us by the developments of the late nineteenth and early twentieth centuries is today very much in flux. Partly this is a result of the intensification of processes that were set in motion more than a century ago: the growth of communication conglomerates has continued and their predatory activities, in many contexts facilitated by the relaxation of government controls, have reached feverish pitch; and the processes of globalization have deepened, as they continue to draw far-flung parts of the globe into ever tighter and more complex webs of interdependency. But there are also new factors at work. Among these are the development of new forms of information processing based on digital systems of codification, and the gradual convergence of information and communication technology on a common digital system of transmission, processing and storage.[16] These developments are creating a new technical scenario in which information and symbolic content can be converted rapidly and with relative ease into different forms. They offer the possibility of much greater flexibility, both in the handling of information and in its transmission. [. . .]

Notes

1   For further discussion of this point, see John B. Thompson, *Ideology and Modern Culture: Critical Social Theory in the Era of Mass Communication* (Cambridge: Polity Press, 1990), pp. 154–62.

2   See Denis McQuail, 'Uncertainty about the audience and the organization of mass communication', in Paul Halmos (ed.), *The sociology of Mass Media Communicators*, Sociological Review Monograph 13 (Keele, Keele University, 1969), pp. 75–84. For a more extended discussion of the ways in which television broadcasting organizations monitor their audiences, see Ien Ang, *Desperately Seeking the Audience* (London, Routledge, 1991).

3   See Helga Nowotny, *Time, the Modern and Postmodern Experience*, trans. Neville Plaice (Cambridge, Polity Press, 1994).

4   See Eviatar Zerubaval, 'The standardization of time: a sociohistorical perspective', *American Journal of Sociology*, 88 (1982), pp. 1–23.

5   See Stephen Kern, *The Culture of Time and Space 1880–1918* (London, Weidenfeld and Nicolson, 1983); Marshall Berman, *All That Is Solid Melts into Air: the Experience of Modernity* (London, Verso, 1983).

6   See J. Crofts, *Packhorse, Waggon and Post: Land Carriage and Communications under the Tudors and Stuarts* (London, Routledge and Kegan Paul, 1967), p. 123 'Coach-journeys were so dreary and exhausting that travellers were thankful to move by short stages, and to reckon their progress in days.'

7   See David Harvey, *The Condition of Postmodernity: an Enquiry into the Origins of Cultural Change* (Oxford, Blackwell, 1989), pp. 240ff. See also Janelle's discussion of the somewhat similar notion of 'time–space convergence': Donald G. Janelle, 'Global interdependence and its consequences', in Stanley D. Brunn and Thomas R. Leinback (eds), *Collapsing Space and Time: Geographic Aspects of Communication and Information* (London, HarperCollins Academic, 1991), pp. 47–81.

8   See E.P. Thompson, 'Time, work-discipline and industrial capitalism', reprinted in his *Customs in Common: Studies in Traditional Popular Culture* (New York, New Press, 1991), pp. 352–403.

9   See Nowotny, *Time*, ch. 2.

10 See Alan J. Lee, *The Origins of the Popular Press in England 1855–1914* (London, Croom Helm, 1976).

11 For a brief selection of relevant works, see George Boyce, James Curran and Pauline Wingate (eds), *Newspaper History from the Seventeenth Century to the Present Day* (London, Constable, 1978); James Curran and Jean Seaton, *Power without Responsibility: the Press and Broadcasting in Britain*, 4th edn (London, Routledge, 1991); Ben H. Bagdikian, *The Media Monopoly*, 4th edn (Boston, Beacon Press, 1992); Jeremy Tunstall and Michael Palmer, *Media Moguls* (London, Routledge, 1991); Alfonso Sánchez-Tabernero, *Media Concentration in Europe: Commercial Enterprise and the Public Interest* (Dusseldorf, European Institute for the Media, 1993). For a summary of the main trends, see Thompson, *Ideology and Modern Culture*, esp. pp. 193–205.

12 'From press baron to media mogul', *Labour Research* (November, 1993), pp. 11–12. The four groups are Rupert Murdoch's News International (which owns the *Sun*, *The Times*, *Today*, *News of the World* and *The Sunday Times*); the Mirror Group (formerly Robert Maxwell's empire, this group owns the *Daily Mirror*, *Sunday Mirror*, *People*, *Sporting Life*, *Sunday Mail* and *Daily Record*); United Newspapers (*Daily Express*, *Sunday Express*, *Daily Star*); and Viscount Rothermere's Daily Mail and General Trust (*Daily Mail*, *Mail on Sunday*). The patterns of concentration vary from country to country and from one sector of the industry to another, reflecting the differing conditions under which the media industries have developed. In the United States, for instance, there are few (if any) national newspapers, but there are around 1,600 locally or regionally based daily newspapers. By the late 1980s, 14 large corporations controlled more than half of the daily newspaper business in the US (see Bagdikian, *The Media Monopoly*, pp. 17ff).

13 The British television industry offers a good example of this coexistence. While the BBC and the major ITV companies remain the dominant organizations and control a large proportion of the resources, there are many small, independent production companies, based primarily in London, which produce programmes on a commissioned basis for Channel Four and, increasingly, for the BBC and ITV. See Jeremy Tunstall, *Television Producers* (London, Routledge, 1993); Scott Lash and John Urry, *Economies of Signs and Space* (London and Thousand Oaks, Calif., Sage, 1994), ch. 5.

14 For further details on the technical innovations, see M. MacLaren, *The Rise of the Electrical Industry during the Nineteenth Century* (Princeton, NJ, Princeton University Press, 1943); D. G. Tucker, Electrical communication', in T. I. Williams (ed.), *A History of Technology*, vol. 6: *The Twentieth Century c.1900 to c.1950* (Oxford, Oxford University Press, 1978).

15 See W. R. Maclauren, *Invention and Innovation in the Radio Industry* (New York, Macmillan, 1949); S.G. Sturmey, *The Economic Development of Radio* (London, Duckworth, 1958).

16 See Peter Hall and Paschall Preston, *The Carrier Wave: New Information Technology and the Geography of Innovation, 1846–2003* (London, Unwin Hyman, 1988), esp. part 4.

Corporate dynamics and broadcasting futures
Graham Murdock

Broadcasting and the politics of representation

Recent years have seen an intensified debate about the nature and scope of rights in complex democracies coupled with an interrogation of established notions of citizenship. As these arguments have unfolded, it has become increasingly clear that questions about communicative rights – rights in relation to the production and circulation of public knowledge and public culture – are central to any definition of full citizenship in a complex democracy. In order to address these issues, however, we first need to work through a thicket of difficult issues to do with the politics of representation.

Questions of representation always involve debates about communicative power as well as cultural form. It is not enough to ask how far the diversity of social experiences, viewpoints, demands and aspirations are presented in the major institutions of public culture and whether the available range of aesthetic forms fosters open debate. We also need to ask who orchestrates these representations? Who is licensed to talk about other people's experience? Who is empowered to ventriloquise other people's opinions? Who is mandated to picture other people's lives? Who chooses who will be heard and who will be consigned to silence, who will be seen and who will remain invisible? Who decides which viewpoints will be taken seriously and how conflicts between positions will be resolved? Who proposes explanations and analyses and who is subject to them? These questions require us to confront the dynamics of social delegation and to interrogate the institutional structures and rationales that underwrite current structures of representation.

As the central public arena for organising complex societies' conversations with themselves, broadcasting, and more particularly television, has become a major focus for the politics of representation. During the

This chapter is taken from *Controlling Broadcasting: Access Policy and Practice in North America and Europe*, eds Meryl Aldridge and Nicholas Hewitt (Manchester, Manchester University Press, 1994), pp. 3–19.

1970s, however, it became clear that the established ways of managing this politics were no longer adequate to the emerging situation. The tectonic plates which had clamped the field of public representations together were moving apart. Cracks were appearing, boundaries were shifting, suppressed forces were re-emerging and new pressures were gathering force. The result was a deepening crisis of public representation. Demands were being made that couldn't be accommodated comfortably within the established programme forms and institutional routines and which directly challenged the rationales that underpinned the historic projects of public service broadcasting.

This crisis of representation coincided with broadcasting's accelerated incorporation into the corporate system. The growing momentum of privatisation not only enlarged the market sector within the television industries by promoting commercially funded expansion in cable and satellite service, it increasingly pulled the public broadcasting organisations into its orbit, both institutionally and ideologically. This chapter sets out to explore this shift and to suggest that corporate dynamics have prompted responses to the crisis of representation that are less and less able to guarantee the communicative rights required for full citizenship.

Citizenship and communicative rights

The problem is that 'citizenship' is subject to competing definitions, some of which are positively unhelpful. There is, for example, the narrow definition which equates citizenship with participation in the formal political process. This leads to claims that the major links between broadcasting and citizenship are to be found primarily (or even exclusively) in those areas of programming that deal with the political process, most notably news and current affairs, leaving drama and entertainment to be subsumed under the signs of 'culture' or 'quality'. Then there is the definition enshrined in John Major's Citizen's Charter which equates citizenship rights with consumer rights. Over and against these attempts to delimit its scope, I want to insist on a general definition of citizenship which identifies it with the right to participate fully in existing patterns of social, political, and cultural life and to help shape their future forms. (This right also carries responsibilities, but my focus here is on rights.)

Following the schema first outlined by T. H. Marshall in the immediate post-war period, and subsequently extended by later writers, we can identify four major clusters of rights that are constitutive of full citizenship.

First, there are civil rights, rights in relation to freedom of action within civil society and freedom from undue coercion by the state. These cover a wide range from freedom of assembly and freedom of belief and religious worship to freedom from arbitrary arrest, detention and torture.

Secondly, and most familiarly, there are political rights. These centre around the right to participate in the formation and application of the laws under which one consents to be governed, which are underpinned in social democracies by the universal franchise and the jury system.

Thirdly, there are social and economic rights, rights in relation to centres of economic power, employee rights and consumer rights for example, coupled with welfare rights in the areas of health, housing, benefits and pensions.

And finally, there are information and cultural rights.

Just as social and economic rights are crucial to guaranteeing the minimum material basis for the exercise of basic civil and political rights, so information and cultural rights play a central role in securing the symbolic and discursive resources for full citizenship.

Information rights can be usefully divided into two sub-sets. First, they require public provision of the full range of information that people need in order to make considered judgements and political choices and to pursue their rights in other areas effectively. In particular, they entail access to comprehensive information on the activities of governmental and corporate agencies with significant power over peoples' lives. But information, in itself, is not enough. To convert it into knowledge that can form the basis for strategies of action requires the availability of the broadest possible array of arguments and conceptual frames through which it can be interpreted and evaluated and its implications traced.

Cultural rights also have a dual character. They clearly involve the right to have one's experiences, beliefs and aspirations represented in the major fora of public culture. As Alberto Melucci has pointed out, this right is fundamental to the construction and reconstruction of social identity since the 'freedom to belong to an identity and to contribute to its definition presumes the freedom to be represented' (Melucci, 1989: 258). This implies, in turn, that democracy in complex societies requires cultural spaces 'which enable individuals and social groups to affirm themselves and be recognised for what they are or wish to be' (Melucci, 1989: 172).

These rights of representation are what Melucci calls 'rights of everyday life' in the sense that they relate to social identities that cannot be neatly subsumed within the master-categories of 'citizen' and 'consumer'. As Elizabeth Jacka has argued, 'allowing these voices of difference to be heard is the true meaning of the words "pluralism" and "diversity" that are bandied around so blithely by the proponents of the free market' (Jacka, 1992: 22). Or rather, one of the 'true meanings'. For cultural rights also involve the negotiation of difference through the provision of communal spaces in which the competing positions and claims of specific communities of interest can be brought together and a workable conception of the public good hammered out. This involves challenging prevailing stereotypes and cherished assumptions coupled with a questioning of habitual grids and a willingness to look from the point of view of the 'other'.

Given these definitions it should be clear, even from this very cursory account, that information and cultural rights can only be guaranteed by open discursive spaces based on certain basic institutional prerequisites.

First, such spaces must be relatively independent of both state and government and major corporate interests to ensure that the field of public representations is not unduly commandeered by either official discourse or commercial speech. Secondly, since questions of representation involve social delegation there must be robust systems to ensure adequate account-ability and participation. Thirdly, since different forms of expression allow different people to speak, about different things, in different ways, and with differing degrees of visibility and legitimacy, an open system must support a diversity of forms and be actively committed to the creation of new ones. And fourthly, since the aim is to create a generalised public space for the exploration of difference it must be universally accessible.

Broadcasting, identity and difference

Public broadcasting's special relationship to the politics of citizenship and the constitution of information and cultural rights was built into the basic fabric of its organisation from its foundation in the 1920s.

This was a decisive moment in which capitalist democracy was shaped by the intersection of two major movements: the emergence of a mass consumer system and the consolidation of a particular notion of citizenship built around the political rights conferred by universal suffrage and the struggle to secure a range of social and welfare rights. These shifts offered two overarching identities, those of 'citizen' and 'consumer'. Both liquidated other identities, one in the imagined community of the nation, the other in the shared experience of the marketplace.

Broadcasting's efforts to situate itself within this emerging field of forces generated two major solutions: the corporate form developed most fully in the United States and the public service form forged by the BBC in Britain (Murdock, 1992a). The first constituted broadcasting organisations as private companies who made profits by packaging audiences for sale to advertisers and beckoned their viewers and listeners to join the democratic community of consumers. The second operated with a public corporation, funded by a licence fee, which didn't take advertising and which addressed audiences as members of a national and imperial community. It advanced a highly selective version of national culture as the symbolic cement binding citizens together in a shared structure of feeling which transcended the allegiances of locality, class and ethnicity. During the thirty years of its monopoly the BBC invented the 'sound of Britain' whose

> function was to make people feel not simply uplifted but patriotic about the Hallé Orchestra or the voice of Laurence Olivier or the Glasgow Orpheus Choir. Such sounds merged with other, more formally national noises: a King fighting his stammer to make his Christmas broadcast, a roar of engines passing overhead at an airshow. (Ascherson, 1992: 21).

With the arrival of television, images were added to these sounds to create a very particular way of looking and of locating oneself, a perspective which reached its height in the reverential tones of Richard Dimbleby's commentary for the live television relay of the Queen's Coronation.

Commercial television, which was introduced a few years later, in the mid-1950s, was a half-way house, a quasi-corporate model. The ITV companies were privately owned, they took advertising, and they set out to make profits, but the full force of corporate logic was interrupted by the imposition of extensive public service requirements, by the stringent controls on advertising, and by the fact that each company was a regional monopoly with exclusive rights to sell advertising in their franchise area.

This peculiar structure generated a specific kind of populist ethos which was more sympathetic to American styles and to the new consumerism, less inclined to defer to cultural and political authorities, more disrespectful, more engaged with popular experience, more responsive to the emerging cultures of youth. Where the BBC's sense of itself was built around notions of national unity and cultural inheritance, ITV enlarged the spaces for voices to speak with the accents of region, class and generation and to speak to the contemporary experience of dislocation and change.

Contested representations

As the 1960s gave way to the 1970s, however, it was clear that this revised map of social differences and identities was less and less adequate to an emerging politics of identity in which a range of groups were staking claims for greater representation within the broadcasting system.

The women's movement was challenging the conventional boundaries separating the personal from the political, the private from the public, and pressing for a redefinition of citizenship rights that included rights in relation to the body. Struggles over public representation were at the centre of these debates as feminism sought to dislodge entrenched notions of femininity and a woman's 'place'. Other groups too – the disabled, the elderly and the young – were pressing for greater representation and attention to their claims and interests. But the most important assault was on the core notion of 'national culture' and on its intimate but suppressed connections with the experience of empire and colonialism (Said, 1993). National minorities within Britain insisted on their cultural distinctiveness with renewed vigour, whilst the jagged transition from imperial power to multi-cultural polity forced a confrontation with plurality and difference which re-drew the mental map of the globe underpinning received notions of national heritage. Reorganising this map, with its divisions between centres and peripheries, metropole and margins, high and low, was a primary focus for the emerging battles around representation. These revolved around three main issues.

The first centred on questions of visibility and legitimacy, on whose lives and interests were shown and talked about within the broadcasting system and how, and foregrounded issues around stereotyping, sexism and racism in language and imagery. The second strand in the debate focused on whether the available forms of expression could accommodate new demands for representation or whether novel forms were needed, whilst the third confronted the issue of social delegation. This last concern generated a number of proposals. Some argued for widening the basis of recruitment into professional production through concerted initiatives on equal opportunities and positive discrimination. Others called for producers working outside the major institutions to be given greater access to the schedules as a way of widening the range of perspectives in play. At the same time there were mounting demands that programme makers, whatever their base, become more responsive to the constituencies they sought to represent by providing spaces for comment and criticism on screen. Others took the case for greater access a step further arguing that more people should be encouraged to make programmes which spoke to their interests and experiences directly, drawing on the facilities and expertise of professionals, but retaining editorial control.

These demands are not unique to Britain. They are signals of a generalised crisis of representation which has confronted the broadcasting systems of a number of complex democracies. But a comparative study is beyond the scope of the present chapter. My purpose here is more modest. I want to show how, in the case of Britain, responses to this crisis have been shaped and circumscribed by the concerted shift towards corporate models of televisual enterprise.

Addressing difference: social interests and niche markets

The lack of fit between the existing institutions of broadcasting and the proliferating demands for representation was a central theme of the Annan Committee's report on the future of broadcasting, published in the spring of 1977. They broke with imagined unities of national culture and embraced a vision of Britain as a fractured cultural formation. In their view: 'Our society is now multi-racial and pluralist: that is to say, people adhere to different views of the nature and purpose of life and expect their own view to be expressed in some form or other. The structure of broadcasting should reflect this variety' (Annan Committee, 1977: 30).

The question was: how? One powerful lobby presented the multi-channel possibilities of cable systems as the best solution. They argued that by abolishing spectrum scarcity and enabling television to move towards a publishing model they opened up multiple spaces for the articulation of interests. One of the most forceful advocates of this solution was the ex-Treasury official, Peter Jay. For him, and other enthusiasts of 'electronic publishing' the crisis of representation arose from the difficulties

> of allocating scarce publishing opportunities between competing interest groups, whether established institutions, financial vested interests, worker vested interests, evangelical producers, Scotsmen, Welshmen, Irishmen, divines, educationalists, ethnic minorities or any other form of man-in-his-organisations as against man-in-his-home-wanting-to-sit-in-his-armchair-and-watch-the-telly (Jay, 1984: 234).

Provide enlarged 'publishing opportunities' and the crisis dissolved.

The Annan Committee (1977: 24) accepted the definition of 'broadcasting as a form of publishing' but remained sceptical about the immediate prospects for significant growth in cable systems. Whilst they recognised the future potential of the new transmission technologies, they felt that they were unlikely to develop on a substantial scale until the 1990s. Moreover, they argued strongly that cable television should develop primarily as a local service addressing demands for greater access and representation at community level and not (as the cable lobby was urging) as a subscription service offering additional general channels. They therefore turned their attention to what could be done on a national basis in the immediate term (1977: 381).

The struggle to enlarge broadcasting's sphere of representation rapidly focused down on the fate of the vacant fourth channel. There were two major proposals. Predictably, the commercial television lobby argued that it should be given to the ITV companies to match the two channels commanded by the BBC and restore a level playing-field in the competition for viewers. In contrast, the counter-proposal engaged directly with the emerging politics of representation. It recommended that the channel be a broadcaster commissioning programmes from a wide range of groups and individuals and financed by an annual sum taken from advertising revenues, topped up with monies from programme sponsorship. The committee embraced this option enthusiastically on the grounds that it would not be a simple 'addition to the plurality of outlets, but a force for plurality in a deeper sense. Not only could it be a nursery for new forms and new methods of presenting ideas, it could also open the door to a new kind of broadcast publishing' (1977: 235).

They hoped that by separating production from distribution and challenging the established structures of representation – both social and aesthetic – it would act as a catalyst for change within existing channels, moving the whole system closer to a publishing model.

This proposal carried the day and a version of Annan's organisational sketch provided the blueprint for the new channel. It was constituted as a non-profit-making corporation not a private company. The bulk of the schedule was to comprise programmes commissioned from a range of independent producers, supplemented by material bought in from overseas. Commissioning and purchasing decisions would be guided by a distinctive remit which emphasised the need to address constituencies of interest who were under-represented in mainstream terrestrial programming and to maintain a positive commitment to innovation and experiment with pro-gramme forms.

At the same time, it was to be financed by advertising revenue not by public funds. This positive endorsement of advertising finance represented a decisive break with the hostile stance of the previous major enquiry into broadcasting (the Pilkington Report) and introduced a permanent tension into the way the channel addressed the construction and representation of difference. The remit clearly works with a conception of social interests whilst advertisers work with a map of market niches.

This tension did not go unnoticed within the Thatcher government. In his account of his time as the channel's first chief executive, Jeremy Isaacs recounts how he was buttonholed at an embassy dinner by Norman Tebbit, a senior minister of the Prime Minister's inner circle:

'You've got it all wrong, you know', he said, 'doing all these programmes for homosexuals and such. Parliament never meant that sort of thing. The different interests you are supposed to cater for are not like that at all. Golf and sailing and fishing. Hobbies. That's what we intended.' (Isaacs, 1989: 65)

Tebbit's opinion chimed neatly with the views of advertisers, who saw the channel as an opportunity to reach specialised markets that had proved difficult to access through ITV. There was a growing consensus, both inside and outside the industry, that targeting was increasingly important in a 'post-Fordist' consumer system in the process of moving from mass to niche markets, from emulation to segmentation, from 'keeping up with the Joneses' to constructing personalised lifestyles. To many commentators, Channel 4 offered an ideal promotional vehicle for the new times (Murray, 1989: 43).

In the channel's first decade, these marketing pressures, though clearly present, did not operate unchecked. Their logic was attenuated by the fact that the channel did not deal directly with advertisers. Air time was sold by the ITV companies who kept the proceeds in return for paying an annual subscription to fund the channel. This created a buffer between the commissioning process and the advertising industry.

Despite Annan's lukewarm response, arguments in favour of expanding cable television were gathering influential support. By the time Channel 4 went on air in November 1982, the committee's cautious evaluation of the industry's prospects during the 1980s, and their resolute rejection of the operator's arguments in favour of subscription services had already been overtaken.

At the beginning of the year, the Information Technology Advisory Panel (which had been set up the previous summer to advise the government) had published a report on cable systems urging significant expansion at the earliest possible date. They argued that although cable's long-term potential lay in the provision of new telecommunications services 'we have to accept that systems will go through an initial period when their attraction will be based on "entertainment" considerations' (Cabinet Office, 1982: 48). In other words, the requirements of business users would be funded by 'revenue from additional popular programming channels' sold to the general public (Cabinet Office, 1982: 48). For this strategy to work, however, new channels would either have to provide more of what people already liked and were prepared to pay extra for (sports and recent films, for example) or cater for niche markets that were under-served by terrestrial services and attractive to targeted advertising (such as young people or major ethnic minorities). This necessarily ruled out any requirements to cater for a diverse range of minorities.

The Government's White Paper of April 1983, laying out its plans for the sector, welcomed the impeccable corporate logic of this position, arguing that because cable systems

> should not be seen as a further instalment of public service broadcasting but as something different from it . . . it is not necessary, or even appropriate, for

[them] to be required to achieve in their programmes a wide range and balance [or to abide by] specific obligations to provide services for minority or specialist interests. (Home Office, 1983: 55)

Although when considering bids for cable franchises the new regulatory body, the Cable Authority, was 'required to take account of the range and diversity of the services proposed and of the arrangements for community programmes and local access' (1983: 55) nobody expected promises in these areas to be anything other than cosmetic, useful for public relations purposes but continually vulnerable to financial exigency. The authority conceded as much in its first *Annual Report and Accounts* arguing that although they hoped 'to see local services developing steadily, this must be undertaken in a properly cautious way consistent with the *need not to jeopardise the main business on which they will inevitably depend*' (Cable Authority, 1986: 19; emphasis added).

[. . .] so far there is little sign that [the development of cable] is likely to provide a viable way of addressing the current crisis of representation. Community programming remains marginal and precarious, a concession not a right, whilst minority channels continue to be defined in terms of niche markets rather than social interests. But even if cable operators had been required to address the politics of difference in a more wholehearted way, two major problems would remain. First, by its nature 'narrowcasting' constitutes its audiences as specific targeted groups. Channels are designed to appeal to their specific interests. This provides spaces in which groups can explore their communality and negotiate internal disagreements, but it does not bring differences into confrontation with each other or contribute to the development of new conceptions of the public good based on the negotiation of shared and sectional interests. Added to which, cable and satellite services are only available to those who can afford the subscriptions and other charges levied by the operators. In a situation where fiscal policies have combined with cuts in welfare provision to produce a steadily widening gap in income inequalities, this inevitably means that many constituencies are permanently barred from representation by their poverty (Murdock and Golding, 1989). These dynamics make the fate of the main terrestrial channels all the more crucial, since it is here that we need to look for services capable of addressing the crisis of representation in its full complexity.

Dismantling public broadcasting

In advancing the case for cable, the authors of the ITAP report were eager to emphasise that they saw 'no reason why the introduction of cable systems should necessarily lead to a reduction in the range and quality of programme services on the public broadcasting network' (Cabinet Office, 1982: 48). In a strict sense they were right, since for most of the 1980s cable (and later) satellite channels made only modest inroads into the revenues and audience shares of established terrestrial services. But the indirect impact was considerable. Cable policy broke the public service consensus that had structured debate until then and offered an alternative model of commercial television built unashamedly around the corporate rationales. This vision proved increasingly attractive to the Thatcher governments as the decade wore on and they became increasingly eager to apply it more generally. Separating programme production from packaging and distribution, the enthusiasm for subscription systems, the advocacy of 'light touch' regulation, and the retreat from public service requirements, all came to play a prominent part in debates about the future of ITV and the BBC.

In the spring of 1985, a committee of enquiry was appointed to look into the future financing of terrestrial broadcasting. It was chaired by Professor Alan Peacock, a vocal supporter of free market mechanisms, and included another prominent enthusiast of the 'hidden hand', Samuel Brittan, *The Financial Times* columnist. Although its main task was to review options for funding the BBC, it soon widened its brief to take in the commercial sector. Its final report, published in July 1986 (Peacock Committee, 1986), made three key suggestions for the immediate reorganisation of the ITV system.

The first, and by far the most radical, was the proposal that in the next round of licence allocations, franchises should be awarded by competitive tender and should usually go to the highest bidder, providing that their programme plans had passed an initial test of minimum quality.

Secondly, they argued that over a ten-year period, the ITV companies 'should be required to increase to not less than forty per cent the proportion of programmes supplied by independent producers' with the aim of increasing competition and encouraging multiple sources of supply (Peacock Committee, 1986: 142). This publisher-broadcaster model, whereby a channel assembles a schedule but commissions or buys in most of its programming from outside suppliers, was already in operation within Channel 4 and the cable industry. However, whereas Channel 4's remit directed it to cater for interests not well served elsewhere in the system, cable channels were free to purchase whatever they thought would maximise interest among audiences and advertisers.

Finally, in a bid to integrate Channel 4 more fully into corporate logic, the committee recommended that it 'should be given the option of selling its own advertising time' (1986: 144). This was a direct response to advertisers' long-standing complaints about the ITV companies' monopoly rights over advertising space within the terrestrial system, and their accusations of over-charging and lack of responsiveness to their needs.

Although, overall, the Peacock Report had a somewhat uneven reception from the government (see Brittan, 1991) the proposals for ITV were largely successful in setting the legislative agenda for the subsequent White Paper, entitled *Broadcasting in the 90s: Competition, Choice and Quality*, published in November 1988 (Home Office, 1988). The proposed changes would be administered by a new regulatory agency, the Independent Television Commission ITC), which would replace both the Independent Broadcasting Authority and the Cable Authority and oversee all commercial television services regardless of how they were delivered. The ITC was to operate with a 'light touch', extending the market-driven regulatory regime developed for cable and satellite services to ITV (renamed Channel 3). The White Paper justified this shift by arguing that 'as viewers exercise greater choice there is no longer the same need for quality of service to be prescribed by legislation or regulatory fiat' (1988: 20). Accordingly, it would be left to 'the operators to decide what to show and when to show it', subject only to the general provisions of the law and some very residual public service requirements (1988: 22).

The ITC's first major task was to preside over the auctioning of the ITV franchises. This proved to be a highly contentious process, with a chorus of disapproval greeting both the arrangements for bidding and the eventual outcome (Murdock, 1992b). Advocates of the original idea of a cash auction were disappointed that incumbents had retained twelve of the sixteen franchises on offer, and that of the thirteen that had been contested, only five had gone to the highest bidder. Supporters of public service ideals with ITV were dismayed that Thames Television (the weekday contractor for London and one of the most respected companies in the system) had been displaced by Carlton Television. And the letter that Mrs Thatcher wrote to Bruce Gyngell, the chief executive of the nationwide breakfast channel, TV-AM, commiserating on his defeat by the Sunrise consortium, amounted to a repudiation of the whole process by the person who had pressed hardest for its institution. As she admitted: 'I am only too painfully aware that I was responsible for the legislation. When I see how some of the other licences have been awarded I am mystified that you did not receive yours, and heartbroken.'

Looking at the outcome of the franchise auction overall we need to ask whether it has created a system that is likely to address the crisis of representation by sustaining and extending the diversity of programming. The answer is almost certainly 'no'. As two prominent business economists argued in 1989, when the debate about the auction process was at its height: 'no amount of regulation . . . can change the fact that the auction method of allocating television franchises will, by increasing the priority given to profit maximisation, make it very difficult to impose non-commercial programme obligations on licensees' (Cheong and Foster, 1989: 121).

Certainly the very substantial annual sums that a number of companies have to return to the Treasury under the new system, coupled with the projections of relatively flat advertising revenues and increasing competition from satellite and cable services, are a massive discouragement to diversity. And in the absence of any clear statutory requirements to produce politically challenging programmes or to provide space for minority experiences and viewpoints, the Channel 3 companies are free to jettison 'difficult' productions altogether. As Anthony Smith has argued, they 'have been placed within a structure so flimsy . . . that the constant temptation will be and is already to offer a narrower, safer range of material, much of it bought in' (Smith, 1992: 47).

In this situation corporate rationales necessarily take priority. As Paul Jackson, director of programmes for Carlton Television (which needs to return 29 per cent of its projected advertising earnings to the Treasury each year) has admitted: 'Given the commercial realities, we won't have the latitude in future to find excuses for programmes that don't earn their keep. Programmes will not survive in the new ITV if they don't pay their way' (Henry, 1992a: 3).

For many senior programme makers who had grown up in the old ITV system, such as the journalist Michael Nicholson, this statement is typical of the new style of executive who care 'nothing for its past reputation' and are 'bereft of public duty and any public concern beyond their shareholders' (Henry, 1992b: 6).

The ascendancy of corporate rationales has been aided by the shift in the regulatory regime. At first sight, the ITC appears to have more sanctions at its disposal. Whereas the IBA's only option was to revoke a company's licences if it broke its programme promises or overstepped the rules (something it was understandably very reluctant to do) the ITC can issue warnings, demand apologies on-screen and impose fines of varying severity before moving to cancel a franchise. But, unlike the IBA, it can only use these disciplines after the event. It no longer has the power to approve Channel 3 programmes and schedules in advance. This withdrawal of prior approval greatly increases the companies' room for manoeuvre and confines the Commission's primary role to damage limitation. As one Channel 3 company director has conceded, given the political and financial realities of the current situation, 'The ITC can't stop the companies doing what they want' (Douglas, 1993: 23).

Moreover, where the ITC has taken a more pro-active role, the effect has generally been to extend the scope of corporate influence on programme making. One of the Commission's first major acts on assuming responsibility for Channel 3 was to publish more permissive guidelines on programme sponsorship giving advertisers access to all programmes except for news and current affairs and those dealing with industrial controversy or current public policies (ITC, 1990: 5). This marks another import of the 'permissive' regime developed for cable into mainstream terrestrial broadcasting and one with significant implications. Despite the ITC's insistence that funders must not seek to influence editorial decisions, the greater hospitality to sponsorship is widely seen within the industry as indicating 'a fundamental change in television culture' (Carter, 1991: 20). By providing a considerably enlarged space for commercial speech – speech produced by and for the major corporations and designed to promote their products and images – the new rules represent a substantial retreat from the ideal of public service broadcasting as an open, imaginative and discursive space (Murdock, 1992c).

Concern has also been expressed about Channel 4's ability to sustain its commitment to diversity and experimentation now that it has to sell its own air-time and the commissioning process is subject to the full force of advertisers' demands. In this situation there is bound to be increased pressure to build programming strategies around market niches rather than social interests. As the distinguished programme-maker Roger Graef, one of the original campaigners for the channel, has put it:

If the channel's remit matters, selling its own airtime moves it in precisely the wrong direction. From the commission and transmission of a distinctive service, Channel 4 now moves into a new business: delivering viewers to advertisers. This is in direct conflict with the essential element of innovation and experiment; trial and error. (Graef, 1991: 22)

Commercial television's increasing capture by corporate rationales makes the maintenance of a strong BBC, concerned to address the current crisis of representation and ensure that all its programming remains universally available, of central importance. Whether these ideals will survive the bruising political battles around the renewal of the Corporation's Royal Charter in 1996 is debatable however. Whilst it makes no firm proposals, the government's consultation document on the BBC's future, published at the end of 1992, includes options that would significantly alter the balance of the Corporation's activities (Department of National Heritage, 1992).

It gives a sympathetic hearing to the Peacock Committee's view that in a multi-channel environment public service broadcasting is best used as a back-stop, compensating for the gaps in commercial provision, arguing that 'with greater choice now available to viewers, the BBC could concentrate on programmes which are unlikely to be broadcast by other organisations' (1992: 18). These would be of two main kinds, those 'which reflect the British way of life, history and culture' and 'more programmes for minorities of all kinds, including ethnic minorities and people with special interests' (1992: 18). The evident tension in this view, between a view of the BBC as a force for conserving 'national' culture and as an arbiter between proliferating claims for representation also marks the Corporation's own outline of its future role, *Extending Choice*, published in the same week as the government's document. Here too we find a commitment 'to portray a multiracial, multicultural society and to respond to the diversity of cultures throughout the UK' coupled with a promise 'to give special prominence to artistic, sporting and ceremonial events that bring the nation together' (BBC, 1992: 19–20). How exactly the competition between the claims and identities offered by the imagined community of the nation on the one hand and the multiple constituencies of difference on the other will be managed, in terms of programme budgets, expressive forms and social delegation, is not addressed. Nor is there any recognition that the unities of national culture have been secured by repressing the claims of cultures rooted in class, region, gender and ethnicity or that the presentation of 'national heritage' cannot be uncoupled from an engagement with the imperial past. It is not enough to provide room for a diversity of cultures alongside a celebration of heritage. It is necessary to work through the problematic relations between them.

There is a significant degree of consensus too on questions of finance. Whilst the government's consultation document presents a generally critical review of the arguments in favour of the BBC taking spot advertising, and cautiously endorses the continuation of the licence fee, it follows the Peacock Committee in presenting a positive evaluation of subscription services as a way of 'reducing the BBC's dependence on the licence fee' and introducing a direct relationship between the Corporation and its customers (Department of National Heritage, 1992: 34). The BBC's dismissal of advertising is more comprehensive and its defence of the licence fee more adamant but it, too, argues strongly 'that the BBC should participate in the development of a subscription television market' to 'enable the creation of new specialist services, primarily on satellite' (BBC, 1992: 65). It could hardly do otherwise since it has already responded to government demands that it exploit the commercial potential of its assets more effectively by establishing a series of scrambled services for specific groups using its terrestrial network at night, when public services have closed down, and by launching a satellite-delivered general entertainment channel, UK Gold, in partnership with Thames Television. These developments are defended on the grounds that they generate revenues that can be used for programming on the main channels. At the same time, there is no doubt that they mark a sharp break with the BBC's historic commitment to universality and the introduction of a two- or three-tier service. *Extending Choice* claims that 'It is entirely consistent with the BBC's public service role for it to supply programming to satellite channels, which supplement and deliver greater depth than is possible on the core licence fee-funded services' (BBC, 1992: 49).

But this is a far cry from John Reith's original promise that 'There need be no first and third class' and that public service broadcasting would provide 'nothing which is exclusive to those who pay more, or who are considered in one way or another more worthy of attention' (Reith, 1924: 218).

The gulf between these statements is a measure of how fully the BBC's strategies have already been shaped by corporate rationales. If this process continues there will be very little chance of developing a public broadcasting system that is capable of addressing the current crisis of representation and contributing the symbolic resources required for the exercise of full citizenship in a complex democracy.

References

Annan Committee, (1977) *Report of the Committee on the Future of Broadcasting*. London: HMSO, Cmnd 6753.

Ascherson, N. (1992) 'How the BBC invented the sound of the nation', *The Independent on Sunday*, 6 September, p. 21.

BBC (1992) *Extending Choice: the BBC's Role in the New Broadcasting Age*. London: British Broadcasting Corporation.

Brittan, S. (1991) 'Towards a broadcasting market: recommendations of the British Peacock Committee', in J.G. Blumler and T. Nossiter (eds), *Broadcasting Finance in Transition*. New York: Oxford University Press.

Cabinet Office (1982) *Cable Systems: a Report by the Information Advisory Panel*. London: HMSO.

Cable Authority (1986) *Annual Report and Accounts*. London: Cable Authority.

Carter, M. (1991) 'Television limbers up for a sponsored run', *Marketing Week*, 11: 20–1.

Cheong, K. and Foster, R. (1989) 'Auditioning ITV franchises', G. Hughes and D. Vines (eds),

Deregulation and the Future of Commercial Television. Aberdeen: Aberdeen University Press.

Department of National Heritage (1992) *The Future of the BBC: a Consultation Document*. London: HMSO, Cm 2098.

Douglas, T. (1993) 'Toothless ITC's crunch time', *Marketing Week*, 5 March, p. 23.

Graef, R. (1991) 'Remit or cash: and epic duel from Channel 4', *The Independent*, 28 August, p. 3.

Henry, G. (1992a) 'ITV's current affairs show "must deliver"', *Guardian*, 6 May, p. 3.

Henry, G. (1992b) 'ITV chiefs "moguls of Mammon placing profits over quality"', *Guardian*, 9 October, p. 6.

Home Office (1983) *The Development of Cable Systems and Services*. London: HMSO, Cmnd 8866.

Home Office (1988) *Broadcasting in the 1990s: Competition, Choice and Quality*. London: HMSO, Cm 517.

ITC (1990) *Draft ITC Code of Programme Sponsorship (October)*. London: Independent Television Commission.

Isaacs, J. (1989) *Storm over 4: a Personal Account*. London: Weidenfeld and Nicolson.

Jacka, E. (1992) 'Remapping the Australian television system', paper delivered to the Cultural Industries Seminar Series, CIRCIT, Melbourne, 17 June.

Jay, P. (1984) 'Electronic publishing', in *The Crisis for Western Political Economy and other Essays*. London: André Deutsch.

Melucci, A. (1989) *Nomads of the Present: Social Movements and Individual Needs in Contemporary Society*. London: Hutchinson Radius.

Murdock, G. (1992a) 'Citizens, consumers and public culture', in M. Skovmand and K.C. Schroder (eds), *Media Cultures: Reappraising Transnational Media*. London: Routledge.

Murdock, G. (1992b) 'Selling the silver: British commercial television after the franchise auction', *Media Perspektiven*, 4/92.

Murdock, G. (1992c) 'Embedded persuasions: the fall and rise of integrated advertising', in D. Strinati and S. Wagg (eds), *Come on Down? Popular Media Culture in Post-war Britain*. London: Routledge.

Murdock, G. and Golding, P. (1989) 'Information, poverty and political inequality: citizenship in the age of privatised communications', *Journal of Communication*, 39 (3): 180–95.

Murray, R. (1989) 'Fordism and post-Fordism', in S. Hall and M. Jacques (eds), *New Times: the Changing Face of Politics in the 1990s*. London: Lawrence and Wishart.

Peacock Committee (1986) *Report of the Committee on Financing the BBC*. London: HMSO, Cmnd 9284.

Reith, J. C. (1924) *Broadcast over Britain*. London: Hodder and Stoughton.

Said, E. (1993) *Culture and Imperialism*. London: Chatto and Windus.

Smith, A. (1992) 'Cash prizes', *New Statesman and Society*, 27 November, p. 47.

The technology and the society   **Raymond Williams**

It is often said that television has altered our world. In the same way, people often speak of a new world, a new society, a new phase of history, being created – 'brought about' – by this or that new technology: the steam-engine, the automobile, the atomic bomb. Most of us know what is generally implied when such things are said. But this may be the central difficulty: that we have got so used to statements of this general kind, in our most ordinary discussions, that we can fail to realise their specific meanings.

For behind all such statements lie some of the most difficult and most unresolved historical and philosophical questions. Yet the questions are not posed by the statements; indeed they are ordinarily masked by them. Thus we often discuss, with animation, this or that 'effect' of television, or the kinds of social behaviour, the cultural and psychological conditions, which television has 'led to', without feeling ourselves obliged to ask whether it is reasonable to describe any technology as a cause, or, if we think of it as a cause, as what kind of cause, and in what relations with other kinds of causes. The most precise and discriminating local study of 'effects' can remain superficial if we have not looked into the notions of cause and effect, as between a technology and a society, a technology and a culture, a technology and a psychology, which underlie our questions and may often determine our answers.

First published in 1974, this chapter is taken from *Television: Technology and Cultural Form* (London, Routledge, 2nd edn, 1989), pp. 9–31.

It can of course be said that these fundamental questions are very much too difficult; and that they are indeed difficult is very soon obvious to anyone who tries to follow them through. We could spend our lives trying to answer them, whereas here and now, in a society in which television is important, there is immediate and practical work to be done: surveys to be made, research undertaken; surveys and research, moreover, which we know how to do. It is an appealing position, and it has the advantage, in our kind of society, that it is understood as practical, so that it can then be supported and funded. By contrast, other kinds of question seem merely theoretical and abstract.

Yet all questions about cause and effect, as between a technology and a society, are intensely practical. Until we have begun to answer them, we really do not know, in any particular case, whether, for example, we are talking about a technology or about the uses of a technology; about necessary institutions or particular and changeable institutions; about a content or about a form. And this is not only a matter of intellectual uncertainty; it is a matter of social practice. If the technology is a cause, we can at best modify or seek to control its effects. Or if the technology, as used, is an effect, to what other kinds of cause, and other kinds of action, should we refer and relate our experience of its uses? These are not abstract questions. They form an increasingly important part of our social and cultural arguments, and they are being decided all the time in real practice, by real and effective decisions.

It is with these problems in mind that I want to try to analyse television as a particular cultural technology, and to look at its development, its institutions, its forms and its effects, in this critical dimension. In the present chapter, I shall begin the analysis under three headings: (a) versions of cause and effect in technology and society; (b) the social history of television as a technology; (c) the social history of the uses of television technology.

Versions of cause and effect in technology and society

We can begin by looking again at the general statement that television has altered our world. It is worth setting down some of the different things this kind of statement has been taken to mean. For example:

1 Television was invented as a result of scientific and technical research. Its power as a medium of news and entertainment was then so great that it altered all preceding media of news and entertainment.

2 Television was invented as a result of scientific and technical research. Its power as a medium of social communication was then so great that it altered many of our institutions and forms of social relationships.

3 Television was invented as a result of scientific and technical research. Its inherent properties as an electronic medium altered our basic perceptions of reality, and thence our relations with each other and with the world.

4 Television was invented as a result of scientific and technical research. As a powerful medium of communication and entertainment it took its place with other factors – such as greatly increased physical mobility, itself the result of other newly invented technologies – in altering the scale and form of our societies.

5   Television was invented as a result of scientific and technical research, and developed as a medium of entertainment and news. It then had unforeseen consequences, not only on other entertainment and news media, which it reduced in viability and importance, but on some of the central processes of family, cultural and social life.

6   Television, discovered as a possibility by scientific and technical research, was selected for investment and development to meet the needs of a new kind of society, especially in the provision of centralised entertainment and in the centralised formation of opinions and styles of behaviour.

7   Television, discovered as a possibility by scientific and technical research, was selected for investment and promotion as a new and profitable phase of domestic consumer economy; it is then one of the characteristic 'machines for the home'.

8   Television became available as a result of scientific and technical research, and in its character and uses exploited and emphasised elements of a passivity, a cultural and psychological inadequacy, which had always been latent in people, but which television now organised and came to represent.

9   Television became available as a result of scientific and technical research, and in its character and uses both served and exploited the needs of a new kind of large-scale and complex but atomised society.

These are only some of the possible glosses on the ordinary bald statement that television has altered our world. Many people hold mixed versions of what are really alternative opinions, and in some cases there is some inevitable overlapping. But we can distinguish between two broad classes of opinion.

In the first – (1) to (5) – the technology is in effect accidental. Beyond the strictly internal development of the technology there is no reason why any particular invention should have come about. Similarly it then has consequences which are also in the true sense accidental, since they follow directly from the technology itself. If television had not been invented, this argument would run, certain definite social and cultural events would not have occurred.

In the second – (6) to (9) – television is again, in effect, a technological accident, but its significance lies in its uses, which are held to be symptomatic of some order of society or some qualities of human nature which are otherwise determined. If television had not been invented, this argument runs, we would still be manipulated or mindlessly entertained, but in some other way and perhaps less powerfully.

For all the variations of local interpretation and emphasis, these two classes of opinion underlie the overwhelming majority of both professional and amateur views of the effects of television. What they have in common is the fundamental form of the statement: 'television has altered our world.'

It is then necessary to make a further theoretical distinction. The first class of opinion, described above, is that usually known, at least to its opponents, as *technological determinism*. It is an immensely powerful and now largely orthodox view of the nature of social change. New technologies are discovered, by an essentially internal process of research and development, which then sets the conditions for social change and progress. Progress, in particular, is the history of these inventions, which 'created the modern world'. The effects of the technologies, whether direct or indirect, foreseen or unforeseen, are as it were the rest of history. The steam-engine, the automobile, television, the atomic bomb, have *made* modern man and the modern condition.

The second class of opinion appears less determinist. Television, like any other technology, becomes available as an element or a medium in a process of change that is in any case occurring or about to occur. By contrast with pure technological determinism, this view emphasises other causal factors in social change. It then considers particular technologies, or a complex of technologies, as *symptoms* of change of some other kind. Any particular technology is then as it were a by-product of a social process that is otherwise determined. It only acquires effective status when it is used for purposes which are already contained in this known social process.

The debate between these two general positions occupies the greater part of our thinking about technology and society. It is a real debate, and each side makes important points. But it is in the end sterile, because each position, though in different ways, has abstracted technology from society. In *technological determinism*, research and development have been assumed as self-generating. The new technologies are invented as it were in an independent sphere, and then create new societies or new human conditions. The view of *symptomatic technology*, similarly, assumes that research and development are self-generating, but in a more marginal way. What is discovered in the margin is then taken up and used.

Each view can then be seen to depend on the isolation of technology. It is either a self-acting force which creates new ways of life, or it is a self-acting force which provides materials for new ways of life. These positions are so deeply established, in modern social thought, that it is very difficult to think beyond them. Most histories of technology, like most histories of scientific discovery, are written from their assumptions. An appeal to 'the facts', against this or that interpretation, is made very difficult simply because the histories are usually written, consciously or unconsciously, to illustrate the assumptions. This is either explicit, with the consequential interpretation attached, or more often implicit, in that the history of technology or of scientific development is offered as a history on its own. This can be seen as a device of specialisation or of emphasis, but it then necessarily implies merely internal intentions and criteria.

To change these emphases would require prolonged and cooperative intellectual effort. But in the particular case of television it may be possible to outline a different kind of interpretation, which would allow us to see not only its history but also its uses in a more radical way. Such an interpretation would differ from technological determinism in that it would restore *intention* to the process of research and development. The technology would be seen, that is to say, as being looked for and developed with certain purposes and practices already in mind. At the same time the interpretation would differ from symptomatic technology in that these purposes and practices would be seen as *direct*: as known social needs, purposes and practices to which the technology is not marginal but central.

The social history of television as a technology

The invention of television was no single event or series of events. It depended on a complex of inventions and developments in electricity, telegraphy, photography and motion pictures, and radio. It can be said to have separated out as a specific technological objective in the period 1875–1890, and then, after a lag, to have developed as a specific technological enterprise from 1920 through to the first public television systems of the 1930s. Yet in each of these stages it depended for parts of its realisation on inventions made with other ends primarily in view.

Until the early nineteenth century, investigations of electricity, which had long been known as a phenomenon, were primarily philosophical: investigations of a puzzling natural effect. The technology associated with these investigations was mainly directed towards isolation and concentration of the effect, for its clearer study. Towards the end of the eighteenth century there began to be applications, characteristically in relation to other known natural effects (lightning conductors). But there is then a key transitional period in a cluster of inventions between 1800 and 1831, ranging from Volta's battery to Faraday's demonstration of electro-magnetic induction, leading quickly to the production of generators. This can be properly traced as a scientific history, but it is significant that the key period of advance coincides with an important stage of the development of industrial production. The advantages of electric power were closely related to new industrial needs: for mobility and transfer in the location of power sources, and for flexible and rapid controllable conversion. The steam-engine had been well suited to textiles, and its industries had been based on local siting. A more extensive development, both physically and in the complexity of multiple-part processes, such as engineering, could be attempted with other power sources but could only be fully realised with electricity. There was a very complex interaction between new needs and new inventions, at the level of primary production, of new applied industries (plating) and of new social needs which were themselves related to industrial development (city and house lighting). From 1830 to large-scale generation in the 1880s there was this continuing complex of need and invention and application.

In telegraphy the development was simpler. The transmission of messages by beacons and similar primary devices had been long established. In the development of navigation and naval warfare the flag-system had been standardised in the course of the sixteenth and seventeenth centuries. During the Napoleonic wars there was a marked development of land telegraphy, by semaphore stations, and some of this survived into peace-time. Electrical telegraphy had been suggested as a technical system as early as 1753, and was actually demonstrated in several places in the early nineteenth century. An English inventor in 1816 was told that the Admiralty was not interested. It is interesting that it was the development of the railways, themselves a response to the development of an industrial system and the related growth of cities, which clarified the need for improved telegraphy. A complex of technical possibilities was brought to a working system from 1837 onwards. The development of international trade and transport brought rapid extensions of the system, including the transatlantic cable in the 1850s and the 1860s. A general system of electric telegraphy had been established by the 1870s, and in the same decade the telephone system began to be developed, in this case as a new and intended invention.

In photography, the idea of light-writing had been suggested by (among others) Wedgwood and Davy in 1802, and the *camera obscura* had already been developed. It was not the projection but the fixing of images which at first awaited technical solution, and from 1816 (Niepce) and through to 1839 (Daguerre) this was worked on, together with the improvement of camera devices. Professional and then amateur photography spread rapidly, and reproduction and then transmission, in the developing newspaper press, were achieved. By the 1880s the idea of a 'photographed reality' – still more for record than for observation – was familiar.

The idea of moving pictures had been similarly developing. The magic lantern (slide projection) had been known from the seventeenth century, and had acquired simply motion (one slide over another) by 1736. From at latest 1826 there was a development of mechanical motion-picture devices, such as the wheel-of-life, and these came to be linked with the magic lantern. The effect of persistence in human vision – that is to say, our capacity to hold the 'memory' of an image through an interval to the next image, thus allowing the possibility of a sequence built from rapidly succeeding units – had been known since classical times. Series of cameras photographing stages of a sequence were followed (Marey, 1882) by multiple-shot cameras. Friese-Greene and Edison worked on techniques of filming and projection, and celluloid was substituted for paper reels. By the 1890s the first public motion-picture shows were being given in France, America and England.

Television, as an idea, was involved with many of these developments. It is difficult to separate it, in its earliest stages, from photo-telegraphy. Bain proposed a device for transmitting pictures by electric wires in 1842; Bakewell in 1847 showed the copying telegraph; Caselli in 1862 transmitted pictures by wire over a considerable distance. In 1873, while working at a terminal of the Atlantic telegraph cable, May observed the light-sensitive properties of selenium (which had been isolated by Berzelius in 1817 and was in use for resistors). In a host of ways, following an already defined need, the means of transmitting still pictures and moving pictures were actively sought and to a considerable extent discovered. The list is long even when selective: Carey's electric eye in 1875; Nipkow's scanning system in 1884; Elster and Geitel's photoelectric cells in 1890; Braun's cathode-ray tube in 1897; Rosing's cathode-ray receiver in 1907; Campbell Swinton's electronic camera proposal in 1911. Through this whole period two facts are evident: that a system of television was foreseen, and its means were being actively sought; but also that, by comparison with electrical generation and electrical telegraphy and telephony, there was very little social investment to bring the scattered work together. It is true that there were technical blocks before 1914 – the thermionic valve and the multi-stage amplifier can be seen to have been needed and were not yet invented. But the critical difference between the various spheres of applied technology can be stated in terms of a social dimension: the new systems of production and of business or transport communication were already organised, at an economic level; the new systems of social communication were not. Thus when motion pictures were developed, their application was characteristically in the margin of established social forms – the sideshows – until their success was capitalised in a version of an established form, the motion-picture *theatre*.

The development of radio, in its significant scientific and technical stages between 1885 and 1911, was at first conceived, within already effective social systems, as an advanced form of telegraphy. Its application as a significantly new social form belongs to the immediate post-war period, in a changed social situation. It is significant that the hiatus in technical television development then also ended. In 1923 Zworykin introduced the electronic television camera tube. Through the early 1920s Baird and Jenkins, separately and competitively, were working on systems using mechanical scanning. From 1925 the rate of progress was qualitatively changed, through important technical advances but also with the example of sound broadcasting systems as a model. The Bell System in 1927 demonstrated wire transmission through a radio link, and the prehistory of the form can be seen to be ending. There was great rivalry between systems – especially those of mechanical and electronic scanning – and there is still great controversy about contributions and priorities. But this is characteristic of the phase in which the development of a technology moves into the stage of a new social form.

What is interesting throughout is that in a number of complex and related fields, these systems of mobility and transfer in production and communication, whether in mechanical and electric transport, or in telegraphy, photography, motion pictures, radio and television, were at once incentives and responses within a phase of general social transformation. Though some of the crucial scientific and technical discoveries were made by isolated and unsupported individuals, there was a crucial community of selected emphasis and intention, in a society characterised at its most general levels by a mobility and extension of the scale of organisations: forms of growth which brought with them immediate and longer-term problems of operative communication. In many different countries, and in apparently unconnected ways, such needs were at once isolated and technically defined. It is especially a characteristic of the communications systems that *all were foreseen – not in utopian but in technical ways – before the crucial components of the development systems had been discovered and refined.* In no way is this a history of communications systems creating a new society or new social conditions. The decisive and earlier transformation of industrial production, and its new social forms, which had grown out of a long history of capital accumulation and working technical improvements, created new needs but also new possibilities, and the communications systems, down to television, were their intrinsic outcome.

The social history of the uses of television technology

It is never quite true to say that in modern societies, when a social need has been demonstrated, its appropriate technology will be found. This is partly because some real needs, in any particular period, are beyond the scope of existing or foreseeable scientific and technical knowledge. It is even more because the key question, about technological response to a need, is less a question about the need itself than about its place in an existing social formation. A need which corresponds with the priorities of the real decision-making groups will, obviously, more quickly attract the investment of resources and the official permission, approval or encouragement on which a working technology, as distinct from available technical devices, depends. We can see this clearly in the major developments of industrial production and, significantly, in military technology. The social history of communications technology is interestingly different from either of these, and it is important to try to discover what are the real factors of this variation.

The problem must be seen at several different levels. In the very broadest perspective, there is an operative relationship between a new kind of expanded, mobile and complex society and the development of a modern communications technology. At one level this relationship can be reasonably seen as causal, in a direct way. The principal incentives to first-stage improvements in communications technology came from problems of communication and control in expanded military and commercial operations. This was both direct, arising from factors of greatly extending distance and scale, and indirect, as a factor within the development of transport technology, which was for obvious reasons the major direct response. Thus telegraphy and telephony, and in its early stages radio, were secondary factors within a primary communications system which was directly serving the needs of an established and developing military and commercial system. Through the nineteenth and into the twentieth century this was the decisive pattern.

But there were other social and political relationships and needs emerging from this complex of change. Indeed it is a consequence of the particular and dominant interpretation of these changes that the complex was at first seen as one requiring improvement in *operational* communication. The direct priorities of the expanding commercial system, and in certain periods of the military system, led to a definition of needs within the terms of these systems. The objectives and the consequent technologies were operational within the structures of these systems: passing necessary specific information, or maintaining contact and control. Modern electric technology, in this phase, was thus oriented to uses of person to person, operator and operative to operator and operative, within established specific structures. This quality can best be emphasised by contrast with the electric technology of the second phase, which was properly and significantly called *broadcasting*. A technology of specific messages to specific persons was complemented, but only relatively late, by a technology of varied messages to a general public.

Yet to understand this development we have to look at a wider communications system. The true basis of this system had preceded the developments in technology. Then as now there was a major, indeed dominant, area of social communication, by word of mouth, within every kind of social group. In addition, then as now, there were specific institutions of that kind of communication which involves or is predicated on social teaching and control: churches, schools, assemblies and proclamations, direction in places of work. All these interacted with forms of communication within the family.

What then were the new needs which led to the development of a new technology of social communication? The development of the press gives us the evidence for our first major instance. It was at once a response to the development of an extended social, economic and political system and a response to crisis within that system. The centralisation of political power led to a need for messages from that centre along other than official lines. Early newspapers were a combination of that kind of message – political and social information – and the specific messages – classified advertising and general commercial news – of an expanding system of trade. In Britain the development of the press went through its major formative stages in periods of crisis: the Civil War and Commonwealth, when the newspaper form was defined; the Industrial Revolution, when new forms of popular journalism were successively established; the major wars of the twentieth century, when the newspaper became a universal social form. For the transmission of simple orders, a communications system already existed. For the transmission of an ideology, there were specific traditional institutions. But for the transmission of news and background – the whole orienting, predictive and updating process which the fully developed press represented – there was an evident need for a new form, which the largely traditional institutions of church and school could not meet. And to the large extent that the crises of general change provoked both anxiety and controversy, this flexible and competitive form met social needs of a new kind. As the struggle for a share in decision and control became sharper, in campaigns for the vote and then in competition for the vote, the press became not only a new communications system but, centrally, a new social institution.

This can be interpreted as response to a political need and a political crisis, and it was certainly this. But a wider social need and social crisis can also be recognised. In a changing society, and especially after the Industrial Revolution, problems of social perspective and social orientation became more acute. New relations between men, and between men and things, were being intensely experienced, and in this area, especially, the traditional institutions of church and school, or of settled community and persisting family, had very little to say. A great deal was of course said, but from positions defined within an older kind of society. In a number of ways, and drawing on a range of impulses from curiosity to anxiety, new information and new kinds of orientation were deeply required: more deeply, indeed, than any specialisation to political, military or commercial information can account for. An increased awareness of mobility and change, not just as abstractions but as lived experiences, led to a major redefinition, in practice and then in theory, of the function and process of social communication.

What can be seen most evidently in the press can be seen also in the development of photography and the motion picture. The photograph is in one sense a popular extension of the portrait, for recognition and for record. But in a period of great mobility, with new separations of families and with internal and external migrations, it became more centrally necessary as a form of maintaining, over distance and through time, certain personal connections. Moreover, in altering relations to the physical world, the photograph as an object became a form of the photography of objects: moments of isolation and stasis within an experienced rush of change; and then, in its technical extension to motion, a means of observing and analysing motion itself, in new ways – a dynamic form in which new kinds of recognition were not only possible but necessary.

Now it is significant that until the period after the First World War, and in some ways until the period after the Second World War, these varying needs of a new kind of society and a new way of life were met by what were seen as specialised means: the press for political and economic information; the photograph for community, family and personal life; the motion picture for curiosity and entertainment; telegraphy and telephony for business information and some important personal messages. It was within this complex of specialised forms that broadcasting arrived.

The consequent difficulty of defining its social uses, and the intense kind of controversy which has ever since surrounded it, can then be more broadly understood. Moreover, the first definitions of broadcasting were made for sound radio. It is significant and perhaps puzzling that the definitions and institutions then created were those within which television developed.

We have now become used to a situation in which broadcasting is a major social institutions, about which there is always controversy but which, in its familiar form, seems to have been predestined by the technology. This predestination, however, when closely examined, proves to be no more than a set of particular social decisions, in particular circumstances, which were then so widely if imperfectly ratified that it is now difficult to see them as decisions rather than as (retrospectively) inevitable results.

Thus, if seen only in hindsight, broadcasting can be diagnosed as a new and powerful form of social integration and control. Many of its main uses can be seen as socially, commercially and at time politically manipulative. Moreover, this viewpoint is rationalised by its description as 'mass

communication', a phrase used by almost all its agents and advisers as well, curiously, as by most of its radical critics. 'Masses' had been the new nineteenth-century term of contempt for what was formerly described as 'the mob'. The physical 'massing' of the urban and industrial revolution underwrote this. A new radical class-consciousness adopted the term to express the material of new social formations: 'mass organisations'. The 'mass meeting' was an observable physical effect. So pervasive was this description that in the twentieth century multiple serial production was called, falsely but significantly, 'mass production': mass now meant large numbers (but within certain assumed social relationships) rather than any physical or social aggregate. Sound radio and television, for reasons we shall look at, were developed for transmission to *individual* homes, though there was nothing in the technology to make this inevitable. But then this new form of social communication – broadcasting – was obscured by its definition as 'mass communication': an abstraction to its most general characteristic, that it went to many people, 'the masses', which obscured the fact that the means chosen was the offer of individual sets, a method much better described by the earlier word 'broadcasting'. It is interesting that the only developed 'mass' use of radio was in Nazi Germany, where under Goebbels' orders the Party organised compulsory public listening groups and the receivers were in the streets. There has been some imitation of this by similar regimes, and Goebbels was deeply interested in television for the same kind of use. What was developed within most capitalist societies, though called 'mass communication', was significantly different.

There was early official intervention in the development of broadcasting, but in form this was only at a technical level. In the earlier struggle against the development of the press, the State had licensed and taxed newspapers, but for a century before the coming of broadcasting the alternative idea of an independent press had been realised both in practice and in theory. State intervention in broadcasting had some real and some plausible technical grounds: the distribution of wave-lengths. But to these were added, though always controversially, more generally social directions or attempts at direction. This social history of broadcasting can be discussed on its own, at the levels of practice and principle. Yet it is unrealistic to extract it from another and perhaps more decisive process, through which, in particular economic situations, a set of scattered technical devices became an applied technology and then a social technology.

A Fascist regime might quickly see the use of broadcasting for direct political and social control. But that, in any case, was when the technology had already been developed elsewhere. In capitalist democracies, the thrust for conversion from scattered techniques to a technology was not political but economic. The characteristically isolated inventors, from Nipkow and Rosing to Baird and Jenkins and Zwyorkin, found their point of development, if at all, in the manufacturers and prospective manufacturers of the technical apparatus. The history at one level is of these isolated names, but at another level it is of EMI, RCA and a score of similar companies and corporations. In the history of motion pictures, capitalist development was primarily in production; large-scale capitalist distribution came much later, as a way of controlling and organising a market for given production. In broadcasting, both in sound radio and later in television, the major investment was in the means of distribution, and was devoted to production only so far as to make the distribution technically possible and then attractive. Unlike all previous communications technologies, radio and television were *systems primarily devised for transmission and reception as abstract processes, with little or no definition of preceding content.* When the question of content was raised, it was resolved, in the main, parasitically. There were state occasions, public sporting events, theatres and so on, which would be communicatively distributed by these new technical means. *It is not only that the supply of broadcasting facilities preceded the demand; it is that the means of communication preceded their content.*

The period of decisive development in sound broadcasting was the 1920s. After the technical advances in sound telegraphy which had been made for military purposes during the war, there was at once an economic opportunity and the need for a new social definition. No nation or manufacturing group held a monopoly of the technical means of broadcasting, and there was a period of intensive litigation followed by cross-licensing of the scattered basic components of successful transmission and reception (the vacuum tube or valve, developed from 1904 to 1913; the feedback circuit, developed from 1912; the neutrodyne and heterodoyne circuits, from 1923). Crucially, in the mid-1920s, there was a series of investment-guided technical solutions to the problem of building a small and simple domestic receiver, on which the whole qualitative transformation from wireless telegraphy to broadcasting depended. By the mid-1920s – 1923 and 1924 are especially decisive years – this breakthrough had happened in the leading industrial societies: the United States, Britain, Germany and France. By the end of the 1920s the radio industry had become a major sector of industrial production, within a rapid general expansion of the new kinds of machines which were eventually to be called 'consumer durables'. This complex of developments included the motor-cycle and motor-car, the box camera and its successors, home electrical appliances, and radio sets. Socially, this complex is characterised by the two apparently paradoxical yet deeply connected tendencies of modern urban industrial living: on the one hand mobility, on the other hand the more apparently self-sufficient family home. The earlier period of public technology, best exemplified by the railways and city lighting, was being replaced by a kind of technology for which no satisfactory name has yet been found: that which served at once mobile and home-centred way of living: a form of *mobile privatisation*. Broadcasting in its applied form was a social product of this distinctive tendency.

The contradictory pressures of this phase of industrial capitalist society were indeed resolved, at a certain level, by the institution of broadcasting. For mobility was only in part the impulse of an independent curiosity: the wish to go out and see new places. It was essentially an impulse formed in the breakdown and dissolution of older and smaller kinds of settlement and productive labour. The new and larger settlements and industrial organisations required major internal mobility, at a primary level, and this was joined by secondary consequences in the dispersal of extended families and in the needs of new kinds of social organisation. Social processes long implicit in the revolution of industrial capitalism were then greatly intensified: especially an increasing distance between immediate living areas and the directed places of work and government. No effective kinds of social control over these transformed industrial and political processes had come anywhere near being achieved or even foreseen. Most people were living in the fall-out area of processes determined beyond them. What had been gained, nevertheless, in intense social struggle, had been the improvement of immediate conditions, within the limits and pressures of these decisive large-scale processes. There was some relative improvement in wages and working conditions, and there was a qualitative change in the distribution of the day, the week and the year between work and off-work periods. These two effects combined in a major emphasis on improvement of the small family home. Yet this privatisation, which was at once an effective achievement and a defensive response, carried, as a consequence, an imperative need for new kinds of contact. The new homes might appear private and 'self-sufficient' but could be maintained only by regular funding and supply from external sources, and these, over a range from employment and prices to depressions and wars, had a decisive and often a disrupting influence on what was nevertheless seen as a separable 'family' project. This relationship created both the need and the form of a new kind of 'communication': news from 'outside', from otherwise inaccessible sources. Already in the drama of the 1880s and 1890s (Ibsen, Chekhov) this structure had appeared: the centre of dramatic interest was now for the first time the family home, but men and women stared from its windows, or waited anxiously for messages, to learn about forces, 'out there', which would determine the conditions of their lives. The new 'consumer' technology which reached its first decisive stage in the 1920s served this complex of needs within just these limits and pressures. There were immediate improvements of the condition and efficiency of the privatised home; there were new facilities, in private transport, for expeditions from the home; and then, in radio, there was a facility for a new kind of social input – news and entertainment brought into the home. Some people spoke of the new machines as gadgets, but they were always much more than this. They were the applied technology of a set of emphases and responses within the determining limits and pressures of industrial capitalist society.

The cheap radio receiver is then a significant index of a general condition and response. It was especially welcomed by all those who had least social opportunities of other kinds; who lacked independent mobility or access to the previously diverse places of entertainment and information. Broadcasting could also come to serve, or seem to serve, as a form of *unified* social intake, at the most general levels. What had been intensively promoted by the radio manufacturing companies thus interlocked with this kind of social need, itself defined within general limits and pressures. In the early stages of radio manufacturing, transmission was conceived before content. By the end of the 1920s the network was there, but still at a low level of content-definition. It was in the 1930s, in the second phase of radio, that most of the significant advances in content were made. The transmission and reception networks created, *as a by-product*, the facilities of primary broadcasting production. But the general social definition of 'content' was already there.

This theoretical model of the general development of broadcasting is necessary to an understanding of the particular development of television. For there were, in the abstract, several different ways in which television as a technical means might have been developed. After a generation of universal domestic television it is not easy to realise this. But it remains true that, after a great deal of intensive research and development, the domestic television set is in a number of ways an inefficient medium of visual broadcasting. Its visual inefficiency by comparison with the cinema is especially striking, whereas in the case of radio there was by the 1930s a highly efficient sound broadcasting receiver, without any real competitors in its own line. Within the limits of the television home-set emphasis it has so far not been possible to make more than minor qualitative improvements. Higher-definition systems, and colour, have still only brought the domestic television set, as a machine, to the standard of a very inferior kind of cinema. Yet most people have adapted to this inferior visual medium, in an unusual kind of preference for an inferior immediate technology, because of the social complex – and especially that of the privatised home – within which broadcasting, as a system, is operative. The cinema has remained at an earlier level of social definition; it was and remains a special kind of theatre, offering specific and discrete works of one general kind. Broadcasting, by contrast, offered a whole social intake: music, news, entertainment, sport. The advantages of this general intake, within the home, much more than outweighed the technical advantages of visual transmission and reception in the cinema, confined as this was to specific and discrete works. While broadcasting was confined to sound, the powerful visual medium of cinema was an immensely popular alternative. But when broadcasting became visual, the option for its social advantages outweighed the immediate technical deficits.

The transition to television broadcasting would have occurred quite generally in the late 1930s and early 1940s, if the war had not intervened. Public television services had begun in Britain in 1936 and in the United States in 1939, but with still very expensive receivers. The full investment in transmission and reception facilities did not occur until the late 1940s and early 1950s, but the growth was thereafter very rapid. The key social tendencies which had led to the definition of broadcasting were by then even more pronounced. There was significantly higher investment in the privatised home, and the social and physical distances between these homes and the decisive political and productive centres of the society had become much greater. Broadcasting, as it had developed in radio, seemed an inevitable model: the central transmitters and the domestic sets.

Television then went through some of the same phases as radio. Essentially, again, the technology of transmission and reception developed before the content, and important parts of the content were and have remained by-products of the technology rather than independent enterprises. As late as the introduction of colour, 'colourful' programmes were being devised to persuade people to buy colour sets. In the earliest stages there was the familiar parasitism on existing events: a coronation, a major sporting event, theatres. A comparable parasitism on the cinema was slower to show itself, until the decline of the cinema altered the terms of trade; it is now very widespread, most evidently in the United States. But again, as in radio, the end of the first general decade brought significant independent television production. By the middle and late 1950s, as in radio in the middle and late 1930s, new kinds of programme were being made for television and there were very important advances in the productive use of the medium, including, as again at a comparable stage in radio, some kinds of original work.

Yet the complex social and technical definition of broadcasting led to inevitable difficulties, especially in the productive field. What television could do relatively cheaply was to transmit something that was in any case happening or had happened. In news, sport, and some similar areas it could provide a service of transmission at comparatively low cost. But in every kind of new work, which it had to produce, it became a very expensive medium, within the broadcasting model. It was never as expensive as film, but the cinema, as a distributive medium, could directly control its revenues. It was, on the other hand, implicit in broadcasting that given the tuneable receiver all programmes could be received without immediate charge. There could have been and can still be a socially financed system of production and distribution within which local and specific charges would be unnecessary; the BBC, based on the licence system for domestic receivers, came nearest to this. But short of monopoly, which still exists in some state-controlled systems, the problems of investment for production, in any broadcasting system, are severe.

Thus within the broadcasting model there was this deep contradiction, of centralised transmission and privatised reception. One economic response was licensing. Another, less direct, was commercial sponsorship and then supportive advertising. But the crisis of production control and financing has been endemic in broadcasting precisely because of the social and technical model that was adopted and that has become so deeply established. The problem is masked, rather than solved, by the fact that as a transmitting technology – its functions largely limited to relay and commentary on other events – some balance could be struck; a limited revenue could finance this limited service. But many of the creative possibilities of television have been frustrated precisely by this apparent solution, and this has far more than local effects on producers and on the balance of programmes. When there has been such heavy investment in a particular model of social communications, there is a restraining complex of financial institutions, of cultural expectations and of specific technical developments, which though it can be seen, superficially, as the effect of a technology is in fact a social complex of a new and central kind.

When old technologies were new:
implementing the future
Carolyn Marvin

Performances by wire

This chapter
appeared as
'Implementing the
future', in When Old
Technologies Were
New: Thinking about
Communications in
the Late Nineteenth
Century (Oxford,
Oxford University
Press, 1988),
pp. 209–31.

[. . .] Perhaps more than any other communications invention, contemporaries considered the telephone the bellwether of a new age. [. . .] As the sole nineteenth-century instrument that transmitted voices across space at the moment of speech, the telephone was both a carrier of point-to-point messages to individuals and a medium of multiple address for public occasions of music, theatre, and politics. The most popular feature of the Paris Exposition Internationale d'Électricité of 1881 was such an arrangement, variously described as the theatrophone and the electrophone. From August to November crowds queued up three evenings a week before two rooms, each containing ten pairs of headsets, in the Palais d'Industrie. In one, listeners heard live performances of the Opéra transmitted through microphones arranged on either side of the prompter's box. In the other, they heard plays from the Théâtre Français through ten microphones placed at the front of the stage near the footlights.[1] Not only were the voices of the actors, actresses, and singers heard in this manner, but also the instruments of the orchestra, the applause and laughter of the audience – 'and alas! the voice of the prompter too'.[2]

[. . .] In London in 1891, the Universal Telephone Company placed fifty telephones in the Royal Italian Opera House in Covent Garden, and another fifty in the Theatre Royal, Drury Lane. All transmitted exclusively to the estate of Sir Augustus Harris at St John's Wood, with an extension to his stables.[3] By 1896 the affluent could secure private connections to a variety of London entertainments for an inclusive annual rent of ten pounds sterling in addition to an installation fee of five pounds.[4] The queen was one of these clients. In addition to having special lines from her sitting room to the Foreign Office, the Home Office, the Board of Green Cloth, and Marlborough House, Her Majesty enjoyed direct connections to her favourite entertainments.[5]

Commercial interest in a larger, less exclusive audience was not far behind. 'Nickel-in-the-slot' versions of the hookups provided by the Theatrophone Company of Paris to its individual subscribers were offered as a public novelty at some resorts. A franc bought five minutes of listening time; fifty centimes bought half as much. Between acts and whenever all curtains were down, the company piped out piano solos from its offices. [. . .]

Informal entertainments were sometimes spontaneously organized by telephone operators during the wee hours of the night, when customer calls were few and far between. On a circuit of several stations, operators might sit and exchange amusing stories. One night in 1891 operators at Worcester, Fall River, Boston, Springfield, Providence, and New York organized their own concert. The *Boston Evening Record* reported:

> The operator in Providence plays the banjo, the Worcester operator the harmonica, and gently the others sing. Some tune will be started by the players and the others will sing. To appreciate the effect, one must have a transmitter close to his ear. The music will sound as clear as though it were in the same room.[6]

[. . .] And, portent of the future, in 1912 the New York Magnaphone and Music Company installed motor-driven phonographs that sent recorded music to local subscribers over a hundred transmitters.[7]

In 1889 a Chicago Telephone Company experiment in transmitting *The Charlatan*, a comic opera playing at the Columbia Theatre, was so successful that its general manager announced plans to furnish subscribers with musical events, comedy, drama, vaudeville, and sermons by prominent preachers.[8] Manager Angus S. Hibbard pointed to the precedent set by the Wisconsin Telephone Company of Milwaukee, which had provided orchestral music from the Palm Garden resort free 'as a compliment to the company's subscribers' every evening and Sunday afternoon for three years. A report six weeks into the Palm Garden experiment described it as 'a distinctively twentieth-century idea'.[9] [. . .] Wisconsin general manager J.D. McLeod described his company as American 'pioneers': 'Judging from the nightly demand upon us, and its popularity, there is a merchantable quantity in such entertainments; and amusement people may ultimately take it up on these lines. But as far as the Wisconsin Telephone company is concerned, it is enough to have broadened its usefulness.'[10]

Telephone entertainments were not limited to musical transmissions. In March 1912 alumni at the annual Chicago Yale Club banquet heard Yale's president address after-dinner remarks to them by long-distance from a comfortable seat in New Haven. Seven hundred newspapermen, gathered at the Waldorf Astoria a few months later for a joint meeting of the Associated Press and the American Newspaper Publishers' Association, were treated to a special after-dinner telephone program. As each guest listened on a special receiver fitted into a watchcase, President Taft spoke from Boston, Canadian premier Robert Borden spoke from Hot Springs, Virginia, a Kipling poem was recited from Daly's Theatre, and a vocalist performed a 'Southern song' from another New York theatre, the Winter Garden.[11]

Sporting events provided occasions for telephone transmission, and had inspired imaginative experiments with the telegraph. In 1884 three Nashville telegraph operators, J.U. Rust, E.W. Morgan, and A.H. Stewart, organized a 'vivid view of the exact situations and plays in a game of baseball played in Chattanooga' for an audience in a Nashville hall.[12] From the playing field, one operator telegraphed each play of the game over a leased line to Nashville, where another operator announced it to the audience. The third operator moved cards bearing the players' names around a ball field painted on poster board that was visible to the entire audience.

In 1886 Detroit, Morgan & Co., as this entrepreneurial team called itself, relayed a Detroit–Chicago game to a Detroit Opera House crowd of more than six hundred [. . .]. The *Detroit Free Press* described the reaction of the audience.

> The audience during the first four or five innings of yesterday's game was wrought up to a very high pitch of enthusiasm. For instance when the operator read – with Dalyrymple's name appearing as batsman – 'foul fly to left', the audience fairly held its breath, and when the next instant the operator called out, 'and out to White', there came a storm of applause, just such as is heard on a veritable ball field. And so it was all through the calling of strikes, balls, long hits and short ones, outs, errors and 'safes', the excitement was intense.[13]

By 1889 the idea had caught on elsewhere. As a gesture of good will to the twenty-four hundred telephone subscribers of the Cleveland Company, its operators were 'always informed regarding the base ball score and always ready to answer questions regarding it. They keep up with the games from inning to inning, and most of them being interested themselves are agreeable in answering all demands on their information so far. Such is the policy of the exchange.'[14] [. . .]

[. . .]

Church services were also an occasion for telephone transmission. From about 1894, telephone wires connected subscribers with local pulpits in towns as large as Pittsburgh and Philadelphia, and as small as Paris, Texas.[15] [. . .]

Telephone pulpits seem to have come earlier to British churches. An account of the inauguration in 1890 of a service in Christ Church in Birmingham with connection to subscribers in London, Manchester, Derby, Coventry, Kidderminster, and Hanley went as follows:

> When the morning service commenced there was what appeared to be an unseemly clamor to hear the services. The opening prayer was interrupted by cries of 'Hello, there!' 'Are you there?' 'Put me onto Christ Church.' 'No, I

don't want the church', etc. But presently quiet obtained and by the time the Psalms were reached we got almost unbroken connection and could follow the course of the services. We could hear little of the prayers – probably from the fact that the officiating minister was not within voice-reach of the transmitter. The organ had a faint, far-away sound, but the singing and the sermon were a distinct success.[16]

[. . .]

An occasion that shared many features of the religious revival was the political campaign. Both events were marked by intense community discussion about the proper kind of society for people to live in, and both were strongly oral in character. Both fell to the blandishments of electricity with no resistance. In 1896, an election year that saw a prolific use of electric media in connection with political news and entertainment, the South Bend Telephone Company of Indiana connected its patrons free of charge one August evening to a tent wherein the Honorable John L. Griffiths of Indianapolis was making a Republican campaign speech to assembled supporters. [. . .] The occasion had been conceived as a two-way affair, with contributions from the crowd as much a part of the event as the speech of the candidate. [. . .]

The telephone could reproduce the heinous as well as the holy, and some communities were interested in both. Public justice pursued in the face-to-face environs of the courtroom was occasionally extended beyond its walls. The sensational murder trial of Reginald Birchall in Woodstock, Ontario, in 1890 attracted people from every neighbouring town to a courtroom scarcely large enough to accommodate the official participants in the trial, alongside journalists from London, the United States, and all Canada. An enterprising local tavern keeper arranged to install a transmitter above the judge's bench in the courtroom. This was connected to twenty receivers in his tavern, each of which he rented for twenty-five cents an hour to the overflow of the curious, and presumably the thirsty. Four tubes were connected to a private room for ladies. All were kept busy.[17]

Systems of electric news

Early in 1889 the *Electrical Review* summarized 'In the Twentyninth Century: The Day of an American Journalist in 2889', a Jules Verne short story that portrayed a great American editor one thousand years thence:

> The editor rules the world; he receives ministers of other governments and settles international quarrels; he is the patron of all the arts and sciences; he maintains all the great novelists; he has not only a telephone line to Paris but a telephote line as well, whereby he can at any time from his study in New York, see a Parisian with whom he converses.
>
> Advertisements are flashed on the clouds; reporters describe events orally to millions of subscribers; and if a subscriber becomes weary, or is busy, he

attaches his phonograph to his telephone, and hears the news at his leisure. If a fire is raging in Chicago, subscribers in New York may not only listen to the description of an eyewitness, but by the telephote may see the fire.[18]

Most predictions of the future of newsgathering were not so dramatically detailed, but the theme of control at a distance so dear to the hearts of scientists and engineers was here extended to the world's understanding of itself through a process of centralized electrical monitoring. The Faustian impulse to embrace the whole world in the nerve net of electricity already had created telegraphic wire services for this purpose. [. . .]

Innovative systems were often recapitulations. Telegraphic news reached nineteenth-century publics not only through the traditional medium of the printed newspaper, but also in bulletins hastily scrawled from the latest dispatches and posted outside newspaper offices. A bulletin board electrically automated for this purpose was exhibited in New York in 1888. It consisted of a row of horizontal windows through which messages were spelled out by a series of separately revolving wheels inscribed with alpha-numeric characters. The electric bulletin board was 'not intended to have a record of the news it conveys, but is designed merely to satisfy the eagerness for news'.[19]

The *New York Times* led its sister newspapers in the regular use of wireless telegraphy. For European stories in its Sunday edition, for which mails were too slow and undersea cables too costly, the *Times* had come to rely on wireless by 1908. Four years later it was receiving 'practically all of its daily foreign news service by wireless telegraphy', a then remarkable stream of about twenty thousand words a week.[20] This exchange between the old world and the new required a cooperative network of cables, telephones, and wireless stations, and was said to have broken a number of speed records in overseas wireless transmission.

The distribution of presidential election returns in the late nineteenth century was the most ambitiously organized American effort to use new electric technologies to deliver the news. Election returns had been distributed by the telegraph since its invention, but the telephone added speed, immediacy, and convenience. Early telephone distribution depended on a backbone of telegraphic returns and used supporting visual technologies such as the stereopticon, the kinetoscope, and the electric searchlight. From 1892, a growing demand for quick and comprehensive election statistics was met and doubtless augmented by unifying old and new networks for increased capacity and flexibility.

The first coordinated system of telephone returns was organized for the presidential election of 1892. During the previous election, American Bell Telephone Company president Howard Stockton had invited guests to his Boston home to hear the returns come in over a special telephone wire on election night.[21] For the 1892 election, the telephone companies of New York and Chicago arranged to forward returns coming in to them from telephone and telegraph wires across the country to all interested New York and Chicago clubs and hotels. Information was systematically exchanged between these two major cities over newly laid circuits through

Milwaukee. Some telephone bulletins were received as much as ninety minutes in advance of bulletins from local telegraph offices.[22]

[. . .]

Not until the presidential election of 1896 were long-distance lines plentiful enough for telephone companies to organize a national network for gathering and distributing election returns. Here, too, extensive telegraphic support was still necessary. [. . .]

For the election of 1900, AT&T collected local returns from telephone companies across the country, compiled summary bulletins, and circulated updated returns back through the same network of local exchanges. In New York City, the New York Telephone Company provided services to thirty-two Manhattan clubs and hotels and thirty-five country clubs, hotels, and associations in Westchester County, and connected individual subscribers to a hundred special stations where operators with the latest information answered their enquiries. Stereopticon bulletins were also displayed at the principal exchanges. In New York, less demand for the return-reporting services of Western Union than in previous elections was attributed to the improved quality of telephone equipment and services.[23]

With the cooperation of AT&T, the telegraph companies, and their local and state networks, the Chicago Telephone Company relayed returns within a minute of receipt to an estimated twenty-five hundred subscribers in hundreds of clubs and houses where private telephone parties were in progress. A General Electric searchlight projected by the *Record* from the top of the Chicago Masonic Temple did not fulfill the fondest hopes of sky-writing enthusiasts, but it did communicate a message:

> It had been announced that McKinley's election would be signaled by a steady horizontal sweep of light from left to right and right to left, while if Bryan were successful the beam was to be swung in a circle around the horizon, with a vertical up-and-down motion. As long as the result was in doubt the agreed signal was a steady, vertical ray. Many watchers throughout Cook County thus received their first news of the result.[24]

In 1912 the distribution of election returns was still provided free of charge and without interruption to regular telephone service, but it had been much refined and perfected. [. . .] The public was notified in the newspapers to call 'Election News' for the latest bulletins, each approximately one page long and requiring two minutes to read. At the end of each bulletin readers announced, 'Please hang up your receivers, another bulletin will be read in ten minutes.'[25] Bulletins were read continuously to one group of subscribers, then another, until new bulletins came in. Special equipment prevented interference or interruption from subscribers attempting to speak or to signal the operator.

What did it mean, this novel network of the latest election intelligence, to its beneficiaries? It did not seem to them to be simply an extension of the telegraph. Dismissing the familiar wire service network as 'very largely a mechanical operation, which a child can comprehend', the

Manchester (New Hampshire) *Union* concluded that 'the collection of the returns from Kickapoo, Arizona; Masardis, Maine; Laredo, Texas, and their dissemination among millions of people before they retire to the privacy of their homes is another matter.'[26] Impressed by estimates that perhaps half a million persons had received telephone returns in their homes and offices, the *Union* marvelled:

> The news was, literally speaking, scooped up in this great telephone net and talked into one's ears from unexpected distances . . . Thousands sat with their ear glued to the receiver the whole night long, hypnotized by the possibilities unfolded to them for the first time . . . If we can hear hundreds of thousands of people scattered over this broad land speak, why can we not in time produce other wonderful results now deemed impossible?[27]

Telephonic news seemed poised to overtake telegraph news, an American electrical journal commented in 1895:

> Already in large cities, the ordinary subscriber uses his telephone ten times a day . . . Moreover, we record this week the use of the long distance telephone wholesale for [political] convention news purposes, thus sapping the vitals of the telegraphic news systems of the Associated and United Press.[28]

Though the picture was not quite that grim, since the telephone and telegraph would learn useful ways of cooperating in the offices of the wire services, newspapers were indeed enamored of the excitement of telephone news. The capacity to communicate the thunder of events directly to an audience with an immediacy greater than that of the telegraph or newspaper alone distinguished the new electric media from the old, even as the new media were pressed into service of the old. In spite of the American Bell Company's policy against permitting private individuals or companies to send news by telephone wire, late nineteenth-century newspapers routinely featured late-arriving telephonic dispatches with bold headings announcing precisely this means of transmission.[29]

By reproducing and simultaneously transforming the telegraphic information network, the telephone distribution of breaking news was part of the transition from a passing world. The crowds that gathered in the streets to celebrate McKinley's victory in 1896 had little inkling in that euphoric moment that their descendants would learn the results of great political contests in sedately familiar living rooms. *Harper's Weekly* described the world that was passing, and, without recognizing them, some of the instruments of its transformation:

> Such a crowd as tramped and cheered and roared up and down Broadway election night, and surged about every building where a calcium-light was throwing election returns upon a screen, has never before been seen in New York . . . The crowds on upper Broadway were entertained as well as instructed; between bulletins on one screen there was an exhibition of the

vitascope, and as the scenes were flashed upon it the shouts of laughter and merriment rose above the din of horns and rattles.[30]

Other efforts to distribute the news were organized from time to time. In the farming country of the Midwest at the turn of the century, weather reports were regularly read over the wires.[31] In April 1898, when all signs pointed to the entry of the United States into Cuba's war against Spain, the general manager of the Chicago Telephone Company promised that every one of the company's fourteen thousand subscribers would be notified by operators within twenty minutes of any official declaration of war. 'Our idea in doing this is to inform our patrons of the declaration probably quicker than they would otherwise get the news', Angus S. Hibbard explained in an official announcement: 'We are a quasi-public corporation and we rather consider it our duty to act this way . . . Of course we will try to guard against any canard, but in no event will we assume responsibility for the news as we send it out. Our operators will simply tell the subscribers that we have received it as news.'[32]

Ways of using the telephone to get the latest news were also improvised without any professional assistance at all. On party line systems one found 'listeners all along the wire for every scrap of conversation going. So a whole countryside may learn that the doctor is on his way to Mrs Brown, Mrs Jones or Mrs Robinson.'[33] Not all of these listeners were interested only in local news. In 1905 *Telephony* reported that every afternoon in Evanston, Illinois, a subscriber called a prominent business house to inquire. 'Well, what's the news today? Somebody just said that the Atlantic won the yacht race, is that so? Has anybody resigned from the cabinet today? How did the Chicago–Pittsburgh game come out? Anybody hurt in the trolley collision? Do you know what day the Cunard liners sail for Europe?'[34]

Telephone diffusion: a proto-broadcasting system

In the late nineteenth century, single events such as a declaration of war, a baseball game, a church service, or a concert were transmitted by new technologies with unprecedented immediacy to scattered audiences *on occasion*. Although modern media transmit content of a similar kind, late nineteenth-century telephone occasions otherwise bear little resemblance to twentieth-century mass media programming. Nineteenth-century telephone occasions were derived transmissions of independently occurring events and were intended to extend the primary audiences of the pulpit, stage, concert hall, and playing field. Wholly invented programming, by contrast, is a distinctive social feature of electronic mass media.

Commercial efforts to enlarge audiences electrically for some regularly repeated occasions in the late nineteenth century were generally of short duration; the audiences they attracted were small. Electrophone parties in Britain were said to be a pastime of the idle rich, not the humble poor.[35] Electrophone Ltd, one of the sturdier British companies to take up regular telephone transmission, piped sermons from the most prestigious pulpits and plays from the most prestigious theatres to London's leading hospitals for the edification of affluent patients, and to occasional private residences as well. Nevertheless, twelve years after its incorporation, Electrophone had a regular subscriber audience of barely six hundred.[36]

But from 1893 until after World War 1, when a number of private companies and national states began to create radio broadcasting systems, an organization in Budapest was a remarkable exception to the usual pattern. This was the Telefon Hirmondó, which for almost a generation transmitted daily programming over telephone wires to supplement the regular telephone service of more than six thousand subscribers. *Hirmondó* was a Magyar term for the crier who shouted the news from the centre of the medieval village for all to hear. Today it denotes a radio announcer. Its semantic transformation followed a path directly through the career of the Telefon Hirmondó. For twenty years Hirmondó's audience received a fully daily schedule of political, economic, and sporting news, lectures, plays, concerts, and recitations. The language of the Telefon Hirmondó was Magyar, the language of Hungarian nationalism. In operation, the Telefon Hirmondó was a closed and exclusive system of cultural communication among the Hungarian elite during the last decades of Magyar power before World War I, a fact that appears to account for both its economic and its cultural staying power.

The Telefon Hirmondó was the brainchild of Tivadar Puskás, a Hungarian engineer who had worked on Thomas Edison's staff of inventors and researchers at Menlo Park. To Puskás, according to Edison, belonged the original credit for suggesting the concept of the telephone switchboard that made the telephone a powerful and practical means of communication. Accounts of the Telefon Hirmondó were followed with interest in the British and American press, and a short-lived imitation of it appeared in the United States. It provided perhaps the only example of sustained and systematic programming in the nineteenth century that truly prefigures twentieth-century broadcasting systems.

The origins of the Telefon Hirmondó lay in the novel and popular theatrophone exhibition that Puskás helped mount at the Paris Exposition Internationale d'Électricité in 1881. The following year he staged his own theatrophone demonstration in Budapest by transmitting a National Theatre opera performance to a nearby grand ball.[37] In the meantime, Puskás's brother, Ferenc, acquired the first telephone concession in Budapest, and the Puskás family hired Nikola Tesla, a longtime friend, to engineer its construction.[38] The Budapest telephone system prospered under Ferenc Puskás, and in 1892 Tivadar Puskás, who had played a minor role in some of the more exciting electrical developments of the age and knew many of its foremost inventors and engineers personally, returned to Budapest to implement his own remarkable idea of a Telefon Hirmondó. The first program was transmitted from the central telephone exchange to one thousand regular telephone subscribers in 1893. Within weeks of the inception of the Telefon Hirmondó, Tividar Puskás was dead. His creation outlived him by almost a quarter of a century.

At first Telefon Hirmondó's programming consisted of news summaries read at the beginning of each hour and immediately repeated. Silence reigned until the next hour's transmission. Five months into the new experiment, *Science Siftings* reported:

> The news collector does his work in the night, and having his budget filled he takes his place in the central office at nine in the morning and begins to tell his story, which is given in a telegraphic style, clear, condensed, and precise. In five minutes after the first delivery the budget of news is repeated, in case some of the subscribers may not have heard. It consists for the most part of home events and news of Hungary. At ten o'clock the foreign news is given, and after eleven the doings of the Hungarian Parliament. Various items of city news are given during the day.[39]

News in the daytime was balanced by cultural programs in the evening – perhaps a report of a lecture at the Hungarian Academy, or the recitation 'with all due emphasis' of a new poem.

Efforts to transmit music met with poor success and provided the first indications of a problem that increased with the listening audience. Simply stated, the addition of subscriber outlets diminished the volume of sound for every subscriber. When control of the Hirmondó passed out of the hands of the Puskás family in 1894, a new distribution system that bypassed the regular telephone network eliminated this and other technical problems.[40] The new company was granted the same right to place its wires as the telephone and telegraph companies. By 1900 the Telefon Hirmondó employed over 150 people in its offices at 22 Megrendelhetö Rákóczi, on one of the 'finest avenues' in Budapest.[41]

The news operation was like that of any newspaper. News from abroad came by telegraph. Local news was assigned to a staff of twelve reporters. A special staff assigned to the galleries of the Hungarian and Austrian Houses of Parliament forward half-hourly reports of the latest developments.[42] Galley proofs of every story were printed by hand roller presses in parallel columns on sheets of paper two feet by six inches. Several sheets constituted the daily program. The work of the 'stentors' who read the news was thought to be so exhausting that they were rotated at ten-minute intervals in groups of four.[43]

[. . .]

Photographs and illustrated advertising posters show that subscribers listened to the Hirmondó through two small round earpieces hanging from a diamond-shaped board mounted on the wall.[44] The audience for which the service was intended apparently possessed wealth, education, and leisure. Its cultural relaxations were those of the opera and the theatre. Its attachment to sport was aristocratic. The latest intelligence from the principal Hungarian and Austrian racetracks, the cycling and automobile track, and the rugby field and billiard table was 'flashed over the wires the moment the results are known'.[45] Its children received proper cultural exposure in a weekly children's program of short stories, songs, recitations, and instrumental music.[46]

The Hirmondó devoted the largest share of its programming to the conditions and exigencies of the financial world. Even on Sundays and during evening programs with an artistic and performing emphasis, due attention was given to the stock exchange. Subscribers were kept posted about developments in the Hungarian and Austrian exchanges and the foreign exchanges, including Wall Street and London.[47] News was also communicated directly from the agricultural districts of the country for speculators in corn and wheat.

[. . .] By 1896 the Hirmondó boasted six thousand subscribers, but this figure represented barely one percent of the population of Budapest.[48] The number of subscribers remained almost constant until 1917, after which reports of the Telefon Hirmondó dropped out of the foreign press. The audience of the Hirmondó was probably larger, since each household may have represented several listeners, and semipublic installations seemed to attract many different listeners. A traveller's account from 1908 explained how this worked.

> You may be seated as I was in the reading-room of one of the hotels or in a large coffee-house, when suddenly a rush is made for a telephone-looking instrument [the Telefon Hirmondó] which hangs from the wall. In time perhaps you will become one of these 'rushers.'[49]

[. . .] Little is known of the Telefon Hirmondó following World War I, during which most of its exterior installations were destroyed. In 1925 the Telefon Hirmondó and Hungarian Radio Broadcasting were combined into a single organization, and the Hirmondó became merely a wire-diffusion agency for studio-broadcast programs.[50]

In the United States at least one brief experiment was directly inspired by the Hirmondó. This was the Telephone Herald of Newark, New Jersey. After sampling the Telefon Hirmondó on vacation in Budapest, a former *New York Herald* advertising manager, M. M. Gillam, set about organizing a similar enterprise in the United States.[51] Gillam and William E. Gun, builder of the battleship *Oregon*, organized the New Jersey Telephone Herald Company with promises of financial backing from a wealthy New York coal magnate. Just as the service was schedule to begin operating, in March 1911, the New York Telephone Company reneged on its contract to lease wires to the Telephone Herald, which it regarded as a competing public utility.[52] After six months of legal wrangling, the New Jersey Public Utilities Commission held the telephone company to its original agreement. The Telephone Herald inaugurated service on October 23, 1911, with the following daily program:

Daily Program of the 'Telephone Herald'

8.00	Exact astronomical time
8.00– 9.00	Weather, late telegrams, London exchange quotations, chief items of interest from the morning papers
9.00– 9.45	Special sales at the various stores; social program for the day
9.45–10.00	Local personals and small items

10.00–11.30	New York Stock Exchange quotations and market letter
11.30–12.00	New York miscellaneous items
Noon	Exact astronomical time
12.00–12.30	Latest general news; naval, military, and Congressional notes
12.30– 1.00	Midday New York Stock Exchange quotations
1.00– 2.00	Reception of the half-day's most interesting news
2.00– 2.15	Foreign cable dispatches
2.15– 2.30	Trenton and Washington items
2.30– 2.45	Fashion notes and household hints
2.45– 3.15	Sporting news; theatrical news
3.15– 3.30	New York Stock Exchange closing quotations
3.30– 5.00	Music, readings, lectures
5.00– 6.00	Stories and talks for the children
8.00–10.30	Vaudeville, concert, opera[53]

The schedule of items presented by the Telephone Herald was faithfully modeled on the Telefon Hirmondó's 'order of the day'. [. . .] The capital reserves of the Telephone Herald proved to be unequal to the popular demand for it, and the legal contest with the telephone company had frightened off investors. With depleted financial resources, the Herald was unable to install equipment fast enough to meet its subscription orders. After three months, twenty-five hundred subscriber contracts had been drawn up, but the number of installations as not much over a thousand.[54] Soon the financial strain began to show. Employees were irregularly paid. The musical service ended abruptly one afternoon when the musicians refused to play any longer without salary. The newsroom staff of two editors and four stentors departed a month later. Lacking capital funds, the service was suspended, and then entirely disbanded.[55]

The history of the Telefon Hirmondó and its admiring imitator, the Telephone Herald, demonstrates that the notion of transmitting regular news and entertainment programming to large audiences existed well before the advent of twentieth-century wireless broadcasting. The existence of these two precursors did not generate any popular shock of recognition, however, or nurture any expert consensus that their efforts marked an inevitable path to the future. While the public was generally confident that something fantastic and all-embracing was germinating among the many remarkable contraptions of electrical communication, the boundaries of immediate possibility appeared much narrower to those closest to the technologies involved.

The historical development of mass broadcasting ahead of cable programming, which the Hirmondó more closely resembled, might have been reversed if radio had not been invented at a time when wire diffusion was still largely experimental. It was not immediately realized how significant a departure from telephony and telegraphy radio would be, however. As late as 1921, Walter Gifford, then four years away from assuming the presidency of AT&T, had difficulty visualizing separate roles for wired and wireless media in the twentieth century. He recalled in 1944:

Nobody knew early in 1921 where radio was really headed. Everything about broadcasting was uncertain. For my own part I expected that since it was a form of telephony, and since we were in the business of furnishing wires for telephony, we were sure to be involved in broadcasting somehow. Our first vague idea, as broadcasting appeared, was that perhaps people would expect to be able to pick up a telephone and call some radio station, so that they could give radio talks to other people equipped to listen.[56]

Late in 1921 an internal Bell Telephone memorandum had projected the future of broadcasting simply as the transmission of important occasions, such as Armistice Day ceremonies or presidential inaugurations:

> We can imagine the President or other official speaking in Washington . . . and that his voice is then carried out over a network of wires extending to all the important centers of the country . . . In each city and larger town there are halls equipped with loud speaking apparatus at which the people in the neighborhood are gathered.[57]

If historical events had occurred in a different order and wire diffusion had been left unchallenged to develop at its own pace, that pace might have been a slow one. Through a combination of technical and economic constraints, wire diffusion might have evolved to suit the needs and interests of privileged minorities, filtering down only gradually to a wider population. By making the delivery of content cheaper and more democratic, wireless communication made mass audiences possible for electric media, and accelerated the development of programming of all kinds.

The Telefon Hirmondó was a hybrid of newspaper practices, conventional modes of oral address, and telephone capabilities that anticipated twentieth-century radio. In operation it was a transitional form using conservative techniques that looked backward to newspaper methods for gathering information, which it presented as spoken newspaper items. In its time it was seen as a novel newspaper form, but it was radically forward-looking in its continuous and regularly scheduled programming, the origination of some programs from its own studios, and the combination of news and entertainment in the same service. No other telephone diffusion experiments embraced a system of regular, timely programming like that of the Hirmondó. Most were limited simply to the reproduction of full-length 'occasions'.

Notes

1   'The electrical exhibition at Paris', *Electrician* (London) 3 December 1881; 'The International Exhibition and the Congress of Electricity at Paris', *Scientific American*, 10 December 1881, p. 377.
2   Edouard Hospitalier, *Modern Applications of Electricity*, trans. Julius Maier (London, Kegan Paul, 1882), p. 392.
3   *Western Electrician* (Chicago), 12 September 1891, p. 155.
4   *Invention* (London), 1 February 1896, p. 66.

5   *Lightning* (London), 9 July 1896, p. 38.
6   'Concert music by telephone', *Scientific American*, 10 October 1891, p. 225.
7   'Phonographic music transmitted by telephone', *Electrical Review and Western Electrician*, 12 September 1912, p. 567.
8   'Comic opera by telephone', *Western Electrician* (Chicago), 4 March 1899, p. 126.
9   'Telephone concerts in Wisconsin', *Western Electrician* (Chicago), 26 December 1896, p. 315.
10   Ibid.
11   'The telephone as entertainer', *Telephony* (Chicago), 18 May, 1912, p. 610.
12   'Base ball by electricity', *Electrical Review*, 24 July 1886.
13   Ibid., quoted from the *Detroit Free Press*.
14   'Long distance telephoning', *Electrical Review*, 3 August 1889, p. 6.
15   *Electrical World*, 5:1. See also 'Church service by telephone', *American Telephone Journal* (Chicago), 30 July 1904, pp. 65–6.
16   'The telephone at Christ Church, Birmingham, England', *Western Electrician* (Chicago), 11 October 1890, p. 195. See also *Electrical Review* (London), 14 (17): 7.
17   'Novel use of the telephone', *Western Electrician* (Chicago), 16 August 1890, p. 185.
18   'How electricity will help out the editor of the future', *Electrical Review*, 2 February 1889, p. 4. Verne's story is reprinted in Jules Verne, *Yesterday and Tomorrow*, trans. I.O. Evans (Westport, Conn., Associated Booksellers, 1965), pp. 107–24.
19   *Electrical Review*, 1 September 1888, p. 10.
20   'Wireless as a news carrier', *Electrical Review and Western Electrician*, 6 April 1912, p. 668.
21   *Electrical Review*, 17 November 1888, p. 5.
22   'Election returns by telephone and telegraph', *Western Electrician* (Chicago), 26 November 1892, p. 275; 'Election returns', *Electrical Review*, 19 November 1892, p. 151.
23   'Use of electricity in announcing election returns', *Western Electrician* (Chicago), 17 November 1900, p. 323.
24   Ibid.
25   M.D. Atwater, 'Distributing national election returns by telephone', *Telephony* (Chicago), 9 November 1912, pp. 721–4.
26   'The telephone and election returns', *Electrical Review*, 16 December 1896, p. 298.
27   Ibid.
28   *Electrical Engineer* (London), 4 September 1895, p. 233.
29   Ibid., 28 August 1895, pp. 206–7.
30   'Election night in New York', *Harper's Weekly*, 14 November 1896, p. 1122.
31   'The farmer and the telephone', *American Telephone Journal* (Chicago), 29 March 1902, pp. 202–3.
32   'War news in Chicago by telephone', *Western Electrician* (Chicago), 9 April 1898, p. 213.
33   'The telephone in the country', *Telephony* (Chicago), July 1905, p. 52.
34   'Telephoning is the national craze', *Telephony* (Chicago), December 1905, p. 52.
35   *Lightning* (London), 5 January 1893, p. 1.
36   Paul Adorjan, 'Wire-broadcasting', *Journal of the Society of Arts* (London), 31 August 1945, p. 514. See also *Electrical Engineer* (London), 19 July 1895, p. 57; *Electrician* (London), 9 June 1899, p. 243.
37   'The telephone in Hungary', *Scientific American*, 2 July 1881, p. 5.
38   John J. O'Neill, *Prodigal Genius: The Life of Nikola Tesla* (New York, Ives Washburn, 1944), pp. 45–6.
39   'The telephone journal', *Science Siftings* (London), 15 July 1893, p. 362.
40   Ferenc Erdei (ed.), 'Radio and television', in *Information Hungary* (New York, Pergamon Press, 1968), p. 645; 'Telephon-Zeitung', *Zeitschrift für Elektrotechnik* (Vienna), 1 December 1896, p. 741.
41   Thomas S. Denison, 'The telephone newspaper', *World's Work*, April 1901, p. 641.
42   W.G. Fitzgerald, 'A telephone newspaper', *Scientific American*, 22 June 1907, p. 507;

Frederick A. Talbot, 'A telephone newspaper', *Littell's Living Age* (Boston), 8 August 1903, pp. 374–5.

43 Denison, 'The telephone newspaper', p. 642.

44 Toth Endréné (ed.), *Budapest Enciklopédia* (Budapest, Corvina Kiadó, 1970), p. 313.

45 Fitzgerald, 'A telephone newspaper', p. 507; Talbot, 'A telephone newspaper', p. 375.

46 'Telephon-Zeitung', *Zeitschrift für Elektrotechnik* (Vienna), pp. 740–1.

47 Talbot, 'A telephone newspaper', p. 507. By 1907 the list of foreign exchanges included New York, Frankfurt, Paris, Berlin, and London.

48 Jules Erdoess, 'Le journal téléphonique de Budapest: l'ancêtre de la radio', *Radiodiffusion* (Geneva), October 1936, p. 37.

49 W.B. Forster Bovill, *Hungary and the Hungarians* (London, Methuen, 1908), p. 111.

50 Erdoess, 'Le journal téléphonique de Budapest', p. 39.

51 Arthur F. Colton, 'Telephone newspaper – a new marvel', *Technical World Magazine* (Chicago), February 1912, p. 668.

52 'Order in the matter of the petition of the New Jersey Herald Telephone Company', *Second Annual Report of the Board of Public Utility Commissioners for the State of New Jersey* (Trenton, MacCrellish and Quigley, 1912), pp. 147–50.

53 Colton, 'Telephone newspaper', p. 669.

54 'An American telephone newspaper', *Literary Digest*, 16 March 1912, p. 529, quoting *Editor & Publisher*.

55 'Phone Herald's short life', *Fourth Estate*, 2 March 1912, p. 23.

56 William Peck Banning, *Commercial Broadcasting Pioneer: the WEAF Experiment, 1922–1926* (Cambridge, Mass., Harvard University Press, 1946), p. 59.

57 Ibid., p. 60.

5

The wireless age: radio broadcasting   **Patrice Flichy**

A vast amount of historiographical literature on the wireless exists. As is often the case in this field, these writings have all tried to determine the true paternity of the invention. The results are, unsurprisingly, largely dependent on each author's nationality. Thus, the great encyclopaedias have attributed five different inventors to the wireless. For the *Lexicon der Deutschen Buchgemeinschaft* Hertz is the father; for the *Malaïa Sovietskaïa Entsiklopedia* it is Popov. The *Nuova Enciclopedia Sonzogno* has naturally given the first place to Marconi, while the *Larousse universel* mentions him, but second to Branly. Finally, the *Encyclopaedia Britannica* has chosen Lodge (see Joos, 1971; Cazenoble, 1981: 2).

In reality the wireless, like numerous other modern technologies, was developed concurrently in several countries. Moreover, it combined the discoveries of a number of different investors. As David Landes (1969: 425) writes, 'the array of scientists and technicians who shared in the early development of the wireless reads like a Unesco committee.'

James Maxwell is generally placed at the head of the procession. In the 1860s this English mathematician unified, within the same theory, existing knowledge on the undulatory characteristics of light, electricity and magnetism. Maxwell's theory constituted one of the great paradigms of nineteenth-century physics. It was, however, only confirmed in 1887 by experiments conducted by the German physicist Heinrich Hertz. Hertz managed to produce (and to detect) electromagnetic waves, which were later given his name.

In view of these facts, one might tend to agree with P. Rousseau (1958) that 'the wireless is a typical example of an invention formed entirely by science, in which empiricism and tinkering played no part, and which advanced guided by theory.' In contrast, another historian Ch. Süsskind (1968), has studied Marconi's experiments and considers that

This chapter is taken from *Dynamics of Modern Communication: the Shaping and Impact of New Communication Technologies* (London, Sage, 1995), pp. 99–116.

'once again, a practical invention has a lead over theory' (see Cazenoble, 1981: 7).

It rapidly becomes apparent that neither of these two contradictory analyses is entirely correct, for there is no unilinear model of the articulation between science and technology. More significantly, the sequence of different stages in the history of the wireless was not a foregone conclusion. Hertz's experiments could well have remained confined to academic physics. In no way were they obviously meant to serve in the creation of a new technological system. Similarly, radio broadcasting was not the inevitable result of radiotelephony.

What appears today as a series of naturally articulated steps is, in reality, the history of a difficult passage from one domain to another; from science to technology (and vice versa), from the military to telecommunications, from commercial information to entertainment, and so forth. It is the history of this movement that I shall now retrace.

From Maxwell to Marconi

Science historians generally compare Maxwell to Hertz. The former is said to have formulated the theory of electromagnetic fields and the electromagnetic theory of light; the latter is said to have verified these theories. It seems, however, that such a clear-cut division never existed between these two scientists' work. According to Salvo d'Agostino (1989: 2), 'Maxwell was convinced of having provided some experimental proof of his theory.' Later, English or German scientists were to try to verify parts of Maxwell's theory. Hertz's originality lay in his attempt to demonstrate the English physicist's 'basic theories', i.e. the existence of 'waves with electric force' in a vacuum or in air. Not content to verify certain predictions in Maxwell's theory, Hertz went further and developed an instrumental theory which he compared to the Maxwell system.

The Maxwell–Hertz relationship was therefore more complex than is often thought. It did not consist merely of the passage from theory to experimentation, but rather of a new intellectual development that was compared to a theory. Even in a case which is often analysed as an intellectual filiation, there was a specific development which integrated the initial theory.

In a teleological conception of the history of science, some authors claim that Branly contributed an effective wave-detecting instrument to Hertz's discovery. This view of Branly's research is, however, inaccurate. Branly was a physicist, a specialist in electricity and a meticulous experimenter. He carried out research on conductors and insulators and studied the development of conductivity with respect to different forms of heat radiation and luminous radiation. In 1890 he noticed that under the effect of a spark, a tube filled with iron filings became a conductor or an insulator alternately. Moreover, when the spark transmitter was moved to another room the effect – later to be called the Branly effect – continued.[1]

Branly's interpretation of this phenomenon is not always very clear. Nevertheless, for Jean Cazenoble, who has made an in-depth study of Branly, there is no doubt that he explained the effect by Hertzian waves. Branly was thoroughly familiar with Hertz's work, on which he had reported in the *Journal de physique*. Moreover, electromagnetic waves constituted the main subject of discussion among physicists in the early 1890s (Cazenoble, 1981: 67). Thus, Branly integrated Hertz's discovery into his own work on conductivity. He remained first and foremost a physicist who readily admitted that he was not the inventor of wireless telegraphy. In 1903 he declared to a journalist: 'Although I did not perform any wireless telegraphy, my experiments, in the very form I described them, contained the germ of all wireless telegraphy' (Monod-Broca, 1990: 179). This assertion, like many retrospective declarations of this kind, is both true and false. True in that the Branly effect was to be used at the start of wireless telegraphy; false in that this effect had to be used by other inventors, with other perspectives, for wireless telegraphy to exist. Wireless telegraphy did not follow directly from the Branly effect.

Unlike other physical effects discovered during the same period, the Branly effect did not contribute significantly to knowledge in the domain of physics. Nor did it serve as a basis for the development of a measuring instrument. It was nevertheless in the laboratory environment that the effect was first to be used. In 1894 the English physicist Lodge built a Hertzian wave receiver with an iron-filing tube (which he called a coherer). In order periodically to destroy the conductivity of the tube, acquired under the effect of Hertzian waves, he used the movement of a Morse recorder. Lodge's receiver had a purely pedagogic function; it clearly demonstrated the existence of Hertzian waves.

But it was not in physics laboratories that microwave transmission was to be born. Rather than being the outcome of a desire to exploit a scientific discovery, it was the result of a technical project to transmit information without wires. A young Italian, Guglielmo Marconi, had attended Augusto Righi's lectures at Bologna University and observed the experiments in which Righi perfected Branly's and Lodge's work.[2] Aware of the existence of Hertzian waves, Marconi developed a project for transmitting these waves over long distances (Aitken, 1976: 183). He built an experimental device and performed tests in the Villa Grifone on his parents' estate (1894–5). His objective was to increase the distance over which the waves could be propagated, so as to transmit them further than the laboratory. As Cazenoble (1981: 78) says: 'One has to have very rudimentary scientific information on the reality of waves to imagine for one moment that they could leave the laboratory. Their properties of dispersion . . . seemed, in informed physicists' eyes, to confine them there forever.'[3] Thus it was, paradoxically, Marconi's relative scientific ignorance which enabled him to appropriate a scientific theory for the technological project of wireless telegraphy.

Was the invention of wireless telegraphy simply the fruit of chance? Was it the result of an encounter in the young inventor's fertile mind between a technological project and a scientific discovery? The answer is no.

It was part of a long tradition of research aimed at freeing telegraphy from the constraints of wires. Cazenoble (1981: 100–8) has shown that from the moment the electric telegraph first appeared, numerous researchers worked on the problem of ridding it of wires (see also Sivowitch, 1971). Morse himself, even before opening his first commercial line, was interested in telegraphy by natural conduction (with transmission by air or water). In 1844 he managed to send a telegraph from one bank of the Susquehanna to the other (1,600 metres). Other experiments were conducted in Europe. Another method, electrostatic telegraphy, was explored in the 1880s, notably by Watson and Edison, but the results were disappointing. Telegraphy by electrodynamic induction, on the other hand, seemed more promising. Finally, Bell, Tainter and Berliner worked on the photophonic transmission of speech. Voice vibrations were transmitted by means of a mirror to a light beam and a receiver coupled to a selenium plaque rendered the sound. All of this work was reported in technical journals in Europe and America.

During its course through the second half of the nineteenth century, this wireless telegraphy project was destined to meet up with Hertzian waves. In 1892, two years before Marconi started his experiments, the English physicist William Crookes noted in the *Fortnightly Review* that electromagnetic vibrations could penetrate mediums such as a wall or the London fog. 'Here, then, is revealed the bewildering possibility of tele-graph without wires' (Barnouw, 1966: 9). As we have already seen, an inventor is never alone;[4] Marconi was part of a technological research movement aimed at realizing wireless telegraphy. It was this movement which was to appropriate Hertz's and Branly's discoveries.

Independently of Marconi, other inventors also exploited these dis-coveries. Alexandre Popov, the Russian maritime engineer, built a Hertzian wave receiver in 1895. By means of his device he was able to detect storms (electric disturbances in the atmosphere). He soon thought of using waves for telegraphic transmission, and in the following years he performed several experiments in wireless telegraphy (Petitjean, 1987: 14–16). The British Admiralty similarly envisaged the use of Hertzian waves for communicating between ships. In December 1895 it asked Captain Henry Jackson to study a device for that purpose. In the following year Jackson tested a maritime wireless telegraphy system (Blond, 1989). In the United States, AT&T undertook research in 1892 (two years before Marconi) on the use of Hertzian waves for wireless telephony (Hoddeson, 1981). However, without an appropriate detector this work never produced any positive results.[5]

Thus, at the end of the nineteenth century, a relatively old techno-logical project (wireless telegraphy) furnished the opportunity for a new scientific invention. The passage from theory to application was not direct, but a technological project did capture a theory. This as not only the work of a brilliant young Italian, for the same process took place throughout a technological community. Marconi's superiority probably lay in the fact that he started a little sooner and pursued his research to improve the reliability and efficiency of his system.

'It was distance that counted for Marconi', wrote the historian Hugh Aitken, 'and not only at the Villa Grifone. For the rest of his life it was to remain his technological obsession' (1976: 191). The British telegraph system's head engineer, William Preece, had the same obsession. His dream was the wireless interconnection of the English and French telegraphs (Aitken, 1976: 213) and he had conducted experiments on telegraphy by induction over several kilometres. In 1896, Marconi went to England with his mother, who was British. There he managed, thanks to her family, to meet Preece who gave him his full support.[6] In 1897 Preece gave the first public lecture on wireless telegraphy. A few days later the text was published in London in *The Electrician* and in Paris in *L'Industrie électrique*. The editor of the French journal considered it to be 'one of the most significant scientific events of the year' (Cazenoble, 1981: 30). Clearly, the advantages of wireless telegraphy had not gone unnoticed and the combination of telegraphy and Hertzian waves was in a sense expected. The waves had finally moved out of physics laboratories and become part of a technological project. The next step was to find a social use for the technology.

Maritime communication

In order to make his system more reliable and to market it, Marconi needed funds. His mother's family suggested he start a company and undertook to help him financially. Preece, aware of Marconi's plans, tried unsuccessfully to convince the British government to buy his patent. Thus, despite the Post Office's support for Marconi – and other forms of public support – wireless telegraphy did not become a state monopoly (Aitken, 1976: 218–28; see also Kieve, 1973: 243).

One of the new company's first markets as providing equipment for isolated lighthouses. Marconi was thereby responding to an existing demand, for which Preece had already performed several experiments with his induction device. During the same year (1898) Marconi also covered, together with the press, a number of spectacular events such as regattas.

However, the main social use of wireless telegraphy in these early years was military communication. In 1898 the British army first used Marconi's equipment during the Anglo-Boer war (Aitken, 1976: 232). The Admiralty, as I have already mentioned, showed a particular interest in this type of communication. Coordination in a modern fleet was more complex than it had been with sailing ships; the ships were faster, more mobile, and difficult to distinguish because of the clouds of smoke they emitted. Jackson and Marconi, who had conducted their research independently, started working together in 1897. Their cooperation spawned radio equipment adapted to a maritime environment. In 1901 a hundred radio stations were operational, of which two-thirds were from Royal Navy workshops and based on Jackson's plans, and a third from Marconi's company (Blond, 1989: 14). In 1903 the Admiralty signed a cooperation agreement which gave it access to all Marconi's patents.

During the same period Marconi also developed a commercial use for wireless telegraphy. Preece had already received requests from the maritime insurance company Lloyd's to transmit information on ships. In 1898 Marconi installed the first system corresponding to Lloyd's requirements. A wireless device was installed between Rathin Island and Ireland (Aitken, 1976: 231) with the purpose of transmitting information on boats approaching the British Isles. Thus Marconi used wireless telegraphy to serve the same social usage as Watson had served 60 years earlier with the semaphore telegraph [. . .].

Cooperation between Marconi and Lloyd's went even further. In 1901 the two companies signed an exclusive cooperation agreement. Lloyd's had a network of over a thousand agents in the main harbours of the world, whose job was to collect and telegraph to London information on the arrival and movement of ships. This network could be mobilized to organize communication with ships. By the end of 1902, 70 merchant ships were equipped with radios and could communicate with 25 coastal stations. In 1907 all the main transatlantic lines were equipped with radios (Aitken, 1976: 235–9).

Communication between ships thus constituted the main function of wireless telegraphy at the start of the century. Like Chappe's first telegraphic link with the Northern army, or electric telegraphy for signalling on the railways, these different uses enabled new telecommunications systems to become operational. They made it possible for the promoter of each invention to start a new activity by responding to an existing demand which had hitherto remained unsatisfied.

The speed with which these three telecommunication technologies (like computers later) got off the ground was partly the result of financing by the military (three cases out of four) or by big companies (railways, maritime insurance). For an innovator, this is a particularly favourable situation as he or she does not have to confront market uncertainty.[7]

The natural monopoly of radio communications

As soon as Marconi wanted to leave the limited, but protected, world of military use, he had to think of another way of marketing his invention. With the army and navy he could simply sell his equipment and leave it up to others to train operators and set up coastal stations. Private shipowners, on the other hand, had no intention whatsoever of organizing a communication system; they simply wanted to use a service.

Marconi's brief cooperation with the Post Office probably made him aware of the organization and economy of a telecommunications network. He decided to become a network manager and rented his equipment with an operator to merchant ships. He also took over the running of coastal stations. 'Marconigrams' were transmitted on the basis of two tariffs: one for passengers and another, lower one, for ship-owners and crew (Barnouw, 1966: 17).

Marconi's new strategy was also a response to English telegraphic legislation. The only activity which did not contravene the Post Office's monopoly in Britain and its territorial waters was internal corporate communication. Whereas boats were legally forbidden to communicate with the coast, Marconi's operators could communicate with one another. Thus, as Aitken notes, the British telegraphic monopoly unwittingly provided Marconi with a legal base for his future commercial monopoly over wireless telegraphy (1976: 234–5). Thanks too to his exclusive alliance with Lloyd's, Marconi could forbid the latter's ground stations from retransmitting messages from boats using competitors' equipment (except in emergencies). Moreover, Marconi did not hesitate to take action for infringement against those industrialists who used his patents. In this way his network monopoly was strengthened by his technical monopoly.

Independently of the commercial development of his company, Marconi also wanted to continue his technological research. As indicated above, his main preoccupation was covering long distances. In December 1901 he managed to transmit a very short telegraphic message consisting of the letter S across the Atlantic (from Cornwall to Newfoundland). This experiment surprised many of his contemporaries, for physicists imagined that the roundness of the earth doomed it to failure. Once again, Marconi seemed to be guided by a major technological project which he tried to realize without any scientific knowledge. It was only in the following year that two physicists were to provide an explanation for the phenomenon: Hertzian waves transmitted in a straight line are reflected by the ionized layers of the upper atmosphere.[8] Marconi took six years to develop a system capable of transmitting telegrams across the Atlantic.

The articulation of Marconi's technical and social objectives (intercontinental transmission and the creation of a telecommunications network) materialized in 1907 with the creation of a regular telegraphic service between Ireland and Canada. This service was gradually extended to Europe, the USA and Australia. In moving from purely maritime to land communication, wireless telegraphy went from a field in which it was the only medium possible to a sector in which it provided an alternative to an older technique, the undersea cable. The Marconi Wireless Telegraph Company became the competitor of the large English undersea cable corporation, Eastern and Associated Telegraph Companies (Crouch, 1989). In 1909 Marconi offered to build the British Empire's radio network in which 18 powerful stations would be established at different strategic spots (Blond, 1989: 17). An embryo of such a network was built just before the First World War.[9]

Marconi's activities were not limited to England; in 1899 he had already established a subsidiary in the United States. American Marconi developed rapidly, albeit in a difficult environment. The company was seen as wanting to fortify British domination over telecommunications, and a number of rival companies were set up. After conflict over patents and internal management problems, these companies disappeared during the course of 1912. Moreover, American Marconi bought out the main opposition (United Wireless), thereby securing a monopoly (Barnouw, 1966: 42).

During the same year, the *Titanic* disaster endowed wireless telegraphy with a new aura; it became the medium capable of directing rescue operations. In fact, the name *Titanic* and wireless telegraphy were to be linked for a long time in the public mind. While the most modern ship in the world was sinking, a new technology – wireless telegraphy – enabled it to continue communicating with the world. The impact of this shipwreck was such that it was decided at an international conference a few months later to make wireless telegraphy compulsory on all ships.[10] Marconi's position was thereby strengthened and, on the eve of the First World War, he had built up a global monopoly of radio communications. On the seas, he controlled the communications network; on land, his device had proved itself over very long distances.

In 1919 John Griggs, President of American Marconi, wrote to his shareholders:

> The principal aim and purpose of the Marconi Telegraph Company of America, during all the period of its existence has been the establishment and maintenance of trans-oceanic communication. Although the company has done no inconsiderable business in minor branches of the wireless, such as the equipping of vessels . . . yet these by the management have always been considered as incidental to the greater and more profitable business of long distance communication. (Mayes, 1972: 11–18)

During the First World War wireless telegraphy became an essentially military affair. The British and, in particular, American navies took over management of maritime radio communications and controlled industrial activity.[11] In 1919 the American Secretary of State for the Navy, Daniels, suggested that his administration take over control of the radio. 'We would lose very much', he told Congress, 'by dissipating it and opening the use of radio communication again to rival companies' (Barnouw, 1966: 53). 'Since there is a natural monopoly', said the defenders of the bill, 'let it rather go to the state.' In the end the bill was not passed by Congress, but it illustrated clearly that 25 years after its invention, wireless telegraphy had become a new universal telecommunications system.[12] Even though the new technology developed independently of the main telecommunications institutions, it was shaped in the same mould.

From radio telegraphy to radio telephony

While the social use of wireless telegraphy was becoming established, technological research progressed. In the USA in 1900 Reginald Fessenden, an academic who had formerly worked with Edison, undertook research on the transmission of speech. Such a project was only realizable if damped waves used in radio telegraphy were replaced by continuous waves. Supported by General Electric's laboratories (Sivowitch, 1971), Fessenden developed the transmitter he needed and performed his first positive experiments in 1906.[13] He was not alone in undertaking such research; the subject also interested the Swedish physicist, Poulsen, and a self-taught American, Stubblefield, among others (Hoffer, 1971; Decaux, 1979; Dieu, 1987).

Another American researcher, Lee De Forest, who had written a thesis on Hertzian waves, set himself two objectives during the first years of the century: replacing Branly's coherer by a more efficient receiving device, and transmitting sound. De Forest's telegraphic devices, which competed with those of Marconi, began to meet with some success around 1902–3. During his work to find an effective receiver for electromagnetic waves, he learned of Fleming's patent on the diode (1904). Fleming, an English academic and Marconi's scientific adviser, noticed that a two-electrode thermionic tube (a heated filament and an anode, or plate) could detect electromagnetic waves. De Forest, in carrying out different tests to improve the sensitivity of the diode, discovered in 1906 that with a third electrode the lamp could serve as both detector and amplifier. He called this triode an 'audion'.

De Forest's discovery of the triode played a fundamental role in the development of the radio and telecommunications; it marked the starting point of electronics. It was also relatively autonomous with respect to other scientific work conducted during the same period on the electron. The flow of current between the filament and the plate in the diode or in the triode was analysed by the physicist Richardson as the consequence of the movement of particles which he called thermoions, hence the name thermionic tubes. It was only around 1920 that the effect of electrons in this phenomenon was first understood (Decaux, 1979: 370).

While Fleming's and De Forest's discoveries were no longer relevant to the radio alone, it was nevertheless within this framework that their research was carried out. Neither of them had been working on an application for electron physics or trying to open a new technical field. They were simply trying to replace Branly's coherer by a more effective device. The De Forest Radiotelephone Company was not to enjoy the same destiny as Marconi's firm. Following serious financial difficulties, De Forest had to sell his audion patents to AT&T in 1914.

The first American inventors of radio telephony thought spontaneously of radio broadcasting. Fessenden conducted his first experiments at the end of 1906. On Christmas Eve, radio operators on a boat in the Caribbean heard 'a human voice coming from their instruments – someone speaking! Then a woman's voice rose in song. It was uncanny! . . . Next someone was heard reading a poem. Then there was a violin solo.' It turned out that the violin player was Fessenden himself (Barnouw, 1966: 20). For Fessenden this was probably more for the show than part of his project of finding a use for the new technology.[14]

De Forest's situation was very different. As a clergyman's son he had a messianic vision of radio usage. A few months after patenting his triode he had started experimenting with radio broadcasting, and wrote in his diary: 'My present task (happy one) is to distribute sweet melody broadcast[15] over the city and sea so that in time even the mariner far out across the silent waves may hear the music of his homeland' (Barnouw, 1966: 20). In 1908 he went with his wife, a pianist,[16] to Paris where they organized a spectacular presentation from the Eiffel Tower. Their transmission of a sound programme was received 800 kilometres away. In the following year, back in New York, De Forest broadcast an appeal for women's enfranchisement. In January 1910 he broadcast, direct from the Metropolitan Opera, a show starring Caruso. He also produced radio news bulletins and presented election results live.

De Forest's experiments remained marginal due to the lack of receivers (the triode had not yet been industrialized) and, in particular, to the absence of a mode of payment for radio programmes. As an inventor he was, however, just as important as Marconi. Both of them developed the basic technology of the radio and defined its social usage. But whereas Marconi, thanks to the support of his mother's family, imagined a way of marketing his invention, De Forest never conceived of anything similar. Hence, the development of the radio took place without him.

A new mass medium

David Sarnoff, one of the technical managers at American Marconi, was first to define an economic base for the development of radio broadcasting. In 1916 he sent a note on a 'radio music box' to his general manager. 'I have in mind', he wrote 'a plan of development which would make radio "a household utility" in the same sense as the piano or phonograph. The idea is to bring music into the house by wireless' (Graham, 1986: 32). Sarnoff was part of a generation of self-made innovators; he started off at American Marconi as a young telegraphist and climbed his way up to the top. An experience he had as a telegraphist in 1912 probably helped him to discover the broadcasting potential of wireless telegraphy. One afternoon in April he received a message from the *Titanic*. For 72 hours he was the sole link between survivors from the ship and the rest of America in its state of shock (Barnouw, 1966: 77). Could this not be seen as the role of future radio reporters? In any event, Sarnoff's proposition in 1916 was considered as ridiculous. In January 1920 he presented his proposal again, this time with economic details. He suggested that people who purchased radios should subscribe to the monthly *Wireless Age* which would provide the programmes. Investments would be offset by profits from the sale of receivers and from the press (subscriptions and advertising) (Barnouw, 1966: 79). Less than a year later radio broadcasting was born.

'Sow broadcasting'

It took only 10 years for wireless telegraphy, whose sole use was point-to-point telecommunication, to become a broadcasting system that was one of the main media for mass culture. This shift from one type of technological and social usage to another took place in relation to two developments which we shall now examine. First, the First World War prompted the industrialization of wireless telegraphy. Secondly, in the United States the radio created a communication environment in which amateurs could operate freely.

Wireless telegraphy was a telecommunication tool particularly well suited to war situations – particularly when the front moved rapidly – and to maintaining contact with aeroplanes and tanks. In France, Colonel Ferrié, who was aware of the principles of De Forest's audion, grasped the opportunity afforded by the war and was one of the first to use the component. He had the triode, called a TM lamp ('type militaire'), developed industrially. Soon military receiving stations were equipped with this lamp and from 1917 it was also used in transmitters. By the end of the war lamps were being mass produced in France where factories had a production capacity of 300,000 lamps. According to Bernard Decaux (1979: 374–5), 'French military radio communication equipment was far superior to British or German equipment.' In 1917 the American contingent in Europe adopted French equipment (see Petitjean, 1985).

The Great War also helped to settle a number of conflicts concerning industrial ownership. In 1916 a New York court outlawed the sale of triodes without permission from American Marconi, owner of the diode patent. On the other hand, Marconi could not use the triode without permission from AT&T (owner of De Forest's patent). Furthermore, General Electric had improved the triode in various ways.[17] When America entered the war the government froze all legal disputes concerning patents. AT&T, General Electric and American Marconi all had to cooperate to produce 80,000 lamps for the armed forces.

We have seen that at the end of the war the American navy almost succeeded in securing a legal monopoly over radio communication. When this did not occur, fears were expressed in American military and political circles that the British would use Marconi to control maritime radio communications. It was therefore decided to Americanize Marconi's US subsidiary. Under heavy pressure, the latter agreed at the end of 1919 to sell its interests to a new company, the Radio Corporation of America (RCA). Both AT&T and GE were shareholders (Barnouw, 1966: 48–9) in RCA, and the American government also had a representative on the governing board. By means of this arrangement intended to exploit inter-oceanic links and compete with British undersea cables, the different partners resolved their quarrels over patents.[18]

Although the war had provided new technological and industrial opportunities, these alone could not lead to the new use of the radio that appeared in the 1920s. It was (as we have seen in other examples throughout this book) the social movement at the origin of broadcasting that was to 'capture' it and set it off in another direction. The relative weakness of this social movement in France, compared to the United States, probably explains why broadcasting took so long to develop there. Although France had gained an effective lead during the war in the industrialization of the radio, it was in America that the use of broadcasting was born.

In the USA wireless telegraphy enjoyed lively public interest from the outset. In 1899 Marconi was received in New York as a hero. When he succeeded in 1901 in transmitting a message across the Atlantic, his achievement made national headlines. Later, American newspapers maintained their interest in wireless telegraphy, as Susan Douglas (1986) observed in her studies of the press at that time. She notes that, contrary to articles on other new technologies, 'there were no speculations on wireless sets of the future . . . Rather, the predictions focused on where the messages might go and on what the wireless would do for society and for individuals' (Douglas, 1986: 38). In these texts wireless telegraphy appeared as the means to instantaneous free communication. The use was autonomous, he or she depended on no operator and had no tax to pay. During the first two decades of the twentieth century there was a considerable discrepancy between the effective commercial use of the radio (maritime communication) and the uses imagined by the media and experimented with by amateurs. Amateur use, which started around 1906, was to develop rapidly. In 1917 the authorities issued over 8,500 broadcasting licences and the number of receivers was estimated at around 125,000 (Barnouw, 1966: 55).[19]

The amateur radio boom was to be sustained by the press and publishing business. Newspapers, technical manuals, books for teenagers or boy-scout manuals provided plans and instructions for building a wireless receiver, while university and college students were taught how to build their own devices. If we relate the number of wirelesses quoted above to the population likely to build a receiver (men between 15 and 35 years old), we see that 0.7 per cent of young Americans actually did so.[20] This high figure gives an idea of the importance of the wireless phenomenon in the United States.

Yet these amateurs' ambitions remained very modest. Transmitting or receiving a Morse message over 10 or 15 miles was a 'thrilling experience', according to one of them (Edgar Love in Douglas, 1986). On the other hand, professionals complained about amateurs congesting the waves. The latter were said to be incapable of deciphering more than a few words a minute. Yet, despite their inexperience, they extended the distance over which they could broadcast and by 1917 were able to send messages from the East Coast across to the West Coast. In the following extract from Francis Collins' book *The Wireless Man*, we see that in 1912 this novelist had already perceived the new dimension of the radio:

> An audience of a hundred thousand boys all over the United States may be addressed almost every evening by wireless telegraph. Beyond doubt this is the largest audience in the world. No football or baseball crowd, no convention or conference, compares with it in size, nor gives closer attention to the business at hand. (Douglas, 1986: 49).

Collins had already grasped the fact that these amateurs were busy tilting usage of the radio from point-to-point telecommunication to broadcasting.

During the years leading up to the First World War a number of amateurs started broadcasting on a more or less regular basis, either in Morse (e.g. the weather report broadcast by Wisconsin University for farmers or the time)[21] or with sound. In California in 1909 Charles Harrold, an academic, broadcast a news bulletin and music once a week (Greb, 1958–9: 3–13). Near Boston in 1915 a group of students launched a university radio with the same type of programme (Barnouw, 1966: 33–6). All these experiments were interrupted in 1917 when the government outlawed the use of wirelesses because of the war.

During the war the American navy established a radio station intended to serve as an instrument for propaganda to Europe (Barnouw, 1966: 51–2). It broadcast calls for armistice to Germany and promoted President Wilson's peace plan.[22]

As soon as the war was over amateurs started experimenting with sound broadcasting again. In 1920 two of them managed to combine their passion for radios with their company's interests. The first, William Scripps, director of the Detroit *News*, was a wireless enthusiast. On 31 August 1920 he started broadcasting a daily news bulletin and recorded music from the newspaper's offices. The day specifically chosen for launching the radio was that of the Detroit primary. His programmes appeared regularly in the *News* but, despite the newspaper's support, audiences were estimated at no more than 500 radio amateurs.

In order to transform broadcasting into a mass media, wireless sets had to be produced on an industrial scale and marketed. Westinghouse was to take this initiative. Another wireless amateur, Frank Conrad, an engineer at Westinghouse, had installed a transmitter in his garage. The company moved the station to its offices in Pittsburg and launched a daily broadcasting service on 2 November 1920, the day of the presidential elections. At the same time Westinghouse, which had gained experience during the war in producing military receivers industrially, decided to market a civil radio set. This plan resembled the one imagined by Sarnoff at RCA, but Westinghouse, relying on Conrad's competence, started earlier. In the following year it created two other stations: one in New York, which concentrated mainly on broadcasting sporting events, and the other in Chicago, which broadcast opera performances in the city.[23] In November 1922 there were still only five stations in the United States; a month later the radio boom began and in eight months 450 new stations appeared (Barnouw, 1966: 91). Growth in such proportions was only possible because a pool of amateurs capable of running these new stations existed. Hence, this social trend provided radio's first audiences as well as its first professionals.

By the 1920s social use of the wireless had changed fundamentally. Its role in maritime communication had declined as it became a mass medium. Contemporary commentators emphasized, as Collins (1912) had done, the mass character of radio audiences. *Radio Broadcast* noted in September 1923 that a speech by President Harding was heard by over a million people; 'no president has ever spoken to such a large audience', it said (Barnouw, 1966: 92). Others remarked on different dimensions of the new medium. Stanley Frost (1922) noted that, thanks to radio, 'all isolation can be destroyed' (see also Douglas, 1986: 54). In a society in which urban change was rapid and cultures with rural origins had disappeared, radio provided a link with society. Unlike the telephone, it was not used to strengthen ties with family or friends, but rather to become a part of society. It soon became an instrument of home entertainment, like the phonograph, for which it provided a substitute for about 20 years [. . .]. It was an alternative source of music for dancing at home.[24]

Creating a commercial use

In order to become established, the social function of radio had to find an economic base. At first Westinghouse had thought that the manufacturers of radio equipment could pay for the programmes. Indeed, without pro-grammes the manufacturers would be unable to sell mass-produced equip-ment. Their financing of the programmes was thus a form of investment. This solution, which amounted to organizing the transfer of funds from equipment to programmes, was appropriate for getting broadcasting off the ground. It was, however, inadequate in a period of maturity. In 1922 the journal *Radio Broadcast* launched the debate: 'How to finance radio broadcasting?', which it continued to feed for a number of years. In 1925 it offered a prize for the best essay on the subject (Barnouw, 1966: 154–8).

Two main types of financing were proposed: taxes and advertising. Although the 'European-style' model of a public tax won the *Radio Broadcast* prize, it did not lead to any specific project. On the other hand, David Sarnoff, who had become RCA's MD, proposed a slightly different plan in which taxes on radios would be managed by the manufacturers. The latter would control a public broadcasting service managed by rep-resentatives from their own companies and from the public. The Sarnoff plan's main drawback was that it sanctioned the RCA/GE/Westinghouse oligopoly.[25]

The telephone companies and AT&T in particular had a totally different vision of radio's economic base. 'We, the telephone company, were to provide no programs. The public was to come in. Anyone who had a message for the world or wished to entertain was to come in and pay their money as they would upon coming into a telephone booth, address the world, and go out' (Lloyd Espenchied in Barnouw, 1966: 106). Between the idea of making users pay for their messages and that of financing through advertising, there was only a short step which AT&T soon took. At the start, opposition to advertising was fierce. The Minister of Trade, Hoover, declared in 1924: 'If a speech by the President is to be used as the meat in a sandwich of two patent medicine advertisements, there will be no radio left' (Barnouw, 1966: 177). But Hoover changed his mind and in the following year decided that the question of advertising had to be settled by the manufacturers themselves. The debate was to take place among private companies.

Behind the opposition between two types of financing, two different cultures confronted each other. For the telephone companies, radio was simply a succession of messages financed by those who supplied them. The coherence of these different messages therefore had no relevance for them. On the other hand, they imagined connecting the different radio stations to form a network. For them radio took on a national dimension. By contrast, radio manufacturers reasoned in terms of audience size. They saw the motor behind the system as being the sale of receivers, which meant that programmes had to be attractive enough to encourage people to buy. The stations financed by these companies soon invented the basic principles of radio programming. Conflict raged between the 'telephone group' led by AT&T (which had withdrawn from RCA in 1923) and the 'radio group' (RCA, GE and Westinghouse) until a compromise was found in 1926. The 'radio group' set up a company specializing in managing and creating the programmes for radio stations: the National Broadcasting Company (NBC). The latter proposed a national programme, structured into a coherent schedule and financed by advertising. Connections between stations were provided by AT&T. In 1927 a number of independent stations formed a second network which was later to become Columbia Broadcasting System (CBS). The basic principles of the American broadcasting system were thus established and were to remain unchanged.

The history of the wireless, compared to that of other [media] inventions [. . .], is probably one of the most complex, one of those with the most inventors and entrepreneurs. In the conclusion to his book, Aitken proposes an interpretation through the concept of translation. Hertz translated Maxwell's abstract theory into one that could be verified in a laboratory. Marconi translated Branly and Lodge's physical experiments into a technological telecommunications device. He also translated his device into a marketable service (Aitken, 1976: 330–1).

The above analysis is, I think, interesting but inadequate. By emphasizing the idea of translation it shows that, rather than continuity from Maxwell to Sarnoff, there was a series of ruptures, of changes of approach. On this level, Aitken's interpretation is far richer than that of most histories of radio in which the succession between inventors took place 'naturally' and 'smoothly'. But by focusing on the intellectual activity of translation, one tends to forget everything that is around the translator: two linguistic systems and a text which has to be adapted from one language to another. In other words, importance is given to the interfaces, while the systems to be interfaced are forgotten.

My approach [. . .], based on the notion of circulation, is different. It examines how a theory, a technological system or a use, migrates from one continent to another. It pays as much attention to the pilot who led this navigation as to the trends which led a technical object from one state to another. The intention is to articulate a specific study of the inventor's work (micro-analysis) with that of the main trends in social and technological change (macro-analysis). Marconi's main success was unquestionably that of giving a technical use to laboratory experiments. But it is as important to show that he was part of a technological tradition, that the project of wireless communication dated back to the birth of the telegraph, that numerous devices had already been tested and that, in parallel with Marconi's work, other inventors performed the same experiments.

The evolution from technological use to social use is always a delicate operation. Marconi's strength, like that of Chappe or Cooke before him, lay in his identification of the first immediate use (military communication). He was thereby able to procure some revenue without having to define a way of marketing the device. When he later marketed wireless telegraphy he borrowed a method from telecommunications. His link with the telecommunication tradition was therefore twofold: both technological (reaching maximal distances) and commercial (making the transmitter of a message pay for the service).

The road from wireless telegraphy to radio was also highly complex. The inventors of radio broadcasting circulated between four different spheres. They came from Marconi's wireless telegraphy tradition. They sought new receivers for Hertzian waves and found them in thermionic lamps. They were also part of a research trend experimenting with free communication. Finally, they bathed in a social movement, that of a turning inwards of the family to the private sphere, of the organization of entertainment at home. By circulating between these spheres, they were to link up the different contributions. Men like De Forest or Sarnoff knew how to tie all these traditions together, although De Forest was only a precursor. Radio broadcasting necessitated mass production of receivers and the required expertise was developed during the war. But commercial form had to be given to this new social use. It was through the combination of several traditions – those of telecommunications, mass industry and the press – that the radio was finally to find its economic base.

On their long road from Hertz to NBC, waves were in a sense transformed. At each stage of this movement there was a new combination, an enhancement. The main actors in this process all 'captured' an innovation and integrated it into their own technological or social project, until a stable system was finally attained. A medium was born; its shape changed little afterwards.

Notes

1   For a description of this experiment, see P. Monod-Broca (1990).
2   This point on Marconi's education, put forward by Hugh Aitken (1976), is contested by other biographers. Nevertheless, the friendship between Righi and Marconi's parents seems to prove that, in one way or another, Marconi was aware of Righi's research.
3   Aitken (1976) indicates that Righi discouraged Marconi. His attempts to use waves over distances of more than 100 metres were hopeless. By trying a number of experimental devices, Marconi did nevertheless find that a wire on the ground captured the waves at greater distances.
4   Some authors, such as Lloyd Moris (1949), consider that Marconi knew about Crookes's article.
5   Later AT&T hesitated several times before resuming this work. Some experts considered that radio telephony was not realizable at the time. It was only towards 1912 that AT&T started to take an interest in the radio.
6   It was the physicist Campbell Swinton who, after having seen Marconi's experiments, obtained an appointment for him with Preece. In 1908 Swinton was one of the first scientists to describe the principle of television.
7   The navy's interest in wireless telegraphy was also evident in other countries. Alexandre Popov, quoted above, experimented with transmitting to ships. In the summer of 1897 the Italian navy invited Marconi to perform tests off the coast of La Spezia. In France, 130 navy vessels were equipped in 1908 (Petitjean, 1987).
8   The existence of these strata was only proved later.

9   Nevertheless, this project gave rise to a number of controversies. The unsuccessful cooperation between Marconi and the Post Office had left some resentment within the British civil service.

10   In 1908 in an international conference the Germans had obtained the ruling that all stations had to accept maritime traffic, irrespective of its origin.

11   In France, it was rather the army, and notably General Ferrié's services, which acted as a driving force in the development of the radio.

12   In England it was also on the occasion of a war (the Russo-Japanese war) that the state obtained a monopoly over wireless telegraphy (Wireless Telegraphy Act of 1904). The monopoly was attributed to the Post Office but in fact real power lay with the Admiralty (Blond, 1989: 15).

13   Cooperation with General Electric was difficult. Heads of laboratories considered the project as unrealistic and gave it to a young engineer considered as being 'crazy enough to undertake it' (Barnouw, 1966: 20). AT&T resumed its work on radio telephony in 1902 and discontinued it when Fessenden registered his patent (Hoddeson, 1981).

14   Bell also retransmitted concerts to promote his telephone.

15   It is interesting to note that the original meaning of the word *broadcast* was 'to sow'.

16   He later divorced and married a soprano. De Forest was an extremely inventive but unsociable man. A library card was once found in some archives indicating that he had borrowed a book entitled *How to Deal with Women* (I owe this anecdote to Pascal Griset).

17   Edwin Armstrong, inventor of a tuning device for receivers (called a 'superheterodyne') declared in 1923 to the US Federal Trade Commission that 'It was absolutely impossible to build the slightest manipulable device without using all, or almost all, the inventions known at the time' (Landes, 1969).

18   In June 1921 Westinghouse joined this cartel again and became a shareholder in RCA.

19   The number of transmitters was certainly higher; in fact, it was only in 1912 that authorization to transmit was required by law, and many amateurs ignored this formality.

20   There was at the time no manufacturer of wireless for the general public.

21   Twenty years earlier weather information had constituted one of the main professional telephone services in rural areas [. . .]. In France, the Eiffel Tower station started broadcasting time signals twice a day from 1910 (Petitjean, 1987: 25).

22   On 29 October 1915, AT&T had already succeeded in broadcasting speech by radio from the USA to the Eiffel Tower station (*AT&T Annual Report*, 1915, p. 31).

23   In France, the first regular transmissions were sent from the Eiffel Tower station from Christmas 1921. In February 1922 the *Ecole Supérieure des PTT* started its transmissions (see Mauriat, 1987).

24   A listener of the Detroit station commented in the *News* (5 September 1920) on one of the first radio programmes: 'We had some of our girl friends up to hear the concert . . . and when "The Naughty Waltz" came on we started to dance. It was great fun' (Barnouw, 1966: 63).

25   Other methods of public financing existed. University radios found patrons and in New York the city financed a station.

References

D'Agostino, S. (1989) 'Pourquoi Hertz, et non pas Maxwell, a-t-il découvert les ondes électriques?', in J. Cazenoble (ed.), *Electricité, il y a cent ans*. Paris: Editions de l'EHESS.

Aitken, H. (1976) *Syntony and Spark: the Origins of Radio*. New York: John Wiley and Sons.

Barnouw, E. (1966) *A History of Broadcasting in the United States*, vol. 1: *A Tower in Babel*. New York: Oxford University Press.

Blond, A.J.L. (1989) 'The development of wireless telegraphy as a competitor to cable in the United Kingdom (1894–1914)', UIT, Conférence de Villefranche-sur-Mer.

Cazenoble, J. (1981) *Les Origines de la télégraphie sans fil*. Paris: CNRS, Centre de documentation des sciences humaines.

Cazenoble, J. (ed.) (1989) *Electricité, il y a cent ans*. Paris: Editions de l'EHESS.

Collins, F. (1912) *The Wireless Man*. New York: Century.

Corn, J. (1986) *Imaging Tomorrow*. Cambridge, Mass: MIT Press.

Crouch, J.H. (1989) 'Historical overview: from pioneers to structures – Cable Wireless', UIT, Conférence de Villefranche-sur-Mer.

Decaux, B. (1979) 'Radiocommunications et électronique', in M. Daumas (ed.), *Histoire générale des techniques*, vol. 5, pp. 343–433. Paris: PUF.

Dieu, B. (1987) 'Un nouveau support pour la parole, la radiotéléphonie', in *La TSF des années folles*. Strasbourg: Les Amis de l'histoire des PTT d'Alsace.

Douglas, S. (1986) 'Amateur operators and American broadcasting: shaping the future of radio', in J. Corn (ed.), *Imagining Tomorrow*. Cambridge, Mass: MIT Press.

Frost, S. (1922) 'Radio dreams that can come true', *Collier's* 69, 10 June.

Graham, M.B.W. (1986) *RCA and the Videodisc: the Business of Research*. Cambridge: Cambridge University Press.

Greb, G.R. (1958–9) 'The golden anniversary of broadcasting', *Journal of Broadcasting*, 3 (1).

Griggs, J.W. (1919) Memo to shareholders in *Wireless Age*, November.

Hoddeson, L. (1981) 'The emergence of basic research in the Bell telephone system, 1875–1915', *Technology and Culture*, 22: 512–44.

Hoffer, T.W. (1971) 'Nathan B. Stubblefield and his wireless telephone', *Journal of Broadcasting*, 15 (3): 317–29.

Joos, L.C.D. (1971) 'La génie n'a pas de patrie: il y a des Popov partout', *Sélection du Reader's Digest*, November.

Kieve, J.L. (1973) *The Electric Telegraph: a Social and Economic History*. Newton Abbot: David and Charles.

Landes, D.S. (1969) *The Unbound Prometheus: Technological Change and Industrial Development in Western Europe from 1750 to the Present*. Cambridge: Cambridge University Press.

Mauriat, C. (1987) 'La naissance de la radio diffusion d'Etat', in *La TSF des années folles*. Strasbourg: Les Amis de l'histoire des PTT d'Alsace.

Mayes, T. (1972) 'History of the American Marconi Company', *The Old Timer's Bulletin*, 13 (1): 11–18.

Monod-Broca, P. (1990) *Branly, au temps des ondes et des limailles*. Paris: Belin.

Moris, L. (1949) *Not So Long Ago*. New York: Random House.

Petitjean, G. (1985) 'Gustave Ferrie et le développement de la TSF militaire', *Toute l'électronique*, September.

Petitjean, G. (1987) 'De l'électricité statique à la TSF', in *la TSF des années folles*. Strasbourg: Les Amis de l'histoire des PTT d'Alsace.

Rousseau, P. (1958) *Histoire des techniques et des inventions*. Paris: Arthème Fayard.

Sivowitch, E.N. (1971) 'A technological survey of broadcasting's prehistory (1876–1920)', *Journal of Broadcasting*, 15 (1): 1–20.

Süsskind, Ch. (1968) 'The Early History of Electronics', *Proceedings IEEE Spectrome*, August, p. 90.

Understanding 'transformations' in media culture

Introduction

In the second part of this book the chapters explore some key issues, approaches and metaphors for understanding media transformation. Their concern is to examine how 'communications revolutions' have been conceived and to evaluate the extent to which contemporary changes can indeed be thought of as revolutionary. The authors of the first three chapters propose and interrogate prominent perspectives on media transformations. They are followed by three chapters which focus on one cardinal dimension in current debates about media transformation – globalization. These three chapters explore what is at stake in theories of globalization and the related dynamics of contemporary media in transforming local, national and worldwide cultures.

Commonly, those who have struggled to explain the significance of new communication technologies have been shown by history to have failed to have grasped their full implications. Clearly, it is not always easy to understand new media and their associated processes of social, cultural and political transformation. Unsurprisingly, images, labels and metaphors derived from understandings of older media are invoked; for example, early newspapers made reference to pre-print forms of news distribution in their titles (*The Messenger* or *The Herald*), while television news has 'headline stories', deploying the terminology and concepts of the earlier medium, the press.

In Chapter 6, Joshua Meyrowitz provides us with an account which attributes to the media profound responsibility for transforming the dynamics of modern culture. His focus is on the cultural consequences of new 'electronic' technologies, by which he means principally broadcast television. He argues forcefully that television has led to a new, reconfigured, social order. He uses the notion of a 'sense of place' which raises questions of identity and mediated versions of space and place to explain the profound change caused by television; identities arise and are shaped in part through changing mediated versions of space and place. Meyrowitz argues that contemporary culture is becoming increasingly 'placeless' in the sense of being dislocated or detached from both physical location and social position, and that this has been a profoundly democratizing phenomenon.

Meyrowitz argues that the effects of the mass media are wide-ranging and extensive; the electronic media have led to a new type and configuration of social order. His account is highly positive about the democratizing impact of electronic media. He argues that electronic media, because they permeate the physical boundaries that once limited communication between people, mean that people commonly learn about what he calls the 'backstage' behaviours of others via the media. This, he argues, means that childhood becomes blurred with the world of adults, masculinity merges with femininity, and political leaders lose their aura as they apparently come closer to the ordinary person. In this way, his account links the electronic media with a set of broad social changes in arguing that television has changed fundamentally the logic of the social order through its restructuring of physical place and social space and the new possibilities it affords for participation and individual and collective identities.

At the heart of a range of analyses of the transformative powers related to media and communications systems are some key metaphors. Indeed, new media themselves are often used as metaphors or slogans to describe and pinpoint current experience. From the 'television age' to the 'computer age', the 'information superhighway' and the 'digital era', metaphors have been fundamental in structuring how public discourses and debates identify and come to terms with transformation and 'the new'. In Chapter 7, Anthony Smith sets out to question the application and adequacy of such metaphors to contemporary conditions. He focuses first on perhaps the most invoked metaphor, asking whether what we are experiencing can usefully be seen, as it is by many, as a 'revolution'. His concern is with broad historical patterns of social change, spanning a century of history, both hemispheres of the world and the breadth of media. The analysis presented is subtle, addressing a complex of causal factors, while avoiding the attribution of determinism to any one in particular. Smith questions the arguments surrounding new media choice and diversity, arguing that the contemporary concern for abundance of choice represents a besetting ideology more than a practical need.

Smith stresses that we should be wary of, and analyse carefully, any metaphors which are used to make sense of, organize and interpret contemporary transformations in media and culture. He suggests that, despite the significance of many of the changes and developments taking place, we remain trapped in what are essentially Victorian ideas and metaphors, analogies rooted in a kind of 'steam-driven' technological determinism. Underlying his analysis, however, is a strong conviction that social orders are undergoing radical forms of transformation, and that there is a need to create new metaphors to do full and effective justice to the transforming information environments of late modernity.

The metaphor of the 'information society' has probably come closest to defining the locomotive and result of recent and contemporary social and cultural change. The 'information society' thesis is probably the main way in which contemporary processes of transformation have been conceived and understood – by politicians, policy-makers, industrialists and the media. It encompasses the rise to pre-eminence of information as a key feature of organizations and production, the growth of information work and the information economy, the rapid development and pervasiveness of information technology, globalization and the shrinking of time as well as space with the growth of global flows, and the phenomenal growth in cultural circulation. So it addresses the shifting boundaries of the private and public spheres, and of work and leisure.

The 'information society' is a term which, on close inspection, however, carries a tremendous diversity of meanings. In Chapter 8, Frank Webster explores five areas in relation to which the notion of the 'information society' has been applied: the technological, economic, occupational, spatial and cultural. He concludes that in each of these five areas there is considerable variation and imprecision in defining and measuring an 'information society'. Further, he problematizes what is meant by 'information', arguing that information needs to be considered in terms of its quality, rather than simply as an amorphous quantity.

Webster's analysis leads him to distinguish between those who see the conditions of today's world as constituting a distinctive rupture with the past – for instance, Daniel Bell's post-industrial society thesis (Bell, 1973), Francis Fukuyama's 'end of history' (Fukuyama, 1992) and Alvin Toffler's 'third wave' (Toffler, 1980) – and those who emphasize continuities between past and present. At the same time as questioning the validity of the thesis as commonly propounded, it is important to understand why it enjoys the credibility it does. Its attractiveness and durability may be due precisely to its flexibility and lack of specificity; and there can be little doubting some of the key trends which it represents. While it is necessary to be critical of the 'information society' as a totalizing explanatory device, it commonly acts to condense a number of processes and phenomena which are of crucial significance for contemporary social and cultural transformation.

There is general consensus that one of the most significant levels of transformation resulting from the expansion of media and communication networks is the emergence of global networks of information, cultural flow and interaction. The next three chapters in Part II examine a range of debates and evidence concerning this growth of worldwide media and communication networks. Debates and definitions of globalization are many, complex, multi-faceted and sometimes contradictory. David Goldblatt et al. (1997) have mapped the field by referring to the 'hyperglobalizers' and the 'sceptics'. The former describe or predict, from various perspectives, the homogenization of the world under the auspices of the industrial might of US popular culture or, less commonly, of Western elite culture. Francis Fukuyama (1992), for example, refers to the fall of the Eastern bloc with the end of the Cold War as the end of alternatives to Western liberal capitalist democracy and culture, the material and hegemonic triumph of the 'First World'. Sceptics, on the other hand, point to the limited and shallow nature of global culture *vis-à-vis* national cultures, and stress the continuing importance of national differences. Anthony D. Smith (1995), for example, contrasts the depth and weight of national cultures, symbols and ideas with those which purport to be global. These, he argues, tend to lack history and depth, and are not anchored or shared in everyday life and experience. As a result, the pronouncement of the passing of the nation-state is viewed as premature. Nations and national cultures are shifting and facing competition from globalizing, trans- and multi-national forces, but continue to exercise power over their local and regional interests, with little evidence of their immediate waning. The relationships between globalization and fragmentation, and the dialectics between 'the global' and 'the local' – and the hybrid 'glocal' – figure centrally in these discussions. Other sceptics argue that those factors now referred to as globalization have existed in previous eras, and that there is little new or exceptionally significant in current developments. In spite of the rhetoric and many of the assumptions of globalization, the world continues to be far from a fully integrated global economy, culture, society or even 'village'.

The globalization of culture is perhaps the most obvious manifestation of globalization, the aspect of globalization most closely connected to daily life. John Tomlinson in Chapter 9 maps some of the key debates about cultural globalization, outlining and evaluating the key positions and arguments. The spread of US and Western cultural goods, tastes and practices is undeniable – in relation to clothes, music, films and television, for instance. In the analysis and the interpretation of these phenomena, however, there is a range of arguments. More popular understandings commonly refer to the 'swamping' effect of US culture: US exports are seen as eroding the integrity or authenticity of local cultures, replacing traditional or indigenous forms with imposed and debased culture in a process of cultural homogenization. These responses and understandings are congruent with a powerful model for explaining the globalization of culture: the 'cultural imperialism' thesis. This is a set of arguments which relates cultural globalization to the context of post-colonialism – a Marxist analysis, but also an approach which has been taken up by UNESCO in its calls for a new communications order. Researchers in this paradigm, notably Herbert Schiller (for example, 1996), see the dramatic expansion and extension of global culture as the latest and logical phase in the exploitative logic of capitalism, as it both challenges and by-passes the nation-state and seeks to extend control and power on to the world stage, from the powerful 'cores' to the dependent 'peripheries'.

The cultural imperialism thesis and its contribution to debates over globalization has not been without its critics. These include those who argue that flows say little about the meanings which are made of television programming and other cultural forms and commodities as they are received around the world – that audiences are active and creative, and read television texts in diverse ways which can contradict the meanings and values which they 'carry' (Liebes and Katz, 1993). Others argue that trans-national corporations have become more powerful than nation-states, developing an inexorable logic of their own; globalization from this perspective elides corporate power with the interests of US and western nation states. Finally, there are arguments that cultural flows today are more complex than suggested and that the argument of cultural imperialism is a US-centric story (Sinclair et al., 1996). Globalization is a complex and shifting set of interconnections and interactions which lead to a decentred network, with diffused rather than concentrated power, and with globalization as a process of creolism (Hannerz, 1990), the mixing, cross-cutting and interplay between nomadic and diasporic cultures – 'digital' or otherwise.

At the core of these debates is the emergence of global commercial media markets and systems which are both required for and have resulted in the restructuring of national media industries. In Chapter 10, Edward Herman and Robert McChesney provide an overview of the dynamics and state of the global media system and its markets at the turn of the twentieth century. They provide a sustained and detailed example of the political economy approach to understanding global media and transformations in the contemporary world order. Their analysis is grounded in an examination of the current trans-national growth and consolidation of global media corporations and their activities across old and new media sectors in recent years. They contend that recent patterns of growth have tended to consolidate the power of existing, especially US, structures and organizations. However, this has not been altogether unproblematic. Multi-national corporations have had to recognize limits to the worldwide marketability of centralized, US, monoglot, productions in the context of the global cultural economy. Not all local audiences and consumers invest in the same things, in the same ways or with the same consequences. As a result, there has been some increase in the export of cultural products from nations outside the US, although this by no means offers a significant challenge to the dominance of US corporations. The global industry has also incorporated some forms of local output, language and cultural inflection, but these local products are often the outcome of American investment behind the scenes of local cultural economies.

Central to any assessment of global trends is their impact on national public service systems and the dilemmas that greatly expanded commercial competition, coupled with new technologies, have forced upon them. Herman and McChesney discuss the contradictions facing public television corporations like the BBC and ABC, as they attempt to compete within the global market while negotiating their legitimacy and authority as public service, subsidized, providers in home, local or domestic markets. The 1990s have been marked by a global trend to 'deregulation', sometimes redefined as 're-regulation', which for many commentators has reinforced and extended the power of commercial market rule over communication and cultural production. Herman and McChesney argue that global media policy in the 1990s has worked in the interests of the largest and most powerful global media players.

Understanding the dynamics and complexities of globalizations, of course, involves more than examining evolving world markets and technologies. Research on the situated contexts and meanings involved in forms of dispersed consumption and reception has begun to ask a range of questions about the prismatic and diverse responses to specific instances of globally mediated culture. Simon During in Chapter 11 distinguishes between globalization and what he terms the 'global popular', arguing that the development of systems which allow for global cultural interchange do not necessarily guarantee the 'global popular'. In this he explicitly attempts to take up the challenge posed by processes of cultural globalization. He distinguishes between what he identifies as globalization – the emergence of large-scale trans-national systems of cultural export and import – and the 'global popular'. This label, he suggests, can be applied only to some of the cultural products which have circulated worldwide since the 1980s: films, television programmes and music and other cultural commodities which have been distributed and apparently enjoyed nearly everywhere in the world. Cultural globalization, he suggests, takes many forms and has many different effects including, paradoxically, 'glocalization', where locally produced materials fail to export well or fare successfully on world markets, and cannot as a result be regarded as achieving the status of the 'global popular'. Although global networks provide the basic conditions for its existence, they cannot guarantee products or stars hit status in many world markets. Transformations in the current phase, designed to compete for the 'global popular', are occurring at the inter-related levels of finance, government regulation, the application of technologies and marketing the appeal of particular stars.

References

Bell, Daniel (1973) *The Coming of Post-industrial Society: a Venture in Social Forecasting*. New York: Basic Books.

Fukuyama, Francis (1992) *The End of History and the Last Man*. London: Hamish Hamilton.

Goldblatt, David, Held, David, McGrew, Anthony and Perraton, Jonathan (1997) 'Economic globalisation and the nation state: the transformation of political power?' *Soundings*, 7: 61–77.

Hannerz, Ulf (1990) 'Cosmopolitans and locals in world culture', *Theory, Culture & Society*, 7: 237–51.

Liebes, Tamar and Katz, Elihu (1993) *The Export of Meaning*. Oxford: Oxford University Press.

Schiller, Herbert I. (1996) *Information Inequality: the Deepening Social Crisis in America*. London: Routledge.

Sinclair, John, Jacka, Elizabeth and Cunningham, Stuart (1996) *New Patterns in Global Television: Peripheral Vision*. Oxford: Oxford University Press.

Smith, Anthony D. (1995) *Nations and Nationalism in a Global Era*. Cambridge: Polity Press.

Toffler, Alvin (1980) *The Third Wave*. London: Collins.

No sense of place: the impact of electronic media on social behavior
Joshua Meyrowitz

No sense of place

For Americans, the second half of the twentieth century has been marked by an unusual amount and type of social change. The underprivileged have demanded equal rights, a significant portion of the visible political elite has weakened or fallen, and many of those in between have been maneuvering for new social position and identity.

Perhaps even more disturbing than the dimensions of the change has been its seeming inconsistency, even randomness. What is the common thread? We have recently witnessed peaceful civil rights demonstrations juxtaposed with violent looting and rioting. We have seen the persecution of the people by the agencies of government transformed into the virtual prosecution of a President by the people and press. And angry talk of social revolution has been transformed into the cool and determined pursuit of 'affirmative action', community control, and a nuclear arms freeze.

Some social observers have comforted themselves by viewing the disruptions of the 1960s as an historical aberration and by pointing gleefully at former hippies who have clipped their locks and joined the materialistic middle class. Nothing has really changed, they seem to suggest. What they fail to see, however, are the male police and hardhats who now wear their hair long, the 'redneck' farmers who let livestock loose in front of the Capitol (echoes of the Yippies?), the wheelchair sit-ins of the disabled, the court battles over returning land to the Indians, and hundreds of other small and large changes in behavior and attitudes. What does it all mean? Are we witnessing constant change and confusion? Or is there a central mechanism that has been swinging the social pendulum to and fro?

Social change is always too complex to attribute to a single cause and too diverse to reduce to a single process, but the theory offered here

This chapter appeared as 'Where have we been? Where are we going?', in *No Sense of Place: the Impact of Electronic Media on Social Behaviour* (Oxford, Oxford University Press, 1985), pp. 307–29.

suggests that one common theme that connects many recent and seemingly diverse phenomena is a change in Americans' 'sense of place'. The phrase is an intricate – though very serious – pun. It is intricate because the word 'sense' and the word 'place' have two meanings each: 'sense' referring to both perception and logic; 'place' meaning both social position and physical location. The pun is serious because each of these four meanings represents a significant concept in the theory. Indeed, their interrelatedness forms the foundations of the two basic arguments presented here: (1) that social roles (i.e. social 'place') can be understood only in terms of social situations, which, until recently, have been tied to physical place, and (2) that the logic of situational behaviors has much to do with patterns of information flow, that is, much to do with the human senses and their technological extensions. Evolution in media, I have suggested, has changed the logic of the social order by restructuring the relationship between physical place and social place and by altering the ways in which we transmit and receive social information.

I have argued that electronic media, especially television, have had a tremendous impact on Americans' sense of place. Electronic media have combined previously distinct social settings, moved the dividing line between private and public behavior toward the private, and weakened the relationship between social situations and physical places. The logic under-lying situational patterns of behavior in a print-oriented society, therefore, has been radically subverted. Many Americans may no longer seem to 'know their place' because the traditionally interlocking components of 'place' have been split apart by electronic media. Wherever one is now – at home, at work, or in a car – one may be in touch and tuned-in.

The greatest impact has been on social groups that were once defined in terms of their physical isolation in specific locations – kitchens, playgrounds, prisons, convents, and so forth. But the changing relationship between physical and social place has affected almost every social role. Our world may suddenly seem senseless to many people because, for the first time in modern history, it is relatively placeless.

The intensity of the changes in the last thirty years, in particular, may be related to the unique power of television to break down the distinctions between here and there, live and mediated, and personal and public. More than any other electronic medium, television tends to involve us in issues we once thought were 'not our business', to thrust us within a few inches of the faces of murderers and Presidents, and to make physical barriers and passageways relatively meaningless in terms of patterns of access to social information. Television has also enhanced the effects of earlier electronic media by providing us with a better image of the places experienced through radio and reached through the telephone.

The widespread social movements and disruptions since the late 1950s, this theory suggests, may be adjustments in behavior, attitudes, and laws to match new social settings. Many of the traditional distinctions among groups, among people at various stages of socialization, and among superiors and subordinates were based on the patterns of information flow that existed in a print society. The new and 'strange' behavior of many individuals or of classes of people may be the result of the steady merging of formerly distinct social environments.

Television has helped change the deferential Negro into the proud Black, merged the Miss and Mrs into a Ms, transformed the child into a 'human being' with natural rights. Television has fostered the rise of hundreds of 'minorities' – people, who in perceiving a wider world, begin to see themselves as unfairly isolated in some pocket of it. Television has empowered the disabled and the disenfranchised by giving them access to social information in spite of their physical isolation. Television has given women an outside view of their incarceration in the home. Television has weakened visible authorities by destroying the distance and mystery that once enhanced their aura and prestige. And television has been able to do this without requiring the disabled to leave their wheelchairs, without asking the housewife to stop cooking dinner, and without demanding that the average citizen leave his or her easy chair.

By merging discrete communities of discourse, television has made nearly every topic and issue a valid subject of interest and concern for virtually every member of the public. Further, many formerly private and isolated behaviors have been brought out into the large unitary public arena. As a result, behaviors that were dependent on great distance and isolation have been undermined; performances that relied on long and careful rehearsals have been banished from the social repertoire. The widened public sphere gives nearly everyone a new (and relatively shared) perspective from which to view others and gain a reflected sense of self. We, our doctors, our police officers, our Presidents, our secret agents, our parents, our children, and our friends are all performing roles in new theaters that demand new styles of drama.

Many formal reciprocal roles rely on lack of intimate knowledge of the 'other'. If the mystery and mystification disappear, so do the formal behaviors. Stylized courtship behaviors, for example, must quickly fade in the day-to-day intimacy of marriage. Similarly, the new access we gain to distant events and to the gestures and actions of the other sex, our elders, and authorities does not simply 'educate' us; such access changes social reality. By revealing previously backstage areas to audiences, television has served as an instrument of demystification. It has led to a decline in the image and prestige of political leaders, it has demystified adults for children, and demystified men and women for each other. Given this analysis, it is not surprising that the widespread rejection of traditional child and adult, male and female, and leader and follower roles should have begun in the late 1960s among the first generation of Americans to have been exposed to television before learning to read. In the shared environment of television, women and men, children and adults, and followers and leaders know a great deal about each other's behavior and social knowledge – too much, in fact, for them to play the traditional complementary roles of innocence vs. omniscience.

[. . .]

The opening of closed situations is a reversal of a trend several hundred years old. As Michel Foucault brilliantly argues in *Discipline and*

Punish, the membranes around the prison, the hospital, the military barracks, the factory, and the school thickened over several centuries. Foucault describes how people were increasingly separated into distinct places in order to homogenize them into groups with single identities ('students', 'workers', 'prisoners', 'mentally ill', etc.). The individuals in these groups were, in a sense, interchangeable parts. And even the distinct identities of the groups were subsumed under the larger social system of internally consistent, linearly connected, and hierarchically arranged units.[1] But Foucault does not observe the current counter-process. The old social order segregated people in their 'special spheres' in order to homogenize individuals into elements of a larger social machine, but the current trend is toward the integration of all groups into a common sphere with a new recognition of the special needs and idiosyncrasies of individuals.

Nineteenth century life entailed many isolated situations and sustained many isolated behaviors and attitudes. The current merging of situations does not give us a sum of what we had before, but rather new, synthesized behaviors that are qualitatively different. If we celebrate our child's wedding in an isolated situation where it is the sole 'experience' of the day, then our joy may be unbounded. But when, on our way to the wedding, we hear over the car radio of a devastating earthquake, or the death of a popular entertainer, or the assassination of a political figure, we not only lose our ability to rejoice fully, but also our ability to mourn deeply. The electronic combination of many different styles of interaction from distinct regions leads to new 'middle region' behaviors that, while containing elements of formerly distinct roles, are themselves new behavior patterns with new expectations and emotions.

Gone, therefore, are many people's 'special' behaviors, those that were associated with distinct and isolated interactions. Gone are the great eccentrics, the passionate overpowering loves, the massive unrelenting hates, the dramatic curses and flowery praises. Unbounded joy and unmitigated misery cannot coexist in the same place and time. As situations merge, the hot flush and the icy stare blend into a middle region 'cool'. The difference between the reality of behaviors in distinct situations versus the reality of behaviors in merged situations is as great as the difference between the nineteenth century conception that a man might have a virtuous wife and a raunchy mistress and the twentieth century notions of open marriages, 'living together', and serial monogamy.

The Victorian era – the height of print culture – was a time of 'secrets'. People were fascinated with the multiple layers and depths of life: secret passageways, skeletons in the closet, masks upon masks. But the fascination with these layers did not drive the Victorians to destroy secrecy, but rather to enhance it as a natural condition of the social order. To a large degree, skeletons were meant to stay in the closet, sex was to remain behind closed doors (perhaps to be spied upon through keyholes), and scandalous acts were to be hidden from peering eyes. The rare exposures and discoveries were titillating, implicit hints of the vastness of undiscovered reality.[2]

Our own age, in contrast, is fascinated by exposure. Indeed, the *act* of exposure itself now seems to excite us more than the content of the secrets exposed. The steady stripping away of layers of social behavior has made the 'scandal' and the revelation of the 'deep dark secret' everyday occurrences. Ironically, what is pulled out of the closets that contain seemingly extraordinary secrets is, ultimately, the 'ordinariness' of everyone. The unusual becomes the usual: famous stars who abuse their children, Presidents with hemorrhoids, Popes who get depressed, Congressmen who solicit sex from pages.

Still we hunger for heroes, and perhaps our search beneath social masks is filled with the hope of finding people whose private selves are as admirable as their public ones. But since most of the people who make enduring contributions to our culture remain under our scrutiny too long to remain pure in our eyes, we have also begun to focus on people who make one grand gesture or who complete a single courageous act that cannot be undermined by scrutiny. Our new heroes are men and women like Lenny Skutnik, who dove into the water – before television cameras – to save an airplane crash survivor, or Reginald Andrews, who saved a blind man's life by pulling him from beneath a New York subway car. Both men were saluted as heroes by the President of the United States.[3] We can admire such isolated heroic acts; the pasts and the futures of such heroes remain comfortably irrelevant and invisible.

While I have concentrated [. . .] on *change*, I realize that behind many obvious social changes much of our social order remains the same. There continue to be many distinctions in roles of group identity, different stages of socialization, and different ranks of hierarchy in spite of the homogenizing trend. (And after the dust of change from the current merging of roles settles, we are also likely to rediscover some of the many differences among us.) Further, while electronic media have merged many social situations, direct physical presence and mutual monitoring are still primary experiential modes. And regardless of media access, living in a ghetto, a prison cell, and a middle class suburb are certainly not 'equivalent' social experiences. Nevertheless, roles and places have changed dramatically and an analysis of how and why they have changed helps to explain many social phenomena that are not otherwise easily understood. While the merging of spheres through electronic media has not given everyone the same knowledge and wisdom, the mystification surrounding other people and places has been pierced. Print still exists and holds many mysteries and secrets for those who master it, but many of the 'secrets of secrecy' have been exposed.

The changing conceptions of secrecy and place, of gender distinctions, of childhood innocence, and of authority can all be seen in a single social event: the birth of a new human being. Not long ago, this scene was marked by highly isolated environments. Pregnant women were to stay out of public view. Husbands were distanced from the pregnancy and sheltered from the birth. During delivery, the father paced nervously in an isolated waiting room; the mother herself was 'removed' from the birthing situation through drugs; young children were kept out of the hospital and were often further isolated through ignorance of the processes of pregnancy and birth. [. . .]

Today, the scene is vastly different. Pregnancy and birth are 'family-centered'; fathers and children are often fully involved. A new phrase has entered the language: '*we* are pregnant', and it is now common practice for fathers to be present at, and assist in, the birth.[4] Siblings as young as two may be involved in the process by attending special 'prepared sibling' classes, taking tours of the hospital, and, in some cases, being present at the birth itself. [. . .] The 'specialness' of the place in which birth now takes place is further diluted by the increasingly popular trend toward photographing, filming, or videotaping the birth – so that the experience is 'taken out' of the hospital and shared with friends, family, and, perhaps later, with the child itself.

Order, not chaos

The analysis here suggests that the new social order is indeed a new *order*, not a random or disorganized variation from the old social system. Certainly, the old structures have broken down, but an understanding of the relationship between situations and behavior suggests that there is both rhyme and reason in the change and in the new structures. Moreover, an analysis of the direction and type of change clearly indicates that the old conventions were not 'natural' or God-given forms of social organization, but rather ones based on arbitrary distinctions among social situations – distinctions fostered, at least partially, by the characteristics of print. Indeed, many of the currently changing roles and institutions were first shaped or strengthened during the same period that saw the spreading of literacy and printing in the vernacular.

The relatively isolated nuclear family with a strong, dominant husband/father figure and an obedient and subservient wife first grew in England in the sixteenth and seventeenth centuries after a millennium of families built around community and kin. Similarly, the conception of the child as a weak creature in need of special attention and instruction first developed in the sixteenth century among the most literate classes and peaked in the nineteenth century along with the spread of literacy and schooling among the lower classes. Finally, the idea of a distant, powerful leader also developed in the sixteenth and seventeenth centuries. Before the sixteenth century, life was much more local and community-based.

The new relationships in each case were at first hostile: harsh, authoritarian patriarchal control over women, fierce desire to break the will of children, and divine monarchs' absolute control over subjects. Later, however, they all became more affectionate: marriages based on mutual attraction and respect, loving care and nurturing of children, and the decline of absolute monarchs in favor of more representative governments. But even this second stage was characterized by 'separate and unequal' statuses. In our time, we are seeing striking reversals of such separatism in the merging rights and roles of husbands and wives and of children and adults and in the renewed ideal of 'community control'.

Thus, while many of the changes in roles I have described are often seen as causes of each other, this analysis suggests that they may all have been influenced by similar forces. The isolation of women in the domestic sphere is sometimes seen as a cause of the intense interest in the needs and protection of the child; sometimes the new image of the child is seen as the cause of the new views of feminine domesticity. Similarly, many conservatives today blame the loss of childhood innocence on working mothers and the feminist movement. But the analysis presented here suggests that both the rise and fall of childhood and the decline and rise in women's rights and involvement in the public sphere may be closely linked to major shifts in communication technology in the past and in our own time. The spread of literacy, with its emphasis on hierarchy and sequence, supported a linear chain of command, from God-the-father, through a strong central national leader, to a father who was a god to his wife and children. The increasingly dependent illiterate child was put in the care of the minimally literate female.[5] As new means of communication blur hierarchy and sequence in our own time, we are experiencing a reintegration of many splintered roles.

The proliferation of new information-systems that followed the spread of literacy allowed for greater separation of backstage and onstage situations. Just as we are experiencing 'sidestage', or 'middle region', behaviors as situations merge, so did the period from the late Middle Ages to the recent past allow for more 'deep backstage' behaviors for many roles and, therefore, for more idealized 'forefront stage' behavior. The new information-systems of literacy created distance between men and women, between adults and children, and between leaders and the common person. Printing fostered the preparation of 'training manuals' for princes and priests (such as those written by Machiavelli and Gracian) and led to the publication of many etiquette manuals aimed at people of different ages and sex.

The sixteenth century also saw a striking change in the sense of place and in the degree of 'permeability' of the domestic sphere. Historians have noted the new sense of 'boundaries' dividing public and private, domestic and political, family and community in the transition between the pre-modern and modern age.[6] In our own time, we have found a dramatic reversal of this trend.

Just as in the late Middle Ages, a husband's power over his wife was muted by the openness of the domestic sphere to public view, so now has the idea of a man's home as his castle declined. For no matter how physically isolated the home is from other homes and people, the parental stress hotline, the rape hotline, a lawyer, and the police are only a few finger pulses away. As telephones, radios, televisions, and computers increasingly link the home to the outside world, external behavioral norms begin to merge into internal ones. The living room, kitchen, and bedroom are being reintegrated into the larger public realm. The politicizing of the personal has redefined housecleaning as 'unpaid labor' for which a wife may demand 'back wages' in a divorce suit. Similarly, the notion of 'marital rape' suggests a new blurring of public and private spheres. What was judged, for several centuries, to be a man's rightful 'correction' of his wife and children in the privacy of his home is now being redefined as criminal abuse. And one recent criminological study of forgery, theft, and assault has examined the following types of 'criminal acts': a child signing a parent's name on a report card, a child taking a dollar from his or her mother's pocketbook without permission, and a brother hitting a sister during a family argument.[7] These are among the many indications of a decreasing tendency to define actions and events in terms of the specific physical sphere in which they take place.

Hunters and gatherers in an information age

To the extent that electronic media tend to reunite many formerly distinct spheres of interaction, we may be returning to a world even older than that of the late Middle Ages. Many of the features of our 'information age' make us resemble the most primitive of social and political forms: the hunting and gathering society. As nomadic peoples, hunters and gatherers have no loyal relationship to territory. They, too, have little 'sense of place'; specific activities and behaviors are not tightly fixed to specific physical settings.[8]

The lack of boundaries both in hunting and gathering and in electronic societies leads to many striking parallels. Of all known societal types before our own, hunting and gathering societies have tended to be the most egalitarian in terms of the roles of males and females, children and adults, and leaders and followers.[9] The difficulty of maintaining many 'separate places', or distinct social spheres, tends to involve everyone in everyone else's business.

Although men and women in hunting and gathering societies usually have division of labor, it is not as sharp as it is in agricultural societies, and doing the work of the opposite sex is not usually considered demeaning. In many hunting and gathering societies, women play an active role in supporting the family, child-care is considered the responsibility of the whole community, and both men and women are expected to be gentle, mild-mannered, and noncompetitive.[10] Because of the inability of hunter and gatherer societies to separate domestic from public spheres, men can not establish aura and distance, and women are involved in public decisions.[11] As in our own society, the lack of privacy in hunting and gathering societies often leads to community control over private arguments between husbands and wives.[12]

Because of the openness of life, hunter and gatherer children are not sharply segregated by age or sex, and they are not usually isolated from adult activities. Sex play among children and adolescents is common and sometimes includes sexual intercourse.[13] Like many of today's parents, hunters and gatherers stress self-reliance rather than obedience to adults, and they do not usually use physical punishment.[14]

In hunting and gathering societies, play and work often take place in the same sphere and involve similar activities. Children observe and play at hunting and gathering.[15] Similarly, work and play have begun to merge in our electronic age. Both children and adults now spend many hours a week staring at video monitors, whether video games or electronic spreadsheets. Further, as the young computer 'hackers' have demonstrated, children's play now often takes place in the same public sphere as their parents' work – the jungle of national and international information networks.

Because leaders in hunting and gathering societies cannot get away from those they lead, leadership – to the extent that it exists – must be gained through persuasion rather than coercion. The leader cannot be easily 'set apart'; leaders have to gain authority by setting 'the best example by working the hardest and sharing the most'.[16] For hunters and gatherers, as for us, exposed leadership is often more of a burden than a privilege. In both societies, even recognized leaders are not expected to make decisions by themselves or to impose their decisions on those who disagree.

There are many other similarities between the norms of hunters and gatherers and our newly developed behavior patterns. In both forms of social organization, marriages are often based on mutual attraction rather than kinship ties, marriages are easily arranged and terminated, and premarital sex and serial monogamy are common. Just as women today are increasingly keeping their birth names after marriage, hunters and gatherers often reckon kinship through the families of both mothers and fathers.[17] And compared to other forms of social organization, both we and hunters and gatherers have few large scale or long-term initiation rites.[18]

One way to characterize ourselves, then, is as 'hunters and gatherers of an information age'. Our shared sphere of interaction is informational rather than physical, but it leads to a similar inability to distinguish clearly among gender, age, and hierarchical statuses. We bypass many previous generations' dependence on physical location as a prime determinant of access to people and information. Unlike tribes with special huts and sacred places, men's domains and women's domains, adult places and children's places, our culture is becoming essentially placeless.

Our advanced technological stage allows us to hunt and gather information rather than food. Like hunters and gatherers who take for granted the abundance of food 'out there' and therefore only hunt and gather enough to consume immediately, we are increasingly becoming a 'subsistence information society'. Rather than engaging in long-term storage of knowledge in their memories or homes, many people are beginning to believe that information is available 'out there' and that individuals do not need to stockpile it. Our children sing 'we don't need no education',[19] and even many scholars have begun to steer away from collecting and storing in their minds the long, linear arguments of literacy that linked new discoveries to old and that pointed to the future. Instead, the computer is increasingly used as an abundant jungle of bits and pieces of 'data' (albeit, a jungle created and stocked by us). Some data are hunted, gathered, and analyzed when an appetite for correlations arises. The connections found are often consumed and digested immediately without being painstakingly linked to other knowledge and ideas.

The notion that we are 'returning' to a primitive era or even to the pre-print period in Western Europe is, of course, much too simple for numerous reasons. Unlike pre-modern civilizations, we remain heavily dependent on literacy in both the way we store information and in the way we think. The electronic age has grown out of and retains many features of a 'print culture'.[20] Differences in literacy skills, therefore, continue to distinguish between children and adults and to divide people into separate social categories. Our less exclusive dependence on print and literacy, however, has muted the social distinctions among people of different stages of literacy. Thus, we are spiralling forward rather than circling backward. We regain some features of the pre-modern world as we advance into a new frontier.

Good or bad?/real or false?

[. . .] By outlining a relationship among media, situations, behavior, I have argued that we cannot have the old role structures and also have electronic media. Controlling the content of electronic media, for example, will not maintain old forms of social organization. Even conservative content may be revolutionary when disseminated in new ways.

Further, by outlining a single process that affects many different social phenomena, this theory indicates that we cannot have *some* of the forces for social change brought about by electronic media without having *all*, or most, of the forces. Because the effects are interrelated and widespread, we cannot easily pick and choose effects. We cannot select uses for new media that advance old goals without often altering the social systems out of which the goals developed. We cannot, for example, 'buy the wife' a television set to ease her boredom with housework without changing her sense of place in the world. We cannot use television to 'educate' our children without simultaneously altering the functions of reading and the structure of the family and the school. When we use *Sesame Street* to advance the speed of children's learning, we also heighten children's entrance into real streets, and for some, perhaps, into real street crime. We cannot have mediated intimacy with our political leaders, in the hope of getting closer to greatness, without losing a belief in heroes. And if we use media to teach many different groups about each other, we also change the lines of social association and the perimeters of group identities.

Any judgments about the new society relative to the old, therefore, must be made with great care. We can selectively condemn and praise, but to see parts of the new environment as disease and other parts as cure may be to misunderstand the unified dynamics involved in social change. Both the things we dislike and the things we like about the new environment may be parts of the same process. If, for example, we lose the extremes of many situation-specific behaviors of the nineteenth century, then we lose not only high manners and quiet 'civilized' clubs, but also many of the extremes of debauchery, poverty, and neglect. If we are to measure accurately the new social order against the old, we must judge both systems as wholes and evaluate *all* the ways in which they differ from each other.

Just as the new environment is neither inherently better nor worse than the old, neither is it inherently more real nor false – though there have been claims in both directions.

Many people feel that they have stopped 'playing roles', that they are now behaving 'naturally' and just 'being themselves'. At the same time, many people have become more aware of the 'staginess' of roles played by *others*, such as politicians, public relations executives, and advertisers. And so they have become more suspicious of what Daniel Boorstin has dubbed 'pseudo events' – events that are created simply to be reported by media.[21]

Yet both of these views may miss the point. Social behavior continues to be based on projecting certain impressions and concealing others, behaving one way here, and another there. What has changed are the dividing lines between here and there; what is different is the number of distinct social settings. People's new 'openness' may be based less on a new basic sense of 'honesty' than on continuing attempts to avoid apparent discrepancies and inconsistencies. Many people are 'revealing' aspects of themselves which were once concealed because it is now more difficult to keep such backstage information secret. For many of the most visible performers – Presidents and other 'personalities' – however, the exposure is so great, the overview of many of their performances so accessible, that even the simplest rehearsed behavior or change in style from one place to another seems 'contrived'.

Contrary to Boorstin's analysis of 'pseudo events', the significance of electronic media may be that the planning and staging of 'media events' cannot be hidden as simply as the planning for face-to-face encounters. A politician, for example, cannot hide his campaign strategists as easily as the average business executive can hide the suggestions of a spouse or hair stylist. Electronic media may be exposing the general 'pseudoness' of events rather than creating it. Boorstin and others may be responding more to the newsness of the *visibility* of staging than to the newness of staging itself. We now have different performances rather than more or less performance; we have a different reality rather than a different measure of reality.

By thrusting the backstage area of life out into the public arena, electronic media have made it more difficult to play traditional formal roles. The behaviors exhibited are still 'roles', though newly patterned to match new staging contingencies. And though 'etiquette' is thought to be passé in some circles, there is still an etiquette implicit in all our expectations of (and disappointments in) the actions of others. And part of the new etiquette is that we no longer should play certain traditional formal roles. As Richard Sennett describes in *The Fall of Public Man*, we have lost the sense of 'distance' that once characterized much of social life. 'The reigning belief today is that closeness between persons is a moral good.'[22]

The 'reciprocal informality' of our time has two sides. It could be said that people are now *allowed* to drop formal communication, or it could be said that we are now *forced* to drop it. In either case, the relationship between access to information and formality remains. In social relations, formality and intimacy seem to be mutually exclusive in any given time or place. Just as formality is a barrier to intimacy, so is intimacy a barrier to formality.

[. . .]

Many people jump [. . .] to the assumption that developments in electronic media are hastening the arrival of an Orwellian nightmare. The evolution of sophisticated surveillance devices and the decline in privacy are seen as concrete manifestations of the type of totalitarianism described by Orwell. Yet these technological developments may actually be signs of a trend in the opposite direction.

Orwell offered a vision of society where Big Brother watched all, but was himself invisible. Orwell conceived of an 'inner party' elite who observed but were unobservable. The Party demanded and received total loyalty and unquestioning obedience. Such a system is conceivable in an electronic age, but if the new technologies have any 'inherent bias', it may be against such a sharply hierarchical system.

[. . .] '[A]uthority' and 'leadership' are unlike mere 'power' in that they depend on performance and appeal. One cannot lead or be looked up to if one is not there to be seen. Yet one of the peculiar ironies of our age is that any person who steps forward into the media limelight and attempts to gain national visibility becomes too visible, too exposed, and is therefore demystified. Electronic media may be used by officials to spy on private citizens, but when an electronic medium such as television is used by leaders as a means of communicating with the people, the medium's expressive bias also often allows citizens to 'spy' on officials.

Further, for a hierarchy to exist, there must be more followers than leaders. In an era of easy and relatively shared access to information about people, one leader may be able to keep a close watch on thousands of followers, but thousands of followers can keep an even closer watch on one leader. The simple mathematics of hierarchy suggests the strong likelihood of an undermining of the pyramid of status in an electronic age.

Electronic media not only weaken authority by allowing those low on the ladder of hierarchy to gain access to much information, but also by allowing increased opportunities for the sharing of information horizontally. The telephone and computer, for example, allow people to communicate with each other without going 'through channels'. Such horizontal flow of information is another significant deterrent to totalitarian central leadership.

There is no doubt that new technologies – like old technologies – may be used by bad governments to bad ends. And once a totalitarian government exists, it can stop or control the flow of information. But the assumption that the new media or the 'lack of privacy' they foster will, in and of themselves, support authoritarian hierarchies is based on a mis-understanding of the relationship between privacy and hierarchy. For it is privacy and distance that support strong central authorities. Our notions of privacy have a very short history in Western civilization, and as we know from studies of hunting and gathering societies and of pre-print Western Europe, the virtual lack of privacy tends to weaken rather than support great distinctions in status. It is the person who tries to stand apart or above, not the average citizen, who is most damaged by lack of privacy.

We may be aesthetically uncomfortable with the thought of full and open access to information, but, all other things being equal, such access would tend to level hierarchies rather than erect them. Even the evidence we have been gathering recently about our leaders' 'abuses of power' may, in this sense, testify more to our relatively increased ability to gather information on leaders than to an absolute increase in the abuse of power. The thing to fear is not the loss of privacy *per se*, but the *nonreciprocal* loss of privacy – that is, where we lose the ability to monitor those who monitor us.

As of now, electronic media may best support a 'hierarchy of the people'. For electronic media give a distinct advantage to the average person. Average people now have access to social information that was once not available to them. Further, they have information concerning the performers of high status roles. As a result, the distance, mystery, and mystification surrounding high status roles are minimized. There are still many 'unusual' people with special knowledge and training, but the average person now knows more about what special individuals know and also more about high status people as 'people'. After seeing so much ordinariness in the close-up views of extraordinary people, we may continue to remain more ignorant and less powerful than they, but we are now more aware of the many things they do not know and cannot do. And even though much of this new information access is reciprocal, the common person has relatively less to lose from exposure and visibility. No one expects the common person to be anything but common. If Joe Smith finds out that the President cheats on his income tax, Joe is likely to be outraged – even if he cheats on his own income tax. Great leaders are not supposed to suffer the frailties of greed, lust, or instability.

At this moment in history, we may be witnessing a political revolution of enormous proportions, a revolution that is masked by the conventions of our language and by the form of our traditional ideals. We are moving from a representative government of de facto elites to a government of direct participation with elected 'administrators'. The change is difficult to see, however, because we refer to both of these systems as 'democracy' and because the new system involves the manifestation of many once unattainable ideals such as true 'public servants' and 'government by and or the people'. Reality does not stay the same, however, when ideals become reality.

Electronic media offer the potential of government by direct referendum, and the growth of interactive television promises the mixed blessing of a political system modeled after the structure of the 'Gong Show' – where performers can be removed from the stage in mid-performance. (A more pleasing metaphor for the same system is the Greek forum.) The new technology fosters the potential of the closest thing the earth has ever witnessed to participatory democracy on an enormous scale – with all the resulting problems and possibilities. Even if this comes to pass, however, we will need some rethinking of our conceptions of authority if we are to see the system for what it is. For whoever steps before us in the role of leader will seem to be a disappointment compared to our hazy, but glowing images of Washingtons, Jeffersons, and Lincolns, and any step taken without our knowledge, any move taken in opposition to a majority 'vote' in a national poll, will be seen as the arrogance of power.

Although the political problems of our age may not be the obvious ones many people fear, there remain many reasons for caution. The decline in trust and faith in authorities is filled with paradox and some danger. The growth in weapons technology and the increase in speed in global communications have led to an enhancement of the raw power of national leaders even as our faith in governments and leaders has declined. Our recent Presidents have had the power to destroy the entire world, but not the authority to convince the majority of the population that they are doing a competent job. There is always the danger of leaders using their massive warmaking powers in attempts to rally the people behind them – or as an excuse for secrecy and information control.

Similarly, our increasingly complex technological and social world has made us rely more and more heavily on 'expert information', but the general exposure of 'experts' as fallible human beings has lessened our faith in them as people. The change in our image of leaders and experts leaves us with a distrust of power, but also with a seemingly powerless dependence on those in whom we have little trust.

Further, the vacuum in our visible political realm of authority may be giving undue power to *in*visible men and women who run large national and multi-national corporations. Unlike governments, corporations have no code of 'openness'. Indeed, competitive business is built on a tradition of secrecy. A business leader who refuses an interview is not viewed as suspiciously as a governor or a President who refuses to speak to the press. We do need to be wary, therefore, of the increasingly complex involvement of many corporations in university research, in government, and in all forms of national and international communication technologies – from book publishing to satellites.

There is also one visible class of 'authorities' who, through their unique positions in our society, have been able to become exceptions to the decline in visible authority. These people have managed to maintain both controlled access to the people *and* controlled performances. They are the television newscasters whose daily performances are tightly controlled and scripted. In an implicit trade code, television news programs do not expose other news programs or new personalities. A few moments of prime time may be used to show a President fall down while skiing, collapse while jogging, or make a serious slip of the tongue, but there are few, if any, intentional television exposures of Tom Brokaw of Dan Rather falling down, cursing, or becoming irritable and tense. Such conventions maintain the fiction that the selectively revealed aspects of newscasters' personalities are representative of their whole selves. But we need to be more aware of the staging contingencies that may be enhancing our trust in journalists just as they weaken our faith in the political process.

New generations of electronic media

Many recent developments in media are likely both to enhance and to retard some of the trends I have described. There is a growing proliferation of sources of information, from personal mini-cassette players, which can create private spaces in the midst of crowded streets, to satellites that embrace the globe in a web of information channels. Such developments splinter the mass audience and largely transform the world of 'broadcasting' we have come to take for granted. Yet [. . .] the new divisions are not a return to the *same* group distinctions that were common in a print era, and the new divisions do not destroy the ability of a medium such as television to draw millions of people into a single event at a single point in time. Nevertheless, the current nightly attendance of nearly half the nation to three network sources will no doubt largely disappear.

The rising importance of the computer to our work and leisure activities is also bringing about many new changes. In some ways, the computer is a hybrid of the book and television. If the computer continues to rely heavily on 'print', it may reinforce the levels of hierarchy associated with writing and reading. Further, computer programming is itself a new 'code' to be mastered. In general, the demands of experience (and money) to gain access to the sophisticated and rapidly expanding capabilities of hardware and software are creating new distinct groupings, grades of socialization, and levels of expertness and authority.

But the effects of the computer on group identity, socialization, and hierarchy are not unidirectional. Although the computer now appears to be reestablishing many divisions in information-systems, its long-term effect may still be to increase the merging of various information-systems and experiences. As costs of hardware and software continue to decrease and as programs become increasingly 'user friendly', the computer may further democratize information access. Just as the automobile involves more complex and expensive technology than the 'technology' of the horse and buggy yet allows for increased mobility for many people who do not know anything about auto mechanics, the 'user friendly' computer is based on sophisticated knowledge that gives the unsophisticated user increased informational mobility. Large corporations and governments may make much more extensive use of computers than the average person, and yet the size of the *gap* between the low and the mighty may nevertheless decrease. (And, of course, many 'average people' work in corporations and have access to the computers used within them.) The teenage 'hackers' who have recently used their inexpensive computers to 'break into' multimillion dollar corporation and government defense information networks have shown that computers not only tend to consolidate power but also to dissipate it.[23]

On the surface, the complexity of computers may seem to separate children and adults further by giving children a new ladder to climb before they reach adulthood. Yet the speed with which many young children seem to master the workings of computers should lead us to question carefully their ultimate effects on adult–child interaction and on stages of learning. Even when the computer is used to store print information, children seem to develop a 'feel' for the computer that surpasses their age (by which we usually mean 'reading age').[24] Operation of a computer is much more difficult than watching television, but the sequence in which one learns to master the computer does not seem to be the same as the sequence through which one masters print. Further, as Seymour Papert has convincingly argued, even 'programming' is not necessarily a complex adult skill, and young children can master it as well, and often better, than their elders.[25]

The fact that the computer involves a type of skill different from reading is most evident in the computer's nonlinguistic uses such as the complex video games that have swept the country (and world). Like television, the video game does not divide its 'audience' into different ages. People of all ages play the games. Further, age and traditional education do not have any direct effect on level of skills. Indeed, many young children master games their parents cannot even fathom. Many video games involve multiple lines of action, increasing speed, and increasing rate of increasing speed. These aspects are all foreign to the one-thing-at-a-time, one-thing-after-another, and take-time-to-think world of reading.

Electronic media have been blamed by many critics for the recent decline in scores on Scholastic Aptitude Tests.[26] Less attention has been paid, however, to the possibility that electronic media may aid the development of other forms of 'intelligence' that we do not yet even know how to name or measure. Traditionally, for example, we attempt to solve complex problems such as the causes of disease or crime by painstakingly *isolating* one set of variables after another and looking for simple, mechanistic cause-effect links. To many people this is the only possible way of 'logically' analyzing phenomena. Such isolating techniques work well in playing chess, but they are of little use in playing video games. It is possible that video and computer games are introducing our children to a different way of thinking that involves the integration of multiple variables and overlapping lines of simultaneous actions. Although the best thing many critics have been able to suggest about video games is that they help the development of 'hand–eye coordination', it is also conceivable that the video game wizards will grow up to find a complex cure for cancer.[27]

In a print society, the graded complexity of print data and the highly compartmentalized nature of print audiences lead to high esteem for 'experts' (the 'top' in a field) and 'specialists' (people whose knowledge is focused in one tiny cluster of information about a particular subject). Indeed, the more highly trained and educated a person is in a print society, the more ensconced they usually become *in* a given body of literature, and, therefore, the more they are trained *out* of awareness of other fields of knowledge. Many of the traditional disciplines are, in this sense, not only bodies of structured knowledge, but also systems of organized ignorance. The specialist's skill is situationally defined. The key to being an 'expert' is not to 'learn everything', but to reduce the size of a 'knowledge situation' until one is able to master all that is in it.

In an electronic society, however, messages from all bodies of knowledge are more equally accessible to all people. While such messages, especially as presented on radio and television, often offer more 'awareness' than 'understanding', the new communication pattern works to undermine the status of authorities whose knowledge and skills are based only on isolated communication networks. Experts and specialists continue to have much more specialized knowledge than the average person, but the new shared forum created by electronic media has affected our evaluation of such specialized knowledge. Because we are now more 'aware' of the many areas that a given specialist knows nothing about, we are gaining a renewed appreciation of a kind of Renaissance generalism. On the one hand, no topic is expected to be so complex that it cannot be explained, at least in broad terms, to the common person; conversely, no authority or leader is fully respected unless he or she appears to have a sense of 'general' social knowledge. Ironically, we are increasingly dependent on specialized knowledge, yet we also have less respect for such knowledge when it is presented in a vacuum.

In one sense, the new notion of 'being smart' involves a dilution of knowledge so that it 'plays well' on television and radio. But in another sense, electronic media offer potential enrichment of our culture's stock of knowledge and understanding. The means of storing and dispensing information through electronic media may, at first, seem disconnected and disorganized. But this perception is probably based on a print-oriented bias. By merging many formerly distinct knowledge situations, electronic media have been breaking down the boundaries among various disciplines, opening new dialogues, and fostering the development of cross-disciplinary areas of study.

Again, the impact of television and radio in this regard is small compared to the potential long-term effects of the computer. At this point, most people still use the computer to store, gain access to, and analyze data in their specialized fields of interest. But unlike books (where one must often go 'bibliography-hopping' through a given field to find 'relevant' sources), the computer gives potentially equal access to data from *all* fields. It may soon be possible for any person with a telephone and a portable terminal to have access to any book in the Library of Congress, any article in any journal, and any data that have been placed in a central research bank. Through a computer search, any mention of a topic (or a given combination of topics) could be located. With such an overwhelming amount of accessible data, a new 'specialty' may develop: the ability to see patterns and interrelationships among various types of data, regardless of their 'field' of origin. The resulting 'specialist in generalism' would be someone who does not 'know' everything about everything but who has a good idea of who knows what, where and how to find things, and how to link together similar questions in diverse fields. This person who would know 'almost nothing about almost everything' could provide a balance for those specialists who, in our increasingly specialized world, know 'almost everything about almost nothing'.

Thus, although the computer may, on the surface, seem to establish a new hierarchy of access based on complex programming skills and on variations in the sophistication and cost of hardware and software, many features of the computer will enhance the merging of information-systems. Further, unless we stop using telephones, radios, and televisions, the spread of computers and other new media will probably not be able to reestablish the distance that once existed in a print culture.[28]

In addition, it is not at all clear that the computer will continue to rely as heavily as it has on abstract written symbols. The increasingly sophisticated use of interactive computer graphics and the drive toward computers that can understand and use human speech, both suggest that mastery of literacy may soon be as irrelevant to the basic operation of computers and computer-controlled machines as it is to the operation of television sets and automobiles. Whether we should applaud or condemn such a 'demotion' of literacy is open to question, but it is clear that such an evolution would further integrate people of different ages and levels of education.

Regardless of which path dominates the evolution of the computer – discursive or presentational symbols – the computer and other new technologies certainly enhance the most significant difference between electronic and all previous modes of communication – the undermining of the relationship between social place and physical place. Anyone's personal computer can now be hooked into any other 'mainframe' or personal computer through the massive telephone system. The computer is also stimulating the integration of various technologies – televisions, telephones, audio/video recorders, satellites, and printers – into one large information network. As more and more work and play in our society is becoming 'informational' rather than 'material', there is a further decline in the difference between here and there and an enhancement of our roles as new-age hunters and gatherers.

Controlling or controlled?

On the surface, the theory presented [. . .] may appear to be part of a wholly 'deterministic' philosophy. Some may wrongly interpret my analysis of the impact of media on human behavior as a suggestion that we are merely bit players in a drama whose script and scenes we do not control. But this is not my intention at all. I do believe, however, that we are each born into a physical and social world in which there are both freedoms and constraints. While we choose our friends, for example, we cannot choose our parents. Further, it is clear that we cannot meet people who are no longer living or not yet alive, and if we marry, we must choose one of the small fraction of living people we happen to meet. We cannot live without food, warmth, and sleep, though we are often free to choose what we eat and where we sleep. Because we cannot be physically in two places at the same time, even our choices of where we go and what we do are themselves limitations in disguise. And finally, regardless of any of the choices we make, we ultimately die (though sometimes we can decide how and when we do so). In studying the human condition, therefore, one can choose to focus on limits or on available options. Just as those who study human choices often take the constraints for granted, I have chosen to study one variable of social constraint while assuming obvious individual and group freedoms.

In many ways, my work parallels that of the anthropologists and psychologists who have studied the effects of interpersonal distances and architectural designs on the style and tone of social interactions.[29] Airport lounges with long rows of fibreglass chairs bolted to the floor obviously foster different types of interactions than do other lounges with soft armchairs loosely arranged in a circle. I argue, similarly, that once invented and used, media affect us by shaping the type of interactions that take place through them. We cannot play certain roles unless the stages for those roles exist.

Such analyses of the structure of interactional settings leave a large number of individual and group freedoms intact. *Individuals* behaving in physical or mediated environments still have a wide range of behavioral choices within the overall constraints. They may behave 'appropriately' in many different personal styles; or they may choose to ignore the social cues and behave 'inappropriately' – provided they are willing to take the social consequences. And finally, they may leave situations in which they feel uncomfortable or avoid them in the first place. On a *group* level, the situation is even less deterministic. For *we* design and use our rooms, buildings, media, rituals, and other social environments. We can redesign them, abandon them, or alter their use.

Ultimately, the most deterministic perspective may be unwittingly embraced by those who refuse to apply our greatest freedom – human reason and analysis – to the social factors that influence behavior. We do not retain free-choice simply because we refuse to see and study those things that constrain our actions. Indeed, we often give up the potential of additional freedom to control our lives by choosing not to see how the environments we shape can, in turn, work to reshape us.

Notes

1   Foucault (1977).
2   For a discussion of the fascination of the Victorians with secrecy, disguise, and masks, see Reed (1975).
3   Goldman et al. (1982); Fritz (1983).
4   For discussions of the changing relationships between health care personnel and patients, as well as the blurring of distinctions between hospital and home, see Hotchner (1979); Van Dyke (1980); Pillitteri (1981); and Gorvine (1982).
5   As Kuhn (1947) notes in her study of New England childhood education, the recognition of the child as a special being in need of special care preceded the recognition of the importance of women and motherhood. Further, the first widespread call for female literacy and education (in the mid-eighteenth century) had as its purpose the education of women sufficiently to be good mothers (for they needed to be able to read the growing literature on child care). There was little initial drive to educate women for their own sake or to teach them beyond the level necessary for 'scientific mothering'.
6   Shorter (1975: 5, 22); Stone (1977: 4–6).
7   Lincoln and Straus (1984).
8   Hunting and gathering societies have differed in form over time and in different locations. I am discussing them here as a Weberian 'ideal type'. I am generalizing about the ways in which nomadic hunting and gathering societies have differed, in broad terms, from other forms of social organization. If a 'return' to a hunting and gathering society seems aberrant, it may be comforting to realize that, according to Lee and Devore (1968: 3) for 99 percent of the estimated two million years that Cultural

Humans have existed, they have lived as hunters and gatherers, and more than half of the people who have ever lived on earth have been hunters and gatherers.

9　O'Kelly (1980: 74–106).

10　O'Kelly (1980: 82–100). See also Turnbull (1961: 154); Goodale (1971: 151–3, 332–8); Draper (1975: 77–94); Marshall (1976: 175–6). Friedl (1975: 18–19) suggests that there are four major forms of division of labor among hunters and gatherers: both men and women gather, men hunt; communal hunting and gathering by both men and women; men hunt, women gather; men hunt, women process the meat and skins. O'Kelly (1980: 91) suggests a fifth pattern; women hunt and gather, men hunt and fish. As Friedl (1975) notes, the degree of overlapping subsistence responsibilities is directly correlated with the degree of sexual equality. Thus, those hunters and gatherers who hunt communally are the most egalitarian, while those in which women only process the men's catch exhibit more sexual asymmetry, including higher incidence of rape and violence against women. The relevance of hunting and gathering societies to changes in male and female roles in our own time was pointed out to me by Candice Leonard. Leonard deals with similar themes in her unpublished paper, 'Sexual equality in the post-industrial society,' University of New Hampshire, 1983.

11　Rosaldo and Lamphere (1974: 39).

12　O'Kelly (1980: 96); see also Turnbull (1961: 124); Marshall (1976: 177).

13　O'Kelly (1980: 97–101).

14　O'Kelly (1980: 98).

15　See, for example, Turnbull (1961: 128–9); Goodale (1971: 151–3); Marshall (1976: 96, 130, 314, 318).

16　O'Kelly (1980: 77–8); see also Turnbull (1961: 124–5); Friedl (1975: 31).

17　O'Kelly (1980: 78–102); see also Turnbull (1961: 127–8); Goodale (1971: 335); Draper (1975: 92); Friedl (1975: 23); Marshall (1976: 261).

18　Friedl (1975: 30). Significantly, when the normally nomadic hunters and gatherers become sedentary and attach themselves to particular places, they lose most of the features that make then resemble our own new norms: women's autonomy, mobility, and influence decrease markedly; work becomes much more clearly sex-typed; the socialization experiences of boys and girls become much more dissimilar; men enter into extra-village politics; and there is increasing household segregation and privacy (Draper, 1975).

19　From 'Another Brick in the Wall (Part II)', lyrics by Roger Waters, Pink Floyd Music Publishers, 1979. This song was number one for four weeks during 1980 and was the fifth most popular song for the year.

20　The continuing significance of print and the literate mind-set to the structure and functioning of our electronic age is a theme that runs through much of the writing of Walter Ong. See, for example, Ong (1977: 82–91).

21　Boorstin (1962).

22　Sennett (1977: 259).

23　Marbach et al. (1983).

24　See, for example, Papert (1980) and Golden (1982).

25　Papert (1980). Papert worked for a time with Piaget. Although Papert builds on many of Piaget's ideas about children 'learning without being taught', Papert argues that the cross-cultural evidence that seems to support the invariance of cognitive stages of growth may not really indicate the universality of such stages. Papert argues that all the cultures studied have been, in a sense, one type of culture: 'pre-computer' cultures. He suggests that what have up till now been 'formal', or abstract, operations may be 'concretized' by the availability of computers (see, for example, pp. 7–28, 174–6).

At least part of the edge that young children now have with computers is likely to disappear with the next generation whose parents may already be experts at computing. What we are witnessing now may be only a transitional phase similar to the period following the introduction of literacy into a society. Initially, literacy among the young, who are first to learn it, undermines the authority of elders, but in the long run literacy strengthens adult authority and causes greater distance between adults and children. The same long-term trend may be true of 'computer literacy'. It is not yet clear, however, how much differentiation in age-related skills the computer will foster compared to literacy. Further, if the rate of change in computer hardware and software remains as high as it is today, the younger generation may always have at least a partial advantage over the older generation (in the same sense that the children of immigrant families often learn the language of the new country better than their parents do). For an excellent discussion of how the increasing rate of social change enhances the status of the younger generation, see Mead (1970).

26   See, for example, Mankiewicz and Swerdlow (1979: 211–17).

27   The potential of the computer to allow for the consideration of multiple variables is already evident in the computer's fostering of the development of 'multivariate analysis', which allows researchers to analyze the interaction of many variables in a manner and with a speed that would be virtually impossible without computers.

28   One of the reasons that the continuing existence of books does not override the existence of television, while the continuing existence of television may override the 'literate' character of computers, is that the distance between two roles is only as great as the shortest informational channel between them. Or, put differently, when they coexist, intimacy overrides distance, but distance cannot override intimacy. Moving in with someone whom you once knew only through business correspondence, for example, overrides the distance fostered by the written medium of letters, but writing letters to the person you share your bed with does not reestablish much distance. In the same way, new 'distancing' forms of interaction, such as discursive text sent by computer, are unlikely to reverse the presentational 'closeness' of the telephone, radio, and television – unless we abandon the older technologies.

29   See, for example, Sommer (1969) and Hall (1966).

References

Boorstin, D.J. (1962) *The Image: Or What Happened to the American Dream*. New York: Atheneum.

Draper, P. (1975) '!Kung women: contrasts in sexual egalitarianism in foraging and sedentary contexts', in Rayna R. Reiter (ed.), *Toward an Anthropology of Women*. New York: Monthly Review Press.

Foucault, M. (1977) *Discipline and Punish: The Birth of the Prison*. Trans. Alan Sheridan. New York: Pantheon. (French edition 1975).

Friedl, E. (1975) *Women and Men: An Anthropologist's View*. New York: Rinehart & Winston.

Fritz, S. (1983) 'Hello, this is Ronald Reagan – yes, really'. *US News and World Report*, 21 March, p. 48.

Golden, F. (1982) 'Here come the microkids', *Time*, 3 May, pp. 50–6.

Goldman, P. et al. (1982) 'The Reagan Gamble', *Newsweek*, 8 February, pp. 24–7.

Goodale, J.C. (1971) *Tiwi Wives: A Study of the Women of Melville Island, North Australia*. Seattle, WA: University of Washington Press.

Gorvine, B. et al. (1982) *Health Care of Women: Labor and Delivery*. Belmont, CA: Wadsworth.

Hall, E. (1966) *The Hidden Dimension*. New York: Doubleday.

Hotchner, T. (1979) *Pregnancy and Childbirth: A Complete Guide to a New Life*. New York: Avon.

Kuhn, A.L. (1947) *The Mother's Role in Childhood Education: New England Concepts, 1830–1860*. New Haven, CT: Yale University Press.

Lee, R.B. and Devore, I. (eds) (1968) *Man the Hunter*. Chicago: Aldine.

Lincoln, A. and Straus, M.A. (1984) *Crime and the Family*. Springfield, IL: Charles C. Thomas.

Mankiewicz, F. and Swerdlow, J. (1979) *Remote Control: Television and the Manipulation of American Life*. New York: Ballantine.

Marbach, W. et al. (1983) 'Beware: hackers at play', *Newsweek*, 5 September, pp. 42–6, 48.

Marshall, L. (1976) *The !Kung of Nyae Nyae*. Cambridge, MA: Harvard University Press.

Mead, M. (1970) *Culture and Commitment: A Study of the Generation Gap*. Garden City, NY: Doubleday.

O'Kelly, C.G. (1980) *Women and Men in Society*. New York: Van Nostrand.

Ong, W.J. (1977) *Interfaces of the Word: Studies in the Evolution of Consciousness and Culture*. Ithaca, NY: Cornell University Press.

Papert, S. (1980) *Mindstorms: Children, Computers and Powerful Ideas*. New York: Basic Books.

Pillitteri, A. (1981) *Maternal-Newborn Nursing: Care of the Growing Family* (2nd ed.). Boston: Little, Brown & Co.

Reed, J.R. (1975) *Victorian Conventions*. Athens, OH: Ohio University Press.

Rosaldo, M.Z. and Lamphere, L. (eds) (1974) *Women, Culture, and Society*, Stanford, CA: Stanford University Press.

Sennett, R. (1977) *The Fall of Public Man*. New York: Knopf.

Shorter, E. (1975) *The Making of the Modern Family*. New York: Basic Books.

Sommer, R. (1969) *Personal Space: The Behaviour Basis of Design*. Englewood Cliffs, NJ: Prentice-Hall.

Stone, L. (1977) *The Family, Sex, and Marriage in England 1500–1800*. New York: Harper & Row.

Turnbull, C.M. (1961) *The Forest People*. New York: Simon & Schuster.

Van Dyke, C. (1980) 'Family-centred health care recognizes needs of patients, families, employees', *Hospital Progress*, August, pp. 54–57 and 68.

Information technology and the myth of abundance
Anthony Smith

Inevitably, the culture within which we live shapes and limits our imaginations, and by permitting us to do and think and feel in certain ways makes it increasingly unlikely or impossible that we should do or think or feel in ways that are contradictory or tangential to it.

Margaret Mead, *Male and Female*[1]

This chapter, originally published in 1982, is taken from *Books to Bytes: Knowledge and Information in the Postmodern Era* (London, British Film Institute, 1993), pp. 3–19.

What really *is* a technological revolution? And who are the revolutionaries? What are the criteria for a historical process to be so described? Where do we *look* for the results? I cannot claim that this essay will answer these questions, nor even that they are precisely enough formulated for useful answers to be provided. But it might be possible to construct a new kind of mental picture of the phenomenon of technological transformation, of its driving motivations and cultural consequences, by looking at certain aspects of current developments in information technology within a historical setting. The advent of printing had obviously 'a great deal to do' with the rise of the nation-state, and Elizabeth Eisenstein's researches and narrative,[2] as well as those of Martin and Febre,[3] have helped to fill out the picture of a late Renaissance 'information revolution'. An age in which a new transforming technology is taking hold must, almost self-evidently, express its most profound social, economic, and political changes in terms of that technology – so closely and complicatedly, that historians inevitably try, but fail, to disentangle the resulting skeins of cause and effect. Was there a drive for empire that altered the technologies of European navigation in the fifteenth and sixteenth centuries? Was imperialism a result of technology-push or economic-pull? Do the processes of 'take-up' of innovation relate to the dominant creative, emotional, and intellectual mindset of an age, so that the tracks may be found again through later research?

Such questions are the permanent concern of social history, but need to be asked also in the present, while the transforming process is under way. The intention of this essay is to suggest that there exists a great unifying social and cultural urge behind a technological revolution, particularly one that relates to information. The search for the emotional satisfactions of the vernacular and the evolution of the feeling of nationhood were indeed tied to the technology of 'moving letters'. The Victorian bourgeois obsession with the perfect mechanical reproduction of images in movement, sound and hue had some psychic link with the evolution of the representational technologies of film, phonograph, telegraph, and the wireless. Today, a surging belief in the perfect development of the individual as consumer is somehow discovering its own confirmation in the development of technologies of information abundance; but that individualism is tied also to a new imperialism or transnationalism in the growth of the phenomenon of cultural dependence of the South upon the North. The new information technology is reconfirming the world vision of the developed world, re-establishing its confidence as the primary subject of culture, as the developing nations fall victim to the cultural pressures of external data flow. Thus, if this argument works, information technology leads towards the displacement of nationhood, of national cultures.

I

We have all become modishly aware that the information environment, so to speak, of the late twentieth-century individual is in the course of being transformed. News columns with titles that play neatly on the words *revolution, age, galaxy, shock*, appear monthly. But we remain prisoners still of an essentially Victorian idea of the requisite constituents of social change, in the sense that we tend to predicate the transformation upon the technology. We relate and chart development according to a measure of machinery, alongside the evolution of inventions. So numerous are the gadgets of the computer age (there goes an example of what is being criticised!) that the designated historic turning points – the number of 'revolutions' per decade – are too numerous to absorb, their effects too shrilly predicted for easy listening. We are paralysed by the dimensions of the transformation, partly because we have internalised a kind of Whiggian principle, by which machines 'produce' social effects of a measurable or, at least, observable variety. The trouble is that technological and social history cannot be related in this way, since the extrapolated trends shoot off the graph every time. Consider the influence of the photocopier, the coaxial cable, television news, teleconferencing, and so on. There are no anchors to cast in each voyage of speculation; every trip rushes straight toward infinity.

We would be greatly helped in the present epoch of speculation if we had available some improved metaphors for social change, something less traumatic and less overworked than 'revolution', something more intermingling of cause and effect, something that suggested less emphasis on technology. New technologies close gaps, resolve tensions, register the temporary shelving of problems, as well as automate jobs out of existence and fill the home with new junk. Above all, in order to reduce the current bewildering hyping of technical history, we need some explanatory models of the inventing process that demonstrate the collective, though concealed, social dialogue that almost invariably precedes the advent of a new device.

The apparatus of the modern media of information has been accumulating steadily through the century; the modern home may possess a telephone and a typewriter, a camera, a record player, a pocket calculator, a pile of disks or cassettes, probably by now a couple of television receivers, possibly a cable TV link, an 8mm film camera and projector, a device for playing video games, for receiving pay TV, for decoding teletext or videotext signals, perhaps even a video camera, and a home computer. Few people, however, are as yet aware of the linkages that exist – or that can exist – between all of these gadgets; the information revolution of the late twentieth century consists very largely of the increased propensity for these text and moving image machines to converge and to interact. That propensity has been latent since Victorian times. Thomas Edison invented the phonograph as a repeating device to aid the telephone, thinking that a central office such as the telegraph bureau would record messages sent down the telephone lines and deliver the disks to the homes and businesses of non-subscribers.[4] It was not a fallacy so much as a prophecy, for we are witnessing today that intermixture of telecommunications with information storage that he envisaged. What happened in the late 1970s was a sudden increase in the potency of telecommunications and in the computing capacity of society that has made it possible for us to reap a whole series of benefits that were impossible when the same technical possibilities existed on a smaller scale. The present 'revolution', if such it is, is one of investment rather than technical innovation, of transformation of scale more than of technological horizon.

All of the devices that have emerged as discrete physical media of information and entertainment have their own industrial housing, so to speak. The century has witnessed the growth of a music industry around the phonograph and radio, a TV industry, a film industry, and telecommunications, computing, and book publishing industries. These great blocks of investment and industrial activity are currently undergoing a transformation, and in every society in which they flourish (surprisingly few, in fact, since most societies are becoming highly import-dependent in respect of media software), there is currently a reconsideration of the regulatory environment in which they operate. In some societies, the process is being labelled 'deregulation', where it is perceived as a process of removing legal constraints against inter-corporate competition. In other societies, the same process is envisaged rather as one of making new and appropriate regulations to stimulate similar releases of enterprise, often accompanied by moves to protect indigenous culture. The new devices of cassettes and disks and the new paid broadcast services entail an extremely complicated re-gearing of all the established industries that hitherto have been device-specific. In other words, it has to be possible for a set of rights and obligations that have been acquired in respect of a given artefact (say, a film made for theatrical release) to be transferred to a wider range of distribution systems (cassettes, cable television). The changing situation is bringing about a gradual alteration in the way we think about the property element in information and entertainment, and about the cultural demarcations between genres. At one level, the change consists in a series of publishing devices and promotional arrangements; at deeper levels, it must alter our ideas about what constitutes a 'book', what separates an 'academic work' from a popular one, indeed what body of data should properly be considered a book or an 'author'.

Let us consider a not unusual career for a modern work of fiction. It may begin as a novel about which an individual writer has pondered for years, or it may originate as a commission conceived by an agent or a publisher and fostered upon a writer of recognised skill. If it seems likely to sustain the investment, the finished work may be promoted, and through dextrous manipulation of the apparatus of literary review and public discussion, forced through a series of different kinds of text distribution. It will come out in hardcover and paperback, in serial fiction and digest form, and then as an even cheaper paperback. But it may also be transmuted into a set of moving images, where its basic authorship will be further dehydrated and industrialised in complex ways. A film designated for cinema distribution may in fact be shown, in widescreen format, only for further promotional purposes; the 70mm image will be seen only by a small fraction of the emerging audience, as the work passes into 35mm and 16mm gauges for distribution in various specialist systems (such as the film society network or the college circuit). It will appear in cassette form (all the framing of the original lost in the transformation to the smaller screen) and videodisk, on cable and pay TV, ending up on 'free' over-the-air television, public or commercial. At later stages in its career, the work may return to one or more of its earlier phases, but it will remain in public consciousness with greater permanency than that bulk of Victorian fiction which failed to become one of the tiny band of classics.

The new work of today faces a wider variety of audiences and enjoys a more finely calculated career. It is commensurately more heavily dependent upon promotion, and, indeed, more and more different kinds of entrepreneurs will speculate upon its possibilities during the course of its complicated life. There is a rush of newcomers to the marketplace, but inevitably, a wave of cartelisation will ensue as soon as this market is rationalised. Thus in this period of convergence of devices, a new division of cultural labour is growing up among them. At the same time, there is a search for new and appropriate forms of material, not dissimilar to that which took place when the telephone and cinematography were evolving, when perception of social role preceded each of a multitude of technical offshoots. The social impact of television and telecommunications has been much subtler and more far-reaching than that of other devices of the same era. Both telephone and cinematography were very slow, however, in gathering around them the aura of transformationism that today envelopes the offshoots of the computer and the television receiver.

In the 1880s it seemed possible that the telephone would become a medium of entertainment. In London and Paris, experimenters were to set up connections between the principal theatres and the central operator, so that subscribers could listen to plays and to the songs of the music hall. Others thought that the new medium would be a useful supplier of general information, supplementing that of the newspaper. As a person-to-person instrument, it suffered from obvious limitations: there were few people with whom one could speak, the costs were high, and established systems of social discourse inhibited subscribers from incorporating the machine into their lives. The telephone was neither intimate nor reliably private. It was often confined to small professional groups, such as the lawyers and doctors of Glasgow, who enjoyed their own separate and mutually incompatible exchanges. As an instrument of business, the telephone suffered from other limitations: it was more expensive than using messenger boys; it created tension within the national telegraph administrations (one of which actually proposed charging for the telephone according to the number of words spoken along the line). It came into use at first through a series of specialist groups: the construction teams on early skyscrapers, the police, doctors, lawyers, and so on. It grew within the interstices of society, later coming to occupy a more general public role.[5] The influence of the telephone on the development of social structures and the physical layout of societies is extremely hard to calculate and has tended to be overlooked.

Road and rail systems are more visible, and the great feats of engineering that made them possible have seized the attention of social historians more tenaciously than the invisible forces of telegraph, telephone and radio. But the areas of influence of the communication devices are themselves different: while transportation facilitated suburbanisation in the present century, communications has had a great deal to do with the changing 'images' of the different parts of a city, the constantly shifting areas of respectability and trend. Suburbanites have not been migrants on the whole; they have desired to retain the advantages of metropolitan life and to remain in constant touch with the centres of the society, while shunning the geographical core. Each device developed in the Victorian era (and later) began life in an aura of a certain vagueness as to its destined purpose. Was the telephone destined for entertainment purposes, or did it fulfil a special role in preserving social order or in providing general information? The purposes have constantly shifted, although each device eventually acquired its own clear purposes, its own 'culture'. Now, all is in doubt again, all the boundaries are moving.

Each fresh wave of new devices has registered and expressed a new stage in the evolution of city structure, in neighbourhood development, and in the structure of the family. Cinemas in the 1920s and 1930s released people from their homes; television in the 1950s re-cemented the home as focus of the family, until in the 1960s, a new politics of the family seemed to break up that tight postwar grouping. Today, the new multiple devices slice up the family and re-individualise it, permitting and encouraging a new microconsumerism, the pursuit of a fresh, but (temporarily) satisfying, illusion of individual gratification through endless freedom and 'choice'.

II

The communication and representation devices of the late Victorians were manifestations of a vast, unarticulated urge; they were an act of ideology expressed again and again, in different versions, of a machine for the perfect reproduction of the lifelike. It is worth dissecting the 'invention' of film in some detail and comparing its tortuous progress, via a complex of interactions between technique and social aspiration, with the phenomenon of today, when it is still difficult to express, in one similarly neat phrase, the nature of the parallel contemporary aspiration. There appears today to exist a latent collectivist, egalitarian consumerist urge, a prompting to break through economic and institutional constraints, toward an abundance of messages, from which a mass of individuals can draw material according to their 'personal' choice. Choice is the chimera of the age, the hypothesis of a new adulthood arising from the opportunity to 'perfect' the self as the basic mechanism of consumption. The Victorians, however, were pursuing, through their technologies of illusionism, an ideal mode in which their desire for a kind of artificial immortality could be assuaged.

The moving image was a substitute for – an extension of – the cemetery. The mass suppliers of early film cameras blatantly exploited this deep need of the age: the retention of the perfect images, in motion, of one's loved ones. One of the newspapers that reported the first public screening by Louis Lumière of his films said: 'When these cameras become available to the public, when all are able to photograph their dear ones, no longer merely in immobile form but in movement, in action, with their familiar gestures, with speech on their lips, death will no longer be final.'[6] The representation and extension through time of the human body was one aspect of the great bourgeois aspiration, but the techniques have their roots in the Renaissance, with the development of anatomical study and the growing importance of perspective as the enabling science that made it possible for the new knowledge to be recorded and imparted.

Marey's discovery of the persistence of vision in the nineteenth century played a similar role in the development of machines to capture, record and dissect the nature of movement.[7] But Marey was not in pursuit of moving pictures as illusions; indeed, he rejected the machines that enabled movement to be synthesised in favour of another line of invention (which included his own chronophotograph – the first camera to employ celluloid strip) that captured movement on a still frame through strobic effects. Marey and his follower Londe were both attempting to overcome deficiencies in human perception rather than create an illusion of reproduced movement that deceived human perception. They wanted to depict reality in a form that slowed down or speeded up true movement. In a sense, Eadweard Muybridge's notions lay along the same line of thought; his Zoopraxiscope succeeded in reanimating a series of still photographs taken in succession by different cameras of a horse in motion. The purpose was scientific – to dissect a natural phenomenon and to reconstitute the movement, in order to prove the correctness of the analysis. Muybridge's images were generally taken to be aesthetically unpleasing. They were to influence painting in due course, but only after delivering a shock to those artists of the traditional schools who thought that the real world corresponded to the idealised images that had been taught academically.

Earlier in the century, a flow of devices demonstrated the other half of the Victorian inspiration – illusionism. Daguerre's invention was a natural development of his skill in *trompe-l'oeil*. At the Great Exhibition of 1851, the stereoscope had drawn fascinated crowds, since it seemed to add a dimension to still photography by supplementing a gap in the pure representation of nature. Baudelaire mocked the hungry eyes 'bending over the peepholes of the stereoscope, as though they were the attic windows of the infinite'. At the same time, the demand for the perfect illusion was being fed through non-photographic devices for creating the sensation of movement or of three-dimensional images, such as the Thaumatrope and the Praxinoscope, which depended on a disk with images that appeared to combine in motion through rapid rotation. These were representational toys dismissed by the more scientific school of Marey, since they demonstrated, but did not analyse, scientific phenomena.[8] Thus the pursuit of the Victorian aspiration for representing an image of life in its perfection veered from one line of development, in which its various manifestations were deemed to be recreational and at best educational, to another line, in which the quest was not to substitute for painting but to serve science.

It was the Lumière moving-picture show that captured the contemporary imagination in the mid-1890s. Writers as far spread as Gorky, Kipling and Henry James witnessed the show as it travelled between Spain and Moscow, Austria and America. They were presented with one-minute scenes of real-life events, unstaged but none the less contrived, through choice of camera angle, location and timing. The train arriving at a station, the workers leaving the factory, the gardener turning the hose upon himself – all became familiar metaphors that impressed upon those pioneer audiences the first collectively experienced moving images that inaugurated the great store of shared allusion which has subsequently accumulated. At the same moment, Edison's laboratory and its breakaway group, the American Mutoscope and Biograph Company, were feeding the same popular drive toward perfect representation with a series of inventions that offered short travel or anecdotal films projected in a machine into which the viewer had to peer. Edison was working to a much grander design that led him to overlook the importance of his silent camera and projecting device; he wanted to link his own phonograph invention with a film and recording technique, with stereoscopic effects added for good measure. Edison wanted to perfect a total system of representation that would perceive, record, and transmit across space, and he thus employed, in a spectacular series of electrical and mechanical inventions, the whole range of sciences that were to be worked on in the course of the following eighty years.[9]

All of the experimenters alluded to, and many others, were technicians primarily, but with a keen eye either on the audience of science or on the audience of contemporary showmanship, sometimes a little of both. The first decade of the twentieth century saw a further group of experimenters who were primarily artists, such as Georges Méliès and Edwin Porter, though both had some technical background. Both saw the possibilities of developing narrative forms by means of the new moving cameras. Méliès had started as a conjuror, and he drew from a line of non-realist illusionism for his film ideas, of which he developed hundreds. His stock – transformations of human beings into animals, of strange apparitions, a Jules Verne-type space journey – was the culmination of the aspirations of a Victorian conjuror. Porter, however, drew upon a realist line of narrative, breaking away from the theatre rather than from popular showmanship. He is famous for having developed the pacing techniques that laid the foundations of modern narrative cinema – the cutting, linking, and transposition of shots, and the suggestion of simultaneity through building-up a chase scene by intercutting events taking place in different locations.[10]

Behind these different lines of artistic and technical development, all of which proved ultimately interactive and intensely creative of technology, was a growing institution, cinema. Behind each movement forward – and many that proved to be culs-de-sac – there lay a shared phenomenon that grew by accretion, based upon an audience whose perception and expectations were being progressively intermingled; each mechanical device depended upon a range of artistic conventions that had to be accepted and internalised by a rapidly growing audience if the institution of cinema was to develop. That institution itself was obliged to follow the contours of contemporary taste, to search for the city locations, the distribution systems, the pricing mechanisms, the patent and copyright devices that would sustain the new medium. The technology that emerged registers as a series of interim readings of the relationships that between them constituted, as they still do, the institution of cinema.

Of course, it is impossible to produce a perfect record of the evolution of a technology by concentrating on the interactions and dependencies – social, artistic, technical, and intellectual – since to do so would entail an analysis of an entire society. Marconi's work on radio was taking place at exactly the same moment as the work of Lumière; Zworykin was working on the basic principles of television in the same decade as the main work of Méliès. Regulatory systems for the telegraph and the telephone were being simultaneously created, and these were greatly to influence the early and continuing institutions of radio and television. And of course, contemporary developments in all of the other sciences – from biochemistry to metallurgy, optics to engineering – played their part in the evolution of the communicating technologies. None the less, those lines of development that led to film, television and radio entailed clusterings of technique that derived their impetus from the same animating aspiration, that of creating a perfect and enduring representation of the perceptual world.

III

It is rather harder to discern the central drive that unites the various new communication media that have been developed in the last and current decades from that earlier aspiration. Certainly, there no longer exists an unsatisfied craving for the mere illusionist representation of reality; perhaps a reverse principle might today be at work, whereby the techniques for suggesting reality are being pushed toward a realm of perfect fantasy in the new potential for, say, computer imaging. But there is some more general demand or perceived demand that is being stimulated and satisfied by the new media – demand for an abundance of supply and an image of the consumer as individual, arising above an ocean of materials. There is the image of a new leisure, a worklife without toil, a textured, variegated career structure. Many of the new devices are concerned with text storage and distribution as much as with still or moving images, with data processing as much as with storage. Some of the new devices appear, in the present stage of their development, to be concerned with supplying a new multiplicity of channels (cable systems, videodisks, satellite broadcasting, cassettes), while others have more to do with adding to the conveniences of the home or reducing information overload (home box office for first-run movies, videotext), or both. The suppliers of new services are breaking down, unconsciously for the most part, old traditional genres, such as the newspaper or magazine, by offering the chance to dial directly a specialist line of information; they are also providing a chance to evade the many constraints of over-the-air broadcasting with its 'paternalistic' overtones of prescribed, preselected patterns of material. The new specialist cable channels are on the whole reworkings of the public broadcasting service model, and offer the chance for a new kind of self-definition on the part of the subscriber into a class or sub-culture type, rather as the newspaper industry did in the era when newspapers of every conceivable stripe flourished.

All of the new services have broken into pre-existing monopolies of some kind, but all are searching for new monopolies of their own in order to survive – monopolies of first-run movies, monopolies of travel or business information, monopolies of high culture material, monopolies over certain geographical zones or certain social groups. With the advent, a decade or so from now, of direct broadcasting by satellite, a wholly new complication will arise, since the satellite, unlike any other transmission system devised hitherto, is capable of equal address across a whole society or group of societies.

Yet these services are, in the main, systems of supply quite separate from the industry providing material to a variety of systems reaching different layers of the audience. Thus a cable offering a cultural channel acquires its content from a multinational industry, programmes that have been created to serve a primary market elsewhere (though with an eye to further sales). The market for software is becoming many-layered, even though various homogenising market forces have already set in. The previous forms of distribution for much of this visual material continue to exist and tend still to be the primary sources of funding – the major national television networks and their independent suppliers. There are half a dozen annual markets and festivals at which the main lines of dealing and the main relationships are built up: Milan, Monte Carlo,

Cannes, Berlin, New York, Los Angeles. Film festivals have created video offshoots, with new video markets in Europe and the East being established. But the dealing on individual projects continues throughout the year by means of bilateral arrangements between banks and production houses, television channels and cable organisations, Hollywood majors and publishing houses. Inevitable rearrangements of capital within the media conglomerates are taking place. A new world industry of moving-image products is emerging, highly diverse, but still dominated by the companies that established their grip over the heartland of the audience in the days of the old national television monopoly.

The material today is beginning to pass through a complex mesh of distribution systems, each one technology-specific, each with a different pricing mechanism and in a different stage of development. A European publishing house owned by an American bank, for example, will initiate a project designed as a series of films and an international book. It will pre-sell the films to a London-based television company for a price that covers a large proportion of the basic production costs. To cover the rest, it will pre-sell the same series to a US public television station or one of the New York cable stations, the London TV company retaining a percentage. The publishing house will then proceed to organise translations that will sell well, on the reputation of the British and American television transmission. The profit to the original publishing house, however, will tend to come from vastly enhanced book sales, since the whole scope of the market for the books has been transformed by the broadcasting operation. Gradually, the materials will flow into other cable and box office systems, while selling in cassette form in the education market. The product will retain strong national overtones; it is owned ultimately by the American bank, but its makers are British, and its accent will tend to be also. The same thing is happening in Paris, Frankfurt, Tokyo and Amsterdam, but five geographical locations in the developed world are coming to play an ever greater role in the world supply of moving images and, indeed, for text materials also.

The five locations are New York, California, London. Frankfurt/Munich and Tokyo,[11] places where there exist strong and sophisticated national audiences for the first-generation television materials, plus the necessary access to capital and the habit of working together on the part of a critical mass of relevant skills and institutions. It is likely that these five centres will remain at the heart of the world market for software in the entertainment and information fields. (Computer translation might eventually enable the Japanese to break also into the world text-information software market, already dominated by Japanese hardware.) There was a similar concentration in the world of book publishing a hundred years after the development of moving type, but the evolution of the newspaper, with its polycentred culture, was quite different. Quite different, too, was cinema, which, though it rapidly became a narrow market, began with a wide variety of supply centres. The developing world contains a number of major centres for film-making (India, the Philippines, Hong Kong), but these have remained largely national in the 1970s. Today, one or more of them could break into the wider world market, but probably only through major investment from the existing centres, since they are 'hampered' by the different musical and literary traditions of the East.

It is clear that two quite distinct developments are taking place. There is a new range of physical artefacts on which are inscribed images and text – cassettes and disks – and these are distributed in roughly the same manner as books and gramophone records. These are, however, to some extent different from their forerunners, in that the material they offer is already familiar to the potential buyer, through the promotion and marketing of a film, of which the cassette or disk constitutes an extended line of supply. The other new media are all services rather than artefacts, although the recipient may, legally or illegally, make a physical copy of the text or image in the home. Thus the new videotext systems are publishing devices, where payment is made through the telephone company for 'pages' of material that have been received on a domestic television receiver. Some of the cable systems are paid for overall by the subscriber, as European public broadcasting systems have always been, while other cable systems or scrambled signal systems oblige the viewer to pay for each selected programme; these leave the recipient without a physical artefact, unless a domestic personal recording has been made. Policing the uses made by individuals of private recordings is, for the rights-holders, something of a nightmare, and pricing mechanisms are having to adjust for the practical impossibility of retaining rights long-term after the distribution of a new product. The owner of those rights has to consider the timing of the whole package of new media outlets, relying on industry-wide organisation for the policing of the multitude of new networks that are springing up.

It is still far too soon to see which technologies will prevail for specific purposes, to discern whether an optic fibre network set up nationwide would eventually take over and swamp all other systems of cables, microwaves, direct satellites, and broadcasting channels, in the establishment of a universal broadband domestic system, a kind of general information ring-main, like the electricity ring-main, linking every individual to the entire national and international system. It does appear, however, that Western societies are on the verge of the development of a system, or collection of systems, that, in their net effect, will tend to negate the basic principles by which information has travelled through society since the Renaissance. Even though the cassette and the videodisk operate in the same mode as books, distributed on the basis of single copy purchase by each user or group of users, the pressure of the non-artefact services is such as to suggest that the artefacts may play a diminished role in the longer term. The Gutenbergian principle is so firmly rooted in our culture that it is hard to imagine a society in which it has been abolished (and, indeed, no one is suggesting that anything like abolition is likely to occur). Rather, we are liable to witness a rapid erosion of the settled notion that information is naturally multiplied in physical copies until the number of copies approximates the number of those wishing to receive it. The Gutenbergian principle has already ceased to function in the case of broadcast material, where the opposite – or what one might call the Alexandrian principle –

operates. There, a single copy exists in the originating tape or live performance, which then reaches its audience in non-material form; a physical
tape can be generated by the individual recipient, but the mass multiplication of physical materials, as in the newspaper and in publishing, is
absent.

One uses the image of Alexandria, because it suggests a great store of
material that is deemed to be fully authentic, but available only to those
who come to it to choose. A modern data base is, in a sense, an electronic
version of the principle where material is added to a central store according
to fixed and accepted methods, and is then available to all who have the
means and skills to unlock it. In the field of moving images, the world is
today steadily building such a store of accredited materials, which have,
most of them, been through the authenticating procedures of network
transmission before becoming available through the newer systems of
distribution. Unlike the materials of a great library or a computerised data
base, these materials have still to be laid out as a programme by a cable
company or satellite distribution company before they can be chosen; but
as broadband systems develop, we are veering slowly toward some new
condition in which an individual can choose electronic dissemination of a
single item that was itself chosen from a vast or total store of video
products. In the field of data, this condition is rather closer, if anything, as
the various videotext systems slowly agree on international technical
standards and interconnections. One further aspect of the steadily dissolving Gutenbergian principle is the part that distance has always played in
fixing the cost of communication of any kind: this has applied equally in
the case of the telephone and telegraph and the printed book. As the
electronic systems emerge, it is becoming increasingly clear that distance is
a rapidly diminishing factor in costs, both of collecting information and of
redistributing it.

We are witnessing, therefore, a subtle transformation of the underlying principle that has sustained the information systems of human society
since the Renaissance. The shift is coming about as a result of a vast
number of quite separate responses of corporations to perceived demand,
responses of technology to science and of science to imagination. There is
no central machine generating this change, no great corporation or con-
spiracy of corporations. There does indeed exist a powerful, almost total
dependence of the whole structure of change upon a number of giant
corporations, but they are tending to grope toward the trend while trying
to influence it. Their corporate needs greatly influence the pace of change,
and while they often choose specific private directions for a period of time,
the central pulse re-establishes its rhythm.

Despite the atmosphere of feverish change that has always beset the
information media, the basic technologies and content forms have changed
very slowly indeed. One may take, for example, the novel and the newspaper as direct emanations of the printing press, and note how each has
changed fundamentally in form not more than, say, once in a century.
Despite the enormous number of attempted means for creating moving
pictures in Victorian times, the celluloid strip, which established itself in

INFORMATION TECHNOLOGY AND THE MYTH OF ABUNDANCE

about 1897, has remained on the same gauge until today. The development of celluloid only took place at the end of the 1880s, and the earliest cameras for shooting a succession of images on a moving strip of celluloid hardly left their experimental stage before 1895. And yet a piece of Victorian film can be taken today to any city on earth and screened. A newspaper printed in any language since roughly the same date will be clearly perceived to be a newspaper in any part of the globe, and many of its chief contents – puzzles, news, editorials, share prices, reviews – apprehended as such in scores of cultures where the language itself may not be known. Radio and television have developed more rapidly, but even with these, each new development – from the valve to the cathode ray tube, from colour signals and transistors to cables – has required about fifteen years to become established within the market. Forms remain stable because the market keeps them so; the public's expectations of any particular device or genre take years to develop, and these expectations, transmuted into listener, viewer, or reader habits, are the capital assets of the publishers and companies that have discovered or nurtured them.

Yet behind the kinds of material and the hardware, important trends do make themselves apparent. Two that have been at work since the beginning of the century are worth emphasising in any attempt to size up the changing information environment. One characteristic of the nineteenth-century systems and devices – from the popular reading room to the peep-show – was that the audience was expected to make no investment in the system itself; revenue was derived either from the purchase of an artefact, such as a newspaper, or from the sale of a right, such as admission to a hall or tent. Indeed, the quest of the age had been so to multiply the product that the mass audience could have access at the lowest coin available. Thus arrived the halfpenny newspaper, created as a result of expensive and diligent development of the mass press, mass distribution system, and the mass transportation system. As the century developed, however, the audience has been expected to indulge in an ever higher proportion of the total investment. Today, most of the investment necessary in maintaining a national television channel is held by the viewer rather than the supplier of the system – compare this with the theatre, or cinema, or the church.

In all of the new media, the audience's share of the investment has gone even higher, and the equipment companies have unsurprisingly been among the chief impresarios of development. The audience has to buy or rent the receiver and the recorder, the cable decoder, the videotex black box and so on. In fact, most of the new media are dependent upon there being several television receivers in a majority of homes; otherwise, there would be little hope of splitting the family as a viewing unit and thereby exploiting the potential for individual choice of material. With the arrival of direct broadcasting by satellite, the cost of each unit audience will rise substantially, since the engineering mechanisms required for switching from satellite to satellite, and thereby obtaining a wider choice, are fairly expensive. The whole expansion of the information sector thus hinges on the general expansion of the consumer economy, on the expansion at a steady rate of the consumer's propensity to invest in new entertainment systems. In the changeover from the old to the new systems, we are thus watching a very considerable switch in total investment in the resources of social communication from the manufacturer and the supplier to the audience at home.

The other important overall trend is for the gradual growth of local monopoly in any system. Information is historically torn between the condition of competition and its condition as a natural monopoly. One may cite the newspaper as a good example. Competition within the market for newspapers seemed natural, inevitable, and desirable in all democratic countries – as it still seems so today in places – so long as political circumstances made this desirable, and so long as the advertising done by mass consumer manufacturers required large slabs of display material. Gradually, television has become the channel for political material and the pre-eminent disseminator of national and regional manufacturer-to-consumer advertising. This has occurred on both sides of the Atlantic, although there are still a few European societies in which television advertising is illegal or minimal. Newspaper circulation has fallen a little in many countries, but seldom dramatically; where the total circulation has in fact fallen, the explanation often lies in the erosion of the habit of purchasing more than one newspaper as papers have become more comprehensive overall.

The markets for advertising have, however, significantly altered throughout the economies of the West. The major area of growth has been in classified advertising, especially in recession-sensitive advertising such as that for jobs and contracts. The market has therefore become more volatile, while television advertising – dependent more upon manufacturers and sellers of commercial services – has tended to be much more resilient to temporary economic trends. There is a natural tendency for a newspaper to be most attractive as a source of advertising (and of news) where it is believed to be most comprehensive in its content, and this tendency, in the context of the changes mentioned, has greatly accelerated the development of natural local monopolies among the printed press. In the United States, this tendency has occurred alongside a growth of chains and of cross-media ownership at the corporate, if not the local, level. The newspaper has thus been coaxed by states into becoming typically a local monopoly. Only a very few countries, such as Britain and Japan, have retained thoroughgoing newspaper competition, and in those cases, the reason has been the institution of national distribution, which has produced monopolisation of another kind – within social strands rather than geographic location. Even in Britain, however, with its highly competitive journalism, the same phenomena have occurred with local newspapers as in Germany, the United States, France and elsewhere.

The processes of monopoly have not set in as far as the electronic media are concerned, where cartelisation is restrained through regulation. It would not be surprising, however, if a certain clarification did not begin – in those markets with a very large number of television outlets as the new media, with their far greater promise of abundant choice – to reach the middle and lower levels of the market. The same tendency toward a single outlet has occurred in the case of cinema, though mitigated by the habit of tripling or quadrupling movie theatres – not to create wider choice, but to provide finer tuning of the audiences for the existing repertoire as they grow and shrink during the run of a given film.

I have deliberately refrained from stressing national differences of trend or of magnitude, in order to bring out the shared phenomena of Western economics. We are witnessing a cultural shift, or set of shifts, that are more subtle and far-reaching than the physical devices, the products of modern electronics, themselves suggest, but that are more deeply rooted in the continuing and the slowly evolving than is often believed. After all, abundance of choice does not in itself constitute a transformation, since an individual will make conditioned choices and will probably not greatly increase the total hours of his exposure. But the role of text in our civilisation and the development of the various skills of text are indeed in all probability today in the course of fundamental change. The management and use of a data base require quite new skills, and will emphasise different aptitudes from those required traditionally in primary education. The computerisation of text suggests that we may absorb smaller quantities of text into our lives, but it will be text that is better ordered and more appropriately selected. The term *book* will probably come to cover a narrower range of products than it now does, and the technical aids to research will soon enable a still wider range of disciplines to benefit from the boon of the computer.

One might take, as an extreme example of the kind of 'book' that is becoming outmoded, the telephone directory, where the form is used, in full Gutenbergian trappings of binding and single copy mass distribution, as the housing for a collection of data, only a tiny fraction of which is required by any individual reader. The time taken to collect the information and to reproduce it is so great that a high proportion of the material required by any individual reader is invalid by the time the finished product reaches him. As the total number of telephone subscribers rises, the proportion whose addresses change more frequently also rises. The directory is an essential body of data in urgent need of an appropriate mode in which to present itself to its readers. Clearly, the format of the traditional book is inappropriate, or will become so as soon as an alternative technology becomes as easily accessible, or where the level of accessibility of the alternative outweighs the disadvantages built into the existing mode. It is thus that the book will 'die', not through sudden technological redundance, but through the prudent choices of those who actually require the information it carries. As the newspaper passes through its own crises of form, many of its traditional elements will probably be lost to the new electronic mode. The pursuit of information 'abundance' in this case is in reality the pursuit of a manageable modicum of relevant information.

But for the most part, the contemporary drive for abundance of choice is a besetting ideology much more than a practical need. It is more like the Victorian illusion of mechanised immortality, providing evidence for the psychic tension of the moment rather than for a social or economic need. The pursuit of plenty in the sphere of information is a psychological analogy to its pursuit in the sphere of nourishment in the developed world, where the use of food has more to do with marketing, fashion, and general culture than with biological need. Information abundance has likewise much to do with cultural identity in the late twentieth century, and little to do with need. None the less, it is a motive force and a justification for an industrial evolution with revolutionary repercussions. An OECD report observes:

> The production, transmission and processing of the most varied information will be at the heart of economic activity and social life . . . through its links with data processing and telecommunications, the electronics complex during the next quarter of a century will be the main pole around which the productive structures of the advanced industrial societies will be reorganised.[12]

There are plenty of documents in circulation that outline the growing disparity in the provision of information, and especially the communications technology, between the countries of the North and those of the developing South. Eighty-five per cent of existing data bases are in the North. The abundance of both hardware and software is the privilege of a tiny group of societies, who are themselves enjoying a continually increasing disparity. Information wealth grows by what it feeds upon.

Studies of the flows of data from computer to computer reveal its increasing internationalisation. International networks are growing in the wake of the establishment of effective national networks. There is a strong tendency for all data flow to be concentrated on capital cities, however, because that is where the main data users are located. But there is also a tendency for data to flow from the less developed to the more developed, where processing facilities are more plentiful and more efficient. In the least advanced countries of Europe, for example, national data flow is toward other countries. The newly emerging techniques of remote sensing and satellite distribution of data are bringing about further exponential growth and further tiltings in the international flow of data from developing to developed worlds. The cultural implications are self-evident, and the political implications easy to deduce. Behind the emblem of information foison there exists a growing phenomenon of global cultural domination, produced not by powerful armies, but by powerful international companies. The greater the stock of expertise in a society, the greater is its ability to make use of the information technology and benefit from its software. The educated society is the one best suited to prosper in the new age, and everything conspires against the society that has a deficit in its national balance of educated talent. The profusion of data through which the Western industrialised consumer indulges his or her choice, and expresses the nuances of a carefully refined and nurtured life-style, is the same oversupply that is drawn from the international data flow and jeopardises the nationhood of developing societies. We may expect in the next decades the lines of international tension to shadow the contours of data abundance.

Notes

1   Margaret Mead, *Male and Female* (London, Gollancz, 1949).
2   Elizabeth Eisenstein, *The Printing Press as an Agent of Change*, 2 vols (Cambridge, Cambridge University Press, 1979); 'The advent of printing and the problem of the Renaissance', *Past and Present*, 45 (1969), pp. 19–89.
3   Henri-Jean Martin and Lucien Febre, *The Coming of the Book: 1450–1800*, trans. David Gerard (London, New Left Books, 1976).
4   Ithiel de Sola Pool et al., 'Foresight and hindsight: the case of the telephone', in Ithiel de Sola Pool (ed.), *The Social Impact of the Telephone* (Cambridge, Mass, MIT Press, 1977), pp. 127–57.
5   Ibid. esp. Ronald Abler, 'The telephone and the evolution of the American metropolitan system', pp. 318–41.
6   This passage draws considerably on several essays in *Afterimage*, 8/9 (spring 1981), esp. Noël Burch, 'Charles Baudelaire *v.* Dr Frankenstein', pp. 4–23.
7   E.J. Marey, *Movement* (London, 1895), listed in *Afterimage*.
8   C.W. Cream, *The Archaeology of the Cinema* (London, Thames and Hudson, 1965).
9   Matthew Josephson, *Edison* (London, Eyre and Spottiswoode, 1959).
10 D.J. Wenden, *The Birth of the Movies* (London, MacDonald, 1975), pp. 19–22.
11 I am indebted for the train of thought in this section to conversations with Mr Stephen Hearst of the BBC.
12 OECD, *Interfutures: Facing the Future, Mastering the Probable and Managing the Unpredictable* (Paris, OECD, 1979).

What information society?   **Frank Webster**

Commentators increasingly talk about information as a defining feature of the modern world. Much attention is now devoted to the informatization of social life: we are told that we are entering an information age, that a new mode of information predominates, that we have moved into a global information economy. Many writers even identify as information societies the United States, Britain, Japan, Germany, and other nations with a similar way of life. Indeed, it appears that information has 'become so important today as to merit treatment as a symbol for the very age in which we live' (Martin, 1988: 303).

Just what sense to make of this symbol has been the source of a great deal of controversy. To some, it constitutes the beginning of a truly professionalized and caring society, while to others, it represents a tightening of control over the citizenry; to some, it heralds the emergence of a highly educated public that has ready access to knowledge, while to others, it means a deluge of trivia, sensationalism, and misleading propaganda; to some, it was the development of the nation state that promoted the role of information, while to others, it was changes in corporate organization that led information to become more critical.

However, a major division of opinion that cuts across interpretations is the separation between thinkers who, on the one hand, subscribe to the notion that in recent times we have seen emerge information societies that are marked by their *differences* from hitherto existing societies. Not all of these are altogether happy with the term 'information society', but insofar as they argue that the present era is special and different, marking a turning point in social development, then I think they can be described as its endorsers. On the other hand, there are scholars who, while happy to concede that information has taken on a special significance in the modern era, insist that the central feature of the present is its *continuity* with the past.

This chapter is taken from The Information Society, 10 (1994), pp. 1–23.

We may separate those who endorse the idea of an information society and those who regard informatization as the continuation of pre-established relations. Toward one wing we may position those who proclaim a new sort of society that has emerged from the old. Drawn to this side are theorists of:

- postindustrialism (Bell, 1973, and a legion of followers)
- postmodernism (e.g. Baudrillard, 1983; Poster, 1990)
- flexible specialization (e.g. Hirschhorn, 1984; Piore and Sabel, 1984)
- the control revolution (Beniger, 1986)
- the informational mode of development (Castells, 1989)

On the other side are writers who place emphasis on continuities. I would include here theorists of:

- neo-Marxism (e.g. Schiller, 1981, 1984)
- regulation theory (e.g. Aglietta, 1979; Lipietz, 1987)
- flexible accumulation (Harvey, 1989)
- national state and violence (Giddens, 1985)
- the public sphere (Habermas, 1962; Garnham, 1990)

None of the latter group denies that information is key to the modern world, but unlike the former group, they argue that the form and function of information is subordinate to long-established principles and practices.

In what follows, I pay particular attention to definitions that under-pin information society theorists. The insistence of these thinkers that our time is one of novelty cries out for analysis, more urgently than those scenarios that contend that the status quo remains. Of course, it is also unavoidable that in examining information society theorists, I shall consider aspects of the latter group, since a good deal of this critique requires expression of their misgivings.

I shall examine definitions of information that are in play. As we shall see – here, in the very conception of the element that underlies all discussion – there are distinctions that echo the divide between information society theorists, who announce the novelty of the present, and informatization thinkers, who recognize the force of the past weighing heavily on today's developments.

Definitions of the information society

In reading the voluminous literature on the information society, many writers operate with undeveloped definitions of their subject. They write copiously about particular features of the information society but are curiously vague about their operational criteria. Eager to make sense of changes in information, they rush to interpret these changes in terms of different forms of economic production, new forms of social interaction, or innovative processes of production. However, they very often fail to set out clearly in what ways and why information is becoming more central today, so critical indeed that it is ushering in a new type of society. Just what is it about information that makes so many think that it is at the core of the modern age?

It is possible to distinguish *analytically* five definitions of an information society, each of which presents criteria for identifying the new. These are:

- technological
- economic
- occupational
- spatial
- cultural

Technological

The most common definition of the information society emphasizes spectacular technological innovation. The key idea is that breakthroughs in information processing, storage, and transmission have led to the application of information technologies (IT) in virtually all corners of society. The major concern is the astonishing reductions in the costs of computers, their prodigious increases in power, and their consequent application anywhere and everywhere.

Because it is now economical and feasible to put computers in typewriters, cars, cookers, watches, factory machines, televisions, and toys, it follows that we are certain to experience social upheaval of such magnitude that we shall enter a new era. Many books, magazine articles, and TV presentations have encouraged the development of a distinct genre that offers this viewpoint: the mighty micro will usher in an entirely new silicon civilization.

Somewhat more sophisticated versions of this technological route to the information society attend to the convergence and imbrication of telecommunications and computing. They argue that cheap information processing and storage technologies (computers) lead to extensive distribution. One of the major areas thus impacted is telecommunications, notably switching centers, which, in being computerized, in effect merge with the general development of computing and impel still more dramatic improvement of information management and distribution. This unification is especially fortuitous because the widespread dissemination of computers means that, for optimum use, they require connection. In short, the computerization of telecommunications means that, increasingly, computer can be linked to computer, hence the prospect of links between terminals within and between offices, banks, homes, shops, factories, schools, the globe itself.

It is tempting to dismiss technological approaches to the information society. Awed by the pace and magnitude of technological change, writers naïvely tell us that 'the computer revolution . . . will have an overwhelming and comprehensive impact, affecting every human being on Earth in every aspect of his or her life' (Evans, 1979: 13). This tone is characteristically full of dire wake-up warnings, shallow analyses of the substantive realm, and the self-assurance that only the author has understood what most others have yet to comprehend. It presents but a poor case for the validity of technological measures (Webster and Robins, 1986: ch. 2).

Nevertheless, if the likes of Alvin Toffler, Christopher Evans, and James Martin impel one toward ready rejection of technological criteria, it has to be acknowledged that many more serious scholars adopt what is at base a similar approach. For instance, Williams (1988: 15), a leading American communications professor, opines that 'it [the information society] is a society where the economy reflects growth owing to techno-logical advances.' And Williams is far from alone. In Britain, for example, a much respected school of thought has devised a neo-Schumpeterian approach to change. Combining Schumpeter's argument that major tech-nological innovations bring about creative destruction with Kondratieff's theme of long waves of economic development, these researchers contend that IT represents the establishment of a new epoch. This new techno-economic paradigm (Freeman and Perez, 1988) constitutes the Information Age that is set to mature early in the next century (Freeman et al., 1982; Freeman, 1987; Hall and Preston, 1988).

Elsewhere, Piore and Sabel (1984) have suggested that new tech-nologies provide the foundation for a radically different way of working called flexible specialization. Thanks to communication and computer technologies, small firms can now quickly assess and adroitly respond to markets. The prospect is for an end to mass production and for its replacement with customized products made by multiskilled and adaptable craftspeople.

Common sense tells us that these technological definitions of the information society do seem appropriate. If it is possible to see a 'series of inventions' (Landes, 1969) – steam power, the internal combustion engine, electricity, the flying shuttle – as characteristic of the industrial society, then why not accept the virtuoso developments in IT as evidence of a new type of society? As Naisbitt (1984: 28) states, 'Computer technology is to the information age what mechanization was to the industrial revolution.' And why not?

Unfortunately, technological definitions of the information society must encounter a number of well-founded objections. These include the following.

(1) If technology is the main criterion for defining a society, then why not just call the emerging era a high tech society or an automated age? Given the variety of ways to describe a society in which IT predominates – silicon society, cybernetic society, robotic age – why choose to designate it an information society? If technology is the key, then why is the prefix 'information' attached? But then 'technological society' scarcely evokes the idea of a new or even significantly different world that 'information society' does.

(2) When one reads of profound and portentous changes that new technology is bringing about, one cannot but be struck by its palpable

presence. There is a self-evident reality about the *hereness* of the new technologies. Since each of us can see it with our own eyes, then it does seem obvious that the technologies are valid as distinguishing features of a new society.

But probing further, one cannot but be struck also by the astonishing vagueness of technology in most of these books. We ask for an empirical measure – in *this* society *now*, how much IT is there and how far does this take us toward qualifying for information society status? How much IT is required in order to identify an information society? Asking simply for a *usable* measure, one quickly becomes aware that a good many of those who emphasize technology are not able to provide us with anything so mundanely real worldly or testable. IT, it begins to appear, is everywhere . . . and nowhere too.

This problem of measurement, and the associated difficulty of stipulating the point on the technological scale at which a society is judged to have entered an information age, is surely central to any acceptable definition of a distinctively new type of society. It is ignored by popular futurists: the new technologies are announced, and it is unproblematically presumed that this announcement in and of itself heralds the information society. This issue is, surprisingly, also bypassed by scholars who yet assert that IT is the major index of an information society. They are content to describe technological innovations in general terms, somehow presuming that this is enough to distinguish the new society.

There are, however, several serious scholars who find that the issue of measurement causes considerable obstacles to progress. They encounter two particularly awkward problems. First, how does one measure the rate of technological diffusion, and second, when does a society cease being industrial and enter into the information category? These are formidably difficult questions and should make enthusiasts for the information society scenario hesitate. For instance, in Britain a decade of social science research by the Programme on Information and Communication Technologies (PICT), one charged with mapping and measuring the information society, has not as yet produced any definitive ways of meeting its objectives (Miles et al., 1990). Certainly, there have been some advances, namely, several studies charting the diffusion of some IT into factories and offices (e.g. Norcott and Walling, 1989). But how is one to assess this diffusion in more general terms: by expenditure on IT (yet given the tumbling prices of the new technologies, how is one to differentiate the economic variable from the more central element of information handling capacity?) or by the amount and range of IT introduced? Ought one to center on IT expenditure or take-up per head, or is it better to examine this on an institutional basis? How is one to quantify the significance of the expansion of microcomputer applications *vis-à-vis* mainframe systems? And, if one opts to focus on the uptake of IT, just what is to count as a relevant technology? For instance, should video equipment come before personal computers, networked systems before robotic applications? Further, while one may be able to imagine a time at which some measures of informatization will have been developed that gain widespread assent, one will still be left with the serious query: where along that graph is the break point that separates the information society from the merely advanced industrial?

(3) The final objection to technological definitions of the information society is frequently made. Critics object to those who assert that, in a given era, technologies are first invented and then subsequently have an impact on the society, thereby impelling people to respond by adjusting to the new. Technology in these versions is privileged above all else; hence, it comes to identify an entire social world: the Steam Age, the Age of the Automobile, the Atomic Age . . .

The central objection here is *not* that this is unavoidably technologically determinist – in that technology is regarded as the prime social dynamic – and as such an oversimplification of processes of change. It most certainly is this, but more important, it relegates into an entirely separate division social, economic, and political dimensions of technological innovation. These follow from, and are subordinate to, the premier league of technology that appears to be self-perpetuating, though it leaves its impress on all aspects of society.

But technology is not aloof from the social realm in this way. On the contrary, it is an integral and, indeed, constitutive part of the social. For instance, research and development decisions express priorities, and from these value judgments, particular types of technology are produced (e.g. military projects received substantially more funding than health work in the twentieth century western world; not surprisingly, a consequence is state-of-the-art weapon systems that dwarf the advances of treatment, say, of the common cold). Many studies have shown how technologies bear the impress of social values, whether it be in the architectural design of bridges in New York, where heights were set that would prevent public transit systems accessing certain areas; the manufacture of cars that testify to the values of private ownership, presumptions about family size (typically two adults, two children), attitudes toward the environment (profligate use of nonrenewable energy alongside pollution), status symbols (the Porsche, the Mini, the Rover), and individual rather than public forms of transit; or the construction of houses that are not just places to live, but also expressions of ways of life, prestige and power relations, and preferences for a variety of lifestyles. Again, market power has an obvious influence on what gets manufactured technologically: corporations think of the customers and potential customers prior to production, so it is not surprising that there are limits to what gets made imposed by ability to pay criteria.

There is extensive literature on this issue, but I do not wish to belabor it *ad nauseam*. All that is required is to state the objection to the *hypostatization* of technology as applied to the issue of defining the information society.

Economic

There is an established subdivision of economics that concerns itself with the economics of information. As a founder of this specialism, the late Fritz Machlup (1902–1983) devoted much of his professional life to the goal of assessing the size and growth of the information industries. Machlup's (1962) pioneering work, *The Production and Distribution of Knowledge in the United States*, has been seminal in establishing measures of the information society in economic terms.

Machlup attempted to trace the information industries in statistical terms. Distinguishing five broad industry groups (two of which are education and media), he attempted to ascribe an economic value to each and to trace its contribution to gross national product (GNP). If the trend is for these groups to account for an increased proportion of GNP, then one may claim to chart the emergence through time of an information economy. This is just what Machlup (1962) proposed in this early study, which calculated that 29 per cent of the GNP of the United States in 1958 came from the knowledge industries, which at the time was a remarkable rate of expansion.

As early as the 1960s, management guru Peter Drucker was contending that knowledge[1] 'has become the foundation of the modern economy' as we have shifted 'from an economy of goods [to] . . . a knowledge economy' (Drucker, 1969: 247, 249). Today it is commonplace to argue that we have evolved into a society where the 'distinguishing characteristic . . . is that knowledge and organization are the prime creators of wealth' (Karunaratne, 1986: 52).

Probably the best known, and certainly the most cited, study of the emergence of an information economy conceived on these lines comes in a nine-volume report from Porat, (1977a, b). In allocating industries to his five categories, Machlup had adopted catholic definitions of 'knowledge production', broadly including both those that created new information and those that communicated it. Porat echoed much of Machlup's approach in his reliance on government statistical sources to design a computer model of the US economy in the late sixties, but divided the economy between the primary, secondary and noninformation sectors. This tripartite schema stemmed from his identification of a weakness in Machlup's work, in which there was a failure to account for information activities that were disguised from initial examination, for example, because they are an in-house element of other industries. Porat included in the primary information sector all those industries that make available their information in established markets or elsewhere, where an economic value can be readily ascribed (e.g. mass media, education, advertising, computer manufacture). Thus,

> The primary information sector includes . . . industries that in some way produce, process, disseminate, or transmit knowledge or messages. The unifying definition is that the goods and services that make up the primary sector must be fundamentally valued for their information producing, processing, or distributing characteristics (Porat, 1978: 8).

However, Porat then sought to identify a secondary information sector, which would allow him to include in his typology important informational activities such as R&D inside a pharmaceutical company, information produced by government departments for internal consumption, and the library resources of an oil corporation. Thus,

> The secondary information sector includes the informational activities of the public bureaucracy and private bureaucracies. The private bureaucracy is that portion of every noninformation form that engages in purely informational activities, such as research and development, planning, control, marketing, and record keeping . . . The public bureaucracy includes all the informational functions of the federal, state, and local governments. (Porat, 1978: 9)

In this way, Porat is able to distinguish the two information sectors, then to consolidate them, separate out the noninformational elements of the economy, and by reaggregating national economic statistics, is able to conclude that over 46 percent of the US GNP is accounted for by the information sector. *Ipso facto*, 'the United States is now an information-based economy.' As such, it is an 'information society [where] the major arena[s] of economic activity are the information goods and services producers, and the public and private [secondary information sector] bureaucracies' (Porat, 1978: 11).

This quantification of the economic significance of information is an impressive achievement. It is not surprising that those convinced of the emergence of an information society have routinely turned to Machlup and, especially, Porat as authoritative demonstrations of a rising curve of information activity, one set to lead the way to a new age.

However, there are difficulties with the economics of information approach (Monk, 1989: 39–63). One is that, behind the weighty statistical tables that are resonant of objective demonstration, there is a great deal of hidden interpretation and value judgment as to how to construct categories and what to include and exclude from the information sector.

For example, Porat is at some pains to identify the quasi-firm embedded within a noninformational enterprise. But is it acceptable, from the correct assumption that R&D in a petrochemical company involves informational activity, to separate this from the manufacturing element for statistical purposes? It is surely likely that the activities are blurred, with the R&D section intimately tied to production wings, and any separation for mathematical reasons is unfaithful to its role. More generally, when Porat examines his secondary information sector, he in fact, splits every industry into the informational and noninformational domains. But such divisions between the 'thinking' and the 'doing' are extraordinarily hard to accept: where does one put operation of computer numerical control systems or the line management functions that are an integral element of production? To be sure, one could say that everything here involves information – and as we shall see, many writers identify the expansion of managers and white collar work *tout court* as reason for the coming of an information society – but that is not the point. The objection here is that Porat divides, arbitrarily, within industries to chart the secondary information sector as opposed to the noninformational realm.

Another difficulty is that the aggregated data inevitably homogenize very disparate economic activities. In the round, it may be possible to say that growth in the economic worth of advertising and television is indicative of an information society, but one is left with an urge to distinguish between informational activities on qualitative grounds. In asking which economically assessed characteristics are more central, are more strategic, to the emergence of an information society, one is requesting scholars to distinguish between, say, information stemming from policy research centers, corporate think tanks, transnational finance houses, manufacturers of 35-mm cameras, software designers, and the copywriters of Saatchi and Saatchi.

The enthusiasm of the information economists to put a price tag on everything has the unfortunate consequence of failing to let us know the really valuable dimensions of the information sector. This search to differentiate between quantitative and qualitative indices of an information society is not pursued by Machlup and Porat, though on a level of common sense, it is obvious that the sales of the *New York Post* cannot be equated with – still less be regarded as more informational, though doubtless it is of more economic value – the circulation of the *Wall Street Journal*. It is a distinction to which we shall return, but one that suggests the possibility that we could have a society in which, as measured by GNP, informational activity is of great weight, but which in terms of the springs of economic, social, and political life is of little consequence.

Of course, these economists are concerned solely with developing quantitative measurements of the information sector, so the issue of the qualitative worth of information would be of limited relevance to them. However, even on their own terms, there are problems. One mentioned earlier, is the question about the point on the economic graph that one enters an information society. Is it when 50 percent of GNP is dedicated to informational activities? This may seem to be a reasonable point, one at which, in straightforward quantitative terms, information begins to predominate. Sadly for information society theorists, however, we are some distance even from that point. Replication studies of Machlup and Porat lead one to qualify any initial sighting of the new age. Rubin and Taylor (1986), in a large-scale update of Machlup's study, concluded that in the United States the contribution of knowledge industries to GNP increased from 28.6 percent to 34.3 percent between 1958 and 1980, with virtually no change since 1970, this constituting an 'extremely modest rate of growth relative to the average rate of growth of other components of total GNP' (Rubin and Taylor, 1986: 3). Furthermore, the same authors' replication of Porat's influential study found little expansion of the information sector during the seventies when compared with other contributors to GNP. These econometric studies scarcely trumpet the arrival of an information society.

Occupational

A popular measure of the emergence of an information society is the one that focuses on occupational change. Put simply, the contention is that we have achieved an information society when the predominance of occupations is found in information work. That is, the information society has arrived when clerks, teachers, lawyers, and entertainers outnumber coal miners, steelworkers, dockers, and builders.

On the surface, the changing distribution of jobs seems an appropriate measure. After all, it appears obvious that as work that demands physical strength and manual dexterity, such as hewing coal and farming the land, declines to be replaced by more and more manipulation of figures and text, such as in education and large bureaucracies, then so we are entering a new type of society. Today 'only a shrinking minority of the labour force toils in factories . . . and the labour market is now dominated by information operatives who make their living by virtue of the fact that they possess the information needed to get things done' (Stonier, 1983: 7, 8).

This trend is seized upon by many reports. For instance, two influential Organization for Economic Corporation and Development (OECD, 1981, 1986) publications produced figures from all member countries, signalling 'continued growth . . . in those occupations primarily concerned with the creation and handling of information and with its infrastructure support' (OECD, 1986). Elsewhere, Porat (1977b: 131) identifies an 'astonishing growth rate' of the 'information work force', which doubled every 18.7 years between 1860 and 1980, thereby propelling the United States toward 'the edge of an information economy' (Porat, 1977b: 204).

The shift in the distribution of occupations is at the heart of the most influential theory of the information society. Here, Daniel Bell (1973) sees in the emergence of white collar society (and, hence, information work) and the decline of industrial labour, changes as profound as the end of class-based political conflict, more communal consciousness, and the development of equality between the sexes.

I consider and critique Bell's theorization elsewhere (Robins and Webster, 1987), but here it is appropriate to raise some general objections to occupational measures of the information society. A major problem concerns the methodology for allocating workers to particular categories. The end product – a bald statistical figure giving a precise percentage of information workers – hides the complex processes by which researchers construct their categories and allocate people to one or another.

Porat, for instance, develops what has become an influential typology to locate occupations that are primarily engaged in the production, processing, or distribution of information. His is a threefold scheme that encompasses more than 400 occupational types that are reported by the US Census and Bureau of Labor Statistics. He explains it as follows:

> The first category includes those workers whose output as primary activity is producing and selling knowledge. Included here are scientists, inventors, teachers, librarians, journalists, and authors. The second major class of workers covers those who gather and disseminate information. These workers move information within firms and within markets; they search, coordinate, plan, and process market information. Included here are managers,

secretaries, clerks, lawyers, brokers, and typists. The last class includes workers who operate the information machines and technologies that support the previous two activities. Included here are computer operators, telephone installers, and television repairers. (Porat, 1978: 5–6)

Jonscher (1983) simplifies this further still, discerning just two sectors of the economy: the first, an information sector, is where people whose prime function is creating, processing, and handling information; the second, a production sector, is where workers are found who chiefly create, process, and handle physical goods.

These distinctions appear reasonable, precise, and empirically valid, but there are difficulties. Not the least is something Porat is well aware of, namely, that 'stating precisely who is an information worker and who is not is a risky proposition' (Porat, 1978: 5). Indeed it *is*, since every occupation involves a significant degree of information processing and cognition. Porat acknowledges this in his attempt to distinguish noninformational from informational labor on the basis of estimating the *degree* to which each type is involved with information. In other words, the categorization is a matter of judging the extent to which jobs are informational or not. Crude percentages of information workers disguise the fact that they are the outcome of the researcher's estimations. As Porat puts it, when 'we assert that certain occupations are primarily engaged in the manipulation of symbols . . . It is a distinction of degree, not of kind' (Porat, 1977b: 3).

For example, the railway signal man must have a stock of knowledge about tracks and timetables and roles and routines; he needs to communicate with other signal men down the line, with station personnel and engine drivers, is required to 'know the block' of his own and other cabins, must keep a precise and comprehensive ledger of all traffic that moves through his area, and has had little need of physical strength to pull levers since the advent of modern equipment. Yet the railway signal man is, doubtless, a manual worker of the industrial age. Conversely, the person who comes to repair the photocopier may know little about products other than the one for which he has been trained, may well have to work in hot, dirty, and uncomfortable circumstances, and may need considerable strength to move heavy machinery and replace damaged parts. Yet he will undoubtedly be classified as an information worker, since his work with new-age machinery suits Porat's interpretations.

The point to be made here is simple: we need to be skeptical of conclusive figures that are the outcomes of researchers' perceptions of where occupations are to be most appropriately categorized. As a matter of fact, social scientists know very little about the detail and complexity of peoples' jobs; there are precious few ethnographies that record the details of working lives (see Terkel, 1977). And researchers trying to label 'information' and 'noninformation' work are just as much in the dark as the rest of their social science colleagues.

One needs also to beware the oversimplifications that can come from allocating a wide variety of jobs to the same pigeonholes. Miles (1991: 917) rightly observes that 'the categories of work subsumed under the different headings are often extremely heterogeneous.' When one considers, for example, that Porat's first category (information producers) lumps together opticians, library assistants, composers, paperback writers, university professors, and engineers, while his second (information distributors) subsumes journalists on quality newspapers with deliverers on the street, and when the OECD puts together, as information producers, physicists, commodity brokers, and auctioneers, then one may well have doubts about the value of this composition of occupations as a means of identifying social change. Further, what of the diversity of occupations, each with the same title? Librarian, for example, can encompass someone spending much of the day issuing for loan and reshelving books, as well as someone routinely involved in advising academics on the best sources of information for progressing state-of-the-art research. Is it really sensible to lump together such diversity?

Finally, an important consequence of this homogenization is a failure to identify the more *strategically* central information occupations. While the methodology may provide us with a picture of greater amounts of information work taking place, it does not offer any means of differentiating the most important dimensions of information work. The pursuit of a quantitative measure of information work disguises the possibility that the growth of certain types of information occupations may have particular consequences for social life.

It has to be said that counting the number of information workers in a society tells us nothing about the hierarchies – and associated variations in power and esteem – of these people. For example, it could be argued that the crucial issue has been the growth of computing and telecommunications engineers, since these may exercise a decisive influence over the pace of technological innovation. A similar, perhaps even greater, rate of expansion in social workers to handle problems of an aging population and increased family dislocation and juvenile delinquency may have little or nothing to do with an information society, though undoubtedly, social workers would be classified with IT engineers as 'information workers'.

Or it may be argued that it is an 'inner circle' (Useem, 1985; Useem and Karabel, 1986) of corporate leaders, quite different from their predecessors, that is the most decisive index of the information society. These are people who are empowered by communicative skills, analytical abilities, foresight, and capacities to formulate strategic policies, who also enjoy privileged educational backgrounds, connections through shared clubs and boardroom affiliations, plus access to sophisticated information and communications technologies. All of this provides them with extraordinary leverage over social, economic, and political affairs at the national and even international level. They are information specialists but radically different from the run-of-the-mill information workers that quantitative methodologists would crudely lump them with.

Perhaps we can better understand this need to qualitatively distinguish between groups of information workers by reflecting on a [. . .] study by social historian Harold Perkin. In *The Rise of Professional Society*, Perkin (1989: 2) argues that the history of Britain since 1880 may be written largely as the rise to preeminence of 'professionals', who rule by virtue of 'human capital created by education and enhanced by . . . the exclusion of the unqualified.' Perkin (1989: 406) contends that certified expertise has been 'the organizing principle of post-war society', the expert displacing once-dominant groups (working class organizations, capitalist entrepreneurs, and the landed aristocracy) and their outdated ideals (of cooperation and solidarity, of property and the market, and of the paternal gentleman) with the professional's ethos of service, certification, and efficiency.

To be sure, professionals within the private sector argue fiercely with those in the public, but Perkin insists that this is an internecine struggle, one within professional society, which decisively excludes the nonexpert from serious participation and shares fundamental assumptions (notably the primacy of trained expertise and reward based on merit).

Gouldner's (1978) discussion of the 'new class' provides an interesting complement to Perkin's. Gouldner identifies a new type of employee that has expanded in the twentieth century, a new class that is 'composed of intellectuals and technical intelligentsia' (Gouldner, 1978: 153), which, while in part self-seeking and often subordinate to powerful groups, can also contest the control of established business and party leaders. Despite these potential powers, the new class is itself divided in various ways. A key division is between those who are for the most part technocratic and conformist, and the humanist intellectuals who are critical and emancipatory in orientation. To a large extent, this difference is expressed in the conflicts identified by Perkin between private and public sector professionals. For instance, we may find that accountants in the private sector are conservative, while there is a propensity for humanistic intellectuals to be radical.

Our main point here is that both Gouldner and Perkin are identifying particular changes within the realm of information work that have especially important consequences for society as a whole. To Gouldner, the new class can provide us with vocabularies to discuss and debate the direction of social change, while to Perkin, the professionals create new ideals for organizing social affairs.

If one is searching for an index of the information society in these thinkers, one will be directed to the quality of the contribution of certain groups. Whether one agrees or not with either of these interpretations, the challenge to the definitions of an information society on the basis of a count of raw numbers of information workers should be clear. To thinkers such as Perkin and Gouldner, the quantitative change is *not* the main issue. Indeed, as a proportion of the population, the groups they lay emphasis upon, while having expanded, remain distinct minorities – tiny in the case of Useem's 'inner circle' and more numerous where the growth of professions is identified, but never more than 20 percent or 25 percent of the workforce.

Spatial

The spatial conception of the information society, while it draws on sociology and economics, has at its core the geographer's distinctive stress on space. Here the major emphasis is on the information *networks* that connect locations and, in consequence, have dramatic effects on the organization of time and space. Goddard (1991) identifies four interrelated elements in the transition to an information society.

1   Information is coming to occupy center stage as the key strategic resource on which the organization of the world economy is dependent. The modern world demands the coordination of globally distributed manufacture, planning across and between sovereign states, and marketing throughout continents. Information is axial to these diverse activities and, thus, is of heightened importance in the contemporary world. It follows too that information management is of exceptional pertinence and that, as a result, we witness the rapid expansion of information occupations.

2   Computer and communications technologies provide the infrastructure that enables information to be processed and distributed. These technologies allow information to be handled on an historically unprecedented scale, facilitate instantaneous and 'real-time' trading, and monitor economic, social, and political affairs on a global stage.

3   There has been an exceptionally rapid growth of the tradable information sector of the economy, by which Goddard means to highlight the explosive growth of services, such as new media (satellite broadcasting, cable, video) and on-line databases providing information on a host of subjects ranging from stock market dealings, commodity prices, patent listings, and currency fluctuations to abstracts of scientific and technological journals.

    Complementing these developments has been the radical reorganization of the world's financial system, which has resulted in the collapse of traditional boundaries that once separated banking, brokerage, financial services, credit agencies, and the like. Inside this bewildering world of high finance – which few people understand and still fewer appear able to control – circulates, in electronic form, dazzling sums of capital (one estimate suggests there are $2 trillion Eurodollars in the system, though there were none just over a generation ago; Harvey, 1989: 163).

4   The growing 'informatization' of the economy is facilitating the integration of national and regional economies.

Courtesy of immediate and effective information processing and exchange, economics has become truly global, and with this has come about a reduction in the constraints of space. Companies can now develop global strategies for production, storage, and distribution of goods and services; financial interests operate continuously, respond immediately, and traverse the globe. The boundaries erected by geographical location are being pushed further and further back – and with them the limitations once imposed by time – thanks to the virtuoso ways in which information can be managed and manipulated in the contemporary period.

Added together, these trends – the strategic importance of information, the establishment of an IT infrastructure, the growth of tradable information, and global integration – emphasize the centrality of information networks, linking together locations within and between towns, regions, nations, continents, and the entire world.

As the electricity grid runs throughout an entire nation, extending down to the individual householder's ring main, so too may we envisage now a wired society (Martin, 1978) operating at the national, international, and global levels to provide an information ring main (Barron and Curnow, 1979) to each home, shop, or office. Increasingly, we are all connected to the network, which itself is expanding its reach and capacities.

Many writers emphasize the technological bases of the information network (e.g. Hepworth, 1989). Perhaps predictably then, with these accounts of an emerging network society, considerable attention is given to advances in and obstacles to the development of an Integrated Services Digital Network (ISDN) infrastructure (Dordick et al., 1981).

However, notwithstanding the importance of technology, and actually providing a salutary reminder of the easily neglected centrality of telecommunications to IT developments, most thinkers concerned with the emergence of a network marketplace place stress on ways in which networks underline the significance of the flow of information (Castells, 1989).

The salient idea here is of information circulating along electronic 'highways'. Interestingly, no one has been able to quantify how much and at what rate information must flow along these routes to constitute an information society. In fact, no one has produced reliable figures capable of giving us an overall understanding of information traffic (cf. Economic Commission for Europe, 1987). We have data on telephone density in relation to population, figures on the expansion of facsimile services, statistics for sales of computer systems, automated telecommunications exchanges, and so on, but lack a clear picture of the size, capacity, and use of the networks.

Nevertheless, all observers are aware of a massive increase in transborder data flows, in telecommunications facilities, in communications between computers at every level from home to transnational organization, in exchanges between stock markets and corporate segments, in access to international databases, in telex messages. Similarly, there is considerable awareness of increases in the global distribution of mass-mediated information, satellite television being the obvious and preeminent example, though one would have to include news gathering and distribution services in any adequate picture. As Mulgan (1991: 1) has it, 'the networks carry an *unimaginable* volume of messages, conversations, images, and commands' (my emphasis).

Why much greater volume and velocity should impel us to think of information flows in terms of the constitution of a new type of society returns us to the geographer's special concern with space. All things happen in particular places and at specific times, but the characteristics of space and time have been transformed with the advent of the network society. Where once trade was cumbersome and slow moving across distances, it can now be effected instantaneously with computerized communications technologies; where once corporate activity had to be coordinated by slow moving letters that took days and even weeks to cross the space that divided the interested parties, now it takes place in real-time, courtesy of sophisticated telecommunications and video conference facilities.

> A world built on networks . . . calls into question older conceptions of space and power. Where the early market economies grew out of the temporal and spatial regularities of city life, today's are built on the logical or 'virtual' regularities of electronic communications, a new geography of nodes and hubs, processing and control centers. The nineteenth century's physical infrastructure of railways, canals and roads are now overshadowed by the network of computers, cables and radio links that govern where things go, how they are paid for, and who has access to what. (Mulgan, 1991: 3)

In short, the constraints of space have been dramatically limited, though certainly not eliminated. And simultaneously, time has itself been shrunk as contact is immediate via computer communications and tele-communications. This 'time/space compression', as Giddens (1990) terms it, provides corporations, governments, and even individuals with hitherto unachievable options.

No one can deny that information networks are an important feature of contemporary societies: satellites do allow instantaneous communications around the globe, databases can be access from Oxford to Los Angeles, Tokyo, and Paris, and facsimile machines and interconnected computer systems are a routine part of modern businesses.

Yet we may still ask: why should the presence of networks lead analysts to categorize societies as information economies? And when we ask this, we encounter the problem of the imprecision of definitions once again. For instance, when is a network a network? Is it two people speaking to one another by telephone, or computer systems transmitting vast data sets through a packet switching exchange; is it when an office block is 'wired', or when terminals in the home can communicate with local banks and shops? The question of what actually constitutes a network is a serious one, and it raises problems not only of how to distinguish between different levels of networking, but also of how we stipulate a point at which we have entered a network/information society.

Finally, one could argue that information networks have been around for a very long time. From at least the early days of the postal service, through to telegram and telephone facilities, much of our economic, social, and political life is unthinkable without such information networks. Given this long-term dependency and incremental, if accelerated, development, why should it be that in the 1980s, commentators begin to talk in terms of information societies?

Cultural

The final conception of an information society is perhaps the most easily acknowledged, yet the least measured. Each of us is aware, from the pattern of our everyday lives, that there has been an extraordinary increase in the information in social circulation. There is simply a great deal more of it about than ever before.

Television has been in extensive use for over thirty years in Britain, but now programs run round-the-clock. There is much more radio output available now than even a decade ago, at the local, national, and international levels. Radios are no longer fixed in the front room, but spread through the home, car, office, and with the Walkman, everywhere. Movies have long been an important part of peoples' information environment, and indeed, attendance at cinemas has declined significantly. But movies today are more prevalent than ever: available at cinema outlets, broadcast on television, readily borrowed from video rental shops, and cheaply purchased from the shelves of chain stores. Walk along any street and it is almost impossible to miss the advertising hoardings, the billboards, the window displays in shops. Visit any railway or bus station and one cannot avoid being struck by the widespread availability of paperback books and inexpensive magazines, their subject matter including such a range as classical, pulp fiction, middlebrow, and self-therapy – a scale and scope without precedent. In addition, audio tape, compact disc, and radio all offer more, and more readily available, music, poetry, drama, humour, and education to the general public. Newspapers are extensively available, and a good many new titles fall on our doorsteps as free sheets. Junk mail is delivered daily . . .

All of this testifies to the fact that we inhabit a media-laden society, but the informational features of our world are more thoroughly penetrative than a short list of television, radio, and other media systems suggests. This sort of listing implies that new media surround us, presenting us with messages to which we may or may not respond. But in truth, the informational environment is a great deal more intimate, more constitutive *of* us, than this suggests. One may consider, for example, the informational dimensions of the clothes we wear, the styling of our hair and faces, the very ways in which we work at our image. From body shape to speech, people are intensely aware of the messages they may be projecting and how they feel about themselves in certain clothes, with a particular hairstyle, etc. A few moments' reflection on the complexities of fashion, the intricacy of the ways in which we design ourselves for everyday presentation, make one well aware that social intercourse involves a greater degree of informational content now than previously.

There has long been adornment of the body, both clothing and make-up being important ways of signalling status, power, and affiliation. But it is obvious that historically the present age has dramatically heightened the symbolic import of dress and the body. When one considers the lack of range of meaning that characterized the peasant smock, which was the apparel of the majority for centuries, and the uniformity of the clothing worn by the industrial working class in and out of work up to the 1950s, then the veritable explosion of meaning in terms of dress since then is remarkable. The availability of cheap and fashionable clothing, the possibilities of affording it, and the accessibility of any amount of groups with similar – and different – lifestyles and cultures (divided by age, gender, race, ethnicity, affluence, region, etc.), all make one appreciate the informational content even of our bodies.

Homes too are information laden in an historically singular way. Furniture, lay out, and decorative design all express ideas and ideals: the G-plan style, the Laura Ashley settee, the William Morris wallpaper – and the mixing of some and all of these according to choice and budget. Certainly, since the days of the Industrial Revolution, homes have signified ways of life; one thinks, for example, of the style of the 'respectable' working class of the late Victorian period or the distinctive design of the professional middle classes between the wars. But it is the explosion in variety in recent decades, and its accessibility to so many people that is most remarkable. With this has come an astonishing vista of signification.

This intrusion of information into the most intimate realms of home, bedroom, and body is complemented by the growth of institutions dedicated to investing everyday life with symbolic significance. One thinks of the global advertising business, of publishing empires, of the fashion industry, of worldwide agencies of media production that bring to the domestic scene reflections of our own ways of life and images of other lifestyles, thereby presenting us with alternative meanings that may be absorbed, rejected, and reinterpreted, but all the while adding to the vocabulary of the symbolic environment.

Readers will recognize and acknowledge this extraordinary expansion of the informational content of modern life. Contemporary culture is manifestly more heavily information laden than any of its predecessors. We exist in a media-saturated environment, which means that life is quintessentially about symbolization, about exchanging and receiving – or trying to exchange and resisting reception of – messages about ourselves and others. It is in acknowledgment of this explosion of *signification* that many writers conceive of our having entered an information society. They rarely attempt to gauge this development in quantitative terms, but rather start from the 'obviousness' of our living in a sea of signs, fuller than at any earlier epoch.

Paradoxically, it is perhaps this very explosion of information that leads some writers to announce the death of the sign. Blitzed by signs, designing ourselves with signs, unable to escape signs wherever we may go, the result is, oddly, a collapse of meaning. As Baudrillard (1983: 95) puts it, 'there is more and more information, and less and less meaning.' Signs once had a reference (clothes, for example, signified a given status, the political statement a distinct philosophy, the TV news was 'what really happened'). However, in this, the postmodern era, we are enmeshed in such a bewildering web of signs that they lose their salience. Signs come from so many directions and are so diverse, fast changing, and contradictory that their power to signify is dimmed. In addition, audiences are creative, self-aware, and reflective, so much so that all signs are greeted with skepticism and a quizzical eye, hence easily inverted, reinterpreted, and refracted from their intended meaning. Thus, the notion that signs represent some reality apart from themselves loses its credibility. Rather, signs are self-referential: they – *simulations* – are all there is. They are, again to use Baudrillard's terminology, the 'hyper reality'.

People appreciate this situation readily enough: they deride the poseur who is dressing for effect but acknowledge that it is all artifice anyway; they are skeptical of the politician who 'manages' the media and his image through adroit public relations but accept that the whole affair is a matter of information management and manipulation. When people do not hunger for any true signs it may be because they believe there are no longer any truths. In these terms, we have entered an age of spectacle, in which people realize the artificiality of signs they may be sent ('It's only Bill Clinton at his latest photo opportunity'; 'It's news manufacture'; 'It's Jack playing the tough guy') and in which they also acknowledge the inauthenticity of the signs they use to construct themselves ('I will just put on my face'; 'There I was adopting the worried parent role').

As a result, signs lose their meaning, and people simply take what they like from those they encounter (usually very different meanings than may have been intended at the outset). And then, in putting together signs for their homes, their work, and themselves, they happily revel in their artificiality, playfully mixing different images to present no distinct meaning but instead to derive pleasure in the parody of pastiche of, say, combining punk and a 1950s Marilyn Monroe facial style. In this information society, we have then 'a set of meanings [which] is communicated [but which] ha[s] no meaning' (Poster, 1990: 63).

Experientially, the idea of an information society is recognized easily enough, but as a definition of a new society, it is considerably more wayward than any of the notions we have considered. Given the absence of criteria we might use to measure the growth of signification in recent years, it is difficult to see how students of postmodernism such as Poster 1990) can depict the present as characterized by a novel mode of information. How can we know this other than from our sense that there is more symbolic interplay going on? And on what basis can we distinguish this society from, say, that of the 1920s, other than purely as a matter of degree of difference? Those who reflect on the postmodern condition have interesting things to say about the character of contemporary culture, but as regards establishing a clear definition of the information society, they are glaringly deficient.

Quality and quantity

Reviewing these varying definitions of the information society, what becomes abundantly clear is that they are either underdeveloped, or imprecise, or both. Whether it is a technological, economic, occupational, spatial, or cultural conception, we are left with highly problematical notions of what constitutes, and how to distinguish, an information society.

It is important that we remain aware of these difficulties. Though as a heuristic device, the term 'information society' has some value in exploring features of the contemporary world, it is far too inexact to be acceptable as a definitive term. Now, however, I want to raise some further difficulties with the language of the information society. The first problem concerns the quantitative versus qualitative measures to which I have already alluded. My earlier concern was chiefly that quantitative approaches failed to distinguish more strategically significant information activity from that which was routine and low level and that this homogenization was misleading. Here I want to raise again the quality/quantity issue insofar as it bears upon the question of whether the information society marks a *break* with previous sorts of societies.

Most definitions of the information society offer a quantitative measure (numbers of white collar workers, percentage of GNP devoted to information, etc.) and assume that, at some unspecified point, we enter an information society when this condition begins to predominate. But there are no clear grounds for designating as a new type of society one in which all we witness is greater quantities of information in circulation and storage. If there is just more information, then it is hard to understand why anyone should suggest that we have before us something radically new. This is a point made well by Giddens, when he observes that all societies, as soon as they are formed into nation states, are information societies insofar as routine gathering, storage, and control of information about population and resources are essential to their operation (Giddens, 1985: 178). On this axis, all that differentiates the present era from, say, seventeenth century England, is much greater quantities of information that are amassed, dissembled, and processed.

Against this, however, it may be feasible to describe as a new sort of society one in which it is possible to locate information of a qualitatively different order and function. Moreover, this does not even require that we discover that a majority of the workforce is engaged in information occupations or that the economy generates a specified sum from informational activity. For example, it is theoretically possible to imagine an information society where only a small minority of information experts hold decisive power. Kurt Vonnegut created this image years ago in his novel *Player Piano*, and it is the basis of an entire subgenre of science fiction. One need look only to the writings of H.G. Wells to conceive of a society in which a knowledge elite predominates, and the majority, surplus to economic requirement, are condemned to dronelike unemployment. On a quantitative measure, say, of occupational patterns, this would not qualify for information society status, but we could feel impelled to so designate it because of the decisive role of information/knowledge to the power structure and direction of social change.

The blunt point is that quantitative measures – simply more information – cannot of themselves identify a break with previous systems, while it is at least theoretically possible to regard small but decisive qualitative changes as marking a system break. After all, just because there are many more automobiles today than thirty years ago does not qualify us to speak of a 'car society'. But it is a systemic change that those who write about an information society wish to spotlight, whether it be in the form of Bell's 'postindustrialism' or in Castells' 'informational mode of development', or in Poster's 'mode of information'.

What is especially odd is that so many of those who identify an information society as a new type of society do so by presuming that this qualitative change can be defined simply by calculating how much information is in circulation, how many people work in information jobs, and so on. What we have here is the assumption that quantitative increases transform, in unspecified ways, into qualitative changes in the social system.

It is noticeable that those scholars such as Herbert Schiller and David Harvey, who stress the continuities of the present with those of the past, while they acknowledge an increasingly central role played by information, have at the forefront of their minds the need to differentiate between categories of information and the purposes to which it is put. In other words, those who insist that the informationalized society is *not* radically different from the past are at pains to differentiate information on qualitative grounds. For instance, they will examine how information availability has been affected by the application of market criteria and contend that the wealthier sectors of society gain access to particularly high-quality information, which consolidates their privileges and powers. Yet, while they emphasize these sorts of qualitative dimensions of informatization, they do so to highlight continuities of the socioeconomic system. Conversely, those who consider that the information society is a radically different system most often resort to quantitative indices to demonstrate a profound qualitative change.

Roszak (1986) provides an interesting insight into this paradox in his critique of information society themes. His examination emphasizes the importance of qualitatively distinguishing information, extending to it what each of us does on an everyday basis when we differentiate between phenomena such as data, knowledge, experience, and wisdom. Certainly, these are themselves slippery terms – one person's knowledge attainment (say, a graduation degree) can be another's information (say, the pass rate of a university) – but they are an essential part of our daily lives. In Roszak's view, the present 'cult of information' functions to destroy these sorts of qualitative distinctions, which are the stuff of real life. It does this by insisting that information is purely quantitative, subject to statistical measurement. But to achieve calculations of the economic value of the information industries, of the proportion of GNP expended on information activities, the percentage of national income going to the information professions, and so on, the qualitative dimensions of the subject (is the information useful? is it true or false?) are laid aside. 'For the information theorist, it does not matter whether we are transmitting a fact, a judgment, a shallow cliché, a deep teaching, a sublime truth, or a nasty obscenity' (Roszak, 1986: 14). These qualitative issues are laid aside as information is homogenized and made amenable to numbering: 'Information comes to be a purely quantitative measure of communicative exchanges' (Roszak, 1986: 11).

The astonishing thing to Roszak is that along with this quantitative measure of information comes the assertion that more information is profoundly transforming social life. Having produced awesome statistics on information activity by blurring the sort of qualitative distinctions we all make in our daily lives, information society theorists then assert that these trends are set to change qualitatively our entire lives.

Roszak vigorously contests these ways of thinking about information. A result of a diet of statistic upon statistic about the uptake of computers, the data-processing capacities of new technologies, and the creation of digitalized networks is that people come readily to believe that information is the essential sustenance of the social system. There is so much of this food that it is tempting to agree with those information society theorists who insist that we have entered an entirely new sort of system. But against this argument of 'more quantity of information to new quality of society', (Roszak, 1986: 91) insists that the 'master ideas' that underpin our civilization are not based upon information at all. Principles such as 'all men are created equal', my country right or wrong', 'live and let live', 'we are all God's children', and 'do unto others as you would be done by' are central ideas of our society, but all come *before* information.

It is important to say that Roszak is not arguing that these and other master ideas are necessarily correct (in fact, some are very noxious, e.g. 'all Jews are rich', 'all women are submissive', 'all blacks have natural athletic ability'). But what he is emphasizing is that ideas, and the necessarily qualitative engagement these entail, take precedence over quantitative approaches to information. And what he especially objects to is that information society theorists reverse that situation at the same time as they smuggle in the (false) idea that more information is fundamentally transforming the society in which we live.

What is information?

Roszak's rejection of statistical measures leads us to consider perhaps the most significant feature of approaches to the information society. We are led here largely because his advocacy is to reintroduce qualitative judgment into discussions of information. Roszak asks questions like the following: is more information necessarily making us a better informed citizenry? Does the availability of more information make us better informed? What sort of information is being generated and stored, and what value is this to the wider society? What sort of information occupations are expanding, why and to what ends?

What is being proposed here is that we insist on examination of the *meaning* of information. And this is surely a common-sense understanding of the term. After all, the first definition of information that springs to mind is the semantic one: information is meaningful; it has a subject; it is intelligence or instruction about something or someone.

If one were to apply this concept of information to an attempt at defining an information society, it would follow that we would be discussing these characteristics of the information. We would be saying that information about *these* sorts of issues, *those* areas, *that* process are what constitutes the new age. However, it is precisely this common-sense definition of information that the information society theorists jettison. What is, in fact, abandoned is a notion of information having a semantic content.

The definitions of the information society I have reviewed perceive information in non-meaningful ways. That is, searching for quantitative evidence of the growth of information, a wide range of thinkers have conceived it in the classic terms of Shannon and Weaver's (1949) information theory. Here, a distinctive definition is used, one that is sharply distinguished from the semantic concept in common parlance. In this theory, information is a quantity that is measured in 'bits' and defined in terms of the probabilities of occurrence of symbols. It is a definition derived from and useful to the communications engineer whose interest is with the storage and transmission of symbols, the minimum index of which is on/off (yes/no or 0/1).

This approach allows the otherwise vexatious conception of information to be mathematically tractable, but this is at the price of excluding the equally vexing, yet crucial, issue of meaning and, integral to meaning, the question of the information's quality. On an everyday level when we receive or exchange information, the prime concerns are its meaning and value: is it significant, accurate, absurd, interesting, adequate, or helpful? But in terms of the information theory that underpins so many measures of the explosion of information, these dimensions are irrelevant. Here, information is defined independently of its content, seen as a physical element as much as is energy or matter. As one of the foremost information society devotees puts it, '*Information exists*. It does not need to be *perceived* to exist. It does not need to be *understood* to exist. It requires no intelligence to interpret it. It does not have to have *meaning* to exist. It exists' (Stonier, 1990: 21). In fact, in these terms, two messages, one that is heavily loaded with meaning and the other pure nonsense, can be equivalent. As Roszak (1986: 13) says, here '*information* has come to denote whatever can be coded for transmission through a channel that connects a source with a receiver, regardless of semantic content.' This allows us to quantify information but at the cost of abandonment of its meaning and quality (cf. Young, 1971).

If this definition of information is the one that pertains in technological and spatial approaches to the information society (where the quantities stored, processed, and transmitted are indicative of the sort of indexes produced), we come across a similar elision of meaning from economists' definitions. It may not be in terms of bits, but at the same time, the semantic qualities are evacuated and replaced by the common denominator of price (cf. Arrow, 1979).

To the information engineer, the prime concern is with the number of yes/no symbols; to the information economist, it is with their vendibility. But as the economist moves from consideration of the concept of information to its measurement, what is lost is the heterogeneity that springs from its manifold meanings. The 'endeavour to put dollar tags on such things as education, research, and art' (Machlup, 1980: 23) unavoidably abandons the semantic qualities of information. Boulding (1966: 13) observed a generation ago that 'The bit . . . abstracts completely from the content of information . . . and while it is enormously useful for telephone engineers . . . for purposes of the social system theorist we need a measure which takes account of significance and which would weight, for instance, the gossip of a teenager rather low and the communications over the hot line between Moscow and Washington rather high.' How odd then that economists have responded to the qualitative problem, which is the essence of information, with a quantitative approach, which being reliant on cost and price, is at best 'a kind of qualitative guesswork' (Boulding, 1966: 13). 'Valuing the invaluable', to adopt Machlup's terminology, means substituting information content with the measuring rod of money. We are then able to produce impressive statistics, but in the process we have lost the notion that information is about something (Maasoumi, 1987).

Finally, though culture is quintessentially about meanings, about how and why people live as they do, it is striking that with the celebration of the nonreferential character of symbols by enthusiasts of postmodernism, we have a congruence with communications theory and the economic approach to information. Here too we have a fascination with the profusion of information, an expansion so prodigious that it has lost its hold semantically. Symbols are now everywhere and generated all of the time, so much so that their meanings have imploded, hence ceasing to signify.

What is most noteworthy is that information society theorists, having jettisoned meaning from their concept of information in order to produce quantitative measures of its growth, then conclude that such is its increased economic worth, the scale of its generation, or simply the amount of symbols swirling around, that society must encounter profoundly meaningful change. We have, in other words, the assessment of information in nonsocial terms – it just is – but we must adjust to its social consequences. This is a familiar situation to sociologists who often come across assertions that phenomena are aloof from society in their development (notably technology and science) but carry within them momentous social consequences. It is demonstrably inadequate as an analysis of social change (cf. Dickson, 1974; Woolgar, 1985).

Doubtless, being able to quantify the spread of information in general terms has some uses, but it is certainly not sufficient to convince us that, in consequence of an expansion, society has *profoundly* changed. For any genuine appreciation of what an information society is like, and how different or similar it is to other social systems, we must surely examine the meaning and quality of the information. What sort of information has increased? Who has generated what kind of information, and for what purposes and with what consequences has it been generated?

Note

1   In the economics literature, 'information' and 'knowledge' tend to be used inter-
changeably.

References

Aglietta, Michel (1979) *A Theory of Capitalist Regulation*. London: New Left Books.

Arrow, Kenneth J. (1979) 'The economics of information', in Michael L. Dertouzos and Joel
Moses (eds), *The Computer Age: a Twenty-year View*, pp. 306–17. Cambridge, Mass.:
MIT Press.

Barron, Iann and Ray Curnow (1979) *The Future with Microelectronics: Forecasting the
Effects of Information Technology*. London: Frances Pinter.

Baudrillard, Jean (1983) *In the Shadow of the Silent Majorities*. New York: Semiotext(e).

Bell, Daniel (1973) *The Coming of Post-Industrial Society: a Venture in Social Forecasting*.
Harmondsworth: Penguin.

Beniger, James R. (1986) *The Control Revolution: Technological and Economic Origins of
the Information Society*. Cambridge, Mass.: Harvard University Press.

Boulding, K.E. (1966) 'The economics of knowledge and the knowledge of economics',
American Economic Review, 56 (2): 1–13 (reprinted in D.M. Lamberton (ed.), *Economics
of Information and Knowledge: Selected Readings*. Harmondsworth: Penguin, 1971).

Castells, Manuel (1989) *The Informational City: Information Technology, Economic
Restructuring and the Urban-Regional Process*. Oxford: Blackwell.

Dickson, David (1974) *Alternative Technology and the Politics of Technical Change*. London:
Collins/Fontana.

Dordick, Herbert S., Bradley, Helen G. and Nanus, Burt (1981) *The Emerging Network
Marketplace*. Norwood, NJ: Ablex.

Drucker, Peter F. (1969) *The Age of Discontinuity*. London: Heinemann.

Economic Commission for Europe (1987) *The Telecommunications Industry: Growth and
Structural Change*. New York: United Nations.

Evans, Christopher (1979) *The Mighty Micro: the Impact of the Micro-Chip Revolution*.
London: Gollancz.

Freeman, Christopher (1974) *The Economics of Industrial Innovation*. Harmondsworth:
Penguin.

Freeman, Christopher (1987) *Technology Policy and Economic Performance*. London:
Frances Pinter.

Freeman, Christopher and Perez, Carlota (1988) 'Structural crises of adjustment, business
cycles and investment behaviour', in Giovanni Dosi et al. (eds), *Technical Change and
Economic Theory*, pp. 38–66, chap. 3. London: Frances Pinter.

Freeman, Christopher, Clark, J. and Soete, L. (1982) *Unemployment and Technical
Innovation: a Study of Long Waves and Economic Development*. London: Frances Pinter.

Garnham, Nicholas (1990) *Capitalism and Communication: Global Culture and the
Economics of Information*. London: Sage.

Giddens, Anthony (1985) *Contemporary Critique of Historical Materialism*, vol. II: *The
Nation-State and Violence*. Cambridge: Polity Press.

Giddens, Anthony 1990) *The Consequences of Modernity*: Cambridge: Polity.

Goddard, John (1991) 'Networks of transactions', *Times Higher Education Supplement*, 22
February, p. vi (an extended version appeared in Kevin Robins (ed.), *Understanding
Information: Business, Technology and Geography*, pp. 178–201. London: Belhaven
Press, 1992).

Gouldner, Alvin W. (1978) 'The new class project 1', *Theory and Society*, 6 (2): 153–203; and
'The new class project 2', *Theory and Society*, 6 (3): 343–89 (published in 1979 as *The
Future of Intellectuals and the Rise of the New Class*. London: Macmillan).

Habermas, Jürgen (1962) *The Structural Transformation of the Public Sphere: an Inquiry into a Category of Bourgeois Society*, trans. Thomas Burger, with Frederick Lawrence. Cambridge: Polity Press, 1989.

Hall, Peter and Preston, Paschal (1988) *The Carrier Wave: New Information Technology and the Geography of Innovation, 1846–2003*. London: Unwin Hyman.

Harvey, David (1989) *The Condition of Postmodernity: An Enquiry into the Origins of Cultural Change*. Oxford: Blackwell.

Hepworth, Mark (1989) *Geography of the Information Economy*. London: Belhaven Press.

Hirschhorn, Larry (1984) *Beyond Mechanization: Work and Technology in a Postindustrial Age*. Cambridge, Mass.: MIT Press.

Jonscher, C. (1983) 'Information resources and economic productivity', *Information Economics and Policy*, 1: 13–35.

Karunaratne, Neil Dias (1986) 'Issues in measuring the information economy', *Journal of Economic Studies*, 13 (3): 51–68.

Landes, David (1969) *The Unbound Prometheus: Technological Change and Industrial Development in Western Europe from 1750 to the Present*. Cambridge: Cambridge University Press.

Lipietz, Alain (1987) *Mirages and Miracles: the Crises of Global Fordism*. London: Verso.

Maasoumi, Esfandias (1987) 'Information theory', in John Eatwell et al. (eds), *The New Palgrave: a Dictionary of Economics*, vol. 2, pp. 846–51. London: Macmillan.

Machlup, Fritz (1962) *The Production and Distribution of Knowledge in the United States*. Princeton, NJ: Princeton University Press.

Machlup, Fritz (1980) *Knowledge: its Creation, Distribution, and Economic Significance*, vol. 1: *Knowledge and Knowledge Production*. Princeton, NJ: Princeton University Press.

Machlup, Fritz (1984) *Knowledge: its Creation, Distribution and Economic Significance*, vol. 3: *The Economics of Information and Human Capital*. Princeton, NJ: Princeton University Press.

Martin, James (1978) *The Wired Society*. Englewood Cliffs, NJ: Prentice-Hall.

Martin, William J. (1988) 'The information society – idea or entity?', *Aslib Proceedings*, 40 (11/12): 303–9.

Melody, William (1987) 'Information: an emerging dimension of institutional analysis', *Journal of Economic Issues*, 21 (3): 1313–39.

Miles, Ian (1991) 'Measuring the future: statistics and the information age', *Futures*, 23 (9): 915–34.

Miles, Ian et al. (1990) *Mapping and Measuring the Information Economy*. Boston, Mass.: British Library.

Monk, Peter (1989) *Technological Change in the Information Economy*. London: Frances Pinter.

Mulgan, Geoff J. (1991) *Communication and Control: Networks and the New Economies of Communication*. Cambridge: Polity Press.

Naisbitt, John (1984) *Megatrends: Ten New Directions Transforming Our Lives*. London: Futura.

Norcott, J. and Walling, A. (1989) *The Impact of Microelectronics*. London: Frances Pinter.

Office of Technology Assessment (1990) *Critical Connections: Communications for the Future*. Washington, DC: US Congress.

Organisation for Economic Co-operation and Development (1981) *Information Activities, Electronics and Telecommunications Activities: Impact on Employment, Growth and Trade*. Information, Computer Communication Policy ICCP Ser. vol. 1. Paris: OECD.

Organisation for Economic Co-operation and Development (1986) *Trends in the Information Economy*. ICCP Ser. no. 11. Paris: OECD.

Perkin, Harold (1989) *The Rise of Professional Society: Britain since 1880*. London: Routledge.

Piore, Michael and Sabel, Charles (1984) *The Second Industrial Divide*. New York: Basic Books.

Porat, Marc Uri (1977a) *The Information Economy: Sources and Methods for Measuring the Primary Information Sector* (detailed industry reports). OT Special Publication 77-12(2). Washington, DC: US Department of Commerce, Office of Telecommunications.

Porat, Marc Uri (1977b) *The Information Economy: Definition and Measurement*. OT Special

Publication 77-12(1) (executive summary and major findings of the study). Washington, DC: US Department of Commerce, Office of Telecommunications.

Porat, Marc Uri (1978) 'Communication policy in an information society', in G.O. Robinson (ed.), *Communications for Tomorrow*, pp. 3–60. New York: Praeger.

Poster, Mark (1990) *The Mode of Information: Poststructuralism and Social Context*. Cambridge: Polity Press.

Robins, Kevin and Webster, Frank (1987) 'Information as capital: a critique of Daniel Bell', in Jennifer Daryl Slack and Fred Fejes (eds), *The Ideology of the Information Age*, pp. 95–117. Norwood, NJ: Ablex.

Robins, Kevin and Webster, Frank (1989) *The Technical Fix: Education, Computers and Industry*. London: Macmillan.

Roszak, Theodore (1986) *The Cult of Information: the Folklore of Computers and the True Art of Thinking*. Cambridge: Lutterworth Press.

Rubin, Michael Rogers and Taylor, Mary (1981) 'The US information sector and GNP:an input–output study', *Information Processing and Management*, 17 (4): 163–94.

Rubin, Michael Rogers and Taylor, Mary (1986) *The Knowledge Industry in the United States, 1960–1980*. Princeton, NJ: Princeton University Press.

Schiller, Herbert I. (1981) *Who Knows: Information in the Age of the Fortune 500*. Norwood, NJ: Ablex.

Schiller, Herbert I. (1984) *Information and the Crisis Economy*. Norwood, NJ: Ablex.

Shannon, Claude and Weaver, Warren (1949) *The Mathematical Theory of Communications*. Urbana: University of Illinois Press.

Stonier, Tom (1983) *The Wealth of Information: a Profile of the Post-industrial Economy*. London: Thames Methuen.

Stonier, Tom (1990) *Information and the Internal Structure of the Universe: an Exploration into Information Physics*. Berlin: Springer-Verlag.

Terkel, Studs (1977) *Working: People Talk about What They Do All Day and How They Feel about What They Do*. Harmondsworth: Peregrine.

Toffler, Alvin (1980) *The Third Wave*. New York: William Morrow.

Toffler, Alvin (1990) *Powershift: Knowledge, Wealth, and Violence at the Edge of the 21st Century*. New York: Bantam.

Useem, Michael (1984) *The Inner Circle: Large Corporations and the Rise of Business Political Activity in the US and UK*. New York: Oxford University Press.

Useem, Michael (1985) 'The rise of the political manager', *Sloan Management Review*, 27: 15–26.

Useem, Michael and Karabel, Jerome (1986) 'Pathways to top corporate management', *American Sociological Review*, 51: 184–200.

Webster, Frank (1995) *Images of the Information Society*. London: Routledge.

Webster, Frank and Robins, Kevin (1986) *Information Technology: a Luddite Analysis*. Norwood, NJ: Ablex.

Williams, Fred (ed.) (1988) *Measuring the Information Society*. London: Sage.

Woolgar, Steve (1985) 'Why not a sociology of machines? The case of sociology and artificial intelligence', *Sociology*, 19 (4): 557–72.

Woolgar, Steve (1988) *Science: the Very Idea*. Chichester: Ellis Horwood.

Young, John F. (1971) *Information Theory*. London: Butterworth.

Cultural globalisation: placing and displacing the West
John Tomlinson

It its relatively short career, the concept of globalisation has accumulated a remarkable string of both positive and negative connotations without having achieved a particularly clear denotation. Both enthusiasm and suspicion arise from often quite vague associations of the term, rather than from a clear consensus on its meaning. Indeed there are many different narratives of globalisation linked not just with different theoretical positions but with different political stances and positions of discursive power. In this study I explore some sensitive political–cultural issues to do with the globalisation process and start by briefly saying what I understand the process *most generally* to involve.

Globalisation here refers to the rapidly developing process of complex interconnections between societies, cultures, institutions and individuals world-wide. It is a social process which involves a compression of time and space, shrinking distances through a dramatic reduction in the time taken – either physically or representationally – to cross them, so making the world seem smaller and in a certain sense bringing human beings 'closer' to one another. As a recent United Nations report puts it, globalisation produces a 'global neighbourhood' (Commission on Global Governance, 1995). At the same time it is a process which 'stretches' social relations removing the relationships which govern our everyday lives from local contexts to 'distanciated' global ones. Thus, at a high level of abstraction, globalisation can be understood as a consequence of the institutional arrangements and technological accomplishments of social modernity, enabling and driving towards ever increasing 'action at distance' (Giddens, 1990, 1994a, b).

Although this may not be a comprehensive definition, it is sufficiently general to make it reasonably uncontroversial. Grasping globalisation in these rather abstract and general terms first has the other advantage of enabling us to see it as a *multidimensional* process which, 'like all significant

This chapter is taken from *The European Journal of Development Research*, 8 (1996), pp. 22–35.

social processes, unfolds in multiple realms of existence simultaneously' (Nederveen Pieterse, 1995: 45). Globalisation is heavy with implications for all spheres of social existence: the economic, the political, the environmental, the cultural. Isolating any one of these dimensions risks misrepresenting the complex interactional effects of the process as a whole but must be done if we are to put flesh on the bones of theoretical abstractions.

What I understand as the cultural dimension of globalisation, or 'cultural globalisation' for convenience, is the particular effects which these general social processes of time–space compression and distanciation have on that realm of practices and experience in which people symbolically construct meaning. I do not suppose that this cultural realm is in practice separable from other social realms and certainly not from the political-economic. Nevertheless, to argue we have to make, albeit artificial, distinctions whilst not losing sight of the points at which processes and logics in other realms become significantly determining: for example, the point at which cultural experiences depend on material resource distribution.

Given these caveats, we can talk of something called 'cultural globalisation'. But in what sort of effects do we recognise it? The first thing to say here is that the most 'obvious' scenario is the least plausible: globalisation does not seem set to usher in a single 'global culture' in the sense of the unification and pacification of humankind dreamed of by utopian thinkers. This is clear for a number of reasons.

To begin with, we should distinguish the two senses in which the general process of globalisation might be said to be 'unifying'. One refers to the way in which complex global interconnectedness makes people throughout the world subject tot he same broad determining forces and processes. For example, the economic fate of local communities – levels of economic activity, employment prospects, standard of living – is increasingly tied to a capitalist production system and market that is global in scope and operation. Similarly, our local environment (and consequently our health and physical quality of life) is subject to risks arising at a global level – global warming, ozone depletion, eco-disasters such as Chernobyl.

These aspects of globalisation represent a rapidly growing context of global interdependence that 'unites' us all, if only in the sense of making us all subject to certain common global influences, processes, opportunities and risks. But clearly this sort of 'structural unity' does not of itself imply the emergence of a common 'global culture' in the utopian sense. Even supposing the world *were* generally grasped in mundane cultural experiences as 'a single place' (Robertson, 1992) or as 'a world in which there are no others' (Giddens, 1990; Beck, 1992), it does not follow that this perception will bind people together, even in the face of mutual threats. As Ulrich Beck (1992: 49) puts it, to assume this would involve 'jumping too casually from the global nature of dangers to the commonality of political will and action'.

There are all sorts of factors inhibiting such a commonality: not least of which is the *unevenness* of the globalisation process itself. Benefits and risks are unevenly distributed and differentially experienced, both geographically and across social divisions of class, gender, age, by what Massey

(1994) refers to as the 'power geometry' of globalisation. We can add to these deeply structured social divisions the antagonisms which arise as globalising processes, such as labour migration, bring diverse cultural traditions into 'enforced proximity'. In the long term and in appropriate conditions of cultural dialogue this might make for increased cultural understanding and tolerance, but in the short term it is just as likely to be felt as the violent *collision* of cultures. As the Commission on Global Governance report (1995: 43) reminds us, 'neighbourhoods' are defined by proximity not by communal solidarity. We do not choose our neighbours so there is no guarantee that the 'global neighbourhood' will be a *good*, peaceful, integrated, *gemeinschaftliche* neighbourhood.

Consequently, there are all sorts of reasons to be sceptical about the emergence of a common global culture in the utopian sense. Yet there is another sense of a movement towards a global culture which seems more plausible to some critics at least. This dystopian version of a global culture supposes the emergence of cultural uniformity (as distinct from unity) as the global expansion of one dominant set of cultural practices and values – one version of how life is to be lived – at the expense of all others. One of the puzzling things about critical responses to globalisation is how this sort of 'pessimistic master scenario' (Hannerz, 1991) attracts adherents who would be extremely (and correctly) sceptical of the utopian view, for both are equally speculative and universalising.

What seems to make the pessimistic scenario more compelling is that it chimes with more general and long-standing critiques of both political– economic and cultural dominance. It is as if the cultural implications of globalisation were prefigured in existing critical discourses, particularly those that conflate global capitalism with Western imperialism. Whilst easy to sympathise with their broad political stance, it is not clear that such critical traditions provide an adequate conceptualisation of the precise cultural 'power geometry' that globalisation entails. In what follows I offer some reasons why we should resist reading cultural globalisation as, inevitably, 'Westernisation' and why we need a more nuanced critique.

Globalisation and Westernisation

The argument that equates globalisation with Westernisation can be out-lined quite briefly though it contains some crucial assumptions which will be unpacked presently. It goes like this. The culture that is currently emerging via globalisation is not a global culture in the utopian sense. It is not a culture that has arisen out of the common experiences and needs of all of humanity and it does not represent a confluence of divergent cultural practices. It does not draw equally on the world's many cultural traditions. It is neither inclusive, integrative, pluralist, balanced nor, in the best sense, synthesising. Rather, globalised culture is the enforced installation, world-wide, of one particular culture, born out of one particular, privileged historical experience. It is, in short, simply the global extension of *Western* culture.

The broad implications of this, and the causes of critical concern, can be understood in, roughly, four ways. First, the process is seen as homogenising; bringing standardised, commodified culture in its wake and threatening to obliterate the world's rich cultural diversity. Second, it is argued that it visits the various cultural ills of the West – its obsession with consumption practices, the fragmentation of cultural identity, its loss of central, stable consensual cultural values – on to other cultures. Third, both of these tendencies are seen as particular threats to what are regarded as the fragile and vulnerable 'traditional' cultures of peripheral, 'Third World' nations. Fourth, the process is viewed as part and parcel of wider forms of domination, such as those involved in the ever-widening grip of transnational capitalism and those involved in the maintenance of post-colonial relations of (economic and cultural) dependency.

These arguments will be recognised as belonging to a familiar critical tradition that predates the current discourse of globalisation: the critique of Western 'cultural imperialism'. Indeed, the discourse of cultural imperialism tended to set the scene for the initial critical reception of globalisation in the cultural sphere, casting the process as 'an aspect of the hierarchical nature of imperialism, that is the increasing hegemony of particular central cultures, the diffusion of American values, consumer goods and lifestyles' (Friedman, 1994: 195). Although, the general concerns of this critique are important and although it established crucial connections between political–economic analysis and cultural critique, the critique of cultural imperialism is a deeply problematic theoretical stance. The various problems arising from this peculiarly ambiguous and often confused critical discourse have since been widely discussed (Boyd-Barrett, 1982; Schlesinger, 1991; Tomlinson, 1991, 1995, 1996; Sinclair, 1992; Thompson, 1995). In so far as the general stance that casts cultural globalisation as 'Westernisation' draws implicitly on the assumptions of the cultural imperialism thesis, it is subject to many of the same objections.

There is not space here to recapitulate all these criticisms, many of which are familiar to cultural studies. Instead I will restrict myself to discussing two of the most common objections to the general idea of Westernisation with a view to distinguishing them from the specific, rather different line of criticism I follow later.

The first is that 'Westernisation' is a rather problematic conceptual category. When people talk about 'Westernisation' they are referring to a whole range of things: the consumer culture of Western capitalism with its now all-too-familiar icons (McDonald's, Coca-Cola, Levi Jeans), the spread of European languages (particularly English), styles of dress, eating habits, architecture and music, the adoption of an urban lifestyle based around industrial production, a pattern of cultural experience dominated by the mass media, a range of cultural values and attitudes regarding personal liberty, gender and sexuality, human rights, the political process, religion, scientific and technological rationality and so on. Whilst all these aspects of 'the West' can be found in various combinations throughout the world today, they do not constitute an indivisible package. Although it is correct to argue, as Cornelius Castoriadis (1991) does, that *social modernity* comes as a package and not as a 'menu' from which cultures may select, this does not imply that the transition from tradition to modernity has to follow, slavishly, the pattern of the West. The 'routes to and through modernity' (Therborn, 1995) and the 'strategies for entering and leaving modernity' (Garcia Canclini, 1995) are clearly not restricted to those taken by Western nation-states. To take but one example, an acceptance of the technological culture of the West and of aspects of consumerism may well co-exist with a vigorous rejection of its sexual permissiveness and its generally secular outlook, as is common in many Islamic societies.

Discriminating between various aspects of what is totalised as 'Westernisation' reveals a much more complex picture: some cultural goods have a broader appeal than others, some values and attitudes are easily adopted while others are actively resisted or found simply odd or irrelevant. And all this varies between societies and between different groupings and divisions within societies such as class, age, gender, urban/rural groups. The first objection to the idea of Westernisation therefore is that it is too broad a generalisation. Its rhetorical force is bought at the price of glossing over a multitude of complexities, exceptional cases and contradictions. This criticism also connects with another one: that ironically the Westernisation/homogenisation/cultural imperialism thesis itself displays a sort of Western ethnocentrism (Hannerz, 1991; Tomlinson, 1991, 1995). Ulf Hannerz puts this point nicely:

> The global homogenisation scenario focuses on things that we, as observers and commentators from the centre, are very familiar with: our fast foods, our soft drinks, our sitcoms. The idea that they are or will be everywhere, and enduringly powerful everywhere, makes our culture even more important and worth arguing about, and relieves us of the real strains of having to engage with other living, complicated, puzzling cultures. (Hannerz, 1991: 109)

A second set of objections concerns the way in which Westernisation suggests a rather crude model of the one-way flow of cultural influence. This criticism has rightly been the one most consistently made of the whole cultural imperialism idea. Culture, it is argued, simply does not transfer in this linear unidirectional way. Movement between cultural/geographical areas always involves translation, mutation and adaptation as the 'receiving culture' brings its own cultural resources to bear, in dialectical fashion, upon 'cultural imports' (Appadurai, 1990; Robins, 1991; Tomlinson, 1991; Garcia Canclini, 1995; Lull, 1995). For Latin America, Jesus Martin-Barbero (1993: 149) describes how 'the steady, predictable tempo of homogenising development [is] upset by the counter-tempo of profound differences and cultural discontinuities.'

A number of things follow from this argument. Most basically it implies that the Westernisation thesis severely underestimates the cultural resilience and dynamism of non-Western cultures, their capacity to 'indigenise' Western cultural imports, imbue them with different cultural meanings, and appropriate them actively rather than be passively swamped. It also draws attention to the *counter-flow* of cultural influence from the periphery to the centre, such as the case of 'world music' (Abu-Lughod, 1991) or some spheres of media production (Sinclair, 1992). Indeed, the 'core–periphery' model itself tends to disguise such counter-flows of cultural (and even political–economic) influence and it is on this basis that the model has recently been questioned by critics from the 'periphery'. For instance, Nestor Garcia Canclini (1995: 232) criticises the concentric figuration of power relations in the model as 'the abstract expression of an idealised imperial system' and calls for a far more nuanced, dialectical view of the processes of cultural interpenetration.

This dialectical conception of culture can be further developed so as to undermine the sense of the West as a stable homogeneous cultural entity. As Nederveen Pieterse (1995: 54) puts it: 'It . . . implies an argument with Westernisation: the West itself may be viewed as a mixture and Western culture as creole culture.' This is an important, if controversial, argument which I do not have the space to explore fully here. However, it is worth noting one aspect of this increasing 'hybridisation' of cultural experience in the West as it becomes more and more connected, via globalisation, with non-Western societies. This is the very practical consequences of the globalisation of capital: its displacement of huge numbers of people from their homes in Asia, Africa or Latin America to the West as either refugees or labour migrants. As Stuart Hall puts this:

> Driven by poverty, drought, famine, economic underdevelopment and crop failure, civil war and political unrest, regional conflict and arbitrary changes of political regime, the accumulating foreign indebtedness of their governments to Western banks, very large numbers of the poorer peoples of the globe have taken the 'message' of global consumerism at face value, and moved towards the places where 'the goodies' come from and where chances of survival are higher. In the era of global communications, the West is only a one-way airline charter ticket away. (Hall, 1992: 306–7)

The political–economic impact of such migrations is a much-discussed feature of the general process of globalisation: presenting Western nation-states with both cheap exploitable labour and the threat of demographic 'invasion'. The growing anxiety in the developed world over these population movements can be seen, for example, in the notoriously heavy policing of the US–Mexican border, and in the current debate about 'Fortress Europe'. However, the cultural implications of such population flows for the West are likely to be more complex and, eventually, more significant.

It has been argued that such flows – and the more general post-colonial diaspora – represent a sense in which the 'Other has installed itself within the very heart of the Western metropolis, [t]hrough a kind of reverse invasion, the periphery has now infiltrated the colonial core' (Robins, 1991: 32). Robins draws the implication that the self-confident, stable cultural identity of the West is being threatened. 'Through this irruption of empire, the certain and centred perspective of the old colonial order is confronted and confused' (1991: 33). The cultural interpenetration that globalisation brings, then, implies a collapse of both the physical and the cultural 'distance' necessary to sustain the myths of Western identity (and superiority) established via the binary oppositions and imaginary geographies (Said, 1978) of the high-colonial era.

While such criticisms, take some of the wind out of the sails of the Westernisation argument, at least in its most dramatic, polemical formulations, they do not entirely resolve the issue of the contemporary cultural power of the West. It can still be argued that, when all is said and done and all these criticisms met, Western cultural practices and institutions remain firmly in the driving seat of global cultural development. No amount of attention to the processes of cultural reception and translation, no anthropological scruples about the complexities of particular local contexts and no dialectical theorising can argue away the manifest power of Western capitalism, both as a general cultural configuration (the commodification of everyday experience, consumer culture) and as a specific set of global cultural industries (CNN, Times-Warner, News International). Is not this evidence of some sort of Western cultural hegemony? What ensues from this is a critical stand-off. Both positions are convincing within their own terms but do not seem precisely to engage. This could be read as another instance of the familiar divergence between political-economy and culturalist approaches but I do not believe we inhabit such discrete theoretical universes. It is surely possible to establish a more sophisticated, hermeneutically sensitive account of cultural globalisation whilst maintaining a keen critical sense of the 'power geometry' involved.

To take the argument a little further, I focus below on one particular, largely implicit, assumption that seems to be embedded in the idea of globalised culture as Westernised culture. This is the assumption that the process of globalisation is *continuous* with the long, steady, historical rise of Western cultural dominance. By this I mean that the sort of cultural power generally attributed to the West today is seen as of the same *order* of power that was manifest in the great imperial expansion of Europe powers from the seventeenth century onwards. Accordingly, this implicit understanding of globalised culture would see the massive and undeniable spread of Western cultural goods – 'Coca-colonisation' – as broadly part of the same process of domination as that which characterised the *actual* colonisation of much of the rest of the world by the West. I do not mean that no distinction is made between the coercive and often bloody history of Western colonial expansion and the 'soft' cultural imperialism of McDonald's hamburgers and Sesame Street. But these and many other instances of Western cultural power are often lumped together – 'totalised' – by the term 'Westernisation', giving rise to an impression of the inexorable advance of Western culture.

This particular totalising assumption needs to be unpacked and critically examined for two reasons. First, because it mistakes the nature of the globalisation process and second because it overstates the general cultural power of the West. I do not deny that the west is in a certain sense 'culturally powerful' but I want to suggest that this power, which is closely aligned with technological, industrial and economic power, is not the whole story. It does not amount to the implicit claim that 'the way of life' of the West is being installed, via globalisation, as the unchallengeable cultural model for all humanity.

In furtherance of this argument, I turn to two accounts which suggest that the globalisation process may be actively problematic for the continuation of Western cultural dominance: to signal not the 'triumph of the West', but its imminent decline.

Globalisation as the decline of the West

This position is advanced in the work of two social theorists, Anthony Giddens and Zygmunt Bauman. In neither case are the arguments developed at great length. I present them simply as suggestive ways of thinking against the grain of the arguments reviewed so far.

Within the broad conceptualisation of globalisation as a 'consequence of modernity', Anthony Giddens (1990, 1994a, b) writes of '[t]he gradual decline in European or Western global hegemony, the other side of which is the increasing expansion of modern influences world-wide', of 'the declining grip of the West over the rest of the world' or of 'the evaporating of the privileged position of the West' (1990: 51–3). What can he mean by this?

Put at its simplest, his argument is that, although the process of 'globalising modernity' may have *begun* in the extension of Western institutions (capitalism, industrialism, the nation-state system), their very global ubiquity now represents a decline in the differentials between the West and the rest of the world. In a sense the West's 'success' in disseminating its institutional forms represents a loss of its once unique social/cultural 'edge'. As Giddens puts the point in a more recent discussion:

> The first phase of globalisation was plainly governed, primarily, by the expansion of the West, and institutions which originated in the West. No other civilisation made anything like as pervasive an impact on the world, or shaped it so much in its own image . . . Although still dominated by Western power, globalisation today can no longer be spoken of only as a matter of one-way imperialism . . . increasingly there is no obvious 'direction' to globalisation at all and its ramifications are more or less ever present. The current phase of globalisation, then, should not be confused with the preceding one, whose structures it acts increasingly to subvert. (Giddens, 1994b: 96)

There are various ways in which this 'loss of privilege' and even the 'subversion' of Western power may be understood. It might be pointed out that certain parts of what we were used to calling the 'third world' are now actually more advanced, technologically, industrially and economically, than some parts of the West. The comparison here might be between the so-called 'Asian Tiger' economies and the economically depressed heavy-industrial regions of Europe or the US. And there might be a complex causal relationship between the rise and decline of such regions connected by a globalised capitalist market, as Giddens (1990: 65, 1994a: 65) suggests. Or, it might be argued that capitalism has no 'loyalty' to its birthplace and so provides no guarantees that the geographical patterns of dominance established in early modernity – the elective affinity between the interests of capitalism and of the West – will continue (Tomlinson, 1996). There are signs of this in the increasingly uneasy relation between the international capitalist markets and the governments of Western nation-states: the periodic currency crises besetting the Western industrial nations – the so-called 'black days' on the international currency markets. And a rather spectacular instance of the global capitalist system's unsentimental attitude to Western institutions could be seen in the débâcle of Britain's oldest merchant bank, Baring Brothers, in February 1995. Barings, founded in 1762 and bankers to the Queen, was destroyed within a few days' trading as a result of its high risk globalising speculations carried out via high speed electronically mediated (distanciated) dealings and this, appropriately enough, took place in Singapore on one of the world's youngest markets, that of South East Asia. The bank was finally sold to the Dutch group ING for one pound. It is hard to resist seeing this as emblematic of the old (complacent?) world of European imperial power finally being overtaken by the new world of decentred global capitalism in which events can be instantaneous and catastrophic.

To take a more broadly cultural example, the loss of privilege of the West can be seen in the shifting orientation and self-understanding of the academic discipline which claims 'culture' as its special province: anthropology. Giddens (1994b: 97f) offers an interesting discussion here arguing that anthropology in its formative stage was a prime example of the West's self-assured assumption of cultural superiority. On account of its 'evolutionary' assumptions, early taxonomising anthropology established itself as a practice to which the West had exclusive rights: the 'interrogation' of all other cultures. Other cultures were there, like the flora and fauna of the natural world, to be catalogued and observed. There was no sense of reflexivity in the project, no thought that they could ever *themselves* engage in the practice; they were categorised as 'if not inert, no more than a "subject" of enquiry' (1994b: 97).

Early anthropology was part of the cultural armoury of an imperialist West during 'early globalisation' precisely because it had not developed its inner logic. With the recognition of the integrity of traditions, the knowledgeability of all cultural agents and the growing sense of 'cultural relativism', anthropology has become both a more modest and humble undertaking and, significantly, a globalised practice. Present-day anthropologists, Giddens suggests, have to approach their study in the role of the *ingénu* – the innocent abroad – rather than as the confident explorer and taxonomist. Without the assurance of a taken-for-granted superior cultural 'home-base', anthropological study becomes a matter of 'learning how to go on' rather than of detached, *de haut en bas* interrogation. Not only this, it becomes clear that in this later phase of globalisation, *all* cultures have a thoroughly reflexive anthropological sensibility: 'In British Columbia the present day Kwakiutl are busy reconstructing their traditional culture using

[Franz] Boas's monographs as their guide, while Australian Aboriginals and other groups across the world are contesting land-rights on the basis of parallel anthropological studies' (Giddens, 1994b: 100). The trajectory of the development of anthropology which 'leads to its effective dissolution today' (1994b: 97) could stand more broadly for the way in which current globalisation subverts and undermines the cultural power of the West from which it first emerged.

Whilst holding on to these ideas, I now want to comment briefly on an interesting distinction that Zygmunt Bauman makes between the 'global' and the 'universal':

> Modernity, once deemed itself *universal*. Now it thinks of itself instead as *global*. Behind the change of term hides a watershed in the history of modern self-awareness and self-confidence. Universal was to be the rule of reason – the order of things that would replace the slavery to passions with the autonomy of rational beings, superstition and ignorance with truth, tribulations of the drifting plankton with self-made and thoroughly monitored history-by-design. 'Globality', in contrast, means merely that everyone everywhere may feed on McDonald's hamburgers and watch the latest made-for-TV docudrama. Universality was a proud project, a Herculean mission to perform. Globality in contrast, is a meek acquiescence to what is happening 'out there' . . . . (Bauman, 1995: 24)

Mapping this on to the distinction which Giddens and others (Hall, 1991) make between early and late phases of globalisation, the key difference becomes that between a Western culture with pretensions to universalism and one without. The globalisation of the West's cultural practices is now simply occurring without any real sense that this is part of its collective project or 'mission', or that these practices are, indeed, the tokens of an ideal human civilisation. Early globalisation involves the self-conscious cultural project of universality, whilst late globalisation – globality – is mere ubiquity.

It may be argued that Bauman erects a rather contrived dualism here between the 'high cultural' project of enlightenment rationalism and some rather specific 'popular cultural' practices. The specific doubts he detects that now 'sap the ethical confidence and self-righteousness of the West' tend to be the preoccupations of the intellectual. These doubts echo those of the Frankfurt School (Adorno and Horkheimer, 1979) about the capacity of the Enlightenment project ever to deliver full emancipation for all human beings; doubts about 'whether the wedlock between the growth of rational control and the growth of social and personal autonomy, that crux of modern strategy, was not ill-conceived from the start' (Bauman, 1995: 29). Whatever reservations we may have about centring the discourse on one particular Western high-cultural narrative, Bauman's stress on the declining cultural self-image and self-confidence of the West is an important one.

We can read the idea of the loss of Western self-confidence in more general and mundane ways. Bauman's description of globality as 'a meek acquiescence to what is happing "out there"' may be a little overstated, but it does grasp something of the spirit in which ordinary people in the West probably experience the global spread of their 'own' cultural practices. Indeed a lot probably hangs on the extent to which Westerners actually feel 'ownership' of the sorts of cultural practices that, typically, get globalised. This is an immensely complicated issue but my guess is that there is only a very low level of correspondence between people's routine interaction with the contemporary 'culture industry' and their sense of having a distinctive *Western* cultural identity, let alone feeling proud or proprietorial about it. It seems more likely that things like McDonald's restaurants are experienced as simply 'there' in our cultural environments: things which we use and have become familiar and perhaps comfortable with, but which we do not – either literally or culturally – 'own'.

In this sense the decline of Western cultural self-confidence may align with the structural properties of globalising modernity referred to in the introduction; the 'disembedding' (to use another of Giddens' terms) of practices and institutions from contexts of local to global control. In a world in which increasingly our mundane 'local' experience is governed by events and processes at a distance, it may become difficult to maintain a distinctive sense of (at least 'mass') culture as 'the way we do things' in the West; to understand these practices as having any particular connection with our specific histories and traditions. Thus, far from grasping globalised culture in the self-assured, 'centred', proprietorial way that may have been associated with, say, the *Pax Britannica*, late-modern Westerners may experience it as a largely undifferentiated, 'de-centred', 'placeless' modernity to which they relate effortlessly, but without much sense of either personal involvement or of 'local' cultural control.

Here I would connect both Bauman's and Giddens' perspectives with a broader perception that globalisation now increasingly 'displaces' or 'deterritorialises' cultural practices and experiences. In Nestor Garcia Canclini's (1995: 229) descriptions, deterritorialisation refers to 'the loss of the "natural" relation of culture to geographical and social territories'. This, of course, refers to the general 'global' case and, in Garcia Canclini's work, to the hybrid cultures of 'border zones' straddling the first and third worlds. But it also has a particular implication for the cultural career of the West. For though cultural production may remain concentrated and centred in the West, and though Western cultural commodities may be globally ubiquitous, it does not follow – as it may have done in an earlier period – that these production and consumption practices serve to reinforce territorially based identities. In so far as the cultural hegemony of Western nation-states has historically depended on such robust constructions of territorial (national-cultural) identity, it could be argued that in one sense they have most to lose from globalisation.

Conclusion

The arguments reviewed in the preceding section are suggestive rather than conclusive ones and they leave many issues unresolved. In particular the complex issue of the phenomenology of cultural identity in a globalised world – and the implications of this for transformations in cultural power – requires far more extensive and nuanced treatment than has been possible here. What has been offered is simply a general sketch of alternative ways of thinking about the difficult cultural issues forced upon us by the globalisation process.

At the risk of labouring the point, it is worth stressing the limitations of the position advanced here. Nothing stated here is meant to deny – or wish away – the present manifest *economic* dominance of Western nation-states, nor even that particular, limited, sense of 'cultural' power that proceeds from this: the power of Western transnational capitalism to distribute its goods around the world. Nor do these arguments entail the idea of a simple 'turning of the tables': the 'decline of the West' does not mean the inevitable 'rise' of any other particular hegemonic power (no matter how tempting it is to speculate about the 'Asian Tigers' and so forth). In the short term at least, much of the 'Third World' will probably continue to be marginalised in the globalisation process (McGrew, 1992; Massey, 1994). Given this, the idea of the 'decline of the West' might well seem rather premature.

But, looking *beyond* the short term, these reflections do suggest that what is happening in globalisation is not a process firmly in the cultural grip of the West and that the global future is much more radically open than the discourses of homogenisation and Westernisation suggest. Moreover, the processes of global modernity seem to possess an inbuilt 'accelerator' – a feature of the reflexivity of modern institutions – which makes cultural transformations much more rapid in their impact: exponentially more rapid than the 'glacial time' of cultural transformation in 'traditional societies'. This amounts to a present historical context of great uncertainty, one in which speculation is particularly risky. But it also suggests that we should not assume that the same patterns of domination of the West over the rest are set to continue, even in the proximate future.

References

Abu-Lughod, J. (1991) 'Going beyond global babble', in A.D. King (ed.), *Culture, Globalization and the World System*, pp. 131–8. London: Macmillan.

Adorno, T. and Horkheimer, M. (1979) *Dialectic of Enlightenment*. London: Verso.

Appadurai, A. (1990) 'Disjuncture and difference in the global cultural economy', in M. Featherstone (ed.), *Global Culture*, pp. 295–310. London: Sage.

Bauman, Z. (1995) *Life in Fragments*. Oxford: Blackwell.

Beck, U. (1992) *Risk Society: Towards a New Modernity*. London: Sage.

Boyd-Barrett, O. (1982) 'Cultural dependency and the mass media', in M. Gurevitch et al. (eds), *Culture, Society and the Media*, pp. 174–95. London: Methuen.

Castoriadis, C. (1991) *Philosophy, Politics, Autonomy*. Oxford: Oxford University Press.

Commission on Global Governance (1995) *Our Global Neighbourhood: the Report of the Commission on Global Governance*. Oxford: Oxford University Press.

Featherstone, M., Lash, S. and Robertson, R. (eds) (1995) *Global Modernities*. London: Sage.

Friedman, J. (1994) *Cultural Identity and Global Process*. London: Sage.

Garcia Canclini, N. (1995) *Hybrid Culture*. Minnesota, MN: University of Minnesota Press.

Giddens, A. (1990) *The Consequences of Modernity*. Cambridge: Polity Press.

Giddens, A. (1994a) *Beyond Left and Right*. Cambridge: Polity Press.

Giddens, A. (1994b) 'Living in a post-traditional society', in U. Beck, A. Giddens and S. Lash (eds), *Reflexive Modernization*, pp. 56–109. Cambridge: Polity Press.

Hall, S. (1991) 'The local and the global: globalization and ethnicities', in A.D. King (ed.), *Culture, Globalization and the World-System*, pp. 19–30. London: Macmillan.

Hall, S. (1992) 'The question of cultural identity', in S. Hall, D. Held and T. McGrew (eds), *Modernity and its Futures*, pp. 274–316. Cambridge: Polity Press.

Hall, S., Held, D. and McGrew, T. (eds) (1992) *Modernity and its Futures*. Cambridge: Polity Press.

Hannerz, U. (1991) 'Scenarios for peripheral cultures', in A.D. King (ed.), *Culture, Globalization and the World System*, pp. 107–28. London: Macmillan.

Lull, J. (1995) *Media, Communication, Culture: a Global Approach*. Cambridge: Polity Press.

McGrew, T. (1992) 'A global society?', in S. Hall, D. Held and T. McGrew (eds), *Modernity and its Futures*, pp. 61–116. Cambridge: Polity Press.

Martin-Barbero, J. (1993) *Communication, Culture and Hegemony*. London: Sage.

Massey, D. (1994) *Space, Place and Gender*. Cambridge: Polity Press.

Nederveen Pieterse, J. (1995) 'Globalization as hybridization', in M. Featherstone, S. Lash and R. Robertson (eds), *Global Modernities*, pp. 45–68. London: Sage.

Robertson, R. (1992) *Globalization: Social Theory and Global Culture*. London: Sage.

Robins, K. (1991) 'Tradition and translation: national culture in its global context', in J. Corner and S. Harvey (eds), *Enterprise and Heritage*, pp. 21–44. London: Routledge.

Said, E. (1978) *Orientalism*. London: Routledge and Kegan Paul.

Schlesinger, P. (1991) *Media, State and Nation*. London: Sage,

Sinclair, J. (1992) 'The decentering of globalization: televisa-ion and Globo-ization', in E. Jacka (ed.), *Continental Shift: Globalisation and Culture*, pp. 99–116. Double Bay, NSW: Local Consumption Publications.

Therborn, G. (1995) 'Routes to/through modernity', in M. Featherstone, S. Lash and R. Robertson (eds), *Global Modernities*, pp. 124–39. London: Sage.

Thompson, J.B. (1995) *The Media and Modernity*. Cambridge: Polity Press.

Tomlinson, J. (1991) *Cultural Imperialism: a Critical Introduction*. London: Pinter.

Tomlinson, J. (1995) 'Homogenisation and globalization', *History of European Ideas*, 20 (4–6): 891–7.

Tomlinson, J. (1996) 'Cultural globalization and cultural imperialism', in A. Mohammadi and R. Johnson (eds), *International Communication in a Postmodern World*. London: Sage.

10

The global media in the late 1990s
Edward Herman and Robert McChesney

In the 1990s, while media systems are still primarily national and local, the media that operate across borders continue to strengthen and have a steadily greater impact on indigenous systems. The dominant players treat the media markets as a single global market with local subdivisions. The rapidity of their global expansion is explained in part by equally rapid reduction or elimination of many of the traditional institutional and legal barriers to cross-border transactions. They have also been facilitated by technological changes such as the growth of satellite broadcasting, video-cassette recorders, fiber optic cable and phone systems. Also critically important has been the rapid growth of cross-border advertising, trade and investment, and thus the demand for media and other communication services. In this chapter we address the state of the global media system at the end of the century and the main characteristics and trajectory of the still rapidly changing global media market.

Overview of media globalization

This chapter is taken from The Global Media: the New Missionaries of Corporate Capitalism (London, Cassell, 1997), pp. 41–69.

Media and entertainment outlays are growing at a faster rate than GDP almost everywhere in the world and significantly faster in the Far East and Central Europe.[1] A 1996 survey of teenagers in television-owning house-holds in forty-one nations finds that they watch on average six hours of television per day, and nowhere in the survey is the figure under five hours.[2] This has been a boon for the US entertainment industry, as it dominates the global market for the production of television programming as well as film. Employment in the entertainment industry in Los Angeles alone has more than doubled from 53,000 in 1988 to 112,000 in 1995.[3] In Germany, for example, the twenty-one most heavily viewed films and nine of the top ten video rentals for 1995 were produced by US film studios.[4] 'The overseas market is a lot like the domestic market was 15 years ago', one media executive states. 'It's wide open.'[5] As the US market is the most mature in media and entertainment consumption, it is the global market that is drawing industry attention. One media industry analyst concludes that 'the long-term growth opportunities overseas dwarf what we think is likely to occur in the United States.'[6]

This growth trend is not without its interruptions; for example, in 1996, after a decade of increased output, the film studios reduced production in the face of a saturated market and some short-term losses.[7] The global music industry too had a sharp fall in its rate of growth in 1996, after years of double digit rates. The dominance of the United States should also not be exaggerated. Some of the key firms producing media and entertainment fare in the United States itself have significant foreign ownership. Non-US media conglomerates, including the Japanese Sony (no. 5), Canadian Seagram (no. 15), Dutch Philips (no. 18), and Australian News Corporation (no. 27) all rank on the top thirty list of the non-US firms with the largest US investments.[8] Many other non-US firms are participating fully in the media and entertainment boom around the world, particularly though not exclusively through the control of TV stations, cable systems, and other distribution channels.

Moreover, a major lesson of the 1990s has been that although Hollywood fare in film, television, and music has considerable appeal worldwide, this appeal has its limits. In Western Europe, the top-rated TV programs are nearly always domestically produced, and there is widespread recognition that audiences often prefer home-grown programs, if these have the resources to compete with Hollywood productions.[9] There has also been an increase in the export of cultural products by nations other than the United States in the 1990s, not only from Europe but from the developing nations.[10] Yet this only qualifies the mainly US domination of the global media market; it does not challenge it. A 1996 advertising industry survey of 20,000 consumers in nineteen nations revealed that 41.5 percent of the respondents considered US cultural fare to be excellent or very good, more than twice the figure for any other nation.[11] The United States enjoyed a trade surplus with Europe in media fare of $6.3 billion in 1995, more than tripling the media trade surplus between the US and Europe for 1988.[12] 'In Europe', one leading Italian film producer acknowledged, with the slight exception of France, 'we've been 90% colonized [by Hollywood] in terms of quantity of product on the market.'[13]

The leading global media firms are producing fare in languages other than English. For example, MTV, the global music television service, has begun to differentiate its content around the world and incorporate local music.[14] After the initial campaign to establish a pan-Asian television service faltered for lack of cultural specificity, its format was changed to incorporate local programming and languages.[15] 'We soon learned that one just can't pour Western programs down people's throats', an executive of News Corporation's Asian Star Television Ltd acknowledged.[16] A

Disney executive states that 'For all children, the Disney characters are local characters and this is very important. They always speak local languages . . . The Disney strategy is to "think global, act local".'[17] As US-based media giants earn a larger share of revenues abroad, they increasingly target different regions and nations of the world, and they enter joint ventures with local producers. Partially as a result, much of the domestically produced media content around the world increasingly has the flavor of Hollywood.[18]

The three media industries that entered the 1990s with the most developed global markets – book publishing, recorded music, and film production – have continued their growth in sometimes booming global oligopolistic markets. Book publishing is less concentrated than film or music, primarily due to language differences, yet the ten largest firms accounted for 25 percent of 1995's global sales of $80 billion. The world's three largest book publishers are owned by Bertelsmann, Time Warner, and Viacom, respectively the world's third, first, and fourth largest media conglomerates. Most of the other global book publishing giants are also affiliated with global media powers like News Corporation, Hachette, and Pearson. The top three book publishers alone accounted for over $10 billion in 1995 sales. The 1990s have been a period of rapid corporate consolidation both globally and in national markets. In Spain, France, and Germany, for example, the three largest book publishers command over 50 percent of the market. Industry analysts expect further consolidation, with the largest global publishers accounting for an increasing share of the market.[19]

Recorded music is the most concentrated global media market. The leading five firms, in order of global market share, are PolyGram (19 percent), Time Warner (18 percent), Sony (17 percent), EMI (15 percent), and Bertelsmann (13 percent). The only other player of any note is Universal (formerly MCA) (9 percent).[20] All but EMI are part of larger global media conglomerates. Some estimates show these six firms' combined sales as accounting for over 90 percent of the global market, while others place it closer to 80 percent.[21] The market boomed in the early and mid-1990s with a 10 percent increase in sales in 1995 to raise global revenues to $40 billion. Recorded music has successfully shifted to digital format as compact discs now account for 70 percent of revenues.[22] Global sales grew by 38 percent from 1992 to 1995. With western markets relatively mature, sales in the developing world are growing more rapidly.[23] A music industry trade publication forecasts that China's market for recorded music will increase by 900 percent between 1994 and 2001, to over $2.1 billion. In anticipation of this shift in demand, the 'big five' music firms and Universal are increasing their number of recording artists in the developing world.[24]

Global film production in the 1990s is dominated by the studios owned by Disney, Time Warner, Viacom, Universal (owned by Seagram), Sony, PolyGram (owned by Philips), MGM, and News Corporation. All but MGM are parts of large global media conglomerates. There are large and sometimes subsidized national film industries, but with only a few exceptions the commercial export market is effectively the province of these eight firms, several of which are not owned by Americans but all of which are part of 'Hollywood'. After the burst of US expansion in the early 1980s, the percentage of non-US revenue for the film industry increased from 33 percent in 1984 to over 50 percent in 1993, where it has remained.[25] 'The international business is exploding', a Hollywood distributor stated in 1995, predicting that by 2000 non-US revenues will account for 60–70 percent of studio income.[26]

Several factors suggest that global growth rates for the film studios will remain high for the foreseeable future. First, there is the construction of thousands of US-inspired (often US-owned) multiscreen theater complexes across the planet. 'Most of the world is severely underscreened', one multiplex builder observed, and multiscreen theaters 'provide an environment that attracts audiences like magnets.' Some of the construction is being carried out by companies like Viacom, Universal, and Time Warner, which also produce films. 'Building theaters is kind of like drilling oil wells, only you get more gushers', a film industry analyst concludes.[27] In Asia, where much of the construction is taking place, Time Warner forecasts annual growth rates of over 20 percent for the coming decade.[28] Second, the widespread diffusion of videocassette players has spurred the home video market, which brought in $8.8 billion, or over half of the film studios' 1995 global income.[29] Some expect the launching of digital video disks in the late 1990s to have the same stimulate effect on film sales in the late 1990s that the launching of CDs had for music sales in the late 1980s and early 1990s.[30] Third, the rise of multichannel commercial television broadcasting has created enormous demand for Hollywood fare. Several multibillion dollar deals signed in 1996 provided nothing short 'of a windfall for major Hollywood studios'.[31] The future may even be brighter; Universal's president states that 'Television in Europe is poised for extraordinary growth.'[32] Indeed, by 1997 Hollywood was in the midst of its greatest expansion in the number of 'sound stages', or production studios for film, television, and video production in its history.[33]

The vast surge in demand may well have laid the foundation for an increase in worldwide film production. At the same time, however, the global film market rewards the largest budgeted films disproportionately. A 1996 *Variety* survey of 164 Hollywood releases concluded that films with budgets greater than $60 million tended to be far more profitable than less expensive film.[34] In 1996 just 13 of the 417 films released by Hollywood studios accounted for nearly 30 percent of total box office.[35] While the main studios are increasing their output to meet demand, they are concentrating upon the production of 'blockbusters'.[36] With the financial stakes so high, the implications for filmmaking tend to be 'homogenization of content and less risk taking', as one Hollywood producer acknowledges.[37]

One entertainment genre that needs little differentiation for global commercial success is violence, and Hollywood has established itself as the preeminent producer of 'action' fare. 'Kicking butt', one US media executive states, 'plays everywhere'. The major US studios find violent fare as close to risk-free as anything they produce, and they have little trouble locating non-US interests willing to cover a share of production costs in return for distribution or broadcasting rights in their nation or region. 'For the US studio it's an excellent deal', the same executive concludes. 'Even if the show bombs, the production cost is not drastic. If it hits, it's all upside.' And with non-US sales playing a larger role in studio planning, violent fare for film and television looks set to command a larger segment of Hollywood output.[38]

The commercialization of global television

It is with this worldwide surge of commercial television that the decisive changes in global media in the 1990s are most apparent. The emergence of satellites and cable distribution of programming have dramatically increased the number of channels available in most nations in the 1990s. In Europe, for example, cable and satellite television revenues increased on average by 30 percent annually from 1990 to 1994, and are expected to grow at 25 percent per annum for the balance of the decade.[39] This is also the trend worldwide. 'The marketplace for subscriber-supported TV is in a vigorous upturn', a Merrill Lynch industry analyst concludes.[40] Goldman Sachs forecasts that the percentage of global TV households with either cable or satellite will increase between 1995 and 2000 from 26 percent to 38 percent.[41] Politically, the strong trend toward deregulation, privatization, and commercialization of media and communication has opened up global commercial broadcasting in a manner that represents a startling break with past practice. Throughout the world the commercialization of national television systems has been regarded as 'an integral part' of economic liberalization programs.[42]

The commercialization and deregulation of national television systems worldwide began in the 1970s and 1980s, but it reached full speed in the 1990s. It has taken place at the expense of the previously dominant state-run systems. One must not exaggerate the decline of public broadcasting systems, as many still earn large audiences in competitive environments.[43] Yet even successful public systems like those in Germany and Sweden saw their audiences cut by nearly half between 1990 and 1995.[44] In the near future most nations with viable public systems will have access to literally hundreds of other channels. In this context it seems inevitable that the public broadcasting service will reach an ever-shrinking audience. If the political environment were different, and there was organized public support for viable nonprofit and noncommercial broadcasting, these services might be able to weather the multi-channel onslaught. But in the current climate, where markets are presumed to 'give the people what they want', and commercial media firms have increasing political power, most public broadcasting systems find themselves under siege.[45] If public broadcasters continue on the current course of shrinking audiences it is just a matter of time before their public subsidy will be terminated. If public broadcasters attempt to mimic commercial broadcasters to increase their audience size, by that route also they lose legitimate claim to a public subsidy.[46] And as public broadcasters lost their public subsidy, it requires them to become commercial enterprises in order to succeed.[47] In the United States, for example, the national Public Broadcasting System now previews its primetime schedule for leading New York advertising agencies in a manner similar to the commercial networks.[48]

The response of the BBC and the Australian Broadcasting Corporation to this dilemma has been to go commercial globally in order to subsidize their domestic public service activities.[49] The BBC's new chairman was selected in 1996 'to spearhead the BBC's international commercial activities', according to the government minister responsible for the appointment.[50] According to *Variety*, the BBC 'has placed an expansionist commercial strategy right at the heart of its survival plan'.[51] The BBC has established alliances with Pearson PLC, Cox Communications, and other firms to produce and distribute global television services.[52] The BBC launched the BBC World Service Television as a global commercial venture in 1991. The point is to capitalize upon the BBC brand name, considered to be the second most famous in the world after that of Coca-Cola. It has already been effectively banned in China and Saudi Arabia, unlike the explicitly commercial television news services, because BBC journalism offended the rulers of those nations.[53] In 1996 the BBC established joint ventures valued at close to $1 billion with TCI-controlled Flextech and the US Discovery Communications (in which TCI has a 49 percent interest) to create over one dozen commercial television channels for global television markets.[54] Whether the BBC will be able to maintain public service standards while becoming an aggressively commercial enterprise remains to be seen. It is clear that the BBC has decided that its survival depends more upon locating a niche in the global media market than in generating political support for public service broadcasting. At any rate, this is an option that only a few public broadcasters from the wealthy (and arguably English-speaking) nations can pursue. For the balance of global public service broadcasters, the future would seem to be one of increasing domestic commercialization, marginalization, or both.

In the late 1990s, the trend toward a global commercial television industry and the consolidation of a global media market is taking a quantum leap with the advance of digital television. Satellites already provide digital television, cable companies are beginning to employ digital converters, and terrestrial broadcasting will eventually switch over, in the next 10 or 20 years as all TV sets become exclusively digital. Although it is unclear what the eventual mix will be between satellite, cable, and terrestrial digital broadcasters, it is clear that digital television is a radical departure from its analogue predecessor. The shift to digital television improves technical quality, lowers production costs, and instantly expands the number of channels by a factor of five or six (and by the year 2000 by a factor of ten). When transmitted by satellite directly to minuscule home dishes, digital broadcasting can provide several hundred channels in 1997, and may deliver several thousand channels within a decade.[55] By the year

2000 nearly twenty million US households are projected to have satellite dishes for digital television, and it will be a $7 billion market.[56] By 2004 Nielsen Media Research projects that nearly thirty million US households will have digital satellite services and another seventy million predominately digital cable.[57] Growth should be comparable in Britain, which is a few years ahead of most of the rest of Europe.[58]

The exact contours of a satellite digital television universe remain unclear, but a few points are evident. First, only a fraction of the channels will have the programming traditionally associated with television. 'Research shows most people only watch eight to ten channels', one executive noted.[59] The precise number will be determined by what is commercially viable, not what is technologically possible. The experience with cable television suggests that a handful of genres will proliferate and the vast majority of the channels will be provided by the very largest media firms.[60] 'Mergers and consolidations', *Variety* observes, 'have transformed the cable-network marketplace into a walled-off community controlled by a handful of media monoliths.'[61] So what will occupy all the channel capacity of these digital satellite systems, or even the 200 or so channels of digital cable television? Many of the channels will be devoted to 'near video on demand', in which one film may be run over a number of channels with starting times separated by only 10 or 15 minutes. This pay-per-view principle is also being widely applied to live sporting events. Many channels will be devoted to home shopping and explicit product marketing. Satellites can also broadcast digital data – such as electronic newspapers, multimedia or World Wide Web Internet sites – to businesses or to home subscribers' computers or TV sets.[62]

Second, within each of these regions the nature of the technology and the market is such that usually only one or two firms control the market. The fixed costs of establishing a digital satellite (or cable) television system are very high; it can only become profitable through covering wide areas and having a large market. Likewise, with current and foreseeable technology there are only a few optimal orbital locations for digital satellite broadcasting for each continent or global region; in the case of the United States and Mexico, for example, four slots at most are available to provide a viable service.[63] Although most digital systems will offer a similar array of commercial cable channels, those firms that are first to develop a marketable service and that can also provide a range of sporting events and films that are unavailable on competitor services have a distinct advantage. This has been the traditional pattern with cable and analogue satellite broadcasting and it appears to hold true for digital broadcasting. Technically, there is no reason that the digital broadcasting service providers need to act as anything more than distributors of other firms' television channels. However, the greatest profit is obtained when the system providers use their position to broadcast their own channels and programming as well.

Accordingly, the major global media firms are in the midst of what has been characterized as a 'winner-take-all battle' of digital star wars'. Although the full development of digital satellite television may take a decade or more, the crucial question of which firms will control these markets will probably be quickly determined.[64] Major joint ventures, usually centered in firms like News Corporation or General Motors' DirecTV, are in locked battle across the planet. In many nations and regions, a single firm already has a monopoly position and will likely scare away challengers. In most other regions or nations there will only be two or three contenders. The most competitive market is the United States. DirecTV has the early lead, but it faces challenges from Primestar, owned by General Electric and the major US cable companies, USSB, owned by Hubbard Broadcasting, Dow Jones and others, and Sky Television, a joint venture of News Corporation, MCI, and Echostar.[65] The logic of this market, however, suggests that digital satellite television systems will soon be regional oligopolies, if not duopolies or even monopolies.

The emergence of global satellite television has led to a rearrangement of the global news industry. The 'big four' western news agencies – AP, UPI, Reuters, and AFP – still dominate the global print market while Reuters TV (formerly Visnews) and Worldwide Television News remain the dominant global television news agencies, but satellite television has brought into existence regional and global news channels. The most prominent is CNN International, owned by Time Warner, which reaches over 200 countries and the vast majority of the world populations. Although subsidized news services like the BBC World Service and the Voice of America still provide global news in numerous languages via the noncommercial and unprofitable channels of shortwave, they are battling to maintain their subsidies in a post-Cold War era; for example, Radio Canada, which broadcast in eight languages to 126 nations over the shortwave, was closed down in March 1997.[66] The commercial satellite news channels are where the growth has been occurring and where much, much more is to be expected.[67] At present they tend to reach a small elite audience, but they are increasingly becoming major providers of global journalism.[68] The BBC through its commercial World Service Television, and the remaining European public broadcasters through Euronews, have attempted to provide alternatives to CNN, with limited success.[69] One executive warns that Euronews may never gain the capital it needs to survive 'unless it decides to "commercialise" itself fully'.[70]

As advertising-supported vehicles, global news channels like CNN, directed at business and the global upper-middle classes, have proved quite lucrative.[71] With the digital increase in the number of channels, CNN faces increased competition, including two more global news channels launched in 1996, one by News Corporation and the other by NBC and Microsoft. As was the case with CNN, both plan to move quickly from the US market to global service by 1997 or 1998.[72] CNN already has a Spanish-language service for Latin America and all the news channels are contemplating plans to broadcast in dominant regional languages as well as English. Roger Ailes, chairman of News Corporation's Fox News Channel, is explicit in stating that it will be directed at the needs of advertisers and the affluent audiences to which advertisers are attracted.[73] These news channels also offer their owners important political leverage in shaping public opinion and dealing with governments.[74] As a TCI executive acknowledges, much of TCI's and News Corporation's interest in a global television news channel is that 'they both know that news means control and a tremendous amount of influence.'[75] In all likelihood only two or three services can survive the anticipated round of competition; a risk factor for potential entrants that evidently caused Disney to cancel its plans to launch a news channel in 1996.

The global trend to deregulation

These rapid changes in the global media system have been based on a 'new information order' of market freedom, and they have strengthened market rule. In the United States, for example, the First Amendment to the constitution has been increasingly interpreted as a statute that protects commercial speech from government interference.[76] Even the limited regulatory standards and enforcement of antitrust statutes to prevent media concentration that existed in the past have lessened to the point of irrelevance.[77] The 1996 US Telecommunications Act, as one observer noted, opened up a 'Pandora's box of consolidation in the media industry', as deregulation was the order of the day.[78] Encouraged by powerful media lobbies, this commercial spirit permeates all national debates concerning media. It also is true for regional bodies like the European Union, the home of outstanding public broadcasting systems but now devoted to establishing a single European market for commercial media. As a rule of thumb, the only basis for substantive media policy debates at the national level is when there are conflicts between powerful media interests. So it is that domestic media interests have been able to get some statutory protection from global media encroachment in the form of quotas and the like. But these campaigns for domestic protection have met with considerable resistance; in every nation there are powerful forces pressing the case for full integration into the global media market.[79]

At the international level, the dominant institutions and trade agreements continue to work toward the elimination of all barriers to the market. When the United States and Mexico signed a pact in 1996 to open up their respective satellite TV markets to the other, Federal Communications Commission Chair Reed Hundt termed the deal 'consistent with the spirit of NAFTA', the regional free trade deal.[80] As the media have become increasingly central to the world economy, media policy matters have become the province of organizations like the IMF and the WTO. The IMF is committed to encouraging the establishment of commercial media globally to better serve the needs of a market economy. The WTO's mission is to encourage a single global market for commercial media, and to oppose barriers to this, however noble the intent.[81] In what may be a precedent-setting case, in January 1997 the WTO ruled that Canada could not impose special taxes or tariffs on US magazine publishers to protect Canadian periodicals. This was interpreted as strengthening 'Washington's case against cultural protection trade policies used by many other countries'.[82] In view of the global nature of the communication industries and technologies, there is an increasing acceptance of reduced national government control over vital areas of communication.[83] As a further case in point, the Geneva-based court of the European Free Trade Association ruled that Norway could not prohibit advertising aimed at children, as is the Norwegian practice,[84] on satellite broadcasts beamed into that country. Similarly, in 1996 the European Court of Justice informed Sweden that it could not ban advertising to children if the broadcasts originated in another EU state.[85] Likewise, EU rules require that France permit TV broadcasts of sporting events with liquor and alcohol advertisements, which violates French practice.[86] For less-powerful nations the prospect of impeding the global commercial market is even less plausible.

If in the 1970s global debate on media centered around the New World Information Order, notions of inequality, and the role of media in a democracy, the most prominent issue of the 1990s may well have become international copyright protection. Media firms lose several billion dollars annually to 'pirated' products; i.e. their films, books, or CDs are reproduced without the originating company and artist receiving compensation. In 1995, for example, it is estimated that China produced $1.8 billion, Russia $726 million, and Italy $515 million-worth of US films, books, and recorded music without compensating the originating film or artist.[87] Over 30 percent of the recorded music sold in Italy in 1995 was reportedly produced without respect to copyright.[88] China is said to account for 40 percent of the world's 'pirate' music market; it is a significant export industry.[89] There is grave concern among media firms that the shift to video compact disks will create 'unprecedented piracy' of films and television programs, 'that will make today's piracy look like petty theft'.[90] Along with pharmaceuticals, media and computer software copyright are the primary topics for global intellectual property rights negotiations.

Western media firms have commissioned their governments to lead the campaign against copyright violation. After threatening trade sanctions, the US government reached an agreement with China in June 1996 for the latter to crack down on the 'pirate' media market.[91] The deal also abolishes China's quota of permitting only ten US films per year to be imported to China, although China reserves the right to block importation if it finds that films violate its censorship standards.[92] Copyright protection is in fact a very complex issue; *The Economist* notes that much of copyright law is 'arbitrary' and designed for powerful interests.[93] Copyright and patents protect monopoly positions, keep prices high, and transfer income from poor to rich countries. The US government aggressively insists upon a protection of intellectuals property that provides maximum income to its own industry, while displaying minimal interest in the concerns of anyone else. The WTO has internalized this perspective, acting at the global level to attempt to enforce copyright protection. It has set the year 2000 as a deadline for nations to enact and enforce intellectual property protection.[94] In sum, the nature of global media policy debates conforms closely to the needs and desires of the largest and most powerful commercial actors.

Global corporate media consolidation

US-based firms – though not necessarily owned by Americans – continue to dominate the global media market, and by all accounts they will do so for a long time to come.[95] In global media markets, US firms can capitalize upon their historic competitive advantage of having by far the largest and most lucrative indigenous market to use as a testing ground and to yield economies of scale. Insofar as Hollywood and Madison Avenue have determined the formats for global commercial entertainment, this also accentuates the US advantage.[96] US-based firms can also take advantage of the widespread and growing international use of the English language, especially among the middle and upper classes.[97] Most of the large US-based media firms are in the process of moving from a 'US-centric production and an international distribution network' model to a more transnational production and distribution model.[98] The increasing need for the media giants to 'localize' their content is encouraging them to 'establish wider international bases'.[99] Another factor in globalizing production is to take advantage of lower costs outside of the United States.[100]

The 1990s have seen an unprecedented wave of mergers and acquisitions among global media giants. What is emerging is a tiered global media market. In the first tier are around ten colossal vertically integrated media conglomerates. Six firms that already fit that description are News Corporation, Time Warner, Disney, Bertelsmann, Viacom, and TCI. These firms are major producers of entertainment and media software and have global distribution networks. Although the firms in the first tier are quite large – with annual sales in the $10–25 billion range – they are a notch or two below the largest global corporate giants, although all of them rank among the 500 largest global firms in annual sales. Four other firms that round out this first group include Polygram (owned by Philips), NBC (owned by General Electric), Universal (owned by Seagram), and Sony. All four of these firms are conglomerates with non-media interests, and three of them (Sony, GE, and Philips) are huge electronics concerns that at least double the annual sales of any first-tier media firm. None of them is as fully integrated as the first six firms, but they have the resources to do so if they wish.

There is a second tier of approximately three dozen quite large media firms – with annual sales generally in the $2–10 billion range – that fill regional or niche markets within the global system.[101] Most of these firms rank among the 1,000 largest global firms in terms of market valuation. These second-tier firms tend to have working agreements and/or joint ventures with one or more of the giants in the first tier and with each other; none attempt to 'go it alone'. As the head of Norway's largest media company stated, 'We want to position ourselves so if Kirch or Murdoch want to sell in Scandinavia, they'll come to us first.'[102] Finally, there are thousands of relatively small national and local firms that provide services to the large firms or fill small niches, and their prosperity is dependent in part upon the choices of the large firms.

In this period of flux all media firms are responding to a general market situation that is *forcing* them to move toward being much larger, global, vertically integrated conglomerates. One media industry observer characterizes the late 1990s as 'an all-out rush to claim global turf', and 'a slugfest the likes of which have never been seen'.[103] A Wall Street media analyst states that 'the name of the game is critical mass. You need buying power and distribution. The ante has been upped. It's a global arena.'[104] 'The minimum hurdle for the size that you have to be has gone up', a media consulting firm executive comments. 'Look, a couple of years ago, a $2 billion to $3 billion company was a well-sized company. Now there is really a concern from the executives of a lot of these companies that they are going to get left behind.'[105] Indeed, even in the current period of high growth it is just as likely that the number of major film and music producers for the global market will decrease rather than increase.

It is when the effects of horizontal and vertical integration, conglomeration, and globalization are combined that a sense of the profit potential emerges. First, there are often distinct cost savings. The media consultant who advised Viacom when it purchased Paramount in 1994 estimated that merely combining the two firms would immediately generate $105 million in cost savings.[106] This comes from fuller utilization of existing personnel, facilities, and 'content' resources. When a giant wishes to launch a new enterprise, it can draw upon its existing staff and resources. NBC or News Corporation, for example, are capable of launching global television news channels because they will use their journalists from their present staffs and other news resources. The marginal cost is quite low.[107] A second source of profitability deriving from conglomeration and vertical integration is the exploitation of new opportunities for cross-selling, cross-promotion, and privileged access. These benefits were given great emphasis in corporate explanations of the benefits of the Disney–ABC and Time Warner–Turner mergers, where they were regularly referred to as 'synergies'. It should be noted, however, that these gains are based on monopoly power, and are not gains to society any more than a firm's greater ability to levy higher prices would be. They are private and 'pecuniary' gains, not social and 'real' gains. The other side of the coin of effective cross-selling (etc.) is the exclusion of others, a reduction of competition, and pressure on rivals to follow the same exclusionary path.

When Disney, for example, produces a film, it can also guarantee the film showings on pay cable television and commercial network television, and it can produce and sell soundtracks based on the film, it can create spin-off television series, it can produce related amusement park rides, CD-Roms, books, comics, and merchandise to be sold in Disney retail stores. Moreover, Disney can promote the film and related material incessantly across all its media properties. Even films which do poorly at the box office can become profitable in this climate. Disney's 1996 *Hunchback of Notre Dame* generated a disappointing $99 million at the US and Canadian box offices. According to *Adweek* magazine, however, it is expected to generate $500 million in *profit* (not just revenues), after the other revenue streams are taken into account. And films that are hits can become spectacularly successful. Disney's 1994 *The Lion King* earned over $300 million at the US box office, yet generated over $1 billion in profit for Disney.[108] In sum, the profit whole for the vertically integrated firm can be significantly greater than the profit potential of the individual parts in isolation. Firms without this cross-selling and cross-promotional potential are at a serious disadvantage in competing in the global marketplace. This is the context for the wave of huge media mergers in the 1990s.

As the Disney example suggested, the 'synergies' do not end with media. Time Warner, Universal, and Disney all have theme parks and likewise, Time Warner, Disney, and Viacom all have chains of retail stores to capitalize upon their media 'brands'.[109] Universal captures the spirit of the times in developing a five-year marketing plan for the 1995 film character 'Babe' to turn it into a 'mass-market cash cow'.[110] There will be a *Babe* film sequel in 1998, an animated *Babe* television series, along with *Babe* toys and books.[111] Universal is also launching 'brand galleries', retail outlets based on its most well-known Universal Studios films and characters at its Florida and California theme parks. It is also designing plans for two other chains of retail stores, one to stand alone and another to be a 'boutique' inside existing chain retailers such as Toys 'Я' Us.[112] Viacom is part of a joint venture to launch a chain of 'Bubba Gump' seafood restaurants to capitalize upon the popularity of its *Forrest Gump* motion picture.[113] Turner Broadcasting aggressively markets its 'brands' from its huge movie and cartoon library to advertisers for use in commercials.[114] Both TCI and Disney are moving into the production of educational material, regarded as a lucrative market as the privatization and commercialization of US schools gathers momentum.[115] Moreover, in view of their experience with commercial programming, media firms may be positioned to profit from the drive to bring advertising-supported fare into schools. The largest US commercial education firm, Channel One, only blossomed after being purchased by media firm K-III.[116] By 1997 Channel One was being 'broadcast' to some 40 percent of all US middle schools and high schools. Reebok, for example, has brought Channel One advertising into the heart of its marketing, using its school advertisements to promote the programs it sponsors over commercial television networks.[117]

The size and market power of the media giants also make it possible to engineer exclusive strategic alliances for cross-promotion with other marketing and retailing powerhouses. In 1996 Disney signed a ten-year deal with McDonald's, giving the fast food chain exclusive global rights to promote Disney products in its restaurants. Disney can use McDonald's 18,700 outlets to promote its global sales, while McDonald's can use Disney to assist it in its unabashed campaign to 'dominate every market' in the world.[118] PepsiCo. signed a similar promotional deal for a 1996 re-release of the *Star Wars* film trilogy, in which all of PepsiCo.'s global properties – including Pepsi-Cola, Frito-Lay snacks, Pizza Hut, and Taco Bell – were committed to the promotion.[119] Universal has taken this process the furthest, by keeping it in-house. In 1997 it began heavily promoting its media fare on parent corporation Seagram's beverage products, including Tropicana orange juice.[120] These link-ups between global marketers and media firms are becoming standard operating procedure, and they do much to enhance the profitability and competitive position of the very largest global firms.

It is important to note that these giant mergers, while enlarging profit opportunities in some respects, can run into difficulties, sometimes quite immense ones at that. The prices paid for the properties may be excessive and/or the interest payments on the debt incurred may prevent necessary capital expenditures and make the firm vulnerable to recession or other unexpected difficulties. Major mergers or acquisitions are often accompanied by the sale of assets to retire debt and refocus the firm's activities in areas where the firm has a large stake. In the late 1990s this process is being encouraged by Wall Street. Many corporate media stock prices have floundered during a bull market, putting severe pressure on corporate media managers to generate earnings growth in the short term. One investment banker observed that the largest media conglomerates will likely 'trim down to focus on businesses that are strong cash flow and high-growth, and get out of the businesses that aren't'.[121] In some cases the anticipated 'synergies' do not materialize or may be more than offset by difficulties in meshing with previously independent operations. Several global electronics giants, including General Electric and Sony, purchased major media firms thinking they could expand their profit potential through the complementary nature of media 'hardware' and 'software'. This has not yet proved to be the case. Matsushita found this route notably unrewarding, unloading (then) MCA to Seagram in 1995 after painful losses.

Firms grow and compete in the global marketplace by internal processes, reinvesting earnings to create new facilities, as well as by mergers and acquisitions. In establishing new ventures, media firms frequently participate in joint ventures with one or more of their rivals on specific media projects. Joint ventures are attractive because they reduce the capital requirements and risk of the participants and permit them to spread their resources more widely. Joint ventures also provide a more flexible weapon than formal mergers or acquisitions, which often require years for negotiation and approval and then getting the new parts assimilated. The ten largest global media firms have, on average, joint ventures with five of the other nine giants. They each also average six joint ventures with second-tier media firms. [. . .] Media giants also use joint ventures as a means of easing entry into new international markets, teaming up with 'local international partners who best understand their own turf'.[122] This is a major route through which the largest national and regional media firms around the world are brought into the global market system. Joint ventures are not without their problems, as media partners can develop differing visions for the joint enterprise; along these lines Universal and Viacom had a dispute over their USA cable television network, and US West has been dissatisfied with its shared operations with Time Warner.[123]

Beyond joint ventures, there is also overlapping direct ownership of these firms. Seagram, for example, owner of Universal, also owns 15 percent of Time Warner and has other media equity holdings.[124] TCI is a major shareholder in Time Warner and has holdings in numerous other media firms.[125] The Capital Group Companies' mutual funds, valued at $250 billion, are among the very largest shareholders in TCI, News Corporation, Seagram, Time Warner, Viacom, Disney, Westinghouse, and several other smaller media firms.[126] The head of Capital Group's media investments, Gordon Crawford, is a trusted adviser to the CEOs of nearly all of these firms. He plays an important role in engineering mergers and joint ventures across the media industry.[127] In particular, through Capital Group's holdings in Seagram and TCI as well as its direct holdings in Time Warner, Crawford is one of the most influential shareholders in Time Warner.[128] More generally, in view of their great merger activity and rapid expansion, the media giants find themselves increasingly reliant on the largest Wall Street commercial and investment banks for strategic counsel and capital. A handful of global institutions like Chase Manhattan, Morgan Stanley, and Salomon Brothers have been key advisers in the major mergers of the mid-1990s.[129]

Competition in media markets is quite different from the notion of competition that dominates popular usage of the term. When politicians, business executives, and academics invoke the term 'competition', they almost invariably refer to the kind found in economics textbooks, based upon competitive markets where there are innumerable players, price competition, and easy entry. This notion of competition has never had much applicability in communication markets. As noted, the 'synergies' of recent mergers rest on and enhance monopoly power. Reigning oligopolistic markets are dominated by a handful of firms that compete – often quite ferociously within the oligopolistic framework – on a non-price basis and are protected by severe barriers to entry. No start-up studio, for example, has successfully joined the Hollywood oligopoly in 60 years.[130] Whether the new studio DreamWorks, formed by Stephen Spielberg, David Geffen, and Jeffrey Katzenbach, succeeds, this is obviously an exceptional case, drawing upon the unique wealth and connections of its founders. If successful, DreamWorks will probably become a second-tier player specializing in providing content to media giants through joint ventures and working agreements.

Rupert Murdoch of News Corporation poses the rational issue for an oligopolist firm when pondering the shakeout in the global media market: 'We can join forces now, or we can kill each other and then join forces.'[131] In this spirit, in 1997 Murdoch contacted Viacom CEO Sumner Redstone, informing him it was time they stopped 'being perceived as adversaries', and that they should 'see what we can do together'.[132] Time Warner CEO Gerald Levin claims that with rapidly expanding economic opportunities 'there is enough new business both domestically and internationally, that there won't be a war of attrition.'[133] And if the giants are pursuing this new business in joint ventures with major rivals in many local and national markets, the likelihood of cut-throat competition recedes markedly. John Malone, the CEO of TCI, whose entrepreneurial drive is often noted, states that 'Nobody can really afford to get mad with their competitors, because they are partners in one area and competitors in another.'[134] The *Wall Street Journal* observes that media 'competitors wind up switching between the roles of adversaries, prized customers and key partners.'[135] In this sense the global media and communication market exhibits tendencies not only of an oligopoly, but of a cartel or at least a 'gentleman's club'. Paine Webber's media analyst terms it the global 'communications kereitsu', in reference to the Japanese corporate system of interlocking ownership and management.[136]

The central role of advertising

With the increasing globalization of the world economy, advertising has come to play a crucial role for the few hundred firms that dominate it. In 1995 the forty largest advertising corporations, all of which were based in Western Europe, Japan, or the United States, spent some $47 billion on advertising worldwide, $26 billion of which was outside the United States, an increase of nearly 20 percent over their spending in 1994. The top eight firms accounted for nearly one-half of the top forty's advertising.[137] As *The Economist* puts it, 'much of the spending in different countries comes from the same companies.' Proctor & Gamble, for example, is among the top ten advertisers in all but two of the ten largest national advertising markets, and number one in three.[138] 'We're in an era of global marketing warfare', an expert on global corporate 'positioning' comments. 'The number one tactical weapon of the age is advertising.'[139] Moreover, global advertising benefits from a stagnant global economy as well as a vibrant one. 'With massive overcapacity in industries worldwide', *Business Week* observes, 'selling products is harder, and differentiating goods more critical.' The development of global commercial broadcasting is an integral part of the creation of a global market. The long experience of the United States highlights how well suited commercial television is to advertising. To help make this commercial bounty global, in 1996 the leading world advertising and broadcasting associations devised a single global standard for the purchase and production of television advertising.[140]

Global advertising is expected to increase at a rate greater than GDP growth for the foreseeable future. US per capita advertising spending in 1995 was $365 while in the UK (second in Europe to Switzerland) it was $258, in Italy $97, and in China and India it was $3 and $1 respectively.[141] The rest of the world is in the process of having its level of advertising elevated toward the US position. In 1970 the United States accounted for 60 percent of global advertising, whereas in 1995 it accounted for 47 percent. McCann-Erickson forecasts that global advertising will increase from $335 billion in 1995 to $2 trillion in 2020, with a further substantial decline in the North American percentage of the global total.[142] Yet the US advertising market is hardly stagnant; it is growing at a pace well in excess of GDP growth in the middle and late 1990s.[143] Asia, Latin America, and

Eastern Europe are where the greatest per capita increases are taking place.[144] The Leo Burnett Agency estimates that China's portion of Asian advertising went from 1 percent in 1991 to 8 percent in 1995, and it is projected to double to 16 percent in 1997.[145] Most of the growth in advertising spending is going toward television, while newspaper and magazine advertising shrinks as a proportion of the whole.[146]

Since the dawn of modern advertising, it has been axiomatic that it must be conducted by agencies independent of both the advertising firm and the media to be effective in the long run. Of the leading global advertising agencies, therefore, only Havas has extensive media holdings, over which it exercises indirect control. The leading advertising organizations also tend to be smaller than leading media firms, whose annual sales are as much as ten times greater.[147] In the 1980s there was a major wave of mergers and acquisitions among advertising agencies, especially in the United States, and global ambitions underlay much of the activity.[148] In the 1990s the trend toward consolidation has continued, only now the global concerns are central to the process. After a series of buyouts and mergers a 'big three' of global advertising organizations, each with a number of agencies around the world, has emerged. The three – the British WPP Group, the US Omnicom Group, and the US Interpublic – had combined gross revenues of $8 billion, and placed over $50 billion of advertising in 1995. The big three are followed by the Japanese Dentsu, British Cordiant, and US Young & Rubicam, each of which is about half the size of the first three. The industry is effectively centered in New York, with a few key agencies based in Tokyo, London, Chicago, and Paris.[149]

In almost all developing countries the leading domestic agencies have sold out to one of the huge global advertising networks for fear of getting cut out of the action. The 'big three' own several agencies and through them maintain offices in over a hundred countries.[150] The US and European advertising agencies ranked below the first five or six firms are now in a hurry to build 'critical mass outside the US', or else see themselves as likely catches 'for any one of the giants as they race to grow ever-bigger'.[151] According to *The Economist*, the 'consensus' is that perhaps one more advertising conglomerate 'will clamber into the first division', while 'the rest will be eaten.'[152] Havas, the world's seventh largest advertising agency with 1995 billings of $6.2 billion, radically overhauled its organization in 1996 to make itself competitive on a global basis. It purchased six Latin American agencies and is expanding operations in Asia and China.[153] The French Publicis likewise has budgeted $350 million for the purchase of Latin American and Asian advertising agencies in 1996 and 1997.[154]

As the *Wall Street Journal* notes, to a considerable extend this global consolidation 'is being driven by the demands of increasingly international clients'.[155] 'Multinationals launching global brands in a strange country', an Indian executive of the WPP Group observes, 'seek a sense of familiarity and sometimes prefer to deal with one agency worldwide.'[156] The clear trend in the 1990s has been for global firms like Colgate-Palmolive, Bayer, Coca-Cola, Intel, and numerous others to consolidate their advertising accounts – that had been spread among as many as fifty different agencies – into a single global agency.[157] Another common option is for transnational firms to consolidate their accounts into a 'club' of three or four huge agencies, as even the largest advertising groups are relatively weak in some regions.[158] 'It's about harnessing the global power of the brand', an Interpublic executive states. 'The common thread is that they [the clients] want control of what their brand stand for, and the ability to develop that on a global scale.'[159]

The largest half-dozen global advertising organizations are also providing a wider range of services for their multinational clients. On the one hand, they complement their advertising services with global direct marketing networks. Non-advertising marketing activities account for half of WPP's income and one-third of Omnicom's income.[160] On the other hand, the largest global advertising agencies now own nine of the twelve largest global public relations (PR) agencies, most of which have offices in scores of nations. Like advertising, PR is a highly concentrated global industry; the top three global firms have as much income as the firms ranked four through sixteen, and the top three firms have twice the income of the firms ranked seventeen through fifty. By dominating global public relations, the global advertising giants can offer their corporate clients expertise in political lobbying, public opinion management, and influencing journalism surreptitiously across the world.[161]

The voracious marketing appetites and changing needs of advertising corporations provide many new opportunities for global media firms. Advertising volume is increasing rapidly both in the United States and globally. US TV networks now broadcast 6,000 commercials per week, up by 50 percent since 1983. Half-hour programs, for example, have had their editorial time cut by as much as 10 percent to make more room for advertising.[162] As *Business Week* observes, 'the buying public has been virtually buried alive in ads.' Desperate to be seen and heard, advertisers are turning to new approaches, including 'stamping their messages on everything that stands still'.[163] In 1996, News Corporation's US Fox television network ran commercial banners along the bottom of the screen during primetime shows, breaking a longstanding taboo, but with mixed results.[164] In 1997, in another precedent-setting example, a Swedish telecommunication firm offered reduced rates on its telephone service if customers would agree to listen to advertisements during their telephone calls.[165]

To circumvent this commercial blizzard, and consumer skepticism of traditional advertising, marketers are working to infiltrate entertainment. On one hand, this means making commercials appear like entertainment. Thirty- and 60-minute infomercials, once the domain of dubious enterprises, are now being employed by firms like Microsoft, Ford, and Eastman Kodak, offering state-of-the-art production values.[166] Infomercials are going global, and they 'sizzle in Asia', according to the *Wall Street Journal*. 'Generally, if it works in America it works in Asia', a Singapore-based US media executive states.[167] The booming US-based Quantum International (1997 sales: $400 million) buys 3,200 half-hours of infomercials in twenty-one different languages in sixty-five nations every week. Almost all of the infomercials are dubbed versions of the US originals, and they 'heavily push the hype of US consumerism'.[168] Another surging development is the effort of television channels like ABC to broadcast entertainment programs featuring products that are sold over the air, with the programs also including explicit commercial breaks for additional paid advertising. MTV has had some success with this format with its program, *The Goods*, but it is still in the infant stage. By 1997 the US Sci-Fi cable channel, owned jointly by Viacom and Universal, had taken this genre the furthest; its weekly 'Sci-Fi Trader' series, which hawks science fiction-related material between interviews with sci-fi authors, is listed as a bona fide program in *TV Guide*, and it raked in advertising dollars from firms like AT&T, Coca-Cola, Procter & Gamble and Philip Morris.[169] As *Adweek* puts it, 'the network that cracks-the-code of marrying entertainment with selling will be richly rewarded.'[170]

This 'marrying' has resulted in further specialization; for example, there are over two dozen consultancies in Los Angeles whose business is linking marketers with film and television producers, usually to get the marketer's product 'placed' and promoted in films and TV programs.[171] In view of the global audience for US films and television shows, this is an important marketing opportunity for leading firms. 'The connections between Madison Avenue and Hollywood have grown so elaborate', *Business Week* concludes, 'that nothing is off-limits when studios and advertisers sit down to hammer out the marketing campaign.' The 1996 hit film *Mission Impossible*, for example, featured an Apple PowerBook Computer as star Tom Cruise's onscreen sidekick. In return, Apple plugged the film in a $15 million advertising campaign.[172] Apple had a similar deal with the 1996 News Corporation blockbuster, *Independence Day*, in which Jeff Goldblum saves the world from an alien invasion using his Apple PowerBook.[173] As an indication of Hollywood's new age, in 1997 Reebok sued Sony's TriStar Pictures, claiming TriStar had reneged on its promise to feature a Reebok commercial prominently in the concluding 'happy ending' scene of the film *Jerry Maguire*. Reebok earned this honor, it claimed, because it had spent $1.5 million in advertising and promotional support for the film. To Reebok, product placement is becoming a central means of selling. 'A great deal about a brand's image gets defined by who's wearing it and using it', a Reebok executive explained. 'That's part of the fabric of who we are.'[174]

The most important method of commercializing films is to specifically produce films that lend themselves to the complementary merchandising of products: the revenues generated here can be greater than those generated by box-office sales or video rentals, as the Disney examples mentioned above highlighted. Time Warner and Disney generate over US$1 and US$2 billion in income respectively from their consumer products divisions. Indeed, Disney now looks to have its 'live-action' films generate the same merchandising revenues that have been associated with its animated films. This is becoming an important criterion for determining which films get made and which do not.[175] The ultimate result of the 'marriage of

Hollywood and Madison Avenue' came with the 1996 release of Time Warner's film *Space Jam*, based upon Nike shoe commercials with Bugs Bunny and Michael Jordan and directed by 'the country's hottest director of commercials'. As *Forbes* magazine puts it, 'the real point of the movie is to sell, sell, sell.' Time Warner 'is looking to hawk up to $1 billion in toys, clothing, books, and sports gear based on the movie characters'. A similar film based on Nike advertisements with basketball star Penny Hardaway is expected to be produced in 1997. Moreover, the style of feature films has increasingly adopted the techniques of television commercials. One 1996 Hollywood film directed by a veteran of advertising – *The Rock*, with Nicolas Cage and Sean Connery – was characterized as 'like a series of vivid, focused, 60-second commercials'.[176]

In short, traditional notions of separation of editorial and commercial interests are weakening. Advertisers have a large and increasing role in determining media content. NBC has agreed to let IBM have final say over content in its new cable program 'Scan', in return for IBM agreeing to sponsor the program on NBC's networks in North America, Asia, Europe, and Latin America. A US advertising executive predicts that 'This is just a forerunner of what we are going to see as we get to 500 channels. Every client will have their own programming tailored to their own needs, based on their ad campaign.'[177] NBC and Viacom finalized a three-year deal in 1996 with Procter & Gamble whereby P&G will provide up to 50 percent of the financing for television series in return for access to advertising time on the show in the US and globally.[178] P&G made a similar deal with Viacom and Bertelsmann to produce movies for European television.[179]

In a striking manifestation of the new era of global media and global advertising practice, in late 1996 Disney's ESPN began offering global buys to advertisers utilizing all its channels and properties around the world, and giving these clients exclusive participation in ESPN programming. No Fear jeans, for example, is to be identified with pivotal plays in replays of games on ESPN networks.[180] Even more sweeping, NBC and Young & Rubicam began negotiations for an unprecedented partnership that would give all the agency's clients integrated marketing and promotional opportunities on all of NBC's global properties, while permitting the agency input on programming decisions. In this way the oligopolistic nature of each industry comes to reinforce the monopoly power of firms in other industries.[181]

It is when one combines the effects of media conglomeration, corporate concentration, and hyper-commercialism upon media content that the nature of the global media system's culture comes into focus. Book publishing, for example, which for decades tended to have a relatively wide ideological and cultural range of output, has been brought squarely into the cross-promotional plans of the media giants.[182] 'The drive for profit', a veteran US book editor observes, 'fits like an iron mask on our cultural output.'[183] Even the most prestigious commercial magazine publishers concede that the traditional autonomy of editorial content has been replaced by a regime where 'everyone keeps an eye on profits.' And few corporate media magazine owners are especially concerned with prestige.[184] Scott Rudin, termed Hollywood's 'most prolific producer', states 'making movies has become so debilitating, so devoid of any enthusiasm for the material, for the talent involved'.[185] Corporate concentration and commercial pressures have also led numerous journalists to leave the corporate press in protest at the compromise of traditional standards.[186] In one example of how journalism fits into the operations of media empires, NBC News made the 1996 Summer Olympics its most frequently covered story for the year, with nearly 20 percent more coverage than that of its second most-covered story. The coverage of the Olympics for the other US networks failed to even make their 'top ten' list of most-covered news stories for the year. Perhaps it was a coincidence, but NBC had the US television rights to the Olympics.[187] Whether the commercial global media system 'gives the people what they want' is a subject [for discussion]. What is crystal clear is that the global media system is giving the largest media firms, their shareholders, and advertisers what they want. 'We're here to serve advertisers', Westinghouse CEO Michael Jordan says. 'That's our *raison d'être*.'[188]

Uneven development of the global media market

Even if the market is becoming the worldwide method for organizing communication, and nonmarket principles and values are playing a much smaller role in determining the nature of media systems, the globalization–commercialization process does not operate at the same pace and to the same extent around the world. Each nation's indigenous commercial and/or noncommercial media system responds somewhat differently to the encroachment of global market forces, leading to continued variation in local markets. Moreover, nation states remain the most important political forces in communication and much else; the pace and course of media market liberalization varies from nation to nation and region to region, though the general trend toward deregulation is clear. In short, each country will have to be understood on its own terms as well as in the context of the global media market for the foreseeable future.

The core tendencies of the global market itself will also tend to produce a highly uneven worldwide media system. Commercial media markets are attracted to people with the money to purchase their products (and the necessary media hardware to use them), and to people with enough money to purchase the products that program sponsors wish to advertise. If global advertisers are interested in a sector of the population or a region, global media firms will move quickly to accommodate them. A nation like India provides a case in point. Over half of its 900 million population is entirely irrelevant to the global media market and, at present rates of change, will continue to be irrelevant for generations. But the prospering middle classes are another matter. 'There are 250 million people in the middle-class in India alone', Disney's Michael Eisner observes, 'which is an enormous opportunity.'[189] And it has only begun to be incorporated into the global media market in any appreciable way in the past decade. The same can be said of upper and middle classes across Asia, the Middle East, and Latin America.

In the context of the market logic guiding global media firms, we can make a few observations about the manner in which the global system will evolve in different regions of the world. Although its share of global media consumption is declining, North America remains the most important market. It is difficult to imagine a firm being a global player without a significant presence there. Western Europe is almost as important, not only because of its wealth but because it still has room to grow to reach US per capita levels of advertising and media consumption. At the other end of the spectrum is sub-Saharan Africa, which, aside from business and affluent classes in South Africa, seemingly has been written off by global media firms as too poor to develop. It does not even appear in most discussions of global media in the business press. Global media firms tend to break the world down to North America, Latin America, Europe, and Asia. When *The Financial Times* published a world map to highlight MTV's global expansion, it simply removed Africa and replaced it with the names of the thirty-eight European nations that carry MTV.[190] In severe economic crises, many African nations have privatized their broadcasting systems, but there is little capital to provide radio and television services.[191] Due in part to 'feeble resources', *The Financial Times* concludes, 'most African television is so excruciating unwatchable.'[192] Even in relatively rich South Africa, half of the homes have no electricity.[193] Left to the global media market, sub-Saharan Africa's media and communication systems will remain undeveloped, and even wither.

Eastern Europe has been the site of a painful transition from a state-dominated economy and media to one with increasing private ownership. As state media subsidies have been eliminated, advertising and subscription income have yet to provide much of a basis for a commercially viable press. As the *New York Times* concluded, the 'Russian press is free, free to go broke.'[194] Those papers that survive have tended to fall into the hands of businessmen and bankers who want to control vehicles of propaganda, and two of the three national TV stations have been acquired by businessmen-banker allies of the Yeltsin government (the other national channel is fully state-owned). One scholar characterized Russian television as 'an instrument to be exploited by criminals and authoritarian politicians'.[195] TV programming is heavily westernized in both direct (imported) content and format – it is also Latinized, with Mexican *telenovas* very popular. Despite strong nationalistic undercurrents, the elites in Russia (and elsewhere in Eastern Europe) are denationalized, and it is reported that 'advertising (not only on TV) quite often used English as a sign of cachet, rather than Russian', and that imported Western objects frequently have foreign language texts 'as a kind of guarantee of "non-Russo-Soviet" authenticity'.[196] Combined with the economic weakness, instability and dependency of the Russian economy and state (also true in varying degrees of other Eastern European countries), this denationalization makes foreign entry and the imposition and advance of the commercial model relatively easy and sure, with uncertain time lags. The main impediment to this foreign penetration is likely to be the continuing authoritarian tendencies of the leadership and, not unrelated, continued economic and political instability. These forces and trends do not bode well for the emergence of a meaningful public sphere over the next decade. The bias of the newly commercializing and state-dominated and state-influenced media during the 1996 presidential election in Russia was so blatant that one Moscow citizen noted plaintively that 'Once again we need shortwave foreign broadcasts to know what's going on.'[197]

The situation is much the same in the rest of Eastern Europe, where the traditional state-subsidized media are disintegrating. The leading film studio of former Czechoslovakia is now used primarily for filming advertisements.[198] In another sign of the collapse of the once-powerful Eastern European film industry, in 1994 Hollywood studios commanded 93 percent of Hungary's film market.[199] While the collapse of the public sector in Africa has failed to rouse much enthusiasm for investment by global media firms, Eastern Europe seemingly holds more commercial promise. The new market-driven economies in Eastern Europe appear to be generating an affluent middle class alongside vast sections of the population mired in brutal poverty, not unlike the cases of Brazil or India. Global media firms have great interest in the new Eastern European middle classes, especially in the wealthier Poland, Hungary, and Czech Republic. Accordingly, media firms have moved into the desirable markets; for example, over half of Czech newspapers are owned by German and Swiss firms.[200] Western firms like Time Warner, Canal Plus, Disney, and Bertelsmann increasingly dominate television in those three nations.[201] 'We believe these countries are integrating more with the European community', a US commercial broadcaster observes, and as these economies recover, advertising in these nations 'will explode'.[202]

'Foreign-owned papers and private television expand the news spectrum' in Eastern Europe, observes the *New York Times*, 'but most show little interest in serious political coverage.'[203] The incorporation of Eastern Europe into the global media market is important in the eyes of Western policy-makers, as it will help to integrate the region into the global economy, and to produce the type of media and political culture where the market domination of society goes unquestioned.[204] *The Financial Times* refers to this as the necessary 'process of de-politicising the economy'.[205]

Latin America is seen as a high-growth area. It has a history of commercial media that, when combined with the continent-wide adoption of neoliberal economic policies, provides major opportunities for global media firms.[206] The region has only two languages, and English is widely understood among the upper and middle classes, making it easier to provide pan-Latin American services. A significant percentage of the region's 430 million people live in abject poverty, but there is a viable middle class, especially in nations like Brazil, Argentina, Mexico, and Colombia. Moreover, these middle classes have shown a fondness for Hollywood programming and advertised international brands.[207] Television sets are in 85 percent of Latin America's 100 million households, and between 11 and

15 percent have pay cable or satellite television.[208] This explains why Latin America has become a prime battleground for digital satellite television. Miami has emerged as the media capital of Latin America; most Latin cable and satellite channels are headquartered there, as is the coordination of Latin American advertising.[209] Latin America is now considered a 'top prospect for future growth' in advertising and marketing. IBM's Latin American marketing director describes the results of its 1995 direct marketing campaigns in Brazil 'as literally like sweeping gold off the street'.[210]

If Miami is the media capital of Latin America, Hong Kong and Singapore share that honor in Asia. Most of the global media giants base their East Asian activities in one of those locales. Asia is unquestionably the most coveted emerging market area for the global media giants. As one report puts it, 'The Asian market for cable and satellite services is huge and relatively untapped, offering practically unrivalled growth opportunities.'[211] The raw population is larger than that of the rest of the world combined, and it has enjoyed the highest rates of economic growth in the world in the 1990s. It is projected to remain the fastest growing region of the world well into the twenty-first century.

Asia's traditional drawbacks for global media firms are that it is far more heterogeneous than, say, Latin America, and Asian nations have had rather strict regulations over media. These regulations are gradually being removed and by all calculations Asia is and will continue to be the fastest growing global commercial media market. Indonesia, the fourth most populous nation in the world, had an entirely 'pirate' video market in 1991. It has now been brought into the global market system.[212] Between 1995 and 2003 India is projected to have a 50 percent increase in television set ownership, China and Indonesia a 33 percent increase, and Thailand and Malaysia a 25 percent increase. By 2003, Asia will have nearly 500 million television households, three times as many as in Western Europe, and nearly 180 million cable and satellite television households.[213] Television advertising revenues are forecast to nearly triple to $20 billion between 1995 and 2003.[214] 'With huge, growing economies, there's a big upside in media and entertainment in Asia', an Australian industry analyst observes. 'We are scouring places looking for opportunities', a US investment manager states.[215] Even Japan, the most developed Asian economy, has considerable room for commercial media growth in comparison to the United States or Western European nations.

The largest jewel in the Asian media crown is China, with its population of 1.2 billion people. Although still a political dictatorship under the Communist Party, China has taken a decided turn toward becoming a market economy. Advertising has become an accepted part of Chinese life, and personal consumption of branded products is markedly increasing in prominence. 'Shanghai', *Advertising Age* notes, 'is quickly embracing the shopping mall culture.'[216] China's slogan for the development of broadcasting is 'Those who invest, should benefit', and by 1992 Chinese media were set on a path of explicit commercialization.[217] Television has exploded in the past decade. The number of channels increased from thirty-two in 1978 to nearly 600 by 1992. In 1994 there were 230 million

TV sets and 800 million viewers in China.[218] Color sets were in 86 percent of China's urban households in 1994, and the number of cable TV customers is expected to increase to between 80 and 100 million by 2000, making it the largest cable market in the world.[219] (The Chinese have encouraged cable over direct-to-home satellite TV as it is easier to regulate content.) The adoption of a market economy has widened class divisions, and in the process has created a viable middle class 'at least 100 million strong'.[220] All evidence suggests that the Chinese commercial television market 'already is taking off', and the future may hold unfathomable riches for global media firms.[221] All the global media giants are working quietly to gain entrance into the Chinese television market, often through delicate negotiations with the Chinese government.[222] Patience is the order of the day. The state-run Chinese Central Television with its five channels still dominates, though it is becoming an increasingly commercial enterprise. 'Once the change in leadership stabilizes', the president of NBC Asia predicts, looking to China's near future, 'and the Government liberalizes, there will be tremendous new demand.'

Conclusion

After another wave of global media deals in the summer of 1996, a leading Wall Street media industry analyst observed, 'It's the ninth inning in a game that began in 1987, and that's the restructuring of the media industry on a global scale.'[223] By 1997, the largest media giants like Disney and Time Warner were increasingly providing their films to their own television networks and cable channels in a privileged manner. This was leaving networks like NBC and CBS that lacked large production studios 'shut out' of the system, and suggested that another wave of mergers may transpire before the dust would settle.[224] How close the global market is to stabilization remains to be seen, but the contours are clearly visible. The firms that sit atop the global media market have transformed themselves seemingly almost overnight. Viacom, for example, a relatively obscure player in the US media industry as recently as the late 1980s, is now one of the firms in the top half of the global first tier, having increased its sales sixfold from 1993 to 1997. Indeed, four of the top six first-tier global media firms did not exist in their present form in the 1980s. The two largest global media firms, Time Warner and Disney, both roughly doubled their annual revenues from 1994 to 1996, partly through internal growth, but mainly via acquisitions. The global media market is being constructed by these and other large firms seeking commercial gain in a congenial political and economic environment. [. . .]

Notes

1   *Media and Entertainment*, Schroder Wertheim & Co. report, 4 October 1995, p. 3.
2   Jane L. Levere, 'Advertising', *New York Times*, 11 June 1996, p. C6.

3   Ted Johnson, 'The upsizing of Hollywood', *Variety*, 18–24 March 1996, p. 65.

4   'A week in the life of German showbiz', *Variety Global Media Report*, 27 May to 2 June 1996, pp. 16, 41.

5   Comment of Ed Wilson, president of Eyemark Entertainment. In Greg Spring, 'Cable, overseas deals beckon', *Electronic Media*, 20 May 1996, p. 12.

6   'Interview with Melissa T. Cook', *Wall Street Transcript*, 18 March 1996, p. 2.

7   Ronald Grover, 'Lights, camera, less action', *Business Week*, 1 July 1996, pp. 50, 52

8   Gustavo Lombo, 'The land of opportunity', *Forbes*, 15 July 1996, pp. 292–4.

9   'European ratings snapshot', *Variety*, 14 October 1996, p. 22.

10   *Our Creative Diversity: Report of the World Commission on Culture and Development* (Paris, World Commission on Culture and Development, 1995), p. 27.

11   Richard Tomkins, 'US tops poll on cultural exports', *The Financial Times*, 4 December 1996, p. 9.

12   'Trade imbalance tops $6bn', *Television Business International*, December 1996, p. 16.

13   David Rooney, 'Filmauro firing up exhib, distrib arms', *Variety*, 25 November to 1 December 1996, p. 29.

14   Mark Landler, 'MTV finds increasing competition for foreign viewers', *New York Times*, 25 March 1996, p. C7.

15   Andrew Geddes, 'TV find no pan-Asian panacea', *Advertising Age*, 18 July 1994.

16   Neel Chowdhury, 'STAR-TV shines in India', *International Herald Tribune*, 16 July 1996, p. 15.

17   Comment of D. Bourse, cited in Doug Wilson, *Strategies of the Media Giants* (London, Pearson Professional, 1996), p. 40.

18   John Tagliabue, 'Local flavor rules European TV', *New York Times*, 14 October 1996, pp. C1, C3; Alice Rawsthorn, 'Hollywood goes global', *The Financial Times*, 27 September 1996, special section, p. x.

19   Alice Rawsthorn, 'World book market "faces further consolidation"', *Financial Times*, 2 October 1996, p. 16.

20   Alice Rawsthorn, 'Out of tune with the times', *The Financial Times*, 25 June 1996, p. 15.

21   Alice Rawsthorn, 'PolyGram is biggest music group', *The Financial Times*, 9 May 1996, p. 6; 'Musical chairs', *The Economist*, 23 December 1995 to 5 January 1996, p. 78.

22   'Music sales', *Variety*, 22–28 April 1996, p. 7.

23   Alice Rawsthorn, 'Recorded music sales bound towards $40bn', *The Financial Times*, 17 April 1996, p. 5.

24   The trade publication is *Music Business International* magazine, cited in Alice Rawsthorn, 'China to lead global music sales growth', *The Financial Times*, 24 January 1996, p. 7.

25   Harold L. Vogel, *Entertainment Industry Economics: a Guide for Financial Analysis*, 3rd edn (New York and Cambridge, Cambridge University Press, 1994), p. 40.

26   Comment of Ted Shugrue of Colombia TriStar Films (owned by Sony), cited in Antonia Zerbisias, 'The world at their feet', *The Toronto Star*, 27 August 1995, p. C1; see also Cäcilie Rohwedder, Lisa Bannon and Eben Shapiro, 'Spending spree by German Kirch Group spells bonanza for Hollywood studios', *Wall Street Journal*, 1 August 1996, p. B1.

27   Quotations of Greg Coote of Village Roadshow and David Davis of Houlihan, Lokey, Howard & Zukin, cited in Leonard Klady, 'US exhibs discover the joy of Plex O'Seas', *Variety*, 8–14 April 1996, pp. 9, 14.

28   Andrew Tanzer and Robert La Franco, 'Luring Asians from their TV sets', *Forbes*, 3 June 1996, p. 41.

29   'Global fast forward', *Variety*, 22–28 April 1996, p. 13.

30   Neil Weinberg, 'The fourth wave', *Forbes*, 20 November 1996, p. 114; Peter M. Nichols, 'A new CD marvel awaits, but the horizon recedes', *New York Times*, 25 August 1996, section 2, pp. 1, 20.

31   Rohwedder et al., 'Spending spree by German Kirch Group', p. B1.

32   Bernard Weinraub, 'MCA in $2.5 billion sale of shows to German TV', *New York Times*, 31 July 1996, p. C1.

33   Linda Lee, 'Film and TV output soars, spurring demand for studio space', *New York Times*, 20 January 1997, pp. C1, C7.

34   Leonard Klady, 'Why mega-flicks click', *Variety*, 25 November to 1 December 1996, p. 1.

35   John Lippman, 'Hollywood reeled record $5.8 billion last year, boosted by blockbuster films', *Wall Street Journal*, 3 January 1997, p. B2.

36   Bernard Weinraub, 'Media', *New York Times*, 6 January 1997, p. C7.

37   Barbara Maltsby, 'The homogenization of Hollywood', *Media Studies Journal*, 10 (2–3) (Spring/Summer 1996), p. 115.

38   Bill Carter, 'Pow! thwack! bam! no dubbing needed', *New York Times*, Week in Review section, 3 November 1996, p. 6.

39   Neil Blackley, Pierre-Yves Gauthier and Guy Lamming, *Pay TV in Europe* (London, Goldman Sachs, 3 March 1995), p. 1.

40   Comment of Jessica Reif, cited in Lee Hall, 'Analysts offer cautious optimism for cable growth', *Electronic Media*, 1 April 1996, p. 30.

41   Neil Blackley and Meg Geldens, 'The broadcast systems market', *Europe Research*, 14 June 1996, p. 14.

42   Manjunath Pendakur and Jvotsna Kapur, 'Think globally, program locally: the privatization of Indian National Television', paper presented to Democratizing Communication: a Comparative Perspective on Information and Power, 23 January 1995, p. 1.

43   Richard Parker, *The Future of Global Television News*, Joan Shorenstein Center on Press, Politics and Public Policy Research Paper R-13, Harvard University, September 1994, p. 5.

44   'Switch it off', *The Economist*, 13 April 1996, p. 15.

45   Heidi Dawley, 'The BBC as we know it is signing off', *Business Week*, 12 August 1996, p. 50.

46   Sandy Tolan, 'Must NPR sell itself?', *New York Times*, 16 July 1996, p. A11.

47   See Helen Bunting and Paul Chapman, *The Future of the European Media Industry: Towards the 21st Century* (London, Pearson Professional, 1996), pp. 35–7.

48   Elizabeth Jensen, 'In funding squeeze, PBS cozies up to Madison Avenue "sponsors"', *Wall Street Journal*, 3 July 1996, p. B1.

49   Don Groves, 'Upping the ante: pubcaster confronts increased competition', *Variety*, 8–14 April 1996, p. 45.

50   Raymond Snoddy, 'BBC seeks bigger international role', *The Financial Times*, 11 January 1996, p. 6.

51   Adam Dawtrey, 'BBC's private predicament', *Variety*, 2–8 September 1996, p. 23.

52   Helen Bunting, *Global Media Companies*, vol. 1 (London, Pearson Professional, 1995), p. 166; Meheroo Jussawalla, 'South East Asia', in *Media Ownership and Control in the Age of Convergence* (London, International Institute of Communications, 1996), pp. 219–20.

53   Erich Broehm, 'Docu disagreement pushes BBC out of Arabian orbit', *Variety*, 15–21 April 1996, p. 52.

54   Raymond Snoddy, 'BBC moves closer to US satellite deal', *The Financial Times*, 28–29 September 1996, p. 4; John Dempsey, 'Discovery goes global with Beeb', *Variety*, 30 September to 6 October 1996, p. 62.

55   'Number of TV channels "may top 4,000 in four years"', *The Financial Times*, 27 February 1996, p. 8.

56   Elizabeth Lesly, Ronald Grover and Neil Gross, 'Cable TV: a crisis looms', *Business Week*, 14 October 1996, p. 103; Christopher Parkes, 'Arizona reaches for the sky with media deal', *Financial Times*, 1 July 1996, p. 4.

57   Christopher Parkes, 'Television finds space to grow', *The Financial Times*, 21 February 1996, p. 13.

58   Raymond Snoddy, 'Broadcasters dish up a revolution', *The Financial Times*, 6 October 1995, p. 13.

59   Neil Weinberg and Robert La Franco, 'Yin, yang and you', *Forbes*, 10 March 1997, p. 104.

60   Aaron Barnhart, 'Cable, cable everywhere but not a thing to watch', *New York Times*, 23 December 1996, p. C7.

61   John Dempsey, 'Cable ops caught in the nets', *Variety*, 17–23 February 1997, p. 1.

62   Raymond Snoddy, 'Information battle enters a new dimension', *The Financial Times*, 10 June 1996, p. 11; Raymond Snoddy, 'News Intl arm plans digital broadcast', *The Financial Times*, 11 June 1996, p. 22.

63   Jeff Cole, 'Mexico's plan to auction satellite system draws attention from US operators', *Wall Street Journal*, 10 March 1997, p. A3.

64   Bronwen Maddox and Raymond Snoddy, 'Media barons line up for digital star wars', *The Financial Times*, 25 April 1996, p. 8.

65   Mark Robichaux, 'As satellite TV soars, big firms crowd the skies', *Wall Street Journal*, 11 March 1996, p. B1; Raymond Snoddy, 'Murdoch empire strikes back in US TV', *The Financial Times*, 26 February 1997, p. 19.

66   'Radio Canada will end its international service', *New York Times*, 8 December 1996, p. 12.

67   Raymond Snoddy, 'Former World Service chief scorns restructuring at BBC', *The Financial Times*, 11 June 1996, p. 8.

68   'This is London, if we can afford it', *The Economist*, 6 January 1996, p. 44.

69   John Ridding, 'Alcatel arm takes Euronews stake', *The Financial Times*, 1–2 April 1995, p. 5.

70   'Euronews courts rival channels to take stakes', *New Media Markets*, 25 July 1996, p. 7.

71   Marc Gunther, 'CNN envy', *Fortune*, 8 July 1996, p. 124.

72   'All news, all the time, any time soon?', *Business Week*, 18 December 1995, p. 42.

73   Chuck Ross, 'Ailes sets out to lead Fox into news business', *Advertising Age*, 1 July 1996, p. 17.

74   Berlusconi's successful and explicit use of his media properties to promote his political agenda is perhaps most striking, though hardly exceptional. See Alexander Stille, 'The world's greatest salesman', *New York Times Magazine*, 17 March 1996, p. 29.

75   Comment of unidentified executive, in Joe Mandese, 'Murdoch digs into more news', *Advertising Age*, 4 December 1995, p. 33.

76   Ira Teinowicz, 'Court further bolsters commercial speech', *Advertising Age*, 27 May 1996, p. 47.

77   Edward S. Herman, 'The media mega-mergers', *Dollars and Sense*, no. 205, May–June 1996, pp. 8–13.

78   Mark Landler, 'In cable TV, more is less', *New York Times*, Week in Review section, 10 November 1996, p. 4.

79   Andy Stern, 'Eurocrats set to clash on quota battleground', *Variety*, 12–18 February 1996, p. 35.

80   Anthony DePalma, 'US and Mexico reach accord over satellite TV transmission', *New York Times*, 9 November 1996, p. 20.

81   Ira Teinowicz and Don Angus, 'US joins the Canada ad fight', *Advertising Age*, 18 March 1996, p. 44.

81   Anthony DePalma, 'World trade body opposes Canadian magazine tariffs', *New York Times*, 20 January 1997, p. C8.

83   'Digital dilemmas', *The Economist*, 23 March 1996, p. 82; 'The revolution that could bring viewers 1,800 new channels', *The Financial Times*, 25 April 1996, p. 8.

84   Diane Summers, 'Norway may lose right to ban satellite advertising', *The Financial Times*, 20 June 1995, p. 1.

85   Neil Buckley, 'EU MPs to demand state TV protection', *The Financial Times*, 18 September 1996, p. 2.

86   Diane Summers and Andrew Jack, 'Brussels warning over French TV's health kick', *The Financial Times*, 3 July 1996, p. 3.

87   Julia Preston, 'With piracy booming in Mexico, US industry's cries get louder', *New York Times*, 20 April 1996, p. 20.

88   Andrew Hill, 'Piracy on the high Cs', *The Financial Times*, 19 March 1996, p. 6.

89   Joyce Barnathan, 'A pirate under every rock', *Business Week*, 17 June 1996, p. 50.

90   Craig S. Smith, 'Counterfeit video compact disks in Asia may dwarf current copyright piracy', *Wall Street Journal*, 18 June 1996, p. A12.

91   Seth Faison, 'US and China agree on pact to fight piracy', *New York Times*, 18 June 1996, pp. A1, A8; Marcus W. Brauchli, 'In a trade war, China takes the bigger hit', *Wall Street Journal*, 17 May 1996, p. A10; Tony Walker, 'Beijing "steps up fight" against pirate CD makers', *The Financial Times*, 22 April 1996, p. 4.

92   Dennis Wharton, 'US, China avert war', *Variety*, 24–30 June 1996, p. 135.

93   Hill, 'Piracy on the high Cs', p. 18.

94   'Retribution for reproduction', *The Economist*, 18 May 1996, p. 73.

95   Doug Wilson, *Strategies of the Media Giants* (London, Pearson Professional, 1996), p. 5.

96   Frank Biondi, 'A media tycoon's take on the 21st century', *Business Week*, 18 November 1994, p. 190.

97   Helen Bunting, *US Media Markets: Leading the World?* (London, Pearson Professional, 1995), p. 98.

98   Mark Landler, 'Think globally, program locally', *Business Week*, 18 November 1994, pp. 186–9.

99   Bunting, *US Media Markets*, pp. 99, 3.

100 'Warner opens animation studio', *The Financial Times*, 22–23 June 1996, p. 4; Julia Flynn and Katherine Ann Miller, 'Tinseltown on the Thames', *Business Week*, 5 August 1996, pp. 47–8.

101 Diane Mermigas, 'Still to come: smaller media alliances', *Electronic Media*, 5 February 1996, p. 38.

102 Marlene Edmunds, 'Vertically integrated Schibsted rises to top', *Variety*, 14–20 October 1996, p. 52.

103 Diane Mermigas, 'Media players mining for global gold', *Electronic Media*, 11 December 1995, p. 18.

104 Comment of Porter Bibb, analyst for Ladenburg Thalmann & Co., cited in Keith J. Kelly, 'Time Warner temblor topples structure', *Advertising Age*, 20 November 1995, p. 6.

105 Comments of Michael J. Wolf, lead partner at Booz, Allen & Hamilton, cited in Rita Koselka, 'Mergermania in Medialand', *Forbes*, 23 October 1995, p. 254.

106 Ibid., p. 258.

107 Christopher Dixon, presentation to Association of Investment Management and Research, New York City, 31 January 1996, p. 4.

108 Marla Matzer, 'Contented kingdoms', *Superbrands '97*, supplement to *Adweek*, 7 October 1996, pp. 30, 33.

109 Jeff Jensen, 'Viacom eyes venues for merchandising', *Advertising Age*, 6 April 1996, p. 3.

110 Jeff Jensen, 'MCA/Universal grooms "Babe" for a new career as mass-market brand', *Advertising Age*, 29 April 1996, p. 16.

111 Diane Mermigas, 'New day dawns for Universal Television', *Electronic Media*, 6 January 1997, p. 24.

112 Jeff Jensen, 'Universal to present new image', *Advertising Age*, 1 July 1996, p. 28.

113 Marla Matzer, 'Contended kingdoms', *Brandweek*, special section of *Adweek*, 7 October 1996, p. 34.

114 Sally Goll Beatty, 'Turner lets some of its treasures moonlight for other marketers', *Wall Street Journal*, 22 May 1996, p. B8; Chuck Ross, 'Heyer steering Turner into marketing alliances', *Advertising Age*, 22 April 1996, p. 53.

115 Larry Dunn, 'Pressure builds when a giant enters a niche', *New York Times*, 16 September 1996, p. C4.

116 Joshua Levine, 'TV in the classroom', *Forbes*, 27 January 1997, p. 98.

117 *Wall Street Journal*, 29 January 1997, p. B2.

118 'Macworld', *The Economist*, 29 June 1996, p. 62.

119 Alice Rawsthorn, 'PepsiCo. to feel force of Star Wars', *The Financial Times*, 17 May 1996, p. 21.

120 Diane Mermigas, 'Seagram eyes global arena for Universal', *Electronic Media*, 13 January 1997, p. 94.

121 Laura Landro, 'Entertainment giants face pressure to cut costs, get into focus', *Wall Street Journal*, 11 February 1997, pp. A1, A17.

122 Diane Mermigas, 'Liberty sees sports as key to global kingdom', *Electronic Media*, 13 May 1996, p. 4.

123 Both the Viacom–Universal conflict over the US cable network and the Time Warner–USWest conflict over Time Warner Entertainment [were] being negotiated and considered by the court system [. . .] in March 1997. [. . .]

124 Bernard Simon, 'Seagram to hold on to 15% stake in Time Warner', *The Financial Times*, 1 June 1995, p. 18.

125 Raymond Snoddy, 'Master of bits at home in the hub', *The Financial Times*, 28 May 1996, p. 17.

126 Catherine E. Celebrezze, 'The man who bought the media', *EXTRA!*, 9 (2) (March–April 1996), pp. 21–2.

127 Mark Robichaux, 'Tim Robertson turns TV's family channel into a major business', *Wall Street Journal*, 29 August 1996, p. A6.

128 Linda Grant, 'Moneyman to the moguls', *Fortune*, 9 September 1996, pp. 37–8.

129 Martin Peers, 'Wall Street looks overseas', *Variety*, 14–20 October 1996, pp. 41–2.

130 Ronald Grover, 'Plenty of dreams, not enough work?' *Business Week*, 22 July 1996, p. 65.

131 Paula Dwyer, 'Can Rupert conquer Europe?', *Business Week*, 25 March 1996, p. 169.

132 Elizabeth Lesly, Gail DeGeorge and Ronald Grover, 'Sumner's last stand', *Business Week*, 3 March 1997, p. 67.

133 Quoted in *Wisconsin State Journal*, 9 February 1996, p. A2.

134 Snoddy, 'Master of bits at home in the hub', p. 17.

135 Elizabeth Jensen and Eben Shapiro, 'Time Warner's fight with News Corp. belies mutual dependence', *Wall Street Journal*, 28 October 1996, p. A1.

136 Dixon, presentation, p. 2.

137 Laurel Wentz and Kevin Brown, 'Global marketers', *Ad Age International*, November 1996, p. 115.

138 'So what was the fuss about?', *The Economist*, 22 June 1996, p. 59.

139 Comments of Jack Trout, cited in advertisement in *Advertising Age*, 22 April 1996, p. 7.

140 Chuck Ross, 'Global rules are proposed for measuring TV', *Advertising Age*, 12 August 1996, p. 3.

141 *Advertising Expenditure Forecasts* (London, Zenith Media, December 1995), pp. 124–9.

142 Robert J. Coen, 'The advertising trends up to 2020', paper presented to Marketing 2020 Conference, New York City, 16 March 1995.

143 Laura Petrecca, 'Coen sees hearty growth in ad spending for 1997', *Advertising Age*, 1 July 1996, p. 10.

144 Calmetta Y. Coleman, 'US agencies expand in Latin America', *Wall Street Journal*, 3 January 1996, p. B2.

145 David Kilburn, 'Asia rising', *Adweek*, 19 August 1996, p. 22.

146 Helen Bunting and Paul Chapman, *The Future of the European Media Industry: Towards the 21st Century* (London, Pearson Professional, 1996), p. 13.

147 'The Global 1000', *Business Week*, 8 July 1996, pp. 46–89.

148 Mark Gleason, 'Big Bang of '86 is still shaping the ad world', *Advertising Age*, 22 April 1996, p. 3.

149 R. Craig Endicott, 'Shops soar on growth of 9.2%, to $17 billion', *Advertising Age*, 15 April 1996, p. s2.

150 Laurel Wentz and Sasha Emmons, '"AAI" charts show yearly growth, consolidation', *Ad Age International*, September 1996, p. 133.

151 Sally Goll Beatty, 'BDDP's management preparing a takeover bid for the agency', *Wall Street Journal*, 13 May 1996, p. B4.

152 'So what was all the fuss about?', *The Economist*, 22 June 1996, p. 59.

153 Anne-Michele Morice, 'Havas hopes new name and look turn heads around world', *Wall Street Journal*, 3 April 1996, p. B10.

154 'Publicis may spend up to $200 million to buy ad agencies', *Wall Street Journal*, 12 September 1996, p. A5.

155 Sally Goll Beatty, 'Global needs challenge midsize agencies', *Wall Street Journal*, 14 December 1995, p. B8.

156 Shiraz Sidva, 'An Indian campaign', *The Financial Times*, 24 November 1995, p. 14.

157 Noreen O'Leary, 'World tours single client', *Adweek*, 5 August 1996, pp. 34–7.

158 'A passion for variety', *The Economist*, 30 November 1996, pp. 68, 71.

159 Greg Farrell, 'The world is their oyster', *Adweek*, 19 February 1996; Stuart Elliott, 'Advertising', *New York Times*, 18 March 1996, p. C9.

160 Sally Goll Beatty, 'Interpublic diversifies further with purchase of direct marketer', *Wall Street Journal*, 17 May 1996, p. B8.

161 Jack O'Dwyer, *O'Dwyer's Directory of Public Relations Firms, 1996* (New York, J.R. O'Dwyer Co. Inc., 1996), p. A7.

162 'Credits spiked to stop surfing', *Variety*, 23 December 1996–5 January 1997, p. 32.

163 Mary Kuntz and Joseph Weber, 'The new hucksterism', *Business Week*, 1 July 1996, pp. 77–84.

164 Chuck Ross, 'Fox-owned station in Chi. breaks program taboo', *Advertising Age*, 26 August 1996, p. 2.

165 Nicholas Denton and Hugh Carnegy, 'Ad breaks may interrupt free Swedish phone calls', *The Financial Times*, 20 January 1997, p. 1.

166 Kuntz and Weber, 'The new hucksterism'.

167 Darren McDermott, 'All-American infomercials sizzle in Asia', *Wall Street Journal*, 25 June 1996, p. B5.

168 P.J. Bednarski, 'A quantum leap in global infomercials', *Electronic Media*, 13 January 1997, pp. EMI-2, EMI-10.

169 Sally Goll Beatty, '"Sci-Fi Trader" on cable channel takes selling to new dimension', *Wall Street Journal*, 29 January 1997, p. B2.

170 'Sci-fi channel launches an entertainment program that sells', *Adweek*, 1996: the infomercial special sourcebook issue, 24 June 1996, p. 34.

171 Michael Schneider, 'Brand name-dropping', *Electronic Media*, 26 August 1996, pp. 1, 30.

172 David Leonhardt, 'Cue the soda can', *Business Week*, 24 June 1996, pp. 64, 66.

173 Bradley Johnson and Kim Cleland, 'Apple, MCI tout "Independence"', *Advertising Age*, 1 July 1996, p. 3.

174 Stuart Elliott, 'The spot on the cutting-room floor', *New York Times*, 7 February 1997, pp. C1–2.

175 Bruce Orwall, 'Disney chases live-action merchandising hits', *Wall Street Journal*, 27 November 1996, pp. B1, B4.

176 Luisa Kroll, 'Entertainomercials', *Forbes*, 4 November 1996, pp. 322, 324.

177 Sally Goll Beatty, 'CNBC will air a show owned, vetted by IBM', *Wall Street Journal*, 4 June 1996, pp. B1, B8.

178 Jenny Holtz, 'NBC joins Paramount, P&G deal', *Electronic Media*, 20 November 1995, p. 32.

179 'Viacom's TV group forms 3-way venture for movie production', *Wall Street Journal*, 26 April 1996, p. A5.

180 'ESPN creates cross-company buy', *Mediaweek*, 2 September 1996, p. 27.

181 Mark Gleason and Chuck Ross, 'Y&R, NBC mull massive linkup', *Advertising Age*, 16 September 1996, pp. 1, 54.

182 Christ Petrikin, 'Is H'wood learning to go by the book?', *Variety*, 16–22 December 1996, pp. 1, 99. For an excellent analysis of this process, see Mark Crispin Miller, 'The crushing power of big publishing', *The Nation*, 17 March 1997, pp. 11–18.

183 Andre Schiffrin, 'The corporatization of publishing', *The Nation*, 3 June 1996, pp. 29–32.

184 Robin Pogrebin, 'At struggling Time Warner, Time Inc. is money', *New York Times*, 3 February 1997, p. C1.

185 Bernard Weinraub, 'Hollywood success, with an aftertaste', *New York Times*, 7 January 1997, p. B1.

186 See Robert W. McChesney, *Corporate Media and the Threat to Democracy* (New York, Seven Stories Press, 1997), pp. 17–29.

187 *Tyndall Report*, 31 December 1996.

188 'Jordan brings the heart of the marketer to CBS-TV', *Advertising Age*, 3 February 1997, p. 18.

189 Bill Carter and Richard Sandomir, 'The trophy in Eisner's deal', *New York Times*, 6 August 1995, section 3, p. 11.

190 'MTV: rocking all over the world', *The Financial Times*, 4 July 1995, p. 17.

191 World Commission on Culture and Development, *Our Creative Diversity* (Paris, UNESCO, 1995), p. 109.

192 Michela Wrong, 'Without a voice of its own', *The Financial Times*, 19 February 1997, p. 11.

193 Donald G. McNeil, Jr, 'A crank-up radio helps Africa tune in', *New York Times*, 16 February 1996, p. A1.

194 Steven Erlanger, 'Russian press is free, free to go broke', *New York Times*, 6 July 1995, p. A5.

195 Brian MacNair, 'Television in post-Soviet Russia: from monolith to mafia', *Media, Culture and Society*, 18 (3) (July 1996), pp. 489–99.

196 John Downing, *Internationalizing Media Theory* (Thousand Oaks, CA, Sage, 1996), pp. 132, 146.

197 'Russia's judgment day', *The Nation*, 8 July 1996.

198 Alan Riding, 'For a Czech film executive, it's all business', *New York Times*, 8 April 1996, p. C9.

199 'US pic domination rankles Eastern Europe', *Variety*, 29 October–3 November 1996, p. 32.

200 Cordelia Becker, 'Mittelstand makes an impression on the news stand', *The Financial Times*, 5 March 1996, p. 19; 'How an astrophysicist became a media mogul', *The Economist*, 3 August 1996, p. 59.

201 Rick Richardson, 'Satellite, cable TV burgeoning in Poland', *Variety*, 15–21 April 1996, p. M26; T.R. Smart, 'A handsome TV station – going once, going twice', *Business Week*, 27 May 1996, p. 58.

202 Mark Landler, 'In Europe, an ex-ambassador's new empires', *New York Times*, 1 April 1996, p. C3.

203 'Eastern Europe's ailing press', *New York Times*, 6 August 1996, p. A10.

204 'Prepared testimony of John Fox, Director, Open Society Institute, before the House International Relations Committee re: foreign aid authorization', Federal News Service, 5 April 1995; Steve Forbes, 'Airwaves for freedom', *Forbes*, 15 July 1996, pp. 23–4.

205 John Thornhill, 'Russia's unfinished revolution', *The Financial Times*, 30 May 1996, p. 13.

206 Elizabeth Fox, 'Latin America', in *Media Ownership and Control in the Age of Convergence* (London, International Institute of Communications, 1996), pp. 157–69.

207 Angus Foster, 'Contenders beam down', *The Financial Times*, 12 September 1995, p. 18; Jeffrey D. Zbar, 'Niche audiences are growing', *Advertising Age International*, July 1996, pp. 118, 121.

208 'Latin American snapshot: a look at key TV markets', *Variety*, 20 November 1995, p. 19.

209 Andrew Paxman, 'Latin cable upsurge', *Variety*, 10–16 June 1996, pp. 23, 28.

210 Jeffrey D. Zbar, 'Conference extols Latin America', *Advertising Age*, 11 March 1996.

211 Andrew Bailes and Neil Hollister, *Asian Cable and Satellite: Unrivalled Growth Opportunities* (London, Pearson Professional, 1996), pp. 44, 1.

212 Don Groves, 'Disney inks Indonesia vid deal', *Variety*, 3–9 June 1996, p. 22.

213 Geoffrey Lee Martin, 'Rival media scions plot growth in Asia-Pacific', *Advertising Age*, 19 September 1996, p. 46.

214 Louise Lucas, 'Asia TV race is a marathon, not a sprint', *The Financial Times*, 27 July 1995, p. 17.

215 Don Groves, 'Asia grows a money tree', *Variety*, 27 May–2 June 1996, p. 13.

216 Janine Stein and Laurel Wentz, 'The new Asia', *Ad Age International*, June 1996, p. 134.

217 Joseph M. Chan, 'Commercialization without independence: trends and tensions of media development in China', in J. Cheng and M. Brosseau (eds), *China Review 1993* (Hong Kong, Chinese University Press, 1993), p. 25.2.

218 Orville Schell, 'Maoism *v.* media in the marketplace', *Media Studies Journal*, Summer 1995, pp. 33–42.

219 'China's TV network to share programs with two concerns', *Wall Street Journal*, 7 February 1996, p. B2; Tony Walker, 'China keeps tight grip on cable TV boom', *The Financial Times*, 20 August 1996, p. 5.

220 Craig Smith, 'China's huge consumer potential prompts industry survey boom', *Wall Street Journal*, 20 March 1996, p. B5.

221 'News corp. tries to forge link with Chinese', *Wall Street Journal*, 31 January 1996, p. A6.

222 Mark Woods, 'Media giants court China TV market', *Variety*, 12–18 February 1996, p. 37.

223 Comment by Christopher Dixon, quoted in David Lieberman, 'Old guard tactic is old brand names', *USA Today*, International edn, 19 July 1996, p. 8A.

224 Geraldine Fabrikant, 'Time Warner is licensing 12 films to its cable outlets', *New York Times*, 16 January 1997, p. C10.

Popular culture on a global scale:
a challenge for cultural studies?
Simon During

[. . .] Since the 1980s some cultural products are indeed globally popular and intentionally so; they are distributed and apparently enjoyed everywhere, at any rate wherever electricity is on line or generators and batteries can be transported and where they are not successfully banned. They belong to what I will call (without any intended Gramscian resonances) the global popular.

As we shall see, the global popular is a category that challenges (though it does not overturn) current cultural studies' welcome to difference, hybridity, and subversion. This chapter takes up that challenge. It attempts to think the global popular affirmatively at the same time as it explores, self-reflexively, interactions between cultural globalization and the new visibility of academic cultural studies. I want to argue that producing academic knowledge of the global popular – its theory, its history – involves a set of new problems and topics, which, perhaps surprisingly, pushes us to consider strong male bodies and special effects. I'll address these issues by referring to Arnold Schwarzenegger, focussing first on his 1990 star vehicle, Paul Verhoeven's *Total Recall*, and then on (the history of) bodybuilding and magic. Why Schwarzenegger? However much of his career may be stalling, he remains a unique phenomenon. Worldwide, he was the most popular movie star during the period in which the contemporary global popular emerged. At least those who have most at stake in such matters think so; the international film exhibitors' trade show, looking back at the 1980s, honored him as 'International Star of the Decade'.[1]

This chapter is taken from *Critical Inquiry*, 23 (1997), pp. 808–21. It should already be apparent that the global popular is not to be identified with cultural globalization (or transnationalization) *tout court*. Cultural globalization takes many forms and has many different effects, some of which work in the opposite direction to the global popular.

Globalized cultural technologies and networks of production and distribution have, paradoxically enough, generated more and more locally produced and consumed works from news shows to soaps (by the logic of what Japanese marketeers apparently sometimes call 'glocalization').[2] Such cultural technologies have also produced new transnational audiences bounded often by language or religion.[3] Some 'glocalized' cultural products appeal to mysteriously disjunct audiences worldwide; how do we account, for example, for the way that the world's largest producer of *telenovelas*, Protele, has been successful in the Swiss and French markets (as well as in Mexico, Turkey, South Korea, and Russia) but a relative failure elsewhere in Europe? How do we account for the way that Bombay movies are popular in Greece but not elsewhere in Europe? To begin to understand these cases, we require site-specific histories. In another mode of cultural globalization, a self-conscious commitment to the global can provide an impetus and marketing platform for new cross-culturally hybridized genres, particularly 'world music'. But such genres are not genuinely popular in many, if any, local markets. More interestingly, commercial cultural production aimed simultaneously at Asian, European, and American markets is itself beginning to form small 'art' or 'independent' niches (long familiar in translated and cosmopolitan 'world literature'). Perhaps the most fertile is that of touring independent rock acts who may be successful if not famous on several continents and prompt various local bands on their circuit to creative imitation. A more obvious example: Japanese money is being put into Hollywood and European art cinema for which there is an increasing audience in Japan as well as in the Indian subcontinent and some Southeast Asian nations. *The Crying Game*, *Howard's End*, and *Naked Lunch*, for instance, were all part-financed by Nikkon Film Development and Finance, which is in turn part-owned by Japan's largest distribution house, Nippon Herald. Last in this partial itemization of globalized culture, geosynchronous broadcasting, whether of 'mega-events' like the Olympics or of day-to-day transmissions like those transmitted by CNN, also belong to the category, even though such broadcasting mainly reaches only elite groups outside of those (relatively few) countries where cabled television sets or satellite dishes are widely distributed.

This list could be extended, but I wish to stress that none of these forms of cultural globalization themselves constitute the global popular that, today, only comes into being when a particular product or star is a hit in many markets. Yet it is impossible simply to sever the global popular from other forms of cultural globalization. The reason is not just that together they form a single, if very loose, globalizing system but that relations between the various kinds of cultural globalization as well as more localized forms of cultural production are constantly changing and transacting. This is especially true at four levels: financing [. . .]; governmental regulations (outside the US national-cultural import policies and, often, censorship tend to be under almost constant negotiation); technology (which can change so quickly as to touch the actual plots of would-be globally popular products – *Jurassic Park*'s plot, for instance, was changed during production to accommodate technological innovations); and, last, the market appeal of particular stars (Arnie being a case in point). Globally popular culture is joined to other modes of cultural globalization within this state of permanent metamorphosis.

Cultural globalization is an element within much larger forces and institutions of globalization. Let us make a relatively simple distinction among economic, financial, and cultural globalization.[4] Economic globalization refers to the transnational decentralization of production and services in a process by which low value-added labor is exported from rich countries or at least the rich regions of rich countries to create the (misnamed) 'international division of labor'.[5] This routinely touches cultural production; *Total Recall*, for instance, was shot in Mexico City to take advantage of low costs, with the highly trained workforce travelling down from California. In the film, the brutalist skyscrapers, which embody Earth's interplanetary imperialism, are in fact monuments to Mexico City's *compradors*. Next, financial globalization denotes capital's increased capacity to flow across national borders. This, too, enables the financing of megabudget movies [. . .], but it connects with cultural globalization in at least two other important ways. Financial globalization helps some non-Western nations and markets become richer and more competitive in relation to the West and so extends the reach of ethico-political judgements based on the once culture-specific assumption that peoples have a right (and a desire) to become comparatively affluent. It extends as well the reach of cultural markets and the state institutions that secure those markets. This process, along with certain anxieties and resistances that flow from it, are often, if indirectly, thematized in globally popular works. This is all the more true because globalization also exerts pressure on all national economies, especially weak ones, to compete in export markets and avoid flights of capital. This draws both rich and poor countries towards social policies regulated by neoclassical economic assumptions and methods (sometimes called the new political economy), policies relatively sensitive to the needs, including the cultural needs, of new export markets.

To understand cultural globalization's conditions of existence we need to make a wider detour into entertainment industry economics. The crucial fact about contemporary cultural markets is the degree to which they are dominated by a single piece of hardware: the television set. In the US, the average household spends 2,500 hours per year watching television[6] and probably less than 10 per cent of that time pursuing other recreational cultural activities. This figure is high in international terms, but leisure the world over is still increasingly dominated by television viewing. More than cinema, television, often connected to a VCR, is the technology that drives contemporary globalization of the audiovisual product. In the US, home video market revenues overtook worldwide theatrical release revenues in the late 1980s, although in some markets (notably in Asia), the construction of cinemas is also proceeding apace.[7] One crucial fallout of the move from domestic cinema into video (and cable) is that movie audiences have become increasingly segmented into niche categories, a process also helped by the development of multiplex cinemas. In the 1970s, new youth markets appeared for a variety of genres and combinations of genres, of which the most successful were teen, horror/slasher, sci-fi, and action movies. This segmentation of the market [. . .] fed into globalization.

It is important to recognize that television software is less globalized than its hardware. Certainly the flows of exports are not symmetrical; in 1988 only about 2 percent of all US programming (excluding Hispanic and 'multicultural' programming) came from abroad, whereas Hollywood – as producer of TV shows as well as films – may well become the US's single biggest export industry.[8] Currently a star can only be established globally by Hollywood cinema, although some global product comes from else-where. Some 'foreign' films are picked up on an *ad hoc* basis by US distributors, such as Cannon or Goldcrest in the 1980s, or occasionally shows and films are created from more localized industries, such as the Hong Kong film or Brazilian and Mexican television industries or by small Canadian and Australian production houses aimed at international television markets (whose most successful players are moving in increasing numbers to the States anyway). Yet only Hollywood produces system-atically for worldwide export. This does not mean, of course, that all Hollywood product is equally globalizable.

Although cultural globalization cannot be thought about simply as local culture's enemy (far from it), and although foreign product may be resisted (China's ban on the private ownership of satellite dishes being a good recent example), still the globalization of VCRs, geosynchronous broadcasting, and the emergence of world stars has attenuated many national cultural industries. Thus US television programs like *Dynasty* and *Santa Barbara* beamed into India on Rupert Murdoch's Star TV have proved popular enough for Doordarshan, the Indian public broadcaster, to buy and transmit more US product. This process has been the more marked because cultural industries are being deregulated worldwide under the influence of the new political economy. In Asia, two of the largest film industries, the Indian and the Indonesian, are losing ground; the Indonesian industry, which produced about eighty feature films annually in the 1980s, is currently producing less than ten because of lack of government support for the local industry. On the other hand, there has been a transnational-ization of US studio ownership, with, most famously, some studios being bought by Japanese hardware manufacturers. Thus *Total Recall* was distributed by Tri-Star, part of Columbia, bought by Sony in 1989. And the conglomerates we call studios are increasingly entering into offshore partnerships. Time Warner, for instance, started a rush in 1990 when, using the satellite PanAmSat (whose footprint covers the Western hemisphere), they joined forces with Omnivisión Latin Entertainment, a Venezuelan company, and formed HBO-Olé to gain access to South American markets, a Spanish and Portuguese broadcasting project in which Time Warner and its partners were later joined by Sony Pictures Entertainment.[9] Time Warner is also building multiplexes in Japan with a Japanese supermarket chain, Nichii.[10] In China, Paramount has entered into similar deals with a Hong Kong company (controlled by members of the mainland politician Chen Yun's family) and a Malaysian company (owned by sons of the Malaysian prime minister).[11] Hollywood also calls on capital that flows in

from a variety of overseas sources: *Total Recall* was produced by Carolco, a now defunct independent, whose investors have included the privately owned French pay television group Canal Plus; Italy's video distributor and media consortium Rizzoli/Corriere della Sera (RCS); the Japanese hardware manufacturer Pioneer (itself part of the Matsushita empire); and the ubiquitous, state-owned French bank Crédit Lyonnais.

It is worth noting as an aside that in 1993 a big share of Carolco was bought by TCI, the largest cable operator in the US and a pioneer in fiber-optic technology, partly on the strength of Carolco's library – which includes the *Terminator* movies and *Basic Instinct*, as well as *Total Recall* – and partly on the promise of another Verhoeven/Schwarzenegger mega-production, *Crusade*.[12] TCI intended to use Carolco to introduce a shift in local distribution that would have had global implications for audiovisual culture. They wished to make certain films available on pay-per-view TV in the US simultaneously with their theatrical release. Here we see what will become a familiar theme in this chapter: the muscled male body – in this case, Schwarzenegger's – being used to join old forms of cultural production and distribution to new and untried ones.

Nonetheless, the ownership of production (or distribution) houses is not a ground for cultural globalization. Production is a localized if diffuse and competitive business, scattered across the talent agencies, the craft unions, the special-effects shops, the costume-hire firms, the CAD (computer assisted design) studios, picture and sound libraries, location search teams, the domestic space of scriptwriters, musicians, and so on. A plethora of individuals and small or large, autonomous or semiautonomous businesses come together in particular productions through a surprisingly informal system of networking, extraordinarily responsive to global market shifts, centered in Los Angeles.

Because globally popular moviemaking is a high-risk, high unit-cost business whose production is localized in Los Angeles, globalization inscribes itself into filmmaking most effectively at the moment of financing, all the more so because the first films consciously aimed at a global market were not produced by the major studios but by independents such as Carolco. In order to be financed, a megabudget, globally oriented, independent film like *Total Recall* will typically require: (1) those involved in its production to take a share of its profits in lieu of up-front payment; (2) presales to foreign distributors, with different deals usually being made in each territory for separate film rental, video, and broadcast television distribution rights; (3) an accounting procedure called cross-collateralization, in which the market performance of a movie in one territory can be discounted against its performance in another, or one movie's performance discounted against another in a package deal; and (4) the purchase of insurance against failure to complete (so-called completion bonds). Local distributors only put up money for films that they believe will sell in their markets; in the mid-1980s, for instance, Goldcrest/Warner failed to meet expectations for *Revolution*, which could not be presold into Germany and Japan, but then exceeded them with *The Mission* and *Dances with Wolves*.[13] So it is at the presale moment that First World production is most directly inscribed by global tastes, and it is probably that the rush of 'postcolonial' films like *The Mission* reflects this. Strange as it may seem, one of the hottest stories in Hollywood in 1989 (finally acquired by David Puttnam) was the story of Chico Mendez – the indigenous Brazilian environmentalist murdered by loggers.[14] 'Globalization' of screen culture, then, means that certain Hollywood films are aimed simultaneously at two markets: home and the rest of the world, with the latter category fragmenting into separate territories (Japan and Germany dominating in terms of income flow) and with an appeal to each built into production at the moment of financing.

It is important to grasp the financial, economic, and technological underpinnings of cultural globalization, but, of course, cultural studies is more interested in the kinds of questions that come next. What is a global culture going to look like? What are its effects? What wants does it fulfil? In answering such questions, the information that I have just outlined helps us move beyond the generalizations of commentators like Jean Baudrillard, for whom cultural globalization simply means the mutation of previously self-governing agents into signifiers of a commodified, homogeneous, self-enclosed world imaginary. But, precisely because the global popular crosses so many cultures, these questions resist easy settlement. We can say, however, that answers will not be found where the West once thought they would be, that is, in those Eurocentric dreams of hegemony traditionally embodied in two forms of universalization: one sacred, the other secular. In particular, the global popular makes it harder than ever for us to imagine a unified world culture under the sway of enlightened universals considered to end irrationality and spread autonomous individuality.

In fact, cultural globalization is occurring along another, much more restricted track – via show business. It is true that one commonly canvassed reason for the transcultural success of video and other global media like satellite broadcasting is the ease with which such means of transmission allow consumers to bypass local state restrictions and control – an explanation that fits liberal and universalist models of the media.[15] Yet convergences in leisure consumption across many communities do not entail convergences in, for instance, familial relations or religious practices – at that level there is little evidence for a large global homogenization of culture thesis.[16] Indeed, I will argue that the appeal of the audiovisual global popular is finally to be read in terms of the limited capacities of particular media to provide for individuals' needs and desires, especially male needs and desires, across the various territories that constitute the world image-market. It is just possible to take films that are globally popular and read from them a set of elements that are universal, in the weak sense that they are culturally translatable to the maximum degree. Even then, given the global-cultural system's constant transformations, it does not follow that these will provide the constituents of a yet-to-be-fully-realized global popular.

As the dominant world star at that moment when nondomestic sales began to become more important than domestic sales in the blockbuster sector of the US film industry. Arnold Schwarzenegger belongs to the global popular. He has been, if anything, more popular in Japan, Indonesia, Eastern Europe (the old Second World), and the Arab countries than in Europe or the Americas. To take just one instance: in Russia, Schwarzy (as the French call him) is, along with Stalin and Hitler, an icon of the fascist People's Socialist Party. His worldwide popularity increased as his movie career progressed through subcultural films into sword and sorcery movies, to the first *Terminator* and thence into *Total Recall*, then into comedies (*Twins* being one of the first comedies to do well in world markets), and most recently into (relatively unsuccessful, self-conscious) comedy-action hybrids.[17] *Total Recall*, the pivotal movie in this sequence because it was directly controlled by the star, cost $60 million and grossed $300 million, of which $180 million came from non-US markets against a then-industry average of a 40/60 domestic/foreign revenue split, while about half the domestic revenue ($63 million) has come from rentals.[18] But, crucially, information about international consumption is, as Momar Kebe N'Diaye puts it, 'fragmentary, incomplete and sometimes contradictory' because, outside OECD nations and despite ever more powerful threats from US government and industry agencies, as well as pressure from GATT, dubbing and 'clandestine' markets abound (*The Terminator*, in particular, being notorious for the number of pirated tapes in circulation around the world).[19] Again, to take just two other examples, Bombay has 8,000 unauthorized cable systems using satellite dishes to grab whatever programming they can; and in Taiwan, where a million households are plugged into unlicensed cables, revenues sometimes estimated in the hundreds of millions are lost to Hollywood annually because of so-called piracy. This is not a 'Third World problem'; Italy heads the international video piracy table.[20]

In general, we know that world markets welcome the intensities attached to what, following Tom Gunning, I'll call a cinema of action-attractions.[21] It's a cinema heavily dependent on special effects and stunts, particularly the presentation of highly stylized, acrobatic violence that revolves around slashing, guns, and hand-to-hand combat, often borrowing from non-Western martial arts. These effects are welded into narratives for which violence is a solution to exploitation. In this, globally popular movies extend generic conventions developed in Western youth markets. In order to acquire more grounded knowledge about what this means, we would need to look towards the situations in which preferences for this kind of movie are enacted. In particular, I would suggest, we should look at how the power to make choices in various local viewing situations is shared between genders, all the more so because outside the core economies, video is not mainly viewed on privately owned VCRs but in video cafés and, as in rural Papua New Guinea, in mobile video trucks that travel from village to village. In the case of Indian video cafés, Ravi Vasudevan has argued that masculinist violence is attractive in part because it helps exclude women from public space – an argument that might well be extendable to other contexts.[22] And it is clear from many sources that video viewing can reinforce extended family socialization in countries where it has been threatened by cinema and other public entertainments.[23] Certainly it is strange that, although romances are popular in many cultures, there is not yet a centralized, globally popular women's cinema based on romance (as there has been, in a relatively restricted mode, for the novel) although the *telenovela* often dominates prime-time broadcasting in countries where women have considerable power over domestic space. Because information about global consumption and its causes is so thin, it is necessary, however, to fall back on interpretation to uncover the cross-cultural wants that globally popular films fulfil. Obviously, this turn to interpretation and speculation runs the risk of substituting our own for other intelligences and feelings. Nonetheless, mindful of that warning, let me analyze in a little more detail two of the crucial features that characterize mainstream contemporary global cinema: male bodies and special effects.

This cinema is marked by a preference for a particular kind of trained male body, not just Schwarzenegger's but many others including Sylvester Stallone's and Jean-Claude van Damme's. These bodies are culturally specific: Schwarzenegger's body, despite his unprecedented mass, the definition of his cuts (to use bodybuilders' lingo), and his V shape (one that became popular in bodybuilding in the 1940s), is still modelled on a classical Greek ideal. In his films, his body is a resource available when everything else – guns, money, status, power – runs out. It's the stuff of survival, there to be identified with by men whose clout is corporeal. Thus it grounds his appeal across the international division of labor.

But this is a little too easy. Unlike most bodies formed in the unconsidered entanglement of heredity, lifeways, and work, Schwarzenegger's body is more alien than natural, the product of a rigorous regime of self-government as well as, so he admits, in the past, steroids. More specifically, training incorporates certain relations that are also embedded in screen spectatorship. As it aims to transform bodies, training requires constant self-inspection – touching, looking, imagining – centered on mirrors. These techniques and their desired outcome – self-specularization and bodily transformation – echo the relation between the viewer and the filmed bodies of actors. These relations flow in two directions. Not only does the training eye see the training body in the mirror somewhat as the spectator sees bodies on screen, but the spectator can also identify or take pleasure in trained bodies on the screen all the more intensely because they are the result of transformative routines based on, and aimed at, being seen. What training does, though, is bring these relations closer to everyday life and the private sphere (into the world of houses and gyms) than they can ever be on screen. And it seems to me that, even for those who do not train, trained bodies carry with them the idea of training and the routine of transforming and observing the body.

It is within the join and disjunction between the body as what nature supplies to all and the body as constructed, visualized object that the Schwarzenegger globally popular effect begins to be generated. This is all the more true because training requires little capital, cultural or otherwise, but does demand work. Workouts mime and personalize labor, especially the kind of (Fordist) labor that is exported in the global economy. Movies like *The Terminator* and *Total Recall* intensify this attachment of the constructed, labored-over body to the body-as-resource by presenting stories about, and images of, bodies that are products as well as controllers of technology. In sum, we can read such films as allegorizing the condition of those for whom the body is, first, a ground to be worked upon; second, a source of labor power for processes of production; and, third, a locus of an undervalued presence in the world but one potentially open to reconstruction and the (learned) pleasures of self-viewing. While it is important to recognize that many lives, especially male lives, from rich white men in expensive gyms to Papua New Guinea's raskals (that is, PNG's powerful urban gang members who often identify with global stars), meet at least the first of these conditions, they bear most pressingly on those with least clout.

Special effects, in the cinema of action-attractions, are generally used to construct magical worlds that exceed everyday causal constraints; indeed, their techniques go back to the artisanal knowledge of conjurers (traditionally among the most cross-culturally peripatetic of popular entertainers). In the context of an analysis of global film's popularity, it is important not to revivify the old ethnographical problem as to whether or not non-Western ontologies and 'magical' ritual actions were 'rational', as if non-Western audiences tended to be inherently more superstitious than Western ones and as if the attraction of special effects were a sign that such irrationalities linger.[24] One of the global popular's promises is that it helps us break with that problematic. In fact, we can say that special effects, especially as linked to violence and psychic communication, construct characters who can engage the world, not just outside of the laws of physics, but outside of messy negotiations with the more powerful – negotiations that are likely to require fewer crippling trade-offs to the degree that one has clout, is educated, and so on. In this sense, the movies can be read as operating within psychic economies so as to compensate for disadvantage. But we can further clarify the relation among special effects, magic, and global film by pausing briefly on a film produced outside the West that also tells a story about a trained body.

In the Egyptian film, *The Man who Befriended the Devil*, the bodybuilder and strongman Alal fights for his people against the corrupt local power élite in scenes using stunts and rudimentary special effects. In a very poor community, by the logic that I have suggested, Alal's body is his most effective tool for reordering both his personal and communal life-conditions. But Alal is overambitious: to maintain justice in the community, he wishes to become immortal. So, taking advice from a sorcerer, he makes a ritual pact with the devil. Despite the pact, he is soon poisoned by a jealous lover and dies. The story's moral is that magic as ritual action is effective only by virtue of a placebo effect. Alal's good deeds, which do indeed survive him, were enabled not by magic powers but by his physical training and his false belief in his contract with the devil. The film instructs audiences in enlightened values by replacing magic as the ritual harnessing of supernatural agency with both training and magic as special effects – a message common enough in the 'modernizing' cultural moment. *Total Recall* shares much with the Egyptian film, but not the latter's antiritual instructions, the clunkiness of its stunts and effects, or its attachment to a localized everyday life. More to the point, with its huge budget, its secure secularity, its capacity to harness technologies that amaze first and instruct second, if at all, *Total Recall* (like other movies of the genre) can increase fictional suspension of disbelief to the point where that suspension is extended to disbelief in magical effects. This means that it can more effectively provide for fantasies and empowerments along the lines that I have suggested. Following a long tradition within Western theatre and film, *Total Recall* uses its remoteness from magic as ritual practice or a set of nonenlightened beliefs to harness magic for narrative and spectacle.

Finally, on filmic globalization, a movie like *Total Recall* consists of more than its attractions. At the level of plot, it performs a balancing act; it must secure its metropolitan and nonmetropolitan appeal simultaneously. How does this dual demand work? The story fictively exaggerates contemporary neocolonialist relations; Earth here is the centre of empire, Mars, Earth's colony. The Schwarzenegger character, Hauser, is an imperialist secret agent who, via a memory implant, becomes Quaid, a construction worker with a yen for a memory-implanted holiday on Mars. Mars is a weird choice for Quaid's holiday because a national liberation struggle is in progress and the planet's atmosphere causes mutations. Mars has been colonized by Earth only because the essential mineral, tribidium, can be mined there. At the movie's end, after a complicated series of betrayals, Quaid rejects his previous identity as Hauser and liberates the colony. In doing so, he also rejects his blonde wife and turns to a dark local woman, in a version of those old colonial romances (especially as written by Pierre Loti) in which the hero is partially indigenized for love of colonialism's victims. This woman plays second fiddle to Quaid but is, like him, violent, strong, and effective (it is worth noting that no equivalent character to this strong woman exists in *The Man who Befriended the Devil*). However, despite appearances, *Total Recall* expresses no anticolonialist revolutionary dream. After all, the Martian miners require a secret agent to win their freedom for them and are portrayed as dehumanized mutants; in this respect, the film is a version of the old freak show, requiring virtuosic makeup and prosthetics. The movie's irredentism finally modulates into a simpler, less focused antistatism. Furthermore, it turns out that Quaid's whole adventure might be implanted, and therefore the whole story of Mars's liberation a simulation.

The film can succeed in various world markets not just by playing with desires for anti-First World insurgency but by supposing in advance that its audiences live inside a global culture. Familiar sci-fi presuppositions clear the way for this; science fiction's planetary perspective maps onto the cultural industries' global scale. Both on Mars and on Earth, political unity is organized at the level of the planet and is secured by ecological finitude. Mars is unified because it does not have enough air, Earth because it does not have enough tribidium. Resource depletion is used to construct a global we. And, in the film, global culture is also tied together by the pervasiveness of the high-quality visual display units (VDUs), as well as futuristic machines that transform digitalized information into virtual reality. Finally, the movie breaks through the horizon of species-being (an effect controlled still more effectively in *Jurassic Park* where dinosaur-terror fuses audiences together by virtue of their sheer humanness). In *Total Recall*, too, because minds can be surgically implanted and mutants can form communities, the species' internal divisions into cultural, national, or ethnic communities seem peripheral. This collapse of difference in the face of non-species-being once again helps fuse a global audience. In sum, by fictively presupposing a world system in which the technology and economic order from which it profits (and which its audiences enjoy) are more firmly embedded then they in fact are, the movie markets the cultural and infrastructural conditions of its own success.

[. . .]

Notes

I would like to acknowledge all those who helped me think through this chapter – not least Homi Bhabha, David Bennett, John Frow, and Lisa O'Connell.

1   The usual measure of a star's appeal is to average the gross takings of his or her movies during the first weekend of their release, over a particular period. See Judy Brennan and Laurence Cohn, 'Star Bright – or Lite?', *Variety Weekly*, 15 March 1993, p. 1.

2   See Roland Robertson, 'Globalisation or glocalisation', *Journal of International Communication*, 1 (1) (June 1994), pp. 33–53.

3   For a discussion of these issues, see Armand Mattelart, Xavier Delcourt and Michèlle Mattelart, *International Image Markets: in Search of an Alternative Perspective*, trans. David Buxton (London, 1984), and Anthony D. Smith, 'Towards a global culture?', in *Global Culture: Nationalism, Globalization and Modernity*, ed. Mike Featherstone (London, 1990), pp. 171–91.

4   See Arjun Appadurai, 'Disjuncture and difference in the global cultural economy', *Public Culture*, 2 (Spring 1990), pp. 1–24.

5   My sense of how what I am calling 'economic globalization' works owes much to my reading of Saskia Sassen, *The Global City: New York, London, Tokyo* (Princeton, NJ, 1991).

6   See Harold L. Vogel, *Entertainment Industry Economics: a Guide for Financial Analysis* (Cambridge, 1990), p. 53.

7   See Don Groves, 'Hollywood wows world wickets', *Variety Weekly*, 22 February 1993, p. 85, for information on cinema construction in South Korea, Singapore, Malaysia, Indonesia and Taiwan.

8   See Vogel, *Entertainment Industry Economics*, p. 49, and Jake Eberts and Terry Ilott, *My Indecision is Final: the Spectacular Rise and Fall of Goldcrest Films, the Independent Studio that Challenged Hollywood* (London, 1990), p. 2.

9   See John Sinclair, 'The decentering of cultural imperialism: televisa-ion and globu-ization in the Latin world', in *Continental Shift: Globalisation and Culture*, ed. Elizabeth Jacka (Sydney, 1992), pp. 99–116. For HBO-Olé, see Peter Besas, 'Yanks seek TV El Dorado', *Variety Weekly*, 12 April 1993, p. 24.

10 See Garth Alexander, 'Warner Bros plexes Japan', *Variety Weekly*, 19 April 1993, p. 36.

11 Don Groves, 'Modern multiplexes to make China smile', *Variety Weekly*, 4 April 1994, p. 12.

12 See Matt Rothman and Judy Brennan, 'TCI's film surprise', *Variety Weekly*, 26 April 1993, pp. 85–6.

13   See Eberts and Ilott, *My Indecision is Final*, p. 435.

14   See Gregg Kilday, 'Guber-Peters: die hards', *Film Comment*, 26 (January–February 1990), p. 33.

15   See, for instance, Douglas A. Boyd, Joseph C. Staubhaar and John A. Lent, *Videocassette Recorders in the Third World* (New York, 1989).

16   See John Tomlinson, *Cultural Imperialism: a Critical Introduction* (London, 1990), for a good discussion of these issues and a review of the literature.

17   See Nicolas Kent, *Naked Hollywood: Money and Power in the Movies Today* (London, 1991), p. 109.

18   See Vogel, *Entertainment Industry Economics*, p. 43.

19   Momar Kebe D'Niaye, 'West Africa', in *Video World-Wide: an International Study*, ed. Manuel Alvarado (London, 1988), p. 235.

20   Mark Lewis, 'Taiwan struggles with piracy', *Variety Weekly*, 22 February 1993, p. 92, and 'Taiwan buyers seek toons 'n' tough guys', *Variety Weekly*, 5 April 1993, p. 91.

21   For 'cinema of attractions', see Tom Gunning, 'The cinema of attractions: early film, its spectator, and the avant-garde', in *Early Cinema: Space, Frame, Narrative*, ed. Thomas Elsaesser and Adam Barker (London, 1990), pp. 56–62.

22   See Ravi S. Vasudevan, 'Glancing off reality: contemporary cinema and mass culture', *Cinemaya*, 16 (Summer 1992), pp. 4–9.

23   See Boyd et al., *Videocassette Recorders in the Third World*.

24   For a recent discussion of this tradition, see Stanley Jeyaraja Tambiah, *Magic, Science, Religion, and the Scope of Rationality* (Cambridge, 1990).

New media for new times

Introduction

Part III focuses on two aspects of the current mediascape and its transformation. The first two chapters examine an old medium in new times – television. In a history of some 60 years, television has become the supremely domesticated modern medium, an omnipresent feature in the textures of household cultures and routines. It has been a key component in processes of privatization, and has been highly successful in weaving itself into what Paddy Scannell (1996) has called the 'dailiness' of social life. Despite its familiar, domesticated and seemingly unchanging appearance, television – like the full range of mass media – has been subject to more or less continuous processes of transformation since its early development.

These transformations have restructured the whole 'circuit' of television encompassing the conditions and practices of production, the generic forms of television, the conditions of reception, and the broader contexts of popular culture and social relations. The arrival of digital television in the late 1990s is only the most recent in a long line of landmark events or new ages in the history of television since the flickering black-and-white images of the pre-war years, including the development and take-up of ITV, the 625-line standard and colour television.

Jeanette Steemers in Chapter 12 provides a timely exploration and assessment of the ways in which digital systems threaten and promise to transform television and of the factors which will have a bearing on the emergent digital television era. She begins by noting some of the ways in which the digital television era is set to contradict the habits and conventions of the old analogue television culture and its regulatory regimes. In her assessment of the potential impact of digital television on the future of broadcasting, she draws not only on examples from the UK but also the German policy context to identify the consequences of the introduction of digital television for European audiovisual plurality and diversity. This analysis leads her to question the appropriateness and applicability of traditional broadcasting policy to today's digital era. Pay-per-view and on-demand systems make broadcasting more like other consumer activities and phenomena. In particular, Steemers warns that the strategies developed by public service broadcasters and policy-makers at both national and European Union level may not be sufficient to counter the emergent threats to plurality and diversity underlying the commercial development and expansion of both terrestrial and satellite digital systems.

Recent years have also seen the restructuring and transformation of central aspects of television production. It can be argued that these changes and innovations have been most strongly experienced and driven by broadcast news cultures and their requirements. News, by definition, has always been a volatile genre, and in television terms has tended to prioritize the up-to-the-minute, immediate reported sounds and images from the news events of the day occurring around the world. In recent years, satellite networks and broadcast systems have transformed the nature of television news and significant aspects of its production and form.

In Chapter 13, Brent MacGregor discusses the changing nature of news and news-gathering and, in particular, the impact of satellite for news producers and the production culture. MacGregor draws on a practitioner's experience and emphasis in his account, providing an added perspective to the concerns of policy-makers, viewers or academic commentators. He notes that satellite communication technologies, like film and video developments before them, have had a range of consequences for broadcast news producers. Most obviously, they have been used to extend dramatically the global reach of news organizations and to increase the speed and quality of worldwide communication. Live or pre-recorded satellite links are now an accepted part of many news programmes. Visual packages can now be transmitted from virtually anywhere in the world – or indeed from outer space – by means of increasingly lightweight portable satellite equipment. Satellite news channels (Sky News and CNN, for instance), operating 24 hours a day, now compete with terrestrial news organizations and in this process the modes of address, news values and points of view involved in news production have shifted from the national to encompass the trans-national. MacGregor analyses the implications of satellite technology for the professional practices, organization and output of television news.

As well as the television screen, 'the computer in the home' has been singled out as particularly significant with regards to contemporary transformations in the media. Chapters 14, 15 and 16 examine new media which are emerging in the context of old media, 'new' communication and media forms converging around the computer screen and terminal, and the linkages via computer-mediated communication with the worlds of the Internet. The notion of displacement is helpful to us in understanding the impact of emerging media and the relationship between these and established media. The significance of new media is not confined to these new media alone: 'new' media have profound impacts on 'old' media.

In focusing on changing television and the computer in the home it is important to remember that some of the most interesting and important contemporary transformations in the media are taking place at the boundaries and intersections between existing and new technologies, forms and institutions: telephone services compete with cable and satellite for the delivery of films; the Internet competes with radio for audio broadcasting; Internet browsing challenges Web TV; on-line newspapers stand beside their paper-based predecessors; the telephone and the Internet compete in providing telephony; and the telephone, teletext and Internet vie with one another to provide interactive services from home shopping to interactive pornography. Enabled by digitization, these changes are spearheading forms of convergence – between old and new media but also between and across media, communication and cultural sectors.

Howard Rheingold, associated with the Californian counter-culture of the 1960s and 1970s, is a well-known advocate of the democracy-enhancing nature of the Internet. In Chapter 14, following Jurgen Habermas (1989), he argues that the public sphere depends on forms of free communication and rational discussion; he sees this as being eroded in the face of the growing manufacture and management of public opinion. For Rheingold, the Internet allows open access, voluntary participation and the (re)generation of public opinion through dispersed assemblies of citizens engaging in rational argument with the freedom to express opinions and to discuss and criticize state policy and power. Internet communication provides almost unlimited information which can be assessed and made available, from anywhere, at any time, by anyone. It is seen as a medium to restore and revitalize community.

Critics argue that real communities involve complex social interaction and a shared history; they cannot simply be subscribed to like an electronic 'community'. Rheingold is seen as presenting 'not an alternative society, but an alternative to society' (Robins, 1996: 100), a withdrawal from the real world. Internet usage is very far from universal, showing a deep bias – to the US, the affluent and men. There is, of course, no reason why *information* should translate into *democracy*. Certainly, the Net reduces the *mediation* of information, and is used by a wide range of progressive organizations. Its growth in the UK, however, is in the context of a reduction in public library services and with government departments, private corporations and even political parties generally wanting *less* rather than more openness and transparency. In this context, the constraints on democratization are hardly technological in nature. The implications of the Internet for local, national and global communication and communities are as yet uncertain. Few commentators, however, suggest other than that it is a technology of considerable significance. Optimists argue that it will provide the electronic *agora*, the public forum in which the democratic voice will be heard; sceptics point to its take-over, domination and absorption by existing media conglomerates and commercialization.

In Chapter 15, Sherry Turkle explores the implications of computer-mediated communication (CMC) for senses of identity. In particular, she explores MUDs (multi-user domains): networked, multi-participant systems on the Net which are accessed via a textual interface from an ordinary 'household' PC terminal. Turkle argues that these have become focal points for thinking about human identities and exploring postmodern notions of decentred and fluid subjectivities. She claims that computers provide access to virtual worlds to live in and argues forcefully that computers enable new and important multiple forms of identities. There are clear links for Turkle and others between the growth of computer networks and the postmodern culture of simulation. Much of this argument about MUDs and identities hinges on the anonymity which they give players, allowing them to express multiple aspects or versions of the self, to experiment with identity and to try out new identities. From this point of view, computer technologies and networks are linked inextricably with notions of fragmenting multiple identities. The self no longer simply plays different roles in different settings at different times, but exists in many, virtual, worlds, playing many roles at the same time.

Critics acknowledge that intense personal relationships can develop via CMC even though there is no face-to-face or non-verbal communication but are doubtful whether anonymity and multiple identities are attainable (Doheny-Farina, 1996). Even though physical characteristics can be made obscure, what interaction can one have on the Net while maintaining an anonymous gender-neutral identity? Developing close relationships, while keeping the particulars of the body anonymous, is a monumental task. Moreover, the cultural biases that exist off-line are likely to be manifest on-line in a variety of discernible ways, so the Net is rarely a refuge from these biases.

Interactivity is one of the major reasons for the claim that television is to be replaced or at least supplemented by the Internet. This is a characteristic of new media which is at the forefront of debates; for example, regarding the commercial viability of service provision via the Internet. Rather like 'community', 'interactivity' is a term which tends to be invested with only positive connotations – who could be against it? What it means, however, varies considerably. First is the interactivity between person and machine. This can range from simply selecting or programming the time at which one can watch or record a film transmitted by digital satellite to ordering groceries from the supermarket, or communicating with others.

Secondly, in the case of MUDs, for example, it is about synchronous communication with geographically isolated and dispersed others. Even with this more extended definition, interactivity is hardly coterminous with democratic debate and influence. Sceptics (for example, Golding, 1998) point to the often banal nature of interactivity: entering a password, completing questionnaires and entering a credit card number; the feedback generated saves the need for corporate customer research. Given the prime requirement of capitalism, technologies are being designed to meet the interests of commercial corporations for private profit rather than to extend public, democratic space; and expressing a viewpoint requires more than just technical capacity. But there are more positive perspectives on interactivity: the electronic *Daily Telegraph* gets 500 e-mails a day (Tough and Parr, 1995); Stern TV viewers in Germany who have logged their preferences can be e-mailed in advance of transmissions in which they are likely to be interested; Internet soaps have developed ways in which users can interact with other users to create and control the story line (van Dusseldorp, 1997); and there are mailing lists, newsgroups, web pages and other interactive services. So the range and meanings of interactivity are broad and growing and are not confined to the new media but intersect, too, with old media.

Computer games are one key area for exploring the parameters and meaning of interactivity. Now a major global industry, in recent times it has rivalled Hollywood and the pop music industries in size, and overtaken television for the leisure time of some male adolescents. In the UK, the video games market is worth £800m per annum; 80 per cent of children aged 11–14 years play video games regularly and 60 per cent have their own consoles. John Keane explains the attraction of video games:

> the popularity of video games among children is chosen by subjects striving, if only intuitively, for the power to co-determine the outcomes of their electronically mediated play . . . Their appeal stems not only from the fact that for brief moments children can escape the demands of household and school by becoming part of an alternate world of bionic men, damsels in distress, galactic invasions, and teenage mutant turtles. Video games also promise interactivity . . . Unlike the process of learning to read books, which reduces children initially to mere readers with no freedom but that of accepting or rejecting the rules of the text, the playing of video games confronts children with a form of hypertext . . . Players are required to choose their own pathways through texts composed of blocks of words, images, and sounds that are linked electronically by multiple paths, chains, or trails that are unfinished and open-ended. Video games blur the boundaries between readers and writers by encouraging their users to determine how they move through a forest of possibilities . . . . (Keane, 1995: 10–11)

In Chapter 16, Leslie Haddon provides an account of the arrival, or emergence, of this new popular medium, the interactive computer game. The story has several unanticipated developments and outcomes in the shift from research mainframe computers to the amusement arcade and then to the home, and he shows the centrality of the consumer in the development of the medium. Early games-players broke down the traditional distinction between producers and consumers. Playing the game was only part of the package of the experience and users also programmed games. In this process of synergy, the profile of games was enhanced by the emergence of television programmes reviewing games alongside film and video releases. There was also the emergence of a new division of labour, as the technical programmer became separated from the 'creative' aspects of game origination, with personnel from film, animation, music and television backgrounds being brought in to undertake the creative role. This led to a diversification of forms and games. The story also raises questions of regulation in discussing concerns and fears aroused by computer games and their public representation and consequences.

References

Doheny-Farina, Stephen (1996) *The Wired Neighbourhood*. New Haven, Conn.: Yale University Press.

van Dusseldorp, Monique (1997) 'Glued to the set: the media battle between TV and PC', *Bulletin of the European Institute for the Media*, 14 (2): 13–15.

Golding, Peter (1998) 'Worldwide wedge: divisions and contradictions in the global information infrastructure', in Daya Kishan Thussu (ed.), *Electronic Empires: Global Media and Local Resistance*. London: Arnold.

Habermas, Jurgen (1989, orig. pub. 1962) *The Structural Transformation of the Public Sphere: an Inquiry into a Category of Bourgeois Society*, trans. Thomas Burger. Cambridge: Polity Press.

Keane, John (1995) 'Structural transformations of the public sphere', *The Communication Review*, 1 (1): 1–22.

Robins, Kevin (1996) *Into the Image: Culture and Politics in the Field of Vision*. London and New York: Routledge.

Scannell, Paddy (1996) *Radio, Television and Modern Life*. Oxford: Blackwell.

Tough, Liz and Parr, Barry (1995) 'Democratic interaction versus making choices: shaping electronic news delivery', *Convergence*, 2 (1): 14–18.

Broadcasting is dead. Long live digital choice
Jeanette Steemers

In common with other communications media, broadcast television has not escaped the excitement surrounding multimedia, interactivity, convergence and the so-called 'information superhighway'. With the prospect of the vast increase in transmission capacity afforded by digital technology, recent years have seen heightened interest, discussion and activity relating to digital television and the policy framework for its introduction. Much of this debate, particularly in the UK, is singularly unexciting for 'real' multi-media enthusiasts, revolving primarily around very traditional television content such as feature films, sport, and entertainment programming. However, the methods of payment under consideration (pay television, pay-per-view), scheduling practices (notably thematic 'niche' channels) and foreseeable distribution mechanisms (near video-on-demand, video-on-demand[1]) are noticeably different from what most, although not all, European viewers have become accustomed to – namely advertising or licence fee funded, universally available, generalist channels.[2]

It could be argued that discussion concerning the future of broadcast television is peripheral, given the multitude of mouth-watering services digital technology promises to deliver, and the prospect of all our individual communication needs being delivered into one multipurpose box from which we select à la carte and on demand.[3] Yet this image of an interactive culture remains a relatively distant vision for most European homes – based on a number of significant technical, financial and creative hurdles that still have to be overcome. For example, the introduction of video-on-demand as opposed to near video-on-demand is dependent on advances and heavy investment in server technology, and all potential operators of digital systems will need to undertake substantial capital investment which may slow down progress.[4] Finally there is little certainty that the public will 'buy into' the new services on offer which demonstrates

This chapter is taken from *Convergence*, 3 (1997), pp. 51–71.

the speculative and uncertain future of digital broadcasting and the promised menu of interactive television services. This is an important point to make because it underlines the continued importance of 'plain old' television as a proven medium and as possibly the first thing that most people will see of the digital 'superhighway' – through satellite, cable, terrestrial or telecommunications delivery systems.

The significance of television at this stage is further underlined by the activities of the major media conglomerates for whom television represents a key component of current digital strategies. The eagerness of companies like the Kirch Group and Bertelsmann in Germany, Canal Plus in France and BSkyB in the United Kingdom both to form alliances in order to control emerging digital markets and to acquire programming rights demonstrates that standard television fare – mainly in the form of feature films and sport – still has a crucial role to play in attracting subscribers and underpinning the economic viability of new digital ventures aimed at the consumer market. On the basis of these intermediate entertainment applications other potentially lucrative applications in the retail, banking and 'interactive' entertainment sector may eventually be driven into the home.

What is different and arguably interactive are the increased opportunities digital technology provides for charging consumers directly for what and how much they consume – through subscription on a per package, product or programme basis. And this further alters the public nature of television to that of a consumer product. Another trend is the continued compartmentalisation of content away from the notion of balanced nationally targeted generic channels towards thematic services. However, evidence suggests that the more established terrestrially delivered generic services will continue to attract the bulk of viewing for some time to come.[5] This shift in the way that television is used and marketed also points to a shift in the balance of power within the media. Rather than a central scheduler or a national broadcaster, it appears increasingly to be those companies who are active on the global stage, across different media, who control rights and the organisation of access through encryption, subscriber management and electronic programme guides, who will set the terms and reap the lucrative revenues of the future.

This scenario of a digital future goes to the heart of the matter because it raises questions about who will eventually control audio-visual media, what effect these developments will have on plurality and cultural diversity, and how traditional public broadcasting organisations such as the BBC in the United Kingdom and ARD and ZDF in Germany can change to survive in a converging media environment. Bearing these questions in mind, the purpose of this chapter is to focus on the side effects and the consequences of the introduction of digital television, and to identify what implications these developments might have for audio-visual diversity. Drawing on examples from Germany and the United Kingdom, it is argued that strategies developed by public service broadcasters and policymakers may not be sufficient to counter longer term threats to the overall plurality and diversity of the audio-visual sector. This state of affairs stems from the lack of a clear role for the public sector and the increasing domination of the emerging digital television market by a small number of companies who are active both at different levels within individual media and across different media.

The outline of this chapter is as follows. 'In Search of a Normative Framework' addresses the problems of applying culture-led broadcasting policy goals to an audio-visual sector which is becoming increasingly intertwined with other forms of communication content and with the computing and telecommunications sectors. 'The Introduction of Digital Television' focuses on current trends associated with the introduction of digital television and the extent to which these developments may affect the diversity and plurality of the audio-visual sector. 'The Role of Public Service Broadcasting in the Digital Era' examines the reaction of public service broadcasters to recent developments and their future role in a digital environment. 'The Role of the Regulator' looks briefly at the problems encountered by regulators at both a national and European level in developing a regulatory framework which takes account of both economic and cultural goals and of the place of broadcasting within a much broader communications context.

In search of a normative framework

Analysis of digital television and of new media generally does present significant difficulties in that the focus of attention has the tendency to move at an alarming rate. This underlines the importance of having some kind of normative base on which to assess new developments. For example, in an age where technology is often assumed to have its own dynamism, there is a set of normative ideals associated with liberal Western style democracies which have traditionally influenced broadcasting policy formulation and implementation. These norms are inevitably optimistic and institutionally have become closely linked with the concept of public service broadcasting, whose practitioners may or may not have lived up to the lofty ideals of public service theory.[6] However, as a counter-tendency to the economic and technological logic which is often assumed to drive the new media, these ideals may still hold value in a converging media environment – because they allow us to gauge what the new developments mean for the realisation of freedom of communication within society.

Traditionally Western media policy has been shaped by normative theories. Such theories see the media's function as one of providing both a forum for and a contribution to a free marketplace of ideas – on the assumption and undertaking that only an informed public can participate in a democratic society.[7] As a result media diversity in the sense of diverse ownership at an economic level, breadth of content and the representation of a wide range of opinions at a content level, and universal public access have been prominent media policy goals, designed to reinforce the media's independence and their contribution to a democratic society.[8] In the case of broadcasting, this freedom has always been interpreted in the institutional sense, because of the original technical and financial barriers which prevented a multiplicity of channels and justified a tighter regulatory framework for what was usually a monopoly public service broadcaster. So in contrast to the press, where the market has been deemed an acceptable mechanism to control diversity, the market alone has not usually been judged adequate to cater for diversity in broadcasting, even allowing for the growth in the number of channels in recent years.[9]

However, there are several problems in implementing traditional regulatory approaches to new forms of television which are arguably becoming more and more indistinguishable in nature from published goods such as books and newspapers. As the differences between the media and telecommunications become blurred in terms of distribution networks, service provision, and ownership, television-like services are emerging which do not fit the traditional perception of broadcasting as a uni-directional point-to-multipoint form of communication. And these new services do not fit into the existing regulatory and institutional structures either. For example, it has been proposed that services available on demand such as video-on-demand, near video-on-demand and even pay-per-view are not broadcasting services at all, and should therefore not be subject to broadcasting rules. Instead they constitute point-to-point communication which is qualitatively different from the point-to-multipoint communication of broadcasting.[10]

With the emergence of new services, there is less certainty about what broadcasting actually is and what should be the justification for regulating it. This is set to become even more challenging when one considers the possibility of multi-directional and truly interactive multipoint-to-multipoint communication of television-type content in real time, as is already happening with radio on the Internet. With increasing calls for more co-ordination between media policy and telecommunications policy, a debate about the degree of regulation and the reasons for applying it is sure to become more of a priority. Although media diversity and pluralism are prominent goals of broadcasting policy – connected with broadcasting's contribution to and influence on public opinion – it could be argued that new services like pay-per-view, video-on-demand, near video-on-demand and home shopping have less influence on public opinion than generalised broadcasting services, and therefore should require only limited content regulation. From this it can also be deduced that different degrees of regulation might apply to different types of content depending on their importance to public debate. For example, the rules relating to market dominance in news and current affairs could be more stringent than those relating to entertainment programming.[11]

However, this approach throws up additional problems. Policy decisions then need to be made about what these levels of content should be, to what degree different forms of content influence public opinion, and to what extent the supply of certain types of content should be allowed to be dominated by a few concerns. Recent disagreements in Germany concerning the legal definition of broadcasting illustrate the sort of difficulties facing regulators in deciding these legal perimeters.[12] Here the policy debate has been complicated by tensions between the federal states (the

Länder) which are constitutionally responsible for broadcasting policy and central government (the *Bund*) which is constitutionally responsible for telecommunications policy. Essentially the conflict boils down to power and control. A narrow definition of broadcasting would limit the future scope of *Länder* activity in broadcasting policy while advancing the interests of central government, whose own draft for a multimedia law embraced both video-on-demand and teleshopping in contravention of *Länder* wishes.[13] Similar tensions of jurisdiction are also becoming evident between the European Union and individual nation states, as EU telecommunications policy increasingly impinges on the cultural concerns of national broadcasting policy.[14]

A further problem in applying traditional broadcasting policy norms stems from the commercialisation and deregulation of broadcasting in recent years which have seen a decline in regulatory resolve to take practical measures to enhance plurality and diversity in favour of regulation by the market.[15] Instead of being viewed as cultural goods which need special regulatory attention for cultural and political reasons, broadcast programmes are now increasingly viewed as economic goods. This combination of the commodification of television together with the technical and economic convergence of broadcasting and telecommunications has served to reinforce the priority of economic over cultural policy goals. And this makes it increasingly difficult for regulators to find a balance between the two. Increasing reliance on competition law to solve difficulties is testimony to this conflict.[16] The old cultural and political values underpinning broadcasting freedom still exist, particularly as they are applied to public service broadcasting (the problems of relying on public service broadcasting are dealt with later in this chapter). However, these values are significantly less relevant for commercial broadcasters in both Germany and the United Kingdom who are now subject to much more relaxed supervision of content than their public service counterparts. However, with the emergence of new audio-visual services there seems to be a lack of clarity on the breadth and depth to which regulatory considerations of plurality and diversity should be applied, particularly with regard to abuses of economic power. Out of this vacuum the major multimedia companies seem to be determining progress both at a national and international level, with governments and regulators forced into playing a reactive role. Yet with increasing reliance on the market as a regulatory framework there is a real danger of monopolistic developments which threaten the principles underpinning the freedom of communication.

The introduction of digital television

With only a few multichannel digital television experiments currently operating in Europe, it is difficult at this stage to produce a definitive list of side-effects and consequences for broadcasting generally.[17] Doubtless more trends will become evident over time, particularly relating to consumer response. However, it could be argued that certain trends associated with the introduction of digital television have far less to do with digital technology itself and much more to do with deregulation and the opening up of the analogue broadcasting sector to commercial operators in recent years. True, digital technology may ultimately allow the public to interact with programme providers and create their own programme content. However, in the short to medium term what digital technology allows is quite simply an increase in the number of services which can be delivered to audiences, just as cable and satellite have done in the analogue sector for many years now (albeit on a more limited scale). This massive increase in transmission capacity has implications for content, funding, distribution, industry structures and the supply of and demand for programming, and changes here may affect the diversity and plurality of the audio-visual sector, but these changes are not exclusive to digital technology. They are already evident in the analogue sector.

Changes in content

As a continuation of trends in the analogue television market, prospective and actual digital television providers – like the Kirch Group in Germany, Canal Plus in France, Nethold's MultiChoice services in Scandinavia and Benelux, and BSkyB and the BBC in the United Kingdom – are all promoting or intending to promote digital packages based predominantly on thematic content in addition to the simulcasting of existing channels. For example, the German digital package *DFI* (*Das Digitale Fernsehen*), launched on 28 July 1996 and majority owned by the Kirch Group, is currently providing a basic palette of 20 channels encompassing documentary, children's, animation, 'classic' (older) film, music and light entertainment services, with more services planned. For an additional subscription two sports channels are available with an option of viewing different camera angles. Canal Plus' *Canal Satellite Numerique*, launched in April 1996, offers a broadly similar basic digital package with additional premium services offering films, music and computer games, and a pay-per-view service providing feature films and individual soccer matches. Similarly BSkyB's less specific plans for a launch of up to 200 digital satellite services at the end of 1997 are focused on a mixture of near video-on-demand films and sport, multiplexed and simulcast versions of existing channels, new niche channels and interactive services.

These efforts to segment and fragment audiences still further, with new forms of narrowcasting and special interest programmes, promise then in theory to reduce the significance of both the generic broadcasting service and the scheduler, and potentially provide viewers with more opportunities to create their own schedules from services available on demand. However, commercial logic suggests that segmented audiences will only be targeted in as far as they have the potential to be profitable. At the same time less attractive and poorer target groups will have to rely more and more on subsidised provision, in all probability by public service providers. Financial considerations and the huge increase in transmission capacity also suggest that narrowcast strategies will involve a heavy reliance on the following: (a) low cost original production, (b) library material, (c) repeats, and (d) high cost feature films and sport for premium channels. This type of strategy does not suggest the type of commitment to high cost 'quality' productions (notably drama) which have traditionally been expected of national terrestrial broadcasters as their contribution to national cultural life.[18]

Changes in funding

Increases in the number of channels and the resulting fragmentation of audiences have shown subscription funding to be more important than advertising as a means of achieving profitability in the UK multichannel market for analogue television. Subscriptions revenues are already estimated to account for 20% of all industry funding.[19] However, the vast majority of these subscription revenues accrue to BSkyB's premium film and sports services, with little evidence that the public is willing to pay extra for other forms of content. However, this shift in the nature of television funding has underpinned the ability of a service provider like BSkyB, with a relatively low total audience share, to out-bid the terrestrial channels with their much larger audiences for sports rights – most notably Premier League football coverage for BSkyB's premium sports channels. In Germany subscription still represents uncharted territory with until recently only one less than moderately successful subscription film channel, Premiere, with 1.2 million subscribers in mid-1996 after five years' operation.[20] It has even been argued that subscription television faces a hard fight for acceptance in the German market because of the large number of 'free' advertiser-supported services available to Germany's 15 million cabled homes.[21] Yet, the emergence of two competing digital platforms, one supported by the Kirch Group (based on the d-box decoder) and one supported by Bertelsmann (based on the Mediabox decoder) testified to the importance of subscription funding and the associated technology in the German market.[22] However, the growing importance of subscription funding has raised concerns about the removal of major sporting events or programming content perceived as being of key cultural or national importance from free-to-air transmission, to be made available only to those who are willing or able to pay.[23]

Changes in distribution

The increase in transmission capacity generated by digital technology and ongoing changes in the way that programmes are marketed and sold (themed content; subscription finance, pay-per-view; near video-on-demand, video-on-demand) are altering the market structure of television. As a consequence it is those players controlling distribution and consumer access who are emerging as the front-runners in the race to control digital developments. This goes some way to explaining the eagerness of the major media groups to cooperate with each other to avoid the risk of exclusion from important markets.[24]

Control of access to consumers through conditional access systems has emerged as a major area of concern, and to some extent this anxiety is based on experience in the analogue television sector. Conditional access systems are important because they form the basis of subscription management and encryption which allows prospective viewers to watch only those programmes to which they have subscribed. The significance of conditional access is illustrated by BSkyB's success in the UK market for analogue satellite pay television. BSkyB holds an exclusive licence to Videocrypt (owned by News Datacom, a subsidiary of BSkyB's main shareholder, News International), the only satellite encryption system to have established itself so far in the UK. It operates a subscriber management system which handles the subscriber lists and authorisations for most of the pay television channels in the UK market. Although credit has been given to BSkyB for taking the risk of investing in satellite transmission and creating a market for pay television in the first place, there has been mounting concern that the main gatekeeper to the distribution system for other programme providers should also be a major provider of rival programme services for that market both as a retailer to satellite and as a wholesaler to cable.[25] The fear is that BSkyB will replicate this dominance in the digital pay market, particularly since the Office of Fair Trading's inconclusive review of BSkyB's position in the analogue pay television sector when it was decided not to refer the BSkyB case to the Monopolies and Mergers Commission, subject to a number of undertakings from BSkyB.[26] However, the issues surrounding diversity and plurality are clearly illustrated by the complaints which first led to the review.[27] The original investigation stemmed from complaints by certain UK cable operators, who had been incensed by BSkyB's long-term supply deals with the two largest cable operators, Nynex and Telewest. In return for preferential rates from BSkyB, Nynex and Telewest undertook not to carry or launch any rival cable-exclusive pay services. This agreement effectively killed off cable's plans to launch rival cable-exclusive sports and film services, which were intended to break BSkyB's dominance over programme supply to cable. In Germany the issues of conditional access and gatekeepers have been equally important and the emergence of the competing proprietary systems of MMBG, involving Bertelsmann, Canal Plus, Deutsche Telekom, and the public broadcasters and the rival d-box system, promoted by the Kirch Group, clearly illustrates what has been at stake in terms of market control.[28]

For consumers the best system would involve a common interface, where decoders are not linked to a particular conditional access system, but this seems unlikely given the amount of investment by pay TV operators in proprietary conditional access systems. Common wisdom supports the view that consumers will only buy one set-top box. This means that a small number of companies may well end up dominating the digital broadcasting market, just as a limited number of operators now dominate the analogue market for subscription television in most European countries. Legislators are not entirely unaware of the dangers of monopolistic abuse which might deter new service providers and reduce choice, competition and innovation, but their responses have been slow and piecemeal. In the UK Department of Trade and Industry (DTI) proposals aim to ensure that all digital programme providers have access to conditional access systems on a fair, reasonable and non-discriminatory basis, in line with a recent European Union directive on standards.[29] Significantly the DTI proposals only relate to digital and not analogue transmission, and the DTI has drawn back from insisting on a common interface capable of supporting different systems, coming down in favour of licensing and regulation by the Office of Telecommunications (OFTEL) instead. At the European Commission there have been attempts to promote the common interface in decoder boxes, but legislative efforts at both a national and EU level are lagging behind developments in the real world where battles are already being fought and won between rival and incompatible systems.[30]

Changing alliances

The prospect of digital distribution, and the emergence of new gateways in particular, is furthering the internationalisation of the audio-visual sector with the emergence of fewer and larger multinational multimedia groupings involved in several territories and across several related media industries. Recent examples in Europe include the merger of CLT and Bertelsmann's TV arm, Ufa, and BSkyB's German digital alliances, first with Bertelsmann and now with the Kirch Group. Eager to maintain their positions in their core markets and as a means of remaining competitive by working in other markets and industry sectors, these groups are establishing various degrees of co-operation. This is reinforcing vertical integration within television and its convergence with other industry sectors. However, this tendency towards transnational operation and collaboration makes regulatory efforts at a national level aimed at preventing abuse of economic power through media ownership and general competition rules much more difficult. Both in Germany and in the UK there have been efforts recently to reassess ownership restrictions in the light of new technological developments and this has led to a relaxation of existing rules. However, to a large degree these changes seem to have been guided more by industry concerns about international competitiveness than by diversity and plurality. There are ownership rules based on television audience share (i.e. viewer hours) and limits on involvement in television by newspaper groups, but the new rules do not adequately address the issue of vertical integration within and across media.[31] This has led Wolfgang Hoffmann-Riem to conclude that:

> The regulatory philosophy of media laws to date will certainly come unstuck when faced by the globally structured multimedia and information society of the future. The actors in this environment can move with relative ease from one level and sphere of action to another, disguise themselves through structural interlocking, submerge in international networks or openly risk

power struggles with supervisory bodies – and usually win on account of the numerous dependencies.[32]

Growing importance of rights acquisition

The acquisition of exclusive rights is essential for the successful implementation of pay-per-view and near video-on-demand strategies. Digital programme providers will need to offer top quality Hollywood feature films and prestige sporting events to encourage consumers to pay a premium price. However, there is a shortage of premium material and as demand exceeds supply, the cost of acquiring it up front is likely to remain the preserve of those commercial organisations with large bank balances or of those who are sufficiently vertically integrated to allow them to draw on their own supply of feature films or long term supply contracts.

The significance of exclusive rights cannot be underestimated. In Germany the Kirch Group's finalisation of a ten-year US$3 billion deal for pay TV rights to films and series from Warner and MCA-Universal was one factor in persuading Bertelsmann to consider cooperating with Kirch on a single digital satellite package for Germany.[33] In the United Kingdom the profitability of BSkyB's analogue satellite package is predicated on the exclusive right to show the English Premier football league on its subscription sports channels. The value of these rights was demonstrated in June 1996 when the contract was renewed and the price is reported to have risen from £300 million for five years coverage in 1992 to £670 million over four years.[34]

However, the acquisition of large packages of sports and feature film rights reinforces the leading role of dominant players like BSkyB and Kirch, who can then use their position to pressure others in the supply chain including cable operators and rival programme providers. This factor is underlined by BSkyB's powerful position as a provider of programming to the UK cable sector which has found it difficult to launch rival services (see above, 'Changes in Distribution'). If control of significant amounts of programming material is combined with control of distribution services, the emergence of alternative distribution systems can be restricted, since control of the distribution system underpins the ability to acquire premium programming in the first place and maintain a dominant position.[35]

The role of public service broadcasting in the digital era

As a consequence of the deregulation and fragmentation of European television markets, public service broadcasters have emerged in theory as the guarantors of old-style normative broadcasting principles. But it is by no means certain that they will have the resources to continue this role indefinitely. They have already had to adapt from a position, in most instances, of monopoly to one of intense competition from less heavily regulated commercial rivals. As a result they have lost audience share and where partially funded by advertising, as is the case in Germany, revenue.

Licence fee revenues have remained static, but production and acquisition costs have risen, affected by the competitive impact of commercial channels. To survive and retain their legitimacy within a dual system, public service broadcasters have adopted a range of responses including changes in programming strategies (more competitive scheduling), closer co-operation with third parties (independent producers, co-producers), the use of supplementary sources of revenue (sponsorship, subscription, programme sales, co-production funding) and rationalisation strategies.[36] Although the effectiveness of these strategies varies from country to country, one certainty remains. Publicly funded public service television will always be financially vulnerable. If it emulates its commercial rivals too closely with populist programming strategies and is deemed to be abandoning its public mission, its right to public funding may be questioned, particularly by its commercial rivals. Equally, if it consistently fails to appeal to the majority of the public by concentrating on programming which commercial channels fail to provide, such as cultural, educational and minority programming, its right to public funding may also be scrutinised.

Notwithstanding the problems outlined above, digital television is forcing public service broadcasters to think once again about their role and how they should put a case for a 'public lane' on the 'information superhighway'. However, as the nature of television itself changes, the questions which need answering are what constitutes the public function of audio-visual media in a democracy and who should perform this role.[37] In a converging environment of mass and individual communication how do you define a public service mission? And should this mission be confined to traditional broadcasting content or extended to cover new types of core services which may at some point be deemed to be indispensable for the public at large? For example, will the educational role of public service broadcasting eventually justify licence fee funding for on-line services and CD-ROMs?[38] Should public service broadcasters have the right to grow with the new technical possibilities or is it time to consider new forms of public provision? Ultimately is it even worth maintaining generalist public service channels, if consumers can eventually choose from hundreds of individual offerings? The answer to these questions lies partly in political willingness to further endow public service broadcasting with a social purpose which, while reflecting changes in society, still accepts some forms of television as universally available public goods which fulfil specific objectives that are noticeably different from the profit-orientated objectives of commercial television companies. The problem, however, lies in deciding what type of activities are covered by these objectives, who should decide the extent of new activities (the broadcasters, politicians or independent bodies?), and the extent to which new activities merit public funding? For public service broadcasting's ability to fulfil a clearly defined mission depends on continued public willingness to give it economic security through the licence fee or some other form of public funding.

In the UK, government proposals for digital terrestrial television have emphasised the merits of public service broadcasting and the wish to safeguard its future into the digital age. The implication seems to be that public service broadcasting does have different objectives from commercial television and can contribute to the diversity and quality of digital television. As the Government stated in its proposals for digital terrestrial television:

> The Government attaches great importance to 'public service' broadcasting – in its broadest sense the services provided by the BBC (television and radio), ITV, Channel 4, S4C and, in the future, Channel 5 – which is a vital part of life in this country. It educates and entertains; it provides extensive and impartial news coverage and stimulates public debate, and it seeks to cater for the interests of the few as well as the many. These channels are the envy of the world, and the Government wants them to have the opportunity to benefit from the new technology.[39]

In Germany the situation is more complex. On the basis of existing Constitutional Court judgements, private broadcasting is permitted to pursue a lower standard of broadcasting practice on the understanding that public service broadcasters will meet a higher standard relating to programme balance and the reflection of different opinions within society. For this reason public service broadcasting has a right to existence and further development and financial support from the licence fee.[40] However, commercial and political interests are loath to see public service broadcasters, ARD and ZDF, expand into digital pay channels, and there is some argument about what further development should entail.[41] Only after significant wrangling for a new inter-*Land* television agreement were ARD and ZDF recently accorded a licence fee increase and the right to launch two publicly funded thematic satellite channels – a children's channel to make up for the failings of private television and a parliamentary channel.[42] Their involvement in digital broadcasting also extends to experimental pilot projects which are predominantly being used to offer existing programming material in different ways.[43]

The BBC too has been looking closely at its role in the forthcoming digital era and has given digital broadcasting a high priority on the assumption that if it fails to react now it will become obsolete.[44] Its plans for a range of 'extended' services alongside BBC1 and BBC2, and a 24-hour television news channel are unproblematic as freely available services. However, plans for subscription-based thematic channels and services to be run by the BBC's commercial arm, BBC Worldwide, represent a significant departure from universal access and the replacement of public service goals with commercial goals. Subscription may represent a welcome boost in revenue for the BBC, but it also represents a dilemma in the form of a longer term threat to the BBC's legitimacy as a universally available publicly funded service. There is always a risk that future governments may be tempted to peg or reduce the licence fee if it can be supplemented with subscription income. And once subscription becomes the norm, the argument for a universally available publicly funded broadcasting service in the midst of channel plenty begins to look much weaker, however strong the social arguments might be.

Although the introduction of digital technology is supposed to herald more choice, the burden of expectation regarding plurality and cultural diversity for television in a converged environment would seem to rest with public service broadcasting. This implies that public service broadcasters should stand out from their commercial rivals, and cultivate a responsiveness to public concerns and needs. However, their ability to fulfil this task depends on a much more clearly defined role in a digital world, combined with the assurance of adequate financial resources to participate in new developments.

The role of the regulator

Convergence between telecommunications and broadcasting arising from digital applications poses decisive and unprecedented challenges for public policy at both a national and European Union level. Policy-makers need to strike a fine balance between the political, social and cultural values traditionally associated with media policy and the predominantly commercial and economic priorities associated with telecommunications policy. Digital technologies may provide more choice for the consumer and may open up new opportunities for business, but whether this develops into real competition and choice depends on an appropriate regulatory framework and on perceptions of its effectiveness.

In the case of audio-visual services the expansion in transmission capacity through digital technology does not remove the need for regulation, although detailed supervision of content has become less effective and less relevant with the large increase in television channels in recent years. However, the special nature of the right to communicate and television's cultural and political role suggest that television cannot be left simply to regulation by the market or competition law. The principles of diversity, pluralism, independence and equality of access that underpin the media's important role in shaping and informing public opinion suggest that, in spite of the promise of bountiful audio-visual services in future, there are still strong grounds for persisting with regulation. This in turn emphasises the importance of these principles.[45] First, the emergence of powerful transnational alliances to distribute, market and sell digital television not only poses a risk to diversity through fewer suppliers, but may also contribute to less economic competition and ultimately less choice for the consumer if a small number of digital gatekeepers are permitted to control the market. Second, conventional analogue broadcasting is likely to remain the dominant force in television for some time to come while digital media become more widely available. This means that safeguarding the plurality of opinion in broadcasting (for example, through stipulations on impartiality in news and current affairs) and regulating access to limited analogue capacity will continue to be regulatory issues until widespread access to digital media allows television to operate more like publishing. Third, the emergence of digital transmission systems will still throw up bottle-necks which require regulation to safeguard diversity and choice (e.g. conditional access systems, electronic programme guides). As the ongoing battles to establish proprietary conditional access have shown, the extent to which companies control access and distribution is much more important than the number of channels they own or services they offer. This is because network access and control determines how the system will be used and to what extent proprietary standards (through set-top boxes) can be imposed.[46] Regulation then is needed wherever there is a threat of market dominance and a threat to diversity of opinion and choice.

Policy-makers, however, face a number of difficulties in constructing a policy framework, not least because legislative activity lags substantially behind developments in the marketplace. The situation is complicated still further by the internationalisation of broadcasting and telecommunications activities which diminishes the importance and effectiveness of national media legislation, and by a continued lack of co-ordination between media and telecommunications policy.[47] This lack of co-ordination is clearly demonstrated in the UK where telecommunications considerations have only figured marginally in the recent debate surrounding the 1996 Broadcasting Act – to the extent that digital terrestrial television appears to be more like an extension of conventional broadcasting. Germany in contrast has experienced a broader debate because the introduction of digital television is closely connected with the use of an existing broadband cable television network with over 15 million subscribers, owned and operated by Deutsche Telekom, Germany's monopoly telecommunications operator. Here the discussion has centred much more on the future operation of the network and its potential for providing a broader array of point-to-point and multipoint-to-multipoint communication services.[48]

While national policy-makers in Germany and the UK grapple with the complexities of regulating television in a converging multimedia environment, the internationalisation of telecommunications and audio-visual policy issues has focused more attention on European activities. The European Commission has tried to promote a common approach to common problems, but most of its audio-visual concerns to date have been guided by industrial and market considerations. Notably this has ensured the creation of an internal market, maintaining competitive safeguards, promoting technical standards and providing support for the European production industry through the Media II programme. Cultural considerations have played a secondary role and this reflects caution about becoming involved in policy areas which exclude harmonisation and reflect national legislative concerns.[49] For example, the *Television without Frontiers* Directive is more concerned with the realisation of a single market; there are no stipulations about the diversity of programme content or the role of public service provision.[50]

Much more important, particularly of late, has been the application of EU competition law in seeking both to promote competitive market structures and to ensure competitive behaviour. In November 1994 Media Service GmbH, a proposed joint pay television venture between the Kirch Group, Deutsche Telekom and Bertelsmann, was ruled incompatible with European competition rules because it would have inhibited the entry of others into the German market.[51] Deutsche Telekom's cable monopoly, together with the dominant position of Kirch and Bertelsmann in the German programming and pay television market, were important factors in the decision. This ruling revealed the inadequacies of national legislation on media control particularly where involvement extends across different stages of the production and distribution chain. However, economic diversity should not be confused with content issues, particularly where they relate to broadcasting's role in contributing to the formation of public opinion, and this would seem to imply that specific rules are needed for ensuring political pluralism of content. A forthcoming Green Paper on audio-visual services, impending Community action on media ownership, and a growing interest in rights issues, conditional access, and common standards points to more EU involvement in broadcasting policy.[52] However, it also points to more controversy as EU activities, particularly in telecommunications, start to impinge on broadcasting issues which have traditionally been national concerns with different goals.[53]

Outlook

Broadcasting is far from dead, but its future health with regard to market dominance, and the safeguarding of plurality and diversity, depends on the outcome of regulatory efforts at both a national and EU level. The fact that there are no easy solutions points to a need to address the changing nature of content and the way that multimedia companies are likely to behave in a converged media environment. There is also a need to address the extent to which the audio-visual industry is unique and to what degree it requires special consideration to safeguard its cultural and political role. This implies a regulatory balance being struck between the need to promote the communications industry on the one hand while safeguarding cultural priorities on the other. However, on the basis of current developments it is not clear that there are sufficient precautions to prevent market dominance and threats to diversity.

In relation to content several decisions need to be made. First there is a need to ascertain what services can be attributed to broadcasting and thereafter be subject to stricter rules on content, and what and when services can be safely left to the market. This in turn demands greater clarity about the cultural and political role of television and who should perform this role. Current trends seem to suggest that regulation of content should be 'light' for commercial broadcast operators or differentiated depending on the potential of different forms of content to influence public opinion. For example, it could be argued that home shopping has less of an impact on public debate than a dedicated news channel. Ultimately the commercial television sector may operate as freely as the publishing sector. Current trends also seem to suggest that public service television should meet higher programme standards to make up for any programme shortfalls by commercial television. However, the role of public service broadcasting is problematic. If public service broadcasting is to make up for shortfalls this assumes that it should be allowed to participate in new developments which go beyond conventional broadcasting. Otherwise its impact may be minimal. The question which then needs to be asked is how far should public service broadcasting be allowed to develop new services, and to what extent should these new services be publicly funded? These are questions which lack clear answers. There is a suspicion that forays into subscription funding and commercial ventures by public service broadcasters are simply a response to budgetary pressures and the need to find alternative funding sources, and that these may ultimately undermine the justification for public funding and ultimately the justification for universal public access.

With regard to content distribution greater attention needs to be paid to bottle-necks in the system and vertical integration. Unsurprisingly companies want to restrict competition and retain and reinforce their dominant positions in individual markets. This goes in the face of competition, consumer choice and the safeguarding of plurality. In addition to media ownership rules, there may also therefore be a need to consider the degree to which the main market players also control production and distribution chains through their domination of content and key rights, delivery systems and consumer access, to the exclusion of other operators and to the detriment of pluralism and the free flow of information.

There are certainly no simple answers for policy-makers seeking to stop anti-competitive behaviour and safeguard diversity and plurality. And the complex developments stemming from the convergence of broadcasting and telecommunications require complex and flexible solutions which take account of the changing structure and operation of emerging communications models. This is clearly an area where work still needs to be done. However, the measures currently undertaken by public service broadcasters and policy-makers suggest a paucity of strategy and strategic thinking which is inadequate for safeguarding diversity and plurality as matters of paramount public interest. [. . .]

Notes

An earlier version of this chapter was presented at the i-TV '96 Conference at the University of Edinburgh, Scotland, on 4 September 1996.

1   Near video-on-demand (NVOD), as the name suggests, is not quite video-on-demand. It involves staggered starts of the same programme, usually feature films, on different channels at regular intervals, and this gives viewers more choice about when they watch a particular programme. True video-on-demand (VOD) offers full access to material at any time and VCR functionality. Most commercial plans for digital television involve NVOD rather than VOD, which so far has been limited to interactive trials only.

2   For example, *New Media Markets'* figures for April 1996 suggest that 22.6 per cent of UK TV homes (5.27m) have access to multichannel television through cable or satellite (6 June 1996), p. 15. In Germany 26.29m households had access to cable or satellite reception, 81 per cent of all TV households, in November 1995. Source: *GfK – Fernsehforschung* cited in *Media Perspektiven Basisdaten – Daten zur Mediensituation in Deutschland 1995*, p. 9.

3   For an overview of interactive TV developments worldwide and their potential, see *TBI (Television Business International)*, 'Special Focus: Interactive TV' (May–June 1996), pp. 36–41.

4   See Klaus Scharpe, Daniel Hürst and Sabine Gafke, *Künftige Entwicklung des Mediensektors: Gutachten im Autftrage des Bundesministeriums für Wirtschaft* (Basel and Berlin: Deutsches Institut für Wirtschaftsforschung/Prognos, December 1995) (available, as at September 1996, at http://www.kp.dlr.de/BMWi/gip/studien/diw). Also Martin Recke, 'Medienpolitik im digitalen Zeitalter', *Kirche und Rundfunk*, 17, 6 March 1996, p. 8.

5   For example, the BBC cites the case of the USA where, in spite of a long history of multichannel television, 70 per cent of prime-time viewing is still with the four main networks. BBC, *Extending Choice in the Digital Age* (London, BBC, 1996), p. 20. The BBC's digital policy is available at: http://www.bbc.co.uk/info/digital (as at September 1996).

6   See also Marc Raboy, 'Public service broadcasting in the context of globalization', in *Public Broadcasting for the 21st Century*, ed. Marc Raboy (Luton, John Libbey Media/University of Luton Press, 1995), pp. 6–10.

7   See Jan van Cuilenberg and Paul Slaa, 'From media policy towards a national communications policy: broadening the scope', *European Journal of Communication*, 8 (1993), p. 151. See also BVerfGe (Bundesverfassungsgericht), 'Urteil des Bundesverfassungsgerichts vom 28. Februar 1961 (Fernsehurteil)', in *Rundfunk und Presse in Deutschland: Rechtsgrundlagen der Massenmedien*, eds Wolfgang Lehr and Klaus Berg (Mainz, Hase and Köhler, 1971), p. 254.

8   Ibid.

9   For a comparison of the different regulatory backgrounds of broadcasting and the press, see Wolfgang Hoffmann-Riem, 'Trends in the development of broadcasting law in Western Europe', *European Journal of Communication*, 7 (1992), pp. 148–54. In Germany the Constitutional Court has been particularly important in emphasising the different safeguards required of the television sector. See BVerfGe (Bundesverfassungsgericht), 'Urteil des Bundesverfassungsgerichts vom 16. Juni 1981', in *Deutsches Press- und Rundfunkrecht*, ed. Wolf-Dieter Ring (Munich, Rehm, undated), pp. 1–25, A-III 3.

10   See Herbert Ungerer referring to the European Commission's proposal to amend the 1990 Television Without Frontiers Directive so that it only applies to point-to-multipoint as opposed to point-to-point services. Herbert Ungerer 'Who should be Europe's digital gate keepers?', paper presented at the 1995 European Cable Communications Conference, London, UK (also available, as at September 1996, at http://europa.eu.int/en/comm/dg04/speech/five/htm/sp95042.htm).

11   For variations of this argument, see Dieter Dörr, 'Vielfaltsicherung durch die EU?', *Media Perspektiven*, 2 (1996), p. 91. Also Wolf Dieter Ring, 'Kein Mangel. Neuordnung der Medien im Markt der Zukunft', *Kirche und Rundfunk*, 16 (2 March 1996), p. 9.

12   See Martin Recke, 'Problem vertagt', *Kirche und Rundfunk*, 42 (1 June 1996), pp. 5–8. Also Manfred Rühle, 'Probleme? Nein! Für eine Neubewertung des Rundfunkbegriffs', *Kirche und Rundfunk*, 34 (4 May 1996), pp. 5–9.

13   As reported in Recke, 'Problem vertagt', p. 6.

14   See Dörr, 'Vielfaltsicherung durch die EU?'

15   See, for example, Tony Prosser, 'Public service broadcasting and deregulation in the UK', *European Journal of Communication*, 7 (1992), pp. 173–93. For Germany, see Silke Ruck, 'Development of broadcasting law in the Federal Republic of Germany', *European Journal of Communication*, 7 (1992), pp. 219–39.

16   For example, BSkyB's position in the UK pay TV market was recently subject to a review by the Office of Fair Trading, based on competition law not media legislation.

17   For an assessment of European digital projects, see Jochen Zimmer, 'Pay TV: Durchbruch im digitalen Fernsehen?', *Media Perspektiven*, 7 (1996), pp. 386–401. For a listing of details of European digital projects, see *New Media Markets,*, 6 June 1996, pp. 8–9 and *Screen Digest*, August 1996, pp. 177–84.

18   Typical budgets at cable and satellite channels range from £3,000 to £6,000 per hour

compared, for example, to £100,000 for a 40-minute top-of-the-range documentary. See also Darren Cockburn and Nick Bertolotti, 'Exploiting rights in a digital age', *Broadcast*, 5 July 1996, p. 15.

19   BBC, *Extending Choice in the Digital Age*, p. 22. Kagan World Media estimate that Pay TV revenues for the UK totalled US$1663m in 1995, compared to US$3640m in advertising revenues and $1878m in licence fee revenues, i.e. approximately 23 per cent (*Kagan's European Television Country Profiles*, 1996, London, p. 26).

20   Zimmer, 'Pay TV', p. 391.

21   Ibid.

22   The rival d-box decoder developed by the Kirch Group seems to have won the German battle following the collapse in September 1996 of the MMBG Mediabox consortium which included Deutsche Telekom, Bertelsmann, CLT, Canal Plus, ARD and ZDF. This followed Bertelsmann's decision to cooperate with the Kirch Group and its partners.

23   These concerns were behind the amendment in February 1996 to the UK Broadcasting Bill, which prevents pay TV services from gaining exclusive rights to eight listed national sporting events ranging from the Olympics to the Oxford and Cambridge Boat Race. See also the comments of Paddy Scannell, 'Public service broadcasting, from national culture to multiculturalism', in Raboy (ed.), *Public Broadcasting for the 21st Century*, p. 37.

24   See *Broadcast*, 'The race to conquer Europe', 5 July 1996, pp. 16–17.

25   OFTEL (Office of Telecommunications), *Submission by the Office of Telecommunications to the Office of Fair Trading review of the pay-TV market* (London, OFTEL, 1996) (available as at September 1996, http://www.open.gov.uk/oftel/paytv/contents.htm).

26   See *New Media Markets*, 'Review leaves key BSkyB issues unanswered', 25 July 1996, pp. 8–10.

27   Office of Fair Trading press release, 1 December 1995.

28   See note 22 above.

29   DTI (Department of Trade and Industry), *The Regulation of Conditional Access Services for Digital Television – Consultation Paper on Detailed Implementation Proposals* (London, DTI, 26 June 1996). See also Directive of the European Parliament and the Council of 24 October 1995 on the use of standards for the transmission of television signals, *Official Journal of the European Communities*, No. L 281.

30   See Ungerer, 'Who should be Europe's digital gate keepers?'; see also *Broadcast*, 'Digital rivals hint at common interface', 14 June 1996, p. 13.

31   For the background to the UK discussion on ownership, see Department of National Heritage, *Media Ownership: the Government's Proposals* (London, HMSO, May 1995), Cm 2872. For an analysis of the proposals see Tim Congden et al., *The Cross Media Revolution: Ownership and Control* (London, John Libbey, 1995). In Germany proposals aimed at relaxing current ownership restrictions are due to be implemented in 1997. However, Hoffmann-Riem believes that German media policy has been wrongly focused on the organisation and provision of services with insufficient attention paid to distribution, production and resale. Wolfgang Hoffmann-Riem, 'New challenges for European multimedia policy', *European Journal of Communication*, 11 (3) (1996), pp. 339, 341.

32   Hoffmann-Riem, 'New challenges for European multimedia policy', p. 330.

33   See *Broadcast*, 'Bertelsmann, Kirch set for digital link-up', 26 July 1996, p. 11.

34   See Emily Bell, 'Coming home – to the City', *The Observer*, Business Section, 7 July 1996, p. 2.

35   See OFTEL, *Submission*.

36   See Yves Achille and Bernard Miege, 'The limits to the adaptation strategies of European public service television', *Media Culture and Society*, 16 (1994), pp. 31–46.

37   See also Cuilenberg and Slaa, 'From media policy towards a national communications policy', p. 167.

38   As suggested by Damian Green, 'Preserving plurality in a digital world', in *The Cross Media Revolution*, ed. Tim Congden et al., p. 30.

39   DNH (Department of National Heritage), *Digital Terrestrial Broadcasting* (London, HMSO, 1995), Cm 2946, p. 4, 1.12.

40   See, in particular, the Constitutional Court Judgement of 1986 – BVerfGe (Bundesverfassungsgericht), 'Urteil des Bundesverfassungsgerichts vom 4. November 1986', in *Funk Korrespondenz Dokumention* (7 November 1996), pp. 19–20. For a detailed discussion of the legal arguments surrounding the public service broadcasters' obligation towards '*Grundversorgung*', or the basic provision of services, see Herbert Bethge, 'Der Grundversorgungsauftrag des öffentlich-rechtlichen Rundfunks in der dualen Rundfunkordnung', *Media Perspektiven*, 2 (1996), pp. 66–72.

41   See, for example, Wolfgang Hoffmann-Riem's arguments for public service involvement in pay television, 'Pay TV im öffentlich-rechtlichen Rundfunk', *Media Perspektiven*, 2 (1996), pp. 73–79; see also Bethge, 'Der Grundversorgungsauftrag'.

42   *Die Welt*, 'Kein Freibrief zur Expansion der Offentlich-Rechtlichen', 8 July 1996.

43   See Zimmer, 'Pay TV', pp. 399–400.

44   BBC, *Extending Choice in the Digital Age*.

45   See also Scharpe et al., *Künftige Entwicklung des Mediensektors*.

46   See Recke, 'Problem vertagt'; also OFTEL, *Submission*.

47   For an account of UK media policy, see Peter Goodwin, 'British media policy takes to the superhighway', *Media, Culture and Society*, 17 (1995), pp. 667–89; also Cuilenberg and Slaa, 'From media policy towards a national communications policy'.

48   Recke, 'Problem vertagt'.

49   Herbert Ungerer, 'EU competition law in the telecommunications, media and information technology sectors', paper presented to the 22nd Annual Conference on International Antitrust Law and Policy, Fordham University School of Law, New York City, 27 October 1995 (available at http://europa.eu.int/en/comm/dg04/speech/five/htm/sp95041.htm).

50   European Commission, Council Directive (1989), *Television without Frontiers* 89/552/EEC.

51   Commission Decision of 9 November 1994 relating to a proceeding pursuant to Council Regulation (EEC) no 4064/89 (iv/m.469 – msg media service), *Official Journal*, no. L364, 31 December 1994. For an explanation of the Commission's findings see Ungerer, 'EU competition law'.

52   See Commission of the European Union/Communities (1994), *Europe's Way to the Information Society: an Action Plan*. Com (94) 347 final.

53   See Dörr, 'Vielfaltsicherung durch die EU?'

Making television news in the satellite age
Brent MacGregor

'Captives of technology'

With the possible exception of the military there is probably no other industry that relies as much on technology as broadcasting does. Its defining technology gives it, in the first instance, an enormous advantage over the print media, but this is a double-edged sword, as greater resources are required simply to do the job at its most basic level. Journalists have always been competitive and the television sub-species are no exception. Getting the story first, a 'beat', the much prized scoop, is a function of two factors: finding the story and then getting it back to base. Whether in the competitive world of the news agencies, newspapers, radio or television, communication technologies are central to the newsgathering process. Nowhere is this more evident than in location-based crisis reporting. In the 30 years from the end of the Second World War to the fall of Saigon, the technology of television news had evolved slowly as the form itself emerged. Television naturally has its own demands, and television reporters, more so than their print and radio colleagues, are 'captives of technology' (Schlesinger, 1978: 270). A telephone line is not good enough to get material back to base, and just creating the story has famously been compared by Fred Friendly to writing a story with a two-ton pencil (Mayer, 1987: 202). Television reporting is harder to do, more time-consuming and expensive simply because of these technical factors, which need to be examined if one is to understand the form itself and why it has become the way it is.

This chapter appeared as 'The technology of newsgathering and production', in *Live, Direct and Biased? Making Television News in the Satellite Age* (London, Arnold, 1997), pp. 174–201.

Film cameras

Cinema newsreels were 'shot silent' by cameramen, with music, sound effects and commentary added later. Location news reporting was done on film, using cumbersome 35 mm cameras. These ranged from three-quarter-ton Biograph monsters used to film the Boer War to hand-held boxes such as the Newman Sinclair. Standard newsreel cameras were large and heavy, typically mounted on the roofs of cars. Such equipment had nevertheless captured such dramatic events as the Hindenburg crash. Although developed before the war, 16 mm film was a long time in arriving as the standard technology of television newsgathering. When television news filming began, NBC used 35 mm, while CBS used 16 mm, which was considered 'not quite professional' (Barnouw, 1970: 42). Eyemo (35 mm) hand-held clockwork cameras could record 1 minute 10 seconds of mute footage. One enterprising NBC stringer rigged six such cameras on a pole, controlled them with a single switch and sold his footage to the five newsreels and the network (Frank, 1991: 34). Bell and Howell and Auricon 16 mm cameras, originally developed for amateurs, were used in Korea (Frank, 1991: 38). The Auricon Cine-Voice could record sound, with the sound recordist needing to be connected to the camera by a thick cable (Cox, 1995: 14, 21 and 66). German Arriflex cameras developed before the war were used for mute work. In spite of these advances, heavy blimped cameras physically linked to tape recorders were still used as late as the Vietnam era (Culbert, 1988: 256).

By 1958 BBC and ITN were using magnetic striped 16 mm to record synchronous sound and picture on film (Cox, 1995: 138), but by the 1960s documentary film-makers in the USA had developed a 16 mm synchronous sound system which didn't require a wired link between camera and sound, which was recorded separately. This way of working required a two-person crew and the use of a clapperboard to enable synchronisation in editing, but there was no longer an umbilical cord between camera and sound.

Reporters had been used in small numbers in newsreels, simply as interviewers, gathering what later came to be called *vox pops* or 'streeters', a practice which was extended into the early days of television (Cox, 1995: 117). Crews would return from location and newsroom sub-editors would write the voice-over commentary from agency copy. The reporter was not seen as a newsgatherer or as the author of the piece. Stand-ups, pieces to camera, were a late arrival as sound recording on location was problematic. Cox attributes their origin in Britain to current affairs programmes such as *Panorama* (1995: 129–30). The *News at Ten* pioneered the British television use of correspondents' commentaries recorded on location. As Nigel Ryan, then Editor of ITN, explains:

> In 1969, we made a seemingly minor alteration to our editing procedure which brought about a sea change, particularly to foreign coverage. Under the old system, film shot on location was edited to a given length dictated by its pictorial value; a writer than prepared a script broadly based on the notes from the reporter on the spot and spoken by a studio voice selected for euphony rather than journalistic merit. The innovation involved reversing this pattern: the reporter sent back his commentary, recorded in the field, so his voice was heard over the film which was then edited to match it . . . The

effect on the screen was electric. Viewers had the taste of being on-the-spot with the action rather than attending an illustrated lecture from a voice out of nowhere; and the reporter was clearly placed in charge of his own report. (Ryan, 1995: 13)

It is hard to imagine that this now universal practice was once considered revolutionary. Its implications are clear, however. Visual imperatives were taking second place to the reporter's script, which was balanced, however, by the extra immediacy of a commentary literally coming from the same place as the pictures.

In domestic newsgathering, crews would have to return to base to have their film processed. Putting this film through 'the bath' would have taken anything from 20 minutes to an hour and a half depending on the film stock being used. The script would generally have been written while the film was being processed. This would then have been recorded, quite often without the reporter or other scriptwriter ever having seen the pictures. This voice-over was then given to a film editor who would insert the pictures over the top of the soundtrack. Journalists, in the early days of television news, came either from radio or from newspaper backgrounds and tended as a consequence to write their reports as self-sufficient pieces with the pictures merely 'wallpaper' inserted over the top of the wordy commentary. Radio was unquestionably the dominant parent of the infant medium in spite of the arrival of certain newsreel figures such as camera-man Ronnie Noble and commentator Leslie Mitchell, who both joined the BBC, and Ray Perrin, who became ITN's chief film-editor. Practice, at NBC, as noted above, was more picture led:

> Our system was to have cameramen film news events, to edit their film into a narrative, then, as a last step, to write a script that included the description of the event and its news relevance. We did not use reporters on the scene, who would speak a script to which pictures would be matched – risking the danger of throwing away the best pictures because they had not been scripted for. So although we had some good reporters, we used them very little, far less than CBS did and perhaps less than we should have. (Frank, 1991: 118)

Newsreel cameramen working abroad would airfreight their film back to base with 'dope sheets' describing what had been shot. These would be used to edit and script the report. When they began to go abroad, television reporters would despatch a soundtrack together with pictures for processing and editing back at base. They would write and record a script to the standard length of a one-, two-, or three-minute news item, not having seen the pictures, although they were usually present when they were filmed. This of course led to a certain unspecific manner both of filming and writing. The unprocessed film, voicetrack and a suggested cutting order would be packaged up and sent to the airport for freighting, with a delay of perhaps two or three days before the material was transmitted. A senior ITN correspondent tells of such an experience when working in Vietnam. During the Tet offensive, Sandy Gall and his cameraman witnessed and filmed the deliberate burning, by the South Vietnamese themselves, of a Saigon building occupied by Vietcong guerrillas. Gall returned from the field to write his script and asked the cameraman what he had actually shot. They were unable to see the pictures and could not, given the tumultuous circumstances, be 100 per cent certain of what exactly had been recorded. All that location journalists in such situations could do was write a general script in the hope that the story would be coherently assembled in London. This despatch of a kit of parts was basically the mode of foreign news operation throughout the 1960s and 1970s. Whether at home or abroad, the film still had to travel back to base and sometimes this was the slowest part of the operation. Whether they took any glee in it, *The Times* reported the following incident in 1964 under the headline, 'Railway film of Duke delayed by railway':

> Associated Television today asked for a British Railways inquiry into the delay of a delivery of a news film showing the Duke of Edinburgh opening the £1,250,000 railways engineering research labs in Derby yesterday. The film was handed to the parcels office at Derby station, with a five shilling tip, but it did not arrive in Birmingham until today. ATV borrowed a BBC film which went by road. (*The Times*, 16 May 1964, p. 10)

The only thing that had changed since Richard Dimbleby despatched his discs of the Fenland floods in 1937 was the efficiency of the national parcel service.

Satellite transmissions

Lightweight cameras using 16 mm film and the arrival of easily recorded synchronous location sound advanced the situation somewhat in the 1960s, but the first great breakthrough in newsgathering came with the advent of telecommunications satellites able to transmit television material instantaneously around the world. Prior to the satellite revolution pictures could be moved by airfreight or over landlines. Transatlantic telephone cable could transmit film but only at the rate of one minute a day (Mayer, 1987: 202). The first commercial telecommunications satellite, Telstar I, was launched in 1962 enabling television pictures to be transmitted instantly across the Atlantic. ITN Editor Geoffrey Cox saw the potential for the news and booked the first available slot, finding the stories to report afterwards (1995: 163). The BBC too made early use of the transatlantic link. As the war in Vietnam ended, the actual newsgathering itself was still conducted on film, but material could be sent by airfreight to Tokyo, where, after processing, it could be satellited to New York and eventually to London where it would have been edited. Pictures would still have been broadcast some time after the event was filmed and well after radio, newspapers and indeed television itself (without pictures) had reported the same story using the telephone and telex to transmit written copy. The technology was very expensive for routine use, with a 1965 price of £3,000 an hour. Stuart

Hood, writing in 1967, commented on the new technology: 'satellites have so far proved disappointing – partly because of the very high costs of transmission, partly because they depend on ground stations for transmission and reception, and there is as yet no system of stations spanning the globe' (1967: 116–17). Even as late as 1980, during the Falklands conflict, it was said that the event was in the wrong hemisphere for satellite links independent of the military. Prior to 1972, ITN still sent film material back to London by airfreight, adding any updates to the commentary later by telephone. Events in the Watergate case were too fast moving for this, and Michael Brunson used the Atlantic satellite sometimes twice nightly to file reports (Potter, 1990: 118). However, this was still far from routine for reasons of cost. In 1976, a 10 minute unilateral US to UK feed cost $1,760 (Schlesinger, 1978: 69).

Videotape

The recording of television images was achieved by John Logie Baird before the arrival of broadcast television. Using vinyl discs to record at a decidedly very low resolution, this material is on display today at Britain's National Museum of Photography, Film and Television in Bradford. Film recording, effectively the result of pointing a film camera at a television, was always possible, but this method incurred the cost of the film stock which then needed time consuming processing.

The ability to record television pictures onto a reusable magnetic medium was not practical until Ampex developed the first videotape machine in 1956. The need to record and replay pictures cheaply and easily arose primarily in the United States, where the networks had the problem of transmitting material across five time zones with different peak viewing periods. Like their domestic equivalents some 20 years later, the first broadcast videotape machines were seen as primarily time-shift devices, recording live programmes for subsequent replay. It was thought that there would need to be three such machines in America and a few more in Europe. Like similar predictions made in the late 1940s about the number of computers the world would need, such predictions were to prove spectacularly wrong.

The huge amount of electronic information which constitute television pictures made magnetic tape recording a substantially greater problem than had been the case with sound. The huge bandwidth could only be recorded onto a substantially sized tape moving at very high speed. Early attempts were unsuccessful as the fast moving tape often broke. The problem was solved by using a rotating head system so that the relative speed between tape and recording head was high but the tape could travel at a mechanically manageable speed. The first machines used two inch wide tape, and the design remained virtually the same from 1958 until 1983, roughly a quarter of a century. This pioneering format was replaced by 'C' format, which used one inch tape and which became an industry standard from the late 1970s until it in turn was replaced in the early

1990s by the first digital formats employing cassette tapes of various widths. The BBC and many commercial broadcasters chose Panasonic's composite digital D-3 machines as the broadcast standard, while 1994 saw the release of the D-5 digital component format, reputedly offering the best quality to date. Channel 4 installed 60 D-5 machines in its new premises and uses them as its standard broadcast machine.

Two inch and one inch were studio tape formats requiring large static machines most often operated by graduate electronic engineers. Various attempts were made at portability but location based video newsgathering was not widespread until the 1970s when Sony's U-matic cassette format was developed for shooting single camera location work. This was the *de facto* industry standard for ENG until it was replaced by another Sony format, Betacam, which in its turn has been superseded by a digital version.

The rate of technological advancement in broadcasting can be witnessed simply by videotape technology. The first format (two inch) was in wide use for 25 years, while its successor, one inch, was a standard for roughly a decade. The Betacam format for ENG was introduced by Sony in 1987, but by 1995 this was well on the way to being replaced by a digital version. Broadcast equipment manufacturers naturally encourage a healthy turnover of technology, as does the inevitable urge on the part of broadcasters to try to stay one crucial step ahead of the competition.

At the 1995 News World Convention in Berlin, a compact new tape format from Panasonic, DVC Pro, was demonstrated to news professionals. The lightweight, broadcast-standard, camera was predicted to revolutionise newsgathering. It was so impressive and so compact that it was stolen. The DVC (digital video cassette) tape (and a Sony competitor) is about the same size as an ordinary audio cassette and should be the last digital tape format before various tapeless recording systems become both feasible and widespread. The first disc recording systems developed by AVID\Ikegami have already been launched, as have Nagra solid-state audio recorders.

Electronic newsgathering

The U-matic videotape format, developed in the early 1970s by Sony, was capable of recording broadcast quality pictures onto three-quarter inch magnetic tape using a portable video cassette recorder. Recordists carried a suitcase-size box linked by an electronic umbilical cord to the camera operator who held a reasonably bulky camera. In operational terms the new technology was a step backward from 16 mm film of the day, requiring the physical linking of sound and vision and the use of a heavier, less robust, camera.

These disadvantages for the crew, however, were far outweighed by the key advantage that there was no longer any need to process the film. Journalistically it was possible therefore to speed up the newsgathering, while logistically crews were no longer tied to the film lab. Journalists had instant playback: they could theoretically shoot a sequence, then stop and look at it immediately played back through the viewfinder of the camera, although in practice they rarely had time to do so. Instead of writing and recording a voice-over blind, reports could return to base and instantly begin editing. Scriptwriting was now done interactively, leading to a much more complementary relationship between words and pictures. Also, a new generation of younger reporters had grown up, many of whom had worked only in television, developing more organic scriptwriting methods, integrating words and pictures, leading to less 'wallpapering'.

The delivery of unedited material from abroad by satellite also changed with the arrival of ENG. Instead of having to process the film and put it into a telecine machine before material could be satellited back to base, the location-recorded tape was instantly transmittable. Already in electronic form, tape could be taken to a 'feedpoint' where it could be played straight out of the machine it was recorded on and sent back to base by satellite. This material was still unedited, however, and the disadvantages of filing material in unassembled pieces were still as great as in the days of film. Dope sheets and precisely written cutting orders which had been traditionally physically despatched with the film had now to be delivered orally on the telephone or, in time, faxed.

In 1975, Alan Protheroe, then a senior BBC News manager and later Assistant Director General, saw the new technology in America, which he described 'like stepping out of a Tiger Moth and on to a Concorde' (*Daily Telegraph*, 1979: 16). At a special event in 1976, ITN had flown a prototype RCA TK 76 over from New York to demonstrate the technology which would complete the revolution begun by the satellite (Potter, 1990: 128). The take-up of ENG technology was not instantaneous. Nearly two years later, Dick Francis, then the BBC's Director of News and Current Affairs, told *The Times* 'you will never get rid of film, even in news production and certainly not in documentary' (*The Times*, 1978a: 3). After trials, trade union resistance delayed implementation and a senior BBC manager lamented that 'it was becoming difficult to work on film in the United States because virtually all television stations had converted to ENG' (*The Times*, 1978b: 4). ITN first used the technology to cover the 1979 visit of the Pope to Poland (ITN, 1995: 32) while the BBC covered the Commonwealth Conference in Lusaka in the same year, prudently and characteristically using both 16mm film and ENG.

Camcorders

ENG technology continued to develop after videotape replaced film as the main medium for news picture acquisition. Continued miniaturisation enabled the development of a broadcast-quality camcorder: all-in-one unit nowhere near as cumbersome as U-matic videotape with its separate camera and recorder unit. RCA developed the camcorder as early as 1977, but it was Sony with the Betacam system that provided the next *de facto* world broadcast ENG standard in 1982. Ironically, the technology was still a generation behind film in terms of handling and actual ease of use, but as is often the case with technology such an issue was not the crucial factor in determining take-up.

Further developments in electronics have already led to additional tape formats which are more compact and still easier to use. Super-VHS (S-VHS) is the electronically enhanced big brother of the domestic format VHS. It has been used by reporters such as Sue Lloyd-Roberts, posing as an ordinary tourist, to work for ITN behind the Iron Curtain.

Hi-8 is yet a further development, another Sony tape format (using 8 mm wide tape) which was used in the Gulf War both by journalists and by the military. The 'smart bomb' footage from combat jets was in fact recorded on this kind of tape.

These developments in picture-acquisition technology bring with them the promise (some journalists would say the threat) of single-person newsgathering based on the idea of multiskilled crewing. The reporter's, camera operator's, sound recordist's and editor's tasks may soon all be performed by one person. This of course has been the norm for radio journalism for some considerable period of time.

'Newshounds' and home movies on air

The VHS videotape format was originally developed for recording in the home and in time became the domestic standard around the world. Cameras and recorders were quickly developed and eventually these were followed by an all-in-one camcorder aimed at the home movie market. The result was a tremendous expansion in the number of units capable of producing television pictures. When 16 mm film was the norm for news-gathering only the staff of large news organisations and their stringers could record pictures for on-air use owing to the cost of the equipment and the film stock. In very special circumstances, such as the Zapruder film of President Kennedy's assassination, 8 mm home movies could be used, but these were hardly a regular source of news pictures. The spread of VHS, and more recently of Hi-8 camcorders, has offered the possibility of a potentially vast number of newsgatherers around the world.

This vast army of eyes is not without its problems. Aside from the person who happens to be passing by the spectacular highway crash or who records an earthquake or some other hard news event which television then uses and acknowledges, there are other problems. News editors are fairly suspicious of the provenance of such material even though sometimes it offers a record of historic events not otherwise captured. Inexpensive, lightweight, camcorders create the possibility that non-professionals could deliberately go about newsgathering. A notable instance of this was during the troubles in the Baltics in January 1991 when Western newsgathering organisations were not allowed to travel to Riga and Vilnius. Soviet citizens, many from the Baltic states themselves, were recording pictures which they were then bringing back to Moscow and selling to Western news organisations. The activities of these 'newshounds' of course raised a number of questions because these people were filming with the sole purpose of showing the horrors of what was going on. They were befriended by the victim peoples and given access, with the result that their material was shot from a certain point of view. Nevertheless they were getting pictures that would not otherwise be available and broadcasters generally acknowledged their provenance. I spoke to a man who went into Kashmir from the Indian side, posing as a tourist. Taking a Hi-8 camcorder, he filmed literally a suitcase full of material with Kashmiris about the atrocities allegedly perpetrated by the Indian army. No one would buy his material, though a major broadcaster did look at it.

Editing in the field

It had always been possible to edit film abroad provided the requisite processing lab was available and editing equipment and skilled staff could be hired locally or flown out. These demands made it rare in British television for editing to be done on location, a situation which changed with the widespread use of video. Unlike film, ENG videotape editing equipment was relatively portable. Hi-band U-matic edit machines could be put in flight cases and taken abroad, leading to the arrival of the edit suite in the hotel room. No longer was the unassembled kit of parts sent from abroad, and there was accordingly less reliance on local facilities. Rather than send back large amounts of unedited video material, news organisations now only needed to book 15 minutes of satellite time to send back a complete cut story. The reporter and crew could now shoot on location, look at the material, edit it virtually *in situ* and despatch a finished package which could be broadcast within minutes of completion. The 1954 prediction [. . .] 'Ultimately films may be obtainable from across the world almost as swiftly as telegrams can be received' (*The Listener*, 1954: 8) had been realised.

Flyaways and satphones

Satellite feeds back to base were originally from a land station, usually an orthodox television station or a telecommunications installation. By 1985 portable land stations had been developed which were capable of being carried by commercial airlines as excess baggage. These 'flyaway' satellite uplinks, weighing as little as 70 pounds, could be put in flight cases and taken abroad. The American network NBC scooped their rivals with such equipment, covering the TWA hijacking live. It was now possible to report live from anywhere in the world, given the requisite equipment. This had to include the old-fashioned telephone for it is not possible to beam material unilaterally up to a satellite. It is necessary first to telephone and book facilities as damage can be done to transponders on the 'bird' by such unannounced uplinks. Therefore, in addition to the 'flyaway' and a generator to power it, there is also the need for telephone communication. This can be provided by a very small umbrella-like satellite dish connected to a telephone which can fit into a briefcase. The satphone connects into the INMARSAT system of maritime communications satellites and makes it possible for reporters to contact base by telephone from virtually anywhere. A fax machine can be connected to a satphone to receive and send hard copy, while a modem linked to a laptop computer means text in digital form can be transmitted. Richard Dowden of *The Independent* (1994) writes of roaming Africa with hand-held technology which enables him to despatch copy to London instantly by the simple expedient of plugging into the cigarette lighter of a car and beaming into the INMARSAT system. A dramatic high-profile use of satellite technology for television was Sandy Gall's live links from inside Afghanistan as the Russians withdrew (1995: 180).

By 1986 the IBA, ITN and Michael Electronics had developed a satellite newsgathering (SNG) unit called Newshawk which used a system of 1.2 metre dishes (ITN, 1995: 32) to uplink television pictures. No longer did tape have to be taken to a television station or telecoms facility, and large telephone company dishes were no longer required in the field. These small trucks have become increasingly common. Starbird Satellite Services, a partnership of the WTN news picture agency and British Aerospace, offers broadcasters not only such uplinks but a dedicated satellite transponder, available 24 hours a day. Until the arrival of such unilateral services, satellite time had to be booked with a series of 'matching orders' faxed between the requesting broadcasters, the national telephone companies at both ends of the link and the international satellite organisation. At a minimum this process took half an hour. Understandably, broadcasters objected to this bureaucracy and as a result a consortium, the European News Exchange (ENEX) was formed between CBS and a number of other commercial stations which leased the exclusive use of a transponder (Hurt, 1996: 24–7). Similarly, in March 1994 ITN signed a deal with British Telecom giving them 24-hour access to a Europewide transponder and therefore no limits on satellite feeds and two-ways (ITN, 1995: 34).

These two-way communications systems are of course not just for filing stories but can be used for receiving advice and information. It is common working practice in American network television news for reporters to write scripts on location using laptop computers before sending them back to base via modem for approval, with New York often suggesting changes. This is not necessarily a bad thing, though all the British journalists spoken to in this sample cringed at the prospect of what they saw as a transatlantic aberration arriving as standard working practice with their organisations. Certainly the increased logistical demands of the new technologies and the relative ease of communication have led to reporters at times spending more time on the telephone to base in London or New York than doing journalism. These greater organisational requirements in turn have led to the arrival of location producers, referred to disparagingly by some journalists as 'fixers'. Thus a full crew can now consist of reporter, camera operator, sound recordist, editor, satellite technician, producer and several first-class tickets worth of excess baggage.

Palm-tree journalism

Satellite links give journalists the ability to report from almost anywhere in the world. Of contemporary news services, CNN particularly makes a fetish of live reporting. They even go so far as to choose their bureau locations strategically to provide rooftop offices with panoramic views. Thus viewers got live pictures of a T-72 tank backfiring in the streets of Moscow in August of 1991, an event which was then duly replayed and discussed. CNN had five reporters in Moscow for the storming of the White House, including one inside the Kremlin, and viewers could watch events unfold live. Reporting of this type is inevitably accompanied by an extensive rhetoric constantly reminding the viewer that they are indeed eyewitnesses viewing history being made; 24-hour services such as CNN constantly stress their ability to 'go live' for as long as necessary to cover a story. This difference between them and the traditional fixed-point bulletins of terrestrial broadcasters has become a unique selling point in a fierce journalistic and commercial competition.

There are serious issues at question according to a former ITN diplomatic editor, himself now a rolling news anchor: 'Live is very dangerous, because in live television, particularly if you have to transmit 24 hours a day, you make mistakes.' He sees these not just as mistakes of fact or emphasis, but serious cases of creating misleading impressions with wider international political consequences:

> The Soviet coup was a good example of how television is distorting something, having television on the spot live was distorting. Western Governments, including certainly Mitterrand and Major, were making very rapid assumptions based on a fixed camera on the CNN office overlooking Kutuzovsky Prospekt where you saw the APCs and the T62s and 72s lined up, that the coup had succeeded, Gorbachev was out and so on. Television is very dangerous.

All momentous events, of course, do not always conveniently occur within range of rooftop cameras. One result is what I call palm-tree journalism. Reporters must remain with their hi-tech installation by the hotel pool to be fed live into the near continuous news system. A BBC foreign correspondent tells of unexpectedly meeting an American counterpart away from the hotel, up-country, in Nicaragua. 'What are you doing here?' he inquired. 'I'm on my day off', came the reply. No longer chained to the satellite dish, the reported could actually go and attempt to see something of the events he had been reporting on 'live' for the previous week. Even on a mainstream general programming channel, as opposed to a 24-hour news network, there are now so many fixed-point bulletins that reporters often have multiple deadlines, needing to file so often that they have restricted time in the field.

Live two-ways and hotel stand-ups

The state-of-the-art technology that makes live satellite broadcasting possible can of course be used to file pre-recorded video material. It is possible to combine the two basic modes of television newsgathering. Edited location recorded pieces, the descendant of the filmed newsreel, can be filed minutes before transmission and the location reporter can be 'injected' live into a programme. Increasingly, one sees the transmission of an edited location report followed immediately by a 'live two-way' with the location reporter. Such interviews by the studio anchor about the 'latest developments' are often redundant. If the reporter has done their job properly there should, in most cases, be nothing more to say. This situation is exacerbated by the fact that the anchor usually will not have seen the ENG piece, as in many cases it will not have arrived until after transmission has begun. As one veteran correspondent remarks,

> in order to give the impression that you're watching news as it's happening they're now doing these two-ways of reporters. The reporters have nothing to add. They've given you their report and very few of them . . . are capable of actually dealing with a live two-way. It's a difficult thing, not just nerves, but technically it's different. This is seen to be live TV – it's happened there, let's go to our man there, show the viewers how clever we are . . . recently when I was in Sarajevo I'd sent over a report, quite a long one, and the newscaster came and said 'What's the latest?' I said 'you've just seen the latest, I've just said it to you, I've got nothing to add to that.' There was a kind of long pause. I won't put up with that crap, if these guys can't sit down for a few minutes and figure out what they're going to say to me, then they can go and jump. But television is going to be hoist by its own petard because of this business of live television. CNN is doing enormous damage.

This reservation about the cult of the live two-way is shared by a senior CNN correspondent who has remarked: 'It's great if you have a Berlin Wall falling, but that doesn't happen very often. Most of the time you've got a parked car.' This same reporter has issued a standing threat to answer the on-air question 'What's happening Richard?' with the reply 'I have no idea what's happening because I've been standing on this hotel balcony for two hours waiting for you to ask me that question' (Rosenblum 1993: 168). A senior BBC journalist with extensive experience of both sides of the two-way condemns it simply as 'a cosmetic contrivance'.

The two-way communications offered by the satellite link can be used to provide the field reporter with information. At its most basic this can consist of the simple reading of wire service copy over the phone to the reporter, who can then repeat it later on-air (Thomson, 1992: 140). The tyranny of the two-way is lamented by many of the journalists who are regularly required to perform them. In this view, such 'live shots' 'originated with some kind of TV witchdoctor in Iowa' (Bell, 1995: 67) and can degenerate into a situation little short of the farcical, where reporters are read material which they hear in their earpiece and which they then duly repeat verbatim on air. This scene from the Hollywood film *Broadcast News* is regularly broadcast in the news and has been described by one reluctant participant 'like a sort of news bypass operation, in which only the ear and mouth were actively engaged – not journalism, or even show business, but puppetry' (Bell, 1995: 209).

While there is no doubt that something can be added by an appropriate two-way, there is an undoubted tendency to overuse them. During its rolling coverage of the August 1996 TWA crash, CNN went live to their reporter on a Long Island beach. Miles from the crash scene offshore, he could only report that the scheduled press conference was now 41 minutes late. He had nothing more to add and, short of actually saying that on-air, gave every indication that that was the case. Earpieces buzzed and he and the Atlanta anchor had no choice but to fill out the time until the top of the hour. The nearly 20 minutes of dialogue that followed was an impressive testament to the calm professionalism of the two broadcasters concerned but added very little to the story which was to be a mystery for some time.

Expensive newsgathering

There have been undoubted positive effects as a result of the deployment of the new technologies. Editing abroad has led to the creation of completed ENG pieces with a better integration of pictures and words. It is no longer the norm to send scrambled kits of unassembled parts back to base for transmission three days after the event. The advantages of the new ways of working are clear, enabling reporters to fully author their own work, producing a script in conjunction with pictures they can see. Indeed, for the first time foreign news reporters are themselves able to view their pieces as finished products. While location-recorded material now inevitably reaches screens sooner and more coherently than it did before, such practices also have their disadvantages. ENG comes to mean 'expensive newsgathering' when 'excess baggage charges can even account for the major part of the cost of overseas news' (Hawker, 1993: 30). A senior BBC news editor has given a figure of £17,500 a week for the maintenance of a fully equipped team with its own satellite uplink (Wallis and Baran, 1990: 223), and BBC Foreign Affairs Editor John Simpson describes a trip to Angola with a crew of six (without a dish) costing £50,000 (Simpson, 1993). Once this costly commitment has been made to send staff – reporter, camera operator, sound recordist, editor, producer and all the kit – the expense incurred often dictates that the material will be used. Similarly, if a satellite feed is pre-booked there is a tendency to use it and, once the reporter has sent their piece, why not use the remaining satellite time to 'get the latest'? To a certain extent logistical, not journalistic, considerations dictate what gets covered and how. One veteran reporter talked of how, when he began his career on film, logistics were 20 per cent of his job and journalism 80 per cent, while now, with the new technologies, those ratios have been reversed.

Television's main advantage over the print media has been its ability to report the news instantly, and this unique selling point has been stressed by the 24-hour dedicated news services such as CNN. The ability to broadcast live from anywhere results from technological factors. Competitive managers in news organisations have always unquestioningly acquired new technologies in an attempt to get an edge on their rivals; purchases which in turn raise the cost of newsgathering. What develops then is a complex competitive dynamic in which technology is a major, but not the only, factor. In the constant search for a competitive journalistic advantage, technology is acquired which in turn changes the nature of the newsgathering and reporting process.

Dupes

Editing tape on location means that instead of having only the unique original film that was sent back to base for processing, video footage can be copied or 'duped'. Such dupes, duplication pictures from a sister news organisation, might arrive in the edit suite, with a reporter not having been present when the pictures were shot and hence knowing nothing of their provenance. They might be inclined to use them because they are powerful and because of the everpresent competitive factor. This could lead to the use of material from unknown sources. The myth of the eyewitness reporter suffers somewhat if he or she uses pictures kindly provided by somebody in the same hotel. An experienced former foreign correspondent, now anchoring, issues a caution:

> If you look at the development of television journalism in its strongest moments, it's about one camera person, one camera crew and a reporter looking at something, filming it from every position that they can manage, but no more, condensing it into their eyewitness account and sending it home. Whatever the story is. That is now a thing of the past. Because somebody else got a better shot of the second element or somebody else got a fifth element that you hadn't though of . . . it was cut in. As a result of course, it becomes less one person's eyewitness report, than merely a sausage machine production of images that you may have seen already on another bulletin on another channel . . . I think you'd be very hard put to find a bulletin today that was shot and reported by one person. I think that almost everything that you see has had the input of perhaps five or six teams all doing different elements.

Cost-cutting has led, particularly in the American networks, to fewer and fewer permanently based foreign correspondents. Equally, 'firemen' are despatched abroad less often than was once the case. The result of these finance-led decisions is that more and more reports consist of agency or third-party tape from abroad, voiced at base. This practice of 'packaging' is fraught with difficulties.

During the Gulf War newsrooms received extraordinary footage from inside occupied Kuwait of resistance fighters in action dropping molotov cocktails from a highway flyover onto an Iraqi military vehicle. The material, shot on domestic VHS, looked authentic and was used. After the war it emerged that over a million dollars were paid by the Kuwaiti government to an American public relations firm to produce 24 video news releases (VNRs) which were sent to news organisations around the world (MacArthur, 1992: 50). No technology can guarantee the authenticity of such material and the explosion in the amount of footage now available makes verification even more difficult.

Even on location there is a worrying tendency to do things by remote control, as one veteran war correspondent reveals:

> Now so much of television is done from feedpoint, the reporters never leave the building . . . In Sarajevo it was all pool, everyone was pooling, so if you didn't want to leave the building you didn't have to . . . I know a bureau correspondent, and he never leaves his bureau. Never, he's too lazy, he never leaves. His cameraman and producer go out and do all the stories . . . They go out and they bring it back . . . and the producer writes a rough script and he rewrites it in his words and broadcasts it, and they say well done fella, great story today.

The obvious question that needs to be asked is have the new technologies and, just as importantly, the working practices that come with them, led to better reporting and a better informed viewing public? For Martin Kalb, a former American television correspondent, the answer is simple: 'as technology has grown more sophisticated, the end product has grown more skimpy' (quoted in Vanden Heuvel, 1993: 15). Is this view shared by those currently using the new technologies?

The possibilities offered for newsgathering in the satellite age cannot help but excite even the most sceptical journalists.

> When the shuttle blew up the first thing I did was pick up the phone and book the satellite for the next 24 hours to secure a line out. Then I realised we could sub-let it after that. The shuttle blew up at 5 o'clock London time, and we had a three and a half minute piece on the air at 5.45. And we'd done a newsflash at about 5.15 with pictures. This was absolutely unheard of.

However, amongst experienced reporters (including the one quoted above) there are undoubted feelings of nostalgia tempered with an air of resignation. The main drawback, to many who grew up with film, is the loss of the 20 or so minutes thinking time while the film was being processed. Instead of a quiet period to make phone calls to base and collect one's thoughts before writing a script, there was now a need to hit the ground running and begin editing instantly. However, younger reporters who had never had this relative luxury did not see the problem. They pointed out that they composed their thoughts as they went along and always began editing with a clear idea of how they were going to craft their piece.

Journalists have always worked to short deadlines. A 'Reuters snap' consisting of the four words 'Ghandi shot, worst expected' flashed around the world in 1947 within minutes of the event. Print reporters covering President Kennedy's press conferences in the early 1960s tell of running out of the room to open phones to dictate pieces that were composed as they spoke. Foreign correspondents shipping unprocessed film by airfreight always had the deadline of the next flight even if their material might be days in arriving on the screen. Nevertheless, some say there is a case to be made for deliberately putting delay into the system:

> Years ago, when the first landline was put between the White House and New York as soon as a press conference was over, reporters came rushing out straight to the live camera and said 'the president has just said this' . . . The first guy to get to the camera was on-air first, but the correspondents were getting it so wrong so often because they hadn't got time to sit down and say 'now he said that . . . what did he mean by that?' . . . The networks and the correspondents were seen to be wrong so often, that all three nets then agreed that there would be a built-in delay, I think it was a 10 minute delay. They all agreed to that so that guys could sit down, reflect and write a proper piece . . . I'd like to see that happening with us.

Picture explosions

The move from film to video has had other effects than shortening deadlines. Videotape costs a fraction of what film did and with ENG there is the danger of shooting too much:

> People are actually terribly ill-disciplined with video now, they just turn it on, shooting three hours on a story which in the old days you shot 10 minutes on. Consequently you end up with hours of material, some of which is never seen by anybody . . . I think it has actually diluted the process of retrieving information and making it consumable to the viewer. Very often the constraints are not journalistic but mathematical and practical, which is crazy. But in the old days it was just a limit to what you could actually find out. Now, added to that is a limit to how much you can actually trawl through on the video screen before your time is up.

This overkill in the field creates enormous problems as proportionally more material comes in to all news organisations. The result is very worrying, claims one experienced hand:

> because of our wanton abuse of the technology all discipline has broken down. People are spraying at anything, recording for hours. They're sitting across all these satellite feeds that are coming in from the outside world and stuff is being thrown onto the air with very little individual research as to

what it actually is really about. It's a third-hand account of what it's really about, often sent in on a dope sheet, by some party who had nothing to do with the shooting of the film in the first place. For example, Visnews or WTN will pick up from some freelance or some local television station. They will have had no conversation with the person who actually shot it. They'll have a conversation with the person who is selling it to them who may never have had a conversation with the person who shot it. There is then maybe another account from Reuters or AP and all this stuff is married up and you end up with a fairly threadbare contact with the original execution of the material. Whereas in the old days, although there was less of it, most of it was generated by someone who had seen it, shipped it and sent the information with it.

Changing circumstances

One reporter spoken to for this chapter called himself one of the luckiest people in the profession as he had only one deadline a day, working as he did for an evening programme only: 'it is wonderful and it is old-fashioned and is civilised.' Unlike some journalists who may have to report to both radio and television or to multiple deadlines either in rolling or fixed-point news, he had the better part of the day to prepare his considered piece. Others of his colleagues are not so fortunate:

> We can now edit on-site, we have little vans with all the machinery in, so you don't have to come back to base with your material, so that means you can get it on more bulletins. In theory you can get on all the bulletins, changing it for each one by editing on site. You have to work much quicker, you must know when to go back and start editing, just because of the deadline and not push your luck. When I first joined ITN the news editor sent me out on a story saying don't bother too much about getting it back for News at One, just aim for the 5.45. And nowadays the first instruction is can you get it back for the 5-to-11 summary and then change it for the One? So everything's moved on in terms of speed and demand on location.

Life is not much easier back at base. Where once film had to be processed, edited and assembled into a transmission roll in the telecine machine, videotape can now arrive when the programme is on-air:

> In the mid-1970s the news was wrapped up before you went on-air. The film had been cut and loaded in the machine ready to roll and you might have one live interview but very rarely . . . Whereas today stuff comes into the programme constantly that I haven't seen because it's been injected live from wherever it comes from. You are writing and editing introductions to the stories when you haven't seen the pictures yet, so you've got to be much more on the ball. I think all news journalists are far more involved now than they ever used to be by the nature of what they are doing.

In what some would regard as a worst-case scenario, bi-media reporting with its almost constant stream of deadlines can lead to a specialist correspondent remaining at base filing for radio and television (using library footage) while, if he is lucky, a producer is free to go out and shoot fresh location footage (Gallagher, 1996: 13). Equally, logistical pressures mean it is easier to have interviewees come to the facilities rather than have crews go to them. Keen-eyed viewers will no doubt have noted the number of interviews that take place in video edit suites and, clearly, the atrium of ITN's magnificent London headquarters is a regular backdrop to talking heads of all kinds. The substantive content of such interviews is of course not changed with the location, fuel costs are saved and fewer silver cases are humped up and down stairs. The danger may be in a long-term loss of contact with the outside world. Viewers may have lost nothing in no longer seeing academic experts stereotypically speaking in front of a row of books but there may be an undue reliance on speakers who can quickly leg it to headquarters or a remote studio. One academic at the London School of Economics told me that his frequent media appearances were not so much a function of the quality of his comment as of his proximity to the central London studios of the various television news organisations. These studios themselves have undergone radical recent change and newsgathering technology is only half of the story, for, once 'gathered', news must be transmitted; intake must be transformed into output.

The traditional newsroom

The traditional broadcast newsroom was a communication system employing an intriguing mixture of high and low technology. State-of-the-art electronic equipment has always been required for television and radio programmes simply to be broadcast. However, the journalistic product that was set before the cameras or read into the radio microphones was traditionally produced using basic technologies such as the typewriter, the telephone, the ballpoint pen and carbon paper. A newsroom has always been a complex information-flow system where input of various kinds is ultimately transformed into electronic broadcast output. Input takes various forms, whether from 'wholesale' (i.e. not available to the general public) sources such as news agency copy arriving on teleprinters or press releases arriving in the post. There are 'retail' sources of information as well, with newspapers and other electronic media being avidly consumed in any newsroom. In addition, the employees of every news organisation generate diverse input into the system.

Not all input is moved directly to output. In all newsrooms there is a considerable amount of forward planning, with certain staff being given responsibility for 'diary' production. Press releases arrive in newsrooms a considerable time before the event announced and a certain percentage of news production concerns such diary stories. The announcement of trade figures or the publication of a major report do not come as surprises and a substantial part of the input to newsrooms concerns future events which must be noted and planned for. Press releases and other announcements of such events are entered into a diary, and prospect sheets are produced for use in planning meetings. The BBC has a central Future Events Unit which acts as a clearing house, receiving press releases and other announcements which are then circulated to output departments with notice of coming events. Agencies equally produce such forward-planning information.

System output

The output of the news system is the programme broadcast on the screen, consisting of the newsreader reading text to camera and introducing location recorded reports. ENG reports are recorded on location with the material being returned to base for assembly into a transmittable package. In addition to these self-generated visual materials, newsrooms receive 'feeds' of still and moving pictures from various external sources which they may use in bulletin creation. The transmitted programme is produced using a script which is written communally over the preparation period prior to the bulletin going on-air. Traditionally, this was by using typewriters and carbon paper. For example, a news agency report would be torn off the teleprinter. A sub-editor would then rewrite the story at a typewriter using a 'four-way' to produce multiple carbon copies. These would be shown to editors and presenters for comment and change. Eventually a script for the whole bulletin would emerge, which was then retyped by typists and reproduced by copying methods such as roneo or mimeograph. In addition, a sheet listing the programme running order and timings would be prepared and printed. Originally, television news presenters read from the paper copy with great skill, looking up periodically to make eye contact with the audience. Prompting devices were later developed enabling anchors to read the script off a screen mounted at first beside then eventually on the front of the camera they were speaking into. This required the retyping of the presenter's script onto a paper roll in large type. This roll simply had a small television camera pointed at it and the output came up on a screen to be read.

Once the paper-produced script had been dealt with by journalists it was passed to the programme director who would 'mark it up', indicating which camera was used for which part of the programme. Timings of item and programme length were arrived at by physically counting the words. Normal broadcast speech is reckoned to be delivered at the speed of three words a second. Scripts were often written with only three words in a line, both to facilitate ease of reading and to make counting the words, and hence the script length, easier.

Digitising the news

This whole paper-based script production chain has been replaced by computer-based electronic newsroom systems (ENSs). Such ENSs are a widespread phenomenon in the media industries. One service provider, Bay Area Systems (BASYS), alone has 450 systems installed worldwide (*Broadcast*, 1995: 9). These systems, which first appeared as direct-input systems in newspaper production, are now fairly common tools in radio and television newsrooms around the world. BASYS was originally developed by independent software developers in the United States who designed a computer newsroom system for KRON-TV in San Francisco. In 1982 ITN chose the system for the news service it was to provide for Britain's new Channel 4. At the time this was the largest installation of the system in the world. Subsequently ITN were to purchase the company, but, unable to undertake the investment required to keep the product up to date, sold BASYS to DEC, who manufactured the hardware the system ran on. Ownership eventually transferred to AVID, a leading provider of digitally based editing systems to broadcasters. Originally designed to run on a VAX minicomputer, BASYS has been ported to the Windows PC environment but most current systems in Britain are still text-based, running on VAX.

An ENS basically consists of a minicomputer with a series of terminals or a network of personal computers linked to a central server into which various forms of 'input' are entered. This input, either from direct entry by journalists or from external sources such as news agency 'wires', is then edited and printed as the script of the radio or television newsroom. It is something of a commonplace that such systems have radically changed the way in which broadcast journalists work, but there has been very little analysis either by the industry itself or by academic observers of the way in which these systems are used and how they have changed working practices. Two recent newsroom studies (Cottle, 1993: 43; Blumler and Gurevitch, 1995) make note of the arrival of computer newsroom systems but don't make an extensive study of their use or effect. This particular technology is one that is new as the vast majority of the academic production studies were conducted in the 1970s and 1980s.

ENS comes and sits on top of the traditional paper-based information flow, not offering a new paradigm but digitising and automating certain parts of that process. Most contemporary ENS systems consist basically of a text-processing and related communications system. Wire copy comes in on-line from news agencies, which can be edited, new text added and then altered by a succession of personnel. At its most basic an ENS is a large, communally accessed word processor whose product is the script. It processes the text of the script, counts the words and therefore gives timings. The programme running order, once displayed on an office white board, is now manipulated on-screen and the system has simple communications and database functions. It can interface with other technology in the system and download text to graphics and the teleprompter. Most current ENS systems (BASYS, Newstar, Newsmaker) interface with videotape library management systems to control the playing of tapes for transmission.

Originally, computer newsroom systems did not deal with the actual audio-visual output of the programme. Picture editing, graphics and the live studio cameras were a production chain almost totally independent of the script system. A television script is a set of printed instructions written in a special language which skilled staff then use to realise a complex time-based audio-visual construct. The use of an ENS is computer-aided design (CAD) but not computer-aided manufacture (CAM), producing a blueprint in the form of a script but not the actual product.

The library management systems, which control the play-in of video tapes, enable running orders to be rearranged instantly, with the changes appearing seamlessly on the teleprompter and in tape play-out. I have observed operations where short regional sub-bulletins, edited by one person, are transmitted by that journalist, a specially trained secretary and the newsreader. There are no technicians or other operating personnel involved. A half-hour live bulletin transmitted twice daily to stations from Australia to California equally exploits such newsroom technology and does so with a remarkably small technical and journalistic team.

At the very least, the effect of the text-only newsroom systems has been to speed up the process. Script production requires less menial manual work, with cleaner and better written scripts being produced. Running orders are more flexible and programmes more responsive as scripts can be changed at the last minute, although some journalists do not see this as a blessing. One newscaster was of the opinion that they were now at 'the limits of how fast you can get'. In terms of content one editor downplayed the effect on substance: 'I don't think journalistically it's changed the way we do things at all, but it's made it easier to find out information and exchange information.'

Newer, more integrated, digital systems are arriving which will more closely link script and actual programme production. Digital video servers will enable newsroom personnel to manipulate visual material as well as text in the same desktop system. Journalists working at their workstation will receive a variety of inputs, all of which they will be able to edit. These developments are signalled by institutional change, with AVID, a leading supplier of digital editing software, purchasing BASYS, while Sony, a traditional provider of videotape editing equipment, has joined forces with the software company Oracle to produce a rival integrated newsroom system. This has been adopted for trials by ITN, while the BBC is developing its own electronic news production system (ENPS) in conjunction with Associated Press.

[. . .]

Conclusions

[. . .] Why [. . .] has news gone down the path it patently has?

> I think one of the real problems is the people who manage television are absolutely, they're completely in love with the 'toys' as they describe them and the toys are lightweight dishes and everything is about technology, nothing is about content. There is no debate about content. The debate is

about the technology. It is about 'how can we do this?', you know, they are already thinking 'what are we going to do about Gorbachev here? Well we could have a link here and a satellite dish there, and we could use a lightweight satellite dish there.' These are the editorial meetings. This is about the how rather than the what. These are the things which drive people in television news, not the content.

Interestingly, 'the people who manage television' are not, have never been, location reporters and hence do not understand first-hand the problems involved. As one former foreign correspondent remarked, 'it's like having an air force where the pilots are barred from command.' [. . .] We may have been able to see tanks rolling live in the streets of Moscow and been told of the liberation of Kuwait City by a reporter with a flyaway, but traditional journalistic considerations still apply. Access is still needed and judgement is still paramount. Media response teams formed during the Gulf War had the satphones and flyaways but what did viewers see as a result? Did we see live war? No, nor were we likely to because the Allied military controlled access. And, one must ask, what would it have added to our understanding if we had? Rooftop shots of tanks in a Moscow street cannot tell us the will of the Russian military. In Bosnia there is no point in having all the kit if you can't get to Goražde and all you can offer the world is hotel stand-ups and shots of a radio receiving messages reputedly from the besieged city but which cannot be verified. Satellite communications, digital technologies and 24-hour global broadcasting didn't stop CNN coming within 20 seconds of announcing that George Bush had died in Tokyo, the victim of a hoax carried out by a disgruntled competitor (Rosenblum, 1993: 181). The consequences of such inadvertent news-making hardly bear thinking about, but then of course 'the marketing people can boast that it was live' (1993: 168). Margins of error are slimmer than ever and no technology has yet been found to improve human judgement. The competitive, management-driven, and often unthinking deployment of technical resources has changed location-based news reporting utterly. In the eyes of those actually doing the reporting, this change has been a mixed blessing and there is a perceived danger that by making the live and the exclusive into primary news values, accuracy and understanding will be lost. While Luddite anti-technology sentiments were muttered by some, these were qualified as soon as they were spoken. There was a near universal plea to use the new technologies properly and not to get seduced by the all too easily measured criterion of being first, being live or having something no competitor has. Equally, by constantly chasing the audience, there is a perceived risk that they might actually be lost, impatient with change for change's sake. As one veteran correspondent laments:

It's this lust that news editors have for taking news one step forward or one step sideways or one step further. I think the old formulae were the best. It's a saleable thing, it's like cornflakes, it's like washing powder, you've got to find a new improved formula . . . It's the new improved news. That irritates me, there's nothing new in television, because there is nothing new in the world situation. Wars look the same, earthquakes look the same, but they're all trying to find new ways of doing it better, covering it better, or in a newer fashion than the guy next door, and I think they're damaging themselves. The viewers aren't impressed by it.

References

Barnouw, E. (1970) *The Image Empire: a History of Broadcasting in the United States from 1953*. New York: Oxford University Press.

Bell, M. (1995) *In Harm's Way: Reflections of a War Zone Thug*. London: Hamish Hamilton.

Blumler, J. and Gurevitch, M. (1995) *The Crisis of Public Communication*. London: Routledge.

Broadcast (1995) 'In-production' supplement, 9 June, p. 9.

Cottle, S. (1993) *TV News, Urban Conflict and the Inner City*. Leicester: Leicester University Press.

Cox, G. (1995) *Pioneering Television News*. London: John Libbey.

Culbert, D. (1988) 'Television's Vietnam and historical revisionism in the United States', *Historical Journal of Film, Radio and Television*, 8 (3): 258–68.

Daily Telegraph (1979) 'Electronics and British trade unionism: how compatible?', 6 July, p. 16.

Dowden, R. (1994) 'Satellite dishes amid the Iron Age spears', *The Independent*, 13 April, p. 9.

Frank, R. (1991) *Out of Thin Air: the Brief Wonderful Life of Network News*. New York: Simon and Schuster.

Gall, S. (1995) *News from the Front: the Life of a Television Reporter*. London: Mandarin.

Gallagher, T. (1996) 'Out of focus: the move away from picture culture in BBC television news under John Birt', unpublished thesis, Institute of Communications Studies, University of Leeds.

Hawker, P. (1993) 'ENG: expensive news gathering?', *Television: the Journal of the Royal Television Society*, 30 (1): 30–1.

Hood, S. (1967) *A Survey of Television*. London: Heinemann.

Hurt, M. (1996) 'TXP 45: The European News Exchange', unpublished thesis, Institute of Communications Studies, University of Leeds.

ITN (1995) *ITN: the First 40 Years*. London: Independent Television News.

The Listener (1954) 'Here is the news', 1 July, p. 8.

MacArthur, J. (1992) *Second Front: Censorship and Propaganda in the Gulf War*. Berkeley, CA: University of California Press.

Mayer, M. (1987) *Making News* (repr. 1993). Boston: Harvard Business School Press.

Potter, J. (1990) *Independent Television in Britain*, vol. 4: *Companies and Programmes 1968–80*. Basingstoke: Macmillan.

Rosenblum, M. (1993) *Who Stole the News?*, New York: John Wiley.

Ryan, N. (1995) 'Calling the shots', *Guardian*, 4 September, p. 13.

Schlesinger, P. (1978) *Putting 'Reality' Together: BBC News* (repr. 1987, 1992). London: Methuen.

Simpson, J. (1993) *Making the News: Huw Weldon Lecture to the 1993 Royal Television Society*, BBC2, 22 September.

Thomson, A. (1992) *Smokescreen: the Media, the Censors, the Gulf*. Tunbridge Wells: Laburnham Books.

The Times (1964) 'Railway film of duke delayed by railway', 16 May, p. 10.

The Times (1978a) 'Electronic news-gatherer looks ahead', 18 July, p. 3.

The Times (1978b) 'Union bar forces BBC to store equipment', 9 October, p. 4.

Vanden Heuvel, J. (1993) 'For the media, a brave (and scary) new world', *Media Studies Journal*, 7: 11–20.

Wallis, R. and Baran, S. (1990) *The Known World of Broadcast News*. London: Routledge.

The virtual community: finding connection in a computerised world
Howard Rheingold

'Daddy is saying "Holy moly!" to his computer again!' Those words have become a family code for the way my virtual community has infiltrated our real world. My seven-year-old daughter knows that her father congregates with a family of invisible friends who seem to gather in his computer. Sometimes he talks to them, even if nobody else can see them. And she knows that these invisible friends sometimes show up in the flesh, materializing from the next block or the other side of the planet.

Since the summer of 1985, for an average of two hours a day, seven days a week, I've been plugging my personal computer into my telephone and making contact with the WELL (Whole Earth 'Lectronic Link) – a computer conferencing system that enables people around the world to carry on public conversations and exchange private electronic mail (e-mail). The idea of a community accessible only via my computer screen sounded cold to me at first, but I learned quickly that people can feel passionately about e-mail and computer conferences. I've become one of them. I care about these people I met through my computer, and I care deeply about the future of the medium that enables us to assemble.

The chapter forms the Introduction to *The Virtual Community: Finding Connection in a Computerised World* (London, Secker and Warburg, 1994), pp. 1–16.

I'm not alone in this emotional attachment to an apparently bloodless technological ritual. Millions of people on every continent also participate in the computer-mediated social groups known as virtual communities, and this population is growing fast. Finding the WELL was like discovering a cozy little world that had been flourishing without me, hidden within the walls of my house; an entire cast of characters welcomed me to the troupe with great merriment as soon as I found the secret door. Like others who fell into the WELL, I soon discovered that I was audience, performer, and scriptwriter, along with my companions, in an ongoing improvisation. A full-scale subculture was growing on the other side of my telephone jack, and they invited me to help create something new.

The virtual village of a few hundred people I stumbled upon in 1985 grew to eight thousand by 1993. It became clear to me during the first months of that history that I was participating in the self-design of a new kind of culture. I watched the community's social contracts stretch and change as the people who discovered and started building the WELL in its first year or two were joined by so many others. Norms were established, challenged, changed, reestablished, rechallenged, in a kind of speeded-up social evolution.

The WELL felt like an authentic community to me from the start because it was grounded in my everyday physical world. WELLites who don't live within driving distance of the San Francisco Bay area are constrained in their ability to participate in the local networks of face-to-face acquaintances. By now, I've attended real-life WELL marriages, WELL births, and even a WELL funeral. (The phrase 'in real life' pops up so often in virtual communities that regulars abbreviate it to IRL.) I can't count the parties and outings where the invisible personae who first acted out their parts in the debates and melodramas on my computer screen later manifested in front of me in the physical world in the form of real people, with faces, bodies, and voices.

I remember the first time I walked into a room full of people IRL who knew many intimate details of my history and whose own stories I knew very well. Three months after I joined, I went to my first WELL party at the home of one of the WELL's online moderators. I looked around at the room full of strangers when I walked in. It was one of the oddest sensations of my life. I had contended with these people, shot the invisible breeze around the electronic watercooler, shared alliances and formed bonds, fallen off my chair laughing with them, become livid with anger at some of them. But there wasn't a recognizable face in the house. I had never seen them before.

My flesh-and-blood family long ago grew accustomed to the way I sit in my home office early in the morning and late at night, chuckling and cursing, sometimes crying, about words I read on the computer screen. It might have looked to my daughter as if I were alone at my desk the night she caught me chortling online, but from my point of view I was in living contact with old and new friends, strangers and colleagues:

I was in the Parenting Conference on the WELL, participating in an informational and emotional support group for a friend who just learned his son was diagnosed with leukemia.

I was in MicroMUSE, a role-playing fantasy game of the twenty-fourth century (and science education medium in disguise), interacting with students and professors who know me only as 'Pollenator'.

I was in TWICS, a bicultural community in Tokyo; CIX, a community in London; CalvaCom, a community in Paris; and Usenet, a collection of hundreds of different discussions that travel around the world via electronic mail to millions of participants in dozens of countries.

I was browsing through Supreme Court decisions, in search of information that could help me debunk an opponent's claims in a political debate elsewhere on the Net, or I was retrieving this morning's satellite images of weather over the Pacific.

I was following an eyewitness report from Moscow during the coup attempt, or China during the Tiananmen Square incident, or Israel and Kuwait during the Gulf War, passed directly from citizen to citizen through an *ad hoc* network patched together from cheap computers and ordinary telephone lines, cutting across normal geographic and political boundaries by piggybacking on the global communications infrastructure.

I was monitoring a rambling real-time dialogue among people whose bodies were scattered across three continents, a global bull session that seems to blend wit and sophomore locker-room talk via Internet Relay Chat (IRC), a medium that combines the features of conversation and writing. IRC has accumulated an obsessive subculture of its own among undergraduates by the thousands from Adelaide to Arabia.

People in virtual communities use words on screens to exchange pleasantries and argue, engage in intellectual discourse, conduct commerce, exchange knowledge, share emotional support, make plans, brainstorm, gossip, feud, fall in love, find friends and lose them, play games, flirt, create a little high art and a lot of idle talk. People in virtual communities do just about everything people do in real life, but we leave our bodies behind. You can't kiss anybody and nobody can punch you in the nose, but a lot can happen within those boundaries. To the millions who have been drawn into it, the richness and vitality of computer-linked cultures is attractive, even addictive.

There is no such thing as a single, monolithic, online subculture; it's more like an ecosystem of subcultures, some frivolous, others serious. The cutting edge of scientific discourse is migrating to virtual communities, where you can read the electronic pre-printed reports of molecular biologists and cognitive scientists. At the same time, activists and educational reformers are using the same medium as a political tool. You can use virtual communities to find a date, sell a lawnmower, publish a novel, conduct a meeting.

Some people use virtual communities as a form of psychotherapy. Others, such as the most addicted players of Minitel in France or Multi-User Dungeons (MUDs) on the international networks, spend eighty hours a week or more pretending they are someone else, living a life that does not exist outside a computer. Because MUDs not only are susceptible to pathologically obsessive use by some people but also create a strain on computer and communication resources, MUDding has been banned at universities such as Amherst and on the entire continent of Australia.

Scientists, students, librarians, artists, organizers, and escapists aren't the only people who have taken to the new medium. The US senator who campaigned for years for the construction of a National Research and

Education Network that could host the virtual communities of the future is now vice president of the United States. As of June 1993, the White House and Congress have e-mail addresses.

Most people who get their news from conventional media have been unaware of the wildly varied assortment of new cultures that have evolved in the world's computer networks over the past ten years. Most people who have not yet used these new media remain unaware of how profoundly the social, political, and scientific experiments under way today via computer networks could change all our lives in the near future.

I have written this chapter to help inform a wider population about the potential importance of cyberspace to political liberties and the ways virtual communities are likely to change our experience of the real world, as individuals and communities. Although I am enthusiastic about the liberating potentials of computer-mediated communications, I try to keep my eyes open for the pitfalls of mixing technology and human relationships. I hope my reports from the outposts and headquarters of this new kind of social habitation, and the stories of the people I've met in cyberspace, will bring to life the cultural, political, and ethical implications of virtual communities both for my fellow explorers of cyberspace and for those who never heard of it before.

The technology that makes virtual communities possible has the potential to bring enormous leverage to ordinary citizens at relatively little cost – intellectual leverage, social leverage, commercial leverage, and most important, political leverage. But the technology will not in itself fulfil that potential; this latent technical power must be used intelligently and deliberately by an informed population. Most people must learn about that leverage and learn to use it, while we still have the freedom to do so, if it is to live up to its potential. The odds are always good that big power and big money will find a way to control access to virtual communities; big power and big money always found ways to control new communications media when they emerged in the past. The Net is still out of control in fundamental ways, but it might not stay that way for long. What we know and do now is important because it is still possible for people around the world to make sure this new sphere of vital human discourse remains open to citizens of the planet before the political and economic big boys seize it, censor it, meter it, and sell it back to us.

The potential social leverage comes from the power that ordinary citizens gain when they know how to connect two previously independent, mature, highly decentralized technologies. It took billions of dollars and decades to develop cheap personal computers. It took billions of dollars and more than a century to wire up the worldwide telecommunication network. With the right knowledge, and not too much of it, a ten-year-old kid today can plug these two vast, powerful, expensively developed technologies together for a few hundred dollars and instantly obtain a bully pulpit, the Library of Congress, and a world full of potential coconspirators.

Computers and the switched telecommunication networks that also carry our telephone calls constitute the technical foundation of *computer-mediated communications* (CMC). The technicalities of CMC, how bits of computer data move over wires and are reassembled as computer files at their destinations, are invisible and irrelevant to most people who use it, except when the technicalities restrict their access to CMC services. The important thing to keep in mind is that the worldwide, interconnected telecommunication network that we use to make telephone calls in Manhattan and Madagascar can also be used to connect computers together at a distance, and you don't have to be an engineer to do it.

The Net is an informal term for the loosely interconnected computer networks that use CMC technology to link people around the world into public discussions.

Virtual communities are social aggregations that emerge from the Net when enough people carry on those public discussions long enough, with sufficient human feeling, to form webs of personal relationships in cyberspace.

Cyberspace, originally a term from William Gibson's science-fiction novel *Neuromancer*, is the name some people use for the conceptual space where words, human relationships, data, wealth, and power are manifested by people using CMC technology.

Although spatial imagery and a sense of place help convey the experience of dwelling in a virtual community, biological imagery is often more appropriate to describe the way cyberculture changes. In terms of the way the whole system is propagating and evolving, think of cyberspace as a social petri dish, the Net as the agar medium, and virtual communities, in all their diversity, as the colonies of microorganisms that grow in petri dishes. Each of the small colonies of microorganisms – the communities on the Net – is a social experiment that nobody planned but that is happening nevertheless.

We now know something about the ways previous generations of communications technologies changed the way people lived. We need to understand why and how so many social experiments are coevolving today with the prototypes of the newest communications technologies. My direct observations of online behavior around the world over the past ten years have led me to conclude that whenever CMC technology becomes available to people anywhere, they inevitably build virtual communities with it, just as microorganisms inevitably create colonies.

I suspect that one of the explanations for this phenomenon is the hunger for community that grows in the breasts of people around the world as more and more informal public spaces disappear from our real lives. I also suspect that these new media attract colonies of enthusiasts because CMC enables people to do things with each other in new ways, and to do altogether new kinds of things – just as telegraphs, telephones, and televisions did.

Because of its potential influence on so many people's beliefs and perceptions, the future of the Net is connected to the future of community, democracy, education, science, and intellectual life – some of the human institutions people hold most dear, whether or not they know or care about the future of computer technology. The future of the Net has become too important to leave to specialists and special interests. As it influences the lives of a growing number of people, more and more citizens must contribute to the dialogue about the way public funds are applied to the development of the Net, and we must join our voices to the debate about the way it should be administered. We need a clear citizens' vision of the way the Net ought to grow, a firm idea of the kind of media environment we would like to see in the future. If we do not develop such a vision for ourselves, the future will be shaped for us by large commercial and political powerholders.

The Net is so widespread and anarchic today because of the way its main sources converged in the 1980s, after years of independent, apparently unrelated development, using different technologies and involving different populations of participants. The technical and social convergences were fated, but not widely foreseen, by the late 1970s.

The wide-area CMC networks that span continents and join together thousands of smaller networks are a spinoff of American military research. The first computer network, ARPANET, was created in the 1970s so that Department of Defense-sponsored researchers could operate different computers at a distance; computer data, not person-to-person messages, were the intended content of the network, which handily happened to serve just as easily as a conduit for words. The fundamental technical idea on which ARPANET was based came from RAND, the think tank in Santa Monica that did a lot of work with top-secret thermonuclear war scenarios; ARPANET grew out of an older RAND scheme for a communication, command, and control network that could survive nuclear attack by having no central control.

Computer conferencing emerged, also somewhat unexpectedly, as a tool for using the communication capacities of the networks to build social relationships across barriers of space and time. A continuing theme throughout the history of CMC is the way people adapt technologies designed for one purpose to suit their own, very different, communication needs. And the most profound technological changes have come from the fringes and subcultures, not the orthodoxy of the computer industry or academic computer science. The programmers who created the first computer network installed electronic mail features; electronic mail wasn't the reason ARPANET was designed, but it was an easy thing to include once ARPANET existed. Then, in a similar, *ad hoc*, do-it-yourself manner, computer conferencing grew out of the needs of US policymakers to develop a communications medium for dispersed decision making. Although the first computer conferencing experiments were precipitated by the US government's wage-price freeze of the 1970s and the consequent need to disseminate up-to-date information from a large number of geographically dispersed local headquarters, computer conferencing was quickly adapted to commercial, scientific, and social discourse.

The hobbyists who interconnect personal computers via telephone lines to make computer bulletin-board systems, known as BBSs, have home-grown their part of the Net, a true grassroots use of technology. Hundreds of thousands of people around the world piggyback legally on the telecom network via personal computers and ordinary telephone lines. The most important technical attribute of networked BBSs is that it is an extremely hard network to kill – just as the RAND planners had hoped. Information can take so many alternative routes when one of the nodes of the network is removed that the Net is almost immortally flexible. It is this flexibility that CMC telecom pioneer John Gilmore referred to when he said 'The Net interprets censorship as damage and routes around it.' This way of passing information and communication around a network as a distributed resource with no central control manifested in the rapid growth of the anarchic global conversation known as Usenet. This invention of distributed conversation that flows around obstacles – a grassroots adaptation of a technology originally designed as a doomsday weapon – might turn out to be as important in the long run as the hardware and software inventions that made it possible.

The big hardwired networks spend a lot more money to create high-speed information conduits between high-capacity computing nodes. Internet, today's US government-sponsored successor to ARPANET, is growing in every dimension at an astonishing pace. These 'data super-highways' use special telecommunication lines and other equipment to send very large amounts of information throughout the network at very high speeds. ARPANET started around twenty years ago with roughly one thousand users, and now Internet is approaching ten million users.

The portable computer on my desk is hundreds of times less expensive and thousands of times more powerful than ARPANET's first nodes. The fiber-optic backbone of the current Internet communicates information millions of times faster than the first ARPANET. Everything about Internet has grown like a bacterial colony – the raw technical capacity to send information, the different ways people use it, and the number of users. The Internet population has grown by 15 percent a month for the past several years. John Quarterman (1990) whose book *The Matrix* is a thick guide to the world's computer networks, estimates that there are nine hundred different networks worldwide today, not counting the more than ten thousand networks already linked by the Internet 'network of networks'.

Real grassroots, the kind that grow in the ground, are a self-similar branching structure, a network of networks. Each grass seed grows a branching set of roots, and then many more smaller roots grow off those; the roots of each grass plant interconnect physically with the roots of adjacent plants, as any gardener who has tried to uproot a lawn has learned. There is a grassroots element to the Net that was not, until very recently, involved with all the high-tech, top-secret doings that led to ARPANET – the BBSers.

The population of the grassroots part of the Net, the citizen-operated BBSs, has been growing explosively as a self-financed movement of enthusiasts, without the benefit of Department of Defense funding. A BBS is the simplest, cheapest infrastructure for CMC: you run special software, often available inexpensively, on a personal computer, and use a device known as a *modem* to plug the computer into your regular telephone line. The modem converts computer-readable information into audible beeps and boops that can travel over the same telephone wires that carry your voice; another modem at the other end decodes the beeps and boops into computer-readable bits and bytes. The BBS turns the bits and bytes into human-readable text. Other people use their computers to call your BBS, leave and retrieve messages stored in your personal computer, and you have a virtual community growing in your bedroom. As the system operator (sysop) of the BBS, you contribute part of your computer's memory and make sure your computer is plugged into the telephone; the participants pay for their own communication costs.

Boardwatch magazine estimates that sixty thousand BBSs operated in the United States alone in 1993, fourteen years after the first BBSs opened in Chicago and California. Each BBS supports a population of a dozen to several hundred, or even thousands, of individual participants. There are religious BBSs of every denomination, sex BBSs of every proclivity, political BBSs from all parts of the spectrum, outlaw BBSs, law enforcement BBSs, BBSs for the disabled, for educators, for kids, for cults, for nonprofit organizations – a list of the different flavors of special-interest BBSs is dozens of pages long. The BBS culture has spread from the United States to Japan, Europe, Central and South America.

Each BBS started out as a small island community of a few people who dialed into a number in their area code; by their nature, like a small-wattage radio station, BBSs are localized. But that's changing, too. Just as several different technologies converged over the past ten years to create CMC – a new medium with properties of its own – several different online social structures are in the process of converging and creating a kind of international culture with properties of its own.

Technical bridges are connecting the grassroots part of the network with the military–industrial parts of the network. The programmers who built the Net in the first place, the scholars who have been using it to exchange knowledge, the scientists who have been using it for research, are being joined by all those hobbyists with their bedroom and garage BBSs. Special 'gateway' computers can link entire networks by automatically translating communications from the mechanical languages used in one network to the languages (known as protocols) used in another network. In recent years, the heretofore separate groups of Internet and BBS pioneers worked together to gateway the more than ten thousand computers of the worldwide FidoNet, the first network of small, private BBSs, with Internet's millions of people and tens of thousands of more powerful computers.

The Net and computer conferencing systems are converging too, as medium-size computer conferencing communities like the WELL join Internet. When the WELL upgraded to a high-speed connection to Internet, it became not just a community-in-progress but a gateway to a wider realm, the worldwide Net-at-large. Suddenly, the isolated archipelagos of a few hundred or a few thousand people are becoming part of an integrated entity. The small virtual communities still exist, like yeast in a rapidly rising loaf, but increasingly they are part of an overarching culture, similar to the way the United States became an overarching culture after the telegraph and telephone linked the states.

The WELL is a small town, but now there is a doorway in that town that opens onto the blooming, buzzing confusion of the Net, an entity with properties altogether different from the virtual villages of a few years ago. I have good friends now all over the world who I never would have met without the mediation of the Net. A large circle of Net acquaintances can make an enormous difference in your experience when you travel to a foreign culture. Wherever I've traveled physically in recent years, I've found ready-made communities that I met online months before I traveled; our mutual enthusiasm for virtual communities served as a bridge, time and again, to people whose language and customs differ significantly from those I know well in California.

I routinely meet people and get to know them months or years before I see them – one of the ways my world today is a different world, with different friends and different concerns, from the world I experienced in premodern days. The places I visit in my mind, and the people I communicate with from one moment to the next, are entirely different from the content of my thoughts or the state of my circle of friends before I started dabbling in virtual communities. One minute I'm involved in the minutiae of local matters such as planning next week's bridge game, and the next minute I'm part of a debate raging in seven countries. Not only do I inhabit my virtual communities; to the degree that I carry around their conversations in my head and begin to mix it up with them in real life, my virtual communities also inhabit my life. I've been colonized; my sense of family at the most fundamental level has been virtualized.

I've seen variations of the same virtualization of community that happened to me hitting other virtual groups of a few hundred or a few thousand, in Paris and London and Tokyo. Entire cities are coming online. Santa Monica, California, and Cleveland, Ohio, were among the first of a growing number of American cities that have initiated municipal CMC systems. Santa Monica's system has an active conference to discuss the problems of the city's homeless that involves heavy input from homeless Santa Monica citizens who use public terminals. This system has an electronic link with COARA, a similar regional system in a remote province of Japan. Biwa-Net, in the Kyoto area, is gatewayed to a sister city in Pennsylvania. The Net is only beginning to wake up to itself.

Watching a particular virtual community change over a period of time has something of the intellectual thrill of do-it-yourself anthropology, and some of the garden-variety voyeurism of eavesdropping on an endless amateur soap opera where there is no boundary separating the audience from the cast. For the price of a telephone call, you can take part in any kind of vicarious melodrama you can dream of; as a form of escape entertainment, the Minitel addicts in Paris and the MUDders of Internet and the obsessive IRC participants on college campuses everywhere have proved that CMC has a future as a serious marketplace for meterable interactive fantasies.

CMC might become the next great escape medium, in the tradition of radio serials, Saturday matinees, soap operas – which means that the new medium will be in some way a conduit for and reflector of our cultural codes, our social subconscious, our images of who 'we' might be, just as previous media have been. There are other serious reasons that ordinary nontechnical citizens need to know something about this new medium and its social impact. Something big is afoot, and the final shape has not been determined.

In the United States, the Clinton administration is taking measures to amplify the Net's technical capabilities and availability manyfold via the National Research and Education Network, France, with the world's largest national information utility, Minitel, and Japan, with its stake in future telecommunications industries, have their own visions of the future. Albert Gore's 1991 bill, the High Performance Computing Act, signed into law by President Bush, outlined Gore's vision for 'highways of the mind' to be stimulated by federal research-and-development expenditures as a national intellectual resource and carried to the citizens by private enterprise. The Clinton–Gore administration has used the example of the ARPA (Advanced Research Projects Agency) venture of the 1960s and 1970s that produced the Net and the foundations of personal computing as an example of the way they see government and the private sector interacting in regard to future communications technologies.

In the private sector, telecommunication companies, television networks, computer companies, cable companies, and newspapers in the United States, Europe, and Japan are jockeying for position in the nascent 'home interactive information services industry'. Corporations are investing hundreds of millions of dollars in the infrastructure for new media they hope will make them billions of dollars. Every flavor of technological futurist, from Alvin Toffler and John Naisbitt to Peter Drucker and George Gilder, base utopian hopes on 'the information age' as a techno-fix for social problems. Yet little is known about the impact these newest media might have on our daily lives, our minds, our families, even the future of democracy.

CMC has the potential to change our lives on three different, but strongly interinfluential, levels. First, as individual human beings, we have perceptions, thoughts, and personalities (already shaped by other communications technologies) that are affected by the ways we use the medium and the ways it uses us. At this fundamental level, CMC appeals to us as mortal organisms with certain intellectual, physical, and emotional needs. Young people around the world have different communication proclivities from their pre-McLuhanized elders. MTV, for example, caters to an aesthetic sensibility that is closely tuned to the vocabulary of television's fast cuts, visually arresting images, and special effects. Now, some of those people around the world who were born in the television era and grew up in the cellular telephone era are beginning to migrate to CMC spaces that better fit their new ways of experiencing the world. There is a vocabulary to CMC, too, now emerging from millions and millions of individual online interactions. That vocabulary reflects something about the ways human personalities are changing in the age of media saturation.

The second level of possible CMC-triggered change is the level of person-to-person interaction where relationships, friendships, and communities happen. CMC technology offers a new capability of 'many to many' communication, but the way such a capability will or will not be used in the future might depend on the way we, the first people who are using it, succeed or fail in applying it to our lives. Those of us who are brought into contact with each other by means of CMC technology find ourselves challenged by this many-to-many capability – challenged to consider whether it is possible for us to build some kind of community together.

The question of community is central to realms beyond the abstract networks of CMC technology. Some commentators, such as Bellah et al. (1985), have focused on the need for rebuilding community in the face of America's loss of a sense of a social commons.

Social psychologists, sociologists, and historians have developed useful tools for asking questions about human group interaction. Different communities of interpretation, from anthropology to economics, have different criteria for studying whether a group of people is a community. In trying to apply traditional analysis of community behavior to the kinds of interactions emerging from the Net, I have adopted a schema proposed by Marc Smith, a graduate student in sociology at the University of California at Los Angeles, who has been doing his fieldwork in the WELL and the Net. Smith focuses on the concept of 'collective goods'. Every cooperative group of people exists in the face of a competitive world because that group of people recognizes there is something valuable that they can gain only by banding together. Looking for a group's collective goods is a way of looking for the elements that bind isolated individuals into a community.

The three kinds of collective goods that Smith proposes as the social glue that binds the WELL into something resembling a community are social network capital, knowledge capital, and communion. Social network capital is what happened when I found a ready-made community in Tokyo, even though I had never been there in the flesh. Knowledge capital is what I found in the WELL when I asked questions of the community as an online brains trust representing a highly varied accumulation of expertise. And communion is what we found in the Parenting Conference, when Phil's and Jay's children were sick, and the rest of us used our words to support them.

The third level of possible change in our lives, the political, derives from the middle, social level, for politics is always a combination of communications and physical power, and the role of communications media among the citizenry is particularly important in the politics of democratic societies. The idea of modern representative democracy as it was first conceived by Enlightenment philosophers included a recognition of a living web of citizen-to-citizen communications known as civil society or the public sphere. Although elections are the most visible fundamental characteristics of democratic societies, those elections are assumed to be supported by discussions among citizens at all levels of society about issues of importance to the nation.

If a government is to rule according to the consent of the governed, the effectiveness of that government is heavily influenced by how much the governed know about the issues that affect them. The mass-media-dominated public sphere today is where the governed now get knowledge; the problem is that commercial mass media, led by broadcast television, have polluted with barrages of flashy, phony, often violent imagery a public sphere that once included a large component of reading, writing, and rational discourse. For the early centuries of American history, until the telegraph made it possible to create what we know as news and sell the readers of newspapers to advertisers, the public sphere did rely on an astonishingly literate population. Neil Postman, in his book about the way television has changed the nature of public discourse, *Amusing Ourselves to Death* (1985), notes that Thomas Paine's *Common Sense* sold three hundred thousand copies in five months in 1775. Contemporary observers have documented and analyzed the way mass media ('one-to-many' media) have 'commoditized' the public sphere, substituting slick public relations for genuine debate and packaging both issues and candidates like other consumer products.

The political significance of CMC lies in its capacity to challenge the existing political hierarchy's monopoly on powerful communications media, and perhaps thus revitalize citizen-based democracy. The way image-rich, sound-bite-based commercial media have co-opted political discourse among citizens is part of a political problem that communications technologies have posed for democracy for decades. The way the number of owners of telecommunication channels is narrowing to a tiny elite, while the reach and power of the media they own expand, is a converging threat to citizens. Which scenario seems more conducive to democracy, which to totalitarian rule: a world in which a few people control communications technology that can be used to manipulate the beliefs of billions, or a world in which every citizen can broadcast to every other citizen?

Ben Bagdikian's often-quoted prediction from *The Media Monopoly* (1983) is that by the turn of the century 'five to ten corporate giants will control most of the world's important newspapers, magazines, books, broadcast stations, movies, recordings and videocassettes.' These new media lords possess immense power to determine which information most people receive about the world, and I suspect they are not likely to encourage their privately owned and controlled networks to be the willing conduits for all the kinds of information that unfettered citizens and nongovernmental organizations tend to disseminate. The activist solution to this dilemma has been to use CMC to create alternative planetary information networks. The distributed nature of the telecommunications network, coupled with the availability of affordable computers, makes it possible to piggyback alternate networks on the mainstream infrastructure.

We temporarily have access to a tool that could bring conviviality and understanding into our lives and might help revitalize the public sphere. The same tool, improperly controlled and wielded, could become an instrument of tyranny. The vision of a citizen-designed, citizen-controlled worldwide communications network is a version of technological utopianism that could be called the vision of 'the electronic *agora*'. In the original democracy, Athens, the *agora* was the marketplace, and more – it was where citizens met to talk, gossip, argue, size each other up, find the weak spots in political ideas by debating about them. But another kind of vision could apply to the use of the Net in the wrong ways, a shadow vision of a less utopian kind of place – the Panopticon.

Panopticon was the name for an ultimately effective prison, seriously proposed in eighteenth-century Britain by Jeremy Bentham. A combination of architecture and optics makes it possible in Bentham's scheme for a single guard to see every prisoner, and for no prisoner to see anything else; the effect is that all prisoners act as if they were under surveillance at all times. Contemporary social critic Michel Foucault, in *Discipline and Punish* (1977), claimed that the machinery of the worldwide communications network constitutes a kind of camouflaged Panopticon; citizens of the world brought into their homes, along with each other, the prying ears of the state. The cables that bring information into our homes today are technically capable of bringing information out of our homes, instantly transmitted to interested others. Tomorrow's version of Panoptic machinery could make very effective use of the same communications infrastructure that enables one-room schoolhouses in Montana to communicate with MIT professors, and enable citizens to disseminate news and organize resistance to totalitarian rule. With so much of our intimate data and more and more of our private behavior moving into cyberspace, the potential for totalitarian abuse of that information web is significant and the cautions of the critics are worth a careful hearing.

The wise revolutionary keeps an eye on the dark side of the changes he or she would initiate. Enthusiasts who believe in the humanitarian potential of virtual communities, especially those of us who speak of electronic democracy as a potential application of the medium, are well advised to consider the shadow potential of the same media. We should not forget that intellectuals and journalists of the 1950s hailed the advent of the greatest educational medium in history – television.

Because of its potential to change us as humans, as communities, as democracies, we need to try to understand the nature of CMC, cyberspace, and virtual communities in every important context – politically, economically, socially, cognitively. Each different perspective reveals something that the other perspectives do not reveal. Each different discipline fails to see something that another discipline sees very well. We need to think together here, across boundaries of academic discipline, industrial affiliation, nation, if we hope to understand and thus perhaps regain control of the way human communities are being transformed by communications technologies. [. . .]

References

Bagdikian, Ben (1983) *The Media Monopoly*. Boston: Beacon Press.
Bellah, Robert N., Madsen, R., Sullivan, W., Swindler, A. and Tipton, S. (1985) *Habits of the Heart: Individualism and Commitment in American Life*. Berkeley, CA: University of California Press.

Foucault, Michel (1977) *Discipline and Punish: the Birth of the Prison*, Trans. Alan Sheridan. New York: Pantheon.

Postman, Neal (1985) *Amusing Ourselves to Death: Public Discourse in the Age of Show Business*. New York: Viking Penguin.

Quarterman, John (1990) *The Matrix: Computer Networks and Conferencing Systems Worldwide*. Bedford, Mass.: Digital Press.

Identity in the age of the internet **Sherry Turkle**

There was a child went forth every day,
And the first object he look'd upon, that object he became.

Walt Whitman

We come to see ourselves differently as we catch sight of our images in the mirror of the machine. A decade ago, when I first called the computer a second self, these identity-transforming relationships were almost always one-on-one, a person alone with a machine. This is no longer the case. A rapidly expanding system of networks, collectively known as the Internet, links millions of people in new spaces that are changing the way we think, the nature of our sexuality, the form of our communities, our very identities.

At one level, the computer is a tool. It helps us write, keep track of our accounts, and communicate with others. Beyond this, the computer offers us both new models of mind and a new medium on which to project our ideas and fantasies. Most recently, the computer has become even more than tool and mirror. We are able to step through the looking glass. We are learning to live in virtual worlds. We may find ourselves alone as we navigate personal oceans, unravel virtual mysteries, and engineer virtual skyscrapers. But increasingly, when we step through the looking glass, other people are there as well.

This chapter appeared as the 'Introduction' to *Life on the Screen: Identity in the Age of the Internet* (London, Weidenfeld and Nicolson, 1996), pp. 9–26.

The use of the term 'cyberspace' to describe virtual worlds grew out of science fiction,[1] but for many of us, cyberspace is now part of the routines of everyday life. When we read our electronic mail or send postings to an electronic bulletin board or make an airline reservation over a computer network, we are in cyberspace. In cyberspace, we can talk, exchange ideas, and assume personae of our own creation. We have the opportunity to build new kinds of communities, virtual communities, in which we participate with people from all over the world, people with whom we converse daily, people with whom we may have fairly intimate relationships but whom we may never physically meet.

[My research] describes how a nascent culture of simulation is affecting our ideas about mind, body, self, and machine. We shall encounter virtual sex and cyberspace marriage, computer psychotherapists, robot insects, and researchers who are trying to build artificial two-year-olds. Biological children, too, are in the story as their play with computer toys leads them to speculate about whether computers are smart and what it is to be alive. Indeed, in much of this, it is our children who are leading the way, and adults who are anxiously trailing behind.

In the story of constructing identity in the culture of simulation, experiences on the Internet figure prominently, but these experiences can only be understood as part of a larger cultural context. That context is the story of the eroding boundaries between the real and the virtual, the animate and the inanimate, the unitary and the multiple self, which is occurring both in advanced scientific fields of research and in the patterns of everyday life. From scientists trying to create artificial life to children 'morphing' through a series of virtual personae, we shall see evidence of fundamental shifts in the way we create and experience human identity. But it is on the Internet that our confrontations with technology as it collides with our sense of human identity are fresh, even raw. In the real-time communities of cyberspace, we are dwellers on the threshold between the real and virtual, unsure of our footing, inventing ourselves as we go along.

In an interactive, text-based computer game designed to represent a world inspired by the television series *Star Trek: the Next Generation*, thousands of players spend up to eighty hours a week participating in intergalactic exploration and wars. Through typed descriptions and typed commands, they create characters who have casual and romantic sexual encounters, hold jobs and collect paychecks, attend rituals and celebrations, fall in love and get married. To the participants, such goings-on can be gripping. 'This is more real than my real life', says a character who turns out to be a man playing a woman who is pretending to be a man. In this game the self is constructed and the rules of social interaction are built, not received.[2]

In another text-based game, each of nearly ten thousand players creates a character or several characters, specifying their genders and other physical and psychological attributes. The characters need not be human and there are more than two genders. Players are invited to help build the computer world itself. Using a relatively simply programming language, they can create a room in the game space where they are able to set the stage and define the rules. They can fill the room with objects and specify how they work; they can, for instance, create a virtual dog that barks if one types the command 'bark Rover'. An eleven-year-old player built a room she calls the condo. It is beautifully furnished. She has created magical jewelry and makeup for her dressing table. When she visits the condo, she invites her cyberfriends to join her there, she chats, orders a virtual pizza, and flirts.

Living in the MUD

The *Star Trek* game, TrekMUSE, and the other, LambdaMOO, are both computer programs that can be accessed through the Internet. The Internet was once available only to military personnel and technical researchers. It is now available to anyone who can buy or borrow an account on a commercial online service. TrekMUSE and LambdaMOO are known as MUDs, Multi-User Domains or, with greater historical accuracy, Multi-User Dungeons, because of their genealogy from Dungeons and Dragons, the fantasy role-playing game that swept high schools and colleges in the late 1970s and early 1980s.

The multiuser computer games are based on different kinds of software (this is what the MUSE or MOO or MUSH part of their names stands for). For simplicity, here I use the term MUD to refer to all of them.

MUDs put you in virtual spaces in which you are able to navigate, converse, and build. You join a MUD through a command that links your computer to the computer on which the MUD program resides. Making the connection is not difficult; it requires no particular technical sophistication. The basic commands may seem awkward at first but soon become familiar. For example, if I am playing a character named ST on LambdaMOO, any words I type after the command 'say' will appear on all players' screens as 'ST says'. Any actions I type after the command 'emote' will appear after my name just as I type them, as in 'ST waves hi' or 'ST laughs uncontrollably'. I can 'whisper' to a designated character and only that character will be able to see my words. As of this writing there are over five hundred MUDs in which hundreds of thousands of people participate.[3] In some MUDs, players are represented by graphical icons; most MUDs are purely text-based. Most players are middle class. A large majority are male. Some players are over thirty, but most are in their early twenties and late teens. However, it is no longer unusual to find MUDs where eight- and nine-year-olds 'play' such grade-school icons as Barbie or the Mighty Morphin Power Rangers.

MUDs are a new kind of virtual parlor game and a new form of community. In addition, text-based MUDs are a new form of collaboratively written literature. MUD players are MUD authors, the creators as well as consumers of media content. In this, participating in a MUD has much in common with script writing, performance art, street theater, improvisational theater – or even *commedia dell'arte*. But MUDs are something else as well.

As players participate, they become authors not only of text but of themselves, constructing new selves through social interaction. One player says, 'You are the character and you are not the character, both at the same time.' Another says, 'You are who you pretend to be.' MUDs provide worlds for anonymous social interaction in which one can play a role as close to or as far away from one's 'real self' as one chooses. Since one participates in MUDs by sending text to a computer that houses the MUD's program and database, MUD selves are constituted in interaction with the machine. Take it away and the MUD selves cease to exist: 'Part of me, a very important part of me, only exists inside PernMUD', says one player. Several players joke that they are like 'the electrodes in the computer', trying to express the degree to which they feel part of its space.

On MUDs, one's body is represented by one's own textual description, so the obese can be slender, the beautiful plain, the 'nerdy' sophisticated. A *New Yorker* cartoon captures the potential for MUDs as laboratories for experimenting with one's identity. In it, one dog, paw on a computer keyboard, explains to another, 'On the Internet, nobody knows you're a dog.' The anonymity of MUDs – one is known on the MUD only by the name of one's character or characters – gives people the chance to express multiple and often unexplored aspects of the self, to play with their identity and to try out new ones. MUDs make possible the creation of an identity so fluid and multiple that it strains the limits of the notion. Identity, after all, refers to the sameness between two qualities, in this case between a person and his or her persona. But in MUDs, one can be many.

Dedicated MUD players are often people who work all day with computers at their regular jobs – as architects, programmers, secretaries, students, and stockbrokers. From time to time when playing on MUDs, they can put their characters 'to sleep' and pursue 'real life' (MUD players call this RL) activities on the computer – all the while remaining connected, logged on to the game's virtual world. Some leave special programs running that send them signals when a particular character logs on or when they are 'paged' by a MUD acquaintance. Some leave behind small artificial intelligence programs called bots (derived from the word 'robot') running in the MUD that may serve as their alter egos, able to make small talk or answer simple questions. In the course of a day, players move in and out of the active game space. As they do, some experience their lives as a 'cycling through' between the real world (RL) and a series of virtual worlds. I say a series because people are frequently connected to several MUDs at a time. In an MIT computer cluster at 2 a.m., an eighteen-year-old freshman sits at a networked machine and points to the four boxed-off areas on his vibrantly colored computer screen. 'On this MUD I'm relaxing, shooting the breeze. On this other MUD I'm in a flame war.[4] On this last one I'm into heavy sexual things. I'm travelling between the MUDs and a physics homework assignment due at 10 tomorrow morning.'

This kind of cycling through MUDs and RL is made possible by the existence of those boxed-off areas on the screen, commonly called windows. Windows provide a way for a computer to place you in several contexts at the same time. As a user, you are attentive to only one of the windows on your screen at any given moment, but in a sense you are a presence in all of them at all times. For example, you might be using your computer to help you write a paper about bacteriology. In that case, you would be present to a word-processing program you are using to take notes, to communications software with which you are collecting reference materials from a distant computer, and to a simulation program, which is charting the growth of virtual bacterial colonies. Each of these activities takes place in a window; your identity on the computer is the sum of your distributed presence.

Doug is a midwestern college junior. He plays four characters distributed across three different MUDs. One is a seductive woman. One is a macho, cowboy type whose self-description stresses that he is a 'Marlboros rolled in the T-shirt sleeve kind of guy.' The third is a rabbit of unspecified gender who wanders its MUD introducing people to each other, a character he calls Carrot. Doug says, 'Carrot is so low key that people let it be around while they are having private conversations. So I think of Carrot as my passive, voyeuristic character.' Doug's fourth character is one that he plays only on a MUD in which all the characters are furry animals. 'I'd rather not even talk about that character because my anonymity there is very important to me', Doug says. 'Let's just say that on FurryMUDs I feel like a sexual tourist.'[5] Doug talks about playing his characters in windows and says that using windows has made it possible for him to 'turn pieces of my mind on and off'.

> I split my mind. I'm getting better at it. I can see myself as being two or three or more. And I just turn on one part of my mind and then another when I go from window to window. I'm in some kind of argument in one window and trying to come on to a girl in a MUD in another, and another window might be running a spreadsheet program or some other technical thing for school . . . And then I'll get a real-time message [that flashes on the screen as soon as it is sent from another system user], and I guess that's RL. It's just one more window.

'RL is just one more window', he repeats, 'and it's not usually my best one.'

The development of windows for computer interfaces was a technical innovation motivated by the desire to get people working more efficiently by cycling through different applications. But in the daily practice of many computer users, windows have become a powerful metaphor for thinking about the self as a multiple, distributed system. The self is no longer simply playing different roles in different settings at different times, something that a person experiences when, for example, she wakes up as a lover, makes breakfast as a mother, and drives to work as a lawyer. The life practice of windows is that of a decentered self that exists in many worlds and plays many roles at the same time. In traditional theater and in role-playing games that take place in physical space, one steps in and out of character; MUDs, in contrast, offer parallel identities, parallel lives. The experience of this parallelism encourages treating on-screen and off-screen lives with a surprising degree of equality. Experiences on the Internet extend the metaphor of windows – now RL itself, as Doug said, can be 'just one more window'.

MUDs are dramatic examples of how computer-mediated communication can serve as a place for the construction and reconstruction of identity. There are many others. On the Internet, Internet Relay Chat (commonly known as IRC) is another widely used conversational forum in which any user can open a channel and attract guests to it, all of whom speak to each other as if in the same room. Commercial services such as

America Online and CompuServe provide online chat rooms that have much of the appeal of MUDs – a combination of real time interaction with other people, anonymity (or, in some cases, the illusion of anonymity), and the ability to assume a role as close to or as far from one's 'real self' as one chooses.

As more people spend more time in these virtual spaces, some go so far as to challenge the idea of giving any priority to RL at all. 'After all', says one dedicated MUD player and IRC user, 'why grant such superior status to the self that has the body when the selves that don't have bodies are able to have different kinds of experiences?' When people can play at having different genders and different lives, it isn't surprising that for some this play has become as real as what we conventionally think of as their lives, although for them this is no longer a valid distinction.

French lessons

In the late 1960s and early 1970s, I lived in a culture that taught that the self is constituted by and through language, that sexual congress is the exchange of signifiers, and that each of us is a multiplicity of parts, fragments, and desiring connections. This was the hothouse of Paris intellectual culture whose gurus included Jacques Lacan, Michel Foucault, Gilles Deleuze, and Félix Guattari.[6] But despite such ideal conditions for learning, my 'French lessons' remained merely abstract exercises. These theorists of poststructuralism and what would come to be called postmodernism spoke words that addressed the relationship between mind and body but, from my point of view, had little or nothing to do with my own.

In my lack of connection with these ideas, I was not alone. To take one example, for many people it is hard to accept any challenge to the idea of an autonomous ego. While in recent years, many psychologists, social theorists, psychoanalysts, and philosophers have argued that the self should be thought of as essentially decentered, the normal requirements of everyday life exert strong pressure on people to take responsibility for their actions and to see themselves as intentional and unitary actors. This disjuncture between theory (the unitary self is an illusion) and lived experience (the unitary self is the most basic reality) is one of the main reasons why multiple and decentered theories have been slow to catch on – or when they do, why we tend to settle back quickly into older, centralized ways of looking at things.

Today I use the personal computer and modem on my desk to access MUDs. Anonymously, I travel their rooms and public spaces (a bar, a lounge, a hot tub). I create several characters, some not of my biological gender, who are able to have social and sexual encounters with other characters. On different MUDs, I have different routines, different friends, different names. One day I learned of a virtual rape. One MUD player had used his skill with the system to seize control of another player's character. In this way the aggressor was able to direct the seized character to submit to a violent sexual encounter. He did all this against the will and over the distraught objections of the player usually 'behind' this character, the player to whom this character 'belonged'. Although some made light of the offender's actions by saying that the episode was just words, in text-based virtual realities such as MUDs, words *are* deeds.

Thus, more than twenty years after meeting the ideas of Lacan, Foucault, Deleuze, and Guattari, I am meeting them again in my new life on the screen. But this time, the Gallic abstractions are more concrete. In my computer-mediated worlds, the self is multiple, fluid, and constituted in interaction with machine connections; it is made and transformed by language; sexual congress is an exchange of signifiers; and understanding follows from navigation and tinkering rather than analysis. And in the machine-generated world of MUDs, I meet characters who put me in a new relationship with my own identity.

One day on a MUD, I came across a reference to a character named Dr Sherry, a cyberpsychologist with an office in the rambling house that constituted this MUD's virtual geography. There, I was informed, Dr Sherry was administering questionnaires and conducting interviews about the psychology of MUDs. I suspected that the name Dr Sherry referred to my long career as a student of the psychological impact of technology. But I didn't create this character. I was not playing her on the MUD. Dr Sherry was (she is no longer on the MUD) a derivative of me, but she was not mine. The character I played on this MUD had another name – and did not give out questionnaires or conduct interviews. My formal studies were conducted offline in a traditional clinical setting where I spoke face-to-face with people who participate in virtual communities. Dr Sherry may have been a character someone else created as an efficient way of communicating an interest in questions about technology and the self, but I was experiencing her as a little piece of my history spinning out of control. I tried to quiet my mind. I told myself that surely one's books, one's intellectual identity, one's public persona, are pieces of oneself that others may use as they please. I tried to convince myself that this virtual appropriation was a form of flattery. But my disquiet continued. Dr Sherry, after all, was not an inanimate book but a person, or at least a person behind a character who was meeting with others in the MUD world.

I talked my disquiet over with a friend who posed the conversation-stopping question, 'Well, would you prefer it if Dr Sherry were a bot trained to interview people about life on the MUD?' (Recall that bots are computer programs that are able to roam cyberspace and interact with characters there.) The idea that Dr Sherry might be a bot had not occurred to me, but in a flash I realized that this too was possible, even likely. Many bots roam MUDs. They log onto the games as though they were characters. Players create these programe for many reasons: bots help with navigation, pass messages, and create a background atmosphere of animation in the MUD. When you enter a virtual café, you are usually not alone. A waiter bot approaches who asks if you want a drink and delivers it with a smile.

Characters played by people are sometimes mistaken for these little artificial intelligences. This was the case for Doug's character Carrot, because its passive, facilitating persona struck many as one a robot could play. I myself have made this kind of mistake several times, assuming that a person was a program when a character's responses seemed too automatic, too machine-like. And sometimes bots are mistaken for people. I have made this mistake too, fooled by a bot that flattered me by remembering my name or our last interaction. Dr Sherry could indeed have been one of these. I found myself confronted with a double that could be a person or a program. As things turned out, Dr Sherry was neither; it was a composite character created by two college students who wished to write a paper on the psychology of MUDs and who were using my name as a kind of trademark or generic descriptor for the idea of a cybershrink.[7] On MUDs, the one can be many and the many can be one.

So not only are MUDs places where the self is multiple and constructed by language, they are places where people and machines are in a new relation to each other, indeed can be mistaken for each other. In such ways, MUDs are evocative objects for thinking about human identity and, more generally, about a set of ideas that have come to be known as 'postmodernism'

These ideas are difficult to define simply, but they are characterized by such terms as 'decentered', 'fluid', 'nonlinear', and 'opaque'. They contrast with modernism, the classical world-view that has dominated Western thinking since the Enlightenment. The modernist view of reality is characterized by such terms as 'linear', 'logical', 'hierarchical', and by having 'depths' that can be plumbed and understood. MUDs offer an experience of the abstract postmodern ideas that had intrigued yet confused me during my intellectual coming of age. In this, MUDs exemplify [. . .] computer-mediated experiences bringing philosophy down to earth.

In a surprising and counter-intuitive twist, in the past decade, the mechanical engines of computers have been grounding the radically non-mechanical philosophy of postmodernism. The online world of the Internet is not the only instance of evocative computer objects and experiences bringing postmodernism down to earth. One of my students at MIT dropped out of a course I teach on social theory, complaining that the writings of the literary theorist Jacques Derrida were simply beyond him. He found that Derrida's dense prose and far-flung philosophical allusions were incomprehensible. The following semester I ran into the student in an MIT cafeteria. 'Maybe I wouldn't have to drop out now', he told me. In the past month, with his roommate's acquisition of new software for his Macintosh computer, my student had found his own key to Derrida. That software was a type of hypertext, which allows a computer user to create links between related texts, songs, photographs, and video, as well as to travel along the links made by others. Derrida emphasized that writing is constructed by the audience as well as by the author and that what is absent from the text is as significant as what is present. The student made the following connection:

> Derrida was saying that the messages of the great books are no more written
> in stone than are the links of a hypertext. I look at my roommate's hypertext

stacks and I am able to trace the connections he made and the peculiarities of how he links things together . . . And the things he might have linked but didn't. The traditional texts are like [elements in] the stack. Meanings are arbitrary, as arbitrary as the links in a stack.

'The cards in a hypertext stack', he concluded, 'get their meaning in relation to each other. It's like Derrida. The links have a reason but there is no final truth behind them.'[8]

Like experiences on MUDs, the student's story shows how technology is bringing a set of ideas associated with postmodernism – in this case, ideas about the instability of meanings and the lack of universal and knowable truths – into everyday life. In recent years, it has become fashionable to poke fun at postmodern philosophy and lampoon its allusiveness and density. Indeed, I have done some of this myself. But [. . .] we shall see that through experiences with computers, people come to a certain understanding of postmodernism and to recognize its ability to usefully capture certain aspects of their own experience, both online and off.

In *The Electronic Word*, the classicist Richard A. Lanham argues that open-ended screen text subverts traditional fantasies of a master narrative, or definitive reading, by presenting the reader with possibilities for changing fonts, zooming in and out, and rearranging and replacing text. The result is 'a body of work active not passive, a canon not frozen in perfection but volatile with contending human motive'.[9] Lanham puts technology and postmodernism together and concludes that the computer is a 'fulfillment of social thought'. But I believe the relationship is better thought of as a two-way process. Computer technology not only 'fulfills the postmodern aesthetic' as Lanham would have it, heightening and concretizing the postmodern experience, but helps that aesthetic hit the street as well as the seminar room. Computers embody postmodern theory and bring it down to earth.

As recently as ten to fifteen years ago, it was almost unthinkable to speak of the computer's involvement with ideas about unstable meanings and unknowable truths.[10] The computer had a clear intellectual identity as a calculating machine. Indeed, when I took an introductory programming course at Harvard in 1978, the professor introduced the computer to the class by calling it a giant calculator. Programming, he reassured us, was a cut and dried technical activity whose rules were crystal clear.

These reassurances captured the essence of what I shall be calling the modernist computational aesthetic. The image of the computer as calculator suggested that no matter how complicated a computer might seem, what happened inside it could be mechanically unpacked. Programming was a technical skill that could be done a right way or a wrong way. The right way was dictated by the computer's calculator essence. The right way was linear and logical. My professor made it clear that this linear, logical calculating machine combined with a structured, rule-based method of writing software offered guidance for thinking not only about technology and programming, but about economics, psychology, and social life. In other words, computational ideas were presented as one of the great modern metanarratives, stories of how the world worked that provided unifying pictures and analyzed complicated things by breaking them down into simpler parts. The modernist computations aesthetic promised to explain and unpack, to reduce and clarify. Although the computer culture was never monolithic, always including dissenters and deviant subcultures, for many years its professional mainstream (including computer scientists, engineers, economists, and cognitive scientists) shared this clear intellectual direction. Computers, it was assumed, would become more powerful, both as tools and as metaphors, by becoming better and faster calculating machines, better and faster analytical engines.

From a culture of calculation toward a culture of simulation

Most people over thirty years old (and even many younger ones) have had an introduction to computers similar to the one I received in that pro-gramming course. But from today's perspective, the fundamental lessons of computing that I was taught are wrong. First of all, programming is no longer cut and dried. Indeed, even its dimensions have become elusive. Are you programming when you customize your wordprocessing software? When you design 'organisms' to populate a simulation of Darwinian evo-lution in a computer game called SimLife? Or when you build a room in a MUD so that opening a door to it will cause 'Happy Un-Birthday' to ring out on all but one day of the year? In a sense, these activities are forms of programming, but that sense is radically different from the one presented in my 1978 computer course.

The lessons of computing today have little to do with calculation and rules; instead they concern simulation, navigation, and interaction. The very image of the computer as a giant calculator has become quaint and dated. Of course, there is still 'calculation' going on within the computer, but it is no longer the important or interesting level to think about or interact with. Fifteen years ago, most computer users were limited to typing commands. Today they use off-the-shelf products to manipulate simulated desktops, draw with simulated paints and brushes, and fly in simulated airplane cockpits. The computer culture's center of gravity has shifted decisively to people who do not think of themselves as pro-grammers. The computer science research community as well as industry pundits maintain that in the near future we can expect to interact with computers by communicating with simulated people on our screens, agents who will help organize our personal and professional lives.

On my daughter's third birthday she received a computer game called The Playroom, among the most popular pieces of software for the pre-school set. If you ask for help, The Playroom offers an instruction that is one sentence long: 'Just move the cursor to any object, click on it, explore and have fun.' During the same week that my daughter learned to click in The Playroom, a colleague gave me my first lesson on how to use the World Wide Web, a cyberconstruct that links text, graphics, video, and audio on computers all over the world. Her instructions were almost identical to those I had just read to my daughter: 'Just move the cursor to any underlined word or phrase, click on it, explore, and have fun.' When I wrote this text in January 1995, the Microsoft corporation had just introduced Bob, a 'social' interface for its Windows operating system, the most widely used operating system for personal computers in the world.[11] Bob, a computer agent with a human face and 'personality', operates within a screen environment designed to look like a living room that is in almost every sense a playroom for adults. In my daughter's screen play-room, she is presented with such objects as alphabet blocks and a clock for learning to tell time. Bob offers adults a wordprocessor, a fax machine, a telephone. Children and adults are united in the actions they take in virtual worlds. Both move the cursor and click.

The meaning of the computer presence in people's lives is very different from what most expected in the late 1970s. One way to describe what has happened is to say that we are moving from a modernist culture of calculation toward a postmodernist culture of simulation.

The culture of simulation is emerging in many domains. It is affecting our understanding of our minds and our bodies. For example, fifteen years ago, the computational models of mind that dominated academic psychology were modernist in spirit: nearly all tried to describe the mind in terms of centralized structures and programmed rules. In contrast, today's models often embrace a postmodern aesthetic of complexity and decentering. Mainstream computer researchers no longer aspire to program intelligence into computers but expect intelligence to emerge from the interactions of small subprograms. If these emergent simulations are 'opaque', that is, too complex to be completely analyzed, this is not necessarily a problem. After all, these theorists say, our brains are opaque to us, but this has never prevented them from functioning perfectly well as minds.

Fifteen years ago in popular culture, people were just getting used to the idea that computers could project and extend a person's intellect. Today people are embracing the notion that computers may extend an individual's physical presence. Some people use computers to extend their physical presence via real-time video links and shared virtual conference rooms. Some use computer-mediated screen communication for sexual encounters. An Internet list of 'Frequently Asked Questions' describes the latter activity – known as netsex, cybersex, and (in MUDs) TinySex – as people typing messages with erotic content to each other, 'sometimes with one hand on the keyset, sometimes with two'.

Many people who engage in netsex say that they are constantly surprised by how emotionally and physically powerful it can be. They insist that it demonstrates the truth of the adage that 90 percent of sex takes place in the mind. This is certainly not a new idea, but netsex has made it commonplace among teenage boys, a social group not usually known for its sophistication about such matters. A seventeen-year-old high school student tells me that he tried to make his erotic communications on the net 'exciting and thrilling and sort of imaginative'. In contrast, he admits that before he used computer communication for erotic purposes he thought about his sexual life in terms of 'trying [almost always unsuccessfully] to get laid'. A sixteen-year-old has a similar report on his cyber-passage to greater sensitivity: 'Before I was on the net, I used to masturbate with *Playboy*; now I do netsex on DinoMUD[12] with a woman in another state.' When I ask how the two experiences differ, he replies:

> With netsex, it is fantasies. My MUD lover doesn't want to meet me in RL. With *Playboy*, it was fantasies too, but in the MUD there is also the other person. So I don't think of what I do on the MUD as masturbation. Although, you might say that I'm the only one who's touching me. But in netsex, I have to think of fantasies she will like too. So now, I see fantasies as something that's part of sex with two people, not just me in my room.

Sexual encounters in cyberspace are only one (albeit well-publicized) element of our new lives on the screen. Virtual communities ranging from MUDs to computer bulletin boards allow people to generate experiences, relationships, identities, and living spaces that arise only through interaction with technology. In the many thousands of hours that Mike, a college freshman in Kansas, has been logged on to his favorite MUD, he has created an apartment with rooms, furniture, books, desk, and even a small computer. Its interior is exquisitely detailed, even though it exists only in textual description. A hearth, an easy chair, and a mahogany desk warm his cyberspace. 'It's where I live', Mike says. 'More than I do in my dingy dorm room. There's no place like home.'

As human beings becoming increasingly intertwined with the technology and with each other via the technology, old distinctions between what is specifically human and specifically technological become more complex. Are we living life *on* the screen or life *in* the screen? Our new technologically enmeshed relationships oblige us to ask to what extent we ourselves have become cyborgs, transgressive mixtures of biology, technology, and code.[13] The traditional distance between people and machines has become harder to maintain.

Writing in his diary in 1832, Ralph Waldo Emerson reflected that 'Dreams and beasts are two keys by which we are to find out the secrets of our nature . . . they are our test objects.'[14] Emerson was prescient. Freud and his heirs would measure human rationality against the dream. Darwin and his heirs would insist that we measure human nature against nature itself – the world of the beasts seen as our forebears and kin. If Emerson had lived at the end of the twentieth century, he would surely have seen the computer as a new test object. Like dreams and beasts, the computer stands on the margins. It is a mind that is not yet a mind. It is inanimate yet interactive. It does not think, yet neither is it external to thought. It is an object, ultimately a mechanism, but it behaves, interacts, and seems in a certain sense to know. It confronts us with an uneasy sense of kinship. After all, we too behave, interact, and seem to know, and yet are ultimately made of matter and programmed DNA. We think we can think. But can *it* think? Could it have the capacity to feel? Could it ever be said to be alive?

Dreams and beasts were the test objects for Freud and Darwin, the test objects for modernism. In the past decade, the computer has become the test object for postmodernism. The computer takes us beyond a world of dreams and beasts because it enables us to contemplate mental life that exists apart from bodies. It enables us to contemplate dreams that do not need beasts. The computer is an evocative object that causes old boundaries to be renegotiated.

[My research has traced] a set of such boundary negotiations. It is a reflection on the role that technology is playing in the creation of a new social and cultural sensibility. I have observed and participated in settings, physical and virtual, where people and computers come together. Over the past decade, I have talked to more than a thousand people, nearly three hundred of them children, about their experience of using computers or computational objects to program, to navigate, to write, to build, to experiment, or to communicate. In a sense, I have interrogated the computers as well. What messages, both explicit and implicit, have they carried for their human users about what is possible and what is impossible, about what is valuable and what is unimportant?

In the spirit of Whitman's reflections on the child, I want to know what we are becoming if the first objects we look upon each day are simulations into which we deploy our virtual selves. In other words, this is not a [study] about computers. Rather, it is a [study] about the intense relationships people have with computers and how these relationships are changing the way we think and feel. Along with the movement from a culture of calculation toward a culture of simulation have come changes in what computers do *for* us and in what they do *to* us – to our relationships and our ways of thinking about ourselves.

We have become accustomed to opaque technology. As the processing power of computers increased exponentially, it became possible to use that power to build graphical user interfaces, commonly known by the acronym GUI, that hid the bare machine from its user. The new opaque interfaces – most specifically, the Macintosh iconic style of interface, which simulates the space of a desktop as well as communication through dialogue – represented more than a technical change. These new interfaces modeled a way of understanding that depended on getting to know a computer through interacting with it, as one might get to know a person or explore a town.

The early personal computers of the 1970s and the IBM PC of the early 1980s presented themselves as open, 'transparent', potentially reducible to their underlying mechanisms. These were systems that invited users to imagine that they could understand its 'gears' as they turned, even if very few people ever tried to reach that level of understanding. When people say that they used to be able to 'see' what was 'inside' their first personal computers, it is important to keep in mind that for most of them there still remained many intermediate levels of software between them and the bare machine. But their computer systems encouraged them to represent their understanding of the technology as knowledge of what lay beneath the screen surface. They were encouraged to think of understanding as looking beyond the magic to the mechanism.

In contrast, the 1984 introduction of the Macintosh's iconic style presented the public with simulations (the icons of file folders, a trash can, a desktop) that did nothing to suggest how their underlying structure could be known. It seemed unavailable, visible only through its effects. As one user said, 'The Mac looked perfect, finished. To install a program on my DOS machine, I had to fiddle with things. It clearly wasn't perfect. With the Mac, the system told me to stay on the surface.' This is the kind of involvement with computers that has come to dominate the field; no longer associated only with the Macintosh, it is nearly universal in personal computing.

We have learned to take things at interface value. We are moving toward a culture of simulation in which people are increasingly comfortable with substituting representations of reality for the real. We use a Macintosh-style 'desktop' as well as one on four legs. We join virtual communities that exist only among people communicating on computer networks as well as communities in which we are physically present. We come to question simple distinctions between real and artificial. In what sense should one consider a screen desktop less real than any other? The screen desktop I am currently using has a folder on it labeled 'Professional Life'. It contains my business correspondence, date book, and telephone directory. Another folder, labeled 'Courses', contains syllabuses, reading assignments, class lists, and lecture notes. A third, 'Current Work', contains my research notes and this [study's] drafts. I feel no sense of unreality in my relationship to any of these objects. The culture of simulation encourages me to take what I see on the screen 'at (inter)face value'. In the culture of simulation, if it works for you, it has all the reality it needs.

The habit of taking things at interface value is new, but it has gone quite far. For example, a decade ago, the idea of a conversation with a computer about emotional matters, the image of a computer psychotherapist, struck most people as inappropriate or even obscene. Today, several such programs are on the market, and they tend to provoke a very different and quite pragmatic response. People are most likely to say, 'Might as well try it. It might help. What's the harm?'

We have used our relationships with technology to reflect on the human. A decade ago, people were often made nervous by the idea of thinking about computers in human terms. Behind their anxiety was distress at the idea that their own minds might be similar to a computer's 'mind'. This reaction against the formalism and rationality of the machine was romantic.

I use this term to analogize our cultural response to computing to nineteenth century Romanticism. I do not mean to suggest that it was merely an emotional response. We shall see that it expressed serious philosophical resistance to any view of people that denied their complexity and continued mystery. This response emphasized not only the richness of human emotion but the flexibility of human thought and the degree to which knowledge arises in subtle interaction with the environment. Humans, it insists, have to be something very different from mere calculating machines.

In the mid-1980s, this romantic reaction was met by a movement in computer science toward the research and design of increasingly 'romantic machines'. These machines were touted not as logical but as biological, not as programmed but as able to learn from experience. The researchers who worked on them said they sought a species of machine that would prove as unpredictable and undetermined as the human mind itself. The cultural presence of these romantic machines encouraged a new discourse; both persons and objects were reconfigured, machines as psychological objects, people as living machines.

But even as people have come to greater acceptance of a kinship between computers and human minds, they have also begun to pursue a new set of boundary questions about things and people. After several decades of asking, 'What does it mean to think?' the question at the end of the twentieth century is, 'What does it mean to be alive?' We are positioned for yet another romantic reaction, this time emphasizing biology, physical embodiment, the question of whether an artifact can be a life.[15]

These psychological and philosophical effects of the computer presence are by no means confined to adults. Like their parents, and often before their parents, the children of the early 1980s began to think of computers and computer toys as psychological objects because these machines combined mind activities (talking, singing, spelling, game playing, and doing math), an interactive style, and an opaque surface. But the children, too, had a romantic reaction, and came to define people as those emotional and unprogrammable things that computers were not. Nevertheless, from the moment children gave up on mechanistic understandings and saw the computer as a psychological entity, they began to draw computers closer to themselves. Today children may refer to the computers in their homes and classrooms as 'just machines', but qualities that used to be ascribed only to people are now ascribed to computers as well. Among children, the past decade has seen a movement from defining people as what machines are not to believing that the computational objects of everyday life think and know while remaining 'just machines'.

In the past decade, the changes in the intellectual identity and cultural impact of the computer have taken place in a culture still deeply attached to the quest for a modernist understanding of the mechanisms of life. Larger scientific and cultural trends, among them advances in psychopharmacology and the development of genetics as a computational biology, reflect the extent to which we assume ourselves to be like machines whose inner workings we can understand. 'Do we have our emotions', asks a college sophomore whose mother has been transformed by taking antidepressant medication, 'or do our emotions have us?' To whom is one listening when one is 'listening to Prozac'?[16] The aim of the Human Genome Project is to specify the location and role of all the genes in human DNA. The Project is often justified on the grounds that it promises to find the pieces of our genetic code responsible for many human diseases so that these may be better treated, perhaps by genetic reengineering. But talk about the Project also addresses the possibility of finding the genetic markers that determine human personality, temperament, and sexual orientation. As we contemplate reengineering the genome, we are also reengineering our view of ourselves as programmed beings.[17] Any romantic reaction that relies on biology as the bottom line is fragile, because it is building on shifting ground. Biology is appropriating computer technology's older, modernist models of computation while at the same time computer scientists are aspiring to develop a new opaque, emergent biology that is closer to the postmodern culture of simulation.[18]

Today, more lifelike machines sit on our desktops, computer science uses biological concepts, and human biology is recast in terms of deciphering a code. With descriptions of the brain that explicitly invoke computers and images of computers that explicitly invoke the brain, we have reached a cultural watershed. The rethinking of human and machine identity is not taking place just among philosophers but 'on the ground', through a philosophy in everyday life that is in some measure both provoked and carried by the computer presence.

We have sought out the subjective computer. Computers don't just do things for us, they do things to us, including to our ways of thinking about ourselves and other people. A decade ago, such subjective effects of the computer presence were secondary in the sense that they were not the ones being sought.[19] Today, things are often the other way around. People explicitly turn to computers for experiences that they hope will change their ways of thinking or will affect their social and emotional lives. When people explore simulation games and fantasy worlds or log on to a community where they have virtual friends and lovers, they are not thinking of the computer as what Charles Babbage, the nineteenth-century mathematician who invented the first programmable machine, called an analytical engine. They are seeking out the computer as an intimate machine.

[. . . It] is computer screens where we project ourselves into our own dramas, dramas in which we are producer, director, and star. Some of these dramas are private, but increasingly we are able to draw in other people. Computer screens are the new location for our fantasies, both erotic and intellectual. We are using life on computer screens to become comfortable with new ways of thinking about evolution, relationships, sexuality, politics and identity. [. . .]

Notes

1 William Gibson, *Neuromancer* (New York, Ace, 1984).
2 For a general introduction to LambdaMOO and MUDding, see Pavel Curtis, 'Mudding: social phenomena in text-based virtual realities', available via anonymous ftp://parcftp.xerox.com/pub/MOO/papers/DIAC92.*; Amy Bruckman, 'Identity workshop: emergent social and psychological phenomena in text-based virtual reality', unpublished manuscript, March 1992, available via anonymous ftp://media.mit.edu/pub/asb/papers/identity-workshop.*; and the chapter on MUDs in Howard Rheingold's *Virtual Community* (New York, Secker & Warburg, 1994). On virtual community in general, see Allucquere Rosanne Stone, 'Will the real body please stand up?: boundary stories about virtual cultures', in *Cyberspace: First Steps*, ed. Michael Benedikt (Cambridge, Mass, MIT Press, 1992), pp. 81–118. The asterisk in a net address indicates that the document is available in several formats.
3 The number of MUDs is changing rapidly. Most estimates place it at over five hundred, but an increasing number are private and so without any official 'listing'. The software

on which they are based (and which gives them their names as MOOs, MUSHes, MUSEs, etc.) determines several things about the game; among these is the general layout of the same space. For example, in the class of MUDs known as AberMUDs, the center of town is similar from one game to another, but the mountains, castles, and forests that surround the town are different in different games, because these have been built specifically for that game by its resident 'wizards'. MUDs also differ in their governance. In MUD parlance, wizards are administrators; they usually achieve this status through virtuosity in the game. In AberMUDs only wizards have the right to build onto the game. In other kinds of MUDs, all players are invited to build. Who has the right to build and how building is monitored (for example, whether the MUD government should allow a layer to build a machine that would destroy other players' property or characters) is an important feature that distinguishes types of MUDs. Although it may be technically correct to refer to being in a MUD (as in a dungeon), it is also common to speak of being on a MUD (as in logging on to a program). To me, the dual usage reflects the ambiguity of cyberspace as both space and program. I (and my informants) use both.

4 A 'flame war' is computer culture jargon for an incendiary expression of differences of opinion. In flame wars, participants give themselves permission to state their positions in strong, even outrageous terms with little room for compromise.

5 I promised Doug anonymity, a promise I made to all the people I interviewed in researching this book. Doug has been told that his name will be changed, his identity disguised, and the names and distinguishing features of his MUD characters altered. It is striking that even given these reassurances, which enable him to have an open conversation with me about his social and sexual activities on MUDs, he wants to protect his FurryMUD character.

6 I immersed myself in these 'French lessons', first in the aftermath of the May 1968 student revolt, a revolt in which Lacan and Foucault became intellectual heroes. Later, in 1973–4, the immersion continued while I studied the intellectual fallout of that failed revolution. That fallout included a love affair with things Freudian and an attack on unitary models of self. While followers of Lacan relied on reinterpretations of Freud that challenged models of a centralized ego, Deleuze and Guattari proposed more radical views that described the self as a multiplicity of desiring machines. See Gilles Deleuze and Félix Guattari, *Anti-Oedipus: Capitalism and Schizophrenia*, trans. Robert Hurley, Mark Seem and Helen R. Lane (Minneapolis, University of Minnesota Press, 1983).

7 Jill Serpentelli, 'Conversational structure and personality correlates of electronic communication', unpublished manuscript, 1992.

8 The student's association of Derrida and hypertext may be unsophisticated, but it is far from outlandish. See, for example, George P. Landow, *Hypertext: the Convergence of Critical Theory and Technology* (Baltimore, MD, Johns Hopkins University Press, 1992), pp. 1–34; and in George P. Landow and Paul Delany (eds), *Hypermedia and Literary Studies* (Cambridge, Mass, MIT Press, 1991).

9 Richard A. Lanham, *The Electronic Word: Democracy, Technology, and the Arts* (Chicago, The University of Chicago Press, 1993), p. 51. George Landow sees critical theory and technology in the midst of a 'convergence'; see Landow, *Hypertext*.

10 I say almost unthinkable because a small number of postmodern writers had begun to associate their work with the possibilities of computer technology. See, in particular, Jean-François Lyotard, *The Postmodern Condition: a Report on Knowledge*, trans. Geoff Bennington and Brian Massumi (Minneapolis, University of Minnesota Press, 1984).

11 *The Wall Street Journal*, 3 January 1995, pp. A3, A4, and *The Wall Street Journal*, 10 January 1995, pp. B1, B3.

12 Here I have changed the name of the MUD (there is to my knowledge no DinoMUD) to protect the confidentiality I promise all informants. I use the real name of a MUD when it is important to my account and will not compromise confidentiality.

13 See, for example, Donna Haraway, 'A manifesto for cyborgs: science, technology, and socialist feminism in the 1980s', *Socialist Review*, 80 (March–April 1985), pp. 65–107.

14   The quotation is from a journal entry by Emerson in January 1832. The passage reads in full, 'Dreams and beasts are two keys by which we are to find out the secrets of our nature. All mystics use them. They are like comparative anatomy. They are our test objects'; see Joel Porte (ed.), *Emerson in his Journals* (Cambridge, Mass., Belknap Press, 1982), p. 81.

15   In a recent review of the place of genetics in contemporary popular culture, Dorothy Nelkin and Susan Lindee have said: 'DNA has taken on the social and cultural functions of the soul'; *The DNA Mystique: the Gene as a Cultural Icon* (San Francisco and New York, W.H. Freeman, 1995), p. 42.

16   Peter Kramer, *Listening to Prozac: a Psychiatrist Explores Mood-altering Drugs and the New Meaning of the Self* (New York, Viking, 1993).

17   Nelkin and Lindee's *The DNA Mystique* documents the degree to which genetic essentialism dominates American popular culture today.

18   Evelyn Fox Keller, 'The body of a new machine: situating the organism between telegraphs and computers', *Perspectives on Science*, 2 (3) (1994), pp. 302–23.

19   For a view of this matter from the perspective of the 1980s, see Sherry Turkle, *The Second Self: Computers and the Human Spirit* (New York, Simon and Schuster, 1984).

The development of interactive games
Leslie Haddon

Towards the end of the 1990s interactive entertainment, the lion's share of which is accounted for by games, was a larger market than video rental in Europe and was almost 80 per cent of the cinema box office. After its emergence within hacker and hobbyist circles, a history of booms and busts and a marginal status alongside toys, games have finally become established within the mainstream culture industries – and for increasing numbers have found a routine, albeit moderate, role within everyday life.

This chapter examines three related histories starting with the development of games hardware, to show how interactive games descended through a number of technological trajectories. The earliest games originated in research computing departments in the early 1960s. Given that the large computers of the 1950s were used mainly for serious purposes, their unlikely origins need some explanation. So too does their subsequent diffusion throughout the computer establishment as they were taken up by microcomputer hobbyists from the mid-70s. Video games machines, the coin-operated machines in amusement arcades and home video games products (especially programmable consoles) were the interactive games' other lineage. Both these routes eventually saw the emergence of an independent games software sector with some of the characteristics of other media industries. However, it was the coin-ops and consoles which laid a basis for the popularity of the micro-computer games of the 1980s, which in turn led the early home computers to become for a time predominantly games machines.

The second section focuses on the evolution of software industries and on specific game texts. A number of genres, such as adventure games, originated on larger mainframe computers. But the most significant type of game was the fast 'action' genre, initially associated with shooting games, which were developed on interactive minicomputers. Both the nature of the

This chapter is based on a paper in *Screen*, 29 (1988), pp. 52–73 and from *Future Visions: New Technologies of the Screen* (London: British Film Institute, 1993), pp. 123–47.

game-play and of these narratives can be understood in terms of the researchers' contemporary interest in interactive computing generally, and the particular tastes of early male game designers. Action games later fitted conveniently in the arcades' coin-ops and home video games attracted interest from other media industries whose licensing deals affected the contents of games. These ties with other media were later re-established when micro-computer games appeared, but only after the early cottage industry of small software producers had been replaced by larger game publishers.

The final section examines the nature of games-playing itself and the frequently negative reception which this activity generated among pressure groups and academics. Moral panics about games – including fears of addiction, the 'effects' of desensitization and of escapism – have spanned a range of political campaigns, media coverage and academic, mainly psychological, analysis. The origin of such concerns is a complex topic in itself, deriving partly from more traditional criticisms of television and partly from more recent anxieties about the experience of computing.

Relevant to this enquiry is why games were initially so interesting to the first computer hobbyists. This group was significant as both early consumers and producers of software, and their whole approach to games as a means of learning about programming shaped the experience of others outside their own community. Computer games were fundamentally different from the previous video games in that users could combine programming with games. Looking into, altering or breaking the copyright protection on programs, as well as creating their own games and special effects, meant that for many playing the game was only part of a package of experience.

To date, many of the commentaries on games-playing have focused on either the nature of games as masculine texts or the masculine appeal of mastering interactive technology. The emphatic interest of young males in games-playing needs to be addressed, but too narrow a focus neglects the history of games-playing as an interactive technology. The crucial stage in the evolution of games was their appearance in arcades where playing became a collective form of leisure among young males. Later, with the advent of the micro-computer, programming expanded the activity of 'games-playing' beyond the moment of sitting at the screen with a joystick, and closer inspection of what constitutes this more complex consumption highlights the particularity of young male interest. It will be argued that any 'masculine' content of games is itself more liable to reflect this interest than to determine it.

Hardware

The first computer games

During the late 1950s and early 1960s, computer science was in the process of being constructed as an academic discipline.[1] MIT introduced the first courses on computing for undergraduates in 1959 and set up an 'artificial intelligence' research department. The military had been funding computer development since the early days of the space programme. When this programme was transferred to the civil body NASA, the military decided to increase its support for computing and basic research projects in particular. The new AI department was able to deploy these funds with a considerable degree of discretion and employed the first enthusiastic students emerging from MIT's new courses. Meanwhile, the university department was developing a close relationship with the young company DEC, then at the forefront of the newly emerging mini-computer industry. DEC provided MIT with a free mini-computer and any assistance that was requested. In return, the mini-computer company benefited from MIT research and advice, received a ranged of free programs from the AI department, and eventually recruited a number of staff from this source. Within these institutional arrangements, the AI department was in the process of developing new forms of computing. At that time, the only model of computing was the batch-processing system dominated by IBM. Anyone wanting access to mainframes had to submit programs to operators and pick up the results later. Using a small research computer and a DEC mini-computer, the MIT unit explored a more direct style of computing with these machines, whereby users could receive immediate feedback. MIT researchers developed a range of facilities to support this new type of 'real-time' computing, formulating some of the principles by which micro-computers were later to operate.

Even prior to the new MIT courses, a male community had evolved in the university's model railway club, where members used their technical expertise to construct and investigate systems – telephone and railway ones in particular. These students continually tried to perfect new 'features' for their systems. The set of values operating in this culture led them to develop their own terminology, in which a key concept was the 'hack': a stylish technical innovation undertaken for the intrinsic pleasure of experimenting – not necessarily fulfilling any more constructive goal. Defining themselves as 'hackers', the students were soon attracted to the new computer systems in the AI department. In the course of displaying their programming skills, these hackers explored and enhanced the capabilities of the new machines.

As 'hacks', projects which tested and demonstrated the computer's abilities were often of little use in themselves. For example, these enthusiasts worked on programs to play chess and to solve puzzles generated by solitaire. This approach to computing was very different from the traditional, 'serious use' of the machine. Rather than treating computers as mundane tools, the hackers played with the machines as if they were toys. While heretical to many of their contemporaries, the AI managers regarded these projects as vehicles for learning about interactive computing. There were also tangible spin-offs. Hackers wrote the operating systems for their first machine, the TX-O and then improved it for DEC's mini-computer, the PDP-I, as well as supplying other programs which would have been very costly to design commercially. More particularly, the hackers produced innovatory software to handle real-time computer graphics and later made considerable contributions to the development of time-sharing.

The first games were just such exploratory projects. Demonstration programs which created visual effects already existed, For example, one such program controlled a row of flashing lights which simulated the motion of a ball in table tennis. Another project entailed the construction of a maze on a VDU in which a mouse would search for cheese. But the start of interactive gaming as we now know it developed with the space battle program *Spacewar*.

In the years between the first *Spacewar* and the advent of the earliest forms of what we now call the PC, games became an established feature on larger computers because of programmers' interest in games-playing and because games were useful to computer manufacturers. In 1962, MIT exhibited *Spacewar* to the general public. DEC requested a copy, and *Spacewar* was soon supplied to all their clients. Apart from their diagnostic utility in checking if machines were in order, games were also used by the DEC salesforce as demonstration pieces. *Spacewar* showed the accessible and friendly face of computers. Later, when graphics capability became an important consideration, games were often used to demonstrate the sophistication of these machines. By the 1970s, games had become established as 'traditional' and legitimate programs.

Arcade games

Nolan Bushnall was mainly responsible for the transfer of games to the arcades.[2] An engineer who had played the original computer games as a student, Bushnall had also worked in amusement parks. Once the price of chip technology fell sufficiently, he attempted a coin-op version of *Spacewar*. Designed in 1971, the game was not an immediate commercial success. But his subsequent effort proved very popular: the electronic table-tennis game *Pong*, made with the help of a colleague. With this product, Bushnall and his colleagues founded the company Atari, a company which was to become the major force in the new games industry.

Other companies entered this new market very quickly. Within a few years there were thirty manufacturers of coin-op video games, reducing Atari's market share to 10 per cent by the end of 1973. But by the late 1970s, Atari, now supported by Warner Communication funds, came to dominate the industry again, producing for both the coin-op and home video games markets. Following the introduction of *Space Invaders* in 1979, the arcade game reached new heights of popularity. This can be measured by sales of game machines which rose from approximately $40 million to $500 million between 1979 and 1981, by which time coin-op games had become an international phenomenon. Their proliferation and profitability attracted growing media attention as well as provoking considerable critical comment.[3]

Coin-op machines were located in American bars and shops as well as the actual arcades from which they took their name. Amusement park owners were particularly motivated to adopt these machines. The new games were part of a widespread attempt to discard the sleazy image of the arcade. These managers felt that the new product would help to introduce respectability to the amusement park, making it a place for family entertainment. The homely table-tennis game may have been particularly attractive from this perspective, but more generally the clean electronic high-tech form of the new games helped to signal the arcade's more modern look. These electronic games specifically appropriated the role which pinball had occupied: within a few years of the introduction of video games, pinball sales had declined by two-thirds. Meanwhile, the major pinball manufacturers were among those companies moving into the production of the new coin-op machines.

Home video games machines

Sanders Electronics, an American defence-orientated company, was responsible for developing the first home video game technology as an alternative use for TV sets.[4] The first commercial product, released in 1972, was licensed to the TV distributor Magnavox. The Odyssey machine was capable of playing twelve games, including simple hockey, tennis and maze games, many of which were similar to each other. Users had to place plastic overlays on the television screen to provide the background setting for the video games. To re-program the machine for different games, players had to plug in circuit cards. These 'TV games' initially had a much lower profile than the coin-ops, although they were reasonably successful in the market as a consumer electronic.

In 1975, Atari released *Pong* for the home market. The home version of *Pong* added new features such as sound effects and ricochets, and introduced integrated circuit technology. These components, otherwise known as silicon chips or semi-conductors, were to be the basis of general micro-electronics developed up to the present day. From 1974, other companies also started to enter the market, with leisure specialists and semi-conductor firms competing with pinball manufacturers. Over thirty new companies started producing for this home market in 1976 alone. The particular appeal to the semi-conductor companies, such as Fairchild and National Semi-conductor, was that video games machines arrived just at the time when they were diversifying from capital goods and in the process of building up a consumer products division. These firms had seen the profitability of utilizing chips in digital watches and calculators and once video games started to use chips, they perceived them as being an ideal product for their new divisions.

After *Pong*, TV games technology consisted of one chip or a combination of chips on which there were fixed programs. By 1976 several companies were working to replace these chips with a micro-processor. This technology had already been introduced into the coin-ops, where the sale price of each unit justified its cost. In 1976, Fairchild Camera and Instruments introduced the Channel F or Video Entertainment System which would accept programmable cartridges. As far as the semi-conductors were concerned, video games provided just the type of dedicated application for the new micro-processor technology that they had been seeking. Soon other programmable consoles were available from RCA, Bally, Magnavox, Coleco and Atari.

This move to micro-processors affected the nature of the video games product. Programmable machines, or consoles, created a flexible division between hardware and software. Thus, a distinct software industry could emerge once video games cartridge manufacturers could sell games separately from the hardware they were played on. Games machines were now potentially 'software players' like hi-fis and other home-based 'delivery systems'. Games software could be bought, collected and compared in the same way as records.

The console market started to boom in the late 1970s, with sales of hardware and software peaking in 1982. Although many of the early manufacturers had already left the field, leaving only Magnavox, Mattel and Atari,[5] as the boom accelerated various companies from the toy industry diversified into this area, Coleco being the most successful newcomer. Atari remained dominant with 80 per cent of the home market by 1980. In that year, 3.5 per cent of American homes had consoles, and by 1981 this had risen to 8 per cent.

There were always dissenting voices which discussed games as a fad, although the general view aired in the trade press in the early 1980s was optimistic. The one cloud on the horizon was the growing home computer industry. Micro-computer products were initially much more expensive, and were thought to cater for a different market, but as home computer prices fell, the new product started to appropriate the role of consoles and distract sales from the video games market. The consensus in the trade press by the end of 1983, a year after video games actually reached peak sales, deemed the video games 'boom' to be over. In fact, sales did not simply disappear. The consoles had now been relegated to toy departments at reduced prices, where they continued to sell steadily but in smaller quantities.[6]

Micro-computer games

Micro-computers had first emerged in the USA as a hobbyist product during the mid-1970s.[7] However some of the leading hardware manufacturers and industry observers foresaw a more lucrative future for this machine as a mass-market consumer electronic. The most ambitious scenarios, such as those cultivated by the semi-conductor giant Texas Instruments, envisaged future PCs which would not only run a variety of software, but which could eventually be connected to telecommunications systems and even have home control facilities. The home computer could become a central part of the household, routinely used by all the family. In the shorter term, difficulties implementing telecoms and control functions meant that American producers pitched these earlier versions of the PC as a more restricted, albeit still versatile, 'software player'.

In fact, the first British home computers, launched in 1980 and 1981 by Sinclair, were a different type of machine, extensively sold as products able to explore the world of computing. This 'computer literacy' theme was to remain stronger in Britain than many had originally expected and it had a significant bearing on the very experience of game-playing. As the boom in home computers expanded, producers for the British market, including the leaders Sinclair, Acorn and Commodore, hoped, along with their American counterparts, that their machines would find more wide-ranging applications. Consequently, these hardware manufacturers maintained an ambivalent attitude towards games.

In their favour, games provided a familiar application for these early machines, requiring no expensive additional equipment such as printers. Some micro-computer firms even recognized the possibility of taking business away from the profitable video games market. On the other hand, too strong a games identity threatened the status of the PC as a more general purpose machine, and indeed pushed the computer towards being a child's toy. Hence, early advertisements for micro-computers never overtly emphasized games as their central function; if anything, the key stress was on the educational potential of the machine. While games were always mentioned in advertisements and fostered by the software support that manufacturers offered, games-playing was depicted as being only one option within a range of applications.

The micro-computer as games machine

By 1983, the sudden entry of a range of new companies culminated in considerable competition and price cutting, straining the profitability of many firms. As a result, a number of manufacturers left the industry or went bankrupt. In 1984, a slight decline in demand occurred just as retailers overstocked for the Christmas sales; price-cutting in the New Year to clear this stock and the consequent fall in retail orders precipitated several company collapses. Acorn had to be rescued, and later even Sinclair ran into difficulties. The national news media which covered these developments suggested that the 'bubble had burst', giving rise to a widely held public perception that the home computer had somehow faded away.

However, assumptions that the home PC had disappeared were incorrect. Hardware and software sales remained at high enough levels to support the fewer companies still operating in the market. The temporary financial problems experienced by many firms were eventually resolved as most companies gradually moved into profit. Although slightly fewer magazines were to be found, the computer press still occupied a firmly established place on the newsagent's shelf. Home computers may have had a lower media profile and commanded less prominence in the multiple retail departments, but the industry was far from dead.

Even by the time of the crisis, the home PC had already become established as the new vehicle for electronic games. The computer had been appropriated by users as a games machine, despite the wishes of manu-facturers. And, by the late 1980s, the peak of interest in games may have passed, but games were still routinely played by many boys and girls.[8]

Nevertheless, the original reservations that games narrowed the PC's potential and devalued it persisted for some years after 1983, together with a disappointment that early ambitions for a more all-purpose machine had not been realized: the technological 'revolution' had gone astray. In order to broaden the identity of the existing computer product, both hardware manufacturers and software publishers (for example, Atari, The Digital Muse) started to promote non-game entertainment software, such as art and music packages (e.g. *Degas Elite, Virtuoso*), and applications derived originally from the business market (chiefly through database, word-processing and spreadsheet software). By the late 1980s other industry commentators saw the route to a more general purpose computer as laying with more powerful machines, exemplified at that time by the Atari ST and Commodore Amiga series. However, such computers also tended to build partly upon the appeal of games rather than challenge their predominance.

Hardware in the 1990s

Probably the most striking development on the hardware front was the 1990s' renewed success of the dedicated video games machines. Nintendo was the chief and original actor to re-establish games consoles from the mid- to late 1980s in Japan and then in the US. So it was not so surprising to see British trade press headlines like 'Home Computer Wars II: the Console Strikes Back' from the late 1980s. In fact, consoles took a little longer to grow in popularity in the UK, reflecting the fact that the home PC had become so established as the games machine in the UK. But eventually the appeal of the games available for consoles, their relative cheapness compared to computers and the fact that their loading was faster all helped to establish them again. For example, by 1994, more than 60 per cent of households with children had the latest 16-bit console technology.[9] In fact, it was actually Nintendo's rival Sega who was initially more successful in the UK. Although a range of other companies, including Commodore, Amstrad and the toy-maker Hornby, added their own brands of console to this market,[10] the two Japanese firms dominated until the mid-1990s.

The strategy introduced by Nintendo seems in part to have taken into account claims that Atari video games failed in the 1990s because too much poor-quality software was available. Nintendo made much more effort to control what type of software was produced.[11] Originally producing this in house (including the very successful *Mario Brothers* game), the company eventually allowed software houses to produce under licence, taking 20 per cent royalty. In fact, software was always the main source of revenue for Nintendo, the hardware being priced relatively low to build an installed base. In addition, Nintendo (and then Sega) used cartridge technology to prevent copying. This not only pushed up the price of software, but software houses had additionally to pay Nintendo to put their games onto its cartridges – creating considerable costs and also risks for software houses, especially when they had to agree to buy large minimum numbers of cartridges. The result was a fair amount of criticism and conflict over unfair business practices, with litigation in Japan and the US, and with

Nintendo coming under the scrutiny of various trading bodies. Both Sega and Nintendo were referred to the Monopolies and Mergers Commission in the UK.[12]

However, in somewhat of a replay of the 1980s' home-computer boom, software sales, which had been growing strongly year on year, declined in 1994–5, as did the companies' profitability, partially reflecting factors such as oversupply of software and discounting.[13] One other factor was the new generation of consoles on the horizon. In fact, with hindsight the mid-1990s' stagnation proved to be a glitch, as consoles and software once again saw impressive growth in sales for the next years as 32-bit consoles, led by the Sony Playstation and Sega's Saturn, proved to be extremely popular. The difference with these machines was the move from cartridge to CD-ROM storage, which was equally difficult to copy but cheaper to produce.

Apart from the rebirth of the console, games developments continued on the home computer. In the late 1980s and early 1990s, games expanded from the early machine formats on to those very PCs that were trying to break away from the image of the games machine. The Amstrad PCW series and PC series of computers started to attract games support, while 1990 saw the release of *PC Leisure*, a magazine for personal computer (i.e. IBM compatible) games. The next few years saw the demise of all other formats, leaving just IBM-compatibles on the mass market (apart from the more up-market Apples) – and at this point all micro-computers were referred to as PCs.

By the mid- to late 1980s, computer sales underwent a further mini-boom, first fuelled by the enthusiasm created for 'multi-media' and then by interest in the Internet. Technologically, the main change was the move to using CD-ROM for storage. This, together with increases in processing power each year, enabling better graphics and the widening of the installed base, meant that PCs once again became attractive for software publishers. By 1997 the retail value of all PC 'entertainment software' sales in the UK was slightly higher than that of consoles, but that category includes more than games.[14] Since games account for at least 70 per cent of the entertainment software market,[15] we can assume that PCs were by this stage once again providing significant competition to consoles as a platform for games.

One final digression in this section concerns a technological trajectory which experienced moderate success but failed to achieve its goals as a mass-market product. This was the 'multi-media' alternative to the PC, which had received considerable attention in the industry in the early to mid-1990s. Led by Philips' CD-*i* (Compact Disc Interactive) but joined by Commodore's less successful CDTV, this was another form of software player. It combined CD storage with micro-processors, but without the keyboard of a PC. In fact, marketing policy deliberately distanced this player from computer products.[16] What is of interest in the light of the above history is the concern of these manufacturers that games would migrate to their new hardware product and take it over so that it would become merely the latest incarnation of a games machine. Therefore, although Philips and Commodore signed up a range of publishers to support their machines, having learnt a lesson from the PC industry, they were still wary of games. Ultimately, both manufacturers wanted their products to become home entertainment centres, occupying a permanent place in the living room and used by all the family – echoing the earlier desire for a general purpose PC – and not just the latest games machines.

Software

Computer games

In *Spacewar*, two spaceships engaged in battle, using torpedoes to shoot at each other. The program operated in real time: the graphics reacted instantly to the players' control, either when turning the spaceship or firing. Action was continuous, leaving little pause to stop and plan. It called on physical reflexes as much as on strategy. Why did the first interactive game take this form? In its narrative content, the space battle reflected the interests of its designer, Steve Russell, who was an avid science fiction reader and a fan of 'space opera' where heroes engage villains in galactic battles. Whereas descriptions of spaceship encounters and space fleet manoeuvres inspired the game's scenarios, the gameplay itself – the action – came from a different source. Russell had wanted to create a more visually stunning 'hack', demonstrating the potential of interactive computing in general, and so translated the fast pace of a written narrative into the rapid physical action of a game. In so doing, he also acknowledged the influence of an existing product which was so important in shaping the later development of games: *Spacewar* reflected the game-play of pinball.

Once *Spacewar* was presented to the hacker community, others added new features such as gravity effects and details of solar systems, and developed the first computer game joysticks to control the motion. There were to be other variations on battle and shooting themes, with *Star Trek* becoming the best-known game on mainframe computers. When alternative types of game were developed, the tastes of game programmers in the male-dominated computing field continued to be reflected in these texts. (For example, simulations had been one of the earlier uses for computers, especially simulations of battles for military purpose. The popular mainframe game *Lunar Landing* was once again located within a space setting, simulating control of a space-craft approaching the moon.)

Mathematically based programs were also popular. One such program, *Game of Life*, simulated ever-changing communities of 'cells' as they formed patterns over generations. The other best-known genre started with the game *Adventure*. Appearing much later, in 1976, this computer game drew on the structure of fantasy war-gaming and, in particular, on the *Dungeons and Dragons* interests of some programmers. The player directed an explorer through an underground world where the protagonist fought off enemies and overcame obstacles through clever tricks in order to find some treasure. This latter genre became, like *Spacewar*, a cult game in computer centres. On the home computer, this adventure format was later to provide the main alternative to the fast-action games predominating on video games machines.[17]

Arcade games

The mix of strategy, speed and physical coordination involved in action games well suited the logic of the arcades – hardly surprising given that this action style of interactive games had been modelled on pinball. The excitement of fast action provided the type of thrill which initially attracted players to the coin-op, while the brevity of games (until skill had been acquired) maximized earnings. Yet the new video games were different from their arcade precursor in one respect: they had at least some narrative content. Albeit 'thin', the storyline of the games allowed commentators to see the new games as being comparable to other media texts. Indeed, it was this feature which so easily enabled concerns about violence on TV and film to be transferred to the new entertainment machines.

This narrative quality, along with a variety of different possible manoeuvres on screen, allowed the rate and form of innovation to be very different from the pinball predecessor. Whereas pinball had evolved very slowly and differences between machines at any one time were often cosmetic,[18] a continuous stream of new arcade video games started to appear by the late 1970s. New releases contained not only different scenarios, but whole new configurations of action: for example, *PacMan*, where players control a blob fleeing from danger through a maze. As this pattern of innovation emerged, video games became part of a 'cultural industry', in much the same way as film and music were.

Video games

Most of the early home video games were variations on the bat-and-ball idea found in the Odyssey machine and in *Pong*. *Pong* itself was an example of a game making the transition from the arcade to the home machine. Driving games also made this transition, but the early chip technology caused a considerable time-lag in any such transfer. The dedicated integrated circuit chip needed for the home games machine could take a year to develop.

The companies which introduced micro-processor-based technology widened the options by adding cartridges containing other game forms besides those found in arcades: noughts and crosses, blackjack and chess. A countervailing tendency arose once software programming enabled a more speedy transfer of games from the coin-ops. Home versions could be released while a game was still in vogue in the arcades. The coin-ops became even more extensive testing grounds for products which might then be cross-licensed to the home market. This relationship bore fruit when one particular arcade game first boosted sales of the domestic machine. *Space Invaders* enjoyed unprecedented success as a coin-op, increasing overall sales in that sector after its introduction in 1978. Once Atari had bought the home licence and was able to offer a version for their consoles, programmable sales also increased considerably. Atari was by now the training ground for many games designers, a number of whom later set up companies to supply the software cartridges for the Atari console and for competing machines.

Besides cross-overs from arcade favourites, a number of film companies, such as 20th Century-Fox, set up software arms and arranged licensing deals. For example, Atari and Lucasfilm arranged joint projects. Games were seen by the film industry both as competition for the same 'entertainment dollar' and as a new outlet for cross-licensing. However, although scenarios and plots of home games became more varied, the action game-play remained a stable product in the industry.

While it lasted, this growth of the video games industry led to innovations in publicity and distribution. The increased rate of new releases was now covered by video games magazines, carrying news and reviews of the latest games available. Meanwhile, existing games producers experimented with novel means of delivering games to players, whereby telephone companies downloaded the games to homes by phone. Both these moves were repeated when games appeared on home computers.

Micro-computer games

Initial interest in micro-computer games came from the hobbyists who both produced and consumed this software. The hobbyist magazines had always devoted some space to games, providing this software genre with respectability. Within a few years of the first home computers being released, a wave of books introducing programming to a more general public relied on games to explain the structure of computer languages. Eventually, even the manuals which were packaged with the hardware adopted this approach.

Micro-computer games soon proved popular outside original hobbyist circles, especially among male youth. Since the previous video games consoles had made less impact in the UK than in the US, computers provided many people with their first chance to play home-based games. This demand encouraged more hobbyists to establish their own part-time mail-order ventures, selling software for the new home computers. Aided by the cheap cassettes technology, these initiatives developed into a small cottage industry. Within a few years, teenagers who had received the early computers as gifts provided a further source of games programmers. Although this software industry was relatively small, the national press carried stories of successful entrepreneurial schoolboys and this fuelled further interest. Consequently, software which aided game design proved to be very popular.

By 1983, several substantial publishing, record and video companies (for example, Mirror Group, Virgin) had entered the computer games field and transformed software production for this increasingly lucrative market into an industry organized on the same model as their other interests. In this restructuring process, a majority of the small start-up firms, as well as others who had tried to cash in on the games boom, went bankrupt, amalgamated or left the market.

The 'burst bubble' coverage which home computers received in 1983–4 made some wonder if games, like the hardware, had also been a fad. But this was certainly not the case. Like hardware, computer games had a lower media profile by the mid-1980s and games were commanding less shelf space. But following the reduction in the number of software houses, the games industry achieved an overall degree of stability which has continued to the present day. Meanwhile, since the early 1980s international sales have become increasingly important to British software houses, the UK becoming a major exporter of games once PCs became popular in other European countries.

Under the new industry regime, games writing became routinized and continuous instead of haphazard and occasional. By the late 1980s, active marketing of the latest product guaranteed sufficient chart hits for profitability, while cheaper 'budget' software gave old products a new life in compilations. There were also some innovations in distribution with software being sold through a wide range of outlets including garages and corner shops.

Finally, the industry started to operate in conjunction with a new type of computer magazine, geared mainly to leisure and entertainment. These journals gave far more coverage to game developments than their hobby-oriented predecessors. These new publicity outlets had the effect of systematically promoting games, often relegating other software to the fringes. Yet the newly emerging magazines also went beyond reviewing games, carrying regular features on how to break into games programs in order to see their inner workings and how to make changes so that the games operated differently. The hobbyist project had infiltrated games-playing, adding a new dimension to the activity for some users.

Software in the 1990s

Despite all these signs of the durability of games, many publishers in the 1980s had still felt that they nevertheless remained a 'fringe' entertainment, rather than a 'mainstream' one like music. Several trade associations were created over the years to promote the industry as a whole. One problem which the games industry identified was its low profile in the mass media, so there were occasional attempts to gain prominence for programmers as media personalities or to obtain newspaper and TV coverage through promotions. But what made more of a difference to the wider visibility of games was the emergence of TV programmes such as *Games Master* and *Bad Influence*, culminating in programmes reviewing games alongside cinema films and videos releases. Films were also made of two of the most popular games: *Mario Brothers* and *Street Fighter*.

Another continuing concern in the industry was the perceived lack of creativity in actual games content. Admittedly, part of the worry about a lack of 'real' innovation relates to the mechanism whereby successful new games are immediately followed by a spate of near copies. This process is not very different from the record and film industries, where producers follow successful formulae.[19] Some of the late 1980s' games, such as *Tetris* and *Little Computer People*, had started to break away from existing genres and there were always new arcade hits to convert and new items to license from the other cultural industries. Occasionally, totally new sub-genres appeared, such as the Kung-Fu, quiz, and horror games. Even the soap opera *EastEnders* found its way on to the games format. Nevertheless, some asked whether this level of innovation was enough. Did changes in scenario and slight changes in the playing skills required provide enough novelty?

One approach to changing the content and nature of games was to separate the role of programmer from games designer. This involved drawing on the expertise of staff from other entertainment media, such as music, television and film, to complement the technological skills of existing games writers. In addition, throughout the 1990s games saw incremental but significant improvements in terms of more detailed and smoother graphics and lifelike sounds and the addition of video clips and digital audio quality music to animation sequences.

The last development was around on-line games. On the one hand, on-line networks provided a new means for distributing games – by downloading them to consoles or PCs. But, in addition, considerable industry interest has been shown in on-line playing, including playing multi-user games. In fact, such on-line games have been in existence for some years – the famous one called MUD was played on the Arpanet before it evolved into the Internet, and British Telecom ran MUD on its videotex service Micronet from 1985 until the whole service was closed down in 1990.[20] But the rise of the Internet helped to generate much more interest in this form of games-playing, with some very optimistic forecasts for the millennium.

The consumption of games: concerns

Moving on to the whole area of consumption, we need to consider the negative reaction to games. Despite hopes that interactive games would give arcades a new image, the new coin-ops began to arouse opposition as early as the end of the 1970s.[21] The criticisms emanating from the anti-games lobby were diverse. In the US, moral panics resulted in some much publicized by-laws to regulate arcades. At a national level, the Surgeon General issued a warning that video games might be dangerous and that children might find them addictive, while the National Coalition on Television Violence extended its area of interest to include the new games. The US was not alone. Perhaps the most vigorous attack on video games came from the Philippines where President Marcos ordered 300 machines to be dismantled, smashed or surrendered to military police within fifteen days because of their detrimental effect on morals and on youth discipline. Even in the UK, the Labour MP George Foulkes led a campaign in 1981 to curb the 'menace' of video games, mainly because of their addictive properties. His 'Control of Space Invaders (and other Electronic Games) Bill' was only narrowly defeated in the Commons.[22]

One set of worries focused on the effect of the technology underlying these games. Critics feared what they saw as the 'compulsive behaviour' engendered by electronic games, an issue previously raised in relation to the 'narcotic' effect of television.[23] This fear of addiction was reinforced by discussions of the 'holding power' attributed to computer environments *per se*, as manifest in earlier concern about the 'unhealthy' attraction of hackers to computer technology.[24] Those opposed to games argued that players were becoming adjuncts of the machine, and thus predisposed to be anti-social. Anxiety intensified because the majority of users were adolescent, and that time of their life was thought necessary for developing interpersonal skills rather than being isolated with 'things'. A number of American psychology studies followed from these commentaries, trying to evaluate whether the use of these electronic devices was addictive or led to lack of social skills. Some studies tackled slightly different concerns about the violent nature of games. Although seemingly about games content and their scenarios, these debates also referred to the underlying technology of the media which was supposed to desensitize users to aggression.

Other critics painted a very different picture, focusing instead on the collective nature of video games culture. Many parents and local community spokespeople recognized that arcade machines were a gathering point for youth.[25] The games were felt to be encouraging young people to 'hang around', a view which tapped into traditional fears about arcades being 'corrupt and corrupting places'.[26] Arcade video games were seen as the new locus for a separate youth culture, distracting young people from more constructive activities. Consequently, a number of studies framed their analyses of arcade life in terms of delinquency.

The location of video games within arcades meant that the new machines were incorporated into the existing social activities of these milieux and thus reactivated old anxieties. Amusement parks and many of the other public sites where coin-op machines were found were part of street culture. They were mainly male, particularly young male, preserves. Some girls were present in these contexts and there were some girl players; after all, the arcade and other public locations were meeting places. Yet observational studies found that the proportion of boys varied between 70 and 90 per cent.[27] So, while the new technology may have been brought in to mark changes, it was soon slotted into a nexus of relations. Very traditional fears about 'deviancy' and working-class, male youth underlay some of the apparently new alarm about video games-playing.[28]

The values, rules and rituals which these young males had built up in the pinball arcades were transferred to the video game. They shaped the whole experience of interactive games-playing. For instance, many would-be players served apprenticeships as spectators. The public display of skill was important. There were times for discussing tactics and giving tips. In sum, while the games were played individually, the activity remained grounded within the social life of the peer group.

Games-playing: gender and games

Just as many of the fears about micro-computer games persisted from the arcade days, so analyses of gender and games have not changed significantly from when they were first formulated in relation to the coin-ops. The most frequent argument has been that the aggressive/destructive/violent/mastery nature of many games is a masculine quality.[29] Early critics also argued that scenarios such as science-fiction settings were male-orientated.[30] Stereotypical male and female characters appeared in the plot, or were offered as roles which players could adopt.[31] The nature of the colour in graphics was also discussed in gender terms (for example, more colourful graphics were more attractive to women).[32] The case against sexist content seems more plausible when some of the more pornographic 'adult' games are considered. For example, the controversial arcade game *Custer's Revenge* had rape as its goal.[33] The next step taken by some of these commentators was to explain the content by reference to the conditions of production – that the vast majority of game designers were male.[34] Clearly, a number of the early male designers of arcade games had come from a background of playing *Spacewar*, which seemed to have severely restricted their creative horizons.

However, the picture was rendered a little more complicated when, in the late 1970s, the game *PacMan* was found to be nearly as popular with women as with men, challenging assumptions about the masculinity of arcade games. Analysts sought explanations in the particular content of *PacMan*. One commentator argued that 'directing the faceless, featureless *PacMan* through its model-home maze is less threatening and more closely related to hide-and-seek games than to nuclear holocaust.'[35]

The few female games designers in the industry suggested a very different mode of analysis, emphasizing the changing context of games-playing.[36] *PacMan* appeared when coin-op games were actually becoming more pervasive than pinball had ever been and when video games had achieved some respectability outside the arcade in places such as lounges and restaurants. These designers argued that whereas the arcade atmosphere had been less comfortable, the new sites were more socially acceptable places for women. A similar point, in fact, had been argued in relation to pinball itself. It was only when American suburban shopping centres decided that it was profitable to allow arcades into the plazas earlier in the 1970s that some of the plusher chains first managed to attract a few women pinball players. The history of pinball thus supports the argument that an important factor in the success of *PacMan* with women was that video games were becoming generally more accessible.

Yet, even this analysis fails to address the nature of the 'interest' which is involved. As in the case of a record, a particular game may be enjoyable to a wide range of people. Alternatively, games-playing may be an activity in which many people would happily engage on an occasional basis. *PacMan* benefited from this less 'committed' form of interest. But the situation where games have a public currency within particular groups of young males is another matter. This involves a continuous interest in games in general, and entails a more regular participation in a collective activity. It was to this core of enthusiasts that the constant flow of new game releases appeared to be principally addressed and it was this level of interest associated with the arcades and other male-dominated locales which formed the basis for a greater enthusiasm among young males for both home video games and the later computer games. The arcade not only provided a familiarity with games-playing skills, but communal practices were carried into the use of domestic machines, despite the image of the isolated games-player in the home.

Games-playing: games and hobby PCs

Although video games-players were very significant, they were not the only key actors shaping the experience of games. We also need to account for the interest of computer hobbyists. As with the hackers who designed the earlier games, the enthusiasts who built and bought the first micro-computers in the mid-1970s sought ways to show this black box in operation. The first demonstrations involved controlling sound, and these were soon followed by programs which produced a display of flashing lights. Games played the sale role, demonstrating the PC in action and illustrating the computer's capabilities. In fact, games became one of the first forms of software to be sold as a product, with some hobbyists converting the classic mainframe and mini-computer games to the smaller machines, as well as copying the arcade favourites.

Games also constituted a new type of programming challenge: squeezing the complex structures designed for minis and mainframes onto the small memory of a micro-computer. More generally, games were still vehicles for learning about the machines. Programs such as *Spacewar* could be justified as an exercise in controlling animated computer graphics, while adventure games involved planning and familiarity with the structure of databases. Moreover, it was possible to program and run games even with very limited equipment.

Finally, these male hobbyists also saw games-playing as being of interest for its own sake for reasons that went beyond the particular narrative content of these products. Games were puzzles within a computerized environment. As such, they were somewhat like programming itself. Thus, early computer magazines presented games-playing as an acceptable activity – as a source of relaxation in the midst of programming. This community never rejected playing as a misuse of machines: games were one of their many applications. These hobbyists were not only to provide a market for the new computer game products, they were also a legitimizing force, pointing to the potentially constructive side of this software genre in contrast to the commentators who later cast games in a dimmer light.

Games-playing: male youth and computer games

Micro-computers reached a far wider audience during the 1980s, especially among male youth.[37] Part of the appeal lay in computing *per se*, part in the fact that these early forms of PC provided a new vehicle for interactive games. But there was always more to games-playing than the moment in front of the screen.[38]

Talking about computers and games, both in and out of school, became an important dimension of boys' discussions. As with music, there was always scope for evaluating the latest releases and, as in the arcades, passing on game-play tips. Moreover, because the computer was programmable, home-brew games and special effects could also be shown to or even developed with peers. Then there was the exchange of software within school, either for copying purposes, or simply to borrow. Nor was school, including computing clubs, the only location for such interaction. Enthusiastic games-players sometimes transformed existing computer clubs and micro-computer shops into alternative arcades. Shop managers shared mixed feelings about such developments with exhibitors at computer shows: hordes of players monopolizing machines might be deterring other, less game-oriented, custom.

All these public settings provided opportunities to try out products, to play in collective settings and to make contact with those who shared an interest – which could mean a chance to exchange games and other software. Moreover, by appropriating these public spaces, boys, albeit perhaps relatively few boys, became very visible to the producers of hardware, software and magazines. Little wonder that these staff and other commentators so easily assumed that PCs and games-playing were a totally male domain, and showed surprise that girls demonstrated any interest at all. The actual situation was far more complex.

One reason for detailing the nature of boys' collective interest is to underline the fact that this social dimension simply did not exist for girls. In contrast to the beliefs of some commentators, available statistics show that girls did actually use computers – mainly for playing games. But behind the figures we need to see the difference in the experience of games. Like boys, girls were not simply isolated users; they played with other family members and with friends who visited their homes. But, unlike boys, that was usually the limit of their interest; for girls the currency which computer talk and games-play had among some young male peers did not exist. Girls would usually rely on brothers to inform them about the latest game and there was simply not the same amount of talk about games, nor the practice of exchanging them. Few girls visited or played games in the various public sites which were geared to micro-computers and, when they did, attendance was not so much with male peers as with family. At home, girls tended to have less say than boys as to which games should be purchased, often playing whatever games were available. Hence, despite all the analysis of masculine games texts, the majority of games played by girls were also of the fast, arcade-style action, reflecting the general predominance of this genre.

Games-playing in the 1990s

For children maturing after the boom of the 1980s, while games might have lost some glamour as a latest innovation, they had become thoroughly established as one more option among a repertoire of activities. But games occupied a modest place on the whole. In one UK survey, where in fact video games-playing was in the top three preferred pastimes of only 20 per cent of children, games were for the majority a time-filler to occupy moments of boredom.[39] Reinforcing the earlier discussions in this chapter of the social nature of games, almost all of those surveyed sometimes played two-player games and two-thirds played at a friend's house, while a number mentioned their pleasure in watching other people play and talking about games. This fits in with observations from other qualitative research I have conducted,[40] as does the finding that many parents (about 40 per cent in that survey) regulated the amount of time their children could play – just as they regulated the amount of time children spend in front of the TV.

While there have always been some adults who play games, the difference as we move through the 1990s and beyond is that there is now a generation effect as the teenagers and young adults of the 1980s grow older. The fact that games are not simply children's toys is underlined by the continuity of games-playing among this cohort who have grown up with games. A mid-1990 UK survey showed that 30 per cent of owners of 16-bit consoles were aged 17–30 years[41] (with 11 per cent older still); and, looking at subsequent 1997 European data, the average age of Sony Playstation owners was 22 years; 45 per cent of them were in employment.[42]

Partly because of the age of this cohort, qualitative research has recorded especially young, single adults using games mostly as a time-filler between other activities, when spare moments arise or as a way of winding down after work.[43] As in the case of children, the novelty of a newly acquired game can lead to more intense playing for a while. On the whole, though, and while enjoyable, games-playing is once again a secondary activity that would not displace, for example, going out with friends. The same qualitative research suggests that there does not appear to be much difference between men and women as regards this way of using games at this stage in their life course.

What changes with the formation of shared households, and especially the arrival of children, is that the moments of individual free disposable time are fewer compared to singles because of new demands and social commitments to others. There are examples of people continuing to play routinely, if not for much time in total, up until the birth of children and then those spare moments are lost, accounted for by childcare responsibilities. That said, it was still possible to find mainly males in their 20s and 30s who could carve out some moments for quick games – or for going on the Internet, which has now emerged as an alternative in some respects. But because of existing gender roles, the demands on, and hence the time structures of, married women with children change dramatically from those of single adult women. Just as such women had found it difficult to find time for, and to justify, exploring computing in general or following up any interest in games in the 1980s,[44] so is it likewise for the next generation.

Lessons to be learnt

While there are now numerous analyses of interactive games as texts,[45] this chapter has offered an account of the social shaping of games as a cultural form. It has charted the complex lineages through which these emerged and developed, including numerous actors and different manifestations. It has explored the various tensions that have existed over the years, uncertainties over whether games were a fad, a marginal form of entertainment or, alternatively, whether they posed a threat to the identity of various hardware products. While a recognizable cultural industry has now evolved, its fortunes have been somewhat volatile, with different business models, changing hardware platforms and continuing concerns about the nature and quality of innovation.

That history has also drawn attention to the different constituencies of users who have played various roles in supporting games from the earliest days: in developing and refining them, in making them visible through demonstration, in using and acquiring them as well as in building a culture of games-playing. In other words, we have seen the social shaping of consumption as well as reactions to how that consumption was represented. In particular, to understand differences in gender, this account has pointed to the need to understand the history and context of consumption as well as the nature of these texts, the different modes of gendered consumption and, into the 1990s, what games-playing means for the first mass-market generation of users as they grow older.

Notes

1   This section is mainly based on Steven Levy, *Hackers: Heroes of the Revolution* (Garden City, NY, Doubleday, 1984); Stewart Brand, 'Spacewar: fanatic life and symbolic death among the computer bums', *Rolling Stone*, 7 December 1972; and Paul Freiberger and Michael Swaine, *Fire in the Valley: the Making of the Personal Computer* (Berkeley, Osborne/McGraw-Hill, 1984).

2   For the history of arcade developments, see T. Perry, C. Truxal and P. Wallich, 'Video games: the electronic big bang', *IEEE Spectrum*, 19 (12) (December 1982), pp. 20–33; Craig Kubey, *The Winners Book of Video Games* (London, W.H. Allen, 1982); John Price, 'Social science research on video games', *Journal of Popular Culture*, 18 (4) (Spring 1985), pp. 111–25; Peter Bernstein, 'Atari and the video games explosion', *Fortune*, 104 (2) (July 1981), pp. 40–6; Judith Larsen and Everett Rogers, *Silicon Valley Fever: Growth of High Technology Culture* (London, Unwin, 1984); Sidney Kaplan, 'The image of amusement arcades and the differences in male and female video game playing', *Journal of Popular Culture*, 1983, pp. 93–8; Sue Smith, 'Coin detected in pocket: videogames as icons', in C. Geist and S. Nachbar (eds), *The Popular Culture Reader* (Bowling Green, Bowling Green University Popular Press, 1983), pp. 145–51; Aaron Latham, 'Videogames star wars', *New York Times Magazine*, 25 October 1981, pp. 100–12.

3   Eric Egli and Lawrence Meyers, 'The role of video game playing in adolescent life: is there reason to be concerned?', *Bulletin of the Psychonomic Society*, 22 (4) (1984), p. 309.

4   For the history of home video games developments, see Ralph Baer, 'Television games: their past present and future', *IEEE Transactions on Consumer Electronics*, CE-23 (4) (November 1979), pp. 496–504; M. Jones, 'Video games as psychological tests', *Simulations and Games*, 15 (2) (June 1984), pp. 133–4; Thomas Murrey, 'The boom in video games', *Dun's Review*, 108 (3) (September 1976), pp. 54–5; 'Video games', *Screen Digest* (July 1977), pp. 127–9; Stephan Bristow, 'The history of video games', *IEEE Transactions on Consumer Electronics* (February 1977), pp. 58–68; J. Perry, C. Truxal and P. Wallich, 'Design case history: the Atari video computer system', *IEEE Spectrum* (March 1983), pp. 45–51; Peter Nulty, 'Why the craze won't quit', *Fortune* (15 November 1982), pp. 114–24.

5   A number of the firms which first entered the market saw a potential in programmable consoles which went beyond games, as a more general entertainment software player. Part of the reason for leaving was that this usage never materialized.

6   Personal interview with Atari management in Britain (8 July 1986).

7   See Leslie Haddon, 'Home computers: the making of a consumer electronic', *Science as Culture*, 2 (1987), 7–51.

8   This is clear from surveys, my own samples and other qualitative research, including a longitudinal study at the Centre for Mass Communications Research in Leicester University: Graham Murdock, Paul Hartmann and Perry Gray, 'Contextualising home computing: resources and practices', in Roger Silverstone and Erich Hirsch (eds), *Consuming Technologies: Media and Information in Private Spaces* (London, Routledge, 1992) and David Skinner's unpublished doctorate research 'Technology Consumption and the Future: the Experience of Home Computing', Brunel University, 1992.

9   Michael Hayes and Stuart Dinsey, *Games War. Video Games: a Business Review* (London, Bowerdean, 1995), p. 12.

10 Many of the details and viewpoints in the following pages are derived from issues of the home computer industry trade press, *Computer Trade Weekly*.

11 David Sheff, *Game Over: Nintendo's Battle to Dominate an Industry* (London, Hodder and Stoughton, 1993).

12 Monopolies and Mergers Commission, *Video Games: a Report on the Supply of Video Games in the UK* (London, HMSO, March 1995).

13 Much of the section on this stage in the life of consoles draws on Eric Lake's current doctorate research on video games development at Cranfield University, 'Mapping the Process of Product Innovation'.

14 'Global interactive entertainment: big growth in spending', *Screen Digest* (February, 1997), p. 34.

15 'Interactive entertainment software: rapid maturing market', *Screen Digest* (June, 1997), p. 130.

16 Alan Cawson, Leslie Haddon and Ian Miles, *The Shape of Things to Consume: Delivering Information Technology into the Home* (Aldershot, Avebury, 1995). Also, Roger Silverstone and Leslie Haddon, 'Design and domestication of information and communication technologies: technical change and everyday life', in R. Mansell and R. Silverstone (eds), *Communication by Design: the Politics of Information and Communication Technologies* (Oxford, Oxford University Press, 1996).

17 Gillian Skirrow provides a history of the adventure genre which traces its features back to previous texts: Gillian Skirrow, 'Hellivision: an analysis of video games', in Colin MacCabe (ed.), *High Theory/Low Culture: Analysing Popular Television and Film* (Manchester, Manchester University Press, 1986), pp. 115–42.

18 Edward Trapanski, *Special When Lit: a Visual History of the Pinball* (New York, Dolphin Books, 1979).

19 M. Litwark, *Reel Power: the Struggle for Influence in the New Hollywood* (London, Sidgwick and Jackson, 1987), p. 100.

20 Cawson et al., *The Shape of Things to Consume*.

21   See Terri Toles, 'Video games and American military ideology', in Vincent Mosco and Janet Wasko (eds), *The Critical Communications Reviews*, vol. III: *Popular Culture and Media Events* (Norwood, Ablex, 1985), pp. 207–23; Nancy Needham, 'Thirty billion quarters can't be wrong: or can they? A look at the impact of video games on American youth', *Today's Education, 1982–3 Annual* (1983), pp. 52–5; Price, 'Social science research on video games', pp. 111–25; Egli and Meyers, 'The role of video game playing in adolescent life', pp. 309–12; *EL News*, 'Anti-video game movement gathering momentum', *Electronic Learning*, 1 (3) (1982), pp. 12–13.

22   Neil Frude, *The Intimate Machine: Close Encounters with New Computers* (London, Century, 1983), p. 68.

23   This same concern has been carried into writing from an overtly socialist perspective, as in Tony Solomonides and Les Levidow, *Compulsive Technology: Computers as Culture* (London, Free Association Books, 1985), p. 6.

24   Discussed in Sherry Turkle, *The Second Self: Computers and the Human Spirit* (London, Granada, 1984).

25   Tom Panelas, 'Adolescents and video games: consumption of leisure and the social construction of the peer group', *Youth and Society*, 15 (1) (September 1983), pp. 51–65.

26   Desmond Ellis, 'Video arcades, youth and trouble', *Youth and Society*, 16 (1) (September 1984), pp. 47–8.

27   There seems to be little public market research available on arcades. These figures are derived from a compilation of small-scale observational studies.

28   This concern about anti-social behaviour and isolation also partly reflects a general reservation about male over-involvement with 'things', and especially with technology.

29   An example of this type of analysis would be Nancy Kreinberg and Elizabeth Stage, 'EQUALS in computer technology', in Jan Zimmerman (ed.), *The Technological Woman: Interfacing with Tomorrow* (New York, Praeger, 1983), p. 255.

30   Needham, 'Thirty billion quarters can't be wrong', p. 54.

31   Toles, 'Video games and American military ideology', p. 214.

32   Perry et al., 'Video games: the electronic big bang', p. 26; Price, 'Social science research on video games', p. 122.

33   D. Talbot, 'Pac-man kills kids: video horrors', *Mother Jones*, April 1983. The game was withdrawn after a campaign by Women Against Pornography.

34   Perry and others estimated that there were about 100 video game designers in the US when they were writing – about four or five of these were women mostly designing home video games. Perry et al., 'Video games: the electronic big bang', pp. 28–9.

35   Smith, 'Coin detected in pocket', p. 150.

36   Perry et al., 'Video games: the electronic big bang', p. 31.

37   As a rough guide, surveys suggest that boys' use of, knowledge of and desire for computers is at least twice as great as that of girls. Boys are by far the biggest users of PCs, followed by girls and then adult males. Details are outlined in Leslie Haddon, 'The Roots and Early History of the British Home Computer Market', unpublished doctoral thesis, University of London, 1988.

38   Based on the author's research which involved interviews with boys and girls and observations in a boys' computer club.

39   Guy Cumberbatch, Andrea Maguire and Samantha Woods, *Children and Video Games: an Exploratory Study* (Birmingham, Aston University, 1993).

40   Leslie Haddon, 'Locating the virtual community in the households of Europe', a report for NCR, 1998.

41   Hayes and Dinsey, *Games War*, p. 13.

42   *Screen Digest*, 'Interactive Entertainment Software' (June 1997).

43   From my Internet study cited above, but also reflected in German research: Daniela Schlütz, 'The Indirect Effects of the Home Computer: a Qualitative Study of How the Use of Computer Entertainment Affects Everyday Leisure Time', unpublished thesis, London School of Economics, September 1997.

44   Leslie Haddon, 'Researching gender and home computers', in K. Sorensen and A. Berg

(eds), *Technology and Everyday Life: Trajectories and Transformations* (Trondheim, University of Trondheim, 1990), pp. 89–108.

45 Apart from Skirrow, 'Hellivision', these include Mary Fuller and Henry Jenkins, 'Nintendo and new world travel writing: a dialogue' and Ted Friedman, 'Making sense of software: computer games and interactive textuality', both in Steven Jones (ed.), *Cybersociety: Computer Mediated Communication and Community* (London, Sage, 1995), pp. 57–72 and pp. 73–89; David Myers, 'Computer games genres', *Play and Culture*, 3 (1990), pp. 286–301; David Myers, 'Computer games semiotics', *Play and Culture*, 4 (1991), pp. 334–45; David Myers, 'Time, symbol transformation and computer games', *Play and Culture*, 5 (1992), pp. 441-57.

IV

Future perfect?

Introduction

The chapters in this final part open up a series of key analyses of how future transformations are being understood. They have been selected to explore the nature of the new and transformed communities and identities which are emerging in response to changing communication environments, systems and relationships. First we explore some questions about the changing spaces, networks and forces which are transforming the old monoliths and monuments of national cultures, especially in a European, trans-national and global context. As earlier chapters have suggested, much discussion of this focuses on the erosion of the old patterns of regulation, control and allegiance by new networks of communication.

Do new information and communication technologies, as it is argued, herald new eras of cultural diversity and freedom? Do they represent a break with historical continuity?

Public service broadcasting is a notion rooted in the nation-state, a key institution of modernity, and something which has been in place as the traditional media have emerged and grown. Mass communications have not simply coincided with the nation-state but have been implicated in the formation of national cultures. Now, however, new communication technologies and regulatory regimes, not to mention new political and cultural organizations, are opening up new forms of association and imagined communities. The development of 'Europe' is pertinent to the UK in this context, with the EU potentially allowing new models or forms of communication, transforming the boundedness of nation-states and national communications.

In Chapter 17, Morley and Robins explore how 'community' can be reimagined or become unstable, and how the new media and communication technologies can be used to create and usher in new forms for public discourse. Their concern is to link a new politics of communication with a politics of space, place and community; and they do this by exploring the re-configuration of what they refer to as 'image spaces', with reference, in particular, to the imagined, mediated community of 'Europe'. Their analysis provides a persuasive account of the possibilities that new communication technologies and regulatory regimes offer for new forms of community and association, crossing the traditional boundaries of communities and nations. Their argument recognizes the demise of public service broadcasting, trends towards privatization, the liberalization of markets and the crisis of Fordism. Within this context they argue that new deregulated broadcasting systems and their corporations reshape image flows, and from these new image markets come new senses of space and place. They point out that tendencies towards cultural homogenization are countered by cultural strategies of localization, through which senses of 'history' and 'community' are articulated and constructed. Their concern is for new forms of association and new identities which are not introverted and nostalgic but look outwards and forwards from the local. So, although apparently rooted in a political economy approach, their concern is with the possibilities of progressive space which are available under emerging reconfigurations.

Individual, group and collective forms of imagination, although powerful, face material and regulatory constraint. Perhaps the key way in which this is taking place today is the ever-growing capacity and deployment of new information and communication technologies for surveillance across a range of physical and virtual social and cultural arenas. This has profound consequences forcitizenship and democracy, and in Chapter 18 David Lyon, focusing on the Internet, explores how surveillance is best understood – specifically, as a capitalist, bureaucratic or panoptic phenomenon. In this he poses a range of important questions regarding the growth and 'normalization' of surveillance technologies, systems and practices.

The conditions of organized surveillance in society and culture have been subject to considerable debate as they have been transformed and sought to keep pace with the modern period. Surveillance, and the control and power derived from monitoring populations, have figured prominently in a range of dystopian visions; as, for example, in Orwell's *1984* with the 'Big Brother' telescreens. Many have argued that the scope and scale of surveillance technologies and practices are best conceived as an electronic panopticon (Lyon, 1993). This image invokes both Jeremy Bentham's plans in the eighteenth century for a model prison and Michel Foucault's influential theoretical analysis of the development of the panoptic form of modern surveillance power, inspection and domination (Foucault, 1977). Bentham's prisons were designed to permit planned surveillance of a specific institutional kind, the 'all-seeing eye and gaze' which enforced discipline by means of the imposition of architecture enabling constant surveillance and no privacy. For Bentham, the early modern, pre-electronic form involved total asymmetry of gaze coupled with conditions of uncertainty, social atomization and unregulated profit-making. For Foucault, the panopticon represents an expanding set of technologies of power and discipline which have become increasingly widespread, pervasive and interconnected in modern times.

In what ways might modern systems of electronic surveillance, recording and monitoring be said to display panoptic features? Anthony Giddens (1990) has noted two inter-related levels of concern and analysis on this question. First is the general rise in the accumulation of coded information and data and its relationships to the modern nation-state. Second is the more direct and active sense of surveillance, as developed in the observing and monitoring of the workplace and production process. To these one might add that many areas of public life are now subject to forms of surveillance with the increasing use of CCTV and video to monitor traffic movement, city centres, shopping malls and other public spaces. New communication and computer technologies have greatly encouraged the growth and convergence of surveillance and databases. While these developments transform the ways in which order is imposed and maintained, the next chapter provides a counterpoint in its emphasis on the disordered nature of contemporary times and conditions.

In Chapter 19, Ien Ang provides an analysis which, perhaps disconcertingly, emphasizes the uncertain and chaotic nature of postmodernity. She draws on McLuhan's metaphor of the 'global village', arguing that this has to be redefined to emphasize not global homogenization but chaos, uncertainty and disorder. She raises some key questions about audiences and media reception in contemporary times. At the heart of the discussion is her suggestion that the transmission paradigm which has underpinned the study of communication until the mid-1980s is now in crisis, out-moded and overtaken by events, including the proliferation of new communication networks and systems at local and global levels. No longer, Ang suggests, can the transparency of meaning in communication be assumed. She argues for the inversion of some of the traditional preoccupations of communication theory. Rather than an emphasis on rational, meaningful communication as a basis for understanding the emergent world social order, she calls for a complete rethink of the 'global village' to take account of its chaotic, dispersed, uneven, indeterminate and uncertain nature. She sees such a shift of position as essential for the development of new critical theorizing to confront the challenge of new, postmodern times.

Ang argues that contemporary transformations in global media and communication systems demand nothing less than a radical rethink in how communication should be conceived. In the place of the old, even obsolete, securities of the mass transmission paradigm, the fractured, excessive and contradictory nature of capitalist postmodernity is held to require new, previously unthinkable, ways of conceiving of the expanding economies and cultures of difference and diversity which are now unleashed in the global capitalist system. If the reconfiguration of 'old' media, together with shifts in media and cultural relations occasioned by new media and communication networks, have challenged thinking about 'communication', they have also had major and related consequences for debates about democracy.

As we have seen, the major fault line in current approaches lies in the divide between 'emancipatory' as opposed to 'repressive' versions of the nature and origins of the shifts underway, in debates of a profoundly polarized nature. Chapter 20 returns to this focus on democracy and the politics of new media and communication technologies. John Street considers the arguments for and against 'electronic democracy', evaluating the democratizing potential of the Internet. His starting point, following Rheingold (Chapter 14), is that recent interest in the Net has revived the debate about 'electronic democracy'. On the one side techno-libertarians and political activists enthuse about extending the possibilities for a virtual polity and renewed public sphere, revitalizing participation and the democratic ideal. On the other side are those who identify the accelerating demise of democracy in these same transformations. Street's discussion examines and summarizes what is at stake in these competing and polarized debates and argues that the politics of electronic democracy demand a renewed politics of technology.

In Chapter 21, the final chapter, Manuel Castells presents an account of the fundamentally new social morphology he sees us as emerging in the network society. For Castells, information and communication technologies are crucial to this new society, although he distances himself from the 'information society theorists' discussed by Frank Webster in Chapter 8. The end of the twentieth century, he argues, is characterized by the very rapid arrival of a new technological paradigm with information machines at its core.

The new world which Castells outlines has its origins in three independent processes: first, a series of developments in information technologies. Although he explicitly rejects technological determinism, he argues that technology has captured all the processes that constitute human societies and has altered fundamentally the terms in which they function. Second are the economic crises which have been experienced by statism and capitalism and the global restructuring to which these have given rise. Third is the growth of social and cultural movements, in which traditional, class-based interests have been replaced by human rights, feminism and environmentalism. These three processes are constituting a new informational and global economy, a new, virtual, culture and a new form of society – the network society. These societies are composed of flows and networks, which he sees as replacing time and space. These networks organize the positions of actors and organizations in societies; the relevance of a social unit is conditioned by its presence or absence in a specific network. There are hierarchical differences between positions in a network, and between networks, but these are unstable and changing. Within networks there are asymmetries between different positions.

The consequences of flows as the basis of society are many. The ability to generate new knowledge or to gather information depends on access to flows of such knowledge or information; so the power of organizations and individuals depends on their positioning. In this sense, we live in a knowledge-based informational society, although Castells argues that there is no single, privileged source of science or information. The productivity and competitiveness of the economic system depends on the position of economic units in the networks of the global economy. Flows of images by new media are fundamental elements in societies and in Castells' analysis. The political system is now dependent on the skilled manipulation of messages and symbols and 'reality' is increasingly mediated: politics that does not exist in the media simply does not exist. Power no longer lies in the barrel of the gun but on the editing consoles of the television network's computers. The materiality of our existence is made up of flows and societies are no longer structured on the basis of work. Finally, Castells' analysis is concerned with identities: recurrent changes of roles and situations in society require people constantly to redefine their identities.

According to Castells' analysis, society is increasingly structured around networks – and individuals, groups, regions and nations are switched on and off according to their relevance to the flow. Transformation has resulted in a new stage wherein flows and information are the basis of the social structure – the beginning of new social orders.

In this final Chapter, Castells ties together the very broad range of phenomena he addresses in his trilogy *The Information Age* (Castells, 1996, 1997, 1998): the IT revolution, the collapse of the Eastern bloc, the restructuring of capitalism, globalization, the growth of the Pacific region, feminism, environmentalism and more. He provides an analysis of contemporary trends in a way that foregrounds the continuities and transformations under way, and the role of the media and communication technologies in these processes.

References

Castells, Manuel (1996) *The Information Age: Economy, Society and Culture*, vol. 1: *The Rise of the Network Society*. Oxford: Blackwell.
Castells, Manuel (1997) *The Information Age: Economy, Society and Culture*, vol. 2: *The Power of Identity*. Oxford: Blackwell.
Castells, Manuel (1998) *The Information Age: Economy, Society and Culture*, vol. 3: *End of Millennium*. Oxford: Blackwell.
Foucault, Michel (1977) *Discipline and Punish*. New York: Vintage.
Giddens, Anthony (1990) *The Consequences of Modernity*. Cambridge: Polity Press.
Lyon, David (1993) 'An electronic panopticon? A sociological critique of surveillance theory', *The Sociological Review*, 41: 653–78.

Reimagined communities? New media, new possibilities
David Morley and Kevin Robins

Very much remains to be done by way of detailed discussions and proposals, but we cannot in any case live much longer with the confusions of the existing 'international' economy and the existing 'nation state'. If we cannot find and communicate social forms of more substance than these, we shall be condemned to endure the accelerating pace of false and frenetic nationalisms and of reckless and uncontrollable global transnationalism.

Raymond Williams, *Towards 2000*, 1983

In the present period, we are seeing processes of political economic restructuring and transformation which involves changes in the historical system of accumulation and social organisation. At the heart of these historical developments is a process of spatial restructuring and reconfiguration. This process is the major concern of the following discussion. It involves at once a transformation of the spatial matrix of society and of the subjective experience of, and orientation to, space and spatiality. Consideration requires a social theory that is informed by the geographical imagination.

Our particular concern is with the media industries, which are implicated in these socio-spatial processes in quite significant and distinctive ways. We want to explore the nature of current transformations, the breaks and continuities, and to assess the implications of the changing configuration of 'image spaces'. Through the prism of geographical analysis it becomes possible to take up some key questions concerning the relationship between economic and cultural aspects of these transformations, to explore the articulations of economic spaces and cultural spaces. Following this line of enquiry, issues around the politics of communication converge with the politics of space and place. Questions of communication

This chapter is taken from *Spaces of Identity: Global Media, Electronic Landscapes and Cultural Boundaries* (London, Routledge, 1995), pp. 26–42.

are also about the nature and scope of community. In a world of 'false and frenetic nationalisms and of reckless and uncontrollable global trans-nationalism', the struggle for meaningful communities and 'actual social identities' is more and more difficult: 'we have to explore new forms of variable societies, in which over the whole range of social purpose different sizes of society are defined for different kinds of issue and decision' (Williams, 1983: 198–9).

Beyond Fordism?

What is the broader context within which the transformation of media industries and markets is taking place? One of the most suggestive ways of looking at the present period of upheaval has been that developed by the Regulation School of political economists (see *inter alia*, Aglietta, 1979; Billaudot and Gauron, 1985; Boyer, 1986a, b; Lipietz, 1987) with their analyses of the decline of the social system they call Fordism. Within this perspective, Fordism is understood in terms of the articulation of a particular 'regime of accumulation', centred around mass production and mass consumption, with an appropriate 'mode of regulation'. 'Social regulation' is a matter of both the organisational and institutional structures, including the apparatuses of the (Keynesian) state, but also the norms, habits, and internalised rules governing the lifeworld – the 'architecture of socialisation' (Billaudot and Gauron, 1985: 22) – which ensure social reproduction and the absorption of conflicts and tensions, always provisionally, over a certain period of time. What is being argued is that Fordism as a mode of capitalist development and as a historically specific coherence of accumulation and regulation, has now reached its limits. The inherent control problems of Fordism – for example, rising wages and declining productivity, overcapacity and market saturation, competition from low-wage countries, increasing costs for public services – have brought the system into crisis. This crisis, moreover, is structural (rather than simply cyclical), and it is a matter of political, social and cultural crisis as much as of economic decline and stagnation. In so far as the resources of Fordism/ Keynesianism have become exhausted, the future of capitalist development demands a fundamental and innovative restructuring of accumulation and regulation.

If the historical nature of Fordism and the dynamics of its crisis are becoming clear enough, the question of its successor regime of accumulation is more problematic and contentious. What lies beyond Fordism? There are many accounts of post-Fordism, increasingly congealing into a new orthodoxy of optimism, which identify a new social coherence centred around what is often referred to as an emergent regime of flexible accumulation. So-called flexible specialisation is manifest in new forms of decentralised production and in the design and product mix aimed at niche markets; demassified enterprises (in which production is no longer concentrated in large factories on a single site) abandon economies of scale in favour of economies of scope; and workers supposedly assume new skills and responsibilities and a new sense of autonomy. This perspective finds its apogee in the work of Michael Piore and Charles Sabel (1984) and other celebrants of the 'Third Italy' and the 'Emilian model' (a somewhat idealistic model of the potential for regional economic development, based on decentralised networks of small, artisan-based companies, using new computer technologies, as occurred in the Emilia-Romagna district in Italy, during the 1970s). These authors see the transcendence of Fordism in terms of a kind of return to feudalism, with the growth of a new class of artisans and the emergence of localised industrial districts. Whilst there are certain important insights here [. . .] there are also strongly ideological elements informing this new myth of flexibility. Post-Fordism is, in effect, imagined as anti-Fordism: it is quite simply the inverse of, and antithesis to, the rigid and massified system of Fordism.

This kind of idealised and teleological account is clearly unsatisfactory. Any real-world transition beyond Fordism will inevitably be a great deal more complex, unruly and uncertain. It cannot be a matter of an evolutionary movement from one distinct social system to another; rather, it is a process that promises to be fraught with turbulence and disruption. Projected futures cannot simply and effortlessly dissolve away the solidity of inherited social structures, infrastructures and relations. The process of transformation is complex and uneven, and it is genuinely difficult to establish whether the present period marks the emergence of a post-Fordist society, whether it should be characterised as neo-Fordist, or whether, in fact, it remains a period of late Fordism. On what basis is, say, flexible specialisation classified as a distinguishing feature of post-Fordism? The basis of definition and periodisation is, in fact, not at all self-evident. In a complex process of change, we have to ask by what criteria we might identify the components of a new phase of accumulation, and also how we do so without falling into the trap of teleologism. We must be clear that, in so far as the direction of change will be a matter of struggle and contestation, neither the emergence nor the nature of any society beyond Fordism is predetermined or inevitable.

The present discussion is concerned with one major area of change centring around the nature and meaning of space. What transformations are taking place in the social production of space, place and spatiality, and what new political logics does this set in motion? Our contention is that space is of paramount importance in this period of transition and restructuring:

> the current crisis is *accentuating spatiality* and revealing more clearly than ever before the spatial and locational strategies of capitalist accumulation and the necessity for labour and all segments of society 'peripheralised' by capitalist development and restructuring to create spatially conscious counter-strategies at all geographical scales, in all territorial locales. (Soja, 1985: 188, our emphasis)

Idealising visions of post-Fordism pick up on this new salience of space, but they do so only very partially. What they perceive is the transmutation of a centralised space economy into new forms of decentralisation and dissemination; they emphasise the increasing importance of localised industrial districts and zones like those described by the economist Alfred Marshall early this century. Reality is more complex and contradictory, however. If the growing significance of neo-Marshallian local economic districts is indeed an identifiable trend, then there are also apparently countervailing tendencies towards a global network economy. Manuel Castells has powerfully described how what he calls the information mode of development, based upon new communications systems and information technologies, is bringing about 'the transformation of spatial *places* into *flows and channels* – what amounts to the *delocalisation of the processes of production and consumption*' (1983: 5, our emphasis). Castells argues that corporate information networks are underpinning the expansion and integration of the capitalist world system, realising the possibility of a world assembly line, and opening up truly global markets. 'The new space of a world capitalist system', he writes, 'is a space of variable geometry, formed by locations hierarchically ordered in a continuously changing network of flows' (1983: 7). What we are moving towards is a fundamentally delocalised world order articulated around a small number of 'concentrated centres for production of knowledge and storage of information as well as centres for emission of images and information' (1983: 6), nerve centres in the cybernetic grids, command and control headquarters of the world financial and industrial system. The consequence, Castells believes, is 'the formation of a new historical relationship between space and society' (1983: 3).

The elaboration of a new spatial order is a consequence, then, of two contrary dynamics. Such complexity, has, of course, always characterised the production of space under capitalism. The historical sequence of capitalist spatialities, which has always manifested itself through the geography of uneven territorial development, has been a consequence of the interplay between centripetal and centrifugal forces, between centralisation and decentralisation, agglomeration and dispersal, homogenisation and differentiation. David Harvey (1985) has identified a fundamental developmental logic underpinning this contradictory process. Capital has always sought to overcome spatial barriers and to improve the 'continuity of flow'. It remains the case, however, that spatial constraints always exist and persist in so far as 'capital and labour must be brought together at a particular point in space for production to proceed' (1985: 145). Mobility and fixity are integrally and necessarily related: 'The ability of both capital and labour power to move . . . from place to place depends upon the creation of fixed, secure, and largely immobile social and physical infrastructures. The ability to overcome space is predicated on the production of space' (Harvey, 1985: 149). There are, then, forces working towards the simultaneous transcendence and disruption of immobility and coherence; both are moments of the same total process of spatial development.

How, then, is this spatial logic working itself out in the present period? On the basis of new information and communications technologies, capital can now be described as hypermobile and hyperflexible, tending towards deterritorialisation and delocalisation. But this is not the only characteristic tendency in the present period. Even if capital significantly reduces the friction of geography, it cannot escape its dependence on spatial fixity. Space and place cannot be annihilated. As Scott Lash and John Urry (1987: 86) argue: 'the effect of heightened spatial indifference has profound effects upon particular places and upon the forms of life that can be sustained within them – contemporary developments may well be heightening the salience of such localities.' The increasing mobility of corporations is associated with the possibility of fractionalising and subdividing operations and situating them in different places, and, in the process, taking advantage of small variations in the nature of different localities. The spatial matrix of contemporary capitalism is one that, in fact, combines and articulates tendencies towards both globalisation and localisation. These new forms of spatial deployment very much reflect the changing organisational structure of accumulation, and, particularly, new patterns of combined corporate integration and disintegration. One developmental logic of capitalist corporations is towards both horizontal and vertical integration, extending the monopolistic logic of concentration that characterised the Fordist regime of accumulation, and this on an increasingly global scale. This continuing integrative process is complemented, however, by certain tendencies towards vertical disintegration, towards the fragmentation of organisational elements into separate and specialised yet functionally interlinked units. This is generally a matter of externalising non-strategic, or, perhaps, unpredictable and variable functions and labour processes – and thereby externalising uncertainty and risk – on the basis of subcontracting or market links.

These emerging organisational transformations take place in and through space and have significant implications for territorial development. Vertical disintegration results in the formation of a localised nexus of small units, often centred around one or a few dominant large companies, and involved in close contractor/subcontractor relationships, continuous information exchange and, thus, spatial proximity. The consequence of the new dynamics of flexible specialisation, with its tendencies towards spatial agglomeration, has been to give a new centrality to local economies (Courlet and Judet, 1986). It is at the level of locality that important new economic and social developments are being worked out. It is precisely this aspect of organisational–territorial transformation that the idealising champions of post-Fordist industrial districts have identified as decisive. They do so in a rather one-sided way, however, disarticulating the local form from its global framework. Territorial complexes of quasi-integrated organisations are extremely vulnerable to external disruptions inflicted by globally mobile and footloose corporations: 'The evolution of flexibility within corporations . . . means that places are created and used up more quickly for the purposes of production or consumption' (Thrift, 1987: 211).

In a context in which 'regions "implode" into localities and nations "explode" into a complex global space' (Albertsen, 1986: 40–5), we have, then, an increasingly direct relationship between the local and the global. And as part of this process, it should be emphasised, the role and significance of the nation state has become ever more problematical and questionable though no less ambitious. For Manuel Castells, the prospects are bleak: 'On the one hand, the space of power is being transformed into flows. On the other hand, the space of meaning is being reduced to microterritories of new tribal communities' (1983: 4). He envisages a new 'space of collective alienation', one in which there is a 'disconnection between people and spatial form', 'the outer experience is cut off from the inner experience' (1983: 7). Castells' prognosis should not be taken lightly. But does the present situation contain other, progressive and hopeful possibilities?

Image spaces

These processes of socio-spatial transformation are the essential context for understanding the nature and significance of developments in the media industries. In this section and the next we want to look at the developing relationships between globalisation and localisation specifically in terms of the logics at work in the audiovisual industries. We want to reorientate the politics of communication towards a politics of space and place. What is the nature of emerging new image markets and image spaces, and what significance do these have for 'imaginary space' (Garnier, 1987), the sense of space and the sense of place? The context for the restructuring of image spaces is the very clear crisis of public service regulation, with its focus on the national arena and national culture. It is a complex process. Thus, whilst it is increasingly clear that technological and economic transformations are surpassing the regulatory capacities of the nation state, there is, at the ideological level, still an obsessive and regressive 'desire to reproduce the nation that has died and the moral and social certainties which have vanished with it . . . to fudge and forge a false unity based on faded images of the nation' (MacCabe, 1988: 29). National ambitions and endeavours will not simply disappear. In this context, none the less, what scope is there for intervention between the global and the local? Castells (1983: 16) again fears the worst: 'the coexistence both of the monopoly of messages by the big networks and of the increasingly narrow codes of local microcultures around their parochial cable TVs'. Is the prospect necessarily and inevitably one of increasing privatism, localism, and 'cultural tribalism' within an electronic global village?

To begin to answer this question, we must look at the new media industries in terms of the complex dynamics of restructuring that we have already discussed in more general terms, particularly the interplay between globalisation and localisation. What is more apparent and remarkable is the accelerating formation of global communications empires, such as those of Murdoch, Berlusconi or Bertelsmann. Internationalisation is not, of course, a new phenomenon but it is now entering a new stage, and the 'maintenance of national sovereignty and identity [is] becoming increasingly difficult as the unities of economic and cultural production and consumption become increasingly transnational' (Collins et al., 1988: 55).

We are seeing the emergence of truly global, decentred, corporations in which diverse media products (film and television, press and publishing, music and video) are being combined into overarching communications empires. Co-financed and co-produced products are made on a global assembly line and are aimed at world markets. Out of a context of collapsing public service traditions, and the consequent deregulation of national broadcasting systems, these mega-corporations are shaping a global space of image flows.

This process of globalisation is very much a function of increasing corporate integration. Various forms of horizontal alignment are apparent, at both national and international levels, with new alliances between broadcasters, film and television producers, publishers, record producers and so on. As a Logica report (1987: 131) makes very clear, it is 'the emergence of new media groups on a vertically integrated scale [that] is the single most important factor in the nature and spread of commercial TV development in Europe.' The progression of Rupert Murdoch, through Fox Broadcasting, 20th Century Fox and Sky Channel, towards the achievement of integrated control over production, distribution and broadcasting is simply the most obvious example. Logica (1987: 268–70) identifies the main functions in the chain of television production as those of originator, programmer, broadcaster, carrier and network operator, and it argues that new media groups are aiming to achieve vertical integration over some or all of the above roles. Total integration is, in fact, likely to be less significant, and less attainable, than the strategic integration of particular functions, and Logica identifies those of carrier/broadcaster, broadcaster/ programmer and programmer/originator as critical to the consolidation of power blocs in the communications industries.

The tendency towards vertical integration is not, then, absolute and encompassing; it is also associated with processes of partial vertical disintegration. Thus, in the case of the American motion picture industry, Michael Storper and Susan Christopherson (1987) suggest that whilst the major studios control and dominate finance, product definition, distribution and marketing, there has been a move towards the externalisation of production and the use of small independent producers. This process of deverticalisation (in which the historical process of vertical integration is reversed) is associated with the externalisation of risk and with the attempt to exploit maximum variety of creative resources. One significant consequence has been a distinctive new pattern of location: independent producers have become spatially concentrated 'because the specialised nature of their services and the constant change in product requires non-routine, frequent market transactions with other firms, such as production companies and major studios' (Christopherson and Storper, 1986: 316). The instability of casualised employment relations and the importance of contact networks generate significant agglomeration tendencies at a local level.

There are many who see this trend towards vertical disintegration and territorial localisation as heralding a benign post-Fordist era of flexible specialisation and cultural industrial districts. It is important, however, to emphasise that vertical disintegration applies primarily to the production sector. As Nicholas Garnham argues: 'It is cultural distribution, not cultural production, that is the key locus of power and profit. It is access to distributions which is the key of cultural plurality' (1986: 31–2). It is also important to emphasise that the logics of integration and disintegration are not contradictory, but, rather, quite complementary. Whilst disintegration and localisation are important, however, integration and globalisation remain the dominant forces (Aksoy and Robins, 1992).

The evolution of localised media production has become a significant issue in Europe, too, assuming distinct and particular forms in specific national and regional contexts (Robins and Cornford, 1994). The case of Britain offers a good example of partial vertical disintegration and, particularly, of its ambiguous and contradictory political implications. Whereas previously the functions of production, editorial and repertoire, and distribution, had been integrated in British broadcasting, with the opening of Channel 4 in 1982 there was a move towards their disaggregation. As with the American film industry, the key innovation was the externalisation of programme-making, which had as its consequence the growth and consolidation of a small-business sector of independent producers. Many of these companies, often involved in politically radical projects, located their activities away from the metropolitan centre, forming into small and localised agglomerations in regional cities (such as Cardiff, Newcastle, Bristol, Leeds, Manchester, Birmingham). These developments succoured real hopes and anticipations for the deconcentration, decentralisation and democratisation of the audiovisual industries. Subsequently, a second wave of deverticalisation emerged, in the context of the government's decision, following the recommendations of the Peacock Report (1986), that the BBC and ITV companies should subcontract 25 per cent of their programmes to independent producers. This new wave of transformation, however, severely undercut idealising expectations and projections. It was increasingly clear that externalisation and subcontracting of production was creating not 'independent' and autonomous programme-makers, but a casualised, segmented and precarious workforce. The creation of an external work-force was above all part of a strategy to break the 'restrictive practices' of the broadcasting unions. 'Flexible working deals', such as those imposed by Tyne Tees, London Weekend Television, TV-AM and Thames Television, were aimed at asserting discipline and control over employees and thereby, of course, strengthening profitability and comparative advantage. Flexibility translates into power: through new contractual relations with internal employees and through the power of market relations with external subcontractors. So-called flexible specialisation combines organisational and functional disintegration or disaggregation with the continued integration of control and co-ordination (Cornford and Robins, 1995).

What, we must now ask, are the political implications of these combined processes of integration and disintegration, globalisation and localisation? What is, in fact, emerging is a certain displacement of national frameworks in favour of perspectives and agendas appropriate to both supra-national and sub-national dynamics. In this process, new questions are being thrown up about the interrelation of economic and market spaces on the one hand, and arenas of cultural consumption and collective identity on the other.

The global politics of communication centres around the international 'war of images' and the struggle between 'image superpowers' (Frèches, 1986). This 'war of position' between transnational corporations is reflected very strongly in the concerns of the European Commission. In a world swamped by television images, the key questions are 'Where will these pictures come from? Who will capture the market – and the employment – for producing and transmitting them?' (Commission of the European Communities, 1986: 3). If US dominance is to be challenged, it is argued, then the construction of a pan-European industry and market is imperative: the common market 'must create conditions for economies of scale to allow European industries to produce in greater quantities, at the lowest possible price, and to recoup their investment costs' (Commission of the European Communities, 1988a: 3). Technical progress is now 'making a mockery of frontiers' and the 'day of purely national audiences, markets and channels is gone': the logic of development must be towards a 'European audiovisual area' (Commission of the European Communities, 1986: 3). In default of this, it is feared that European audiovisual markets are likely to be dominated by the output of American, Japanese or Brazilian corporations.

This strategy is very much aimed at supporting, and integrating, large European corporations. Open skies and network flows are seen as fundamental to the creation of a single large market that will underpin a European industrial and economic renaissance. In this context, 'television without frontiers' (Commission of the European Communities, 1984) is also very much implicated in opening up global advertising markets and spaces. As yet, 'the restrictions and constraints on television advertising across Europe mean that the television set is still relatively unexploited as an advertising medium' (Tydeman and Kelm, 1986: 63). The future of the image industries is very much embedded in that of global advertising; a European audiovisual area is intended to support and facilitate freedom of commercial speech in Europe (Hondius, 1985).

This pan-European space of accumulation is also projected as a space of culture and identity: 'the creation of a large market establishes a European area based on common cultural roots as well as social and economic realities' (Commission of the European Communities, 1987: 3). It is a matter of 'maintaining and promoting the cultural identity of Europe', of 'improving mutual knowledge among our peoples and increasing their consciousness of the life and destiny they have in common' (Commission of the European Communities, 1988b: 3, 11). A transnational politics of culture is worked out in terms of the articulation of European affiliations and allegiances as against, particularly, an Atlanticist cultural identity. But there are problems with what such a 'people's Europe' might be. What is the meaning of this 'sense of belonging to a community composed of countries which are different yet partake of a deep solidarity'

(Commission of the European Communities, 1988b: 4)? Is it possible to translate a multinational administrative unity into any meaningful identity and solidarity? Perhaps it is the differences, what the Commission (1986: 8) recognises as 'richness' and 'cultural diversity', which are more significant in the creation of positive attachments and identities? What must be recognised is that there are forces also working against cultural homogenisation and transnationalism. In the context of centripetal tendencies brought about by the globalisation of communications, there are also centrifugal tendencies to protect and preserve native languages and cultures (Gifreu, 1986). The 'globalisation of social transactions', experienced as an 'internationalisation process' which is gradually robbing Europe of its originality and demobilising its citizens so that European cultural differences are disintegrating (Bassand, 1988: 72), also conspires to produce localised and particularised communities and identities.

Working both against and within a supra-national politics of communication and culture, there is a growing sub-national agenda focused around local and urban cultural identities. Local media are seen as 'regional building tools not only in traditional cultural terms (regional awareness, cultural identity, linguistic crystallisation), but also in terms of economy (provision of jobs, sensitisation of the public to communication technologies, dynamisation of local markets, etc.)' (Crookes and Vittet-Philippe, 1986: 4). As Torsten Hägerstrand argues, in the context of a system society, in which many activities have 'released themselves from the bonds and fetters of place', and in which the media 'have contributed very little to the local and regional content of world-pictures', there arise countervailing tendencies to explore the 'possibility space' of local media, to establish localised arenas for public debate and cultural expression, to elaborate, in fact, meaningful local public spheres (Hägerstrand, 1986: 10, 16, 18).

The British case is again instructive. Tendencies in the organisation of the audiovisual industries towards partial disintegration and the externalisation of production, in a society historically characterised by a national framework of centralised and metropolitan cultural influence, became in the 1980s associated with the elaboration of significant local cultural initiatives. In a number of urban and local contexts, the image industries have been at the forefront of local economic and cultural development strategies. Glasgow ('European City of Culture'), Sheffield, Birmingham, Liverpool, Newcastle, Bradford, Cardiff ('Media City') were prominent in launching initiatives. Following the model of the Greater London Council in the early 1980s, these strategies moved towards the elaboration of localised cultural industrial districts, along neo-Marshallian lines. In many cases, this question of local industrial and cultural public spheres raised questions about public space, and issues of the quality of working and leisure time became translated into policies for the urban fabric and the design of the built environment.

It was not simply a story of economic and cultural radicalisation, however: the local sphere is a contested terrain. Neither was the culture of locality a concern only of progressive local authorities. It was also high on the agenda of communications conglomerates seeking to combine global marketing with the targeting of local and regional consumers. The cultural industries are not just about programme-making, but also and crucially about distribution, and so long as the new conduits of distribution, such as cable and microwave systems, are closed to democratic access, then aspirations for cultural radicalism will remain an empty ideal.

Local initiatives have also been shaped by external political intervention: local autonomy and accountability have been undermined by centrally imposed development strategies. Whilst 'the official story from the centre has been one of rolling back the state and freedom from bureaucratic control', it is in fact the case that 'the "market freedom" supposedly represented by Free Enterprise Zones and Urban Development Corporations is supported by an almost unprecedented level of state subsidy and support' (Duncan and Goodwin, 1988: 272). What we have in the combined strategies of the development corporations for industry, leisure and the urban fabric is an opportunist inflection and incorporation of that earlier localist politics. The arts and cultural industries have been drawn into the heart of this entrepreneurial initiative. Cable is envisaged as a means 'to tackle multifarious difficulties being faced in inner city areas and to achieve successful regeneration' (Cable Authority, 1987). And, according to the Arts Council (1988: 2), the arts

> are essential ingredients in the mix of cultural, environmental and recreational amenities which reinforce economic growth and development. They attract tourism and the jobs it brings. More importantly, they can serve as the main catalyst for the wholesale regeneration of an area. They provide focal points for community pride and identity.

The new culture of enterprise enlists the enterprise of culture to manufacture differentiated urban or local identities. These are centred around the creation of an image, a fabricated and inauthentic identity, a false aura, usually achieved through 'the recuperation of "history" (real, imagined, or simply re-created as pastiche) and of "community" (again, real, imagined, or simply packaged for sale by producers)' (Harvey, 1987: 274). The context for this is the increased pressure on cities and localities to adopt an entrepreneurial stance in order to attract mobile global capital. The marketing of local identities and images is a function of intensified inter-urban competition, and success 'is often short-lived or rendered moot by competing or alternative innovations arising elsewhere' (Harvey, 1987: 278). Under such conditions, local economies are precarious and local identities and cultures may be false and fragile.

Reimagined communities?

So far, we have approached recent developments in the media industries in terms of broader political economic transformations, associated with the dual tendency towards globalisation and localisation of image spaces. We want now to approach these same processes from a different perspective, to look at the media in terms of cultural transformations. As Fredric Jameson argues, 'the locus of our new reality and the cultural politics by which it must be confronted is that of space' (Stephanson, 1987: 40). This concerns spatial processes and structures, but also the subjective side of space, orientation within space and experience of space. And it is also a matter of both global space and local space: 'what is wanted is . . . a new relationship between a global cultural style and the specificity and demands of a concrete local or national situation' (Stephanson, 1987: 40). How do we position ourselves within the new global cultural space? How do we reconcile our cognitive existence in hyperspace, in the virtual space of electronic networks, with our bodily existence in localised space? Can we reposition ourself in local space without falling into nostalgic sentiments of community and *Gemeinschaft*? In Raymond Williams's (1983) terms, what new forms of identity and of bonding are possible and appropriate?

Contemporary cultural theory has been concerned with the disorientating experience of global space, and fundamental to this concern is the impact of global-image space. Richard Kearney (1988: 1–2) describes a world in which the image reigns supreme, a 'Civilisation of the Image' in which 'reality has become a pale reflection of the image . . . The real and the imaginary have become almost impossible to distinguish'. With 'the omnipresence of self destructing images which simulate each other in a limitless interplay of mirrors', argues Kearney, 'the psychic world is as colonised as the physical world by the whole image industry' (1988: 1, 5). This globalisation of image flows and spaces is fundamentally transforming spatiality and sense of space and place. Fredric Jameson (see Stephanson, 1987: 33) refers to the 'existential bewilderment in this new postmodern space', a 'culture in which one cannot position itself'.

This aspect of 'postmodernisation' is most apparent in the writings of Jean Baudrillard. In the society of the image, he argues, the individual is 'now only a pure screen, a switching centre for all the networks of influence' (Baudrillard, 1985: 133). With the television image, 'our own body and the whole surrounding universe become a control screen': 'the simple presence of the television changes the rest of the habitat into a kind of archaic envelope, a vestige of human relations whose very survival remains perplexing . . . as soon as behaviour is crystallised on certain screens and operational terminals, what's left appears only as a large useless body, deserted and condemned' (Baudrillard, 1985: 129). This is the world of screen and network, the 'smooth operational surface of communication'; it is a world of 'absolute proximity, the total instantaneity of things, the feeling of no defence, no retreat' (1985: 133).

This hyperspace is very much the cultural echo of that logic of transnational networks and communicating flows which Manual Castells sees as characterising the globalisation and cybernation of accumulation. However, whilst Castells (1983: 4) sees the consequence of this as 'the destruction of human experience, therefore of communication, and therefore of society', Baudrillard (1985: 132) comes to celebrate 'a state of fascination and vertigo linked to this obscene delirium of communication'.

He is seduced by the new communications networks, by the information and image flows, and by the decentred and disorientated identities associated with them. This new space of flows is shaped and controlled by transnational capital: it is the space of IBM and AT&T, of Murdoch and Berlusconi. It is their evolving network marketplace of commodity flows and advertising spectacle that generates Baudrillard's 'ecstasy of communication'. It is their screens and networks and simulations and cybernetic systems that produce his awe before the technological sublime.

This does, of course, engage with important developments in the late twentieth century. We should not devalue this moment of truth; it may even be exhilarating to know it. But the point must be to push it further. As Richard Kearney (1988: 380) argues, 'it is not sufficient to merely know that the technological colonisation of images is a symptom of a globally computed network of "third stage" multinational capital'. Knowing this, we must ask a more difficult question: 'Where are we to find a place of critical distance where we may begin to imagine alternative projects of social existence capable of counteracting the paralysis which the "technological sublime" induces in us?'

What is significant about this kind of postmodernist culture and theory is its preoccupation with mediation: image, simulation, network, screen, spectacle. Marike Finlay (quoted in Young, 1989: 86) suggests that postmodernism is 'a psychotic defence against the loss of referential identity'. Technological mediation is associated with estrangement from the real. In philosophical terms, this psychotic derealisation is an ultimate consequence of the logic of scientific and administrative rationality, the totalising ambitions of abstract and formal reason. In more social terms, it is a 'culturally generalised psychosis' appropriate to a rationalised, bureaucratic and technocratic society of indirect relationships and large-scale system integration, now on a global scale; a society in which space-transcending information and communications technologies allow 'the creation of organisations sufficiently complex and "impersonal" that they are readily reified', and conceived 'not as products of human action but as autonomous systems' (Calhoun, 1988: 5).

Rationalisation in both its bureaucratic and psychotic forms is characterised by what Michael Rustin (1987: 31) calls abstract universalism, with its 'denial of the particular location of human lives in place and time', its placeless and non-referential sense of identity. Rustin argues that cultural and political intervention needs, rather, to take account of social texture, density, difference. What is needed is 'a new particularism', a 'recognition that collective identities are formed through the common occupancy of space, and constituted in relations of particularist kinds' (1987: 34). This is about the reclamation or reimagination of a sense of referential identity, the revaluation of concrete and particular experience. In Richard Rorty's terms, it is about solidarity, as opposed to objectivity, as a way of placing one's life in a larger context. According to the Enlightenment ideal of objectivity, the individual 'distances himself [sic] from the actual persons around him . . . by attaching himself to something which can be described without reference to any particular human beings'

(Rorty, 1985: 3). The desire for solidarity, on the other hand, is referential and contextualised: the individual tells the story of his or her contribution to a community, be it 'the actual historical one in which they live, or another actual one, distant in time or place, or a quite imaginary one'. This process of bonding can occur in the context of attachment to bounded territorial locations, though it should not be thought that this is about an ambition to return to the parochial world of *Gemeinschaft*. Solidarity and collectivity should also have aspirations directed beyond the locality. In terms of the global-image space, Richard Kearney calls for 'a practice of imagination capable of responding to the postmodern call of the other reaching towards us from the mediated gaze':

> On the far side of the self-reflecting looking glass, beyond the play of masks and mirrors, there are human beings who suffer and struggle, live and die, hope and despair. Even in those televisual images which transmit events from the furthest corners of our globe, we are being addressed, potentially at least, by living others . . . Are not those of us who witness such images . . . obliged to respond not just to surface reflections on a screen but to the call of human beings they communicate? (Kearney, 1988: 387–8)

What does this mean for European identities? Refuge in some simple and coherent national, and nationalist, identity cannot be easily sustained. In a European context, at least, the 'imagined communities' of nationalism are increasingly problematical. Whilst a protracted and fierce rearguard action will, no doubt, be waged in the embittered defence of nations, and nationhood, it is clear that socio-spatial transformations in the late twentieth century call for new orientations and new forms of bonding. The most obvious response to these new conditions has, of course, been the attempt to build a European Community: 'a common market', a 'citizens' Europe', a 'Europe of Culture'. The attempt to cope with simultaneous fragmentation and globalisation here produces a political compromise whereby national cultures are subsumed and preserved in a spurious, administrative–bureaucratic internationalism. Defined as it is against the American and Japanese 'threats', this really amounts to a kind of supra-nationalism (and perhaps super-nationalism?).

But what, then, are the conditions and requirements for genuinely reimagined communities? As Raymond Williams argues in *Towards 2000* (1983), we must explore new forms of variable societies and variable identities. Postmodern culture must be elaborated out of differential and plural identities, rather than collapsing into some false cohesion and unity. It must be about positions and positioning in local and global space: about contexts of bodily existence and about existence in mediated space. At one level, it is about bounded and localised spatial arenas which bring individuals into direct social contact, about revaluing public places and recreating a civic culture. But it must be recognised, as Craig Calhoun (1988: 27–8) argues, that 'however desirable decentralised communities might be, they are at most complements to system integration and not alternatives to it'. It is necessary to improve the way large-scale systems work, and this means learning how to use the mass media and the new communications technologies to create 'a new forum for public discourse'.

Much of this discussion has emphasised the stifling power of global-image corporations. However, emergent transformations in the space of accumulation and in the spatial disposition of cultural forms do open up some new possibilities for reimagined solidarities. The recent growth in decentralised programme-making opens up at least the possibility of local media spaces. It is possible to envisage 'an amplification of the internal flows of communication in regions and localities' that might 'establish platforms for public debate and distinctive cultural expression' (Häger-strand, 1986: 18). Public discourse, grounded in a spatial framework, could be elaborated in a local public sphere. In this context, media culture must be seen as part of a much broader strategy for local development through the stimulation of cultural innovation, identity and difference (Bassand et al., 1986). Whilst such localism could, of course, degenerate into introverted and nostalgic historicism and heritage fixation, local attachment can be seen in more radical and innovative terms. New conditions of mobility make local attachment not a matter of ascribed and determined identity but increasingly a question of choice, decision and variability. Local cultures are, moreover, permeated and suffused by external influences. As Kenneth Frampton argues, local cultures can only be constituted now as locally inflected manifestations of global culture. What is called for, in his view, is a strategy of Critical Regionalism 'to mediate the impact of universal civilisation with elements derived indirectly from the peculiarities of a particular phase' (Frampton, 1985: 21). A critical regional or local culture must necessarily be in dialogue with global culture.

But contemporary cultural identities must also be about internationalism in a direct sense, about our positions in transnational spaces. At one level, this can be a matter of supra-national language and cultural communities: for example, 'francophone identities' (Jouanny, 1988) or, more radically, a 'latin audiovisual space' (Mattelart et al., 1984). But it must also transcend a Eurocentric perspective to achieve other forms of dialogue and collectivity. Fundamental here are solidarities with Third World cultures: those outside Europe, but also Third World communities, in all their diversity, now installed within European territories. European identity can no longer be, simply and unproblematically, a matter of Western intellectual and cultural traditions. As a consequence of its belligerent, imperialistic and colonialist history, Europe now contains a rich diversity of cultures and identities. The question is whether ethnic (and also gendered) differences are disavowed and repressed, or whether they can be accepted – and accepted, moreover, in their difference.

References

Aglietta, M. (1979) *A Theory of Capitalist Regulation: the US Experience* London: New Left Books.

Aksoy, A. and Robins, K. (1992) 'Hollywood for the 21st century: global competition for critical mass in image markets', *Cambridge Journal of Economics*, 16 (1): 1–22.

Albertsen, N. (1986) 'Towards post-Fordist localities? An essay on the socio-spatial restructuring process in Denmark', paper presented to the XIth World Congress of Sociology, New Delhi, August.

Arts Council, (1988) *An Urban Renaissance*. London: Arts Council of Great Britain.

Bassand, M. (1988) 'Communication in cultural and regional development', in M. Ernste and C. Jaeger (eds), *Information Society and Spatial Structure*. London: Belhaven.

Bassand, M., Hainard, F., Pedrazzani, Y. and Perrinjaquet, R. (1986) *Innovation et changement social: actions culturelles pour un développement local*. Lausanne: Presses Polytechniques Romandes.

Baudrillard, J. (1985),'The ecstasy of communication', in H. Foster (ed.), *Postmodern Culture*. London: Pluto.

Billaudot, B. and Gauron, A. (1985) *Croissance et crise: vers une nouvelle croissance*, 2nd edn. Paris: La Découverte.

Boyer, R. (1986a) *La Théorie de la régulation: une analyse critique*. Paris: La Découverte.

Boyer, R. (1986b) *Capitalismes fin de siècle*. Paris: Presses Universitaires de France.

Cable Authority (1987) *Cable and the Inner Cities*. London: Cable Authority.

Calhoun, C. (1988) 'Communications technology and the transformation of the urban public sphere', paper presented to the International Conference on Information, Technology and the New Meaning of Space, International Sociological Association, Research Committee 24, Frankfurt, 15–19 May.

Castells, M. (1983) 'Crisis planning, and the quality of life: managing the new historical relationships between space and society', *Environment and Planning D: Society and Space*, 1 (1): 3–21.

Christopherson, S. and Storper, M. (1986) 'The city as studio: the world as back lot: the impact of vertical disintegration on the location of the motion picture industry', *Environment and Planning D: Society and Space*, 4 (3): 305–20.

Collins, R., Garnham, N. and Locksley, G. (1988) *The Economics of Television: UK Case*. London: Sage.

Commission of the European Communities (1984) *Television without Frontiers*. Brussels: Commission of the European Communities.

Commission of the European Communities (1986) 'Television and the audiovisual sector: towards a European policy', *European File*, 14/86, August–September.

Commission of the European Communities (1987) *A Fresh Boost for Culture in the European Community*. Brussels: Commission of the European Communities.

Commission of the European Communities (1988a) 'Towards a large European audiovisual market', *European File*, 4/88, February.

Commission of the European Communities (1988b) 'The European Community and culture', *European File*, 10/88, May.

Cornford, J. and Robins, K. (1995) 'Beyond the last bastion? Industrial restructuring and the labour force in the British television industry', in G. Sussman and J. Lent (eds), *Communication Workers of the World: the New International Division of Labour*. Boulder, Colo.: Westview Press.

Courlet, C. and Judet, P. (1986) 'Nouveaux éspaces de production en France et en Italie', *Annales de la recherche urbaine*, 29: 95–103.

Crookes, P. and Vittet-Philippe, P. (1986) *Local Radio and Regional Development in Europe*. Manchester: European Institute for the Media.

Duncan, S. and Goodwin, M. (1988) *The Local State and Uneven Development: Behind the Local Government Crisis*. Cambridge: Polity Press.

Frampton, K. (1985) 'Towards a critical regionalism: six points for an architecture of resistance', in H. Foster (ed.), *Postmodern Culture*. London: Pluto.

Frèches, José (1986) *La Guerre des images*. Paris: Denoël.

Garnham, N. (1986) 'Concepts of culture: public policy and the cultural industries', *Cultural Studies*, 1 (1): 23–38.

Garnier, J.-P. (1987) 'L'éspace mé diatique ou l'utopie localisé', *Espaces et sociétés*, 50.

Gifreu, J. (1986) 'From communication policy to reconstruction of cultural industries', *European Journal of Communication*, 1 (4): 463–76.

Hägerstrand, T. (1986) 'Decentralisation and radio broadcasting: on the "possibility space" of a communication technology', *European Journal of Communication*, 1 (1): 7–26.

Harvey, D. (1985) 'The geopolitics of capitalism', in D. Gregory and J. Urry (eds), *Social Relations and Social Structures*. London: Macmillan.

Harvey, D. (1987) 'Flexible accumulation through urbanisation: reflections on "postmodernism" in the American city', *Antipode*, 19 (3): 260–86.

Hondius, F.W. (1985) 'Freedom of commercial speech in Europe', *Transnational Data Report*, 8 (6): 321–7.

Jouanny, Robert (1988) 'Espaces et identités francophones', *Acta geographica*, 73: 12–23.

Kearney, R. (1988) *The Wake of Imagination*. London: Hutchinson.

Lash, S. and Urry, J. (1987) *The End of Organised Capitalism*. Cambridge: Polity Press.

Lipietz, Alain (1987) *Mirages and Miracles: the Crises of Global Fordism*. London: Verso.

Logica (1987) *Television Broadcasting in Europe: Towards the 1990s*. London: Logico Consultancy.

MacCabe, Colin (1988) 'Those golden years', *Marxism Today*, 32 (4): 24–31.

Mattelart, A., Delcourt, X. and Mattelart, M. (1984) *International Image Markets*. London: Comedia.

Piore, M. and Sabel, C. (1984) *The Second Industrial Divide: Possibilities for Prosperity*. New York: Basic Books.

Robins, K. and Cornford, J. (1994) 'Local and regional broadcasting in the new media order', in A. Amin and N. Thrift (eds), *Globalisation, Institutions and Regional Development in Europe*. Oxford: Oxford University Press.

Rorty, Richard (1985) 'Solidarity or objectivity?', in J. Rajchman and C. West (eds), *Post-Analytic Philosophy*. New York: Columbia University Press.

Rustin, M. (1987) 'Place and time in socialist theory', *Radical Philosophy*, 47: 30–6.

Soja, E. (1985) 'Regions in context: spatiality, periodicity and the historical geography of the regional question', *Environment and Planning D: Society and Space*, 3 (2): 175–90.

Soja, E. (1989) *Postmodern Geographies: the Reassertion of Space in Critical Social Theory*. London: Verso.

Stephanson, A. (1987) 'Regarding postmodernism – a conversation with Fredric Jameson', *Social Text*, 17: 29–54.

Storper, M. and Christopherson, S. (1987) 'Flexible specialisation and regional industrial agglomerations: the case of the US motion picture industry', *Annals of the Association of American Geographers*, 77 (1): 104–17.

Thrift, N. (1987) 'The geography of the late twentieth century class formation', in N. Thrift and P. Williams (eds), *Class and Space: the Making of Urban Society*. London: Routledge and Kegan Paul.

Tydeman, J. and Kelm, E.J. (1986) *New Media in Europe: Satellites, Cable, VCRs and Videotex*. London: McGraw-Hill.

Williams, R. (1983) *Towards 2000*. London: Chatto and Windus/Hogarth Press.

Young, R.M. (1989) 'Postmodernism and the subject: pessimism of the will', *Free Associations*, 16: 81–96.

The world wide web of surveillance: the internet and off-world power flows
David Lyon

Much is made of the enabling character of the Internet. We are told that this amazing tool liberates us to do things hitherto undreamed of. The idea of a 'World Wide Web' suggests a global network of interconnected electronic nodes that make possible a new level of communication, that goes beyond the older broadcasting mode, into a sphere of interchange that promises to better even the democratic structure of the telephone system. The decentralized character of telephones, and the interchangeable positions of sender and receiver, are augmented and enriched in the Internet, with the potential for new communicative relations within a burgeoning cyberspace (see, e.g., Poster, 1995).

Webs can have other purposes, of course. The spider spins the web in order to entangle and entrap the unsuspecting fly. The more the fly struggles, the more it is stuck. Without disputing whatever inherently democratizing possibilities lie latent in the Internet, it is worth exploring the capacity of the 'Web' to capture and control, to target and to trap, to manage and to manipulate. Although much has changed since the birth of the Internet's precursor as a Cold War military communications system, power has not simply been discarded as an infantile trait. Rather, power is now bound up with an extensive, increasingly integrated, surveillance technology.

'Personal' data caught in the Web are of many kinds. The Internet makes possible new levels of surveillance-integration, relating to work-situations, government administration, policing and, above all, marketing. You may see a surveillance camera in the shopping mall, or even suspect that someone else is listening in to your cellular phone call. But Internet-based surveillance is far more subtle. You are part of a user group? 'People-finding' tools such as Alta Vista or Dejanews gather personal data from them. You visit Websites? Many such sites automatically create visitors'

This chapter is taken from *Information, Communication & Society*, 1 (1998), pp. 91–105.

registers, collecting directly from the user's computer data such as the kind of computer you own, your e-mail address and the previous page you visited. The fine threads are almost imperceptible, and although each 'fly' movement creates more entanglement, the 'fly' remains blissfully unaware of what is happening.

In order to understand the World Wide Web of surveillance, first, some background is needed. The precursors to contemporary surveillance are many, but the Internet helps to shift such activity into a different register, a different plane. Where once the monitoring of place was significant, now surveillance data flows in a kind of 'off-world' sphere. 'Off-world' real estate is advertised in the movie, *Bladerunner*. Here, my use of the term echoes Manuel Castells' (1989) reference to economic 'flows', uncoupled from physical places, enabled by communication and information technologies (CITs). Such flows are essential to the 'remote control' exercised by corporations over aspects of geographically dispersed production and, increasingly, consumption. The various forms of such 'cyberspace surveillance' activity generated on the Internet are explored in the second section, and common traits are noted.

Third, the question is asked, how should these surveillance practices be understood? Are they an extension of capitalist control, or further evidence of our identity-less incarceration in an electronically enhanced 'iron cage' of bureaucratic organization? Or are they better understood as a form of panoptic power, where an unseen observer oversees a regime of truth and knowledge? Or should social theory attempt to go beyond these modern/postmodern tensions? Lastly, comment is made on the prospects for critical social research, given both the need for, and the difficulty of, such inquiry.

Surveillance: a modern growth industry

Watching others' activities, as a means of monitoring and supervising them, is hardly a new practice. The most ancient records – say of Egypt or Babylon – indicate that surveillance has been carried out to keep tabs on populations for taxation or military purposes, or to ensure that work was carried out satisfactorily. In modern times, however, surveillance became much more routine and general, involving whole national populations, across a range of activities and life situations. Births, marriages and deaths were recorded systematically, individual persons were listed as being of an age and status to vote in democratic elections, and workers were assembled under one roof to facilitate supervision.

In the twentieth century, these processes intensified. Government administration undertook surveys of populations, and departments such as health, welfare, immigration, taxation, customs, housing, vehicle and driver licensing kept more and more detailed records. Rational mechanisms for bureaucratic organization, analysed *par excellence* by Max Weber, employed a panoply of methods for creating and maintaining files, and ensuring that a hierarchy of rule-observing officials kept control thereby.

The logic of capitalist development also entailed supervision and monitoring in order to maximize productivity and profit. Scientific management represented this trend towards greater surveillance-intensity, with its focus on detailed time-and-movement analyses. By the mid-twentieth century it had become clear that surveillance was constitutive of modern organization.

However, the term 'surveillance' was still reserved mainly for intelligence and security services, not the routine business of everyday life. 'Surveillance' was really only popularized as a social research area in its own right in the mid-1980s, for several interesting reasons. One was that organizations of all kinds started to computerize, from the 1960s onwards. The massive collection of personal data, begun during the Cold War era, when state socialist societies still exerted tight political control over their citizens, generated fears of Orwellian police states and Kafkaesque faceless bureaucratic machines. Investigations of the social implications of electronic technologies suggested to some the advent of 'surveillance societies' (Marx, 1985; Flaherty, 1989).

At the same time as widespread and accelerating computerization occurred, enthusiasm was mounting for Michel Foucault's ground-breaking studies of modern forms of discipline. These appeared in a series of related books, but most famously for present purposes in his *Discipline and Punish* (1977). In that book, the architectural plan for the 'panopticon' prison was elevated to exemplary status for modern disciplinary techniques that subject the human body to regular and predictable regimes. What Foucault did not attempt, however, was an extension of his analysis to electronic forms of surveillance. Those analysts who have done so tend to focus on the panopticon as the key to the power of networked databases, perhaps at the expense of other conceptual candidates such as 'biopower'. I return to this below.

At least two major debates began concerning surveillance. The first focuses on whether electronic technologies contribute to a qualitatively different kind of surveillance from that characterized by paper files and classic bureaucratic organization. Analysts such as James Rule (1973) and Gary T. Marx (1988) argue that they do, and present sociological explanations of how this happens. The second question, however, is how far Foucault's work can be applied to electronic surveillance (see Lyon, 1993). Analysts such as Frank Webster and Kevin Robins (1986), Shoshana Zuboff (1988) and Diana Gordon (1987) were early exponents of the relevance of panopticism, while others were less sure.

The two debates now converge in the area of most rapid expansion, consumer surveillance. The use of the newer technologies raises the question of how far database marketing goes beyond older styles of mass advertising, coupon delivery and 'loyalty' club memberships. So-called 'mass customization' creates incentives for collection of personal data for use in the production-marketing process. Manufacturers or retailers wish to establish a service-type relationship with customers, collecting, storing and manipulating information about them in order to control their behaviours (Samarajiva, 1994: 91).

Database marketing works by clustering consumers by social type and location, and by more and more tightly trying to personalize advertising and consumer advice. This is linked directly with the question of Foucaldian analysis. The panopticon works by both classification and observation. Webster and Robins explain the attempt more closely to influence consumers as 'social management' – an extension of Taylorist practices of scientific management. This is elaborated and refined in Oscar Gandy's work on what he calls the 'panoptic sort', where database marketing is seen as a 'discriminatory technology' for grading and guiding consumers (Gandy, 1993, 1996). In each case, personal data are gleaned from public sources, or from information provided, wittingly or unwittingly, by the consumer.

Consumer surveillance uses many of the same techniques as other forms of dataveillance, such as profiling, record linkage, and so on, but in North America operates largely beyond the reach of regulatory limits placed on government use of these practices (Québec is the exception). This, coupled with the apparent effectiveness of the crude behaviourist sociology involved in channelling choice and directing desire, means that database marketing has mushroomed in a few short years. Until recently, the only other brake on its progress was the relative lack of communicative means for transmitting data, not only within, but also between countries and continents. Enter the Internet.

Cyberspace surveillance

The term 'World Wide Web of surveillance' is more a metaphor than a precise indicator. 'Internet-based surveillance' comes closer to designating the field, but even this, technically speaking, would not encompass e-mail systems, despite the fact that many refer casually to e-mail as being 'on the Net' or their e-mail accounts as 'Internet addresses'. Perhaps 'cyberspace surveillance' would serve better, referring to any forms of surveillance that occur in computer-mediated communications. From the viewpoint of the data-subject, all these are part of the Web whose weaving is triggered at the keyboard and which can be seen – if one knows where to look – on the screen.

Three main categories of cyberspace surveillance may be discerned, relating to employment, to security and policing, and to marketing. These categories blur in practice, for at least two reasons. One is that the very existence of electronic networks makes it easier in principle for data to be shared between different agencies, even though in most countries regulatory regimes limit this. The other is that the same network used by large and powerful bodies, such as governments or corporations, can also be used by individuals or groups with far less power. At the very least this means that cyberspace surveillance is not necessarily centralized. As William Bogard (1996: 134) observes, this is not just a global system, 'but an orbital and cellular network linking the macro and micro levels of information-gathering'.

In employment situations, monitoring and supervisory forms of surveillance are common, so it is hardly surprising that increasing use of the Internet, and above all e-mail, by employees has created new challenges. In December 1996 a Canadian federal scientist at the Department of Defence was arrested for allegedly downloading more than 20,000 pictures and video clips of child pornography, using his office computer (MacLeod, 1997). Also in 1996, Compaq Computer in Houston, Texas, fired twelve employees for using worktime to visit sex sites. With respect to e-mail, concerns have arisen among employers about the use of company time and resources for private correspondence, within and beyond the organization.

Responses to such practices generally take the form of technical measures to minimize the risk of recurrence. Software is installed to record and report all activities entailing use of the Internet and e-mail. All company information technology services divisions have the capacity to track the use of electronic network use, and to monitor the content of e-mail messages. In most of North America, whether they do so or not is a matter of company or organizational policy. A few years ago, a US survey of managers revealed that 22 per cent had searched employees' computer files, voice-mail, e-mail and other electronic communications (Pillar, 1993: 7). The results are sometimes dramatic. A Los Angeles police officer, Laurence Powell, got into deep water after sending an e-mail to a friend, describing his involvement with Rodney King; 'I haven't beaten anybody this bad in a long time' (Weisband and Reinig, 1995: 41).

These examples, from work-situations, also spill over into the area of policing and security. Part of the policing is private, as when Canadian service-provider i-STAR removes certain risqué groups in the alt.sex hierarchy from public access. But another part is public, when Internet-based surveillance is undertaken by legally constituted police services. In 1995, for instance, the American FBI undertook 'Operation Innocent', an undercover sting involving the interception of America On-Line (AOL) e-mails of people who had responded to messages purporting to be from paedophiles. Raids were conducted on 125 homes and offices in fifty-seven cities and many arrests were made (*New York Times*, 16 September 1995, cited in Zuijdwijk and Steeves, 1995).

The best-known effort to enable widespread 'security' surveillance on the Internet is the so-called Clipper Chip. In 1994 the US government proposed to introduce a uniform encryption standard, that would effectively prohibit the proliferation of codes designed to protect the privacy of electronic communications. While individual users could rest assured that their messages would remain private, the one exception was that, in the interests of 'national security', government agents would be able to listen in, when appropriate and necessary. Needless to say, the controversy aroused by this proposal has been fierce – on and off-line – and is, as yet, unresolved (see Levy, 1994).

While the preceding examples of cyberspace surveillance in employment and policing are interesting and, for many, alarming, they are on a small scale when compared with the massive armoury of commercial surveillance used by marketers. Many suspect that Netscape itself tracks the virtual movement of its users, and Netscape admits that they know each time a browser of theirs is in use. Curiously enough, when in May 1996 a new 'Communicator Suite' was being launched by Netscape, a Danish software firm discovered that Website operators could read anything on the hard drive of a computer logged onto the Website, this was described merely as a 'bug' (CNN, 1996). Many other companies are certainly engaged in extensive profiling of Internet users. Some of these use the well-worn ploy of registration – as when one fills a warranty form for an appliance, thus giving extensive personal data to the company – to profile visitors to Websites. In this case, some informed consent is required of netsurfers.

In many other cases, however, no such consent is sought or required. Websites frequently send automatic messages back to their owners, providing data about users' needs, habits and purchases, based on their visits to the site in question. Some transactional information is passively recorded, such that the Webmaster can determine what files, pictures or images are of interest to the user, how long was spent with each, and where the user was before and after visiting that site. Internet Profiles, known better as I/PRO, indicates just how well and by whom a site is used. I/PRO's clients include Yahoo!, Compuserve, Netscape, and others such as CMP Publications and Playboy (Stagliano, 1996).

So-called 'Cookies' (Client-Side Persistent Information) give extensive tracking capacities to companies, eager to exploit commercially the valuable segmented personal data on discrete individuals. Cookies allow Websites to store information about visited sites on the user's hard drive, then they read the drive each time a site is visited to discover if the user has been there before. The latest marketing techniques applaud these practices, as offering benefits to the consumer, of customized advertising, tailored to their needs. But the title of one such manual – *Strategic Marketing for a Digital Age* (Bishop, 1996) – also leaves little doubt about who else will benefit from the 'military' manoeuvre.

Recently, much has been made of the potential for using 'intelligent agents' to short-circuit the often tedious process of deploying Internet search engines to find usable data. Not without irony, the 'agents' that now use increasingly sophisticated tracking processes, including 'mapping techniques', are called 'spiders'. NetCarta Corporation, that makes mapping technologies, stresses the enhanced productivity of these spiders. Though little evidence is as yet available of their use in consumer tracking and profiling, the potential is obvious (see Elmer, 1997: 185). Another technique, known as data mining, is used with increasing frequency on the Internet. The Chicago Tribune Company, for instance, used data mining to analyse the behaviour of consumers as they move from site to site. While it is true that many data gathered via the Internet are available to any user with a credit card, the fact is that only large corporations can afford large scale techniques such as data mining.

A so called 'privacy panic' arose, in late 1996, over the activities of Lexis-Nexis and their P-TRAK system, designed to help police and lawyers locate litigants, witnesses, shareholders, debtors, heirs and beneficiaries. In response to an outcry regarding the availability of Social Security numbers along with names, addresses and telephone numbers, the US Federal Trade Commission (FTC) called for broader privacy protection, and Lexis-Nexis eliminated access to Social Security numbers. As it happens, other companies offer much fuller services than P-TRACK, also for fixed fees per datum. Information Resources in Fullerton CA, for example, offers items such as criminal and court records, Social Security numbers, driving records and employment background checks.

Although one cannot obtain such information directly from the Web, all such companies – Information Resources, CDB Infotech, Information America, and so on – have Websites for marketing purposes (<isworld@listserv.hea.ie>). Some companies do, however, offer handbooks for sale, that give details on how to use Internet search engines for finding personal data, gleaned from multifarious sources, including 'private' bulletin boards (e.g. the 'Snoop Collection' from 'Background Investigation Division' in Chico, California). One might be forgiven for asking why such companies often accompany their statements with claims about commitment to 'freedom of information'.

Much uncertainty still surrounds the Internet use of personal databases and personal information sources. No one seems to object to having national white-pages directories available as a means of locating people and businesses (such as Canada411: <http://canada411.com>). Yet when the city of Victoria put its tax-assessment rolls on the Internet, British Columbia Privacy Commissioner David Flaherty announced an investigation. The fear was that people could be located when they may have legitimate reasons for withholding details of their whereabouts. The site proved extremely popular but the mayor closed it down after the investigation was announced (McInnes, 1996).

Theorizing the surveillance web

What John Beniger (1986) calls the 'control revolution' extends through all modern organizations. Especially in the police, the military, and in business corporations, a bureaucratic drive is evident, pushing towards tighter predictability as a means to greater control. For Beniger, such control is understood as increasing the probability of a desired outcome. This is the logic behind surveillance of many kinds. All contemporary institutions in the so-called advanced societies are characterized by an internal imperative to obtain, store, produce and distribute data for use in the risk management for and of their respective populations.

The examples given earlier show how this works in practice. Employers try to reduce risk – of workers using office time or equipment for their own purposes, for instance – in employment situations. The police, in concert with other institutions, work towards preventing the risks of crimes being committed, or, more generally, of threatening behaviours. And marketers do all in their power to avoid risks of lost opportunities, market niches, and, ultimately, profit. All engage in data gathering

procedures to try to pinpoint risks (or opportunities) and to predict outcomes. So surveillance spreads, becoming constantly more routine, more
intensive (profiles) and extensive (populations), driven by economic,
bureaucratic and now technological forces. Within the latter, we refer
particularly to CITs, and thus to the internal logics of such systems that
serve to render as 'real' the risks in question.

The surveillance literature becomes fuzzy at this point. Two of the
main concerns have to do with the outcomes of surveillance situations.
One refers to social participation, the other to personhood. The first sees
surveillance outcomes in terms of social division and inequality, and thus
social access and exclusion. The second focuses on questions of 'invasions
of privacy', on identity and, sometimes, on human dignity. Unfortunately,
some theorists seem so concerned with the one that they ignore or
minimize the significance of the other. Yet the two dimensions overlap,
indeed, are two sides of the same coin. Identification and identity, for
example, may be the means of inclusion and exclusion. Personhood is
therefore realized in participation.

Surveillance is clearly implicated in the maintenance of social
inequality and division. The panoptic sort (Gandy) distinguishes between
different classes of consumers, which has the effect of reinforcing the
lifestyle patterns and expectations of each group, and maintaining an
invisible but effective barrier between consumers and non-consumers. The
latter form marginal populations – due to their age, ethnicity, income,
neighbourhood and so on – that are in part constituted by the workings of
surveillance systems that concentrate on the more rich and respectable
echelons of society. Such marginal groups have their own surveillance, that
tend to be much more punitive, found in health, welfare and penal systems
(Lyon, 1994; cf. Ericson, 1993).

Surveillance also deepens questions of identity, when – from the
perspective of the data-subject – the capacity to control communication
about oneself is wrested from the individual. This is one strand in the
debate over privacy, the right to which is often held to entail taking – or
being given back – such control by various means. Legal recourse through
privacy and data protection legislation is one means, the proliferating
technical panoply of encryption devices and 'privacy enhancing technologies – PETs', is another. Analyses of surveillance that start from a
premise of privacy are really focusing on fairly philosophical questions of
personhood, and, in particular, what sorts of expectations one might have
for communicative self-determination. Such analyses tend to assume that
autonomous, individuated 'selves' are threatened by intensified surveillance.

These issues are clearly ones of considerable political and ethical
import, and that is why they should be discussed in relation to the
burgeoning practices of cyberspace surveillance. However removed from
daily life and remote from public control these practices seem to be, the
drives behind them are very powerful, and their material consequences are
all too real. As Stephen Graham says, many of these systems are directly
'geared to the protection and fortressing of affluent consumer neighbour-

hoods and corporate districts . . . and to the exclusion, enforcement and control of the groups and areas that are marginalised by labour market and welfare restructuring' (1998: 28). The distribution of life-chances and of communal and personal well-being are increasingly dependent on the increasingly efficient systems of advanced surveillance.

Beyond these questions of participation and personhood, however, lie some further concerns about the nature of contemporary cyberspace surveillance. The kinds of issues just discussed assume that modern discourses of human rights or social justice still hold good in the world of the Internet. Yet the Internet is implicated in certain cultural shifts that call in question just those kinds of categories. Mark Poster, for instance, argues that the way that today's 'personal' databases function makes them more like a 'superpanopticon' (1995). Surveillance practices are not so much a threat to the 'privacy' of an individual subject, but are actually involved in the very constitution of subjects. This puts a new slant on surveillance, that is glossed in some other treatments of the 'superpanopticon' (e.g. Mehta and Darier, 1997).

The 'new slant' may be observed in more conventional settings. In the case of medical practices, notes Robert Castel, there has been a shift of emphasis away from face-to-face examination of the patient and towards an examination of records 'compiled in varying situations by diverse professionals and specialists interconnected solely through the circulation of individuals dossiers' (Castel, 1991: 282). This process has, he believes, crossed a threshold and taken the character of a mutation, a new form of surveillance that has prevention of risk at its core. Individual subjects are now less significant than statistical correlations; autonomized management becomes the order of the day. If one can guide and assign individuals rather than take responsibility for them, then the management strategy has worked. This could even be seen, argues Castel, as a 'post-disciplinary' situation, where the quest of efficiency has become paramount. To 'forward plan social trajectories from a "scientific" evaluation of individual abilities' is the new – maybe mythical – goal (1991: 296).

The focus on risk management may also lead theory beyond the panopticon, and towards Foucault's notion of 'biopower', which is discussed not in *Discipline and Punish*, but in his *History of Sexuality* (1978). What Richard Ericson and Kevin Heggarty say of police-related biopower may equally be applied, on a broader scale, to cyberspace surveillance: 'Biopower is the power of human biography, of constructing biographical profiles of human populations for risk management and security provision . . . aimed at fabricating people into the social body . . . according to the logic of the norm' (1997: 91–2). Space forbids expansion of this point, but it does connect nicely the social logic (beyond the panoptic disciplining of bodies) and the techno-logic of surveillance.

The idea that there might be a 'mythical goal' of surveillance is explored by William Bogard (1996). He argues that a 'simulation' of surveillance is contributing to 'hypercontrol' in societies infused with communication and information technology networks. The 'mutation' described by Castel seems to have wider relevance. Bogard adds the work of Jean Baudrillard to that of Foucault to try to obtain theoretical leverage on the simulated or virtual aspects of surveillance. Where the panopticon originally dealt with real time and physical space – it is, essentially, an architecture – today's 'hyperpanoptics' exist in a realm of electronic environments, where time is asynchronous and speed of flows is crucial, and where distance and proximity are blurred in 'cyberspace'. Existing surveillance literature often speaks of data-images or data-shadows, and of blurring boundaries between images and realities, but Bogard's work suggests that this is central rather than epiphenomenal to today's situation.

Bogard stresses that the simulation of surveillance does not mean it is illusory, unreal. Indeed, 'the better a simulation, the less awareness there is of the artifice that identifies it as a simulation' (1996: 31). This connects with the idea of a 'mythical goal' of surveillance, namely, that the problem of perceptual control over a distance is solved through new electronic means. Knowing in advance who is likely to engage in welfare fraud, buy Benetton or vote Liberal is seen as the means of maintaining order, normalizing populations, maximizing efficiency.

Unlimited surveillance is the unspoken goal (and it is attractive to politicians, police, marketers and high-tech companies alike) but it is, as Bogard says, 'actual only in simulation' (1996: 49). Alongside older forms of monitoring and supervision (such as the use of software for checking on employees or children's use of the Internet) are these newer methods, that more and more involve the subjects of surveillance, now part of the total surveillance scene. And the Internet serves only to make the mythical goal more (seemingly) realizable.

These reflections aid analysis insofar as they help theory to move beyond the confines of physical space and real time – a task already accomplished in the virtual realm of cyberspace. But it would be a mistake to pull Wittgenstein's ladder up behind us as we rise through the clouds into this next level of surveillant simulation. The danger of discourses that inhabit a world of simulations is to forget the realness of the 'real world' (see, e.g., Robins, 1995). This demands that whatever constructive insights are gleaned from Foucault and Baudrillard, they be articulated with those of access, inclusion/exclusion and participation on the one hand, and identity, dignity and personhood on the other. As Graham reminds, in respect of the city, 'webs of simulated surveillance system become woven into supporting and constructing the fabric of "real" urban life, just as the "real" landscapes of cities themselves become transformed into a realm of surveillant simulation' (1998: 38; see also Robins, 1995). Much work remains to be done to understand how these systems work.

Bringing cyberspace surveillance down to earth

The World Wide Web of surveillance exists as a means of control, enhancing through electronic networks already existing forms of surveillance. Exactly how that control is sought and is achieved – panopticism?

biopower? – remains debatable, although it is clear that on present showing, existing inequalities of power and access are reinforced, and, for those who are aware of their digital transparency, fears of being held in an unseen gaze are unrelieved.

The foregoing discussion suggests that modern surveillance, based in the so-called control revolution, has evolved rapidly in new directions since the inception of computer-power. While such computerization started as a way to enhance and augment already existing systems of surveillance, its technical possibilities have provided opportunities for novel practices, geared to coping with risk by pre-empting and preventing or by managing and manipulating. The convergence of computing with telecommunications, seen for example in the Internet, has enabled the growth of virtual surveillance, off-world data-flows, detached from their erstwhile moorings in time and space, but with real enough effects in those settings.

Surveillance theories have struggled with these changes, and the classic work of Marx and Weber has been augmented by that of Foucault, and now, Baudrillard. However, theory is still in a somewhat rudimentary condition. Yet if the preceding argument is correct, surveillance, including surveillant stimulation, has all too real social, material, spiritual effects. Understanding these, and thus developing some critical discourses to deal with them, is of paramount importance.

As use of the Internet expands rapidly among the well-heeled communities of the so-called advanced societies, so the scope of newer surveillance methods will also grow. At present, most 'critical' debate is couched in terms of 'privacy' concerns, in which rights to be left alone (protected by law), or to 'free speech' (guaranteed by encryption security) are voiced most stridently. Resistance is all too often understood in terms of charging royalties on the use of personal data, which simply falls back on market solutions. Some encourage at least voluntary compliance with data protection conventions, but it appears that companies may do this and continue their surveillance practices.

Some theories of privacy, recognizing classic liberal conceptions as a cul-de-sac, have attempted to introduce a social dimension to the argument. Priscilla Regan's (1995) work is exemplary in this respect. David Flaherty, also going beyond individualized solutions, appeals to the Internet community to promote a culture in which digital tracking is illegal, unethical and immoral without informed consent (Flaherty, 1997: 6). This places the onus of responsibility on the surveillor rather than on the data-subject.

But until the inequality-reinforcing and personhood-threatening aspects of contemporary surveillance are seen together, and until these dimensions are understood in relation to the virtualizing of surveillance, the real issues of contemporary surveillance will continue to elude us. Whatever the social benefits of the Internet – and, stripped of hype, there are many – their realization cannot responsibly be theorized in isolation from the existence of the World Wide Web of surveillance. This is not something added to or different from the 'rest of' the Internet, but an aspect intrinsic to its constitution.

Note

This chapter is a revised version of a paper presented at the Canadian Association for Information Science, meeting in St John's, Newfoundland, June 1997.

References

Beniger, J. (1986) *The Control Revolution*. Cambridge, Mass.: Harvard University Press.

Bishop, B. (1996) *Strategic Marketing for a Digital Age*. Toronto: HarperCollins.

Bogard, W. (1996) *The Simulation of Surveillance: Hypercontrol in Telematic Societies*. Cambridge and New York: Cambridge University Press.

Castel, R. (1991) 'From dangerousness to risk', in G. Burchell, C. Gordon and P. Miller (eds), *The Foucault Effect: Studies in Governmentality*. Brighton: Wheatsheaf.

Castells, M. (1989) *The Informational City*. Oxford: Blackwell.

CNN (1996) http://cnnfn.com/archive/news/9605/20/netscape/index.htm>

Elmer, G. (1997) 'Spaces of surveillance: indexicality and solicitation on the Internet', *Critical Studies in Mass Communication*, 14: 182–91.

Ericson, R. 1993) 'Review of Steven Nock, "The Costs of Privacy"', *American Journal of Sociology*, 100 (1) (July 1994): 294–6.

Ericson, R.V. and Heggarty, K.D. (1997) *Policing the Risk Society*. Toronto: University of Toronto Press.

Flaherty, D. (1989) *Protecting Privacy in Surveillance Societies*. Chapel Hill, NC: University of North Carolina Press.

Flaherty, D. (1997) 'Privacy on the Internet', <http://latte.cafe.net/gv...ns/internet_privacy.html>

Foucault, M. (1977) *Discipline and Punish*. New York: Vintage.

Foucault, M. (1978) *The History of Sexuality*. New York: Vintage.

Gandy, O. (1993) *The Panoptic Sort: a Political Economy of Personal Information*. Boulder. CO: Westview.

Gandy, O. (1996) 'Coming to terms with the panoptic sort', in D. Lyon and E. Zureik (eds), *Computers, Surveillance and Privacy*. Minneapolis, MN: University of Minnesota Press.

Gordon, D. (1987) 'The electronic panopticon: a case-study of the development of the national criminal records system', *Politics and Society*, 15: 483–511.

Graham, S. (1998) 'Surveillant simulation and the city', *Environment and Planning D: Society and Space*, 16: 483–504.

Levy, S. (1994) 'The battle of the clipper chip', *New York Times Magazine*, 12 June: 44, 51, 60, 70.

Lyon, D. (1993) 'An electronic panopticon? A sociological critique of surveillance theory', *Sociological Review*, 41: 653–78.

Lyon, D. (1994) *The Electronic Eye: the Rise of Surveillance Society*. Minneapolis, MN: University of Minnesota Press.

McInnes, C. (1996) 'Victoria data site pulled off Internet', *Globe and Mail*, Toronto, 27 September.

MacLeod, I. (1997) 'Cyber-shirking alarms companies', *Kingston Whig-Standard*, 16 January.

Marx, G.T. (1985) 'The surveillance society: the threat of 1984-style techniques', *The Futurist* (June): 21–6.

Marx, G.T. (1988) *Undercover: Police Surveillance in America*. Berkeley, CA: University of California Press.

Mehta, M. and Darier, E. (1997) 'Virtual control and disciplining on the Internet: electronic governmentality and the global superpanopticon', *The Information Society*, 14 (2): 107–116.

Pillar, C. (1993) 'Bosses with X-ray eyes', *MacWorld*, July.

Poster, M. (1995) *The Second Media Age*. Cambridge: Polity Press.

Regan, P. (1995) *Legislating Privacy*. Chapel Hill, NC: University of North Carolina Press.

Robins, K. (1995) 'Cyberspace and the world we live in', *Body and Society*, 1 (3–4): 135–55.

Rule, J. (1973) *Private Lives, Public Surveillance*. London: Allen Lane.

Samarajiva, R. (1994) 'Privacy in electronic public space: emerging issues', *Canadian Journal of Communication*, 19: 87–99.

Stagliano, R. (1996) 'Publicité du troisième type', in *L'Internet: l'ecstase et l'effroi*. Paris: Le Monde Diplomatique.

Webster, F. and Robins, K. (1986) *Information Technology: a Luddite Analysis*. Norwood, NJ: Ablex.

Weisband, S. and Reinig, B. (1995) 'Managing user perceptions of e-mail privacy', *Communications of the ACM*, 38: 12.

Zuboff, S. (1988) *In the Age of the Smart Machine*. New York: Basic Books.

Zuijdwijk, T. and Steeves, V. (1995) *The Protection of Privacy on the Internet*. Ottawa: Immigration and Refugee Board.

19

In the realm of uncertainty: the global village and capitalist postmodernity
Ien Ang

Speaking about the present condition of the world, or 'today', has become a thoroughly messy and capricious matter. The collapse of official communism in Eastern Europe and the subsequent ending of the Cold War, the Gulf War, the gradual decline of American hegemony, the rise of Japan to world economic might, the spread of the AIDS virus, and the environmental crisis are only some of the major historical events which signal a reshuffling of geopolitical relations whose eventual outcomes remain deeply uncertain. Indeed, as Immanuel Wallerstein has noted, the capitalist world-system is in mutation now; we have arrived 'in the true realm of uncertainty' (1991: 15).

I cannot dissociate myself from this condition of uncertainty. Indeed, what I would like to do here is take this uncertainty on board – not only as to the state of the world 'today' but also regarding the current state (and status) of 'theory', let alone 'communication theory'. The very idea of a book on 'communication theory today' – in which this chapter first appeared (Crowley and Mitchell, 1994) – assumes that such an entity exists or should exist (despite its undoubtable internal plurality and diversity), that it can be proposed and formulated, and that it matters. But this assumption cannot be unquestioned. Of course 'communication' is, and should be, a crucial site of critical intellectual reflection if we are to understand contemporary social, political and cultural relations, although the very notion of 'communication' itself, encompassing such a mixed bag of events and processes, is hardly specific enough to be used as a starting point for theorizing the complicated entanglements between peoples, powers and cultures in the world 'today'.

At any rate, what I will try to explicate here is that if we are to understand Wallerstein's true realm of uncertainty, we have to go beyond the concerns of communication theory, however defined. This is because

This chapter is taken from *Living Room Wars: Rethinking Media Audiences for a Postmodern World* (London, Routledge, 1996), pp. 162–80.

communication theory, founded as it is on the logic of reduction, if not elimination, of uncertainty, cannot deal with uncertainty as a *positive* force, and a necessary and inevitable condition in contemporary culture, the condition of *capitalist postmodernity*.

One of the most popular metaphors used to describe this condition has been McLuhan's 'global village'. However, this very popularity tends to foreclose a closer engagement with exactly what it means when we say that today's world is a 'global village'. Often the unwarranted (but strangely reassuring) assumption is made that the creation of the 'global village' implies the progressive homogenization – through successful communication – of the world as a whole.[1] However, as George Marcus has noted, the fact 'that the globe generally and intimately is becoming more integrated . . . paradoxically is not leading to an easily comprehensible totality, but to an increasing diversity of connections among phenomena once thought disparate and worlds apart' (1992: 321). In other words, the global village, as the site of the culture of capitalist postmodernity, is a thoroughly paradoxical place, unified yet multiple, totalized yet deeply unstable, closed and open-ended at the same time. I will propose here a theorization of capitalist postmodernity as a *chaotic* system, where uncertainty is a built-in feature.

The global village and the fallacy of communication

Communication theory has traditionally used metaphors of transport and flow to define its object. In the resulting transmission models of communication, as James Carey has remarked, 'communication is [seen as] a process whereby messages are transmitted and distributed in space for the control of distance and people' (1989: 15). In putting it this way, Carey foregrounds the deeply political nature of epistemological choices. In Carey's words, '[m]odels of communication are . . . not merely representations of communication but representations *for* communication: templates that guide, unavailing or not, concrete human interaction' (1989: 32). In historical and economic terms, the instances of human interaction Carey refers to pertain primarily to the geographical expansion of modern capitalism, with its voracious need to conquer ever more extensive and ever more distant markets. Such was the context for the creation and spread of a spatially biased system of communication, epitomized by the parallel growth of the railroad and the telegraph in the nineteenth century, which privileges speed and efficiency in the traversing of space. Spatial integration was the result of the deployment of these space-binding communication technologies, first at the level of the nation, then extending over increasingly large parts of the globe. Following Canadian theorist Harold Innis, Carey describes modern capitalist culture as a 'space-binding culture': 'a culture whose predominant interest was in space – land as real estate, voyage, discovery, movement, expansion, empire, control' (1989: 160). In this respect, McLuhan's 'global village', a world turned into a single community through the annihilation of space in time, represents nothing other than (the fantasy of) the universal culmination of capitalist modernity. In short, what I want to establish here is the intimate inter-connection between the transmission paradigm of communication, the installation of high communication systems and the logic of capitalist expansion.

But the control effected by communication-as-transmission does not only pertain to the conquest of markets for the benefit of economic gain; it is also a control over people. In social terms, then, communication-as-transmission has generally implied a concern with social order and social management; hence, for example, the longstanding interest in commu-nication research, particularly in the United States, in the 'effects' of messages: persuasion, attitude change, behavioural modification. What is implicit in this social psychological bias in communication research is an (unstated) desire for a compliant population, and therefore a belief in the possibility of an ordered and stable 'society'. In this sense, communication research has evolved as a branch of functionalist sociology, for which the question of social integration (e.g. through the dissemination of a 'central value system' throughout the entire social fabric) is the main concern. The effects tradition was a specification of this concern in relation to the media: are the media (dys)functional for social integration? This concern did not remain restricted to the population *within* a society; it has also been envisaged beyond the societies that make up the core of modern capitalism, as in the information diffusion theories of Third World 'development' and 'modernization' of the 1950s and 1960s where mass communication processes were thought to play a vital role. Here, the making of the 'global village' can be rewritten as the transformation, or domestication, of non-Western others in the name of capitalist modernity, the civilization which was presumed to be the universal destiny of humankind: global spatial integration is equated with global social and cultural integration.

It should be clear that in theoretical terms transmission models of communication inherently privilege the position of the Sender as legitimate source and originator of meaning and action, the centre from which both spatial and social/cultural integration is effectuated. Communication is deemed successful if and when the intentions of the Sender, packaged in the Message, arrive unscathed at the Receiver, sorting the intended effects. But the hegemony of such linear and transparent conceptions of com-munication has been severely eroded in the last few decades. This erosion was simultaneously an epistemological and a political one. A telling case is Everett Rogers' declaration, in 1976, of the 'passing' of the 'dominant paradigm' of the diffusion model of development. As author of *The Diffusion of Innovations* (1962), Rogers had to submit almost fifteen years later that the model's weakness lies precisely in its emphasis on linearity of effect, in its reliance on hierarchy of status and expertise, and on rational (and presumably benevolent) manipulation from above (see Rogers, 1976).

Not coincidentally, the same period saw the ascendancy of alterna-tive, critical accounts of development, often framed within theories of cultural imperialism and dependency. The rise of such accounts can be understood in the light of the growing force of anti-systemic, new social movements in the West which have challenged the unquestioned hegemony of capitalist modernity's 'central value system', as well as the increasing desire for self-determination in postcolonial, developing nations. As John Tomlinson has argued, 'the various critiques of cultural imperialism could be thought of as (in some cases inchoate) protests against the spread of (capitalist) modernity' (1991: 173). However, Tomlinson continues, 'these protests are often formulated in an inappropriate language of domination, a language of cultural imposition which draws its imagery from the age of high imperialism and colonialism' (1991: 173). I would add here that this inappropriate language is symptomatic of the fact that most theories of cultural imperialism remain firmly couched within transmission models of communication. Indeed, the marked emphasis within the notion of cultural imperialism on the dimension of power operating in the relation between Sender and Receiver importantly exposes the illusion of neutrality of the transmission paradigm. But because it conceptualizes those relations in terms of more or less straightforward and deliberate imposition of dominant culture and ideology, they reproduce the mechanical linearity of the transmission model. Such a vision is not only theoretically, but also historically inadequate: in a world-system where capitalism is no longer sustained through coercive submission of colonized peoples (as in nineteenth-century high imperialism) but through the liberal institutions of democracy and the sovereign nation-state, equation of power with imposition simply will not do. The problem, rather, is to explain how capitalist modernity 'imposes' itself in a context of formal 'freedom' and 'independence'. In other words, how are power relations organized in a global village where everybody is free and yet bounded? It is in order to grasp the ramifications of this question that we need to develop new theoretical tools.

For the moment, I would like to stress how the crisis of the transmission paradigm was not just an internal, academic affair,[2] but ran parallel with developments in the 'real' world, where the spread of modern capitalism from core to periphery, which was very much undergirded by the increasingly global deployment of ever more sophisticated space-binding media, has been found to have led not to the creation of an ordered global village, but to the multiplication of points of conflict, antagonism and contradiction. Never has this been clearer than in today's new world (dis)order, Wallerstein's 'true realm of uncertainty'. In short, the crisis of the transmission paradigm takes the shape here of a deep uncertainty about the *effectiveness* of the Sender's power to control. For Sender, read (the media of) modern capitalism. In this context, it shouldn't surprise that the transmission paradigm was particularly hegemonic in communication theory during the high period of American hegemony as the superpower within the modern capitalist world. Neither is it surprising that the crisis of the paradigm erupted when that hegemony started to display cracks and fissures.

Within communication theory, this crisis has led to a proliferation of *semiotic* models of communication, which foreground the ongoing construction of meaning as central to communicative practices. What such models reject is the assumption of transparency of meaning which underlies the idea of communication as transmission; instead, communication is conceived as a social practice of meaning production, circulation and exchange. James Carey's rich and important work epitomizes this shift by adopting such a semiotic model in his formulation of a ritual view of communication, which he defines as 'the production of a coherent world that is then presumed, for all practical purposes, to exist' (1989: 85). From this perspective, communication should be examined as 'a process by which reality is constituted, maintained, and transformed' (1989: 84), the site of 'symbolic production of reality' (1989: 23). In Carey's view, this social reality is a 'ritual order' made up by 'the sharing of aesthetic experience, religious ideas, personal values and sentiments, and intellectual notions' through which a 'common culture' is shaped (1989: 34–5).

The gist of Carey's theoretical argument is that communication *is* culture. Without communication, no culture, no meaningful social reality. However, there are problems with Carey's emphasis on ritual *order* and *common* culture, inasmuch as it invokes the suggestion that such an order of common meanings and meaningfulness can and should be securely created. Carey's proposal to build 'a model of and for communication of some restorative value in reshaping our common culture' (1989: 35) stems from a genuine critique of the instrumentalist values of capitalist modernity, but his longing for *re*storing and *re*shaping cultural sharing suggests a nostalgia for a past sense of 'community', for a local-bound, limited and harmonious *Gemeinschaft*. But it is difficult to see how such a (global?) common culture can be created in the ever-expanding and extremely differentiated social reality constructed by capitalist modernity. To put it differently, Carey's concern with the time-binding functions of communication – its role as social cement through the construction of continuity and commonality of meanings –seems ironically to perpetuate the concern with social integration which is implicit in the transmission paradigm. Carey's position implies that a global village which is integrated in both spatial and social/cultural terms can and should be brought about not through the dissemination of pregiven meanings from Sender to Receiver, but by enhancing rituals of mutual conversation and dialogue. In this sense, he unwittingly reproduces the assumption of capitalist modernity as a universal civilization, at least potentially. The (democratic) promotion of communication-as-ritual is the recipe for it.[3]

Carey's model, then, privileges the *success*, both theoretically and politically, of communication-as-ritual. In so doing, he tends to collapse communication and culture, as the title of his book, *Communication as Culture*, suggests. For Carey, communication studies and cultural studies are one and the same thing. In this sense, Carey's solution to the crisis of the transmission paradigm is a conservative one in that it ends up securing 'communication', and thus communication theory, as a privileged theoretical object for cultural studies.

I would suggest, however, that it is the *failure* of communication that we should emphasize if we are to understand contemporary (postmodern) culture. That is to say, what needs to be stressed is the fundamental *uncertainty* that necessarily goes with the process of constructing a meaningful order, the fact that communicative practices do not necessarily have to arrive at common meanings at all. This is to take seriously the radical implications of semiotics as a theoretical starting point: if meaning is never given and natural but always constructed and arbitrary, then it doesn't make sense to prioritize meaningfulness over meaninglessness. Or, to put it in the terminology of communication theory: a radically semiotic perspective ultimately subverts the concern with (successful) communication by foregrounding the idea of 'no necessary correspondence' between the Sender's and the Receiver's meanings. That is to say, not success, but failure to communicate should be considered 'normal' in a cultural universe where commonality of meaning cannot be taken for granted.

If meaning is not an inherent property of the message, then the Sender is no longer the sole creator of meaning. If the Sender's intended message doesn't 'get across', this is not a 'failure in communications' resulting from unfortunate 'noise' or the Receiver's misinterpretation or misunderstanding, but because the Receiver's active participation in the construction of meaning doesn't take place in the same ritual order as the Sender's. And even when there is some correspondence in meanings constructed on both sides, such correspondence is not natural but is itself constructed, the product of a particular articulation, through the imposition of limits and constraints to the openness of semiosis in the form of 'preferred readings', between the moments of 'encoding' and 'decoding' (see Hall, 1980). That is to say, it is precisely the existence, if any, of correspondence and commonality of meaning, not its absence, which needs to be accounted for. Jean Baudrillard has stated the import of this inversion quite provocatively: '[M]eaning . . . is only an ambiguous and inconsequential accident, an effect due to ideal convergence of a perspective space at any given moment (History, Power, etc.) and which, moreover, has only ever really concerned a tiny fraction and superficial layer of our "societies"' (Baudrillard, 1983: 11). What we have here is a complete inversion of the preoccupations of communication theory, of meaningful human interaction as the basis for the social – or, for that matter, for the global village. As I will try to show below, this theoretical inversion, which is one of the fundamental tenets of poststructuralist theorizing, allows us to understand the global village not as a representation of a finished, universalized capitalist modernity (characterized by certainty of order and meaning), but as a totalized yet fundamentally dispersed world-system of capitalist *post*modernity (characterized by radical uncertainty, radical *indeterminacy* of meaning).

New revisionism?

Such a move is not merely a theoreticist game but is essential if we are to develop a *critical* theorizing of the new world (dis)order. I will clarify this by briefly looking at the presumptions at work in the recent controversy around what some authors have called the 'new revisionism' in mass communication research (Curran, 1990; see also, e.g., Schlesinger, 1991). This so-called 'new revisionism', I should say at the outset, is a fiction, born of a rather conservative wish to retain 'mass communication' as a separate field of study, on the one hand, and a misrecognition of the radical potential of the idea of indeterminacy of meaning, on the other. Although I will not spend too much time deconstructing this fiction, I think it is important to counter some of its assertions in order to clarify precisely what that radical potential involves. What should be resisted, I think, is the theoretical and political closure which the fiction of the new revisionism imposes on our understanding of what 'mass communication' means in today's world.

According to James Curran, this so-called 'new revisionism' has fundamentally transformed what he calls 'the radical tradition' of mass communication scholarship. This transformation is exemplified, says Curran, in the well-known ethnographic studies of media audiences in cultural studies [. . .]. As Curran would have it, these studies revise the classic radical stance, which was informed by a (neo-)Marxist pessimism towards the all-powerful role of the mass media as transmitters of dominant ideology (and which also undergirds most theories of cultural imperialism). But now that audiences are conceived as active producers of meaning and produce a diversity of readings, that 'oppressive' role of the media has been considerably diminished, to the point that there might be no dominant ideology at all. Curran claims that 'radical researchers' now stress 'audience autonomy' and have implicitly concluded 'that the media [have] only limited influence' (1990: 145–6). In this sense, Curran concludes, previously radical critics have presumably moved towards a more moderate, pluralist position, so that 'the critical tradition in media research has imploded in response to internal debate' (1991: 8). But this is an utterly mistaken conclusion. Curran could only come to such a conclusion by adopting a narrow conceptualization of power, as if evidence of diversity in readings of media texts could be equated with audience freedom and independence from media power! In other words, while the semiotic notion that meaning is constructed rather than given is now widely recognized throughout the discipline, Curran retains the mechanical, distributional notion of power of the transmission paradigm. This, however, is a rather truncated rendering of the radical scope of indeterminacy of meaning, made possible by objectifying 'communication', 'media' and 'audience', lifting them out of their larger social and historical contexts.

If anything, Curran's rendering of 'the new audience research' indicates that merely replacing a transmission model for a semiotic model of communication is not enough. The problem with communication models in general is that they describe the world in terms of closed circuits of senders, messages and receivers. That the unidirectionality of such circuits is complicated by feedback loops, processes of exchange and interaction, or intermediary moments of meaning construction doesn't make the circuit less closed: there is no 'outside' to the communication. As a result, it becomes impossible to think about the relation of power and meaning in more multidimensional terms, to recognize the operation of multiple forms of power at different points in the system of social networks in which both 'senders' (e.g. media) and 'receivers' (e.g. audiences) are complexly located and produce meanings. Instead, power becomes a fixed entity which simply changes hands from senders to receivers and vice versa. And since, again according to Curran, critical scholars now acknowledge that audiences are not passive absorbers of 'dominant ideology' transmitted by the media but actively produce their own meanings with the help of the predispositions they bring to texts, a paradigmatic consensus can now be declared which favours the liberal pluralist idea that '[t]here are no dominant discourses, merely a semiotic democracy of pluralist voices' (1990: 151). Here again is another invocation of a unified and integrated global village, now as a space in which power is so evenly diffused that everybody is happily living ever after in a harmonious plurality of juxtaposed meanings and identities.[4]

This is what I mean by the closure imposed by Curran's misappropriation of 'the new audience research' and invention of a 'new revisionism'. It is a closure which expels any sense of and or uncertainty, with no place for unresolved ambiguity and contradiction. It is also a closure which revels in a confidence of having repudiated any notion of cultural imperialism, any idea of unequal power relationships between 'core' and 'periphery' in the global village. And to be sure, certain tendencies within critical work on audiences have facilitated this misappropriation, precisely for their lack of clarity about the theoretical status of this work. Thus, John Fiske's (in)famous celebration of the semiotic power of audiences to create their own meanings and pleasures has been widely interpreted as a confirmation of the liberal pluralist paradise (e.g. Curran, 1990: 140). What is more, Fiske's excessive romanticism and populism has been severely criticized *within* cultural studies for its connivance in free market ideologies of consumer sovereignty (e.g. Morris, 1988a). What is important to note here, however, is not so much the apologetic political consequences of Fiske's position, but the theoretical underpinnings of his discourse, particularly his theory of the relationship of power and meaning.

For example, in *Television Culture* he describes the relation between television and its audiences as an antagonism between 'top-down power' opposed by 'bottom-up power' (Fiske, 1987: 314). The latter is predominantly a semiotic power operating within a more or less autonomous cultural economy, to be differentiated from the economic power held by the 'top', for example the executives of the television industries, operating within the financial economy. Fiske is right in wanting to differentiate between these two forms of power – indeed, I would argue that it is precisely by making this kind of theoretical differentiation that we might begin to overcome the simplistic, one-dimensional concepts of power inherent in the transmission paradigm (and reproduced by Curran). The problem, however, is that Fiske tends to exaggerate the strength of the semiotic democracy by seeing the struggle as a 'two-way force' in which the partners are implicitly considered separate but equal. Again, this rosy conclusion could only be arrived at by isolating the communication between television and its audiences from the broader contexts in which both are shaped. Fiske's radical inclination is thus contained by his holding on to the familiar topography of communication: the Sender's sphere (production and distribution) is opposed by the Receiver's sphere (reception and consumption). Again, a closed circuit, despite the struggle taking place within it. Again, theoretical closure, systemic certainty. In this sense, Curran's liberal pluralism and Fiske's more radical pluralism tend to collude. In emphasizing this apparent collusion Curran has rushed towards the conclusion that the 'new revisionism' has led critical theorists to abandon their 'radical' concerns. This, however, is a very uninformed miscomprehension of the current state of affairs in critical theorizing.

In the last two decades or so, a transformation in the theorization of power has taken place in critical theory – largely through post-Althusserian elaborations of Gramsci's notion of hegemony and Foucault's concept of power/knowledge – not because it no longer believes in domination but because, in the words of Mark Poster, 'it is faced with the formidable task of unveiling structures of domination when no one is dominating, nothing is being dominated and no ground exists for a principle of liberation from domination' (1988: 6). This, of course, is another way of evoking the contradictory condition of 'free-yet-bounded-ness' which I noted earlier as characteristic of living in the global village. In this context, John Tomlinson's suggestion that the notion of cultural imperialism should be replaced by the much less deterministic (but no less determining) one of 'globalization' is particularly relevant:

> [T]he idea of imperialism contains, at least, the notion of a purposeful project: the *intended* spread of a social system from one centre of power across the globe. The idea of 'globalisation' suggests interconnection and interdependency of all global areas which happens in a far less purposeful way. It happens as the result of economic and cultural practices which do not, of themselves, aim at global integration, but which nonetheless produce it. More importantly, the effects of globalisation are to weaken the cultural coherence of *all* individual nation-states, including the economically powerful ones – the 'imperialist powers' of a previous era. (Tomlinson, 1991: 175)

In other words, critical theory has changed because the structure of the capitalist order has changed. What it has to come to terms with is not the certainty of (and wholesale opposition to) the spread of a culturally coherent capitalist modernity, but the uncertainty brought about by the disturbing incoherence of a globalized capitalist postmodernity, and the mixture of resistance and complicity occurring within it. The critical import of audience ethnography, placed within the larger theoretical project of critical cultural studies, should be seen in this context: it is to document how the bottom–top, micro-powers of audience activity are both complicit with and resistive to the dominant, macro-forces within capitalist postmodernity. It has nothing to do with the complacency of Curran's liberal pluralism; on the contrary, it radicalizes the 'radical concerns' of critical theorizing. To elaborate on this point, we need to do away with any notion of the closed circuit of communication, and to embrace fully the primacy of indeterminacy of meaning which, I would argue, is essential for understanding how and why capitalist postmodernity is a 'true realm of uncertainty'.

Beyond order and meaning: the global village deconstructed

I can begin to explain this by taking issue with the simplistic idea that existence of diversity is evidence of freedom from power and domination. That is to say, variation – e.g. in audience readings and pleasures – is not the result of autonomy and independence, as the liberal pluralists would have it, but emerges out of the inescapably overdetermined nature of any particular instance of subjective meaning production. The latter is traversed by a multiplicity of power relations, the specifics of which cannot be known ahead of time precisely because their articulations are always irreducibly context-bound. They are not determined by fixed predispositions but take shape within the dynamic and contradictory goings-on of everyday life, of history. In this sense, the existence of different readings is by no means evidence of 'limited' power. On the contrary, it only points to the operation and intersection of a whole range of power relations at any one time, going far beyond linear 'influence'. This is one way in which the idea of indeterminacy of meaning can be concretely qualified: indeterminacy is not grounded in freedom from (external) determinations, but is the consequence of *too many*, unpredictable determinations. Nor does a concern with specific pleasures that people get out of particular media forms 'totally displace a concern with power', as Philip Schlesinger claims (1991: 149); on the contrary, theorizing pleasure enables us to develop a much more complex understanding of how certain forms of power operate by paying attention to the intricate intertwinings of pleasure and power – an especially important issue today where 'the pleasure principle' has been incorporated in the very logic of consumer capitalism.[5]

But I am running ahead of my argument. The point I want to make about the liberal pluralist account of variation and difference is that it implicitly assumes a closed universe of readings, making up a contained diversity of audience groupings with definite identities, equivalent to the liberal pluralist conception of electoral politics where voters are distributed over a fixed repertoire of parties. It is in this sense that liberal pluralist discourse conjoins the marketing discourse of market segmentation (where consumers are neatly divided up and categorized in a grid of self-contained demographic or psychographic 'segments'), which is not so surprising given that both discourses are two sides of the coin of 'democratic capitalism'. This concept of diversity presupposes that 'society' is a finite totality, a 'unity in diversity', or, more precisely, a unity of a diversity of meanings and identities. This concept of social totality is conceived as 'the structure upon which its partial elements and processes are founded', that is to say, as 'an underlying principle of intelligibility of the social order' (Laclau, 1991: 90–1). In this sense, difference and diversity refers to the structured partition of that unitary order – say, the imaginary global village – into fixed parts, such as identifiable readings and audience groupings (to be uncovered by 'audience research').

The idea of indeterminacy of meaning, however, enables us to put forward a much more radical theorization of difference and diversity, one that does away with any notion of an essence of social order, a bounded 'society' which grounds the empirical variations expressed at the surface of social life. Not order, but chaos is the starting point. Variation does not come about as a result of the division of a given social entity into a fixed range of meaningful identities, but represents the infinite play of differences which makes all identities and all meanings precarious and unstable. Any relative fixation of those identities and meanings is not the expression of a structural predetermination within a social order. On the contrary, it is the (temporary and provisional) outcome of, in Laclau's (1991) terms, the attempt to limit the infinite play of differences in the site of the social, to domesticate the potential infinitude of semiosis corroborated by the principle of indeterminacy of meaning, to embrace it within the finitude of an order, a social totality which can be called a 'society'. From this perspective, this ordered social totality is no longer a pregiven structure which establishes the limits within which diverse meanings and identities are constituted. Rather, since the social is the site of potentially infinite semiosis, it always *exceeds* the limits of any attempt to constitute 'society', to demarcate its boundaries. This is why, as we all know, a 'society' can accomplish only a partial closure, a partial fixing of meanings and identities, a partial imposition of order in the face of chaos.[6] That is, any containment of variation and difference within a limited universe of diversity is always-already the product of a determinate ordering by a structuring, hegemonizing power, not, as the functionalist discourse of liberal pluralism would have it, evidence of a *lack* of order, absence of power. In this sense, the question to ask about the complex relation between media and audiences is not why there isn't more homogeneity, but why there isn't more heterogeneity!

To illuminate how this altered notion of difference effectively subverts the closure of liberal pluralist discourse, let me briefly return to the argument I have put forward in *Desperately Seeking the Audience* (Ang, 1991), where I have discussed the history of the corporate practice of 'audience measurement', or, more popularly, 'ratings'. Over the years, there has been a progressive sophistication of measurement methods and technologies, aimed at the ever more detailed and accurate determination of size and demographic composition of the audience at any particular moment, for any particular programme or channel. [. . .] [T]he latest device currently being tested in this respect is the so-called 'passive people meter', a kind of computerized eye roaming people's living rooms in order to catch their gaze whenever it is directed to the TV screen. The industry's hope is that this technology will deliver ratings statistics that can tell the television companies exactly who is watching what at any split second of the day. However, this very search for the perfect measurement method, which I have characterized as desperate, is based on the implicit assumption that there is such a thing as an 'audience' as a finite totality, made up of subdivisions or segments whose identities can be synchronically and diachronically 'fixed'. I have suggested that this assumption is a fiction, but a *necessary* fiction for a television industry which increasingly experiences the audience as volatile and fickle. A hegemonic, empowering fiction which is positively constructed as true by the creation of simulations of order in the ranks of the audience in the form of ratings statistics and other market research profiles.

The paradox of the passive people meter, however, is that it is propelled by a desire to produce a fully precise representation, a completely accurate map of the social world of actual audience practices. This progressive rapprochement of representational strategies and the social, I suggest, is bound ultimately to reveal chaos rather than order. That is to say, it will turn out that the universe of television-viewing practices can only be represented as an ordered totality by imposing (discursive) closure on it, because these infinite, contradictory, dispersed and dynamic everyday practices will always be in excess of any constructed totality, no matter how 'accurate'. In attempting to determine the identity of this universe we will, as Laclau puts it, 'find nothing else but the kaleidoscopic movement of differences' (1991: 92), which will probably only result in further, more insistent and more desperate attempts to map it.

In concrete, historically specific terms, the chaos I am referring to relates to the enormous proliferation of possible television-viewing practices in the last few decades, possibilities which have been created by the expansion of the television industries in capitalist modernity in the first place. From transnational 24-hour satellite channels (e.g. CNN and MTV) to a myriad of local or regional cable channels dishing up unmanageable volumes of specialized programming, from video recorders and remote control devices (which have encouraged 'zipping' and 'zapping') to TVs watched in 'uncommon' places (laundries, campsites, airports, and so on), and, above all, the very ubiquitousness of television which makes it bleed into every corner of day-to-day social life – all this can surely only make for an endless, unruly and uncontrollable play of differences in social practices related to television viewing: continuous social differentiation bordering on chaos. It is this chaos which the discourse of liberal pluralism cannot account for, and which the functionalist rationality of audience measurement technology is designed to suppress and tame in the form of a statistical order. But it is precisely this chaos which I suggest we need to take into consideration in understanding the logic of power relations in capitalist postmodernity. Capitalist postmodernity may have constructed a spatially integrated, interconnected global village, but at the same time it encourages social *dis*integration.

Capitalist postmodernity as a chaotic system

But it is important to properly theorize 'chaos'. Often chaos is associated with loss of control, lack of order. Such a conception of chaos – or, in our context, the infinitude of the social, infinite semiosis – leads to a romanticized view of the practices of everyday life (such as audience practices) as always evading the structures – institutional, ideological – imposed upon them, that is to say, as the site of resistance *per se*. This, of course, is the position taken up by Fiske. But such a position is informed by a negative theory of chaos: chaos as lack.

It is instructive here to draw comparisons with the emergence of chaos theory in the physical sciences. Katherine Hayles, author of *Chaos Bound* (1990), has given a, for our purposes, rather fortuitous example of how chaos can be acknowledged as a positive force in our experience as media consumers: 'Every time we keep a TV or radio going in the background, even though we are not really listening to it, we are acting out a behavior that helps to reinforce and deepen the attitudes that underwrite a positive view of chaos' (Hayles, 1990: 7). This *positive* view of chaos implies transvaluation of chaos as having primacy over order. However, Hayles continues, chaos theory does not *oppose* chaos to order; rather, it sees chaos as 'the engine that drives a system toward a more complex kind of order' (1990: 23). This is not dissimilar to Laclau's idea of how 'society', or, for that matter, 'audience' (as a functional sub-totality within 'society'), is created out of the attempt to put an order to the (chaotic) infinitude of the social. In this sense, 'society' (or 'audience') is, in Hayles's terms, a chaotic system, or a complex kind of order, an order whose ultimate suture is impossible because it is a system born out of the precarious structuration of chaos. If chaos is ultimately impossible to domesticate it is because it is, as chaos theory would have it, 'an inexhaustible ocean of information' rather than a lack, 'a void signifying absence' (1990: 8). The more chaotic a system is, the more information it contains, and the more complex the order established out of it. In other words, what characterizes chaotic systems – and, by extension, social systems – is not so much that they are poor in order, but that they are rich in information (1990: 6). This formulation illuminates why the passive people meter is likely to be counterproductive (in creating order in the audience measurement field): it is because it will elicit *too much*, not too little information. Too much information will only aggravate the possibility of constructing the (simulated) orderliness of the 'audience', therefore threatening to foreground the return of the repressed: chaos.

Chaos theory is in fact one more example of the recognition that we live in a 'true realm of uncertainty'. In this sense, Hayles rightly brings the emergence of chaos theory in the physical sciences into connection with the increasing importance of poststructuralist and postmodern theory in the humanities and the social sciences, not least in cultural studies. As Hayles puts it, '[d]ifferent disciplines are drawn to similar problems because the concerns underlying them are highly charged within a prevailing cultural context' (1990: xi). This context, we can add, is precisely the context of capitalist postmodernity. It is in capitalist postmodernity that the presence of chaos constantly lurking behind any institution of order has become a systemic force. Capitalist postmodernity, in other words, is a truly chaotic system.

What, then, is the historical specificity of this system, and how can we theorize the structural uncertainty engendered by and within it? It is illuminating here to reinvoke the demise of the transmission paradigm of communication theory, as it finds its parallel, at the level of the social, in the demise of the paradigm of the modern. The modern paradigm was predicated, as I have said earlier, upon the assumption that modernity, under the aegis of the expansion of capitalism, is a universal destination for the whole world, so that history could be conceived as a linear development in which the modern is designated as the most advanced end-point – literally the End of History – towards which the less modern, those termed 'traditional' or 'less-developed', must and will of necessity evolve. The postmodern paradigm, however, has shattered the certainty of this universalizing evolutionary discourse. It challenges the assumptions of modern discourse by questioning the binary counterposing of the modern/Western/present/Sender/self and pre-modern/non-Western/past/Receiver/other. The modern and the Western do not necessarily coincide, and the present has many different, complex and contradictory faces, projecting many different, uncertain futures. It is this overdetermined, convoluted and contradictory heterogeneity of the present – characterized by a multiplicity of coeval, overlapping and conflicting cultural self/other relationships[7] – which is foregrounded in postmodernity.

It is important to be precise about the character of this heterogeneity of the present, and it is here that the notion of chaos, as outlined above, and the force of the infinitude of the social takes effect. This heterogeneity of the present does not just refer to the juxtaposed coexistence of a liberal plurality of distinct, mutually independent cultures and societies (which could be said to have existed to a certain extent before the Europeans imposed capitalism on the rest of the world). In the capitalist postmodern world, heterogeneity is not based on foundational essences, but is a contingent articulation of the fluid and moving play of differences in which 'cultures' and 'societies', tumbled as they are into endless interconnections (to paraphrase Clifford Geertz, 1988: 147), constantly construct, reconstruct and deconstruct themselves. Any identity of a 'culture', a 'society', and any other social entity ('nation', 'ethnicity', 'gender', 'audience', 'the people', and so on) is merely the conjunctural articulation of constantly changing positionalities, a precarious positivity formed out of a temporary fixation of meaning within the capitalist world-system. Paradoxically, then, heterogeneity arises precisely as a result of the hegemonizing, globalizing, integrating forces of the modern capitalist order. It is for this reason that this system, this totalizing system of global capitalism in which we are all trapped, is nevertheless a profoundly unstable one, whose closure can never be completed.

Crucially, however, this postmodern heterogeneity is not *just* the consequence of the excessive flux of the social which produces a surplus of meaning that the system is unable to master, that is, put in order. To assert this would be tantamount to making a romantic metaphysical statement. What is historically particular about capitalist postmodernity's 'true realm of uncertainty' has to do with the system's ambiguous stance towards the infinitude of the social itself: as much as it wants to control it, it also depends on exploiting it. It is in the very nature of capitalism, particularly consumption capitalism, to inscribe excess in its very mode of (re)production.

The dynamic of perpetual change is of course characteristic of capitalism *per se*, not just consumption capitalism. But what distinguishes the latter is the way in which perpetual *cultural* (de)construction, perpetual (de)construction of meanings and identities through for example the fashion system and planned obsolescence, has become the linchpin of the economy. That is to say, the culture of consumerism is founded on the idea that constant transformation of identities (through consumption) is pleasurable and meaningful. This exploitation of the pleasure principle implies that consumption capitalism is, as Jon Stratton has remarked, based on the excess of desire: in contrast with earlier, production-oriented capitalism, which catered to given, and thus *limited*, needs and demands, consumption capitalism relies on providing for socially produced, and therefore in principle *limitless*, needs and wants (Stratton, 1990: 297–8). This occurs not only at the level of consumption, where the consumer is constructed as always 'wanting'. In postmodern culture the poststructuralist dictum that subjects do not have fixed identities but are always in process of being (re)constructed and (re)defined is not just a theoretical axiom, but has become a generalized cultural principle. The historical institutionalization of excess of desire in the culture of capitalist postmodernity (most directly for example through the discourses of advertising and marketing) exploits the fundamental excessiveness of the social in the creation of an escalating, and ultimately uncontrollable, proliferation of difference and identity, or identities-in-difference. Excess of desire opens up the cultural space for the formulation and proliferation of unpredictable needs and wants – i.e. meanings and identities – not all of which can be absorbed and incorporated in the postmodern order of the capitalist world-system (see, e.g., Ahmed, 1992). In other words, at the heart of capitalist postmodernity is an extreme contradiction: on the one hand, its very operation depends on encouraging infinite semiosis, but, on the other hand, like every systemic order, it cannot let infinite semiosis go totally unchecked.

So, the capitalist world-system today is not a single, undifferentiated, all-encompassing whole, but a fractured one, in which forces of order and incorporation (e.g. those of globalization, unification and 'Westernization') are always undercut (though not necessarily subverted) by forces of chaos and fragmentation (e.g. localization, diversification and 'indigenization'). In this world-system there are still dominant forces (it would be ludicrous to deny this), although there is never a guarantee in advance that their attempts to impose order – which is what the dominant will always do – will be successful: think only of former President Bush's failure to create a 'New World Order' – now a quaint idea! Nor does relative failure to impose order mean that the dominant are any less powerful; on the contrary: it only means that the effectivity of their resources and forms of exercise of power is uncertain. Stronger still, it is precisely because of this uncertainty that order is consciously conceived as a task, a problem, an obsession; a matter of design, management, engineering, policy (Bauman, 1991: 6). In this sense, the very insecurity of order in capitalist post-modernity – contradictorily based as it is on both fixing and unfixing meanings and identities, both the delimitation and the instrumental expansion of the social – only encourages the dominant to feverishly step up both the intensity and the range of their ordering practices. But the work will never be done: in the capitalist world-system the moment of absolute order will never come. Even worse, precisely because global capitalism becomes ever more totalizing, the task of order making will become ever more grandiose and complex, the suturing of the fragments of the system into a totality an ever more unfinishable, Sisyphean labour. As Zygmunt Bauman puts it, '[p]roblems are created by problem-solving, new areas of chaos are generated by ordering activity' (1991: 14). For one thing, this is how we can interpret the ceaseless search for better measurement methods and technologies in the ratings industry, or the frantic, never-ending quest for new advertising and marketing strategies to capture the elusive consumer.

But if the forces of order are continuously deployed without ever achieving complete order (ultimate closure, a finite and finished totality, totalized structure), then the forces of chaos are also continuously impinging on the system without ever resulting in total chaos (inexhaustible openness, unbounded infinitude, unfettered process). Instead, capitalist postmodernity is an orderly disorder, or disorderly order, whose hegemony rests on the setting of structural limits, themselves precarious, to the possibilities of random excess. It is within these limits that 'resistance' to the dominant takes place (except in the rare situations of 'revolutions', which are temporary moments of limitlessness). In Wallerstein's words:

> Universalism [of capitalist modernity] is a 'gift' of the powerful to the weak which confronts the latter with a double bind: to refuse the gift is to lose; to accept the gift to lose. The only plausible reaction of the weak is neither to refuse nor to accept, or both to refuse and to accept – in short, the path of the seemingly irrational zigzags (both cultural and political) of the weak that has characterized most of nineteenth- and especially twentieth-century history. (Wallerstein, 1991: 217)

In other words, the negotiations and resistances of the subordinate, bounded as they are within the boundaries of the system, unsettle (but do not destroy) those boundaries.

It is convenient at this point to return to John Fiske and to recontextualize his celebration of the bottom-up power that television audiences evince in the construction of their own meanings and pleasures. To be fair to Fiske, his writings are much more complex than the simplified reiterations would have us believe. In no way is he simply an apologist for liberal pluralism. On the contrary, he derives his relative optimism from his analysis of (mainly US) commercial television as 'the prime site where the dominant have to recognize the insecurity of their power, and where they have to encourage cultural difference with all the threat to their own position that this implies' (1987: 326). The problem is that Fiske tends to overestimate (and romanticize) precisely that threat. This threat simply makes the task of the television industries to retain their dominance more complicated and expensive (but not impossible), just as the dispersion and proliferation of viewing practices makes the task of audience measurement more complicated and expensive – and therefore, it should be said, more wasteful, more nasty, more aggressive. Furthermore, it should be noted that the encouragement of cultural difference is, as I have argued above, part and parcel of the chaotic system of capitalist postmodernity itself. In this sense, it would be mistaken to see the acting out of difference unambiguously as an act of resistance; what needs to be emphasized, rather, is that the desire to be different can be simultaneously complicit with and defiant against the institutionalization of excess of desire in capitalist postmodernity. At most, the resistive element in popular practices is, as Michel de Certeau (1984) has suggested in *The Practice of Everyday Life*, a matter of 'escaping without leaving'.

Meaghan Morris has criticized the fact that the idea of what she terms 'excess of process over structure' has led to 'a cultural studies that celebrates "resistance" as a programmed feature of capitalist culture', and to 'a theoretical myth of the Evasive Everyday' (1992: 464–5). Indeed, such a celebration can easily take place when the acts of 'evasive every-dayness' are taken at face value, in the context, say, of closed circuits of communication (where departure from 'preferred readings' can be straight-forwardly read as 'evasion', this in turn heroized as 'resistance'). However, if we place these acts in the more global and historical context of the chaotic system of capitalist postmodernity, then their 'political' status becomes much more ambivalent. Then we have to take into account their significance in a system which already incorporates a celebration of limit-less flux as a mechanism within its ordering principle. What is built-in in the culture of capitalist postmodernity is not 'resistance', but uncertainty, ambiguity, the chaos that emanates from the institutionalization of infinite semiosis.

This, then, is how the true realm of uncertainty which characterizes the 'global village' should be specified – if we still want to retain that metaphor. It should be clear, finally, that the unstable multiplicity of this 'essentially deconstructive world' (Marcus, 1992: 327) no longer makes it possible, as modern discourse would have it, to tell a single, total story about the world 'today'. As Stratton has put it, in the postmodern episteme 'there is no fixed site of truth, no absolute presence; there are just multiple representations, an infinite number of rewritings' (1990: 287). Theorizing in the postmodern context has to give up on the search for totalizing and universalizing forms of knowledge and truth. Put more positively, if there is no position from which a fixed and absolute truth (i.e. a Grand Theory) can be put forward, then we can only strive for the construction of 'partial truths', to use James Clifford's (1986) term. Critical theorizing, then, always has to imply an acknowledgement of its own open-endedness, its own partiality in its inevitable drive towards narrative closure, in its attempts to impose order in the stories it tells. At the very least, a critical understanding of what it means to live in the true realm of uncertainty that is capitalist postmodernity must take on board a positive uncertainty about its own 'communicative' effect, its own attempts to construct meaningful discourse in which the chaos of the world 'today' is rendered in 'sceptical, if not paranoid assessment' (Morris 1988b: 197). Or in the words of Laclau: 'Utopia is the essence of any communication and social practice' (1991: 93).

Notes

1   This sense of reassurance (and thus of certainty) applies to both the proponents and the opponents of the 'global village'.
2   As is well known, the passing of the dominant paradigm has been widely felt within the discipline as a 'ferment in the field', as documented in the special issue of the *Journal of Communication* (1983).
3   In this respect, Carey aligns himself with the liberal pragmatism of American philosophers such as John Dewey and Richard Rorty. It should be noted that the scope of Carey's 'Great Community' never seems to become thoroughly global: his 'we' remains firmly located within the boundaries of the United States of America.
4   The most well-known exemplar of such a liberal pluralist inflection of the 'new audience research' is Tamar Liebes and Elihu Katz (1990).
5   This idea, of course, was first developed by Herbert Marcuse in his *One-Dimensional Man* (1964).
6   This exposition draws heavily on Ernesto Laclau's concise essay 'The impossibility of society', in his *New Reflections on the Revolution of our Time* (1991).
7   For a further elaboration of the concept of coevalness in contemporary global culture, see Johannes Fabian (1983).

References

Ahmed, A.S. (1992) *Postmodernism and Islam: Predicament and Promise*. London: Routledge.
Ang, I. (1991) *Desperately Seeking the Audience*. London/New York: Routledge.
Baudrillard, J. (1983) *In the Shadow of the Silent Majorities*, trans. P. Foss, P. Patton and J. Johnston. New York: Semiotext(e).
Bauman, Z. (1991) *Modernity and Ambivalence*. Cambridge: Polity Press.
Carey, J. (1989) *Communication as Culture*. Boston: Unwin Hyman.
de Certeau, M. (1984) *The Practice of Everyday Life*, trans. S. Randall. Berkeley, CA: University of California Press.
Clifford, J. (1986) 'Introduction: partial truths', in J. Clifford and G.E. Marcus (eds), *Writing Culture: the Poetics and Politics of Ethnography*. Berkeley/Los Angeles/London: University of California Press.
Crowley, D. and Mitchell, D. (eds) (1994) *Communication Theory Today*. Cambridge: Polity Press.
Curran, J. (1990) 'The new revisionism in mass communication research: a reappraisal', *European Journal of Communication*, 5 (2–3): 135–64.
Curran, J. (1991) 'Introduction', in J. Curran and M. Gurevitch (eds), *Mass Media and Society*. London and New York: Oxford University Press.
Fabian, J. (1983) *Time and Other*. New York: Columbia University Press.
Fiske, J. (1987) *Television Culture*. London: Methuen.
Geertz, C. (1988) *Works and Lives: the Anthropologist as Author*. Cambridge: Polity Press.

Hall, S. (1980) 'encoding/decoding', in S. Hall, D. Hobson, A. Lowe and P.Willis (eds), *Culture, Media, Language*. London: Hutchinson.

Hayles, N.K. (1990) *Chaos Bound: Orderly Disorder in Contemporary Literature and Science*. Ithaca, NY: Cornell University Press.

Laclau, E. (1991) *New Reflections on the Revolution of our Time*. London: Verso.

Liebes, T. and Katz, E. (1990) *The Export of Meaning: Cross-cultural Readings of Dallas*. New York: Oxford University Press.

Marcus, G.E. (1992) 'Past, present and emergent identities: requirements for ethnographies of late twentieth-century modernity worldwide', in S. Lash and J. Friedman (eds), *Modernity and Identity*. Oxford: Basil Blackwell.

Marcuse, H. (1964) *One-Dimensional Man*. Boston: Beacon Press.

Morris, M. (1988a) 'Banality in cultural studies', *Block*, 14: 15–25; reprinted in P. Mellencamp (ed.), *Logics of Television: Essays in Cultural Criticism*. Bloomington, Ind.: Indiana University Press, 1990.

Morris, M. (1988b) 'Things to do with shopping centres', in S. Sheridan (ed.), *Grafts*. London: Verso.

Morris, M. (1992) 'On the beach', in L. Grossberg, C. Nelson and P. Treichler (eds), *Cultural Studies*. New York/London: Routledge.

Poster, M. (1988) 'Introduction', in J. Baudrillard, *Selected Writings*, ed. M. Poster. Stanford, CA: Stanford University Press.

Rogers, E.M. (1962) *The Diffusion of Innovations*. Glencoe, Ill.: Free Press.

Rogers, E.M. (1976) 'Communication and development: the passing of a dominant paradigm', *Communications Research*, 3: 213–40.

Schlesinger, P. (1991) *Media, State and Nation*. London: Sage.

Stratton, J. (1990) *Writing Sites: a Genealogy of the Postmodern World*. Hemel Hempstead: Harvester Wheatsheaf.

Tomlinson, J. (1991) *Cultural Imperialism*. London: Pinter.

Wallerstein, I. (1991) *Geopolitics and Geoculture*. Cambridge: Cambridge University Press.

20

Remote control? Politics, technology and 'electronic democracy'
John Street

This chapter is taken from the *European Journal of Communication*, 12 (1997), pp. 27–42.

There are technology fashions just as there are fashions in everything else. And the processes that mark the rise and fall of styles in clothes, foods or pop stars, also order the acclaim awarded to technologies. In 1994, the hot news was the CD-ROM; in 1995, it was the Internet. Not surprisingly, therefore, politicians have been clambering aboard the Internet campaign bus. In February 1995, the G7 nations met to discuss 'the information society'. Bill Clinton's White House boasted that it could be reached by the click of a keyboard, as could endless other political information resources (see Harrison, 1994). Even the British Civil Service tentatively opened itself to the gaze of travellers on the superhighway. In the 1994 Congressional mid-term elections, an 'on-line political activist' from California was quoted as saying: 'I think that by 1996, we will begin to see some number of campaigns either won or lost because campaign operations either use or fail to use network communications and organisation' (*International Herald Tribune*, 9 November, 1994). In 1995 one presidential hopeful, Lamar Alexander, began his campaign on the Internet (*Guardian*, 1 March 1995). In the UK, the Labour Party's (1995) guide to the Internet promises that 'we will be able to get more information about central and local government, and participate in decision-making'.

These relatively modest developments have, however, prompted a grander rhetoric that heralds the dawning of a new democratic order. As one writer proclaimed recently: 'The Net is the world's only functioning political anarchy but it could soon become a major tool for democracy. By allowing anyone, everywhere access to the information and opinions of anyone else, anywhere else, a morsel is being given to mankind with one instruction: "Eat Me", so that we may grow' (Fenchurch, 1994: 11). A similar spirit seemed to inform Newt Gingrich's dream of a 'virtual Congress' and Al Gore's talk of the 'electronic town meeting'. The Clinton administration has set itself the goal of creating 'a seamless web of communication networks, computers, databases and consumer electronics' that will protect and preserve democracy (quoted in Glencross, 1993: 3). Implied in all this is the idea that we are creating the conditions for an electronic democracy. With the networks in place and interactive technology to hand, people can vote on issues, inform themselves on government policy, interrogate their representatives; they can become active, effective citizens of the democratic dream.

Among advocates of these new possibilities, two different underlying agendas can be detected. For some, the technology represents a way of improving the existing form of (liberal) democracy. For others, though, it constitutes an opportunity to create a *new* form of democracy – or rather, the revival of an old one: the direct democracy of Ancient Athens. Electronic polling offers the chance to get 'Back to Greece' (Adonis and Mulgan, 1994).

This talk of electronic democracy (whatever its form) is not just a product of Internet fever. It is part of a long argument, one which follows the course of communications technology generally (Carey, 1989). As information technology has developed, so it has been incorporated into the debate about, and the rhetoric of, democracy. Throughout the late 1970s and early 1980s, there were excited reports of experiments in new participatory technologies. This in turn prompted an academic literature devoted to the idea and practice of electronic democracy (Barber, 1984; Arterton, 1987; Abramson et al., 1988; McLean, 1989; van de Donk et al., 1995). This acknowledgement and incorporation of new technologies has not, however, created the conditions for a fresh consensus.

The current interest in the Internet has, therefore, simply served to add conviction to the old arguments and to turn distant possibilities into more proximate probabilities. In this chapter, I want to make some sense of this recent bracketing of electronic democracy with the Internet. I want, in particular, to make explicit the connection between the theory of (electronic) democracy and the technology used to give effect to it. Arguments about electronic democracy, or democracy in general, cannot be considered only in philosophical hyperspace.

Democracy and the new technology

It makes little sense to talk of 'free speech' without reference to the methods by which (mass) communication occurs. This ability to speak freely depends on access to the main means of communication, and this is not a necessary or natural state of affairs. It has to be organized or created. A coherent political theory must also be attached, I want to suggest, to an account of the process by which (1) the technology itself is developed and directed; and by which (2) the technology is implicated in the ideas, values and opportunities that may be imagined. Arguments about the virtue of electronic democracy, or about the relative merits of competing versions of it, must rest upon some assumption about the ability to control technical change, to direct it in ways that help realize particular ends. Only with such control will it be possible to advance or delay certain forms of electronic democracy. If no such control is possible, if technical change is autonomous, then arguments about the *kind* of democracy become largely irrelevant. At the very least, arguments about electronic democracy must assume some degree of control over the use to which the technology is put.

This, though, cannot be the end of the story. Supplementing arguments about electronic democracy with discussion of theories of technical change creates an artificial divide between theory and practice. What I want to suggest is that technical systems and political values are not discrete entities; rather they are each extensions of the other. We live through our technology; our values and our identities both shape and are shaped by it. In this sense, technology is cultural. And so is political theory; it is embedded in our forms of life in the same way that technology is (Winner, 1986). If this is true, then arguments about electronic democracy must go beyond questions of theory and technique, to look at the ways in which the technology constructs the kind of people and places that will form this new democracy; it must ask: what kind of citizen, what kind of public will inhabit these 'seamless webs'?

Much recent discussion has argued that both public space and the notion of citizenship are being transformed by emergent forms of communication. Developments in delivery systems (satellite, cable, etc.), the proliferation of channels and the tendency towards narrowcasting, are seen as creating a political order in which politics is being domesticated and citizenship being privatized (Keane, 1991; Habermas, 1992; Silverstone, 1994). This process is reinforced by those, like Steve Jones (1995: 28–9), who argue that by breaking down existing boundaries, the new forms of communication are simultaneously dissolving the communities that ground a notion of a common good/general will. The result is a political life marked by instrumental, individualistic self-interest in which a democracy based on public participation is impossible. Equally, there are those who argue that this same technology is creating ideal conditions for a new democratic order (e.g. Rheingold, 1992).

What these competing claims represent is the intimate connection between political ideas and technical forms. Arguments about electronic democracy must engage with both. Thus, this chapter is divided into three sections. The first reviews the existing political arguments about electronic democracy. The second addresses the notion of technical change that underlies the argument, but which is rarely made explicit. The third tries to reconcile these two dimensions – the political and the technical – in advocating a different approach to the debate about electronic democracy.

The political theory of electronic democracy

The argument for electronic democracy

Although advocates differ over their preferred model of democracy, they are linked by a shared belief in the ability of electronic technology to create the conditions for political participation. As one enthusiast writes: 'Modern communications technology can provide the means to broadly educate and enlighten citizens, to engage them in discussions of the public good and the means to achieve it, and to empower citizens in their quest for self-determination' (Staton, 1994: 31–2). Underlying such claims is the thought that attempts to guarantee full participation in modern democracies have been wrecked by four, previously insurmountable, problems: *time, size, knowledge* and *access*. Participation, the argument runs, is limited by the problems of assembling large numbers of people, of the ignorance of ordinary citizens, and of the inequalities in the distribution of resources which affect people's capacity for involvement. Taken together, these difficulties make direct participation impractical and undesirable.

Electronic democracy seems to offer a solution to all these problems, thereby opening up the possibility of full participation. A wired-up world would solve the difficulties of *time* because communication and participation become instantaneous. Citizens can participate at the push of a button. They do not need to meet in cold halls or travel to polling booths. Similarly, problems of *size* are solved because physical space becomes irrelevant. It is no longer necessary to gather people in a single place. And so it is with problems in the distribution of *knowledge*. It is now widely available through networks, which also remove the problems of *access*. The costs of information and access are dramatically reduced, and as Jon Bing argues: 'Groups which up to now have had organisational problems will find it easier to become a political pressure group' (quoted in Lloyd, 1983: 634). The use of the Internet to generate international petitions is an obvious example. Seen like this, electronic democracy seems to offer a solution to the problems of liberal democrats (Becker and Staton, 1981) and direct democrats (Barber, 1984). It hardly seems to matter what kind of democracy you favour, electronic technology can guarantee its success. But it is precisely this sort of reasoning which critics of electronic democracy revolt against.

The argument against electronic democracy

There are four main lines of criticism directed at electronic democracy. The first concentrates upon the inherent theoretical difficulties within the idea of democracy. As Iain McLean (1989) points out, there are some 'problems of democracy' that cannot be solved by the application of technology. Democratic decisions are not just the product of citizen choices. It depends how you register those choices. As the argument about proportional representation makes abundantly clear, the character of the electoral system can crucially affect the result. You get different majorities and different winners depending on whether you use single-transferable votes or a list system. What counts as 'the best' will depend upon judgements about how democracy ought to work, what interests ought to feature and what results ought to be produced. These obstacles are exacerbated by the thought that there may not be a majority among any given population. There are instead 'cycling majorities', in which any given majority is the product of agenda-setting and voting rules. Once again, the problem cannot be solved by the expedient of the Internet and the computer. Technology does nothing to solve the conceptual problems that democracy generates.

A second line of criticism derives from the assumption that by increasing access to, and the availability of, data, information technology improves the quality of democracy. While there are powerful reasons for seeing freedom of information as a central tenet of democracy, it does not follow that all information in itself enhances democracy. Democratic decisions are not equivalent to mathematical calculations. Decisions are not necessarily improved by the simple expedient of acquiring more data. All decisions are ultimately matters of judgement, and the art of judgement may, in fact, be hampered by an excess of information (Vickers, 1965; Dennett, 1986).

These first two lines of criticism lead to a third: that the kind of democracy being proposed is a debased, impoverished version of the true ideal. Democracy becomes a mere device for registering preferences. 'Modern technology', writes Michael Walzer (1985: 306–7):

> makes possible something like this . . . we might organize push-button referenda on crucial issues, the citizens alone in their living rooms, watching television, arguing only with their spouses, hands hovering over their private voting machines . . . But is this the exercise of power? I am inclined to say, instead, that is only another example of the erosion of value – a false and ultimately degrading way of sharing in the making of decisions.

Like Walzer, Jean Elshtain (1982: 108) argues that electronic political participation is equivalent to making consumer choices on the shopping channel. The key element of democracy – deliberative, public policy choices – is replaced by privatized. instrumental decisions: 'advocates of interactive television display a misapprehension of the nature of real democracy, which they confuse with the plebiscite system'. 'A true democratic polity', she continues, 'involves a deliberative process, participation with other citizens, a sense of moral responsibility for one's society and the enhancement of individual possibilities through action in, and for, the *res publica*' (Elshtain, 1982: 109).

The thought that electronic democracy is promoting a particular, degenerate form of democracy links to a final criticism. This is the complaint that the technologies of electronic democracy actually serve to promote the interests of the powerful. Such arguments draw on the gap between promise and practice in the operation of actual systems of electronic participation. But they also draw on the claim that the problems of access that beset previous forms of democracy are reproduced in the new electronic order. The same imbalances and inequality of resources continue to distort participation. It is, furthermore, possible to read into the rhetoric and practice of electronic democracy the interests and ambitions of dominant groups, to see it as part of a larger project to depoliticize politics, transforming the citizen into the consumer (Weizenbaum, 1984; Zolo, 1992). Imagining such a future electronic democracy, Kevin Davey

(*New Times*, 3 February 1996: 3) creates a scenario in which the system already knows how the citizen is going to vote because it has complete information on everyone and everything. Voting itself becomes entirely redundant because it is entirely predictable.

Summing up current debate about electronic democracy, Calabrese and Borchert (1996: 264–5) observe that while 'the discourse on electronic democracy is aesthetically pleasing', it has to be treated cautiously: 'visions of empowerment are illusory or manipulative if they do not rest on the foundation of a clearly articulated vision of government.' On this basis, there is, I think, a strong inclination to side with the critics in this debate. Democracy is not simply a method for registering votes. The application of a more efficient technology is not, therefore, an adequate response. Equally, democracy requires more than the collection of information. It is an opportunity to deliberate about the conflicting claims of public and private goods. But to assert such things is not, by the same token, an adequate response either. The discussion of electronic democracy cannot be reduced to a formal debate about the relative merits of competing models of democracy. As the preceding discussion should indicate, the debate is not just about abstract ideas, but also about the conditions for their realization. The debate has, therefore, to engage with the technology itself and its effects.

The technology of electronic democracy

A coherent response to the possibility of electronic democracy must avoid three traps. These are set by any attempt to make sense of the development and impact of technology, and can be captured in three mistaken claims about technology: that it is neutral, that it is autonomous and that it can be selected freely.

Proponents of electronic democracy seem most vulnerable to the first of these, the idea that the technology is neutral. For them, information technology provides a 'technical fix'. The 'problems' of democracy are seen as merely practical, and to be solved by the application of technology.

But technical fixes are only 'fixes' because of the way the problem is defined. They do not constitute 'the' answer but 'an' answer. Technical fixes are less about fixing a problem, rather they are *imposing a particular definition* of what the problem is (and to which the technology represents a happy solution). If democracy's problems are practical, then technology may solve them, but if they are not, then technology merely reproduces them in a different form. The technical fix is, in fact, a 'political' solution, in the sense that it seeks to propagate a particular view of the world and of the methods appropriate to ordering it.

It is partly out of recognition of the problem of the 'technical fix' that critics of electronic democracy focus upon the interests behind the technology. For them, the technology represents a deliberate attempt by powerful interests to deskill and depoliticize citizens (Campbell and Connor, 1986; Lyon, 1994). It is the commercial and political incentives of the powerful that create the rhetoric of electronic democracy. But this version of technical change, which sees it as the product of political choice, overlooks the question of how the technology itself is brought into being. The Internet was not created by sheer act of will. Drawing attention to the commercial, political and military interests linked to it (Calabrese and Borchert, 1996), while important, does not in itself establish them as the intentional authors of the technology. As Thomas Hughes (1987) demonstrates in his study of the development of the electricity grid, technical change has a momentum which is often independent of those who appear to control it. They are as often forced to cope with the many unanticipated consequences of technical change as they are able to plan that change.

This leads to the third of the three traps which threaten accounts of technical change. This is the idea that technology is autonomous, that it is directed by a technical rationality which is not only independent of centres of political power, but actually dictates to them. Such a view can inspire technological dystopianism (Ellul, 1964) or utopianism (Pool, 1990), both of which suggest that we can do little more than accept the inevitable technological (and subsequent social) revolution. More modestly, it can be detected in the fear that electronic democracy signals an era of 'political consumerism' in which participation is an extension of shopping (shipping being a lesser form of activity than political involvement) (Sartori, 1989). The key idea is that the technology produces efforts in its users, and that these effects are the consequence of an inescapable technical logic.

The problem with this approach is, in part, that the argument works only by assuming that technology produces harmful or deleterious effects, that consumption *is* a lesser activity than political participation. This is clearly a claim that is open to debate. More importantly, though, the autonomous technology argument rests on a strong notion of determinism. This, too, is open to debate. The same technology has a different meaning and different effects according to its place in space and time. The culture in which it is embedded also constitutes it. (For a fuller version of this argument, see Street, 1992).

In short, the three views of technology – as neutral, chosen or autonomous – are flawed to the extent that they overlook the combination of political, scientific and cultural processes that construct the technology. Avoiding the three traps means, I think, that we must respond to the debate about electronic democracy by recognizing the mutual dependence of political argument and technology.

The core ideas within the political argument are themselves the product of our relationship with technology. At one level, the technology is the embodiment of certain interests and possibilities, but at another it is the bearer of effects: it changes what we can imagine and what we can want, it alters our politics. Though we can identify the interests and choices around a technology, they do not automatically become the authors of that technology. The technology is not something that exists as a simple object for our use. It acts to structure our choices and preferences, but not in a wholly determinist way. The relationship is in constant flux: political processes shape technology; and it then shapes politics. What possibilities and alternatives exist at any one time is a matter of empirical investigation, an investigation that does not end either with the technology or the political interests promoting it. Debate about electronic democracy has to avoid theoretical idealism and technological determinism; it has to acknowledge the complex interplay of political ideas and technical practices. I want now to explore further the implications of this injunction.

Rethinking electronic democracy

Debates about democracy are debates about information, about how it is distributed and how it is used (see, for example, Lively, 1975; Arblaster, 1987). Any attempt to think about electronic democracy must, therefore, consider how information technologies do (and should) structure access to, and use of, political knowledge.

As I noted earlier, there are those who argue that the current forms of mass communication threaten democracy by 'distorting' political knowledge, adversely affecting people's ability to perform the role of the democratic citizen and to exercise political judgement. Elshtain's (1982) talk of the citizen being transformed into a consumer is based on the thought, to misquote Oscar Wilde, that the consumer knows the price of everything and the value of nothing. In the process, politics becomes a form of market exchange; it is 'privatized', and hence what is called 'public opinion' is merely a summation of private desires (Sartori, 1989). The citizen ceases to exist as a self-conscious actor. 'The real electors', writes Danilo Zolo (1992: 163–4),

> see themselves replaced by their own demoscopic and televisual projection, which anticipates them and leaves them the passive observers of themselves. Individual citizens, despite being the true holders of the right to vote, find themselves subjected to the pressure of public predictions which tend circularly to be self-fulfilling by edging them out of the electoral event.

For such critics, the form of mass communication has erased the possibility of rational political decisions.

These gloomy prognostications recall the familiar story that accompanies almost all new technologies, and are most common in reflections upon the general effects of television. Equally familiar are the rebuttals which offer a defence founded in the notion of the active audience. These arguments parallel those around technology, in which the alternative is between choice and determinism, between activism and passivism. But in both cases this is a false dichotomy (see Ang, 1996). The citizen's relationship to politics cannot be read off some general account of audience behaviour or programme content, but instead has to be understood in terms of context and forms of address – 'the contingency of meaning', in Corner's words (1995: 136). Writers like Silverstone (1994: ch. 3) focus on the viewer's changing relationship to politics through the twin effects of domestication and suburbanization. The implication of this is that we need to recognize the way in which different media systems construct different opportunities for political engagement and different levels of thought. As Schickler (1994) observes, different formats can produce different types of participation. The phone-in, for example, 'seems conducive to prejudiced, sloppy thinking, and to extremely simple views of the social and political process' (Schickler 1994: 194). Similarly, Langdon Winner (1994) argues that the tendency to present information in restless 'bitesize' chunks (along the lines pioneered by MTV) fragments political understanding, while others contend that the political 'community' is itself a product of the organization of communication networks (Friedland, 1996). The implications of these claims – whether or not we accept their particular formulation – is that the way information is presented and organized is correlated with forms of political discourse. In other words, the citizen's capacity to make political judgements is dependent upon the way in which political information is delivered and received. Thinking about electronic democracy has to be sensitive to these issues.

But such elements of electronic democracy do not exist independently. They have to fit within a larger setting. As Blumler and Gurevitch (1995: 98) argue: 'the media can pursue democratic values only in ways that are compatible with the socio-political and economic environment in which they operate. Political communication arrangements follow the contours of and derive their resources from the society of which they are a part.' Compatibility cannot be guaranteed. Brants et al. (1996: 246) point to one potential cause of tension in their study of communication networks in the Netherlands: 'Network technology has the potential to create a new public sphere which fits the social structure better . . . However, politics does not yet fit the new technology. Politicians feel uncomfortable with the different role they play in such a challenging direct democracy.' The organization of electronic democracy has to be made to accord with the way in which representation and legitimation operate within the wider political system.

It is not enough, however, just to draw attention to the way the design of the forms of address may effect participation, or to the tensions between different interests within the political system. These matters are overlaid by the question as to what *kind* of democracy is being sought. It is clear from the current debate about electronic democracy that competing notions of democracy are in play. There are those who favour a direct form of democracy and those who advocate a representative one. This division has consequences for the organization of the technology as well as for political practice. So in arguing about electronic democracy and the potential represented by the Internet, we have to connect various issues through the competing notions of democracy, between those that seek to aggregate preferences and those that aim to create a forum for deliberative decision-making.

Much of the literature on electronic democracy tends to assume that it is intended to serve the first of these goals. The technology is used to furnish individuals with more information about issues that relate to their personal interests. The objection to this form of electronic democracy is expressed, as we saw earlier, in terms of its treatment of politics as a form of market exchange and its creation of a citizen who is a privatized consumer. Although this objection is presented as a general critique of electronic democracy, it does not have this force. It is, in fact, just an objection to one way of organizing electronic democracy and one kind of democracy. Or to put it another way: if electronic democracy is organized differently or a different model of democracy is defended, then these objections collapse.

There is no reason why electronic democracy should not take another form. It could, for instance, be used to support a system of deliberative democracy. There are powerful reasons (Fishkin, 1991; Miller, 1992) for supposing that democracies in which citizens are required to deliberate on the choices which face a society, rather than simply registering their preferences, produce better decisions. The point of the deliberative process is to allow people to *form* opinions, rather than just to *express* them (Miller, 1992: 67). If this is the purpose allotted to democracy, then the forms of communication must accord with it. Citizens must not only be able to interrogate databases and acquire an expertise of their own, they must be able to reflect upon this knowledge in dialogue with their fellow citizens. This means that the hierarchies which tend to protect forms of expertise have to be broken down. At the same time, it is not just a matter of increasing access to information and allowing for discussion. There also needs to be the opportunity for *deliberation*. There need to be networks which enable both discussion *and* deliberation. People have to make decisions, not just exchange thoughts.

If we are persuaded by this version of democracy, then a further set of issues are raised, among which is the question of the type of collectivity that is to deliberate. The terms that define the community depend again, as with the choice between types of democracy, on political judgement. Do we want, for instance, to enshrine the notion of 'community' as the rule-bound 'club' or as some form of 'commonwealth'? (Bellamy and Hollis, 1995). These questions have to be settled both in terms of their political desirability and in terms of the conditions that make them possible. As we have already noted, the Internet can, on the one hand, create different types of community (Friedland, 1996) and on the other, it can destroy community (Jones, 1995).

These questions require political debate and judgement, but they are not confined to the realm of political theory. They also engage with the ways in which forms of communication are organized. Political relationships depend upon the forms of communication that enable them to occur. This is not just a function of the political economy of communication, although this is clearly important, but it also depends upon the forms of address which are allowed for. These questions cannot, therefore, be answered by political theorists alone. We need to integrate political theory, technical change and cultural practice. We have to see arguments about 'democracy' not as abstract ideas, but as contingent upon, and bound up with, the technology that helps constitute those ideas. Equally, the technology itself must be seen as part of the political and cultural realm, not as an instrument to be used or as an independent force to which we must be reconciled. It is not enough simply to identify a form of democracy as desirable, and to sketch out the role that the technology has to play in fulfilling it. The technology is itself the product and expression of competing and contradictory political interests. One example of this fact was provided by the city of Norwich. Following a fire in its central library, the city council devised a plan to create an information infrastructure with a view to attracting EU funding. The EU criteria emphasized an element of active citizen participation. When Brussels failed to provide funding, a new source of cash was sought: the National Lottery. The project changed to become a heritage site, offering historical tableaux in virtual reality. The worthy, democratic aims were lost from view.

Conclusion

If the debate about electronic democracy is to move beyond the crude dichotomy established by those who advocate it and those who decry it, and if we are to reflect cogently upon the experiments in such democracy which are emerging, then we need to be explicit about what kind of democracy is being advocated. If deliberative democracy is the preferred option, then it is important to state and defend this, but the argument cannot end there. It is not just a matter of applying the technology to this particular ideal. Rather we have to think through the implications of deliberative democracy for both the forms of address and the political economy of the means of communication. At the same time, the possibility of such a democracy cannot be attributed simply to acts of political will. That kind of control over the technology is not possible because technological change is not simply the product of political choice. So the idea of democracy to which we aspire must be understood as partly a product of the technology that surrounds it. Political ideas cannot be separated from the medium in which they are thought, and hence it makes little sense to talk of returning to Ancient Greek democracy via new technology, or of simply 'improving' an existing democratic form. Technical change brings with it new ideas and possibilities, and new notions of democracy; at the same time, these possibilities have themselves to be subject to critical political analysis, informed by a particular notion of democracy. The politics of electronic democracy are also the politics of technology.

Note

Earlier version of this chapter were presented at seminars in Leicester and Glasgow, and at the 1996 Political Studies Association conference. Each audience was very helpful, and I owe particular thanks to Jay Blumler, Simon Frith, Karen Lury, Keith Negus and Charles Raab.

References

Abramson, J.B., Arterton, F.C. and Orren, G.R. (1988) *The Electronic Commonwealth*. New York: Basic Books.

Adonis, A. and Mulgan, G. (1994) 'Back to Greece: the scope for direct democracy', *Demos Quarterly*, 3: 2–9.

Ang, I. (1996) *Living Room Wars*. London: Routledge.

Arblaster, A. (1987) *Democracy*. Milton Keynes: Open University Press.

Arterton, C. (1987) *Teledemocracy*. London: Sage.

Barber, B. (1984) *Strong Democracy: Participatory Politics for a New Age*. San Francisco: University of California Press.

Becker, T. and Staton, C.D. (1981) 'Hawaii televote', *Political Science*, 33 (1): 52–6.

Bellamy, R. and Hollis, M. (1995) 'Liberal justice: political and metaphysical', *The Philosophy Quarterly*, 45 (178): 1–19.

Blumler, J. and Gurevitch, M. (1995) *The Crisis of Public Communication*. London: Routledge.

Brants, K., Huizenga, M. and van Meerten, R. (1996) 'The new canals of Amsterdam: an exercise in local electronic democracy', *Media, Culture and Society*, 18 (2): 233–48.

Calabrese, A. and Borchert, M. (1996) 'Prospects for electronic democracy in the United States: rethinking communication and social policy', *Media, Culture and Society*, 18 (2): 249–68.

Campbell, D. and Connor, S. (1986) *On the Record*. London: Michael Joseph.

Carey, J. (1989) *Communication as Culture*. London: Unwin Hyman.

Corner, J. (1995) *Television Form and Public Address*. London: Edward Arnold.

Dennett, D. (1986) 'Information, technology, and the virtues of ignorance', *Daedalus*, 115 (3): 135–53.

van de Donk, W., Snellen, I.Th.M. and Tops, P.W. (eds) (1995) *Orwell in Athens*. Amsterdam: IOS Press.

Ellul, J. (1964) *The Technological Society*. New York: Vintage.

Elshtain, J.B. (1982) 'Democracy and the QUBE tube', *The Nation*, 7–14 August, pp. 108–9.

Fenchurch, R. (1994) 'Network wonderland', *Demos Quarterly*, 4: 11.

Fishkin, J. (1991) *Democracy and Deliberation*. New Haven, Conn.: Yale University Press.

Friedland, L. (1996) 'Electronic democracy and the new citizenship', *Media, Culture and Society*, 18 (2): 185–212.

Glencross, D. (1993) 'Convergence at Aspen', *Spectrum* (Autumn), p. 3.

Habermas, J. (1992) *The Structural Transformation of the Public Sphere*. Cambridge: Polity Press.

Harrison, M. (1994) 'Exploring the information superhighway: political science and the Internet', Keele Research Paper, no. 6.

Hughes, T. (1987) *Networks of Power*. Baltimore, MD: Johns Hopkins University Press.

Jones, S. (ed.) (1995) *Cybersociety*. London: Sage.

Keane, J. (1991) *The Media and Democracy*. Cambridge: Polity Press.

Labour Party (1995) *The Net Effect*. London: Labour Party.

Lively, J. (1975) *Democracy*. Oxford: Basil Blackwell.

Lloyd, A. (1983) 'Europe examines electronic democracy', *New Scientist*, 2 June, p. 634.

Lyon, D. (1994) *The Electronic Eye*. Cambridge: Polity Press.

McLean, I. (1989) *Democracy and the New Technology*. Cambridge: Polity Press.

Miller, D. (1992) 'Deliberative democracy and social choice', *Political Studies*, 40 (special issue): 54–67.

Pool, I. (1990) *Technologies without Boundaries*. Boston, Mass.: Harvard University Press.

Rheingold, H. (1992) *Virtual Community*. London: Mandarin.

Sartori, G. (1989) 'Video power', *Government and Opposition*, 24 (1): 39–53.

Schickler, E. (1994) 'Democratizing technology: hierarchy and innovation in public life', *Polity*, 27 (2): 175–99.

Silverstone, R. (1994) *Television and Everyday Life*. London: Routledge.

Staton, C.D. (1994) 'Democracy's quantum leap', *Demos Quarterly*, 3: 31–2.

Street, J. (1992) *Politics and Technology*. London: Macmillan.

Vickers, G. (1965) *The Art of Judgment*. London: Chapman and Hall.

Walzer, M. (1985) *Spheres of Justice*. Oxford: Basil Blackwell.

Weizenbaum, J. (1984) *Computer Power and Human Reason*. London: Penguin.

Winner, L. (1986) *The Whale and the Reactor*. Chicago, Ill.: University of Chicago Press.

Winner, L. (1994) 'Three paradoxes of the information age', in G. Bender and T. Druckrey (eds), *Culture on the Brink: Ideologies of Technology*, pp. 191–7. Seattle, WA: Bay Press.

Zolo, D. (1992) *Democracy and Complexity*. Cambridge: Polity Press.

An introduction to the information age
Manuel Castells

In the last decade I was struck, as many have been, by a series of major historical events that have transformed our world/our lives. Just to mention the most important: the diffusion and deepening of the information technology revolution, including genetic engineering; the collapse of the Soviet Union, with the consequent demise of the international Communist movement, and the end of the Cold War that had marked everything for the last half a century; the restructuring of capitalism; the process of globalization; emergence of the Pacific as the most dynamic area of the global economy; the paradoxical combination of a surge in nationalism and the crisis of the sovereign nation-state; the crisis of democratic politics, shaken by periodic scandals and a crisis of legitimacy; the rise of feminism and the crisis of patriarchalism; the widespread diffusion of ecological consciousness; the rise of communalism as sources of resistance to globalization, taking in many contexts the form of religious fundamentalism; last, but not least, the development of a global criminal economy that is having significant impacts in international economy, national politics, and local everyday life.

I grew increasingly dissatisfied with the interpretations and theories, certainly including my own, that the social sciences were using to make sense of this new world. But I did not give up the rationalist project of understanding all this, in a coherent manner, that could be somewhat empirically grounded and as much as possible theoretically oriented. Thus, for the last 12 years I undertook the task of researching and understanding this wide array of social trends, working in and on the United States, Western Europe, Russia, Asian Pacific, and Latin America. Along the way, I found plenty of company, as researchers from all horizons are converging in this collective endeavour.

This chapter is taken from *City*, 7 (1997), pp. 6–16. It was originally an address to the Conference on 'Information and the City' held at Oxford University, March 1996.

My personal contribution to this understanding is the book in three volumes that I have now completed, *The Information Age*. [. . .] The first volume analyses the new social structure, the network society. The second volume studies social movements and political processes, in the framework of and in interaction with the network society. The third volume attempts an interpretation of macro-social processes, as a result of the interaction between the power of networks and the power of identity, focusing on themes such as the collapse of the Soviet Union, the emergence of the Pacific, or the ongoing process of global social exclusion and polarization. It also proposes a general theoretical synthesis.

I will take this opportunity to share with you the main lines of my argument, hoping that this will help a debate that I see emerging from all directions in the whole world. I see coming a new wave of intellectual innovation in which, by the way, British researchers are at the forefront.

Trying to summarize a considerable amount of material within one hour, I will follow a schematic format. I will focus on identifying the main features of what I consider to be the emerging, dominant social structure, the network society, that I find characteristic of informational capitalism, as constituted throughout the world. I will not indulge in futurology: everything I say is based on what I have perceived, rightly or wrongly, already at work in our societies. I will organize my lecture in one disclaimer, nine hypotheses, and one conclusion.

Disclaimer

I shall focus on the structure/dynamics of the network society, not on its historical genesis, that is how and why it came about, although in my book I propose a few hints about it. For the record: in my view, it resulted from the historical convergence of three *independent* processes, from whose interaction emerged the network society:

- The Information Technology Revolution, constituted as a paradigm in the 1970s.

- The restructuring of capitalism and of statism in the 1980s, aimed at superseding their contradictions, with sharply different outcomes.

- The cultural social movements of the 1960s, and their 1970s aftermath (particularly feminism and ecologism).

The Information Technology Revolution *did not* create the network society. But without Information Technology, the Network Society would not exist.

Rather than providing an abstract categorization of what this Network Society is, let me summarize its main features and processes, before attempting a synthesis of its embedded logic in the diversity of its cultural/institutional variations. There is no implicit hierarchy in the sequence of presentation of these features. They all interact in, guess what, a network.

1 An informational economy

It is an economy in which sources of productivity and competitiveness for firms, regions, countries, depend, more than ever, on knowledge, information, and the technology of their processing including the technology of management, and the management of technology. This is not the same as a service economy. There is informational agriculture, informational manufacturing, and different types of informational services, while a large number of service activities, e.g. in the developing world, are not informational at all.

The informational economy opens up an extraordinary potential for solving our problems, but, because of its dynamism and creativity, it is potentially more exclusionary than the industrial economy if social controls do not check the forces of unfettered market logic.

2 Global economy

This is not the same as a world economy. That has existed, in the West, at least since the sixteenth century. The global economy is a new reality: it is an economy whose core, strategically dominant activities have the potential of working as a unit in real time on a planetary scale. This is so for financial and currency markets, advanced business services, technological innovation, high technology manufacturing, media communication.

Most economic activity in the world, and most employment are not only national but regional or local. But, except for subsistence economies, the fate of these activities, and of their jobs, depends ultimately on the dynamics of the global economy, to which they are connected through networks and markets. Indeed, if labor tends to be local, capital is by and large globalized – not a small detail in a capitalist economy. This globalization has developed as a fully fledged system only in the last two decades, on the basis of information/communication technologies that were previously not available.

The global economy reaches out to the whole planet, but it is not planetary, it does not include the whole planet. In fact, it excludes probably a majority of the population. It is characterized by an extremely uneven geography. It scans the whole world, and links up valuable inputs, markets, and individuals, while switching off unskilled labour and poor markets. For a significant part of people around the world, there is a shift, from the point of view of dominant systemic interests, from exploitation to structural irrelevance.

This is different from the traditional First World/Third World opposition, because the Third World has become increasingly diversified, internally, and the First World has generated social exclusion, albeit in lesser proportion, within its own boundaries. Thus, I propose the notion of the emergence of a Fourth World of exclusion, made up not only of most of Africa, and rural Asia, and of Latin American shanties, but also of the

South Bronx, La Courneuve, Kamagasaki, or Tower Hamlets of this world. A fourth world that, as I document extensively in volume three, is predominantly populated by women and children.

3 The network enterprise

At the heart of the connectivity of the global economy and of the flexibility of informational capitalism, there is a new form of organization, characteristic of economic activity, but gradually extending its logic to other domains and organizations: the *network enterprise*. This is not the same as a network of enterprises. It is a network made either from firms or segments of firms, or from internal segmentation of firms. Multinational corporations, with their internal decentralization, and their links with a web of subsidiaries and suppliers throughout the world, are but one of the forms of this network enterprise. But others include strategic alliances between corporations, networks of small and medium businesses (such as in Northern Italy or Hong Kong), and link-ups between corporations and networks of small businesses through subcontracting and outsourcing.

So, the network enterprise is the specific set of linkages between different firms or segments, organized *ad hoc* for a specific project, and dissolving/reforming after the task is completed, e.g. IBM, Siemens, Toshiba. This ephemeral unit, The Project, around which a network of partners is built, is the actual operating unit of our economy, the one that generates profits or losses, the one that receives rewards or goes bust, and the one that hires and lays off, via its member organizations.

4 The transformation of work and employment: the flexi-workers

Work is at the heart of all historical transformations. And there is no exception to this. But the coming of the Information Age is full of myths about the fate of work and employment.

With the exception, and an important one, of Western Europe, there is no major surge of unemployment in the world after two decades of diffusion in information technology. Indeed, there is much higher unemployment in technologically laggard countries, regions, and sectors.

All evidence and analysis points to the variable impact of technology on jobs depending on a much broader set of factors, mainly firms' strategies and governments' policies. Indeed, the two most technologically advanced economies, the US and Japan, both display a low rate of unemployment. In the US in the last four years there is a net balance of 10 million new jobs, and the educational content for these new jobs is significantly higher than that of the pre-existing social structure: many more information-intensive jobs than hamburger flippers jobs have been created. Even manufacturing jobs are at an all time high on a global perspective: between 1970 and 1989, manufacturing jobs in the world increased by 72 per cent, even if OECD countries, particularly the US and the UK, have indeed de-industrialized.

There is certainly a major unemployment problem in the European Union, as a result of a combination of rigidities in the institutional environment, strategies of global redeployment by firms and, more importantly, the restrictive macroeconomic policies induced by an insane obsession with fitting in the Maastricht criteria that nobody, and particularly not Germany, will be able to qualify for, in an incredible example of collective alienation in paying respect to gods of economic orthodoxy that have taken existence independently from us.

There is indeed a serious unemployment problem in the inner cities of America, England, or France, among the uneducated and switched off populations, or in low technology countries around the world, particularly in the rural areas.

For the majority of people in America, for instance, unemployment is not a problem. And yet, there is tremendous anxiety and discontent about work. There is a real base for this concern:

(a) There is the transformation of power relationships between capital and labour in favour of capital, through the process of socio-economic restructuring that took place in the 1980s, both in a conservative environment (Reagan, Thatcher), and, to a lesser but real extent, in a less conservative environment (Spain, France). In this sense, new technologies allowed business to either automate or shift production offshore or out-source supplies or to subcontract to smaller firms or to obtain concessions from labour or all the above.

(b) The development of the network enterprise translates into down-sizing, subcontracting, and networking of labour, inducing flexibility of both business and labour, and individualization of contractual arrangements between management and labour. So, instead of layoffs what we often have are layoffs followed by subcontracting of services on an *ad hoc*, consulting basis, for the time and task to be performed, without job tenure and without social benefits provided by the firm.

This is indeed the general trend, exemplified by the rapid growth in all countries of self-employment, temporary work, and part-time, particularly for women. In England, between 40 and 45 per cent of the labour force seems to be already in these categories, as opposed to full time, regularly salaried employment, and is growing. Some studies in Germany project that in 2015, about 50 per cent of the labour force would be out of stable employment. And in the most dynamic region in the world, Silicon Valley, a study we have just completed shows that, in the midst of a job creation explosion, in the last ten years, between 50 per cent and 90 per cent of new jobs, most of them highly paid, are of this kind of non-standard labour arrangements.

The most significant change in work in the information age is the reversal of the socialization/salarization of labour that characterized the industrial age. The 'organization man' is out, the 'flexible women' is in. The individualization of work, and therefore of labour's bargaining power, is the major feature characterizing employment in the network society.

5 Social polarization and social exclusion

The processes of globalization, business networking, and individualization of labour weaken social organizations and institutions that represented/ protected workers in the information age, particularly labour unions and the welfare state. Accordingly, workers are increasingly left to themselves in their differential relationship to management, and to the market place.

Skills and education, in a constant redefinition of these skills, become critical in valorizing or devaluing people in their work. But even valuable workers may fall down for reasons of health, age, gender discrimination, or lack of capacity to adapt to a given task or position.

As a result of these trends, most societies in the world, and certainly OECD countries, with the US and the UK at the top of the scale, present powerful trends towards increasing inequality, social polarization and social exclusion. There is increasing accumulation of wealth at the top, and of poverty at the bottom.

In the US inequality has regressed to the pre-1920s period. In the limit, social exclusion creates pockets of dereliction with various entry points, but hardly any exits. It may be long-term unemployment, illness, functional illiteracy, illegal status, poverty, family disruption, psychological crisis, homelessness, drugs, crime, incarceration, etc. Once in this underworld, processes of exclusion reinforce each other, requiring a heroic effort to pull out from what I call the black holes of informational capitalism, that often have a territorial expression. The proportion of people in these black holes are staggering, and rapidly growing. In the US, it may reach above 10 per cent of the population, if you consider that simply the number of adults under the control of the justice system in 1966 was 5.4 million, that is almost 3 per cent of the population, while the proportion of people below the poverty line is 15 per cent.

The Information Age does not have to be the age of stepped-up inequality, polarization and social exclusion. But for the moment it is.

6 The culture of real virtuality

Shifting to the cultural realm, we see the emergence of a similar pattern of networking, flexibility, and ephemeral symbolic communication, in a culture organized around electronic media, including in this communication system the computer-mediated communication networks. Cultural expressions of all kinds are increasingly enclosed in or shaped by this world of electronic media. But the new media system is not characterized by the one-way, undifferentiated messages through a limited number of channels that constituted the world of mass media. And it is not a global village.

Media are extraordinarily diverse, and send targeted messages to specific segments of audiences and to specific moods of the audiences. They are increasingly inclusive, bridging from one to another, from network TV to cable or satellite TV, radio, VCR, musical video, walkman type of devices, connected throughout the globe, and yet diversified by cultures, constituting a hypertext with extraordinary inclusive capacity. Furthermore, slowly but surely, this new media system is moving towards interactivity, particularly if we include CMC networks, and their access to text, images, sounds, and will eventually link up with the current media system.

Instead of a global village we are moving towards mass production of customized cottages. While there is oligopolistic concentration of multimedia groups around the world, there is at the same time, market segmentation, and increasing interaction by and among the individuals that break up the uniformity of a mass audience. These processes induce the formation of what I call *the culture of real virtuality*. It is so, and not virtual reality, because when our symbolic environment is, by and large, structured in this inclusive, flexible, diversified hypertext, in which we navigate every day, the virtuality of this text is in fact our reality, the symbols from which we live and communicate.

7 Politics

This enclosure of communication in the space of flexible media does not only concern culture. It has a fundamental effect on *politics*. In all countries, the media have become the essential space of politics. Not all politics takes place through the media, and image making still needs to relate to real issues and real conflicts. But without significant presence in the space of media, actors and ideas are reduced to political marginality. This presence does not concern only, or even primarily, the moments of political campaigns, but the day-to-day messages that people receive by and from the media.

I propose the following analysis:

- To an overwhelming extent people receive their information, on the basis of which they form their political opinion, and structure their behaviour, through the media, particularly television and radio.

- Media politics needs to simplify the message/proposals.

- The simplest message is an image. The simplest image is a person. Political competition revolves around personalization of politics.

- The most effective political weapons are negative messages. The most effective negative message is character assassination of opponents' personalities. The politics of scandal, in the US, in Europe, in Japan, in Latin America etc. is the predominant form of political struggle.

- Political marketing is the essential means to win political competition in democratic politics. In the information age it involves media advertising, telephone banks, targeted mailing, image making, image unmaking, image control, presence in the media, staging of public appearances etc. This makes it an excessively expensive business, way beyond that of traditional party politics, so that mechanisms of political financing are obsolete, and parties use access to power as a way to generate resources to stay in power or to prepare to return to it. This is the fundamental source of political corruption, to which intermediaries add a little personal twist. This is also at the source of systemic corruption, that feeds scandal politics. The use of scandal as a weapon leads to increased expense and activity in intelligence, damage control, and access to the media. Once a market is created, intermediaries appear to retrieve, obtain, or fabricate information, offering it to the highest bidder. Politics becomes a horse race, and a soap opera motivated by greed, backstage manoeuvres, betrayals, and, often, sex and violence, becoming hardly distinguishable from TV scripts.

- Those who survive in this world become politically successful, for a while. But what certainly does not survive, after a few rounds of these tricks, is political legitimacy, not to speak of citizens' hope.

8 Timeless time

As with all historical transformations, the emergence of a new social structure is necessarily linked to the redefinition of the material foundations of life, *time and space*. Time and space are related, in society as in nature. Their meaning, and manifestations in social practice, evolve throughout histories and across cultures, as Giddens, Thrift, Harvey, Adams, Lash, and Urry, among others, have shown.

I propose the hypothesis that the network society, as the dominant social structure emerging in the Information Age, is organized around new forms of time and space: timeless time, the space of flows. These are the dominant forms, and not the forms in which most people live, but through their domination, they affect everybody. Let me explain, starting with time, then with some greater detail on space, given the specific interests of many in this conference.

In contrast to the rhythm of biological time of most of human existence, and to the clock time characterizing the industrial age, a new form of time characterizes the dominant logic of the network society: *timeless time*. It is defined by the use of new information/communication technologies in a relentless effort to annihilate time, to compress years in seconds, seconds in split seconds. Furthermore, the most fundamental aim is *to eliminate sequencing of time*, including past, present and future in the same hypertext, thus eliminating the 'succession of things' that, according to Leibniz, characterizes time, so that without things and their sequential ordering there is no longer time in society. We live, as in the recurrent circuits of the computer networks in the encyclopedia of historical experience, all our tenses at the same time, being able to reorder them in a composite created by our fantasy or our interests.

David Harvey has shown the relentless tendency of capitalism to eliminate barriers of time. But I think in the network society, that is indeed a capitalist society, but something else at the same time, all dominant processes tend to be constructed around timeless time. I find such a tendency in the whole realm of human activity. I find it certainly in the split second financial transactions of global financial markets, but I also find it, for instance, in instant wars, built around the notion of a surgical strike that devastates the enemy in a few hours, or minutes, to avoid politically unpopular, costly wars. Or in the blurring of the life cycle by new reproductive techniques, allowing people a wide range of options in the age and conditions of parenting, even storing their embryos to eventually produce babies later either by themselves, or through surrogate mothers, even after their procreators are dead. I find it in the twisting of working life by the variable chronology of labour trajectories and time schedules in increasingly diverse labour markets. And I find it in the vigorous effort to use medical technology, including genetic engineering, and computer-based medical care to exile death from life, to bring a substantial proportion of the population to a high level of life-expectancy, and to diffuse the belief that, after all, we are eternal, at least for some time.

As with space, timeless time characterizes dominant functions and social groups, while most people in the world are still submitted to biological time and to clock time. Thus, while instant wars characterize the technological powers, atrocious, lingering wars go on and on for years, around the planet, in a slow-motion destruction process, quasi-ignored by the world until they are discovered by some television programme.

I propose the notion that a fundamental struggle in our society is around the redefinition of time, between its annihilation or desequencing by networks, on one hand, and, on the other hand, the consciousness of glacial time, the slow-motion, inter-generational evolution of our species in our cosmological environment, a concept suggested by Lash and Urry, and a battle undertaken, in my view, by the environmental movement.

9   The Space of Flows

Many years ago (or at least it seems to me as many) I proposed the concept of Space of Flows to make sense of a body of empirical observation: dominant functions were increasingly operating on the basis of exchanges between electronic circuits linking up information systems in distant locations. Financial markets, global media, advanced business services, technology, information. In addition, electronically based, fast transportation systems reinforced this pattern of distant interaction by following up with movements of people and goods. Furthermore, new location patterns for most activities follow a simultaneous logic of territorial concentration/decentralization, reinstating the unity of their operation by electronic links, e.g. the analysis proposed in the 1980s on location patterns of high tech manufacturing; or the networked articulation of advanced services throughout the world, under the system labelled as 'global city'.

Why keep the term of space under these conditions? Reasons: (1) These electronic circuits do not operate in the territorial vacuum. They link up territorially based complexes of production, management and information, even though the meaning and functions of these complexes depend on their connection in these networks of flows. (2) These technological linkages are material, e.g. depend on specific telecommunication/ transportation facilities, and on the existence and quality of information systems, in a highly uneven geography. (3) The meaning of space evolves – as the meaning of time. Thus, instead of indulging in futurological statements such as the vanishing of space, and the end of cities, we should be able to reconceptualize new forms of spatial arrangements under the new technological paradigm.

To proceed with this conceptualization I build on a long intellectual tradition, from Leibniz to Harold Innis, connecting space and time, around the notion of space as coexistence of time. Thus, my definition: space is the material support of time-sharing social practices.[1]

What happens when the time-sharing of practices (be it synchronous or asynchronous) does not imply contiguity? 'Things' still exist together, they share time, but the material arrangements that allow this coexistence are inter-territorial or transterritorial: *the space of flows is the material organization of time-sharing social practices that work through flows.* What concretely this material organization is depends on the goals and characteristics of the networks of flows, for instance I can tell you what it is in the case of high technology manufacturing or in the case of global networks of drug traffic. However, I did propose in my analysis some elements that appear to characterize the space of flows in all kinds of networks: electronic circuits connection information systems; territorial nodes and hubs; locales of support and social cohesion for dominant social actors in the network (e.g. the system of VIP spaces throughout the world).

Dominant functions tend to articulate themselves around the space of flows. But this is not the only space. *The space of places continues to be the predominant space of experience*, of everyday life, and of social and political control. Places root culture and transmit history. (A place is a locale whose form, function, and meaning, from the point of view of the social actor, are contained within the boundaries of physical contiguity.)

In the network society, a fundamental form of social domination is *the prevalence of the logic of the space of flows over the space of places.* The space of flows structures and shapes the space of places, as when the differential fortunes of capital accumulation in global financial markets reward or punish specific regions, or when telecom systems link up CBDs to outlying suburbs in new office development, bypassing/marginalizing poor urban neighbourhoods. The domination of the space of flows over the space of places induces intra-*metropolitan dualism* as a most important form of social-territorial exclusion, that has become as significant as regional uneven development. The simultaneous growth and decline of economies and societies within the same metropolitan area is a most fundamental trend of territorial organization, and a key challenge to urban management nowadays.

But there is still something else in the new spatial dynamics. Beyond the opposition between the space of flows and the space of places. As information/communication networks diffuse in society, and as technology is appropriated by a variety of social actors, segments of the space of flows are penetrated by forces of resistance to domination, and by expressions of personal experience. Examples:

(a)   Social movements. *Zapatistas* and the Internet (but from the Lacandona forest). But also American Militia.

(b)   Local governments, key agents of citizen representation in our society, linking up through electronic networks, particularly in Europe (see research by Stephen Graham).

(c)   Expressions of experience in the space of flows.

Thus, we do witness an increasing penetration, and subversion, of the space flows, originally set up for the functions of power, by the power of experience, inducing a set of contradictory power relationships. Yes, it is still an elitist means of communication, but it is changing rapidly. The problem is to integrate these observations in some theory, but for this we still lack research, in spite of some insightful elaborations, such as the one by Sherry Turkle at MIT.

The new frontier of spatial research is in examining the interaction between the space of flows, the space of places, function, meaning, domination, and challenge to domination, in increasingly complex and contradictory patterns. Homesteading in this frontier is already taking place, as shown in the pioneering research by Graham and Marvin, or in the reflections of Bill Mitchell, but we are clearly at the beginning of a new field of study that should help us to understand *and to change* the currently prevailing logic in the space of flows.

Conclusion: the Network Society

So, what is the Network Society? It is a society that is structured in its dominant functions and processes around networks. In its current manifestation it is a capitalist society. Indeed, we live more than ever in a capitalist world, and thus an analysis in terms of capitalism is necessary and complementary to the theory of the network society. But this particular form of capitalism is very different from industrial capitalism, as I have tried to show.

The Network Society is not produced by information technology. But without the information technology revolution it could not be such a comprehensive, pervasive social form, able to link up, or de-link, the entire realm of human activity.

So, is that all? Just a morphological transformation? Well, historically, transformation of social forms has always been fundamental, both as expressions and sources of major social processes, e.g. standardized mass production in the large factory as characteristic of the so-called Fordism, as a major form of capitalist social organization; or the rational bureaucracy as the foundation of modern society, in the Weberian conception.

But this morphological transformation is even more significant because the network architecture is particularly dynamic, open-ended, flexible, potentially able to expand endlessly, without rupture, bypassing/ disconnecting undesirable components following instructions of the networks' dominant nodes. Indeed, the February 1997 Davos meeting titled the general programme of its annual meeting 'Building the Network Society'.

This networking logic is at the roots of major effects in our societies. Using it:

- capital flows can bypass controls
- workers are individualized, outsourced, subcontracted
- communication becomes at the same time global and customized
- valuable people and territories are switched on, devalued ones are switched off.

The dynamics of networks push society towards an endless escape from its own constraints and controls, towards an endless supersession and reconstruction of its values and institutions, towards a meta-social, constant rearrangement of human institutions and organizations.

Networks transform power relationships. Power in the traditional sense still exists: capitalists over workers, men over women, state apparatuses still torture bodies and silence minds around the world.

Yet, there is a higher order of power: the power of flows in the networks prevails over the flows of power. Capitalists are dependent upon uncontrollable financial flows; many workers are at the same time investors (often unwillingly through their pension funds) in this whirlwind of capital; networkers are inter-related in the logic of the network enterprise, so that their jobs and income depend on their positioning rather than on their work. States are bypassed by global flows of wealth, information, and crime. Thus, to survive, they band together in multilateral ventures, such as the European Union. It follows the creation of a web of political institutions – national, supranational, international, regional, and local – that becomes the new operating unit of the information age: the network state.

In this complexity, the communication between networks and social actors depends increasingly on shared *cultural codes*. If we accept certain values, certain categories that frame the meaning of experience, then the networks will process them efficiently, and will return to each one of us the outcome of their processing, according to the rules of domination and distribution inscripted in the network.

Thus, the challenges to social domination in the network society revolve around the redefinition of cultural codes, proposing alternative meaning and changing the rules of the game. This is why the affirmation of *identity* is so essential, because it fixes meaning autonomously *vis-à-vis* the abstract, instrumental logic of networks. I am, thus I exist. In my empirical investigation I have found identity-based social movements aimed at changing the cultural foundations of society to be the essential sources of social change in the information age, albeit often in forms and with goals that we do not usually associate with positive social change. Some movements, that appear to be the most fruitful and positive, are proactive, such as feminism and environmentalism. Some are reactive, as in the communal resistances to globalization built around religion, nation, territory, or ethnicity. But in all cases they affirm the preeminence of experience over instrumentality, of meaning over function, and, I would dare to say, of use value of life over exchange value in the networks.

The implicit logic of the Network Society appears to end history, by enclosing it into the circularity of recurrent patterns of flows. Yet, as with any other social form, in fact it opens up a new realm of contradiction and conflict, as people around the world refuse to become shadows of global flows and project their dreams, and sometimes their nightmares, into the light of new history making.

Note

1   Leibniz: 'Space is something purely relative, like time; space being an order of coexistences as time is an order of successions. For space denotes in terms of possibility and order of things that exist at the same time, in so far as they exist together . . . When we see several things together we perceive this order of things among themselves.'

Atari, 308, 309, 310, 312, 315–16
audience research, 372–3, 376–7, 381–2
Australian Broadcasting Corporation, 183
Australian News Corporation, 179
authority, 110, 111, 112
AVID, 269, 270

Bagdikian, Ben, 284
Bain, Alexander, 48
Baird, John Logie, 49
Bakewell, 48
Baran, S., 262
Barber, B., 386, 388
Baring Brothers, 173
Barnouw, E., 76, 79, 80, 81, 82, 83, 85, 86, 251
Barron, Iann, 152
Bassand, M., 350
Baudelaire, Charles, 127
Baudrillard, Jean, 139, 155, 156, 347, 348, 362, 371
Bauman, Zygmunt, 172, 174–5, 381
Bay Area Systems (BASYS), 269, 270
BBC, 31, 32, 40, 183, 242, 251, 256, 270
BBC World Service, 185
BBC Worldwide, 185, 242
Beck, Ulrich, 166
Becker, T., 388
Bell, Alexander Graham, 76
Bell Corporation, 11
Bell, Daniel, 95, 147, 158
Bell, M., 262
Bellah, Robert N., 283
Bellamy, R., 394
belonging, sense of, 20
Beniger, James R., 139
Beniger, John, 359
Bentham, Jeremy, 285, 333
Berliner, Emile, 76
Berman, Marshall, 20
Bertelsmann, 180, 188, 232, 237, 238, 239, 244, 245
Berzelius, J., 48

Betacam videotape format, 255, 256
Billaudot, B., 337
Bing, Jon, 388
biopower, 361
Birchall, Reginald, 61
Blond, A.J.L., 76, 77, 79
Blumler, J., 269, 393
bodybuilding, 218–19
the body, 154–5
Bogard, William, 356, 361–2
book publishing, 180, 197
books, 124, 131, 135
Boorstin, Daniel, 108, 109
Borchert, M., 390, 391
Boulding, K.E., 161
Boyd-Barratt, Oliver, 168
Boyer, R., 337
Branly, E., 74–5, 87
Brants, K., 393
Braun, Ferdinand, 49
Brittan, Samuel, 37
broadcasting, 11, 25–6, 28–41, 52–3, 54–7, 81, 82–8, 131–2
  legal definition of, 234–5
  and politics of representation, 28–9
  public service see public service broadcasting
  regulation of, 10, 37–8, 39, 53, 234, 235, 243–5
  telephone as proto-broadcasting system, 11, 65–70, 81
  see also radio; television
Brunson, Michael, 254
BSkyB, 236, 237, 238, 239, 240
bulletin-board systems (BBSs), 278–80
Bushnall, Nolan, 308

cable systems, 15, 33–4, 35–7, 129, 131, 182, 183, 184, 202, 346
Calabrese, A., 390, 391
Calhoun, C., 348, 349
camcorders, 256–7
cameras, film, 250–3
Campbell, D., 390
Canada, 185, 186
Canal Plus, 215, 232, 236, 238
capital flows, 339–40